Macroeconomics
Principles and Tools
Third Edition

Macroeconomics
Principles and Tools
Third Edition

Arthur O'Sullivan
Lewis and Clark College

Steven M. Sheffrin
University of California, Davis

Upper Saddle River, New Jersey

Library of Congress Cataloging-in-Publication Data

O'Sullivan, Arthur.
　　Macroeconomics : principles and tools / Arthur O'Sullivan, Steven M. Sheffrin.—3rd ed.
　　　　p. cm.
　　A variety of multi-media instructional tools, including a Web site, is available to
　　　　supplement the text.
　　Includes bibliographical references and index.
　　ISBN 0-13-035811-8
　　1. Macroeconomics.　I. Sheffrin, Steven M.　II. Title.
HB172.5.O85 2002
339—dc21

2001059333

Executive Editor: Rod Banister
Editor-in-Chief: P.J. Boardman
Managing Editor (Editorial): Gladys Soto
Assistant Editor: Marie McHale
Editorial Assistant: Lisa Amato
Media Project Manager: Victoria Anderson
Executive Marketing Manager: Kathleen McLellan
Marketing Assistant: Christopher Bath
Managing Editor (Production): Cynthia Regan
Production Assistant: Dianne Falcone
Permissions Coordinator: Suzanne Grappi
Associate Director, Manufacturing: Vincent Scelta
Production Manager: Arnold Vila
Design Manager: Patricia Smythe
Designer: Steve Frim
Cover Ilustration: Nancy D'Urso
Multimedia Artists: Sarah Arkin and John Hagopian
Print Production Liaison: Suzanne Duda
Composition/Illustrator (Interior): UG / GGS Information Services, Inc.
Full-Service Project Management: UG / GGS Information Services, Inc.
Printer/Binder: R.R. Donnelley/Willard

Credits and acknowledgments borrowed from other sources and reproduced, with permission, in this textbook appear on appropriate page within text and on page P-1.

Pearson Education LTD.
Pearson Education Australia PTY, Limited
Pearson Education Singapore, Pte. Ltd
Pearson Education North Asia Ltd
Pearson Education, Canada, Ltd
Pearson Educación de Mexico, S.A. de C.V.
Pearson Education–Japan
Pearson Education Malaysia, Pte. Ltd

10 9 8 7 6 5 4 3 2 1
ISBN 0-13-035811-8

To Our Children: Conor, Maura, Meera, and Kiran

About the Authors

Arthur O'Sullivan

Arthur O'Sullivan is a professor of economics at Lewis and Clark College in Portland, Oregon. After receiving his B.S. Degree in economics at the University of Oregon, he spent two years in the Peace Corps, working with city planners in the Philippines. He received his Ph.D. degree in economics from Princeton University in 1981 and has taught at the University of California, and Davis and Oregon State University, winning several teaching awards at both schools. He recently accepted an endowed professorship at Lewis and Clark College, where he teaches microeconomics and urban economics. He is the author of the best-selling textbook, *Urban Economics*, currently in its fifth edition.

Professor O'Sullivan's research explores economic issues concerning urban land use, environmental protection, and public policy. His articles appear in many economics journals, including Journal of Urban Economics, Journal of Environmental Economics and Management, National Tax Journal, Journal of Public Economics, and Journal of Law and Economics.

Professor O'Sullivan lives with his family in Lake Oswego, Oregon. He enjoys outdoor activities, including tennis, rafting, and hiking. Indoors, he plays chess, foosball, and ping-pong with his two kids, and is lucky to win one of five games.

Steven M. Sheffrin

Steven M. Sheffrin is dean of the division of social sciences and professor of economics at the University of California, Davis. He has been a visiting professor at Princeton University, Oxford University, and the London School of Economics, and served as a financial economist with the Office of Tax Analysis of the United States Department of Treasury. He has been on the faculty at Davis since 1976 and served as the chairman of the department of economics. He received his B.A. from Wesleyan University and his Ph.D. in economics from the Massachusetts Institute of Technology.

Professor Sheffrin is the author of eight other books and monographs and over 100 articles in the fields of macroeconomics, public finance, and international economics. His most recent books include *Rational Expectations* (Second Edition) and *Property Taxes and Tax Revolts: The Legacy of Proposition 13* (with Arthur O'Sullivan and Terri Sexton), both from Cambridge University Press.

Professor Sheffrin has taught macroeconomics at all levels, from large lectures of principles (classes of 400) to graduate classes for doctoral students. He is the recipient of the Thomas Mayer Distinguished Teaching Award in economics.

He lives with his wife Anjali (also an economist) and his two children in Davis, California. In addition to a passion for current affairs and travel, he plays a tough game of tennis.

Brief Contents

Contents

A CLOSER LOOK

FEATURES

Preface

Our Story

When we set out to write an economics text, we were driven by the vision of the sleeping student. A few years ago, one of the authors was in the middle of a fascinating lecture on monopoly pricing when he heard snoring. It wasn't the first time a student had fallen asleep in one of his classes, but this was the loudest snoring he had ever heard—it sounded like a sputtering chain saw. The instructor turned to Bill, who was sitting next to the sleeping student and asked, "Could you wake him up?" Bill looked at the sleeping student and then gazed theatrically around the room at the other students. He finally looked back at the instructor and said, "Well professor, I think you should wake him up. After all, you put him to sleep."

That experience changed the way we taught economics. It highlighted for us a basic truth—for many students, economics isn't exactly exciting. We took this as a challenge—to get first-time economics students to see the *relevance* of economics to their *lives*, their *careers*, and their *futures*.

In order to get students to see the relevance of economics we knew that we had to *engage* them. With the first and second editions of *Macroeconomics: Principles and Tools*, we helped professors to do that by emphasizing an active learning approach. We engaged students by teaching them how to do something—economic analysis. We kept the book **brief, lively, and to the point,** and used the **five key principles** of economics as an organizing theme. The result was that the first and second editions were a success in classrooms across the country, and we strove in this edition to do even better.

Key Changes

We knew that our text's brevity and student accessibility were key strengths and we worked to enhance and preserve them in the third edition. We also found that professors and students truly appreciated our concerted effort to use economic principles to explain current and topical events. For the third edition, we made a systematic attempt to refine this feature of the book. We made a special effort to enhance our chapter opening stories, Economic Detective exercises, and Closer Look boxes. The result is a text that applies economic reasoning to the most current economic controversies and debates.

In macroeconomics, we use the tools of growth accounting to assess the growth of productivity in the late 1990s and discuss whether or not we are experiencing a "new economy." We also take a more in-depth look at the problems facing the Japanese economy through the last decade and the role that two extraordinary chairmen of the Federal Reserve played in promoting economic stability. Some of our new features include the elusive link between money and happiness, whether committees make more or less effective economic decisions than individuals, and the role that climate and economic

geography play in economic growth. In addition to these new topics, we added more historical material on our experiences with monetary and fiscal policy and how our economic thinking has changed over time.

The September 11, 2001 terrorist attack impacted the economy in many different ways. In this edition, we have updated our discussion of the recent performance of the U.S. economy, the status of the federal budget, and monetary and fiscal policy in light of this event. In particular, we provide an extended discussion of the key role that the Federal Reserve played in calming financial markets directly after the attack, and discuss changes in fiscal policy that occurred as well.

In addition to these changes, we undertook a thorough review of our test bank to ensure accuracy and to provide a more focused range of questions for instructors' use. A totally new test bank was added to the supplement package to give instructors even greater flexibility in creating quizzes and exams. We incorporated the *Active Learning* aspect of the text into the questions in the supplement package—focusing new questions on asking students to create graphs, rather than just interpreting them. The Active Learning CD-ROM also was enhanced in this fashion through the addition of a Graphing Tool and Tutorial. In addition, we added videos to the CD-ROM so that students could see the economic experiments referred to in the text in action.

Teaching Philosophy

We began with the idea that an introductory economics course should be taught as if it is the last economics class a student will ever take. Because this is *true* for most students, we have just one opportunity to teach them how to use economics. The best way to teach economics is to focus on a few key concepts and ideas and apply them repeatedly in different circumstances.

We start the book with the five key principles of economics and then apply them throughout the book. This approach provides students with the big picture—the framework of economic reasoning. We make the key concepts unforgettable by using them repeatedly, illustrating them with intriguing examples, and giving students many opportunities to practice what they've learned.

Our book is designed to be accessible to students. We have kept the writing lean, the examples lively and topical, and the visuals exciting.

Principles and Tools

In keeping with the themes of relevance and student accessibility, we have once again organized our text around the **five key principles** of economics. Throughout the text, every point of theory is tied back to the five key principles and is indicated by the key symbol (see margin).

1. **The Principle of Opportunity Cost.** The opportunity cost of something is what you sacrifice to get it.
2. **The Marginal Principle.** Pick the level of an activity at which the marginal benefit equals the marginal cost.
3. **The Principle of Diminishing Returns.** If we increase one input while holding the other inputs fixed, output will increase, but at a decreasing rate.
4. **The Spillover Principle.** In some circumstances, decision makers do not bear all the cost or experience all the benefits from their decision.
5. **The Reality Principle.** What matters to people is the real value of money or income—its purchasing power—not the face value of money or income.

We use these principles to explain the logic underpinning the most important tools of economics. By using these five principles repeatedly, we reveal the logic of economic reasoning and demystify the tools of economics. Students see the big picture and also learn how to use the tools of economics properly.

"What I Do, I Understand"—Confucius

Our book is based on **Active Learning,** a teaching approach based on the idea that students learn best by doing. Our book engages students by letting them do activities as they read. We implement **Active Learning** with the following features:

- **Economics Detective** exercises provide a few clues and then ask the student to solve the economic mystery.

- **Using the Tools** questions at the end of each chapter give students opportunities to do their own economic analysis. Complete answers appear at the end of each chapter.

- **Economic Experiments** actively involve the student in role-playing as consumers, producers, and policymakers. All these activities are designed to be fun for students and easy for professors, who decide when and how to use them.

- **Test Your Understanding** questions help students determine whether they understand the preceding material before continuing. These are straightforward questions that ask students to review and synthesize what they have read. Complete answers appear at the end of each chapter.

- **Chapter-Opening Stories** open each chapter and motivate the chapter's subject matter.

- Each chapter starts with a list of **practical questions** that are answered in the chapter.

- **Lively Examples** are integrated throughout the text and help bring economic concepts to life. We have hundreds of fresh, new examples in this edition.

- **A Closer Look** boxes are featured throughout the text and provide brief, interesting examples of the tools and concepts discussed in the text.

The Mystery of the Three-Clock Tower

Economic Detective

Back in the days before the inexpensive wristwatch, most people did not carry their own timepieces. Many towns built clock towers in the center of town so that their citizens could know the time. The towns paid for the clock towers with voluntary contributions from citizens. One town in the northeastern United States built a four-sided tower but put clock faces on only three sides of the tower. To most people, this seems bizarre. If you build a clock tower, why not put clock faces on all four sides?

The key to solving this puzzle is the fre   turns out that one of the

Using the **TOOLS**

This chapter introduced several new tools of economics, including four different elasticities and a formula that can be used to predict the change in price resulting from a change in supply or demand. Here are some opportunities to use these tools to do your own economic analysis.

APPLICATIONS

1. Projecting Transit Ridership

As a transit planner, you must predict how many people ride commuter trains and how much money is generated from train fares. According to a recent study,[9] the short-run price elasticity of demand for commuter rail is 0.62 and the long-run elasticity is 1.59. The current ridership is 100,000 people per day. Suppose fares increase by 10%.

a. Predict the changes in train ridership over a one-month period (short run) and a five-year period (long run).

b. Over the one-month period, will total revenue increase or decrease? What will happen in the five-year period?

2. Bumper Crops

Your job is to predict the total revenue generated by the nation's corn crop. Last year's crop was 100 million bushels, and the price was $4.00 per bushel. This year's weather was favorable throughout the country, and this year's crop will   bushels, or   % larger than last year's. The price elasticity of dem

                the effect

TEST Your Understanding

1. Money solves the problem of double coincidence of wants that would regularly occur under a system of _____.

2. Why is money only an imperfect store of value?

3. What is the problem associated with the double coincidence of wants?

4. Because we measure all prices in monetary units, money serves as a unit of account. True or false? Explain.

5. Why are checks included in the de   of money?

Book Organization

Throughout most of the 1990s, the U.S. economy performed very well—low inflation, low unemployment, and rapid economic growth. This robust performance contributed to an increasing interest by economists in understanding the processes of economic growth. Our theories of economic growth address the fundamental question of how long-term living standards are determined and why some countries prosper while others do not. This is the essence of economic growth. As one noted economist says, "Once you start thinking about growth, it is hard to think of anything else."

Yet, the great economic expansion of the 1990s came to an end in 2001, as the economy started to contract. Difficult economic times remind us that macroeconomics is also concerned with understanding the causes and consequences of economic fluctuations. Why do economies experience recessions and depressions, and what steps can be taken to stabilize the economy? This has been a constant theme of macroeconomics throughout its entire history.

A key dilemma confronting economics professor has always been how much time to devote to classical topics such as growth and production, versus more Keynesian topics such as economic fluctuations. Our book is designed to let professors *choose*. It works like this: to pursue a classical approach, professors should initially concentrate on the first four chapters, followed by the first four chapters in the macroeconomics section. To focus on Keynesian themes, start with Chapters 1 through 4, cover the first two chapters in macroeconomics, and then turn to the chapter on aggregate demand and supply.

The Active Learning Package

Each component of the teaching and learning package has been carefully reevaluated to ensure that it is consistent with the changes made to this edition and with the needs of our audience.

Print Supplements

New Two-Volume Test Bank

Our team of instructors has striven to write, edit, review, and accuracy check the over 9,000 questions in both of the microeconomics and macroeconomics test banks.

Test Bank #1—The test bank for *Macroeconomics: Principles and Tools,* prepared by Mary Lesser of Iona College, offers approximately 3,000 multiple-choice, true/false, short answer, and graphing questions. The questions are referenced by topic and are presented in sequential order. Each question is keyed by degree of difficulty as *easy*, *moderate*, or *difficult*. Easy questions involve straightforward recall of information in the text. Moderate questions require some analysis on the student's part. Difficult questions usually entail more complex analysis and may require the student to go one step further than the material presented in the text. Questions are also classified as *fact*, *definition*, *conceptual*, and *analytical*. A question labeled Fact tests student's knowledge of factual information presented in the text. A Definition question asks the student to define an economic concept. Conceptual questions test a student's understanding of a concept. Analytical questions require the student to apply an analytical procedure to answer the question.

The test bank includes tables and a series of questions asking students to solve for numerical values, such as profit or equilibrium output. It also contains numerous questions based on graphs. The test bank includes examples of all of the graphs that students have seen in the textbook. The questions ask the students to interpret the information that is presented in the graph.

There are also many questions in the test bank that are not referenced by a graph, but which require students to sketch out a graph on their own to be able to answer the question. The author worked to create many new questions focused on testing the graphing ability of student and their ability to *actively* answering each question.

Test Bank #2—This new addition to the supplement package, prepared by Linda S. Ghent of Eastern Illinois University, will serve as another important resource for instructors. This new test bank for *Macroeconomics: Principles and Tools* contains over 1,500 multiple-choice, true/false, and short answer questions. Each question is also keyed by degree of difficulty (*easy*, *moderate*, or *difficult*), topic reference, and type of question (*definition*, *fact*, *conceptual*, or *analytical*).

Instructor's Manual

The instructor's manual to accompany *Macroeconomics: Principles and Tools,* prepared by Stephen Perez of California State University, Sacramento, follow the textbook's organization, incorporating policy problems in case studies, exercises, extra questions, and useful Internet links. The manual also provides detailed outlines (suitable for use as lecture notes) and solutions to all questions in the textbook. The instructor's manual is also designed to help the instructor incorporate applicable elements of the supplement package.

The instructor's manual contains by chapter: a summary, objectives, an outline, opening questions, examples for class discussion, teaching tips, extended examples, problems and discussion questions, Test Your Understanding questions, Internet exercises, and tips for classroom experiments.

Study Guide

The study guide to accompany *Macroeconomics: Principles and Tools*, prepared by Janice Boucher Breuer of University of South Carolina, emphasize the practical application of theory. This study guide is a practicum designed to promote comprehension of economic principles and develop each student's ability to apply them to different problems.

Integrated throughout this study guide are Performance Enhancing Tips (PETs), which are designed to help students understand economics by applying the principles and promoting analytical thinking.

Two practice exams, featuring both multiple-choice and essay questions, are included at the end of each chapter. Both exams require students to apply one or more economic principles to arrive at each correct answer. Full solutions to the multiple-choice questions are included, not only listing each correct answer but also explaining in detail why one answer is correct and the others are not. Detailed answers to the essay questions are also provided.

This study guide contains by chapter: an overview of the corresponding chapter in the textbook, a checklist to provide a quick summary of material covered in the textbook and lectures, a list of key terms and their definitions, practice exams, and the detailed answer keys.

Using Experiments, Cases, and Activities in the Classroom

Prepared by Dirk Yandell of the University of San Diego, this manual contains experiments that illustrate topics such as positive versus normative economics and monopoly. The experiments include tables and charts, in addition to an overview, learning objectives, a list of preparations and materials needed, a detailed what-to-do section, an analysis of the results, and questions that require students to interpret and analyze the material.

Color Transparencies

All figures and tables from the text are reproduced as full-page, four-color acetates.

E-Commerce Guide

Electronic commerce is playing an increasingly important role in how business is conducted. Prentice Hall's *Guide to E-Commerce and E-Businesses* provides readers with background on the history and direction of E-Commerce, the impact it has on the economy, and how to use it as a source of economic information and data. This guide can be shrink-wrapped free with a new copy of the third edition.

Technology Supplements

Active Learning CD-ROM

An interactive learning tool for students, the CD-ROM begins with detailed outlines that guide the student through all the key concepts of each chapter. Over 35 Active Graphs (referenced in the text) allow students to change the value of variables and see the effects in the movement of the graphs. New to this edition are seven videos of selected Economic Experiments from the textbook; a Graphing Tutorial and an electronic Graphing Tool. Graphing questions, concept checks, and end-of-chapter quizzes provide ample opportunity for self-assessment. The Active Learning CD-ROM is free with every new copy of the textbook.

TestGen–EQ Software

New for this edition, the print Test Banks are designed for use with the TestGen-EQ test-generating software. This computerized package allows instructors to custom design, save, and generate classroom tests. The test program permits instructors to edit, add, or delete questions from the test banks; edit existing graphics and create new graphics; analyze test results; and organize a database of tests and student results. This new software allows for greater flexibility and ease of use. It provides many options for organizing and displaying tests, along with a search and sort feature. The software can prepare 25 versions of a single test.

Mastering Economics CD-ROM

This CD-ROM, developed by Active Learning Technologies, is an integrated series of 12 video-enhanced interactive exercises that follow the people and issues of CanGo., an

e-business start-up. Students use economic concepts to solve key business decisions, including how to launch the start-up company's initial public offering (IPO), enter new markets for existing products, develop new products, determine prices, attract new employees, and anticipate competition from rivals. The videos illustrate the importance of an economic way of thinking to make real-world business decisions. Every episode includes three separate video segments: The first video clip introduces the episode topics by way of a current problem or issue at CanGo. After viewing the first clip, students read more about the theory or concept and then work through a series of multi-layered exercises. The exercises are composed of multiple-choice, true/false, fill-in, matching, ranking choices, comparisons, and one- or two-sentence answers. After completing the exercises, students watch another video clip. This resolution video illustrates one of the possible resolutions to the problem or decision faced by CanGo's management team. A correlation guide that links the Mastering Economics segments with chapters of the book is included in the *Mastering Economics Instructor's Manual* available at *http://www.prenhall.com/osullivan*.

Instructor's Resource CD-ROM

The Instructor's Resource CD-ROM includes the computerized test banks, instructor's manuals, and PowerPoint Presentation. It is dual platform for both PC and Macintosh.

Companion Web Site
(http://www.prenhall.com/osullivan)

The Companion Web site is a content-rich, multidisciplinary Web site with Internet exercises, activities, and resources related specifically to the third edition of *Macroeconomics: Principles and Tools*. It includes the following features:

The Online Study Guide, prepared by Fernando and Yvonn Quijano, offers students another opportunity to sharpen their problem-solving skills and to assess their understanding of the text material. The Online Study Guide for O'Sullivan/Sheffrin now contains three levels of both multiple-choice and essay quizzes. Each level includes 10 to 15 questions per chapter. The new third level of questions is focused on testing the students' ability to draw and interpret graphs. The Online Study Guide grades each question submitted by the student, provides immediate feedback for correct and incorrect answers, and allows students to e-mail results to up to four e-mail addresses.

Current Events Articles and Exercises, related to topics in each chapter, are fully supported by group activities, critical-thinking exercises, and discussion questions. These articles, from current news publications to economics-related publications, help show students the relevance of economics in today's world.

Internet Exercises—New Internet resources are added every two weeks by a team of economics professors to provide both the student and the instructor with the most current, up-to-date resources available. The Companion Web site also links the student to the **Take It to the Net** exercises featured in the textbook. These Web-destination exercises are keyed to each chapter and direct the student to an appropriate, updated, economics-related Web site to gather data and analyze a specific economic problem.

Syllabus Manager—For the instructor, the Companion Web site offers resources such as the answers to Current Events and Internet exercises, and a Faculty Lounge area including teaching resources and faculty chat rooms.

Downloadable Supplements—From the Companion Web site, instructors can also download supplements and lecture aids. Instructors should contact their Prentice Hall sales representative to get the necessary username and password to access the faculty resources. The supplements including the following:

- **The PowerPoint Presentation**—This lecture presentation tool, prepared by Fernando Quijano and Yvonn Quijano, offers outlines and summaries of important text material, tables and graphs that build, and additional exercises. The PowerPoint Presentation is included in the instructor's resource CD-ROM and is downloadable from the O'Sullivan/Sheffrin Web site. Many important graphs "build" over a sequencing of slides so that students may see the step-by-step process involved in economic analysis. The package will allow for instructors to make full-color, professional-looking presentations while providing the ability for custom handouts to be provided to the students.

- **The Instructor's Manual**

- **Mastering Economics Instructor's Manual**

Prentice Hall Video Library

A comprehensive video ancillary is available to help bring the major concepts covered in the textbook to life. The Video Library offers a resource for feature and documentary-style videos related to the chapters in the text. The programs have extremely high production quality, present substantial content, and are hosted by well-versed, well-known anchors.

Video Guide

The integrated Video Guide provides a summary of each of the clips in the Video Library. For each video, the guide also supplies running time, teaching notes, and discussion questions, as well as useful tips on how to use the clip in class. Each video is keyed to the appropriate topic in the text.

Online Course Offerings

WebCT

Developed by educators, WebCT provides faculty with easy-to-use Internet tools to create online courses. Prentice Hall provides the content and enhanced features to help instructors create a complete online course. For more information, please visit our Web site located at *http://www.prenhall.com/webct*.

Blackboard

Easy to use, Blackboard's single template and tools make it easy to create, manage, and use online course materials. Instructors can create online courses using the Blackboard tools, which include design, communication, testing, and course management tools. For more information, please visit our Web site located at *http://www.prenhall.com/blackboard*.

CourseCompass

This customizable, interactive, online course-management tool powered by Blackboard provides the most intuitive teaching and learning environment available. Instructors can communicate with students, distribute course material, and access student progress online. For further information, please visit our Web site located at *http://www.prenhall.com/coursecompass*.

CourseCompass with Ebook

This online course provides the features of CourseCompass along with an electronic version of the textbook. The addition of a digital textbook to CourseCompass gives instructors greater choice and flexibility as they design and build their online courses. With this feature, students can remain online and use an eBook for all of their online assignments.

Subscription Options

The Wall Street Journal Print and Interactive Editions Subscription

Prentice Hall has formed a strategic alliance with *The Wall Street Journal*, the most respected and trusted daily source for information on business and economics. For a small additional charge, Prentice Hall offers your students a 10-week subscription to *The Wall Street Journal* print edition and *The Wall Street Journal* Interactive Edition. Adopting professors will receive a free one-year subscription of the print and interactive version as well as weekly subject-specific *Wall Street Journal* educators' lesson plans.

Economist.com Subscription

Through a special arrangement with *Economist.com* for a small additional charge, Prentice Hall offers your students a 12-week subscription to *Economist.com*. Adopting professors will receive a free six-month subscription. Please contact your Prentice Hall representative for further details and ordering information.

The Financial Times Subscription

We are pleased to announce a special partnership with *The Financial Times*. For a small additional charge, Prentice Hall offers your students a 15-week subscription to *The Financial Times*. Adopting professors will receive a free one-year subscription. Please contact your Prentice Hall representative for details and ordering information.

A World of Thanks

There is a long distance between the initial vision of an innovative principles text and the final product. Along the way we participated in a structured process to reach our goal.

We wish to acknowledge the assistance of the many individuals who participated in this process. First we want to thank the participants who took part in the focus groups for the first and second editions; they helped us see the manuscript from a fresh perspective:

Carlos Aquilar, El Paso Community College

Jim Bradley, University of South Carolina

Thomas Collum, Northeastern Illinois University

David Craig, Westark College

Jeff Holt, Tulsa Junior College

Thomas Jeitschko, Texas A & M University

Gary Langer, Roosevelt University

Mark McCleod, Virginia Polytechnic Institute and State University

Tom McKinnon, University of Arkansas

Amy Meyers, Parkland Community College

Hassan Mohammadi, Illinois State University

John Morgan, College of Charleston

Norm Paul, San Jancinto Community College

Nampeang Pingkaratwat, Chicago State University

Scanlan Romer, Delta Community College

Barbara Ross-Pfeiffer, Kapiolani Community College

Virginia Shingleton, Valparaiso University

Zahra Saderion, Houston Community College

Jim Swofford, University of South Alabama

Linda Wilson, University of Texas–Arlington

Janet West, University of Nebraska–Omaha

Michael Youngblood, Rock Valley Community College

A special acknowledgment goes to the instructors who were willing to class-test drafts in different stages of development. They provided us with instant feedback on parts that worked and parts that needed changes:

Sheryl Ball, Virginia Polytechnic Institute and State University

John Constantine, University of California, Davis

James Hartley, Mt. Holyoke College

John Farrell, Oregon State University

Kailash Khandke, Furman College

Peter Lindert, University of California, Davis

Louis Makowski, University of California, Davis

Stephen Perez, California State University, Sacramento

Barbara Ross-Pfeiffer, Kapiolani Community College

Many people read all or parts of the manuscript at various stages. For their helpful criticisms, we thank:

Christine Amsler, Michigan State University

Karijit K. Arora, Le Moyne College

Alex Azarchs, Pace University

Kevin A. Baird, Montgomery County Community College

Donald Balch, University of South Carolina

Collette Barr, Santa Barbara Community College

Mahamudu Bawumia, Baylor University

Charles Scott Benson Jr., Idaho State University

Jay Bhattacharya, Okaloosa–Walton Community College

John Payne Bigelow, Louisiana State University

Scott Bloom, North Dakota State University

Janice Boucher Breuer, University of South Carolina

Kathleen K. Bromley, Monroe Community College

Cindy Cannon, North Harris College

Katie Canty, Cape Fear Community College

David L. Coberly, Southwest Texas State University

John L. Conant, Indiana State University

Ana-Maria Conley, DeVry Institute of Technology

Ed Coulson, Penn State University

Lee Craig, North Carolina State University

Peggy Crane, San Diego State University

Albert B. Culver, California State University, Chico

Norman Cure, Macomb Community College

Irma de Alonso, Florida International University

Sel Dibooglu, Southern Illinois University

Martine Duchatelet, Barry University

Mousumi Duttaray, Indiana University

Ghazi Duwaji, University of Texas, Arlington

David Eaton, Murray State University

Duane Eberhardt, Missouri Southern State College

Carl Enomoto, New Mexico State University

David Figlio, University of Oregon

Dan Georgianna, University of Massachusetts–Dartmouth

Linda Ghent, East Illinois University

Hossein Gholami, Fayetteville Tech Community College

Susan Glanz, St. John's University

Randy R. Grant, Linfield College

Paul C. Harris, Jr., Camden County College

James E. Hartley, Mount Holyoke College

Rowland Harvey, DeVry Institute of Technology

John Henry, California State University, Sacramento

Robert Herman, Nassau Community College

Charles W. Haase, San Francisco State University

Charlotte Denise Hixson, Midlands Technical College

Jeff Holt, Tulsa Community College

Brad Hoppes, Southwest Missouri State University

Calvin Hoy, County College of Morris

Jonathan O. Ikoba, Scott Community College

John A. Jascot, Capital Community Technical College

Thomas Jeitschko, Texas A & M University

George Jensen, California State University, Los Angeles

Taghi T. Kermani, Youngstown State University

Rose Kilburn, Modesto Junior College

Philip King, San Francisco State University

Steven F. Koch, Georgia Southern University

James T. Kyle, Indiana State University

Gary Langer, Roosevelt University

Susan Linz, Michigan State University

Marianne Lowery, Erie Community College

Melanie Marks, Longwood College

Jessica McCraw, University of Texas, Arlington

Bret McMurran, Chaffey College

Thomas J. Meeks, Virginia State University

Jeannette Mitchell, Rochester Institute of Technology

Rahmat Mozayan, Heald College

William Neilson, Texas A & M University

Alex Obiya, San Diego City College

Paul Okello, University of Texas, Arlington

Charles M. Oldham, Jr., Fayetteville Technical Community College

Jack W. Osman, San Francisco State University

Carl Parker, Fort Hays State University

Randall Parker, East Carolina University

Stephen Perez, California State University, Sacramento

Stan Peters, Southeast Community College

Chirinjev Peterson, Greenville Technical College

Nampeang Pingkarawat, Chicago State University

L. Wayne Plumly, Jr., Valdosta State University

Fatma Abdel-Raouf, Cleveland State University

Dan Rickman, Oklahoma State University

John Robertson, University of Kentucky

Barbara Ross-Pfeiffer, Kapiolani Community College

George Schatz, Maine Maritime Academy

Kurt Schwabe, Ohio University

Mark Siegler, Williams College

Terri Sexton, California State University, Sacramento

Dennis Shannon, Belleville Area College

Virginia Shingleton, Valparaiso University

Garvin Smith, Daytona Beach Community College

Noel Smith, Palm Beach Community College

Xiaochuan Song, San Diego Mesa College

Ed Sorensen, San Francisco State University

Abdulwahab Sraiheen, Kutztown University

Rodney Swanson, University of California–Los Angeles

James Swofford, University of South Alabama

Evan Tanner, Thunderbird, The American Graduate School of International Management

Robert Tansky, St. Clair County Community College

Denise Turnage, Midlands Technical College

Tracy M. Turner, Kansas State University

Fred Tyler, Fordham University

James R. VanBeek, Blinn College

Daniel Villegas, Cal Polytechnic State University

Chester Waters, Durham Technical Community College, Shaw University

Irvin Weintraub, Towson State University

Donald Wells, University of Arizona

James Wheeler, North Carolina State University

Gilbert Wolfe, Middlesex Community College

Virginia York, Gulf Coast Community College

Our greatest appreciation goes out to Carlos Aguilar and his economics students from El Paso Community College, who gave us their feedback and evaluations with comparable textbooks. The students provided us with positive feedback and constructive criticism that helped us prepare the third edition:

Erik Acona

Erica Avila

Jaime Bermudez

Israel Castillo

Maribell Castillo

Sarah Davis

Rebekah Dennis

Michele Donohoe

Emmanuel Eck	Harmony Lopez
Patrick Espinoza	Stacey Lucas
Edward Estrada	Maria Lynch
Kim Gardner	Sindy McElvany
Aleisa Garza	Roger Mitchell
Daniel Heitz	Benny Ontiveros
Laura Herebia	Louie Ortega
Hilda Howard	Karen Seitz
Melanie Johnson	Ana Smith
Brenda Jordan	Beverly Stephens
Eugene Jordan	Adrian Terrazas
Vanessa Lara	Chris Wright

From the start, Prentice Hall provided us with first-class support and advice. P.J. Boardman, Marie McHale, Gladys Soto, Lisa Amato, Victoria Anderson, Cynthia Regan, Kathleen McLellan, David Theisen, and Christopher Bath of Prentice Hall contributed in myriad ways to the project. We want to single out two people for special mention. Our Development Editor, Mike Elia, worked patiently with us to make our prose clean and lively, and our presentation utterly clear. Finally, we are deeply indebted to Rod Banister, Executive Editor at Prentice Hall, who used a combination of great organizational skill and a good sense of humor to guide the project from start to finish.

Last but not least, we must thank our families, who have seen us disappear, sometimes physically and other times mentally, to spend hours wrapped up in our own world of principles of economics. A project of this magnitude is very absorbing, and our families have been particularly supportive in this endeavor.

ARTHUR O'SULLIVAN

STEVEN SHEFFRIN

Introduction:
What Is Economics?

Picture the following scenes:

- Betsy was studying for a midterm when someone invited her to a party. Should she go to the party or stay home and study?
- The Rentz family is tired of paying rent every month to the landlord. Should they buy their own home?
- The young entrepreneurs who started scour.com, an Internet search engine for video and music, have been offered $4 million for a 51% share in their company. Should they accept the offer?
- The California legislature is discussing the governor's proposed budget. Should the legislators accept it or should they give more money to the state's universities?
- The Federal Reserve Board is meeting in Washington, D.C. Should the board cut interest rates?

What do the people in these scenes have in common? Each person or group will make a decision, and each decision will require some economic reasoning.

What is Economics?
Scarcity and Production
   Possibilities
Markets and the Invisible Hand

The Economic Way of Thinking
Positive and Normative
   Economics
Use Assumptions to Simplify
Explore the Relationship
   Between Two Variables
Think Marginal

Preview of Coming Attractions: Microeconomics
Understand Markets and Predict
   Changes
Make Personal and Managerial
   Decisions
Evaluate Public Policies

Preview of Coming Attractions: Macroeconomics
Understand How a National
   Economy Operates
Understand the Grand Debates
   over Economic Policy
Make Informed Business
   Decisions

Appendix: Using Graphs and Formulas

1

conomic reasoning involves a careful evaluation of alternative actions. Betsy can have some party fun, but she might get a lower grade on the midterm as a result. The Rentz family can buy a home, but to come up with the down payment, they may sacrifice a family vacation or a new car. The young entrepreneurs can take $4 million now or they can continue to operate on their own and wait for a better offer. The California legislature can give more money to universities, but that means there will be less money for other programs such as prisons. The Federal Reserve Board can cut interest rates and help people who want to borrow money, but the lower interest rates might heat up the economy and cause inflation. Because there are alternative courses of action, people face trade-offs, and economic reasoning helps people think carefully about these trade-offs and then make decisions.

What is Economics?

Economics: The study of the choices made by people who are faced with scarcity.

Scarcity: A situation in which resources are limited and can be used in different ways, so one good or service must be sacrificed for another.

Economics is the study of the choices made by people when there is scarcity, that is, when there are limits to what they can get. **Scarcity** is a situation in which resources—the things we use to produce goods and services—are limited in quantity and can be used in different ways. Because resources are limited, we must sacrifice one good or service for another. Here are some examples of scarcity:

- Like everyone else, you have a limited amount of time today. If you play video games for an hour, you have one less hour to spend on other activities such as studying, exercising, or working.
- A city has a limited amount of land. If the city uses an acre of land to build a park, there is one less acre for apartments, office buildings, or factories.
- A nation has a limited number of people, so if it forms an army, it has fewer people to serve as teachers, scientists, and police officers.

Because of scarcity, people must make choices. You must decide how to spend your time; the city must decide how to use its land; and we as a nation must decide how to divide our people among teaching, science, law enforcement, and the military.

Decisions are made at every level in society. Individuals decide what products to buy, what occupation to pursue, and how much money to save. Firms decide what products to produce and how to produce them. Governments decide what projects and programs to complete and how to pay for them. The choices made by individuals, firms, and governments answer three basic questions:

1. What products do we produce? There are trade-offs in the choice among alternative products. For example, if a hospital devotes its resources to producing more heart transplants, it has fewer resources for caring for premature infants.
2. How do we produce these products? There are alternative ways to produce the products we desire. For example, utility companies can produce electricity with oil, solar power, or nuclear power. Professors can teach college students in large lectures or in small sections.
3. Who consumes the products? We must decide how the products of society are distributed among people. If some people earn more money than others, should they consume more goods? How much money should be taken from the rich and given to the poor?

Scarcity and Production Possibilities

Factors of production: The resources that are used to produce goods and services.

Let's take a closer look at the first question. What products do we produce? The resources that are used to produce products are known as the **factors of production**. Economists have identified five factors of production:

1. **Natural resources** are created by acts of nature. Natural resources—for example, arable land, mineral deposits, oil and gas deposits, and water—are used to produce goods and services. Some economists refer to all types of natural resources as land.

2. **Labor** is the human effort—including both physical and mental effort—used to produce goods and services. Labor is scarce because there are only 24 hours in each day: If we spend time in one activity, such as work, we have less time for other activities, such as recreation.

3. **Physical capital** is made by human beings and is used to produce goods and services; some examples of physical capital are machines, buildings, equipment, roads, pencils, computers, and trucks.

4. **Human capital** is the knowledge and skills a worker acquires through education and experience; human capital, like physical capital, is used to produce goods and services, although not in the same way. Every job requires some human capital: To be a surgeon, you must learn anatomy and acquire surgical skills; to be an accountant, you must learn the rules of accounting and acquire computer skills; to be a taxi driver, you must know the city's streets; to be a musician, you must know how to play an instrument well enough to be paid for playing it. One of the reasons for getting a college degree is to increase your human capital, widening your employment opportunities.

5. **Entrepreneurship** is the effort used to coordinate the production and sale of goods and services. An entrepreneur comes up with an idea for a good or a service and decides how to produce it. The entrepreneur takes risks, committing money and time without any guarantee of profit, hoping of course for success and big profits.

Natural resources: Things created by acts of nature and used to produce goods and services.

Labor: Human effort, including both physical and mental effort, used to produce goods and services.

Physical capital: Objects made by human beings to produce goods and services.

Human capital: The knowledge and skills acquired by a worker through education and experience and used to produce goods and services.

Entrepreneurship: Effort used to coordinate the production and sale of goods and services.

Before we can decide what products to produce, we must determine which combinations of products are possible, given our productive resources and our technological know-how. A production possibilities graph shows an economy's production options, the different combinations of products the economy can produce. The two-dimensional graph can show the production options with two general categories of goods, such as farm goods and factory goods or capital goods and consumer goods. The graph can also show the production options for any pair of specific goods, such as guns and butter, computers and space missions, or houses and automobiles.

Figure 1.1 shows a production possibilities graph for an economy that produces farm goods and factory goods. The possible or feasible combinations of these two types of goods are shown on the curve and in the shaded area. For example, one option is point *b,* with 700 tons of factory goods and 10 tons of farm goods. Another option is point *i,* with 300 tons of factory goods and 20 tons of farm goods. The set of points on the border between the shaded and unshaded area is called the **production possibilities curve** (or production possibilities frontier) because it separates the combinations that are attainable (the shaded area within the curve and the curve itself) from the combinations that are not attainable (the unshaded area outside the curve).

What is the difference between points inside the curve and points on the curve? For any point inside the curve, we can find a point on the curve that generates more of both goods. For example, at point *i* the economy can produce 300 tons of factory goods and 20 tons of farm goods. But we know from point *d* that the economy could produce more of both products: 400 tons of factory goods and 50 tons of farm goods. Producing at point *i* is clearly inferior to producing at point *d.* In general, an economy that is producing at a point inside the production possibilities curve could do better: It could produce more of both goods.

Production possibilities curve: A curve that shows the possible combinations of goods and services available to an economy, given that all productive resources are fully employed and efficiently used.

Figure 1.1

Scarcity and the Production Possibilities Curve

The production possibilities curve (or frontier) illustrates the notion of scarcity: With a given amount of resources, an increase in farm goods comes at the expense of factory goods. The curve is bowed outward because resources are not perfectly adaptable to the production of the two goods.

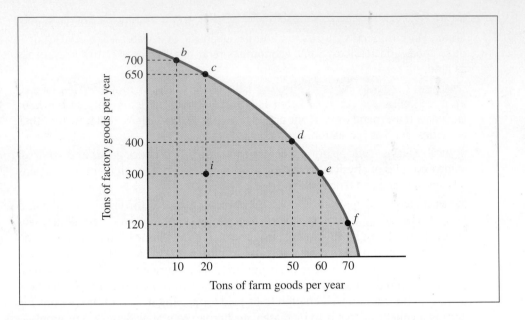

An economy might be at a point below the curve for the following reasons:

- Resources are not fully employed. For example, some workers could be idle, or some production facilities could be idle or underused.

- Resources are used inefficiently. Products can be produced with different mixtures of inputs, and some mixtures produce more output than others. If businesses pick the wrong input mixture, the economy won't produce as much output as it could.

In contrast, when an economy reaches a point on the production possibilities curve, it would be impossible to increase the production of both goods. For every point on the curve, the society's resources are fully employed and used in an efficient manner.

The production possibilities curve illustrates the notion of scarcity. At a given time, an economy has a fixed amount of each factor of production. That means we can produce more of one product only if we produce less of another product. To produce more farm goods, we take resources away from factories. As we move resources out of factory production, the quantity of factory goods will decrease. For example, if we move from point *b* to point *c* on the production possibilities curve in Figure 1.1, we sacrifice 50 tons of factory goods (700 tons − 650 tons) to get 10 more tons of farm goods (20 tons − 10 tons).

Compare the move from point *b* to point *c* with the move from point *e* to point *f*. Starting at point *b,* a 10-ton increase in farm goods decreases factory goods by 50 tons. Starting at point *e,* a 10-ton increase in farm goods decreases factory goods by 180 tons. On the lower part of the curve, we sacrifice more factory goods to get the same 10-ton increase in farm goods. Why?

The answer is that resources are not perfectly adaptable for the production of both goods. Some resources are more suitable for factory production, while others are more suitable for farming. Starting at point *b,* the economy uses its most fertile land to produce farm goods. A 10-ton increase in farm goods reduces the quantity of factory goods by only 50 tons because plenty of fertile land is available for conversion to farming. As the economy moves downward along the production possibilities curve, farmers will be forced to use land that is progressively less fertile. To increase farm output by 10 tons, farmers will need more land and more of the other inputs. As progressively larger quantities of resources are diverted from factory goods, the sacrifice of factory goods becomes

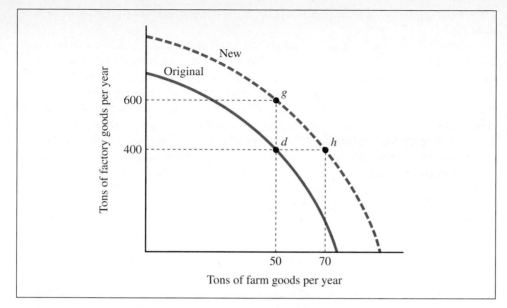

Figure 1.2

Shifting the Production Possibilities Curve
The production possibilities curve will shift outward as a result of an increase in the economy's resources (natural resources, labor, physical capital, human capital, and entrepreneurship) or a technological innovation that increases the output from a given amount of resources.

larger and larger. In the move from point *e* to point *f*, the land converted to farming is so poor that to increase farm output by 10 tons, so much land and other resources are diverted to farms that factory output drops by 180 tons.

What sort of changes would shift the entire production possibilities curve? The curve shows the production options available with a given set of productive resources, so an increase in an economy's resources will shift the entire curve outward. If an economy acquires more resources—natural resources, labor, physical capital, human capital, or entrepreneurial ability—the economy can produce more of both products. As a result, the production possibilities curve will shift outward, as shown in Figure 1.2. For example, if we start at point *d* and the economy's resources increase, we can produce more factory goods (point *g*), more farm goods (point *h*), or more of both goods (points between *g* and *h*). The curve will also shift outward as a result of technological innovations that allow us to produce more output with a given quantity of resources.

The production possibilities frontier could shift inward as well. Suppose a hurricane destroys factories, roads, and train tracks. The economy will have fewer resources available for production, so the production possibilities curve will shift inward. That means the nation will produce fewer factory goods, fewer farm goods, or fewer of both. Similarly, recent wars in Iraq and Afghanistan—which caused widespread destruction of roads, factories, bridges, electricity generation facilities, and housing—shifted the production possibilities frontiers of those economies inward.

Markets and the Invisible Hand

Let's look at how a market-based economy answers the three basic economic questions. A **market** is an arrangement that allows buyers and sellers to exchange things, trading what they have for what they want. For example, the labor market allows workers and firms to exchange time and money. A software firm has money and wants workers to design programs, while the worker has time and wants income to support the family. Similarly, the car market allows consumers and producers to exchange cars and money. A consumer has money and wants a car, while a producer has a car and wants money. By providing opportunities to trade goods and services, markets help society to answer the

Market: An arrangement that allows buyers and sellers to exchange things: A buyer exchanges money for a product; a seller exchanges a product for money.

three basic questions of what to produce, how to produce it, and who gets the products produced.

Markets determine the prices of goods and services, and these prices guide decisions about what and how much to buy and sell. Consider a hurricane in Florida that disrupts the electric power supply and disables refrigerators, so people must use ice to preserve their food. The sudden increase in the demand for ice will increase its price. The higher price will cause consumers to use ice wisely and to switch to foods that don't require refrigeration. At the same time, the higher price will encourage profit-seeking firms to produce more ice to accommodate the greater demand. On both sides of the market, the higher price helps the state to deal with the power disruption caused by the hurricane.

The decisions made in markets result from the interactions of millions of people, each acting in his or her own self-interest. Adam Smith used the metaphor of the invisible hand to explain that people acting in their own self-interest may actually promote the interest of society as a whole.

> *It is not from the benevolence of the butcher, the brewer, or the baker that we expect our dinner, but from their regard to their own interest. We address ourselves, not to their humanity but to their self-love, and never talk to them of our own necessities but of their advantages. [Man is] led by an invisible hand to promote an end which was no part of his intention. . . . By pursuing his own interest he frequently promotes that of the society more effectually than when he really intends to promote it.*

Adam Smith, *Wealth of Nations* (New York: Modern Library, 1994)

In the last sentence Smith said "frequently," not "always." Smith recognized that individuals pursuing their own self-interest will not necessarily promote the social interest. Later in the book we'll discuss situations in which the pursuit of self-interest will be contrary to the interest of society as a whole. In these cases it is sensible for the government to guide people's decisions to promote the social interest.

In modern economies, most of the decisions about how much to produce, how to produce it, and who gets the products are made in markets. Of course, no economy relies exclusively on markets to make these economic decisions. Later in the book we'll look at how government regulates markets, provides goods and services, imposes taxes to pay for the goods and services it provides, and redistributes income.

TEST Your Understanding

1. List the three basic questions that we can ask about a society's economy.

2. Which of these three questions does the production possibilities curve help to answer?

The Economic Way of Thinking

How do economists think about problems and decision-making? This economic way of thinking is best summarized by noted economist John Maynard Keynes: "The Theory of Economics does not furnish a body of settled conclusions immediately applicable to policy. It is a method rather than a doctrine, an apparatus of the mind, a technique of thinking which helps its possessor to draw correct conclusions." Let's look at some of the elements of the economic way of thinking.

Positive and Normative Economics

The focus of most modern economic reasoning is on positive analysis. **Positive economics** concerns the forces that affect economic activity, and predicts the consequences of alternative actions. Here are some questions answered by positive economics:

Positive economics: Analysis that answers the questions, What is or what will be?

- How will an increase in the price of Internet access affect the number of subscribers?

- How will an increase in the wage for fast-food workers affect the number of workers hired?

- What fraction of an income-tax cut will be spent on consumer goods, and what fraction will be saved?

- How will an increase in interest rates affect investment in factories?

In other words, positive economics answers the questions, What is? or What will be?

A second type of economic reasoning is normative in nature. **Normative economics** answers the question, What ought to be? Here are some examples of normative questions:

Normative economics: Analysis that answers the question, What ought to be?

- Should the government increase the minimum wage?

- Should a commuter who drives to work during the rush hour pay a congestion tax of $5 per day?

- Should the government provide free prescription drugs to senior citizens?

- Should NASA stage a manned mission to Mars?

Although most economists shy away from normative questions and instead focus on positive analysis, economic reasoning is an important part of most policy debates. Economists contribute to the debates by doing positive economic analysis about the consequences of alternative actions. For example, an economist could predict how a $5 congestion tax would affect the number of rush-hour vehicles, and then tell us how much faster traffic would flow. This positive analysis sets the stage for citizens and policymakers to decide whether or not to impose the congestion tax. Similarly, an economist would remind us that a mission to Mars would use resources that could be used for other programs such as college loans, and tell us how a cut in student-loan programs would affect the number of people attending college. After an economist quantifies the trade-offs, citizens and policymakers can make a choice.

To summarize, most modern economic analysis is positive in nature, but is often focused on the question relevant for normative concerns. Nassau Senior, the first professor of political economy at Oxford, summarizes the role of economic analysis in public policy.

> *But the economists' conclusions, whatever be their generality and their truth, do not authorize him in adding a single syllable of advice. That privilege belongs to the writer and statesman who has considered all the causes which may promote or impede the general welfare of those whom he addresses, not to the theorist who has considered only one, though among the most important, of those causes. The business of a Political Economist is neither to recommend nor to dissuade, but to state general principle.*

As you go through this book, you'll find plenty of positive economic analysis relevant to today's policy debates.

Use Assumptions to Simplify

Economists use assumptions to make things simpler and to focus on what really matters. Most people use simplifying assumptions in their everyday thinking and decision-making. For example, suppose you want to travel from Seattle to San Francisco by automobile. If you use a road map to pick a travel route, you are using two assumptions to simplify your decision-making:

- The earth is flat: The flat road map does not show the curvature of the earth.
- The highways are flat: The standard road map does not show hills and mountains.

These two assumptions are abstractions from reality. But they are useful because they simplify your decision-making without affecting your choice of a travel route. You could plan your trip with a globe that shows all the topographical features of the alternative travel routes between Seattle and San Francisco, but you would probably pick the same travel route because the curvature of the earth and the topography of the highways are irrelevant for your trip. In this case, the assumptions underlying the standard road map are harmless.

What if you decide to travel by bicycle instead of by automobile? Now the two assumptions are not harmless unless you want to pedal up mountains. If you use the standard road map and assume that there are no mountains between Seattle and San Francisco, you are likely to pick a mountainous route instead of a flat one. In this case, the simplifying assumption makes a difference. The lesson from this example is that we must think carefully about whether an assumption is truly harmless.

In this book, we use simplifying assumptions to help make it easier to learn a concept or to analyze something. Most of the assumptions will be harmless in the sense that they simplify the analysis by eliminating irrelevant details. Although many of the assumptions are unrealistic, that does not mean that the analysis based on the assumption is incorrect. Just as we can use an unrealistic road map to plan a trip, we can use unrealistic assumptions to do economic analysis. When we use an assumption that actually affects the analysis, we'll alert you to this fact and explore the implications of alternative assumptions.

Most of the economic analysis in this book is based on two assumptions, both of which are realistic in most circumstances:

- **Self-interest.** We'll assume that people act in their own self-interest, without considering the effects of their actions on other people. We assume that a pizza consumer doesn't care about other people who might want to buy the pizza, but only about his or her own well-being. Similarly, we assume that a pizzeria owner doesn't care about how his or her decisions affect other people, but only about the owner's profit. There is solid evidence that most people act in their own self-interest in most situations, so the economic analysis in this book is relevant for a wide range of decisions.
- **Informed decisions.** We'll assume that people make informed decisions. We assume that a consumer deciding what to eat for lunch knows the price of pizza, the prices of alternative foods, and the relevant characteristics of the foods (taste, amount of fat, number of calories). With this information, the consumer can make an informed decision about what to eat. Similarly, the manager of a pizzeria knows the cost of producing pizza, and this information leads to an informed decision about how many pizzas to produce and what price to charge. In most cases, consumers and producers have enough information to make informed decisions. Later in the book, we'll discuss situations in which one side of the market is poorly informed.

Explore the Relationship Between Two Variables

Economic analysis often involves variables and how they affect each other. A **variable** is a measure of something that can have different values. For example, consider a student who has a part-time job and also receives a fixed weekly allowance from her parents. Her weekly income is a variable whose value is determined by the values of the other variables: the number of hours she works, the hourly wage she is paid, and the weekly allowance she gets from her parents.

To explore the relationship between any two variables, such as the hours worked and weekly income, we must assume that the other variables do not change. For example, the student might say, "If I work one more hour this week, my income will increase by $8." In making this statement, the student is exploring the relationship between two variables (work time and income), assuming that the other two variables (wage and allowance) do not change. To be complete, the statement must say, "If I work one more hour this week, my income will increase by $8, assuming that my wage and my allowance do not change."

This book contains many statements about the relationship between two variables. For example, the number of pizzas a person eats depends on the price of pizza, the price of burgers, and that person's income. Suppose we say, "A decrease in the price of pizzas increases the quantity of pizzas consumed." This is a statement about the relationship between two variables—the price of pizzas and the quantity of pizzas—implicitly assuming that the other two variables, the price of burgers and the person's income, do not change in value. Sometimes we will make this assumption explicit by adding a warning label: "A decrease in the price of pizzas increases the quantity of pizzas consumed, **ceteris paribus**." The Latin words mean "other things being equal to what they were before." In the present context, the phrase means "other variables being fixed." From now on, whenever we refer to a relationship between two variables, we assume that the other relevant variables are held fixed.

Variable: A measure of something that can take on different values.

Ceteris paribus: Latin, meaning "other things being equal." In economics, the phrase indicates that all other variables are held fixed.

Think Marginal

Economists often need to consider how a small change in one variable causes a change in another variable. A small change in value is called a **marginal change**. The marginal question is, If we increase one variable by one unit, by how much will the other variable change? The key feature of this marginal question is that one variable increases by a single unit. For the student who is concerned about income, the marginal question is, If I work one more hour per week, by how much will my income increase?

Marginal change: A small change in value.

You will encounter marginal thinking throughout this book. Here are some other marginal questions:

- If I spend one more year in school, by how much will my lifetime income increase?
- If I buy one more CD, how many tapes will I sacrifice?
- If a table producer hires one more carpenter, how many more tables will be produced?
- If national income increases by $1 billion, by how much will spending on consumer goods increase?

Answering a marginal question like any of these is the first step in deciding whether or not to pursue a particular activity. You will see more about this as we move along in this book.

Preview of Coming Attractions: Microeconomics

Microeconomics: The study of the choices made by consumers, firms, and government and of how their choices affect the market for a particular good or service.

There are two types of economic analysis: microeconomics and macroeconomics. **Microeconomics** is the study of the choices made by households, firms, and government and of how these choices affect the markets for goods and services. Let's look at three ways we can use microeconomic analysis.

Understand Markets and Predict Changes

One reason for studying microeconomics is to understand better how markets work. Once you know how markets operate, you can use economic analysis to predict changes in the price of a particular good and changes in the quantity of the good sold. In this book we answer dozens of practical questions about markets and how they operate. Let's look at a practical question that can be answered with some simple economic analysis.

How would a tax on beer affect the number of highway deaths among young adults? A tax on beer will make it more expensive, and young adults, like other beer consumers, will consume less of it. Alcohol consumption contributes to highway accidents, and the number of highway fatalities among young adults is roughly proportional to the total beer consumption by young adults. Therefore, a tax that decreases beer consumption by 10% will decrease highway deaths among young adults by about 10%.

Make Personal and Managerial Decisions

We use economic analysis, on the personal level, to decide how to spend our time, what career to pursue, and how to spend and save the money we earn. As workers, we use economic analysis to decide how to produce goods and services, how much to produce, and how much to charge for them. Let's use some economic analysis to look at a practical question confronting someone considering starting a business.

If the existing music stores in your city are profitable and you have enough money to start your own music store, should you do it? If you enter this market, the competition between the stores for consumers will heat up, leading to lower prices for tapes and CDs. In addition, your costs may be higher than the costs of the stores that are already established. It will be sensible to enter the market only if you expect a small drop in price and a small difference in cost. Of course, there is the risk that the existing stores may try to protect their market shares by cutting prices and increasing their advertising. Indeed, entering what appears to be a lucrative market may turn out to be a financial disaster.

Evaluate Public Policies

Although modern societies use markets to make most of the decisions concerning production and consumption, the government has several important roles in a market-based society. We can use economic analysis to determine how well the government performs its roles in the market economy. We can also explore the trade-offs associated with various public policies. Let's look at a practical question about public policy.

Is it sensible for the government to pay part of the cost of your college education? Think about who benefits from your education. You get many benefits yourself, including higher lifetime income, more career options, and the thrill of learning. But other people also benefit from your education. In the modern workplace, teamwork is important, and the productivity of a team of workers depends in part on the education level of the team members. A college education is likely to make you a better team worker, allowing your fellow workers to be more productive and earn more income. In addition, your college education will make you a more intelligent citizen, which means that you'll

The standard of living has increased dramatically in the last several decades. We eat better food and live in better houses.

make better choices on election day. It is sensible for the government to help pay for your college education because taxpayers (your fellow workers and citizens) benefit from your education.

Preview of Coming Attractions: Macroeconomics

Macroeconomics is the study of the nation's economy as a whole. In macroeconomics we learn about important topics that are regularly discussed in newspapers and on television, including unemployment, inflation, the budget deficit, and the trade deficit. Macroeconomics explains why economies grow and change, and why economic growth is sometimes interrupted.

Macroeconomics: The study of the nation's economy as a whole.

In the 1930s, over 25% of the workers in the United States could not find jobs. Many banks were closed, thousands of factories were shut down, and the economy nearly ground to a halt. In terms of the production possibilities curve described earlier in the chapter, the U.S. economy was inside the production possibilities curve: Our resources were not fully employed, and we didn't produce as many goods and services as we could. Macroeconomics explains the forces that cause the economy to malfunction in this way and provides insights into how we might fix the economy to allow it to grow.

John Maynard Keynes (pronounced "Canes"), known as the father of "Keynesian" economics, was a renowned economist who taught at Cambridge University in England. During the dismal 1930s, Keynes wrote a book, *The General Theory of Employment, Interest, and Money.* Writing at a time of massive unemployment, Keynes emphasized the short-run benefits of government spending to stimulate the economy and put people back to work. Some examples of government spending that could decrease unemployment are building highways and hiring more public-school teachers.

Modern macroeconomics goes beyond dealing with short-term crises such as high unemployment and considers the issue of growth over the long term. Because of economic growth in the last several decades, people in the United States today enjoy a much higher living standard than that experienced by their grandparents. We drive better cars and live in houses with more amenities, and even many middle-class Americans travel routinely across the country and around the world. We can consume more of all goods and services because the economy has more of the resources needed to produce these goods and services, as indicated by an outward shift of the possibilities frontier. Macroeconomics explains why some of these resources increase over time and how an increase in these resources translates into a higher standard of living.

Macroeconomic issues are at the heart of many national political debates. Every candidate for president of the United States must convince voters that he or she understands the concepts of macroeconomics. Once elected, the prospects for reelection depend crucially on how well the economy performs during his or her term as president. If the public believes that the economy has performed well, the president is likely to be reelected. But if the public thinks that the economy has not performed well, they are unlikely to support the incumbent. In recent years, several presidents—including Jimmy Carter and George Bush—were not reelected because the economy performed poorly during their terms as president.

For a preview, let's think about three ways we can use macroeconomic analysis.

Understand How a National Economy Operates

One purpose of studying macroeconomics is to understand how the entire economy works. We can answer the following question with some macroeconomic analysis: Why do some countries grow much faster than others?

In the fastest-growing countries, citizens save a large fraction of the money they earn, and the workforce is well educated. Saving money provides funds that firms can use to purchase machines and equipment. An economy with a well-equipped workforce will grow faster than an economy whose workers are poorly equipped. A country with a well-educated workforce is able to quickly adopt new technologies that increase the productivity of its workforce.

Understand the Grand Debates over Economic Policy

Macroeconomics developed as a separate branch of economics during the 1930s, when the entire world suffered from massive unemployment. With a knowledge of macroeconomics, you can make sense of all sorts of policy debates, including the debate over the wisdom of policies designed to reduce the unemployment rate.

Should Congress and the President do something to reduce the unemployment rate? If unemployment is very high, the Congress and the President may want to reduce it. However, it is important not to reduce the unemployment rate too much, because as we'll see later in the book, a low unemployment rate will cause inflation. Moreover, unemployment can't be reduced overnight. Therefore, it is sensible to take action only if we believe that inaction will lead to persistent unemployment. In macroeconomics, we study the trade-offs associated with policies designed to combat unemployment and inflation.

Make Informed Business Decisions

A third reason for studying macroeconomics is to make informed business decisions. A manager who understands how the national economy operates will make better decisions involving interest rates, exchange rates, the inflation rate, and the unemployment rate. A manager who intends to borrow money for a new production facility could use her knowledge of macroeconomics to predict the effects of current public policies on interest rates and then decide whether to borrow the money now or later. Similarly, a manager must keep an eye on the inflation rate to help decide how much to charge for his firm's products and how much to pay workers. A manager who studies macroeconomics will be better equipped to understand the complexities of unemployment, interest rates, and inflation.

TEST Your Understanding

Summary

This chapter explains what economics is and why it is useful. Economics is about choices made by individuals, organizations, governments, and society as a whole. We can use economic analysis to understand how these choices affect the world around us. We can also use economics to make our own choices as consumers, workers, managers, and voters. Here are the main points of the chapter.

1. The production possibilities curve shows the combinations of goods and services available to an economy and illustrates the notion of scarcity: the production of one product comes at the expense of another. The curve will shift outward as a result of an increase in the economy's productive resources or an improvement in technology.

2. We use microeconomics to understand how markets work, predict changes in prices and quantities, make personal or managerial decisions, and evaluate the merits of public policies.

3. Macroeconomics explains how an economy works and helps us to understand the grand debates over economic policy.

4. To think like an economist, we (a) use assumptions to simplify what we are analyzing; (b) explore the relationship between the values of two variables, holding fixed the values of any other related variables; and (c) think in marginal terms.

5. Two assumptions are used extensively in economics: People act in their own self-interest, and people make informed choices.

Key Terms

ceteris paribus, 9
economics, 2
entrepreneurship, 3
factors of production, 2
human capital, 3
labor, 3

macroeconomics, 11
marginal change, 9
market, 5
microeconomics, 10
natural resources, 3
normative economics, 7

physical capital, 3
positive economics, 7
production possibilities curve, 3
scarcity, 2
variable, 9

Problems and Discussion Questions

1. For some goods and services, the assumption that people have enough information to make informed choices is unrealistic. Provide a brief list of some of these goods and services.

2. For some decisions, you act altruistically rather than acting in your own self-interest. Provide a brief list of such decisions.

3. "If I study one more hour for my economics exam, I expect my grade to increase by 3 points." List the variables that are implicitly assumed to be fixed in that statement.

4. It's your first day on your job in the advertising department of a baseball team. Your boss wants to know whether it is sensible to run one more television advertisement encouraging people to attend an upcoming game. List the relevant marginal questions.

5. Complete the statement: As we switch resources from the production of one good to another, we _____ the production possibilities curve; as we add resources to an economy, we _____ the curve.

6. **Web Exercise.** Visit the Web site for the CIA's World Fact Book *(http://www.odci.gov/cia/publications/factbook/)*. Pick a country and get some data about its factors of production (labor, human capital, natural resources).

7. **Web Exercise.** Visit the Web site of the IndUS Entrepreneurs, a nonprofit organization for entrepreneurs *(http://www.tie.org)*. Access the page describing the organization's programs *(http://www.tie.org/prog.html)*. What does this organization do and how might it be helpful for aspiring entrepreneurs?

Take It to the Net

We invite you to visit the O'Sullivan/Sheffrin page on the Prentice Hall Web site at: **http://www.prenhall.com/osullivan/** for additional World Wide Web exercises for this chapter.

Model Answers for Questions

Test Your Understanding

1. What goods and services do we produce? How do we produce the goods and services we select? Who consumes the goods and services we produce?

2. The production possibilities curve shows the combinations of goods that are available to the economy, so it helps us to answer the first question.

3. People act in their own self-interest; people make informed decisions.

4. "If I attend one more lecture, by how much will my exam grade increase?"

APPENDIX

Using Graphs and Formulas

In this appendix, we review the mechanics of graphing. You'll recognize most of the simple graphs and formulas in this appendix, because they were covered in your high-school mathematics. We'll review them here to prepare you to use them as you begin your own economic analysis.

Using Graphs to Show Relationships

A graph is a visual representation of the relationship between two variables. As we saw earlier in Chapter 1, a variable is a measure of something that can take on different values. For example, suppose that you have a part-time job and you are interested in the relationship between the number of hours you work and your weekly income. The relevant variables are the hours you work per week and your weekly income.

We can use a table of numbers such as Table 1A.1 to show the relationship between time worked and income. Let's assume that your weekly allowance from your parents is $20 and your part-time job pays $4 per hour. For example, if you work 10 hours per week, your weekly income is $60 ($20 from your parents and $40 from your job). The more you work, the higher your weekly income: If you work 22 hours, your weekly income is $108; if you work 30 hours, it is $140.

Table 1A.1 Relationship Between Hours of Work and Income

Hours worked per week	0	10	22	30
Income per week	$20	$60	$108	$140

Drawing a Graph

A graph makes it easier to see the relationship between time worked and income. To draw a graph, we perform seven simple steps.

1. Draw a horizontal line to represent the first variable. In Figure 1A.1 we measure time worked along the horizontal axis (also known as the x axis). As we move to the right along the horizontal axis, the number of hours worked increases, from zero to 30 hours. The numbers along the horizontal axis are spaced equally.

2. Draw a vertical line intersecting the first line to represent the second variable. In Figure 1A.1 we measure income along the vertical axis (also known as the y axis). As we move up along the vertical axis, income increases from zero to $140.

3. Pick a combination of time worked and income from the table of numbers. From the second column, for instance, time worked is 10 hours and income is $60.

4. Find the point on the horizontal axis with that number of hours worked—10 hours worked—and draw a dashed line vertically straight up from that point.

5. Find the point on the vertical axis with the income corresponding to those hours worked ($60) and draw a dashed line horizontally straight to the right from that point.

6. The intersection of the dashed lines shows the combination of those hours worked and the income for working those hours. Point b shows the combination of 10 hours worked and $60 income.

7. Repeat steps 3 through 6 for different combinations of work time and income from the table of numbers. Once you have a series of points on the graph (b, c, and d), you can connect them to draw a curve that shows the relationship between hours worked and income.

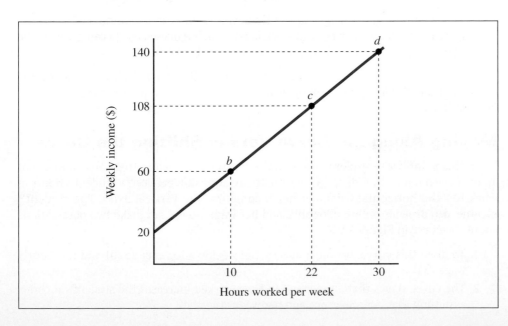

Figure 1A.1
Relationship Between Hours Worked and Total Income
There is a positive relationship between the amount of work time and income. The slope of the curve is $4: Each additional hour of work increases income by $4.

Positive relationship: A relationship in which an increase in the value of one variable increases the value of another variable.

There is a **positive relationship** between two variables if an increase in the value of one variable increases the value of the other variable. An increase in the time you work increases your income, so there is a positive relationship between the two variables. As you increase the time you work, you move upward along the curve shown in Figure 1A.1 to higher income levels.

Negative relationship: A relationship in which an increase in the value of one variable decreases the value of another variable.

There is a **negative relationship** between two variables if an increase in the value of one variable decreases the value of the other variable. For example, there is a negative relationship between the amount of time you work and your performance in school. Some people refer to a positive relationship as a direct relationship and to a negative relationship as an inverse relationship.

Computing the Slope

Slope of a curve: The change in the variable on the vertical axis resulting from a one-unit increase in the variable on the horizontal axis.

How sensitive is one variable to changes in the other variable? We can use the slope of the curve to measure this sensitivity. The **slope of a curve** is the change in the variable on the vertical axis resulting from a one-unit increase in the variable on the horizontal axis. Once we pick two points on a curve, we can compute the slope as follows:

$$\text{slope} = \frac{\text{vertical difference between two points}}{\text{horizontal difference between two points}}$$

To compute the slope of a curve, we take four steps:

1. Pick two points on the curve: for example, points b and c in Figure 1A.1.
2. Compute the vertical distance between the two points (also known as the rise). For points b and c, the vertical distance between the points is $48 ($108 − $60).
3. Compute the horizontal distance between the same two points (also known as the run). For points b and c, the horizontal distance between the points is 12 hours (22 hours − 10 hours).
4. Divide the vertical distance by the horizontal distance to get the slope. The slope between points b and c is $4 per hour:

$$\text{slope} = \frac{\text{vertical difference}}{\text{horizontal difference}} = \frac{48}{12} = 4$$

In this case, a 12-hour increase in time worked increases income by $48, so the increase in income per hour of work is $4, which makes sense because this is the hourly wage.

Because the curve is a straight line, the slope is the same at all points along the curve. You can check this yourself by using the values between points c and d to calculate the slope.

Moving Along the Curve Versus Shifting the Curve

Up to this point, we've explored the effect of change in variables that cause movement along a given curve. In Figure 1A.1 we see the relationship between a student's hours of work (on the horizontal axis) and her income (on the vertical axis). The student's income also depends on her allowance and her wage, so we can make two observations about the curve in Figure 1A.1.

1. To draw this curve, we must specify the weekly allowance ($20) and the hourly wage ($4).
2. The curve shows that an increase in time worked increases the student's income, assuming that her allowance and her wage are fixed.

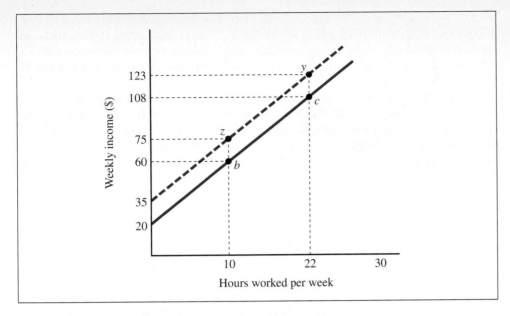

A change in the student's weekly allowance will shift the curve showing the relationship between time worked and income. In Figure 1A.2, when the allowance increases from $20 to $35, the curve shifts upward by $15. For a given time worked, the student's income increases by $15. Now the income associated with 10 hours of work and the higher allowance is $75 (point z), compared to $60 with 10 hours of work and the original allowance (point b). In general, an increase in the allowance shifts the curve upward and leftward: For a given amount of time worked, the student will have more income (an upward shift as a result of the increased allowance). To reach a given amount of income, the student needs fewer hours of work (a leftward shift).

This book uses dozens of two-dimensional curves, each of which shows the relationship between only two variables. That is all a single curve can show. A common error is to forget that a single curve tells only part of the story. In Figure 1A.2 we needed two curves to show what happened when we looked at three variables (work time, allowance, and income). Here are some simple rules that will help to avoid this error:

- A change in one of the variables shown on the graph causes movement along the curve. In Figure 1A.2 an increase in work time causes movement along the curve from point b to point c.

- A change in one of the variables that is not shown on the graph (one of the variables held fixed in drawing the curve) shifts the entire curve. In Figure 1A.2 an increase in the allowance causes the entire curve to shift upward.

Negative and Nonlinear Relationships

We can use a graph to show a negative relationship between two variables. Consider a consumer who has a monthly budget of $150 to spend on CDs (at a price of $10 per CD) and cassette tapes (at a price of $5 per tape). Table 1A.2 shows the relationship between

Table 1A.2   Relationship Between CDs and Tapes

Number of CDs purchased	0	5	10	15
Number of tapes purchased	30	20	10	0

the number of CDs purchased and the number of tapes purchased. If the consumer buys 5 CDs in a certain month, he will spend a total of $50 on CDs, leaving $100 to spend on tapes. With the $100 he can buy 20 tapes at a price of $5 per tape. As the number of CDs increases, the number of tapes decreases, from 20 tapes and 5 CDs, to 10 tapes and 10 CDs, to 0 tapes and 15 CDs.

Using the seven-step process outlined earlier, we can use the numbers in Table 1A.2 to draw a curve showing this negative relationship. In Figure 1A.3 the curve is negatively sloped: The more the consumer spends on CDs, the fewer tapes he can buy. We can use points e and f to compute the slope of the curve. The slope is −2 tapes per CD: A five-unit increase in CDs (the horizontal difference, or the run) decreases the number of tapes by 10 (the vertical difference, or the rise):

$$\text{slope} = \frac{\text{vertical difference}}{\text{horizontal difference}} = \frac{-10}{5} = -2$$

The curve is a straight line with a constant slope of −2 tapes per CD.

We can use a graph to show a nonlinear relationship between two variables. Panel A of Figure 1A.4 shows the relationship between study time and the exam grade that results from study time. Although the exam grade increases as study time increases, the grade increases at a decreasing rate; that means the increase in grade is smaller and smaller for each additional hour of study. For example, the second hour of study increases the grade by 4 points (from 6 points to 10 points), but the ninth hour of study increases the grade by only 1 point (from 24 points to 25 points). This is a nonlinear relationship: The slope of the curve changes as we move along the curve. In Figure 1A.4 the slope decreases as we move to the right along the curve: The slope is 4 between points g and h but only 1 between points i and j.

Another possibility for a nonlinear curve is that the slope increases (the curve becomes steeper) as we move to the right along the curve. This is shown in panel B of Figure 1A.4. The slope of the curve increases as the amount of grain increases, meaning that total production cost increases at an increasing rate. If the producer increases production from 1 ton to 2 tons, the total cost increases by $5 (from $10 to $15). On the upper portion of the curve, if the producer increases production from 10 to 11 tons, the total cost increases by $25 (from $100 to $125).

Figure 1A.3

A Negative Relationship Between CD Purchases and Tape Purchases

There is a negative relationship between the number of CDs purchased and the number of cassette tapes purchased. Because the price of CDs is $10 and the price of tapes is $5, the slope of the curve is −2 tapes per CD: Each additional CD decreases the number of tapes by 2.

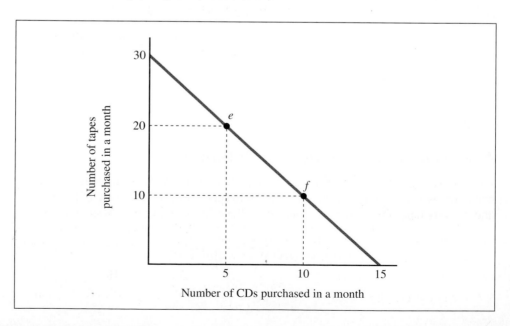

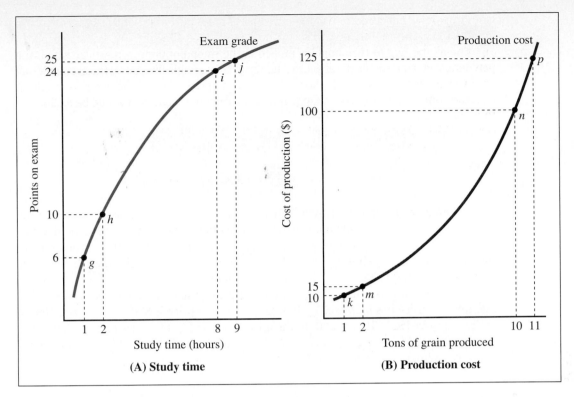

(A) Study time

(B) Production cost

Figure 1A.4

Nonlinear Relationships

(A) Study Time There is a positive and nonlinear relationship between study time and the grade on an exam. As study time increases, the exam grade increases at a decreasing rate. For example, the second hour of study increases the grade by 4 points (from 6 points to 10 points), but the ninth hour of study increases the grade by only 1 point (from 24 points to 25 points).

(B) Production Cost There is a positive and nonlinear relationship between the quantity of grain produced and total production cost. As the quantity increases, total cost increases at an increasing rate. For example, to increase production from 1 ton to 2 tons, production cost increases by $5 (from $10 to $15), but to increase production from 10 to 11 tons, total cost increases by $25 (from $100 to $125).

Using Formulas to Compute Values

Economists often use formulas to compute the values of the relevant variables. Here is a brief review of the mechanics of formulas.

Computing Percentage Changes

In many cases, the formulas that economists use involve percentage changes. In this book we use the simple approach to computing percentage changes: We divide the change in the variable by the initial value of the variable and then multiply by 100. For example, if the price of pizzas increases from $20 to $22, the percentage change is 10%: The change ($2) divided by the initial value ($20) is 0.10; multiplying this number by 100 generates a percentage change of 10%:

$$\text{percentage change} = \frac{\text{absolute change}}{\text{initial value}} = \frac{2}{20} = 0.10 = 10\%$$

Going in the other direction, if the price decreases from $20 to $19, the percentage change is −5%: The change (−$1) divided by the initial value ($20) is −0.05, or −5%.

The alternative to the simple approach is the midpoint approach, under which the percentage change equals the absolute change in the variable divided by the average value or the midpoint of the variable. For example, if the price of pizza increases from $20 to $22, the computed percentage change under the midpoint approach would be 9.52381%:

$$\text{percentage change} = \frac{\text{absolute change}}{\text{average value}} = \frac{2}{(20 + 22)/2}$$

$$= \frac{2}{21} = 0.0952381 = 9.52381\%$$

If the change in the variable is relatively small, the extra precision associated with the midpoint approach is usually not worth the extra effort. The simple approach allows us to spend less time doing tedious arithmetic and more time doing economic analysis. In this book we use the simple approach to compute percentage changes: If the price increases from $20 to $22, the price has increased by 10%.

If we know a percentage change, we can translate it into an absolute change. For example, if a price has increased by 10% and the initial price is $20, then we add 10% of the initial price ($2 is 10% of $20) to the initial price ($20), for a new price of $22. If the price decreases by 5%, we subtract 5% of the initial price ($1 is 5% of $20) from the initial price ($20), for a new price of $19.

Using Formulas to Compute Missing Values

It will often be useful to compute the value of the numerator (the top half of a fraction) of a particular formula. To do so, we must have values for the other two parts of the formula. For example, consider the relationship between time worked and income. Suppose the slope of the curve showing this relationship is $4 per hour. If you decide to work 7 more hours per week, how much more income will you earn? In this case we can compute the change in income by looking at the formula for the slope of the curve:

$$\text{slope} = \frac{\text{difference in income}}{\text{difference in work time}}$$

$$4 = \frac{\text{difference in income}}{7}$$

Because we know two of the three parts of the slope formula (the slope is $4 and the difference in work time is 7 hours), we can figure out the third part (the difference in income) by plugging in different numbers for the numerator until we find the value that satisfies the formula. In this case the answer is $28: Plugging $28 into the numerator, the difference in income is four times the difference in work time, which is consistent with a slope of $4.

There is a more direct approach to computing the value of the numerator or denominator of a formula. We can rearrange the three parts of the formula to put the missing variable on the left side. For example, to compute the difference in income resulting from a change in work time, we can rearrange the slope formula as follows:

$$\text{difference in income} = \text{slope} \times \text{difference in work time}$$

When we plug in the slope (4) and the difference in work time (7 hours), the change in income is $28 = $4 times 7 hours. We can use the same process to compute the value of the denominator, given values for the two other variables.

Key Terms

negative relationship, 16   **positive relationship**, 16   **slope of a curve**, 16

Exercises and Discussion Questions

1. Suppose you belong to a tennis club that has a monthly fee of $100 and a charge of $5 per hour for court time to play tennis.
   a. Use a curve to show the relationship between the monthly bill from the club and the hours of tennis played.
   b. What is the slope of the curve?
   c. If you increase your monthly tennis time by 3 hours, by how much will your monthly bill increase?

2. Suppose that to make pizza, Terry uses three ingredients: tomato sauce, dough, and cheese. Terry initially uses 100 gallons of tomato sauce per day, and the cost of other ingredients (dough, cheese) is $500 per day.
   a. Draw a curve to show the relationship between the price of tomato sauce and the daily cost of producing pizza (for prices between $1 and $5).
   b. To draw the curve, what variables are assumed to be fixed?
   c. What sort of changes would cause movement upward along the curve?
   d. What is the slope of the curve?
   e. What sort of changes would cause the entire curve to shift upward?

3. Compute the percentage changes for the following changes:

Initial Value	New Value	Percentage Change
10	11	_____
100	98	_____
50	53	_____

4. The price of jeans decreases by 15%. If the original price was $20, what is the new price?

5. Suppose the slope of a curve showing the relationship between the number of burglaries per month (on the vertical axis) and the number of police officers (on the horizontal axis) is −0.50 burglaries per police officer. Use the slope formula to compute the change in the number of burglaries resulting from hiring eight additional police officers.

6. Complete the statement: A change in one of the variables shown on a graph causes movement _____ a curve, while a change in one of the variables that is not shown on the graph _____ the curve.

Key Principles of Economics

Your student film society is looking for an auditorium to use for an all-day Hitchcock film program and is willing to pay up to $200 for one. Your college has a new auditorium that would be perfect for your event. According to the campus facility manager, "The daily rent on the auditorium is $450, an amount that includes $300 to help pay for the cost of building the auditorium, $50 to help pay for insurance, and $100 to cover the extra costs of electricity and janitorial services for a one-day event." How should you respond to the facility manager? As we'll see, if you could persuade the facility manager to use the marginal principle—one of the five key principles of economics—you could rent the facility for only $101.

Principle: A simple truth that most people understand and accept.

n this chapter, we introduce five key principles that provide a foundation for economic analysis. The dictionary defines a **principle** as a simple, self-evident truth that most people readily understand and accept. For example, most people readily accept the principle of gravity. The five principles of economics provide the underlying logic of economic analysis and also help explain the tools of economic analysis. As you go through the book, you will see these principles again and again as you do your own economic analysis. Here are some practical questions we answer in this chapter:

1. What is the cost of producing military goods such as bombs and warships?
2. When is it sensible to tighten the emissions standards on cars, reducing the allowable volume of pollution per mile driven?
3. As a firm hires more workers, what happens to the total output of its factory?
4. If a paper producer dumps chemical waste into a river, what is the true cost of paper?
5. Suppose your wage doubles and at the same time the prices of consumer goods double, too. Are you better off, worse off, or equally well off?

The Principle of Opportunity Cost

The principle of opportunity cost incorporates the notion that no matter what we do, there is always a trade-off. We must trade off one thing for another because resources are limited and can be used in different ways: By acquiring something, we use up resources that could have been used to acquire something else. The notion of opportunity cost allows us to measure this trade-off.

PRINCIPLE of Opportunity Cost

The opportunity cost of something is what you sacrifice to get it.

Opportunity cost: What you sacrifice to get something.

Most decisions involve several alternatives. For example, if you spend an hour studying for an economics exam, you have one less hour to pursue other activities. To determine the opportunity cost of something, we look at what you consider the best of these other activities. For example, suppose the alternatives to studying economics are studying for a history exam and playing a video game. If you consider studying for history a better use of your time than video play, then the opportunity cost of studying economics is what you sacrifice by not studying history. We ignore the video game because that is not the best alternative use of your time.

How can we measure the opportunity cost of an hour spent studying for an economics exam? Suppose an hour of studying history—instead of economics—would increase your grade on a history exam by 4 points. In this case the opportunity cost of an hour studying economics is 4 points lost on the history exam. If the best alternative to studying economics were playing video games, then the opportunity cost would be the pleasure you would get from an hour in the video arcade.

The principle of opportunity cost can be applied to decisions about how to spend a fixed money budget. For example, suppose that you have a fixed budget to spend on recorded music and CDs cost twice as much as audio tapes. If you buy a CD, you must sacrifice two tapes: The opportunity cost of one CD is two audio tapes. A hospital with a fixed salary budget can increase the number of doctors only at the expense of nurses or physician's assistants. If a doctor costs five times as much as a nurse, the opportunity cost of a doctor is five nurses.

In some cases, a good that appears to be free actually has a cost. That's why economists are fond of saying, "There's no such thing as a free lunch." Suppose someone offers to buy you lunch if you agree to listen to a sales pitch for a time-share condominium. Although you don't pay any money for the lunch, there is an opportunity cost because you could spend that time in another way. The lunch isn't free because you sacrifice an hour of your time to get it.

Opportunity Cost and Production Possibilities

The production possibilities curve illustrates the principle of opportunity cost for an entire economy. As you saw in Chapter 1, this curve shows all the possible combinations of goods and services available to an economy, assuming that all its productive resources are fully employed. The principle of opportunity cost explains why the production possibilities curve is negatively sloped. At a given time an economy has fixed amounts of productive resources, so the production of one product comes at the expense of another product.

To illustrate the notions of opportunity cost and production possibilities, consider the trade-offs associated with allocating electricity between competing uses. The Pacific Northwest gets about three-fourths of its electric power from hydroelectric dams, and is therefore heavily dependent on rain and snow to fill the rivers to generate power for homes, offices, factories, and farms.

Figure 2.1 shows a production possibilities curve for the production of aluminum and wheat. In drawing this production possibilities curve, one of the resources held fixed is the amount of electric power. The production of aluminum requires enormous amounts of power for the smelting process, and wheat farming in the Pacific Northwest requires irrigation, with water pumps powered by electricity. Given a fixed amount of

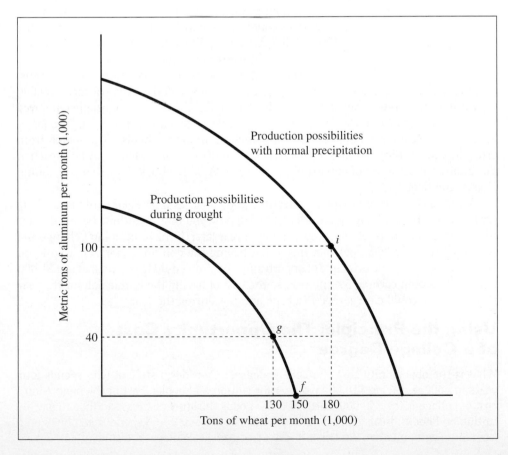

Figure 2.1

Electricity and the Production Possibilities Curve
A drought decreases the amount of electric power available for aluminum smelting and irrigation, shifting the production possibilities curve inward. The region's economy moved from point *i* to point *f*, with aluminum production dropping to zero.

power—and fixed amounts of the other factors of production—there is a trade-off between producing aluminum and wheat. Suppose the region initially chooses point *i*, with 100,000 metric tons of aluminum and 180,000 tons of wheat.

A prolonged drought in 2000–2001 reduced the flow of water through the region's hydroelectric turbines, reducing the amount of power by about 3,000 megawatts.[1] As shown in Figure 2.1, the drought shifted the production possibilities curve inward, forcing the region to make some difficult choices between aluminum and wheat production. In response to the decrease in hydroelectric power, Bonneville Power Administration (BPA) paid aluminum manufacturers to shut down the region's 10 smelters, so the quantity of aluminum produced dropped to zero. BPA also paid farmers $330 for each acre of land they did not irrigate. Farmers took 90,000 acres out of wheat production, reducing the quantity of wheat produced. In Figure 2.1, the BPA programs moved the region from point *i* on the production possibilities curve to point *f*, with zero aluminum and 150,000 tons of wheat.

In this case, the region chose to shut down the aluminum industry, but there were other options. The region could have allocated some of its electric power to aluminum smelting, but given the fixed quantity of hydroelectric power, such a decision would have required a larger reduction in wheat production. In Figure 2.1, the region could have chosen point *g*, with some aluminum production but less wheat.

Using the Principle: Military Spending, Collectibles

We can use the principle of opportunity cost to explore the cost of military spending. Malaysia bought two warships in 1992, paying a price equal to the cost of providing safe drinking water for the 5 million Malaysians who lacked it.[2] In other words, the opportunity cost of the warships was safe drinking water for 5 million people. In the United States, the opportunity cost of warships could be spending on housing programs for the homeless. When the Soviet Union fell apart and military tensions around the world diminished, citizens in the United States and Western Europe called for massive cuts in defense spending, with the idea of spending the "peace dividend" on social programs. The French cut their annual defense budget by billions of dollars and withdrew 50,000 troops stationed on German soil.[3] In the United States, the number of people employed by the military has decreased, and the Pentagon developed a new program, "Troops to Teachers" to help former soldiers get jobs teaching in local schools.[4] The switch from army duty to teaching reminds us that the opportunity cost of a soldier may be a teacher. For another illustration of opportunity cost, read "A Closer Look: Plowshares, Pruning Hooks, and Ecotels?"

What is the cost of buying a collectible good such as a baseball card, an antique Barbie doll, a Beanie Baby, or a work of art? Suppose you buy an antique Barbie doll for $1,000, intending to resell it for more money a year later. If the price doesn't change and you resell it for $1,000, does that mean that having the doll for a year didn't cost you anything? Applying the principle of opportunity cost, you could have invested the $1,000 in a bank account earning 5% interest, so the cost of having the Barbie doll for the year is the $50 you could have earned in a bank account during the year.

Using the Principle: The Opportunity Cost of a College Degree

What is the opportunity cost of a college degree? Consider a student who spends four years in college, paying $10,000 per year for tuition and books. Part of the opportunity cost of college is the $40,000 worth of other goods the student must sacrifice to pay for tuition and books. Instead of going to college, the student could spend this money on a car, stereo equipment, or ski trips. If instead of going to college, the student could have

worked as a bank clerk for $20,000 per year, the other part of the opportunity cost of college is $80,000 that could have been earned during the four years. That makes the total opportunity cost of the student's college degree $120,000:

Tuition and books (4 years at $10,000 per year)	$ 40,000
Opportunity cost of college time (4 years at $20,000 per year)	80,000
Total opportunity cost	$120,000

We haven't included the costs of food or housing in our computations of opportunity cost. That's because a student must eat and live somewhere even if he or she doesn't go to college. But if housing and food are more expensive in college, then we would include the *extra costs* of housing and food in our calculations of opportunity cost.

There are other things to consider in a person's decision to attend college. As we'll see later, a college degree can increase a person's earning power, so there are benefits from a college degree. In addition, there is the thrill of learning and the pleasure of meeting new people. To make an informed decision about whether to attend college, we must compare the benefits to the opportunity costs.

The Marginal Principle

The marginal principle provides a simple decision-making rule that helps individuals, firms, and governments make decisions. Economists think in marginal terms, considering how a one-unit change in one variable affects the value of another variable. When we say marginal, we're considering a small change or an incremental change.

Marginal **PRINCIPLE**

Increase the level of an activity if its marginal benefit exceeds its marginal cost; reduce the level of an activity if its marginal cost exceeds its marginal benefit. If possible, pick the level at which the activity's marginal benefit equals its marginal cost.

The marginal principle enables us to fine-tune our decisions. We can use the principle to determine whether a one-unit increase in a variable would make us better off. For example, a barber could decide whether to keep his or her shop open for one more hour. You could decide whether to study one more hour for a psychology midterm.

The marginal principle is based on a comparison of the marginal benefits and marginal costs of a particular activity. The **marginal benefit** of some activity is the extra benefit resulting from a small increase in the activity, for example, the extra revenue generated by keeping a barbershop open for one more hour. Similarly, the **marginal cost** is the additional cost resulting from a small increase in the activity, for example, the additional costs incurred by keeping a shop open for one more hour. According to the marginal principle, you should continue to increase the activity as long as the marginal benefit is greater than the marginal cost. When you've reached the level where the marginal benefit equals the marginal cost, your fine-tuning is done. It's worth emphasizing that the marginal principle is based on marginal benefits and costs, not total benefits and total costs.

> **Marginal benefit:** The extra benefit resulting from a small increase in some activity.
>
> **Marginal cost:** The additional cost resulting from a small increase in some activity.

Example: Pedaling for Television Time

To illustrate the marginal principle, consider an experiment conducted by researchers at St. Luke's Roosevelt Hospital in New York City.[6] The researchers addressed the following question, "If a child must pedal a stationary bicycle to run a television set, will he watch less TV, and if so, how much less?"

The researchers randomly assigned sedentary children, age 8 to 12, to two types of TVs. The first had a stationary bicycle in front of the TV, but the TV operated independently of the bicycle: No pedaling was required to operate the TV. In contrast, the second type of TV worked only if the child pedaled a bike facing the TV. The kids in the control group (no pedaling required) watched an average of 20 hours of TV per week, while the kids in the treatment group (pedaling required) watched just a few hours per week.

We can use the marginal principle to explain the results of the experiment. Figure 2.2 shows the marginal benefit of TV time for the control group. The marginal-benefit curve is negatively sloped, reflecting the idea that each hour of TV is worth less than the previous hour: The first hour of TV time is worth more than the second hour; the second hour is worth more than the third; and so on. Specifically, the first hour generates a benefit of $1.30 (shown by point *b*), while the second hour generates a benefit of $1.20 (point *m*). The marginal benefit decreases by $0.05 for each additional hour, reaching $0.35 for 20 hours of TV time (point *n*).

To determine the marginal cost of TV time, we can use the notion of opportunity cost. Suppose that for the typical kid, the value of the next-best alternative use of time is $0.35 per hour. This could be the value of an hour spent playing with friends, reading, studying, or playing videogames. In Figure 2.2, the marginal cost of TV time is constant at $0.35 per hour. Using the marginal principle, we would predict that the typical kid in the control group (no pedaling) would choose point *n*, watching 20 hours of TV per week. It is not sensible to watch the twenty-first hour because the extra benefit exceeds the opportunity cost.

In Figure 2.2, the marginal cost of TV time is higher for the treatment group because pedaling requires effort. To compute the marginal cost of TV for the treatment

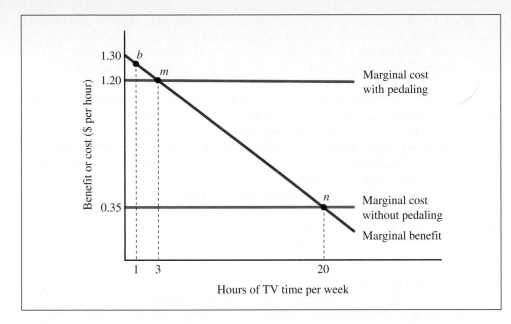

Figure 2.2
The Marginal Principle and TV Time
If the opportunity cost of TV time is $0.35 per hour and pedaling is not required for TV time, the marginal principle is satisfied at point *n*, and the child will watch 20 hours of TV per week. If pedaling is required and the discomfort of pedaling is $0.85 per hour, the marginal cost of TV time is $1.20 (equal to $0.35 + $0.85), and the marginal principle is satisfied at point *m*, with only 3 hours of TV time per week.

group, we must add the discomfort of pedaling to the opportunity cost of TV time. In Figure 2.2, we assume that the discomfort is measured as $0.85 per hour of pedaling, so the marginal-cost curve is horizontal at $1.20 (equal to $0.35 + $0.85). The marginal principle is satisfied at point *m*, with only 3 hours of TV time. For a pedaling kid, the first hour of TV has a benefit of $1.30 and a cost of $1.20, so it is worthwhile. Similarly, the benefit of the second hour of TV exceeds the marginal cost. For the third hour, the marginal benefit equals the marginal cost, so the marginal principle is satisfied with 3 hours. For the fourth hour of TV time, the marginal benefit is only $1.15, which is less than the marginal cost. Therefore, it would not be sensible to pedal for the fourth hour of TV time.

Using the Marginal Principle: Renting College Facilities, Emissions Standards

Recall the chapter opener about renting a college auditorium to a student film society. If the student group offers to pay $200, should the college accept the offer? The college could use the marginal principle to make the decision.

To decide whether to accept the group's offer, the college should determine the marginal cost of renting out the auditorium. The marginal cost equals the extra costs the college incurs by allowing the student group to use an otherwise vacant auditorium. In our example, the extra cost is $100 for extra electricity and janitorial service. It would be sensible for the college to rent the auditorium because the marginal benefit ($200 from the student group) exceeds the marginal cost ($100). In fact, the college should be willing to rent the facility for any amount greater than $100.

Most colleges do not use this sort of logic. Instead, they use complex formulas to compute the perceived cost of renting out a facility. In most cases, the perceived cost includes some costs that are unaffected by renting out the facility for the day. In our example, the facility manager included $300 worth of construction cost and $50 worth of insurance cost as part of the cost of the auditorium, computing a cost of $450 instead of $100. Because many colleges include costs that aren't affected by the use of a facility, they overestimate the actual cost of renting out their facilities, missing opportunities to serve student groups and make some money at the same time.

We can use the marginal principle to analyze emissions standards for automobiles. The government specifies how much of each pollutant a new car is allowed to emit. For example, the rules specify the maximum volume of carbon monoxide to be emitted per mile of travel. The marginal question is, Should the standard be stricter, with fewer units of carbon monoxide allowed? On the benefit side, a stricter standard reduces the health costs resulting from pollution: If the air is cleaner, people whose respiratory ailments are worsened by air pollution will have fewer visits to doctors and hospitals, lower medication costs, and will lose fewer work days. On the cost side, a stricter standard requires more expensive control equipment on the cars and may also reduce fuel efficiency. Using the marginal principle, the government would make the emissions standard stricter as long as the marginal benefit (savings in health costs) exceeds the marginal cost (the cost of additional equipment and extra fuel).

The marginal principle can be used to think about all sorts of decisions involving how much of an activity to undertake. For an example of decisions involving food and exercise, read "A Closer Look: Why Are We Getting Bigger?"

TEST Your Understanding

1. The cost of a master's degree in engineering equals the tuition plus the cost of books. True or false? Explain.

2. Suppose a nation picks 1,000 young adults at random to serve in the army. What information do you need to determine the cost of using these people in the army?

3. Explain the logic behind the economist's quip, "There is no such thing as a free lunch."

4. If a bus company adds a third daily bus between two cities, the company's total costs will increase from $500 to $600 per day and its total revenue will increase by $150 per day. Should the company add the third bus?

5. Suppose you can save $50 by purchasing your new car in a different city. If the trip requires only $10 in gasoline, is the trip worthwhile?

The Principle of Diminishing Returns

Principle of diminishing returns: As one input increases while the other inputs are held fixed, output increases but at a decreasing rate.

Xena has a small copy shop, with one copying machine and one worker. When the backlog of orders piled up, she decided to hire a second worker, expecting that doubling her workforce would double the output of her copy shop, from 500 pages per hour to 1000. She was surprised when output increased to only 800 pages per hour. If she had known about the **principle of diminishing returns**, she would not have been surprised.

PRINCIPLE of Diminishing Returns

Suppose output is produced with two or more inputs and we increase one input while holding the other input or inputs fixed. Beyond some point—called the point of diminishing returns—output will increase at a decreasing rate.

Xena added a worker (one input) while holding the number of copying machines (the other input) fixed. Because the two workers shared a single copying machine, each worker spent some time waiting for the machine to be available. As a result, although adding the second worker increased the output of the copy shop, output did not double. With a single worker and a single copy machine, Xena has reached the point of dimin-

In the last few decades, the percentage of Americans who are at least 20 pounds overweight has increased steadily, reaching about one-third of the population. In fact, obesity is increasing around the world.[7] We can use the marginal principle to explain the worldwide increase in obesity.

A person gains weight when his or her calorie intake from food exceeds his or her calorie expenditure from physical activity. Over the last hundred years, innovations in agriculture and food processing have reduced the price of food, decreasing the marginal cost of consuming calories. A decrease in the marginal cost of consuming calories will increase food consumption, increasing obesity. Although cheaper food is a factor behind the increase in obesity, the increase in consumption has been relatively small, too small to explain the huge increase in obesity.

What about the expenditure side of the calorie equation? Another factor in the increase in obesity is a widespread decrease in physical activity.[8] Several decades ago, most workers had physically demanding jobs (for example, in factories and farms) and were paid to burn calories: The harder they worked, the more money they earned. In other words, one of the benefits of burning calories was higher income. In recent decades, workers have switched from physically demanding jobs to sedentary jobs in offices. The income from a sedentary job is not related to the worker's physical effort, so one of the benefits of burning calories has disappeared. A decrease in the marginal benefit of burning calories will decrease the number of calories burned, increasing obesity.

What about recreational exercise such as snowboarding, biking, tennis, and basketball? Although we can use recreational exercise to burn those calories that used to be burned on the job, recreational exercise has a cost. In addition to the cost of equipment and club membership, there is the opportunity cost of time spent exercising rather than working, studying, or engaging in other leisure activities.

It appears that changes on the expenditure side of the calorie equation are responsible for the bulk of the recent increase in obesity. Calorie burning has been transformed from a beneficial activity (working harder led to a higher income) into a costly activity (it takes time and money to burn calories off the job). This has naturally led to a decrease in calorie expenditure and increases in obesity.

ishing returns: As she increases the number of workers, output increases but at a decreasing rate. The first worker increases output by 500 pages (from zero to 500), but the second worker increases output by only 300 pages (from 500 to 800).

This principle of diminishing returns is relevant when we try to produce more output in an existing production facility (a factory, a store, an office, or a farm) by increasing the number of workers sharing the facility. When we add a worker to the facility, each worker becomes less productive because he or she works with a smaller piece of the facility: There are more workers to share the machinery, equipment, and factory space.

Table 2.1 Diminishing Returns for Pizza

Number of workers	Total product: pizzas produced	Marginal product
1	12	12
2	18	6
3	21	3
4	22	1

As we pack more and more workers into the factory, total output increases, but at a decreasing rate.

Table 2.1 shows fictitious but convenient data for representing the production of pizza at a particular facility. The production facility is the pizzeria premises, the pizza oven, and all the machines and equipment used to produce pizza. If the pizzeria has a single worker, the single worker assembles 12 uncooked pizzas per hour and pops them into the oven as soon as they are assembled. Suppose he is joined by a second worker, who could also assemble 12 pizzas per hour. Because this second worker shares the pizza oven with the first worker, he will occasionally have to wait before he can pop his assembled pizzas into the oven. Similarly, once the second worker's pizzas are in the oven, the first worker will have to wait to get another batch of his assembled pizzas into that oven. Therefore, we wouldn't expect output to double just because the number of workers has doubled. If total output is only 18 pizzas, adding workers increases output, but at a decreasing rate: Hiring the first worker increased output by 12 pizzas (from zero to 12); hiring the second increased output by only 6 pizzas.

Total product curve: A curve showing the relationship between the quantity of labor and the quantity of output.

Figure 2.3 shows the pizzeria's **total product curve**, which shows how many pizzas are produced with different quantities of labor. As the pizzeria adds workers, total product increases but at a decreasing rate. Hiring a second worker increases output by 6 pizzas, while hiring a third worker increases output by only 3 pizzas, and hiring a fourth worker increases output by only 1 pizza. It's possible that hiring a fifth worker would not increase output at all or may even reduce output because the workers will get into each others' way.

Figure 2.3

Total Product Curve and Diminishing Returns

As the number of workers increases, the number of pizzas produced per hour increases but at a decreasing rate. The second worker increases output by 6 pizzas (from 12 pizzas to 18 pizzas), but the fourth worker increases output by only 1 pizza (from 21 pizzas to 22 pizzas). Diminishing returns occur because workers share a pizza oven.

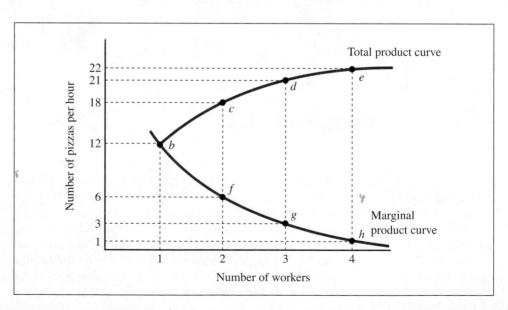

The **marginal product of labor** is defined as the change in output from one additional worker. As shown in the third column in Table 2.1 and Figure 2.3, the marginal product of the first pizza worker is 12 pizzas, and the marginal product of the second worker is 6 pizzas. In a three-worker pizzeria even more time would be spent waiting for an empty oven, and the marginal product of the third worker is only 3 pizzas. When there are diminishing returns, the marginal product of labor decreases as the number of workers increases.

Marginal product of labor: The change in output from one additional worker.

Diminishing Returns in the Short Run

Later in the book, we use the principle of diminishing returns to explore the decisions made by a firm in the short run. The **short run** is a period of time over which one or more factors of production is fixed. In most cases, the short run is defined as a period of time over which a firm cannot modify an existing facility or build a new one. The length of the short run varies across industries, depending on how long it takes to build a production facility. The short run for a hot-dog stand lasts just a few days: That's how long it takes to get another hot-dog cart. In contrast, if it takes a year to build a computer factory, the short run for a computer manufacturer is one year. Diminishing returns occur in the short run because adding workers to an existing facility means that each worker gets a smaller piece of the facility, and each becomes less productive.

Short run: A period of time over which one or more factors of production is fixed; in most cases, a period of time over which a firm cannot modify an existing facility or build a new one.

What About the Long Run?

The principle of diminishing returns is not relevant in the long run. The **long run** is defined as a period of time long enough for a firm to change all its factors of production, meaning that it can modify its existing facility or build a new one. To increase output in the long run, a firm can build an additional production facility and hire workers for the new facility. In the long run, the firm will not suffer from diminishing returns because workers won't have to share a production facility with more and more workers. For example, if the firm builds a second factory that is identical to the first and hires the same number of workers, the firm's output will double. Because firms can duplicate or replicate their production facilities in the long run, the principle of diminishing returns is irrelevant for long-run decisions.

Long run: A period of time long enough that a firm can change all the factors of production, meaning that a firm can modify its existing production facility or build a new one.

The Spillover Principle

In Chapter 1, we discussed the role of markets in determining what goods are produced, how they are produced, and who gets what is produced. The metaphor of the invisible hand suggests that the decisions of millions of consumers and producers, each acting in his or her own self-interest, will frequently promote the interests of society as a whole. Let's consider some circumstances under which we cannot rely on individuals to make choices that are socially desirable.

The **spillover** principle suggests that the costs or benefits of some decisions "spill over" onto people who are not involved in making those decisions. A spillover occurs when people who are external to a decision are affected by the decision. Another word for spillover is *externality*.

Spillover: A cost or benefit experienced by people who are external to the decision about how much of a good to produce or consume.

Spillover **PRINCIPLE**

> **For some goods the costs or benefits associated with producing or consuming those goods are not confined to the person or organization producing or consuming them.**

Let's examine spillover costs first and then turn to spillover benefits. Consider a paper mill that dumps chemical waste into a river, and these wastes make the water unhealthy for drinking. The manager of the paper firm decides how much paper to produce, but some of the costs of producing paper are incurred by people who live in a city downstream from the mill. For example, the city might spend extra money to clean the water before its citizens can safely drink the water. Suppose for each ton of paper produced, the city's water-treatment costs increase by $10. In this case, the spillover cost of paper is $10 per ton. In deciding how much paper to produce, the paper firm will consider the cost of the inputs it buys—for example, it may pay $30 per ton for labor and raw materials—but won't consider the $10 spillover cost incurred by people downstream.

Here are some other examples of spillover costs:

- When Freon leaks from a car air conditioner, it is released into the atmosphere, where it depletes the protective ozone layer and increases the number of cases of skin cancer. A person deciding whether to repair a leaky air conditioner might not consider the effects of releasing freon on the number of cancer cases.

- Your neighbor throws a loud party while you are trying to study. In deciding whether to have the party, the neighbor doesn't consider the consequences for your exam grade.

- Secondhand smoke from cigarettes is bothersome and causes health problems for people who breathe it in.

In each example, the decision-maker incurs some—but not all—of the costs associated with the decision. As we'll see later in the book, the challenge for policymakers is to ensure that everyone who bears the costs of a decision is involved in the decision-making process.

Some goods generate spillover benefits instead of spillover costs. Suppose a farmer is thinking about building a dike or small flood-control dam on a river, at a cost of $100,000. If the farmer's benefit from the dike is only $40,000, he or she won't build it. If three other farmers would experience the same benefit, the total benefit would be $160,000, and it would be sensible for them to get together and build the dike. To make the right decision, we must get all the potential beneficiaries to participate in the decision-making process. If each of the four farmers contributed $25,000 to a dike-building fund, the dike could be built.

There are many goods that generate spillover benefits. Here are some examples:

- If a person contributes money to public television, everyone who watches public television benefits from that contribution. A person deciding whether to contribute doesn't necessarily consider the benefits experienced by others.

- If a scientist discovers a new way to treat a common disease, everyone suffering from the disease will benefit. In deciding what problem to work on, the scientist doesn't necessarily consider the benefits experienced by society as a whole.

- If you get a college degree, you may become a better team worker, so your fellow workers will be more productive and earn more income. In your decision to complete college, you probably didn't consider the benefits to be experienced by your fellow workers.

- If you buy a fire extinguisher, it is less likely that a fire that starts in your apartment will spread to other apartments. In deciding whether to buy an extinguisher, you probably don't consider the benefits to your neighbors.

In each case, some of the benefits spill over onto people who are not involved in the decision-making process, so a decision-maker might decide against taking an action

There are spillover benefits from scientific research. In considering what problems to work on, scientists don't necessarily consider the spillover benefits from their research.

that would be beneficial to society. For example, scientists might not spend their time on a project that could reduce disease. Your high-school friends might decide to forgo college because the cost they incur exceeds the benefits they will experience.

If people do not face the full costs and benefits of their actions—including the spillover costs and spillover benefits—we cannot rely on unregulated markets to make decisions that are in the general interests of society. But there are ways for the government to intervene in markets to ensure that decision-makers bear the full costs or experience the full benefits of their actions. Later in the book, we'll discuss some of the ways in which government can solve spillover problems.

TEST Your Understanding

6. When a table producer hired its twentieth worker, the output of its factory increased by five tables per month. If the firm hires two more workers—a twenty-first and a twenty-second worker—would you expect output to increase by ten tables per month?

7. According to the principle of diminishing returns, an additional worker decreases total output. True or False? Explain.

8. For each of the following examples, is there a spillover benefit or a spillover cost?

- Your roommate plays loud, obnoxious music.
- Strip mining causes oil and gas to enter the underground water system, making smoking in your bathtub hazardous to your health.
- A person in a residential neighborhood collects and restores old cars on his front lawn.
- A family contributes $5,000 to an organization that provides holiday meals to the poor.
- A landowner preserves a large stand of ancient trees and thus provides a habitat for the spotted owl (an endangered species).

The Reality Principle

One of the key ideas in economics is that people are interested not just in the amount of money they have, but also in how much their money will buy.

Reality **PRINCIPLE**

What matters to people is the real value of money or income—its purchasing power—not the face value of money or income.

To illustrate this principle, suppose you work in the college bookstore to earn extra money to pay for movies and newspapers. If your take-home pay is $10 per hour, is this a high wage or a low wage? The answer depends on the prices of the goods you buy. If a movie costs $4 and a newspaper costs $1, with one hour of work you could afford to see two movies and buy two papers. The wage may seem high enough for you. But if a movie costs $8 and a newspaper costs $2, an hour of work would buy only one movie and one paper, and the same $10 wage doesn't seem so high. This is the reality principle in action: What matters is not how many dollars you earn but what those dollars will purchase.

The reality principle can explain how people choose the amount of money to carry around with them. Suppose you typically withdraw $40 per week from an ATM to cover your normal expenses. If the prices of all the goods you purchase during the week double, you would have to withdraw $80 per week to make the same purchases. The amount of money people carry around depends on the prices of the goods and services they buy.

Economists use special terms to express the ideas behind the reality principle:

Nominal value: The face value of an amount of money.

Real value: The value of an amount of money in terms of the quantity of goods the money can buy.

- The **nominal value** of an amount of money is simply its face value. For example, the nominal wage paid by the bookstore is $10 per hour.

- The **real value** of an amount of money is measured in terms of the quantity of goods the money can buy. For example, the real value of your bookstore wage would fall as the prices of movies and newspapers increase even though your nominal wage stayed the same.

Using the Reality Principle: Government Programs and Statistics

Government officials use the reality principle when they design public programs. For example, Social Security payments are increased each year to ensure that the checks received by the elderly and other recipients will purchase the same amount of goods and services even if prices have increased.

The government also uses the reality principle when it publishes statistics about the economy. For example, when the government issues reports about changes in "real wages" in the economy over time, these statistics take into account the prices of the goods purchased by workers. Therefore the real wage is stated in terms of its buying power, rather than its face value or nominal value.

TEST Your Understanding

9. Average hourly earnings in the United States increased between 1970 and 1993, but real wages fell. How could this occur?

10. Suppose your wage doubles and so do the prices of all consumer goods. Are you better off, worse off, or just as well off?

11. Suppose your bank pays you 4% per year on your savings account: Each $100 in the bank grows to $104 over a one-year period. If prices increase by 3% per year, how much do you really gain by keeping $100 in the bank for a year?

Using the TOOLS

We've explained the five key principles of economics, which provide the foundation of economic analysis. Here are some opportunities to use the principles to do your own economic analysis.

1. ECONOMIC EXPERIMENT: Producing Foldits

Here is a simple economic experiment that takes about 15 minutes to run. The instructor places a stapler and a stack of paper on a table. Students produce "foldits" by folding a page of paper in thirds and stapling both ends of the folded page. There is an inspector who checks each foldit to be sure that it is produced correctly. The experiment starts with a single worker, who has one minute to produce as many foldits as possible. After the instructor records the number of foldits produced, the process is repeated with two students, three students, four students, and so on. The question is, "How does the number of foldits produced change as the number of workers increases?"

APPLICATIONS
2. What's the Cost?

Consider the following statements about costs. Are they correct? If not, provide a correct statement about the relevant cost.

- One year ago, I loaned $100 to a friend, and she just paid me back the whole $100. The loan didn't cost me anything.
- Our sawmill bought five truckloads of logs a year ago for $20,000. Today we'll use the logs to make picnic tables. The cost of using the logs is $20,000.
- Our new football stadium was built on land that a wealthy alum donated to our university. The university didn't have to buy the land, so the cost of the stadium equals the amount the university pays to the construction company that builds the stadium.

3. How Much RAM?

You are about to buy a personal computer and must decide how much random-access memory (RAM) to have in the computer. Suppose each 32-megabyte block of RAM costs $40. For example, a computer with two blocks of memory (64 MB) costs $40 more than a computer with one block (32 MB). The marginal benefit of memory is $320 for the first block and decreases by half for each additional block, to $160 for the second block, $80 for the third block, and so on. How many blocks of memory should you get in your computer? Illustrate your answer with a graph.

 **Summary**

This chapter covers five key principles of economics, defined as simple, self-evident truths that most people would readily accept. If you understand these principles, you are ready for the rest of the book, which will show you how to do your own economic analysis. In fact, if you've done the exercises in this chapter, you're already doing economic analysis.

1. **Principle of opportunity cost.** The opportunity cost of something is what you sacrifice to get it.

2. **Marginal principle.** Increase the level of an activity if its marginal benefit exceeds its marginal cost: reduce the level if its marginal cost exceeds its marginal benefit. If possible, pick the level at which the marginal benefit equals the marginal cost.

3. **Principle of diminishing returns.** Suppose that output is produced with two or more inputs and that we increase one input while holding the other inputs fixed. Beyond some point—called the point of diminishing returns—output will increase at a decreasing rate.

4. **Spillover principle.** For some goods, the costs or benefits associated with the good are not confined to the person or organization that decides how much of the good to produce or consume.

5. **Reality principle.** What matters to people is the real value of money or income—its purchasing power—not the face value of money or income.

Key Terms

long run, 33	**nominal value**, 36	**real value**, 36
marginal benefit, 28	**opportunity cost**, 24	**short run**, 33
marginal cost, 28	**principle**, 24	**spillover**, 33
marginal product of labor, 33	**principle of diminishing returns**, 30	**total product curve**, 32

Problems and Discussion Questions

1. Suppose another year of college will increase your lifetime earnings by $30,000. The costs of tuition and books add up to only $8,000 for an additional year. Comment on the following statement: "Because the benefit of $30,000 exceeds the $8,000 cost, you should complete another year of college."

2. To celebrate its fiftieth anniversary, a gasoline station sells gasoline at the price it charged on its first day of operation: $0.10 per gallon. As you drive by the gasoline station, you notice a long line of people waiting to buy gasoline. What types of people would you expect to join the line?

3. You are the mayor of a large city, and you must decide how many police officers to hire. Explain how you could use the marginal principle to help make the decision.

4. Consider a city that must decide how many mobile cardiac arrest units (specially equipped ambulances designed to treat people immediately after a heart attack) to deploy. Explain how you could use the marginal principle to help make the decision.

5. Explain why the principle of diminishing returns does not occur in the long run.

6. You are the manager of a firm that makes computers. If you had to decide how much output to produce in the next week, would you use the principle of diminishing returns? If you had to decide how much output to produce ten years from now, would you use the principle of diminishing returns?

7. Your coffee shop has a single espresso machine. As the firm adds more and more workers, would you expect output (espressos per hour) to increase at a constant rate? Why or why not?

8. Use the spillover principle to discuss the following examples. Are there spillover costs or spillover benefits?

   • Logging causes soil erosion and stream degradation, harming fish.

   • An environmental group buys 50 acres of wetlands to provide a habitat for migrating birds.

   • Your office mate smokes cigarettes.

   • A person buys a dilapidated house in your neighborhood and fixes it up.

9. Explain this statement: The salaries of baseball players have increased in both real and nominal terms.

10. **Web Exercise.** Visit the Web site of the U.S. Environmental Protection Agency, accessing the page with answers to frequently asked questions [*http://www.epa.gov/history/faqs/index.htm*]. What is the EPA's mission, what are its goals, and how does it try to achieve these goals? Why do we need an organization like the EPA?

11. **Web Exercise.** The price of a gallon of gasoline was $0.42 in 1973 and had risen to $1.33 by 1999. How does the change in the price of gasoline compare to the cost of other goods? To answer, go to the

Web site of the Bureau of Labor Statistics [*http://www.bls.gov/cpi/*] and get information on the consumer price index (CPI). The CPI measures the cost of a standard market basket of goods in different years. The value of the CPI is 100 in the base year, and as prices increase, the value of the CPI increases. For example, a value of 123 means that prices have risen to the point where the cost of the standard market basket of goods is 23% higher than it was in the base year. How does the CPI figure for 1973 compare to that of 1999? Has the price of gasoline increased or decreased compared to the cost of other consumer goods?

Take It to the Net

We invite you to visit the O'Sullivan/Sheffrin page on the Prentice Hall Web site at: **http://www.prenhall.com/osullivan/** for additional World Wide Web exercises for this chapter.

Model Answers to Questions

Chapter-Opening Questions

1. To get a warship, we sacrifice something else, such as safe drinking water for 2.5 million Malaysians.
2. According to the marginal principle, the standard should be made stricter if the marginal benefit (the savings in health costs from a cleaner environment) exceeds the marginal cost (the cost of additional equipment and extra fuel).
3. According to the principle of diminishing returns, output will eventually increase at a decreasing rate.
4. The true cost (or what economists refer to as the economic cost) of paper equals the firm's cost (for material, labor, and the paper mill) and the cost associated with the pollution generated as a byproduct of paper.
5. Your income will buy the same quantity of goods and services, so you will be equally well off.

Test Your Understanding

1. False. This statement ignores the opportunity cost of time spent in school.
2. We need the opportunity cost of using the people in the army instead of in the civilian economy. One measure of the opportunity cost is the wages the people could have earned as engineers, teachers, doctors, lawyers, or factory workers.
3. One of the costs of a lunch is the time spent eating it. Even if someone else pays for your lunch, it is not truly free.
4. The marginal benefit is $150, and the marginal cost is only $100 (equal to $600 − $500), so it would be sensible to add the third bus.

5. It will be worthwhile if the opportunity cost of the time spent traveling is less than $40.
6. No. If the factory experiences diminishing returns, the additional output from the twenty-first worker will be smaller than the output from the additional output from the twentieth worker, and the extra output from the twenty-second worker will be even smaller than the output from the twenty-first worker. Therefore, hiring two more workers will increase total output by less than 10 tables.
7. False. The principle says that output increases but at a decreasing rate. Its does not say that hiring another worker decreases output, although this is a possibility with a very crowded factory.
8. *Obnoxious music:* Spillover cost. You must listen to what you consider awful music chosen by your roommate.

   Contaminated water: Spillover cost. People who bathe in the contaminated water risk being burned.

   Yard cars: Spillover cost. For most people, a bunch of partly restored cars (cars jacked up on the street or on the front lawn) is an eyesore.

   Food for the poor: Spillover benefit. Even noncontributors are happy if the poor receive holiday meals.

   Endangered species: Spillover benefit. Many people like the idea of preventing a species from becoming extinct.
9. The price of consumer goods increased faster than wages.
10. Your real wage hasn't changed, so you are just as well off.

Figure 2.A
How Much RAM?

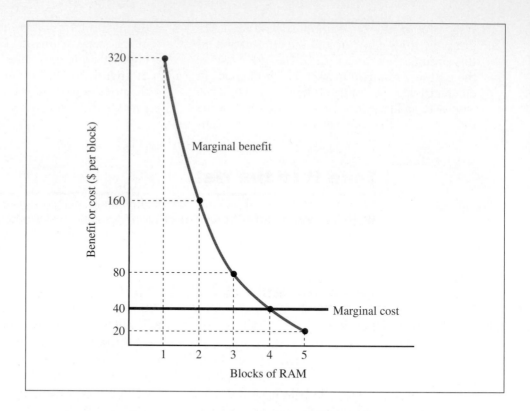

11. A set of goods that cost you $100 will cost you $103 today, so you must use $3 of your $4 interest earnings to cover the higher costs, leaving you with only $1 as actual interest earnings.

Using the Tools

2. **What's the Cost?** The opportunity cost of the loan to the friend is the interest the person could have earned if the $100 were in a bank account instead.

The opportunity cost of the logs is the amount of money the firm could get by selling the logs on the log market today. The opportunity cost of the land is the value of land in its next-best alternative, for example, a classroom building, a library, or a student center.

3. **How Much RAM?** See Figure 2.A. The marginal benefit of RAM equals the marginal cost at 4 blocks (128 MB).

 **Notes**

1. Gail Kinsey Hill, "Aluminum Industry Powering Down," *The Oregonian*, March 11, 2001, page C1; Gail Kinsey Hill, "Paying the Price for Power," *The Oregonian*, May 20, 2001, page A1; Gail Kinsey Hill and Alan Brettmann, "Alcoa OKs Deal with BPA," *The Oregonian*, May 17, 2001, page A1.

2. United Nations Development Program, *Human Development Report 1994* (New York: Oxford University Press, 1994).

3. Alan Riding, "The French Seek Their Own 'Peace Dividend,'" *New York Times,* July 15, 1990, p. 6.

4. Eric Schmitt, "Peace Dividend: Troops Turn to Teaching," *New York Times,* November 30, 1994, p. B1.

5. Jose de Cordoba, "Panama Has Plans for U.S. War Stuff: Turn It Into Hotels," *Wall Street Journal*, January 11, 2000, p. A1.

6. *USA Today*, April 19, 1999, p. 1.

7. World Health Organization, "Obesity: Preventing and Managing the Global Epidemic" (Geneva, 1997).

8. Virgina Postrel, "Economic Scene: Waistlines Are Now Victims of Economic Progress," *New York Times*, March 22, 2001; Tomas Philipson and Richard A. Posner, "Long Run Growth in Obesity as a Function of Technological Change," National Bureau of Economic Research Working Paper, 1999.

Markets and Government in the Global Economy

Imagine a housecleaning race between Shaquille O'Neal and his house cleaner. Shaq wouldn't have to stop vacuuming to move furniture; he could just lift up the chair or sofa with one hand and operate the vacuum with the other hand. With his massive hands and long reach, he could clean a window with one or two quick swipes. Given his 7-foot height and big vertical leap, he wouldn't need a stepladder to reach cobwebs in the ceiling corners.

If Shaq could clean his house faster than anyone else, why would he hire someone to do it? Although Shaq is a more productive cleaner than his house cleaner, he is also a more productive basketball player, and the difference in their basketball skills is enormous compared to the difference in their cleaning skills. Shaq will be better off specializing in the activity that is most productive relative to other people (basketball) and then using his basketball income to hire someone to clean his house. Stated another way, Shaq's opportunity cost of cleaning—the income he could earn playing basketball instead—is higher than his house cleaner's, so it is sensible for Shaq to play basketball and hire a cleaner.

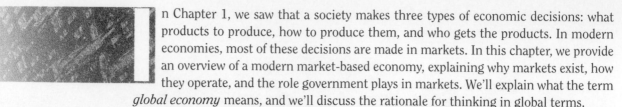

I n Chapter 1, we saw that a society makes three types of economic decisions: what products to produce, how to produce them, and who gets the products. In modern economies, most of these decisions are made in markets. In this chapter, we provide an overview of a modern market-based economy, explaining why markets exist, how they operate, and the role government plays in markets. We'll explain what the term *global economy* means, and we'll discuss the rationale for thinking in global terms.

The material we cover in this chapter will help you to understand how a market-based economy operates in today's global environment. Here are some of the practical questions we answer:

1. Why do markets exist?
2. Why do both rich and poor nations benefit from trade?
3. How do governments restrict international trade?
4. What are GATT, NAFTA, and the World Trade Organization?

Why Do Markets Exist?

In Chapter 1, we saw that a market is an arrangement that allows buyers and sellers to exchange things. A buyer exchanges money for a product (a good or service), while a seller exchanges a product for money. Before we explore how a market operates, let's think about why markets exist in the first place.

In the words of Adam Smith, "Man is the only animal that makes bargains: one dog does not exchange bones with another dog." We use markets to make our bargains, exchanging what we have for what we want. If each person were self-sufficient, producing everything he or she consumed, there would be no need for markets. Markets exist because we aren't self-sufficient but instead consume many products produced by other people. To get the money to pay for these products, each of us produces something to sell. Some people grow food; others produce goods such as clothing and bicycles; and others provide services such as medical care or legal advice. Because each of us specializes in one or two products, we need markets to sell what we produce and to buy other

The typical person is not self-sufficient but instead specializes by working at a particular job and uses his or her income to purchase goods and services.

products. Most of us use the labor market to sell our work time to employers and then use our labor income to buy food, housing, appliances, and other products.

Specialization and the Gains from Trade

Why do people specialize and trade? We can explain the rationale for specialization and trade with an example involving two people and two products: bread and shirts. The first two rows of Table 3.1 show how much of each good Brenda and Sam can produce in one hour. Brenda can produce either six loaves of bread or two shirts, while Sam can produce either one loaf of bread or one shirt.

We can use the principle of opportunity cost to explain the benefits from specialization and trade.

PRINCIPLE of Opportunity Cost

The opportunity cost of something is what you sacrifice to get it.

Opportunity cost is defined in terms of one unit of the good or, in our example, in terms of one shirt or one loaf of bread. The opportunity costs are shown in the third and fourth rows of Table 3.1.

1. Brenda's opportunity cost of one shirt is three loaves of bread; that's how many loaves of bread she could produce in the time it takes her to produce one shirt. She needs half an hour to produce a shirt, and during that half hour, she could produce three loaves of bread instead.
2. Brenda's opportunity cost of a loaf of bread is one third of a shirt; that's how many shirts she could produce in the time it takes her to produce a loaf of bread. She needs one sixth of an hour to produce a loaf of bread, and during that one sixth of an hour, she could produce one third of a shirt instead.
3. Sam's opportunity cost of a shirt is one loaf of bread.
4. Sam's opportunity cost of a loaf of bread is one shirt.

Each person could be self-sufficient. Brenda could produce all the bread and shirts she wants to consume, and Sam could produce everything for himself too. But what would happen if they decided to specialize and trade? Suppose they agree to trade at the rate of two loaves of bread for each shirt.

- Brenda could specialize in bread and trade for shirts. Instead of producing one shirt for herself, Brenda could use the time it would take to produce one shirt to produce three loaves of bread; that's her opportunity cost of a shirt. If she then trades two loaves of bread for one shirt, she will have one loaf of bread left over. Specialization and trade make Brenda better off because she gets the same number of shirts and one extra loaf of bread.

Table 3.1 Production per Hour and Opportunity Cost

	Brenda	Sam
Bread produced per hour	6	1
Shirts produced per hour	2	1
Opportunity cost of one loaf of bread	1/3 shirt	1 shirt
Opportunity cost of one shirt	3 loaves of bread	1 loaf of bread

- Sam could specialize in shirts and trade for bread. Instead of producing one loaf of bread for himself. Sam could use the time it would take to produce a loaf of bread to produce one shirt: that's his opportunity cost of a loaf of bread. If he trades the shirt for two loaves of bread, he will have two loaves of bread instead of the one he could have produced himself. Specialization and trade make Sam better off because he gets the same number of shirts and one extra loaf of bread.

This example shows the benefit of specialization and trade. By specializing and trading, each person can consume more.

Opportunity Cost and Comparative Advantage

Comparative advantage: The ability of one person or nation to produce a good at an opportunity cost that is lower than the opportunity cost of another person or nation.

We say that a person has a **comparative advantage** in producing a particular good if he or she has a lower opportunity cost than another person in producing that good. It is sensible for each person to produce the good for which he or she has a comparative advantage.

- **Shirts.** Sam's opportunity cost for shirts (one loaf) is lower than Brenda's (three loaves), so it is sensible for Sam to specialize in shirts and trade for bread.

- **Bread.** Brenda's opportunity cost for bread (one-third shirt) is lower than Sam's (one shirt), so Brenda should specialize in bread and trade for shirts.

As we saw in Table 3.1 specialization and trade—with each person producing the good for which he or she has a comparative advantage—allows each person to consume more.

Absolute advantage: The ability of one person or nation to produce a particular good at a lower absolute cost than that of another person or nation.

You may have noticed that Brenda is more productive than Sam in producing both goods. Economists say that she has an **absolute advantage** in producing both goods. Despite her absolute advantage, Brenda gains from specializing in bread and trading some of her bread for shirts produced by Sam. In an hour Brenda can produce twice as many shirts as Sam, but she can produce *six* times as many loaves of bread. Brenda relies on Sam to make some of her shirts because that frees her to spend more time producing bread, the good for which she has the greatest productivity advantage over Sam and therefore a comparative advantage. The lesson is that trade results from comparative advantage (lower opportunity costs), not from absolute advantage.

TEST Your Understanding

1. Tim's opportunity cost of producing one chair is five tables, while Carla's opportunity cost of producing one chair is one table. Compute each person's opportunity cost of tables. Which person should produce chairs, and which should produce tables?

2. In an hour, a financial planner can either produce three financial statements or answer twelve phone calls. What is the opportunity cost of a financial statement? What is the opportunity cost of a phone call?

3. Wally is the manager of a car wash and is more productive at washing cars than are any of the potential workers he could hire. Does that mean he should wash all the cars himself?

How Do Markets Operate?

Now that we know why markets exist, we're ready to discuss how they operate. In a modern economy, direct trade between two individuals is rare. Rather than producing one consumer good and trading directly with other consumers/producers, most exchanges occur in markets involving firms and other organizations. Markets allow us to exchange what we have for what we want. Most of us work in firms or other organizations for a paycheck, which we then use to buy goods and services from other firms.

The Circular Flow

Figure 3.1 is a **circular flow diagram** of a simple market-based economy. Exchanges occur in two markets:

Circular flow diagram: A diagram showing the flow of money and goods between markets.

- **Factor or input market.** The owners of the factors of production—natural resources, labor, physical capital (machines, buildings, and equipment), and human capital (the knowledge and skills acquired by a worker)—sell these inputs to organizations that use the inputs to produce goods and services.

- **Product or output market.** The organizations that produce goods and services sell their products to consumers.

There are two types of decision-makers in the circular flow model: households and firms.

Households as Sellers and Buyers

Households own the factors of production (inputs) and firms have the knowledge and the ability required to transform inputs into outputs. As shown by arrows B and J in Figure 3.1, the factor markets allow households and firms to exchange inputs and money: Households supply inputs to the factor market (arrow B), and firms pay households for these inputs (arrow J). There are three types of factor markets:

- In the labor market, firms hire workers, paying them wages or salaries in exchange for the output produced by the workers. In the United States, about three-fourths of the income earned by households comes from wages and salaries.

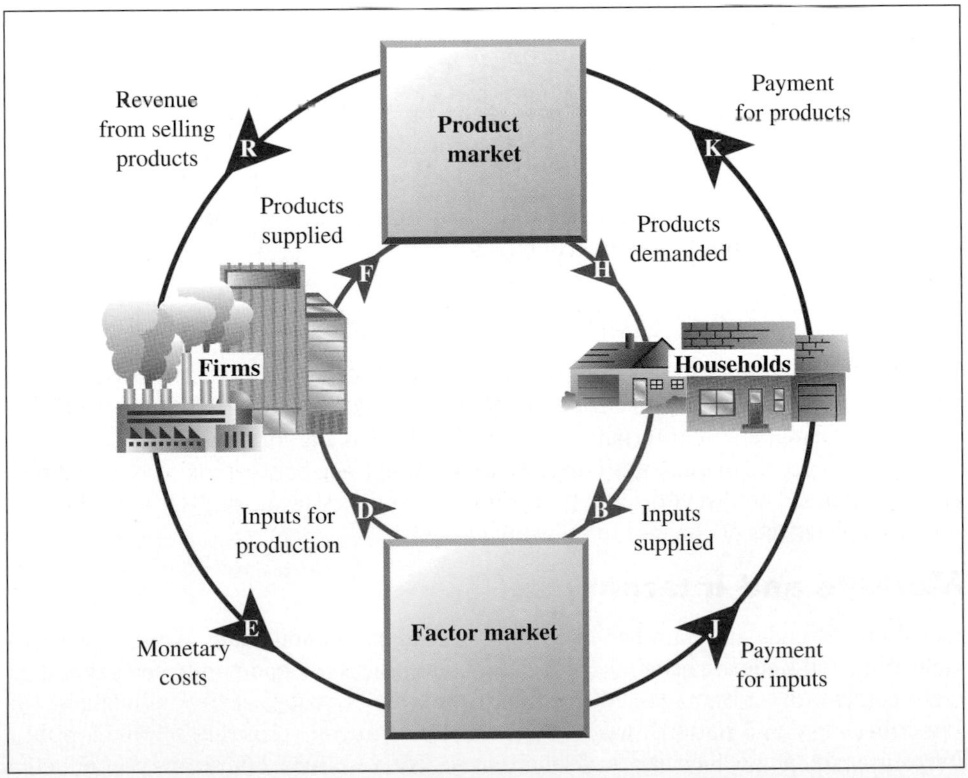

Figure 3.1
Circular Flow Diagram
The circular flow diagram shows the interactions between households (the suppliers of factors of production, or inputs) and firms (the producers of products) in the factor and product markets.

- In the capital market, households use their savings—money in bank accounts, mutual funds, and stock investments—to provide the funds that firms use to buy physical capital, for example, machines, buildings, and equipment. In exchange for the use of their savings, households receive interest payments or some portion of the firm's profits. In the United States, about 20% of the income earned by households comes from interest payments and profits.

- In the natural resource market, households own natural resources (for example, land, minerals, or oil) or own the firms that control the natural resources. These natural resources are sold to firms to use as inputs in the production process.

Households are also involved in the product market, where they purchase goods and services from firms. This interaction between households and firms is shown by arrows H and K in Figure 3.1: Households consume the products produced by firms (arrow H) and pay firms for these products (arrow K). To summarize, households are sellers in factor markets and buyers in product markets.

Firms as Sellers and Buyers

The purpose of a firm is to transform inputs into outputs—products—and then sell the products. Before a firm can produce anything, it must get the inputs required for production. As shown by arrow D in Figure 3.1, inputs flow from the factor markets to the firm, where they're used to produce output. As shown by arrow E, the money to pay for the inputs flows from the firm to the factor market on its way to households. In other words, the firm is a buyer in the factor markets. Once the firm produces a product, it brings it to the product market (shown by arrow F) and receives money when consumers buy it (arrow R).

Figure 3.1 shows that economic activity is circular. The inner circle shows physical flows (products and inputs), and the outer circle shows monetary flows (money exchanged for inputs or products). Firms pay money to households for their inputs. In the other direction, households pay money to firms when they buy the firms' products.

This circular flow diagram is a starting point for describing how an economy works, but it is incomplete for two reasons. First, the diagram does not show the role of government in the economy. As we'll see throughout the book, the government is a big part of a market-based economy: Government provides some goods and services, buys inputs, redistributes income, collects taxes, and regulates firms. Second, the diagram does not show the effects of international trade, which, as we'll see later in the chapter, is a large and growing part of most modern economies.

The Global Economy and Interdependence

In today's global economy, many products are produced in one country and sold in another. International trade is one component of the global economy. After introducing some of the language of international trade, we discuss the foreign-exchange market, which allows people to exchange currency, facilitating trade between nations with different currencies. Then we'll discuss global interdependence, exploring some of the economic ripple effects of changes in individual nations.

Markets and International Trade

Recall how Brenda and Sam benefited from specialization and trade. We saw that specialization and trade are beneficial if there are differences in opportunity costs that generate comparative advantages. Although our example consisted of two individuals, the same ideas apply to nations, which differ in their natural resources, climate, public infrastructure, physical capital, and labor forces. The resulting differences in productiv-

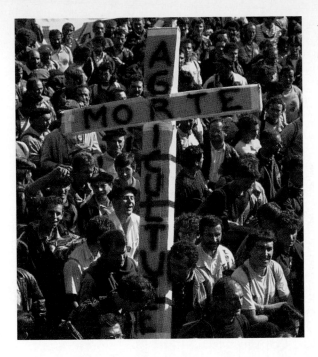

A proposal to lift trade restrictions is often met with opposition from people employed in protected domestic industries. French farmers protested against GATT.

ity mean that, like an individual, a nation has a comparative advantage in the production of particular products. When a nation specializes in production and engages in trade, it gives its citizens an opportunity to consume larger quantities of goods and services.

A nation will specialize in the product for which it has a comparative advantage. Like trade between individuals, international trade results from comparative advantage, not absolute advantage. This explains why a rich nation trades with a poor nation, even though a rich nation is more productive and has an absolute advantage in all products. For example, suppose the United States is more efficient than India in producing both computers and clothing but that the United States has a comparative advantage in computers while India has a comparative advantage in clothing. Both countries would be better off if each country specialized—the United States in computers and India in clothing—and traded. Remember, it is comparative advantage that matters. Even if the United States were absolutely more efficient in producing clothing, both countries would still benefit from specialization and trade.

International Trade: Exports and Imports

From the perspective of the United States, an **export** is a good produced in the United States and sold in another country, while an **import** is a good produced elsewhere and purchased in the United States. As shown in Figure 3.2, the leading U.S. exports are agricultural commodities, electrical machinery, and chemicals, while the leading imports are automated data-processing equipment (ADP) and office machinery, electrical machinery, vehicles, and crude oil. Figure 3.3 shows the volumes of trade between the United States and its major trading partners. The three largest partners are Canada, Japan, and Mexico.

Protectionist Policies

Despite the advantages from global specialization, most nations use trade barriers to restrict international trade. Why? Trade barriers are often designed to protect domestic firms from competition from foreign firms and to protect the jobs of workers in industries that would be adversely affected by trade. These industries are often very successful

Export: A good produced in the "home" country (for example, the United States) and sold in another country.

Import: A good produced in a foreign country and purchased by residents of the "home" country (for example, the United States).

Figure 3.2
Major Imports and Exports of the United States, 1999

Source: Statistical Abstract of the United States 2000 (Washington, DC: U.S. Government Printing Office, 2001).

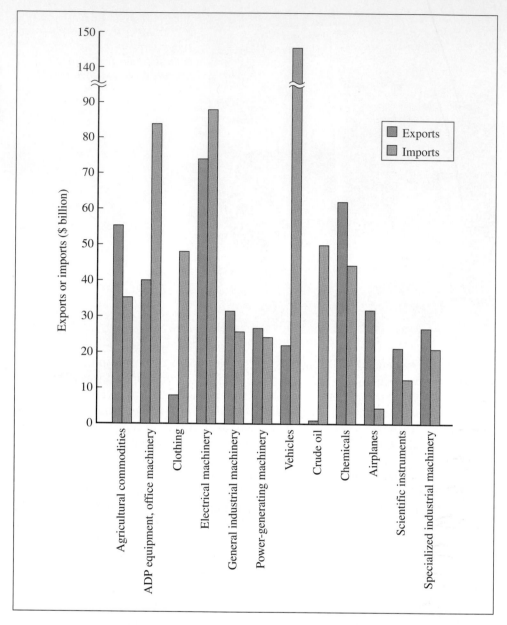

in lobbying politicians to obtain protections from trade. Policies that restrict trade are known as **protectionist policies**.

There are three common forms of protection:

- A quota is an absolute limit on the volume of a particular good that can be imported into a country. If a country imposed a quota on steel imports of 200,000 tons, only 200,000 tons of steel could enter that country.

- Under a voluntary export restraint, one country agrees to limit the volume of exports to another country. For example, the Japanese government agreed to limit the number of Japanese cars sold in the United States and Europe. Many nations use voluntary export restraints to avoid explicit quotas, which are often prohibited by treaties.

- A tariff is a special tax on imported goods. For example, a 10% tariff on imported television sets means that the tax on a $300 imported TV set is $30.

Protectionist policies: Rules that restrict the free flow of goods between nations, including tariffs (taxes on imports), quotas (limits on total imports), voluntary export restraints (agreements between governments to limit imports), and nontariff trade barriers (subtle practices that hinder trade).

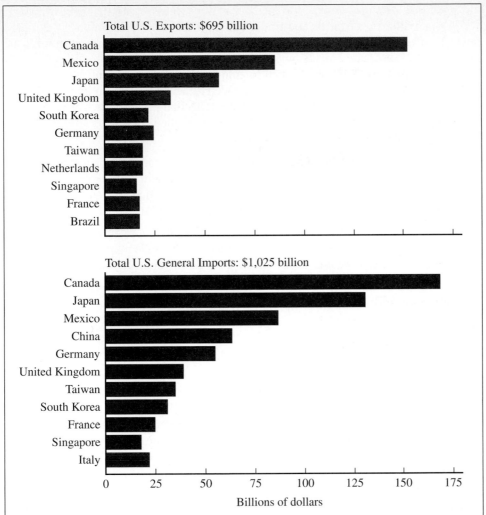

Total U.S. Exports: $695 billion

Total U.S. General Imports: $1,025 billion

Billions of dollars

Figure 3.3

Major Trading Partners of the United States, 1999

Source: Statistical Abstract of the United States 2001 (Washington, DC: U.S. Government Printing Office, 2001).

There are other ways a nation can limit imports without an official trade barrier. One way is to target imports for extra-strict enforcement of health and safety laws. A foreign firm that is faced with stricter standards than domestic firms may decide to stay out of the market. Another way a country can restrict imports is to design or allow its customs system to be inefficient and sluggish. If it takes a lot of time and effort to pass imported goods through customs, foreign firms may drop out of the market. These are examples of nontariff trade barriers, practices that do not show up as official laws but have the same effects as tariffs and quotas.

History of Tariff and Trade Agreements

Since 1980, the average U.S. tariff has been about 5% of the value of imported goods, a rate that is close to the average tariffs in Japan and most European nations but very low by historical standards. Under the Smoot-Hawley tariffs of the 1930s, the average tariff in the United States was a whopping 59% of value. Tariffs are lower today because of several international agreements that reduce tariffs.

The first major trade agreement following World War II was the **General Agreement on Tariffs and Trade [GATT]**. This agreement was initiated in 1947 by the United States and 23

General Agreement on Tariffs and Trade [GATT]: An international agreement that has lowered trade barriers between the United States and other nations.

other nations and now has over 100 member nations. There have been eight rounds of GATT negotiations over tariffs and trade regulations, resulting in progressively lower tariffs for the member nations. The last set of negotiations, the Uruguay round, completed in 1994, decreased tariffs by about one-third of the previous level. In 1995 the **World Trade Organization [WTO]** was formed to enforce GATT and other international trade agreements. As explained in "A Closer Look: Video Piracy in China," an important international issue for WTO nations is the piracy of intellectual property such as videos.

In recent years, various groups of nations have formed trade associations to lower trade barriers and promote international trade.

- The **North American Free Trade Agreement [NAFTA]**. This agreement took effect in 1994 and will be implemented over a 15-year period. The agreement will eventually eliminate all tariffs and other trade barriers between Canada, Mexico, and the United States. NAFTA may soon be extended to other nations in the Western Hemisphere.

- A total of 15 nations have joined the **European Union [EU]**, an organization designed to remove all trade barriers within Europe and create a single market. Eleven of these nations have already committed to using a single currency, called the euro.

- The leaders of 18 Asian nations formed an organization called **Asian Pacific Economic Cooperation [APEC]** and in 1994 signed a nonbinding agreement to reduce trade barriers between their nations.

World Trade Organization [WTO]: An organization that oversees GATT and other international trade agreements.

North American Free Trade Agreement [NAFTA]: An international agreement that lowers barriers to trade between the United States, Mexico, and Canada (signed in 1994).

European Union [EU]: An organization of European nations that has reduced trade barriers within Europe.

Asian Pacific Economic Cooperation [APEC]: An organization of 18 Asian nations that attempts to reduce trade barriers between their nations.

Foreign exchange market: A market in which people exchange one currency for another.

Currency Markets and Exchange Rates

The **foreign exchange market** allows people to exchange one nation's currency for another nation's currency, such as U.S. dollars for Japanese yen. Because each nation uses a different currency, international trade would not be possible without a foreign exchange market. A U.S. firm that sells computers in Japan is paid in yen but must pay its U.S. workers with dollars. The foreign exchange market allows the U.S. firm to exchange the

A CLOSER LOOK   VIDEO PIRACY IN CHINA

The heart of China's home entertainment is the video compact disk (VCD), the analog of the videocassette used widely in the United States. Consumers rent disks from thousands of neighborhood video outlets. About 95% of the VCDs in China are pirated versions—illegal copies made from laserdisks or with handheld video cameras in theaters.[2] The copies made with video cameras—which often feature audience laughter and big heads blocking the screen—are released just days after the film is first screened in the United States or Hong Kong. At a price of $1 to $2, the pirated versions of movies like *The Grinch*, *Gladiator*, and *Mission Impossible-2* are bargains compared to the $20 price tag for legitimate versions.

The piracy problem is straining China's relations with its trading partners as the nation prepares to join the World Trade Organization (WTO). Once China joins the WTO, the member nations are expected to apply pressure on China to reduce the piracy problem.

yen it receives for dollars. The **exchange rate** is defined as the rate at which we can exchange one currency for another. At an exchange rate of 90 yen per dollar, if the U.S. firm sells a computer in Japan for 90,000 yen, it can exchange the yen for 1,000 U.S. dollars.

Many newspapers publish information on foreign exchange rates. As shown in Table 3.2, exchange rates are quoted in two equivalent ways. First, the "value in dollars" indicates how many dollars a single unit of the foreign currency will buy. For example, the value in dollars of a German mark was $0.4332, meaning that 1 mark could be exchanged for $0.4332. Second, "the units per dollar" indicates how many units of the foreign currency are needed to buy 1 dollar. To get 1 dollar, you needed 2.3079 marks.

We can use the exchange rate between two currencies to determine the actual cost of a good produced in another nation. Suppose you are planning a trip to Mexico and want to determine the cost of staying in a hotel. If a hotel room in Mexico costs 450 pesos per night and the exchange rate is 9 pesos per dollar, the hotel room will cost you $50: To get the 450 pesos to pay for the room, you must sacrifice $50. If the exchange rate were 10 pesos per dollar instead, the hotel room would cost you only $45 a night: To get the 450 pesos, you would need only $45. The greater the exchange rate (pesos per dollar), the cheaper the hotel room in Mexico.

Global Interdependence

In the modern global economy, the nations of the world are intertwined. The fortunes of one nation affect those of its trading partners. Suppose the German economy goes through a bad spell and faces severe economic difficulties, including a high unemployment rate. As a result, German consumers will purchase fewer goods and services, including fewer imported goods from countries like Belgium. Firms in Belgium will produce less output and will hire fewer workers. The unemployment that began in Germany thus spreads to Belgium. Through international economic linkages. Germany's bad times can be transmitted to Belgium.

While trade brings the advantages of world specialization, it also creates vulnerabilities. The benefits of increased world productivity come at the cost of increased reliance

Table 3.2   Exchange Rates in July 2001

Nation	Currency	Value in Dollars (U.S. $ equivalent)	Units per Dollar (Currency per U.S. $)
Australia	Dollar	0.51	1.96
Brazil	Real	0.41	2.41
Britain	Pound sterling	1.41	0.71
Canada	Dollar	0.66	1.51
France	Franc	0.1291	7.74
Germany	Mark	0.4332	2.3079
Hong Kong	Dollar	0.1282	7.799
Ireland	Punt	1.07	0.92
Israel	Shekel	0.24	4.19
Japan	Yen	0.0079	125.75
Mexico	Peso	0.1095	9.12
Saudi Arabia	Rial	0.27	3.75

on the economic fortunes of economic neighbors. Large economic powers such as the United States, Germany, and Japan can have a large effect on the economies of other nations. The saying "When the U.S. sneezes, Canada catches a cold" expresses this idea. Countries that produce key raw materials, such as oil, can also have very large effects. During the 1970s, the oil-producing countries raised the world price of oil and inflicted much economic hardship on large countries such as the United States, Japan, and the countries of Western Europe.

The economies of the world are linked through the financial system as well as through trade in goods and services. One of the most important developments of the last decade has been the increase in the financial linkages between countries. For example, the residents of the United States can now routinely invest in firms in Asia and Latin America. A firm in Thailand that wants to undertake a major new venture might borrow funds in Western Europe, Japan, or the United States. Large banks in Japan have routinely made loans to firms throughout the world. In the past, many governments limited the ability of their citizens and businesses to borrow or lend in foreign countries. But in recent years, many economies have undergone a process of **financial liberalization**, opening up their financial markets to participants from foreign countries.

Financial liberalization creates many new opportunities for countries. They no longer need to rely on their own residents to finance important projects but instead can tap the resources from the entire world. Similarly, financial liberalization allows investors to scout the world for new and profitable investment opportunities and does not restrict them to their own country. In general, financial liberalization facilitates global specialization and leads to a more efficient world economy.

Financial liberalization creates opportunities and creates new vulnerabilities. Suppose investors have a bad experience in one developing country and become convinced that the economic prospects of that country have deteriorated. They begin to cut back on their loans to that country, slowing down economic activity there. At the same time, they may conclude, perhaps inaccurately, that similar difficulties plague a neighboring country, causing them to pull funds from that country too, also causing economic difficulties in the neighboring country. Before financial liberalization, neither country would have attracted the funds necessary to grow as rapidly as they did. But they would not have been subject to the changing opinions of the international financial markets either.

Because of the tighter linkages in product and financial markets, the economies of the world are becoming more and more interdependent. The greater flow of products across national boundaries and the increases in international financial transactions have increased the need for international institutions to help make the system work. The **International Monetary Fund**, headquartered in Washington, D.C., works closely with the governments of the world to promote efficient and effective financial policies to facilitate the growth in world trade and commerce.

Financial liberalization: The opening of financial markets to participants from foreign countries.

International Monetary Fund: An organization that works closely with national governments to promote financial policies that facilitate world trade.

TEST Your Understanding

4. What fraction of household income comes from wages and salaries?

5. What do firms do?

6. Nation T can produce either 3 tons of wheat or 9 tons of steel, while nation H can produce either 4 tons of wheat or 8 tons of steel. Which nation has a comparative advantage in wheat? Which has a comparative advantage in steel?

7. Complete the statement with *more* or *less*: If the exchange between U.S. dollars and French francs went from 5 francs per dollar to 3 francs per dollar, this would tend to make French goods _____ expensive to U.S. citizens.

Government in a Market Economy

Now that we know how markets operate, we can consider the role of government in a market-based economy. In most modern societies, the government has five general responsibilities.

1. Providing goods and services. The government provides all sorts of goods and services, including streets and highways, education, parks, public safety, national defense, and space exploration.
2. Redistributing income. In a market-based economy, some people earn much more income than others, and the government redistributes income to the poor.
3. Taxation. The government uses taxes on various goods and services to support its spending programs.
4. Regulation of business practices. The government uses regulations to control pollution, encourage competition among firms, and improve the safety of consumer goods.
5. Trade policy. The government uses various policies to control international trade, promoting some types of trade and restricting others.

Although it's convenient to speak of "the government," it's important to recognize that there are thousands of governments in the United States, and each citizen deals with at least three levels of government. Local governments pave the streets and run the primary and secondary schools, while state governments pave the highways and run the colleges and universities. The national government provides goods and services for the nation as a whole, including national defense and space exploration. In addition, the national government has the primary responsibility for income redistribution. All three levels of government impose taxes to pay for their spending programs, and all three regulate business practices.

Government Spending Programs

How do governments in the United States spend the money they collect from taxpayers? Figure 3.4 shows the budget breakdown for the three levels of government.

1. There are more than 80,000 local governments in the United States, including municipalities (city governments), counties, school districts, and special districts responsible for providing services such as water, fire protection, and libraries. Local governments spend most of their money on education (kindergarten through high school), public welfare and health (payments to poor households and support for public hospitals), highways, and police protection.
2. For states, the biggest spending programs are education (including colleges and universities), public welfare, highways, health and hospitals, and corrections (state courts and prisons).
3. For the federal government, the biggest spending programs are national defense, programs for the elderly (Social Security and Medicare), income security (payments to the poor), and interest on the national debt.

Criteria for a Tax System

If the government is to play a role in the market-based economy, taxes are necessary. The practical policy question is whether our current tax system is the best we can do. To most people, a good tax system is fair and easy to understand, and does not disrupt markets that otherwise operate effectively. Let's take a closer look at each one of these criteria.

Figure 3.4

**Percentages of
Government
Spending on
Various Programs**

*Source: Statistical Abstract of
the United States, 2000: Economic Report of the President*
(Washington, DC: U.S. Government Printing Office, 1998).

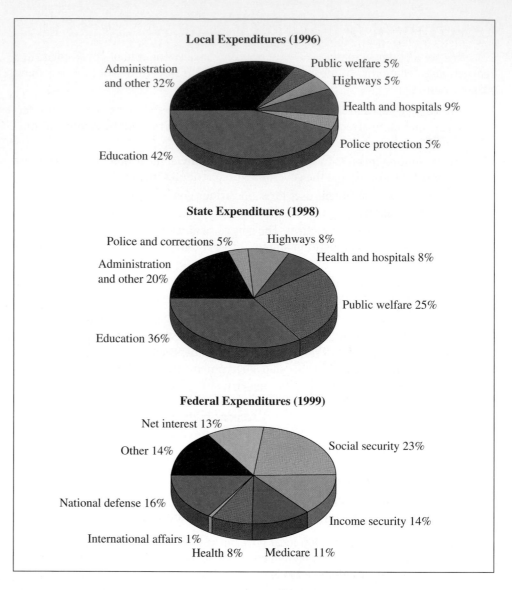

Local Expenditures (1996)

Administration
and other 32%

Public welfare 5%

Highways 5%

Health and hospitals 9%

Police protection 5%

Education 42%

State Expenditures (1998)

Police and corrections 5%

Highways 8%

Administration
and other 20%

Health and hospitals 8%

Public welfare 25%

Education 36%

Federal Expenditures (1999)

Net interest 13%

Other 14%

Social security 23%

National defense 16%

Income security 14%

International affairs 1%

Health 8%   Medicare 11%

Benefit-tax approach: The idea
that a person's tax liability
should depend on his or her
benefits from government
programs.

There are two perspectives on the issue of fairness. The **benefit-tax approach** suggests
that a person's tax liability should depend on his or her benefits from government programs. For example, the revenue from the gasoline taxes in the United States supports
the construction and maintenance of highways. The more you drive, the more you use
the highway system *and* the more gasoline taxes you pay. For many government programs, however, it would be difficult, if not impossible, to determine just how large a
benefit a particular citizen receives. For example, all law-abiding citizens benefit from
the criminal justice system (police, courts, prisons), but because we don't know how
much each person benefits from the system, it would be impossible to determine just
how much each person should pay for it.

Horizontally equity: The idea
that people in similar economic
circumstances should pay
similar amounts in taxes.

Vertical equity: The idea that
people with more income or
wealth should pay higher taxes.

The second perspective on fairness focuses on a citizen's ability to pay. A tax is
horizontally equitable if people in similar economic circumstances pay similar amounts in
taxes. For example, under a pure income tax, each person with a given amount of
income would pay the same income tax. In contrast, the idea of **vertical equity** is that people with more income or wealth should pay higher taxes. The practical policy question is

how much more they should pay. A tax system that is vertically equitable in the eyes of one citizen may be inequitable in the eyes of another.

The second criterion for evaluating a tax system is simplicity. If you've ever filled out an income tax form, you know that the tax system in the United States is very complex. The average household devotes about 27 hours per year to federal tax preparation. In addition, each household must contend with state and local taxes. Firms spend large sums of money to comply with the tax code, and pass on these costs to consumers in the form of higher prices. Despite the frequent calls for tax simplification, there is no sign that it will get any easier to comply with the tax system.

The third criterion for the tax system concerns its effects on market decisions. If a particular market does not generate any spillover benefits or costs, there is no reason to disrupt the market. When a tax is imposed, many people try to avoid the tax by changing their behavior. Taxes distort people's choices and disrupt markets, and one of the objectives of tax policy is to minimize these disruptions. One implication is that taxes should be spread over many goods and services rather than just a few. For example, a special tax on electricians would discourage people from becoming electricians and disrupt the market for electricians. In contrast, a general income tax would have roughly the same effect on occupations that generate the same income, so the market disruptions will be smaller.

There are many trade-offs associated with designing a tax system. A tax system that is pretty simple may not be equipped to deal with the many different circumstances of taxpayers, leading to horizontal inequities. A simple tax system may also be vertically inequitable in the eyes of many taxpayers, with high-income people paying either too much or too little. A tax that is considered vertically equitable is likely to distort peoples' decisions, causing disruptions in many markets. The challenge for policymakers is to develop a system with the appropriate balance among the three criteria.

The Revenue Sources of Local, State, and Federal Governments

Now that we know the criteria for a tax system, let's look at the tax structures of the three levels of government. Figure 3.5 shows the revenue sources for localities, states, and the federal government.

1. The major revenue source for local governments is the property tax. The property tax is a flat percentage of the value of residential, commercial, or industrial property. For example, if the tax rate is 2% and you own a property with a market value of $100,000, your annual tax would be $2,000 (0.02 times $100,000).
2. The major revenue sources for the states are sales taxes and individual income taxes. The sales tax is a fixed percentage of the purchase price of a consumer good. A person's state income tax liability is based on how much he or she earns, with tax rates that typically increase as income increases.
3. The major revenue sources for the federal government are individual income taxes and "social insurance and retirement receipts," which are taxes collected to support Social Security, Medicare, and workers' compensation.

To see how tax rates in the United States compare to those in other industrialized nations, read "Tax Rates in Different Nations."

Government Regulation of Markets

It is possible to imagine a world in which the government plays no role in the economy. In such a world, all economic decisions (what products to produce, how to produce them, and who gets the products) would be made in unregulated markets. This is

Figure 3.5

Percentages of Government Revenue from Different Sources

Source: Statistical Abstract of the United States, 2000: Economic Report of the President (Washington, DC: U.S. Government Printing Office, 1998): Census Bureau data at *http://www.census.gov/govs/www/*.

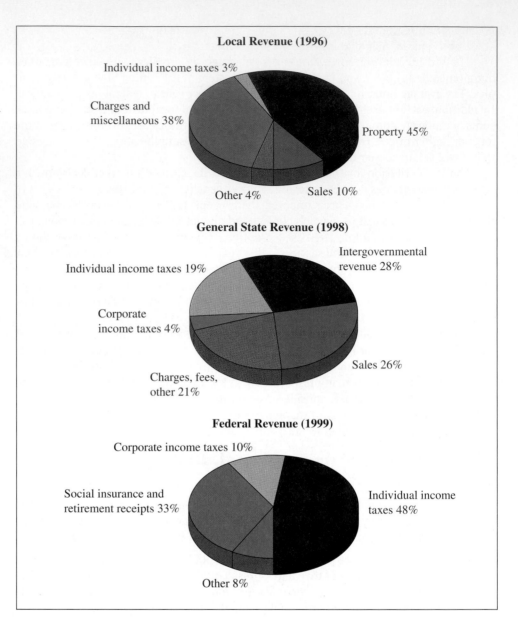

Local Revenue (1996)

Individual income taxes 3%

Charges and miscellaneous 38%

Property 45%

Other 4%   Sales 10%

General State Revenue (1998)

Individual income taxes 19%

Intergovernmental revenue 28%

Corporate income taxes 4%

Sales 26%

Charges, fees, other 21%

Federal Revenue (1999)

Corporate income taxes 10%

Social insurance and retirement receipts 33%

Individual income taxes 48%

Other 8%

referred to as laissez-faire, which translates from French roughly as "let it happen." In modern economies, however, the government plays an important role in many markets.

The government establishes a legal system to enforce property rights. If you buy land to build a house, you must register your purchase with the appropriate government agency and ensure that you are buying the land from the rightful owner and that no one else has a claim on that property. The government's legal system also makes it possible for one person to write a binding contract with another. A contract facilitates a transaction because each person involved in the transaction can be confident that the other person will fulfill his or her part of the deal. Without the legal system to enforce contracts, it would be nearly impossible to conduct business.

Governments at all levels also regulate economic activity. At the national level, the government regulates the purchase and sale of stocks and bonds, promotes competition among firms by blocking some corporate mergers, promotes safety in food products and

TAX RATES IN DIFFERENT NATIONS

How does the United States rank in terms of tax revenue as a fraction of total income? The Figure shows tax rates for OECD nations, including the United States. The United States is at the low end, with only four nations (Turkey, Japan, Korea, and Mexico) with lower tax rates. One reason for the relatively low tax rate in the United States is that the government pays a relatively small share of its citizens' health-care costs.

Tax Rates in OECD Nations, 1998

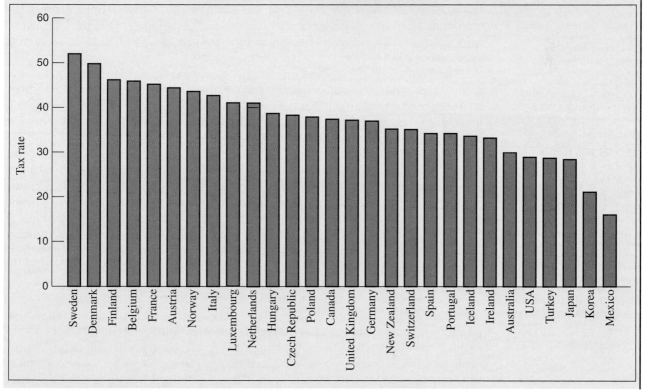

workplaces, and limits air and water pollution. The states regulate banking, transportation, education, land use, and many professions (physicians, lawyers, pharmacists, and house builders). Local governments use zoning and other regulations to control land use. It is difficult to think of a single area in which the government does not influence markets.

Because government plays such an important role in most modern market-based economies, most countries have what economists call **mixed economies**. Although most economic decisions are made in markets, these markets are regulated by the government, and the regulations differ from nation to nation and from state to state.

Mixed economy: A market-based economic system in which government plays an important role, including the regulation of markets, where most economic decisions are made.

Alternative Economic Systems

Centrally planned economy: An economy in which a government bureaucracy decides how much of each good to produce, how to produce the goods, and how to allocate the products among consumers.

An alternative to a market-based economy is a **centrally planned economy**, an economic system under which production and consumption decisions are made by a central government, not by individual producers and consumers in markets. In a pure centrally planned economy, there is no private property: everything is owned by the government.

In a centrally planned economy, a central bureaucracy makes all the decisions about what products to produce, how to produce them, and who gets the products. Bureaucrats tell each firm how much it should produce. One challenge for bureaucrats is to ensure that each firm has enough raw materials and workers to meet the firm's production goals. Another challenge for bureaucrats is to accurately assess the preferences of consumers so that the goods that are produced are actually desired by consumers.

Until the late 1980s, central planners ran the economies of the Soviet Union, most nations in Eastern Europe, and China. While some of these economies were effective in developing heavy industry, there were several major problems. The fundamental problem was that the bureaucrats lacked the information needed to make the millions of decisions required to allocate raw materials and other inputs to thousands of production facilities in the economy. The result was inefficiency and waste. Moreover, these economies lacked the flexibility of market economies. As computers and the information revolution transformed market economies throughout the world, planned economies were slow to adapt.

Many nations that had relied on centrally planned economies have recently shifted to mixed economic systems, with prices and private property. Two challenges are associated with the **transition** to economic systems in which markets play a much greater role in making economic decisions about production and consumption: the establishment of property rights and privatization of state-run firms.

Transition: The process of shifting from a centrally planned economy toward a mixed economic system, with markets playing a greater role in the economy.

The first challenge is to establish clear property rights and the rule of law. If property rights are uncertain, entrepreneurs will not be willing to make large investments and take risks because there will be no guarantee that they will benefit from successful projects. Entrepreneurs need law and order to prevent criminals from stealing the profits from legitimate enterprises. Russia has had severe problems with organized crime, making it difficult for ordinary businesses to exist without paying large sums for "protection." Entrepreneurs also need a legal system that prevents the government from unduly interfering with their everyday business activities. It will take time to develop the legal culture necessary to support a market-based economy.

Privatizing: The process of selling state firms to individuals.

A second challenge in the transition to a mixed economy is to **privatize** state-owned firms, that is, to sell the firms to individuals. Once a firm is sold off, it is allowed to compete with other firms in the marketplace. One problem with privatizing is that only the profitable production facilities will continue to operate. No one will want to buy unprofitable facilities, so many people will lose their jobs. Of course, other job opportunities will eventually appear as successful operations are expanded, but there may be a period when total employment drops. Another problem with privatizing is that there may be only one or two firms in a certain market, so even after the firms are privatized, there will be little competition between the privatized firms.

The difficulties for societies making the transition to a mixed economy make one thing clear. To have a successful market-based economy, the government must establish property rights, enforce laws, and provide a framework of regulation. Modern Western market economies have developed the roles of government gradually over many decades. Economies making the transition need to develop these roles more rapidly.

TEST Your Understanding

8. Match each trade restriction with its description.

Restriction	Description
A. Tariffs	1. Limits on total imports.
B. Quotas	2. Hidden impediments to trade.
C. Voluntary export restraints	3. Agreements between nations to restrict trade.
D. Nontariff trade barriers	4. Taxes on imports.

9. Complete the statement with GATT or NAFTA: _____ is a worldwide trade agreement, while _____ applies to a single continent.

Summary

This chapter has provided an overview of a market-based economy. In the factor markets, households provide labor and capital to firms in exchange for money. In the product markets, firms provide goods and services to households in exchange for money. In recent years, international trade agreements have lowered the barriers to trade, hastening the move to a global economy. Here are the main points of the chapter:

1. Most people are not self-sufficient but instead specialize to earn income, which they use to buy goods and services from others.

2. A system of international specialization and trade is sensible because people and nations have different opportunity costs of producing goods, giving rise to comparative advantage.

3. The foreign exchange market allows people to exchange one currency for another, facilitating international trade.

4. The free flow of goods can be hampered by barriers to trade, including tariffs, quotas, voluntary export restraints, and nontariff trade barriers. There are many international agreements designed to reduce trade barriers, including GATT, NAFTA, and the European Union.

Key Terms

absolute advantage, 44
Asian Pacific Economic Cooperation [APEC], 50
benefit-tax approach, 54
centrally planned economy, 58
circular flow diagram, 45
comparative advantage, 44
European Union [EU], 50
exchange rate, 51

export, 47
financial liberalization, 52
foreign exchange market, 50
General Agreement on Tariffs and Trade [GATT], 49
horizontal equity, 54
import, 47
International Monetary Fund, 52

mixed economy, 57
North American Free Trade Agreement [NAFTA], 50
privatizing, 58
protectionist policies, 48
transition, 58
vertical equity, 54
World Trade Organization [WTO], 50

Problems and Discussion Questions

1. Recall the example of Brenda and Sam shown in Table 3.1. Suppose a technological innovation increases shirt productivity of both people: Brenda can now produce three shirts per hour, while Sam can now produce two shirts per hour. Their produc-tivity for bread has not changed. Suppose they agree to trade one shirt for each loaf of bread. Will both people gain from specialization and trade?

2. Consider two financial planners, Phil and Frances. In an hour Phil can either produce one financial

statement or answer ten phone calls, while Frances can either produce three financial statements or answer twelve phone calls. Does either person have an absolute advantage in producing both products? Should the two planners be self-sufficient (each producing statements and answering phones) or should they specialize?

3. Professor A is a better teacher than professor B for both an undergraduate course (U) and a graduate course (G). As the chair of the department, you measure teaching performance as the average grade received by students on standardized exams. How would you decide which course the professors should teach? Assume that students in course G will get 90 points if Professor A teaches it or 45 if Professor B teaches it. Students in course U will get 90 points if Professor A teaches it or 60 if Professor B teaches it.

4. Use the notion of comparative advantage to explain why two countries, one of which is less efficient in producing all products, will still find it advantageous to trade.

5. Suppose the prices of goods in Mexico and the United States remain unchanged while the exchange rate increases from 10 pesos per dollar to 20 pesos per dollar. Take the perspective of a U.S. consumer. Are Mexican goods more or less attrac-

tive? Take the perspective of a Mexican consumer. Are U.S. goods more or less attractive?

6. Some studies have suggested that industries in countries that receive protection from foreign trade are less efficient than the same industries in other countries that do not receive protection. Can you explain this finding?

7. **Web Exercise.** Visit the Web site of the Organization of Economic Cooperation and Development (OECD), an international organization of industrialized, market-economy countries (*http://www.oecd.org*). The site has all sorts of data on OECD countries, including data on trade at *http://www.oecd.org/publications/figures/*. Use the data to get figures for imports and exports of goods and services for the following countries: United States, Canada, Germany, France, Japan, and the Netherlands. In which of these countries do exports exceed imports? In which countries do imports exceed exports?

8. **Web Exercise.** Visit the Fortune Web site [*http://www.pathfinder.com/fortune/fortune500/500list.html*] and get a list of the world's largest corporations. How many corporations in the top 20 are U.S. firms?

9. **Web Exercise.** Visit the Web site of Accu-Rate Foreign Exchange Corporation [*http://www.accurate.ca/index.html*] to check the most recent exchange rates. If a hotel room in Lisbon costs 4,500 escudos, how much is that in dollars?

Take It to the Net

We invite you to visit the O'Sullivan/Sheffrin page on the Prentice Hall Web site at: **http://www.prenhall.com/osullivan/** for additional World Wide Web exercises for this chapter.

Model Answers to Questions

Chapter-Opening Questions

1. Markets exist because most people are not self-sufficient but instead specialize in producing one or two products and then buy other products from other people.

2. Comparative advantage makes trade between rich and poor nations beneficial for both.

3. The most common forms of protection are quotas, voluntary export restraints, and tariffs.

4. GATT is an international agreement that has lowered trade barriers between the United States and

other nations. NAFTA is an international agreement that lowers barriers to trade among the United States, Mexico, and Canada (signed in 1994). The WTO is the new organization that oversees GATT and other international trade agreements.

Test Your Understanding

1. Tim's opportunity cost of one table is one-fifth of a chair, while Carla's opportunity cost of one table is one chair. Carla has a lower opportunity cost of chairs, so she should produce chairs. Tim has a

lower opportunity cost of tables, so he should produce tables.

2. The opportunity cost of a financial statement is four phone calls, and the opportunity cost of a phone call is one-fourth of a financial statement.

3. No. If he has a comparative advantage at managerial tasks such as doing the books or marketing, he should hire some workers to wash the cars, allowing him to specialize in the tasks for which he has a comparative advantage.

4. About three-fourths.

5. They transform inputs into outputs—products— and then sell the products.

6. The opportunity cost of wheat is 2 tons of steel in H and 3 tons of steel in T. Therefore, H has a comparative advantage in wheat. The opportunity cost of steel is 1/2 ton of wheat in H and 1/3 ton of wheat in T. Therefore, T has a comparative advantage in steel.

7. More.

8. A4, B1, C3, D2.

9. GATT, NAFTA.

 **Notes**

1. Rone Tempest, "Barbie and the World Economy," *Los Angeles Times,* September 22, 1996, page A1.

2. AP Worldstream, "In Time for Christmas, Chinese Video Piracy Thriving," December 12, 2000; *Los Angeles Times*, "Widespread DVD Piracy in China a Blow to Hollywood," August 31, 2000.

California Department of Health Services. Funded by the Tobacco Tax Initiative.

"Your scent is intoxicating..."

"Yours is carcinogenic."

Supply, Demand, and Market Equilibrium

In 1998, cigarette makers in the United States signed agreements with all 50 states to settle lawsuits over smoking-related health-care costs. Over the next 25 years, the states will receive $246 billion from the tobacco makers. The agreement includes new restrictions on advertising and marketing of cigarettes, including the elimination of billboard ads, poster ads in buses and trains, and cigarette logos on jackets, T-shirts, and caps. Although the Marlboro man will continue to appear in ads, Joe Camel is retiring. A few weeks after the agreement was announced, the price of cigarettes increased by 40 cents per pack.

As a budget analyst for your state government, you monitor health-care programs dealing with tobacco-related illness. The annual budget for these programs equals the revenue from the tobacco settlement ($80 million per year) plus the revenue collected from the state's cigarette tax ($200 million in the year before the tobacco settlement). Two years after the tobacco settlement, you discover that the revenue from the state is only $250 million, or $30 million less than you expected. What happened? This sounds like a case for the economic detective.

e know that a market is an arrangement that allows buyers and sellers to exchange money and products. In this chapter we use a model of supply and demand—the most important tool of economic analysis—to see how markets work. We can use the model of supply and demand to see how the prices of goods and services are affected by all sorts of changes in the economy, such as bad weather, higher income, technological innovation, taxes, regulation, and changes in consumer preferences. This chapter will prepare you for the applications of supply and demand you'll see in this book. You'll also learn how to be an economic detective, using clues from the market to explain past changes in market prices. The first case for the economic detective is the puzzling revenue shortfall for health-care programs.

We will use the model of supply and demand to explain how a perfectly competitive market operates. A **perfectly competitive market** has a very large number of firms, each of which produces the same standardized product and is so small that it does not affect the market price of the good it produces. The classic example of a perfectly competitive firm is a wheat farmer, who produces a tiny fraction of the total supply of wheat. No matter how much wheat the farmer produces, the market price of wheat won't change.

Perfectly competitive market: A market with a very large number of firms, each of which produces the same standardized product and is so small that it does not affect the market price of the good it produces.

This chapter includes many applications of supply and demand analysis. Here are some practical questions we answer:

1. Would there be fewer travel deaths if parents traveling by airplane with infants were required to strap the infants into safety seats?

2. Ted Koppel, host of the ABC news program *Nightline,* once suggested that the prices of illegal drugs had fallen because the supply of illegal drugs had increased. Was he correct?

3. Some data published in your local newspaper seem to suggest that gasoline consumers violate the law of demand, buying more gasoline at higher prices. Should you be skeptical about the data?

4. Over the last few decades the consumption of chicken and turkey has increased. Why?

The Demand Curve

On the demand side of a product market, consumers buy products from firms. The main question concerning the demand side of the market is, How much of a particular product are consumers willing to buy during a particular period? A consumer who is "willing to buy" a particular product is willing to sacrifice enough money to purchase it. The consumer doesn't merely have a desire to buy the good but is willing to sacrifice something to get it. Notice that demand is defined for a particular period, for example, a day, a month, or a year.

We'll start our discussion of demand with the individual consumer. How much of a product is an individual willing to buy? It depends on a number of variables. Here is a list of the variables that affect a consumer's decision, using the pizza market as an example:

- The price of the product, for example, the price of a pizza

- Consumer income

- The price of substitute goods such as tacos or sandwiches

- The price of complementary goods such as beer or lemonade

- Consumer tastes and advertising

- Consumer expectations about future prices

Together, these variables determine how much of a particular product an individual consumer is willing to buy. We'll start our discussion of demand with the relationship between the price and quantity demanded, a relationship that is represented graphically by the demand curve.

The Individual Demand Curve and the Law of Demand

The starting point for a discussion of individual demand is a **demand schedule**, a table of numbers that shows the relationship between price and quantity demanded, ceteris paribus (the Latin phrase for "everything else held fixed"). The variables that are held fixed in the demand schedule are income, the prices of substitutes and complements, consumer tastes, advertising, and expectations about future prices. Table 4.1 shows Al's demand schedule for pizza. At a price of $2, Al buys 13 pizzas per month. As the price rises, he buys fewer pizzas: 10 pizzas at a price of $4, 7 pizzas at a price of $6, and so on, down to only 1 pizza at a price of $10.

The **individual demand curve** shows the relationship between the price and the **quantity demanded** by a consumer, ceteris paribus (everything else held fixed). To draw the curve, we assume that everything else that affects a consumer's demand for pizza (income, prices of substitutes, prices of complementary goods, his tastes, advertising, expectations about future prices) does not change. The only variable that changes is the price of pizza, and we use the numbers from the demand schedule to draw the individual demand curve. Figure 4.1 shows Al's demand curve for pizza.

The demand curve is negatively sloped, reflecting the **law of demand**. This law is not a legal restriction that sends violators to jail, but is a pattern of behavior that we observe in most consumers.

LAW OF DEMAND

The higher the price, the smaller the quantity demanded, ceteris paribus (everything else held fixed).

The words "ceteris paribus" provide a reminder that to isolate the relationship between price and quantity demanded, we assume that the other determinants of demand are unchanged. In Al's case we see that as the price of pizza increases, he consumes fewer pizzas. A movement along the demand curve is called a **change in quantity demanded**, a change in the quantity a consumer is willing to buy when the price of the good changes. For example, if the price increases from $8 to $10, we move along the demand curve from point *c* to point *b*, and the quantity demanded decreases from 4 pizzas per month to 1 pizza per month.

Demand schedule: A table of numbers that shows the relationship between price and quantity demanded by a consumer, ceteris paribus (everything else held fixed).

Individual demand curve: A curve that shows the relationship between price and quantity demanded by a consumer, ceteris paribus (everything else held fixed).

Quantity demanded: The amount of a good a consumer is willing to buy

Law of demand: The higher the price, the smaller the quantity demanded, ceteris paribus (everything else held fixed).

Change in quantity demanded: A change in the amount of a good demanded resulting from a change in the price of the good; represented graphically by movement along the demand curve.

Table 4.1 Al's Demand Schedule for Pizzas

Price ($)	Quantity of pizzas per month
2	13
4	10
6	7
8	4
10	1

Figure 4.1

The Individual Demand Curve

According to the law of demand, the higher the price, the smaller the quantity demanded, everything else being equal. Therefore, the demand curve is negatively sloped: When the price increases from $6 to $8, the quantity demanded decreases from 7 pizzas per month (point *d*) to 4 pizzas per month (point *c*).

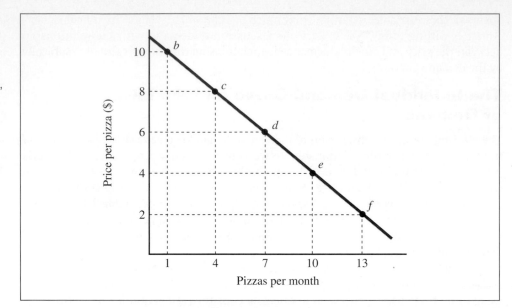

Substitution affect: The change in consumption resulting from a change in the price of one good relative to the price of other goods.

Income affect: The change in consumption resulting from an increase in the consumer's real income.

Market demand curve: A curve showing the relationship between price and quantity demanded by all consumers together, ceteris paribus (everything else held fixed).

To see why the law of demand is sensible, think about how Al might react to an increase in the price of pizza.

- **Substitution effect**. The more money Al spends on pizza, the less he has to spend on other products such as tacos, music, books, and travel. The price of pizza determines exactly how much of these other goods he sacrifices to get a pizza. If the price of pizza is $6 and the price of tacos is $1, Al will sacrifice 6 tacos for each pizza he buys. If the price of pizza increases to $8, he'll now sacrifice 8 tacos for each pizza. Given the larger sacrifice associated with buying pizza, he is likely to buy fewer pizzas, substituting tacos for pizza.

- **Income effect**. Suppose Al has a food budget of $100 per month and buys 10 pizzas at a price of $6 each (a total cost of $60) and spends $40 on other food. If the price of pizza rises to $7 each, the cost of his original food choices will be $110 ($70 for pizza and $40 on other items), well above his $100 food budget. To avoid exceeding his budget, Al must cut back on something and will probably cut back on pizza as well as other items. This is called the income effect because when the price of pizza increases, the purchasing power of Al's income (or budget) decreases, forcing him to consume smaller quantities.

From Individual to Market Demand

The **market demand curve** shows the relationship between the price of the good and the quantity that all consumers together are willing to buy, ceteris paribus (everything else held fixed). As in the case of the individual demand curve, when we draw the market demand curve, we assume that the other variables that affect individual demand (income, the prices of substitute and complementary goods, tastes, and price expectations) are fixed. In addition, we assume that the number of consumers is fixed. The market demand curve shows the relationship between price and the quantity demanded by all consumers, everything else being equal.

Figure 4.2 shows how to derive the market demand curve when there are only two consumers. Panel A shows Al's demand curve for pizza, and panel B shows Bea's demand curve for pizza. At a price of $8, Al will buy 4 pizzas (point *c*) and Bea will buy 2 pizzas (point *g*), so the total quantity demanded at this price is 6 pizzas (4 + 2). In panel C, point

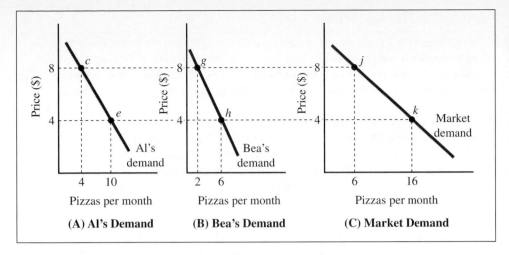

Figure 4.2

From Individual to Market Demand
The market demand equals the sum of the demands of all consumers. In this case there are only two consumers, so at each price, the market quantity demanded equals the quantity demanded by Al plus the quantity demanded by Bea. At a price of $8, Al's quantity is 4 pizzas (point c) and Bea's quantity is 2 pizzas (point g), so the market quantity demanded is 6 pizzas (point j). Each consumer obeys the law of demand, so the market demand curve is negatively sloped.

j shows the point on the market demand curve associated with a price of $8; at this price, the market quantity demanded is 6 pizzas. At a price of only $4, Al buys 10 pizzas and Bea buys 6 pizzas, for a total of 16 pizzas (shown by point k on the market demand curve).

The market demand is negatively sloped, reflecting the law of demand. This is sensible because if each consumer obeys the law of demand, consumers as a group will too. When the price increases from $4 to $8, there is a change in quantity demanded as we move along the demand curve from point k to j. The movement along the demand curve occurs if the price of pizza is the only determinant of demand that has changed.

The Supply Curve

On the supply side of a perfectly competitive market, firms sell their products to consumers. The main question for the supply side of the market is, How much of a particular product are firms willing to sell?

Here are the variables that affect the decisions of sellers, using the market for pizza as an example:

- The price of the product, such as the price of pizza
- The cost of the inputs used to produce the product, such as the wage paid to workers, the cost of electricity, and the cost of equipment
- The state of production technology, such as the knowledge used in making pizza
- The number of producers, such as the number of pizzerias
- Producer expectations about future prices
- Taxes or subsidies from the government

Together, these variables determine how much of a particular product producers are willing to sell. We'll start our discussion of market supply with the relationship between price of a good and quantity of that good supplied, a relationship that is represented graphically by the supply curve.

The Marginal Principle and the Output Decision

A perfectly competitive market has dozens or perhaps hundreds of firms, and we'll start our discussion of the supply curve with an individual firm. Nora's supply curve shows how many pizzas she is willing to produce at each price. Her decision about how many pizzas to produce is based on the marginal principle.

Marginal **PRINCIPLE**

Increase the level of an activity if its marginal benefit exceeds its marginal cost; reduce the level of an activity if its marginal cost exceeds its marginal benefit. If possible, pick the level at which the activity's marginal benefit equals its marginal cost.

Nora's activity is producing pizzas. If the price of pizza is $8, the marginal benefit of producing a pizza is the $8 Nora gets from selling it. In Figure 4.3 when the price is $8, the marginal benefit curve for pizza is horizontal at $8. Recall that marginal cost is the increase in total cost resulting from producing one more unit. In Figure 4.3 the marginal-cost curve for pizza is positively sloped, indicating that the more pizzas Nora produces, the higher the marginal cost of production.

When the price of pizza is $8, Nora satisfies the marginal principle at point p. She produces exactly 300 pizzas because that's the quantity at which the $8 marginal benefit equals the marginal cost of producing pizza. She stops at 300 pizzas because the marginal cost of producing the 301st pizza exceeds the $8 she could get from selling it. For example, if the marginal cost of the 301st pizza is $8.02. she would lose $0.02 on the 301st pizza.

How would Nora react to an increase in the price of pizza? If the price of pizza increased to $10, the marginal benefit of pizza production will increase to $10. At the higher price, it makes sense to produce the 301st pizza because the $10 benefit exceeds the $8.02 cost of producing it. In fact, when Nora applies the marginal principle with the higher price, she will increase production to 400 pizzas because that's the quantity at which the $10 marginal benefit equals the marginal cost. In Figure 4.3 the marginal-benefit curve for a price of $10 intersects the marginal cost curve at 400 pizzas (point q).

Individual Supply and the Law of Supply

Supply schedule: A table of numbers that shows the relationship between price and quantity supplied, ceteris paribus (everything else held fixed).

Quantity supplied: The amount of a good a firm is willing to sell.

A firm's **supply schedule** is a table of numbers that shows the relationship between price and the **quantity supplied** by the individual firm, ceteris paribus (everything else held fixed). The variables that are held fixed are input costs, technology, expectations, and government taxes or subsidies. Table 4.2 shows Nora's supply schedule for pizza. At a

Figure 4.3
The Marginal Principle and the Output Decision

The marginal benefit curve is horizontal at the market price. To satisfy the marginal principle, the firm produces the quantity at which the marginal benefit equals the marginal cost. An increase in the price shifts the marginal-benefit curve upward and increases the quantity at which the marginal benefit equals the marginal cost.

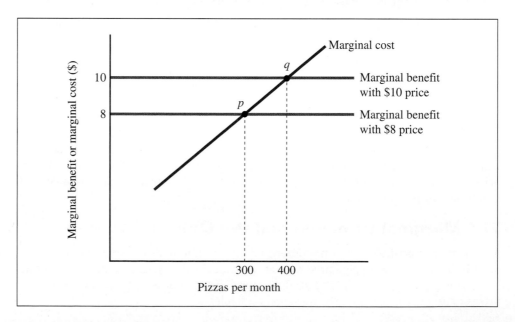

Table 4.2 Nora's Supply Schedule for Pizza

Price ($)	Quantity of pizzas per month
4	100
6	200
8	300
10	400
12	500

price of $4, she supplies 100 pizzas per month. As the price rises, she supplies more pizza: 200 pizzas at a price of $6, 300 pizzas at a price of $8, and so on, up to 500 pizzas at a price of $12.

The **individual supply curve** shows the relationship between the price and the quantity supplied by a single firm, ceteris paribus (everything else held fixed). To draw the curve, we assume that everything else that affects the supply of pizza (input costs, technology, price expectations, government taxes and subsidies) does not change. The only variable that changes is the price of pizza, and we use the numbers from the supply schedule to draw a supply curve. Panel A of Figure 4.4 shows Nora's supply curve for pizza.

Nora's supply curve is positively sloped, reflecting the **law of supply**, a pattern of behavior that we observe in producers.

> **Individual supply curve:** A curve that shows the relationship between price and quantity supplied by a producer ceteris paribus (everything else held fixed).

> **Law of supply:** The higher the price, the larger the quantity supplied, ceteris paribus (everything else held fixed).

LAW OF SUPPLY

The higher the price, the larger the quantity supplied, ceteris paribus (everything else held fixed).

The words "ceteris paribus" remind us that to isolate the relationship between price and quantity supplied, we assume that the other determinants of supply are unchanged. As the price of pizza increases, Nora produces a larger quantity of pizza. A

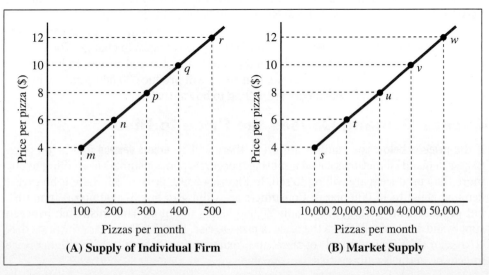

(A) Supply of Individual Firm

(B) Market Supply

Figure 4.4
Individual and Market Supply Curve
(A) Supply of individual firm. Nora supplies 300 pizzas at a price of $8 (point *p*) but 400 pizzas at a price of $10 (point *q*).
(B) Market supply. There are 100 identical pizzerias, so the market quantity equals 100 times the quantity supplied by Nora's, the typical pizzeria. At a price of $8, Nora supplies 300 pizzas (point *p*), so the market quantity supplied is 30,000 pizzas (point *u*).

Change in quantity supplied: A
change in the quantity supplied
resulting from a change in the
price of the good; represented
graphically by movement along
the supply curve.

movement along the supply curve is called a **change in quantity supplied**, a change in the quantity a producer is willing to sell when the price of the good changes. For example, if the price increases from $8 to $10, Nora moves upward along her supply curve from point p to point q, and the quantity supplied increases from 300 pizzas per month to 400 pizzas per month.

Individual Supply to Market Supply

Market supply curve: A curve
showing the relationship
between price and quantity
supplied by all producers
together, ceteris paribus
(everything else held fixed).

The **market supply curve** for a particular good shows the relationship between the price of the good and the quantity that all producers together are willing to sell, ceteris paribus (everything else held fixed). To draw the market supply curve, we assume that the other variables that affect individual supply are fixed. In addition, we assume that the number of producers is fixed.

Panel B of Figure 4.4 shows the market supply curve when there are 100 producers, each of which has the same individual supply curve as Nora. At a price of $8, Nora supplies 300 pizzas per month (point p), so the 100 firms together produce 30,000 pizzas (300 pizzas per firm times 100 firms), as shown by point u. If the price increases to $10, Nora supplies 400 pizzas (point q), so the quantity supplied by the market is 40,000 (point v).

The market supply curve is positively sloped, reflecting the law of supply. This is sensible because if each firm obeys the law of supply, firms as a group will too. When the price increases from $8 to $10, there is a change in quantity supplied as we move along the market supply curve from point u to point v. The movement along the supply curve occurs if the price of pizza is the only determinant of supply that has changed.

TEST Your Understanding

1. Complete the statement with "increase" or "decrease": When a price increases, the law of demand suggests that the quantity demanded will _____, while the law of supply suggests that the quantity supplied will _____.

2. List the variables that are held fixed in drawing a market demand curve.

3. List the variables that are held fixed in drawing a market supply curve.

Market Equilibrium

Market equilibrium: A situation
in which the quantity of a
product demanded equals the
quantity supplied, so there is no
pressure to change the price.

When the quantity of a product demanded equals the quantity supplied, this is called a **market equilibrium**. When a market reaches an equilibrium, there is no pressure to change the price. For example, if pizza firms produce exactly the quantity of pizza consumers are willing to buy, there will be no pressure for the price of pizza to change. The equilibrium price is shown by the intersection of the supply and demand curves. In Figure 4.5. at a price of $8, the supply curve shows that firms will produce 30,000 pizzas, which is exactly the quantity that consumers are willing to buy at that price.

Excess Demand Causes the Price to Rise

Excess demand: A situation in
which, at the prevailing price,
consumers are willing to buy
more than producers are willing
to sell.

If the price is below the equilibrium price, there will be **excess demand** for the product. Excess demand (sometimes called a shortage) occurs when consumers are willing to buy more than producers are willing to sell. In Figure 4.5 at a price of $6, there is an excess demand equal to 17,000 pizzas: Consumers are willing to buy 37,000 pizzas (point d), but producers are willing to sell only 20,000 pizzas (point c). This mismatch between supply and demand will cause the price of pizza to rise. Firms will increase the price they charge for their limited supply of pizza, and anxious consumers will pay the higher price to get one of the few pizzas that are available.

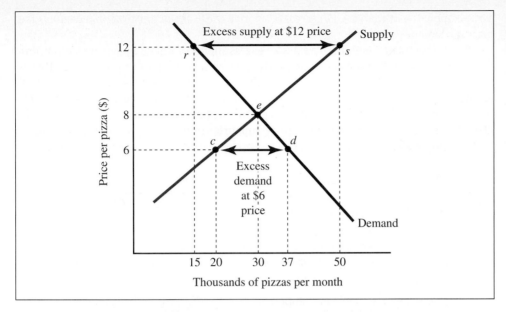

Figure 4.5

Supply, Demand, and Market Equilibrium

At the market equilibrium (point *e*, with price = $8 and quantity = 30,000), the quantity supplied equals the quantity demanded. At a price lower than the equilibrium price ($6), there is excess demand (the quantity demanded exceeds the quantity supplied). At a price above the equilibrium price ($12), there is excess supply (the quantity supplied exceeds the quantity demanded).

An increase in price eliminates excess demand by changing both the quantity demanded and quantity supplied. As the price increases, there are two effects.

- The market moves upward along the demand curve (from point *d* toward point *e*), *decreasing* the quantity demanded.

- The market moves upward along the supply curve (from point *c* toward point *e*), *increasing* the quantity supplied.

Because quantity demanded decreases while quantity supplied increases, the gap between the quantity demanded and the quantity supplied narrows. The price will continue to rise until excess demand is eliminated. In Figure 4.5, at a price of $8, the quantity supplied equals the quantity demanded.

In some cases, government creates an excess demand for a good by setting a maximum price (sometimes called a price ceiling). If the government sets a maximum price that is less than the equilibrium price, the result is a permanent excess demand for the good. The most prominent example in the United States is rent control, a maximum price for apartments. During World War II the federal government instituted a national system of rent controls. Although New York City was the only city to retain rent control after the war, rent control returned to dozens of cities in the 1970s. Since then several states have passed laws that have weakened rent control.

Excess Supply Causes the Price to Drop

What happens if the price is above the equilibrium price? **Excess supply** (sometimes called a surplus) occurs when producers are willing to sell more than consumers are willing to buy. This is shown by points *r* and *s* in Figure 4.5. At a price of $12, the excess supply is 35,000 pizzas: producers are willing to sell 50,000 pizzas (point *s*), but consumers are willing to buy only 15,000 pizzas (point *r*). This mismatch will cause the price of pizza to fall as firms cut the price to sell their pizza. As the price drops two things happen:

- The market moves downward along the demand curve, *increasing* the quantity demanded.

- The market moves downward along the supply curve, *decreasing* the quantity supplied.

Because the quantity demanded increases while the quantity supplied decreases, the gap between quantity supplied and demanded narrows. The price will continue to drop until

Excess supply: A situation in which, at the prevailing price, producers are willing to sell more than consumers are willing to buy.

excess supply is eliminated. In Figure 4.5, at price of $8, the quantity supplied equals the quantity demanded.

The government sometimes creates an excess supply of a good by setting a minimum price (sometimes called a price floor). If the government sets a minimum price that is greater than the equilibrium price, the result is a permanent excess supply. For several decades, the U.S. government set minimum prices for dozens of agricultural products such as corn and dairy products. These agricultural price-support programs ended in 1996. The European Community has price supports (minimum prices) for grains, dairy products, livestock, and sugar, and Japan has price supports for dairy products and sugar.

TEST Your Understanding

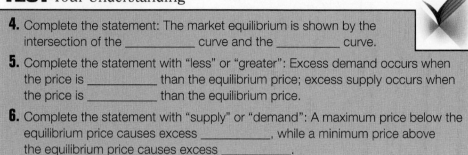

4. Complete the statement: The market equilibrium is shown by the intersection of the _____ curve and the _____ curve.

5. Complete the statement with "less" or "greater": Excess demand occurs when the price is _____ than the equilibrium price; excess supply occurs when the price is _____ than the equilibrium price.

6. Complete the statement with "supply" or "demand": A maximum price below the equilibrium price causes excess _____, while a minimum price above the equilibrium price causes excess _____.

Market Effects of Changes in Demand

We've seen that a market equilibrium occurs when the quantity supplied equals the quantity demanded, shown graphically by the intersection of the supply curve and the demand curve. In this part of the chapter, we'll see how changes on the demand side of the market affect the equilibrium price and equilibrium quantity.

Change in Quantity Demanded Versus Change in Demand

Earlier in the chapter we listed the variables that determine how much of a particular product consumers are willing to buy. One of the variables is the price of the product, and the law of demand summarizes the negative relationship between price and quantity demanded. We're ready to take a closer look at the other variables that affect demand—income, the prices of related goods, tastes, advertising, and the number of consumers—and see how changes in these variables affect the demand for the product and the market equilibrium.

If any of these other variables change, the relationship between price and quantity—shown numerically in the demand schedule and graphically in the demand curve—will change. That means we will have an entirely different demand schedule and a different demand curve. To convey the idea that changes in these other variables change the demand schedule and the demand curve, a change in any of these variables causes a **change in demand**. In contrast, a change in the price of the good causes *a change in quantity demanded*.

Change in demand: A change in the amount of a good demanded resulting from a change in something other than the price of the good; represented graphically by a shift of the demand curve.

Increases in Demand

We'll start with changes in the pizza market that increase the demand for pizza. An increase in demand means that at each price, consumers are willing to buy a larger quantity. In Figure 4.6 an increase in demand shifts the market demand curve from D_2 to D_3. At the initial price of $8, the quantity demanded increases from 30,000 pizzas

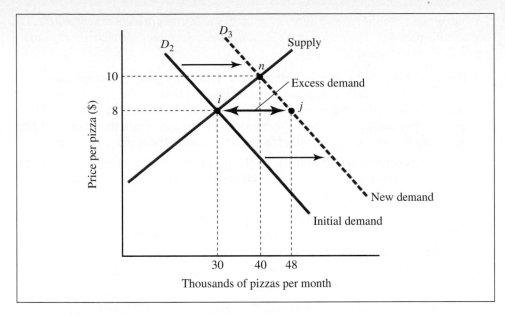

Figure 4.6
Market Effects of an Increase in Demand
An increase in demand shifts the demand curve to the right: At each price, the quantity demanded increases. At the initial price ($8), the shift of the demand curve causes excess demand, causing the price to rise. Equilibrium is restored at point *n*, with a higher equilibrium price ($10, up from $8) and a larger equilibrium quantity (40,000 pizzas, up from 30,000 pizzas).

(point *i*) to 48,000 (point *j*). An increase in demand like the one represented in Figure 4.6 can occur for several reasons, which are listed in the first column of Table 4.3.

- **Increase in income.** Consumers use their income to buy products, and the more money they have, the more money they spend. For a **normal good** there is a positive relationship between consumer income and the quantity consumed.

- **Increase in price of a substitute good.** When two goods are **substitutes**, an increase in the price of the first good causes some consumers to switch to the second good.

Normal good: A good for which an increase in income increases demand.

Substitutes: Two goods that are related in such a way that an increase in the price of one good increases the demand for the other good.

Table 4.3   Changes in Demand Shift the Demand Curve

An increase in demand shifts the demand curve to the right when	A decrease in demand shifts the demand curve to the left when
The good is normal and income increases	The good is normal and income decreases
The good is inferior and income decreases	The good is inferior and income increases
The price of a substitute good increases	The price of a substitute good decreases
The price of a complementary good decreases	The price of a complementary good increases
Population increases	Population decreases
Consumer tastes shift in favor of the product	Consumer tastes shift away from the product
Favorable advertising	Unfavorable publicity
Consumers expect a higher price in the future	Consumers expect a lower price in the future

Tacos and pizzas are substitutes, so an increase in the price of tacos increases the demand for pizzas as some consumers substitute pizza for tacos, which are now more expensive relative to pizza.

Complements: Two goods that are related in such a way that an increase in the price of one good decreases the demand for the other good.

- **Decrease in price of a complementary good.** When two goods are **complements**, they are consumed together as a package, and a decrease in the price of one good decreases the cost of the entire package. As a result, consumers buy more of both goods. Pizza and beer are complementary goods, so a decrease in the price of beer decreases the cost of a beer and pizza meal, increasing the demand for pizza.

- **Increase in population.** An increase in the number of people means that there are more pizza consumers—more individual demand curves to add up to get the market demand curve—so market demand increases.

- **Shift in consumer tastes.** Consumers' preferences or tastes change over time, and when consumers' preferences shift in favor of pizza, the demand for pizza increases.

- **Favorable advertising.** The purpose of an advertising campaign is to shift consumers' preferences in favor of a product, so a successful pizza advertising campaign will increase the demand for pizza.

- **Expectations of higher future prices.** If consumers think next month's pizza price will be higher than they had initially expected, they may buy a larger quantity today (and a smaller quantity next month). That means that the demand for pizza today will increase.

Market Effects of an Increase in Demand

We can use Figure 4.6 to show the effects of an increase in demand on the equilibrium price and equilibrium quantity. An increase in the demand for pizza shifts the demand curve to the right, from D_2 to D_3. At the initial price of $8 (the equilibrium price with the initial demand curve), there will be an excess demand, as indicated by points i and j: Consumers are willing to buy 48,000 pizzas (point j), but producers are willing to sell only 30,000 pizzas (point i). Consumers want to buy 18,000 more pizzas than producers are willing to supply, so there is pressure to increase the price.

As the price rises, the excess demand shrinks because the quantity demanded decreases while the quantity supplied increases.

- The market moves upward along the supply curve to a larger quantity supplied.

- The market moves upward along the new demand curve to a smaller quantity demanded.

The supply curve intersects the new demand curve at point n, so the new equilibrium price is $10 (up from $8), and the new equilibrium quantity is 40,000 pizzas (up from 30,000).

Decreases in Demand

What sort of changes in the pizza market will decrease the demand for pizza? A decrease in demand means that at each price, consumers are willing to buy a smaller quantity. In Figure 4.7, a decrease in demand shifts the market demand curve from D_2 to D_1. At the initial price of $8, the quantity demanded decreases from 30,000 pizzas (point i) to 12,000 pizzas (point k). A decrease in demand like the one represented in Figure 4.7 can occur for several reasons, which are listed in the second column of Table 4.3.

- **Decrease in income.** A decrease in income means that consumers have less to spend, so they buy a smaller quantity of each normal good.

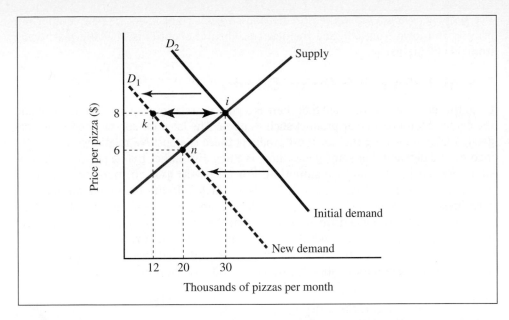

Figure 4.7

Market Effects of a Decrease in Demand
A decrease in demand shifts the demand curve to the left: At each price, the quantity demanded decreases. At the initial price ($8), the leftward shift of the demand curve causes excess supply, causing the price to fall. Equilibrium is restored at point *n*, with a lower equilibrium price ($6, down from $8) and a smaller equilibrium quantity (20,000 pizzas, down from 30,000 pizzas).

- **Decrease in price of a substitute good.** A decrease in the price of a substitute good such as tacos makes pizza more expensive relative to tacos, causing consumers to demand less pizza.

- **Increase in price of a complementary good.** An increase in the price of a complementary good such as beer increases the cost of a beer and pizza meal, decreasing the demand for pizza.

- **Decrease in population.** A decrease in the number of people means that there are fewer pizza consumers, so the market demand for pizza decreases.

- **Shift in consumer tastes.** When consumers' preferences shift away from pizza in favor of other products, the demand for pizza decreases.

- **Expectations of lower future prices.** If consumers think next month's pizza price will be lower than they had initially expected, they may buy a smaller quantity today, meaning the demand for pizza today will decrease.

Market Effects of a Decrease in Demand

We can use Figure 4.7 to show the effects of a decrease in demand on the equilibrium price and equilibrium quantity. The demand for pizza shifts the demand curve to the left, from D_2 to D_1. At the initial price of $8 (the equilibrium price with the initial demand curve), there will be an excess supply, as indicated by points *i* and *k*: Producers are willing to sell 30,000 pizzas (point *i*), but given the lower demand, consumers are willing to buy only 12,000 pizzas (point *k*). Producers want to sell 18,000 more pizzas than consumers are willing to buy, so there is pressure to decrease the price.

The excess supply means that there is pressure to reduce prices, and as the price falls, the excess supply shrinks because the quantity demanded increases while the quantity supplied decreases.

- The market moves downward along the supply curve to a smaller quantity supplied.

- The market moves downward along the new demand curve to a larger quantity demanded.

The supply curve intersects the new demand curve at point n, so the new equilibrium price is $6 (down from $8), and the new equilibrium quantity is 20,000 pizzas (down from 30,000 pizzas).

Normal Versus Inferior Goods

Inferior good: A good for which an increase in income decreases demand.

Up to this point, we've assumed that there is a positive relationship between income and the demand for a particular product such as pizza. The label for such a good is normal good, a label indicating that for most products there is a positive relationship between income and demand. For some goods there is a negative rather than a positive relationship between income and consumption. For an **inferior good** an increase in income decreases demand, shifting the demand curve to the left. In most cases an inferior good is an inexpensive good such as margarine that has an expensive alternative (butter). As income increases, some consumers switch from the inexpensive good to the expensive one, for example, buying less margarine and more butter. As a result, the demand for margarine decreases and the demand curve shifts to the left. Some other examples of inferior goods are potatoes, intercity bus travel, and used clothing.

TEST Your Understanding

7. Which of the following go together?
  a. Change in demand
  b. Change in quantity demanded
  c. Change in price
  d. Movement along the demand curve
  e. Shifting the demand curve
  f. Change in income

8. What's wrong with the following statement? "Demand increased because the demand curve shifted."

9. Complete the statement with "right" or "left": An increase in the price of cassette tapes will shift the demand curve for CDs to the _____; an increase in the price of CD players will shift the demand curve for CDs to the _____.

10. In the following list of variables, circle the ones that change as we move along the demand curve for pencils, and cross out the ones that are assumed to be fixed; quantity of pencils demanded, number of consumers, price of pencils, price of pens, consumer income.

Market Effects of Changes in Supply

We've seen that changes in demand shift the demand curve and change the equilibrium price and quantity. In this part of the chapter, we'll see how changes on the supply side of the market affect the equilibrium price and equilibrium quantity.

Change in Quantity Supplied Versus Change in Supply

Earlier in the chapter we listed the variables that determine how much of a particular product firms are willing to sell. One of the variables is the price of the product, and the relationship between price and quantity supplied is shown by the law of supply. We're ready to take a closer look at the other variables that affect supply—input costs, technology, the number of firms, and price expectations—and see how changes in these variables affect the supply of the product and the market equilibrium.

If any of these other variables changes, the relationship between price and quantity—shown numerically in the supply schedule and graphically in the supply curve—will change. That means that we will have an entirely different supply schedule and a different supply curve. To convey the idea that changes in these other variables change the supply schedule and the supply curve, a change in any of these variables causes a **change in supply**. In contrast, a change in the price of the good causes *a change in quantity supplied* (defined earlier in the chapter).

Change in supply: A change in the amount of a good supplied resulting from a change in something other than the price of the good; represented graphically by a shift of the supply curve.

Increases in Supply

We'll start with changes in the pizza market that increase the supply of pizza. An increase in supply means that at each price, producers are willing to sell a larger quantity. In Figure 4.8, an increase in supply shifts the market supply curve from S_2 to S_3. At the initial price of $8, the quantity demanded increases from 30,000 pizzas (point i) to 45,000 (point m). An increase in supply like the one represented in Figure 4.8 can occur for several reasons, which are listed in the first column of Table 4.4.

- **Decrease in input costs.** A decrease in the cost of labor or some other input will make pizza production less costly and more profitable at a given price, so producers will supply more.

- **Advance in technology.** A technological advance that makes it possible to produce pizza at a lower cost will make pizza production more profitable, so producers will supply more.

- **An increase in the number of producers.** The market supply is the sum of the supplies of all producers, so the larger number of producers, the greater the supply.

- **Expectations of lower future prices.** If firms think next month's pizza price will be lower than they had initially expected, they may be willing to sell a larger quantity today (and a smaller quantity next month). That means that the supply of pizza today will increase.

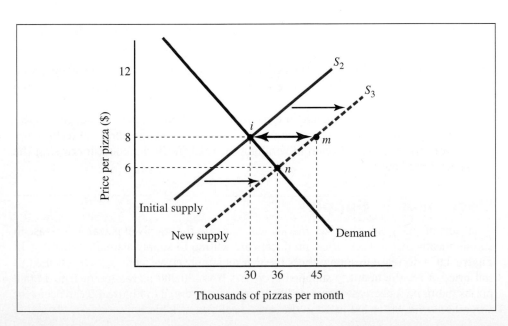

Figure 4.8
Market Effects of an Increase in Supply
An increase in supply shifts the supply curve to the right: At each price, the quantity supplied increases. At the initial price ($8), the rightward shift of the supply curve causes excess supply, causing the price to drop. Equilibrium is restored at point n, with a lower equilibrium price ($6, down from $8) and a larger equilibrium quantity (36,000 pizzas, up from 30,000 pizzas).

Table 4.4 Changes in Supply Shift the Supply Curve

An increase in supply shifts the supply curve to the right when	A decrease in supply shifts the supply curve to the left when
The cost of an input decreases	The cost of an input increases
A technological advance decreases production costs	
The number of firms increases	The number of firms decreases
Producers expect a lower price in the future	Producers expect a higher price in the future
Subsidy	Tax

- **Subsidy.** If the government subsidizes the production of the product (pays firms some amount for each unit produced), the subsidy will make the product more profitable, so firms will produce more.

Market Effects of an Increase in Supply

We can use Figure 4.8 to show the effects of an increase in supply on the equilibrium price and equilibrium quantity. An increase in the supply of pizza shifts the supply curve to the right, from S_2 to S_3. At the initial price of $8 (the equilibrium price with the initial supply curve), there will be an excess supply, as indicated by points i and m: Producers are willing to sell 45,000 pizzas (point m), but consumers are willing to buy only 30,000 (point i). Producers want to sell 15,000 more pizzas than consumers are willing to buy, so there is pressure to decrease the price.

As the price decreases, the excess supply shrinks because the quantity supplied decreases while the quantity demanded increases.

- The market moves downward along the new supply curve to a smaller quantity supplied.
- The market moves downward along the demand curve to a larger quantity demanded.

The new supply curve intersects the demand curve at point n, so the new equilibrium price is $6 (down from $8) and the new equilibrium quantity is 36,000 pizzas (up from 30,000).

How has technological change in electricity generation affected the supply of electricity from alternative sources, including wind power? To see the effects of technological innovation in the production of wind power, read "A Closer Look: Increasing the Supply of Wind Power."

Decreases in Supply

What sort of changes in the pizza market will decrease the supply of pizza? A decrease in supply means that at each price, producers are willing to supply a smaller quantity. In Figure 4.9, a decrease in supply shifts the market supply curve from S_2 to S_1. At the initial price of $8, the quantity supplied decreases from 30,000 pizzas (point i) to 14,000 pizzas (point p). A decrease in supply like the one represented in Figure 4.9 can occur for several reasons, which are listed in the second column of Table 4.4.

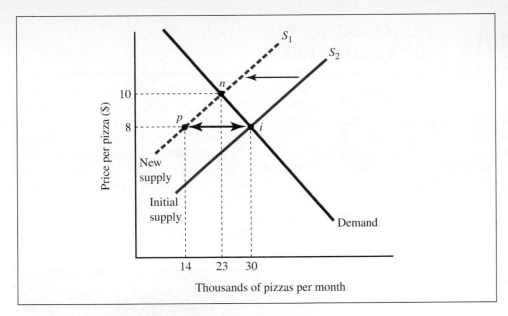

Figure 4.9

Market Effects of a Decrease in Supply
A decrease in supply shifts the supply curve to the left: At each price, the quantity supplied decreases. At the initial price ($8), the leftward shift of the supply curve causes excess demand, causing the price to rise. Equilibrium is restored at point *n*, with a higher equilibrium price ($10, up from $8) and a smaller equilibrium quantity (23,000 pizzas, down from 30,000 pizzas).

- **Increase in input costs.** A increase in the cost of labor or some other input will make pizza production more costly and less profitable at a given price, so producers will supply less.

- **A decrease in the number of producers.** The market supply is the sum of the supplies of all producers, so a decrease in the number of producers decreases supply.

- **Expectations of higher future prices.** If firms think next month's pizza price will be higher than they had initially expected, they may be willing to sell a smaller quantity today (and a larger quantity next month). That means that the supply of pizza today will decrease.

- **Tax.** If the government imposes a tax on producers (a firm pays the government some amount for each unit produced), the tax will make the product more costly and less profitable, so firms will supply less.

Market Effects of a Decrease in Supply

We can use Figure 4.9 to show the effects of a decrease in supply on the equilibrium price and equilibrium quantity. A decrease in the supply of pizza shifts the supply curve to the left, from S_2 to S_1. At the initial price of $8 (the equilibrium price with the initial supply curve), there will be an excess demand, as indicated by points *i* and *p*: Consumers are willing to buy 30,000 pizzas (point *i*), but producers are willing to sell only 14,000 pizzas (point *p*). Consumers want to buy 16,000 more pizzas than producers are willing to sell, so there is pressure to increase the price.

As the price increases, the excess demand shrinks because the quantity demanded decreases while the quantity supplied increases.

- The market moves upward along the demand curve to a smaller quantity demanded.

- The market moves upward along the new supply curve to a larger quantity supplied.

The new supply curve intersects the demand curve at point *n*, so the new equilibrium price is $10 (up from $8), and the new equilibrium quantity is 23,000 pizzas (down from 30,000).

INCREASING THE SUPPLY OF WIND POWER

The year 2001 may be remembered as the year of the wind. Every few weeks, newspapers announced the development of another huge windfarm, a collection of turbines propelled by the wind and hooked up to the electric power system or electric grid. The United States Energy Department expects the supply of electricity from wind to double in just one year.[1]

The explosion in wind electricity resulted from technological innovations that decreased the cost of producing electricity from the wind. In the 1980s, the cost of wind electricity was about 50 cents per kilowatt hour. Several design innovations—including the replacement of small rapid rotors with large slow-moving blades and the development of monitoring systems that permit the turbines to change their direction and blade angle to more efficiently harness the wind—have decreased the cost of maintaining the turbines and increased the electricity output per hour. By 2001, the cost of wind power had dropped to about 4 cents per kilowatt hour, compared with 2.5 to 3 cents for electricity generated by conventional sources (natural gas and coal). Because the producers of wind power receive a fed-

eral tax credit of 1.5 cents per kilowatt hour, wind power is often competitive with conventional power sources.

In graphical terms, the technological innovations in the design of wind turbines decreased production costs, shifting the supply curve for wind electricity to the right, increasing the equilibrium quantity and decreasing the price. The federal tax credit amplified the rightward shift of the supply curve, leading to an even larger increase in quantity and decrease in price.

Market Effects of Simultaneous Changes in Demand and Supply

What happens to the equilibrium price and quantity when both supply and demand increase? It depends on which change is larger. In panel A of Figure 4.10, the increase in demand is larger than the increase in supply, meaning the demand curve shifts by a larger amount than the supply curve. The market equilibrium moves from point *i* to point *d*, and the equilibrium price increases from $8 to $9. This is sensible because an increase in demand tends to pull the price up, while an increase in supply tends to push the price down. If demand increases by a larger amount, the upward pull will be stronger than the downward push, and the price will rise.

We can be certain that when supply and demand both increase, the equilibrium quantity will increase. That's because both changes tend to increase the equilibrium quantity. In panel A of Figure 4.10, the equilibrium quantity increases from 30,000 to 44,000 pizzas.

Panel B of Figure 4.10 shows what happens when the increase in supply is larger than the increase in demand. The equilibrium moves from point *i* to *s*, meaning that the price falls from $8 to $7. This is sensible because the downward pull on the price resulting from the increase in supply is stronger than the upward pull from the increase in demand. As expected, the equilibrium quantity rises from 30,000 to 45,000 pizzas.

What about simultaneous *decreases* in supply and demand? In this case the equilibrium quantity will certainly fall because both changes tend to decrease the equilibrium

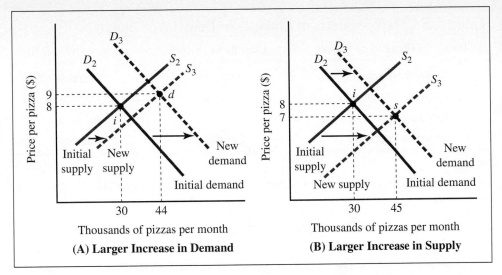

Figure 4.10

**Market Effects
of Simultaneous
Changes in Supply
and Demand**
**(A) Larger increase in
demand.** If the increase in
demand is larger than the
increase in supply (if the shift
of the demand curve is larger
than the shift of the supply
curve), both the equilibrium
price and the equilibrium
quantity will increase.
**(B) Larger increase in sup-
ply.** If the increase in supply
is larger than the increase in
demand (if the shift of the
supply curve is larger than
the shift of the demand
curve), the equilibrium price
will decrease and the equilibrium quantity will increase.

quantity. The effect on the equilibrium price depends on which change is larger, the decrease in demand, which pushes the price downward, or the decrease in supply, which pulls the price upward. If the change in demand is larger, the price will fall because the force pushing the price down will be stronger than the force pulling it up. In contrast, if the decrease in supply is larger, the price will rise because the force pulling the price up will be stronger than the force pushing it down.

TEST Your Understanding

11. Which of the following items go together?
   a. Change in quantity supplied
   b. Change in input cost
   c. Change in price
   d. Shifting the supply curve
   e. Movement along the supply curve
   f. Change in supply

12. An increase in the wage of computer workers will shift the supply curve for computers to the left. True or false? Explain.

13. In the following list, circle the variables that change as we move along the market supply curve for housing, and cross out the variables that are assumed to be fixed: quantity of housing supplied, number of potential consumers, price of wood, price of houses, consumer income.

Applications

We can use the lessons from the pizza market to explore the effects of changes in other markets on equilibrium prices and quantities. Table 4.5 summarizes the effects of changes in demand and supply on equilibrium prices and quantities. When demand changes and the demand curve shifts, price and quantity change in the same direction.

- **Increase in demand.** Both the equilibrium price and the equilibrium quantity increase.

- **Decrease in demand.** Both the equilibrium price and the equilibrium quantity decrease.

Table 4.5 Market Effects of Changes in Demand or Supply

Change in Demand or Supply	Change in Price	Change in Quantity
Increase in demand	Increase	Increase
Decrease in demand	Decrease	Decrease
Increase in supply	Decrease	Increase
Decrease in supply	Increase	Decrease

When supply changes and the supply curve shifts, price and quantity change in opposite directions.

- **Increase in supply.** The equilibrium price decreases, but the equilibrium quantity increases.

- **Decrease in supply.** The equilibrium price increases, but the equilibrium quantity decreases.

Changes in Demand: Population Growth, Product Safety, Travel Modes

How will an increase in enrollment at a university affect the equilibrium price of apartments in the university town? In Figure 4.11, the initial equilibrium is shown by point *i*, with a monthly rent of $400 per apartment. An increase in university enrollment increases the number of students seeking apartments, shifting the demand for apartments to the right. The new equilibrium is shown by point *n*, with a price of $600 per apartment. The increase in demand increases the equilibrium price and the equilibrium quantity of apartments.

How does public information about the safety of products affect equilibrium prices and quantities? In 1999 a controversial report suggested that pesticide residue on apples made them unsafe for infants and small children. Although many experts disputed the report, it decreased the demand for apples. In Figure 4.12, the initial equilibrium is shown by point *i*, with a price of $0.60 per pound and a quantity of 26,000 pounds per

Figure 4.11

University Enrollment and Apartment Rent

An increase in university enrollment will increase the demand for apartments in the university town, shifting the demand curve to the right. Equilibrium is restored at point *n*, with a higher price ($600, up from $400) and a larger quantity (4,000 apartments, up from 3,000 apartments).

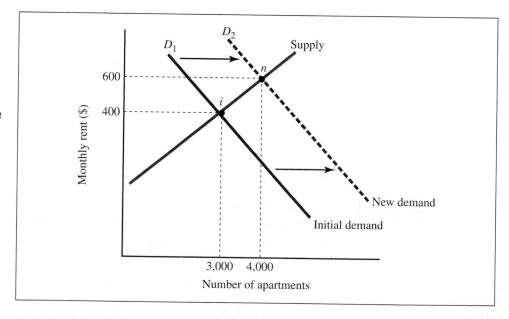

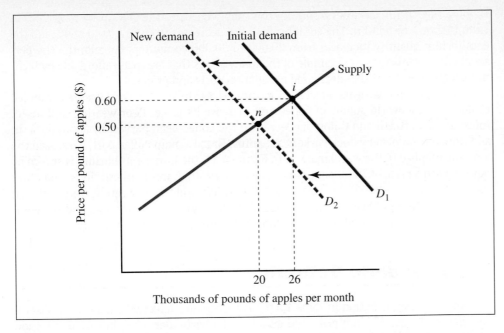

Figure 4.12
Market Effects of Pesticide Residue
A report of pesticide residue on apples decreases the demand for apples, shifting the demand curve to the left. Equilibrium is restored at point *n*, with a lower price ($0.50, down from $0.60) and a smaller quantity (20,000 pounds, down from 26,000 pounds).

month. The pesticide report shifted the demand curve to the left, leading to a new equilibrium at point *n*, with a lower equilibrium price ($0.50) and a smaller equilibrium quantity (20,000 pounds). The decrease in demand decreased the equilibrium price and the equilibrium quantity of apples.

How does an increase in the price of air travel affect automobile travel and highway deaths? For the answer, read "A Closer Look: Infant Airline Seats and Safety."

Changes in Supply: Technology, Weather

How do technological innovations affect equilibrium prices? Recent innovations in electronics have decreased the cost of producing personal computers. In Figure 4.13, the initial equilibrium is shown by point *i*. The decrease in production costs increases the

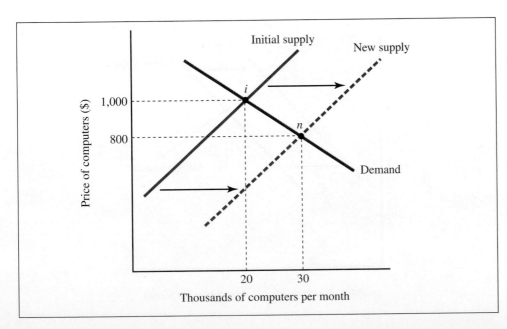

Figure 4.13
Technological Innovation and the Computer Market
Technological innovation decreases production costs, increasing supply and shifting the supply curve to the right. The equilibrium price decreases, and the equilibrium quantity increases.

supply of personal computers, shifting the supply curve to the right. The new equilibrium is shown by point *n*: The equilibrium price decreases from $1,000 to $800, and the equilibrium quantity increases from 20,000 to 30,000 computers per month. The personal computer is just one example of the many goods that are made affordable by technological innovations that decreased production costs and prices.

How does poor weather affect equilibrium prices? In 1992, several events combined to decrease the world supply of coffee and increase its price. Poor weather and insect infestations in Brazil and Colombia decreased the coffee-bean harvest by about 40%. In addition, a slowdown by dockworkers at Santos, Brazil's main coffee port, decreased the amount supplied to the world market. In Figure 4.14, the initial equilibrium is shown by point *i*, with a price of $0.60 per pound. The poor weather, insect infestations, and other supply disruptions shifted the supply curve to the left, and the new equilibrium is shown by point *n*. The equilibrium price of coffee increased to $0.72 per pound, and the equilibrium quantity decreased from 30 million to 22 million pounds per month.

The Economic Detective

We can use the information in Table 4.5 to play economic detective. Suppose we observe changes in the equilibrium price and quantity of a particular good, but we don't know what caused these changes. It could have been a change in demand or a change in supply. We can use the information in Table 4.5 to work backwards, using what we observe about changes in prices and quantities to discover the reason for the changes. We discuss three cases for the economic detective: an increase in the consumption of poultry products, a decrease in the price of illegal drugs, and the budgetary effects of the tobacco settlement.

The Mystery of Increasing Poultry Consumption
Why has the consumption of poultry (chicken and turkey) increased so much over the last several decades? One possibility is that consumers have become more health conscious and have switched from red meat to poultry as part of an effort to eat health-

Figure 4.14
Bad Weather and the Coffee Market
Bad weather decreases the supply of coffee beans, shifting the supply curve to the left. Equilibrium is restored at point *n*, with a higher price ($0.72, up from $0.60) and a smaller quantity (22 million pounds, down from 30 million pounds).

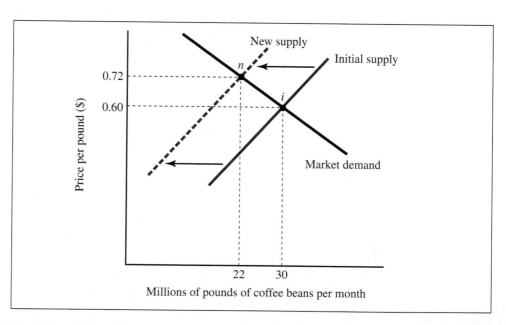

Should parents traveling by airplane be allowed to hold their infants in their laps? Or should they be required to buy a ticket for each infant and strap them into safety seats? A law requiring separate tickets and seats for infants would generate good news and bad news.

- Good news: Fewer infants would die in airline crashes because infants are safer in their own seats on aircraft.

- Bad news: More people would die in car crashes. A law requiring parents to buy tickets for infants would increase the cost of traveling by air, causing some parents to switch from flying to driving. Driving is actually more dangerous than flying: The number of people injured or killed per 100,000 miles traveled is much higher in cars.

There is an ongoing dispute between two federal agencies over infant safety seats for air travel. Since 1979 the National Transportation Safety Board has recommended that safety seats be mandatory, while the Federal Aviation Administration has used its regulatory authority to prevent such rules. Ultimately, the Congress will resolve this dispute.

The lesson from this example is that consumers respond to changes in prices. An increase in the price of one good (air travel) causes some consumers to switch to a substitute good (highway travel), leading to some unexpected results.

Source: "Effort Under Way to Revamp Laws on Child Safety," *Oregonian*, March 23, 1997, p. A20.

An increase in the price of air travel will cause some consumers to switch to highway travel, which is actually more dangerous.

ier food. In other words, the demand curve for poultry may have shifted to the right, increasing the equilibrium quantity of poultry. Of course, an increase in demand will increase the price too, so if this explanation is correct, we should also observe higher prices for poultry.

According to the U.S. Department of Agriculture, this popular explanation is incorrect.[2] In fact, the increase in poultry consumption was caused by an increase in supply, not an increase in demand. This conclusion is based on the fact that poultry prices have been decreasing, not increasing. Between 1950 and 1990, the real price of poultry (adjusted for inflation) decreased by about 75%. As shown in Figure 4.15, an increase in supply causes the market equilibrium to shift from point *i* (price = $2 and quantity = 50 million pounds) to point *n* (price = $0.80 and quantity = 90 million pounds). The increase in supply decreases the equilibrium price. The supply of poultry increased because innovations in poultry processing decreased the cost of producing poultry products. The lesson here is that we shouldn't jump to conclusions based on limited infor-

Figure 4.15

The Mystery of Increasing Poultry Consumption

Because the price of poultry decreased at the same time the quantity of poultry consumed increased, we know that the increase in consumption resulted from an increase in supply, not an increase in demand. Innovations in poultry processing decreased production costs, shifting the supply curve to the right.

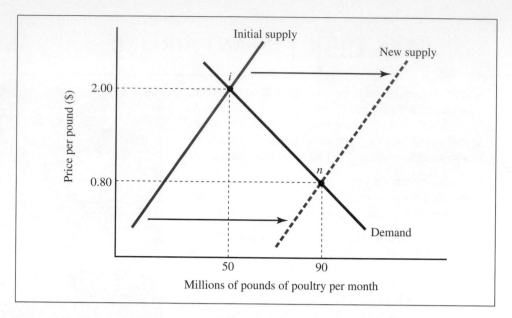

mation. A change in the equilibrium quantity could result from either a change in supply or a change in demand. To draw any conclusions, we need information about both price and quantity.

There may be a grain of truth in the popular explanation. It is possible that both demand and supply increased, shifting both curves to the right. Because the price of poultry decreased, however, we know that the shift of the supply curve (which tends to decrease the price) overwhelmed any shift of the demand curve (which tends to increase the price). Although changes in consumer preferences might contribute to increasing poultry consumption, the changes in consumption were caused largely by changes on the supply side of the market.

The Mystery of Falling Cocaine Prices

Ted Koppel, host of the ABC news program *Nightline*, once said. "Do you know what's happened to the price of drugs in the United States? The price of cocaine, way down, the price of marijuana, way down. You don't have to be an expert in economics to know that when the price goes down, it means more stuff is coming in. That's supply and demand."[3] According to Koppel, the price of drugs dropped because the government's efforts to control the supply of illegal drugs had failed. In other words, the lower price resulted from an increase in supply. According to the U.S. Department of Justice, the quantity of drugs consumed actually decreased during the period of dropping prices.[4] Is Koppel's economic detective work sound?

In this case, both the price and the quantity decreased. As shown in the second row of Table 4.5, when both the price and the quantity decrease, that means demand has decreased. In Figure 4.16, a decrease in demand shifts the demand curve to the left, and the market moves from point *i* (price = $15 and quantity = 400 units per day) to point *n* (price = $10 and quantity = 300 units per day). Koppel's explanation (an increase in supply) would be correct if the quantity of drugs increased at the same time that the price decreased. Because the quantity of drugs consumed actually decreased during the period of dropping prices, Koppel's explanation is incorrect. Lower demand—not a failure of the government's drug policy and an increase in supply—was responsible for the decrease in drug prices.

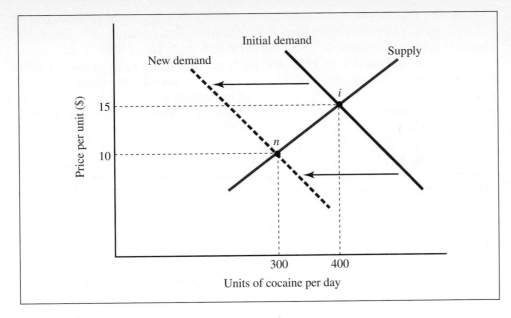

Figure 4.16

The Mystery of Lower Drug Prices
Because the quantity of cocaine consumed decreased at the same time the price of cocaine decreased, we know that the decrease in price resulted from a decrease in demand, not an increase in supply. A decrease in the demand for cocaine decreased the price and decreased the quantity consumed.

The Tobacco Settlement and Revenue for Health-Care Programs

At the beginning of this chapter, we presented a puzzle for a state budget analyst. The analyst expected the state support for programs dealing with tobacco-related illness to be $280 million per year, including $80 million from the tobacco settlement and $200 million from the state's cigarette tax. In fact, the state provided only $250 million. What happened?

The key to solving this mystery is the fact that the agreement will decrease the quantity of cigarettes purchased. Cigarette producers responded to the agreement by increasing the price of cigarettes by about 40 cents per pack. Consistent with the law of demand, the increase in price decreased the quantity demanded, decreasing the revenue from the cigarette tax. In Figure 4.17 an increase in price from $3.00 to $3.40 causes movement upward along the initial demand curve from point i to point p, decreasing the

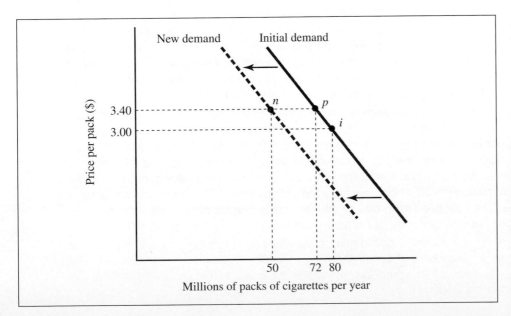

Figure 4.17

The Mystery of the Tobacco Money
The tobacco settlement increases the price of cigarettes from $3.00 to $3.40, causing movement upward along the original demand curve from point i to point p, decreasing the quantity consumed from 80 million to 72 million packs. The reduction in advertising and marketing shifts the demand curve to the left, reducing the quantity demanded at the new price ($3.40) from 72 million (point p) to 50 million packs (point n).

quantity sold from 80 million to 72 million packs per year. The agreement also required cigarette makers to reduce their advertising and marketing activities. As a result, the demand curve shifted to the left, as shown in Figure 4.17. The cutback in advertising reduced the quantity sold from 72 million packs per year (point p) to 50 million packs per year (point n). The net effect of the agreement is to decrease the quantity of cigarettes sold—and taxed—from 80 million to 50 million packs per year. With a tax of $1 per pack, that means that the state's revenue from the cigarette tax falls from $80 million to $50 million.

TEST Your Understanding

14. Complete the statement with "supply" or "demand": If the price and quantity change in the same direction, _____ is changing; if the price and quantity change in opposite directions, _____ is changing.

15. Suppose a freeze in Florida wipes out 20% of the orange crop. How will this affect the equilibrium price of Florida oranges? Defend your answer with a graph.

16. Suppose that between 2000 and 2001, the equilibrium price and the equilibrium quantity of amber both decrease. Draw a supply-demand diagram that explains these changes.

Using the TOOLS

In this chapter you learned how to use two tools of economics—the supply curve and the demand curve—to find equilibrium prices to predict changes in prices and quantities. Here are some opportunities to use these tools to do your own economic analysis.

1. ECONOMIC EXPERIMENT: MARKET EQUILIBRIUM

This simple experiment takes about 20 minutes. We start by dividing the class into two equal groups: consumers and producers.

- The instructor provides each consumer with a number indicating the maximum amount he or she is willing to pay (WTP) for a bushel of apples: The WTP is a number between $1 and $100. Each consumer has the opportunity to buy 1 bushel of apples per trading period. The consumer's score for a single trading period equals the gap between his or her WTP and the price actually paid for apples. For example, if the consumer's WTP is $80 and he or she pays only $30 for apples, the consumer's score is $50. Each consumer has the option of not buying apples. This will be sensible if the best price the consumer can get exceeds his or her WTP. If the consumer does not buy apples, his or her score will be zero.

- The instructor provides each producer with a number indicating the cost of producing a bushel of apples (a number between $1 and $100). Each producer has the opportunity to sell 1 bushel per trading period. The producer's score for a single trading period equals the gap between the selling price and the cost of producing apples. So if a producer sells apples for $20 and his or her cost is only $15, the producer's score is $5. Producers have the option of not selling apples, which is sensible if the best price the producer can get is less than his or her cost. If the producer does not sell apples, his or her score is zero.

Once everyone understands the rules, consumers and producers meet in a trading area to arrange transactions. A consumer may announce how much he or she is willing to pay for apples and wait for a producer to agree to sell apples at that price. Alternatively, a producer may announce how much he or she is willing to accept for apples and wait for a consumer to agree to buy apples at that price. Once a transaction has been arranged, the consumer and producer inform the instructor of the trade, record the transaction, and leave the trading area.

There are several trading periods, each of which lasts a few minutes. After the end of each trading period, the instructor lists the prices at which apples sold during that period. Then another trading period starts, providing consumers and producers another opportunity to buy or sell 1 bushel of apples. After all the trading periods have been completed, each participant computes his or her score by adding the scores from each trading period.

APPLICATIONS

2. Using Data to Draw a Demand Curve

The following table shows data on gasoline prices and gasoline consumption in a particular city. Is it possible to use these data to draw a demand curve? If so, draw the demand curve. If not, why not?

Year	Gasoline Price (per gallon)	Quantity Consumed (millions of gallons)
1999	1.20	400
2000	1.40	300
2001	1.60	360

3. Foreign Farm Workers and the Price of Berries

Current law allows thousands of Mexican workers to work on farms in the United States during harvest season. Suppose a new law outlaws the use of foreign farm workers. Assume that the resulting excess demand for labor increases the wage paid to farm workers by 20%. Use a supply-demand graph to predict the effects of the higher wage on the price of berries.

4. Market Effects of an Import Ban on Shoes

Consider a nation that initially imports half the shoes it consumes. Use a supply-demand graph to predict the effect of a ban on shoe imports on the equilibrium price and quantity of shoes.

5. The Mystery of Free Used Newspapers

In 1987 you could sell a ton of used newspapers for $60. Five years later, you could not sell them at any price. In other words, the price of used newspapers dropped from $60 to zero in just five years. Over this period the quantity of used newspapers bought and sold increased. What caused the drop in price? Defend your answer with a supply-demand graph.

Summary

In this chapter we've seen how supply and demand determine prices. And we saw how to predict the effects of changes in demand or supply on prices. Here are the main points of the chapter.

1. To draw a demand curve, we must be certain the other variables that affect demand (consumer income, prices of related goods, tastes, expectations, and number of consumers) are held fixed.

2. To draw a market supply curve, we must be certain the other variables that affect supply (input costs, technology, the number of producers, expectations, taxes and subsidies) are held fixed.

3. An equilibrium in a market is shown by the intersection of the demand curve and the supply curve. When a market reaches an equilibrium, there is no pressure to change the price.

4. A change in demand changes price and quantity in the same direction: An increase in demand increases the equilibrium price and quantity; a decrease in demand decreases the equilibrium price and quantity.

5. A change in supply changes price and quantity in opposite directions: An increase in supply decreases price and increases quantity; a decrease in supply increases price and decreases quantity.

Key Terms

Change in demand, 72
Change in quantity demanded, 65
Change in quantity supplied, 70
Change in supply, 77
Complements, 74
Demand schedule, 65
Excess demand, 70
Excess supply, 71

Income effect, 66
Individual demand curve, 65
Individual supply curve, 69
Inferior good, 76
Law of demand, 65
Law of supply, 69
Market demand curve, 66
Market equilibrium, 70

Market supply curve, 70
Normal good, 73
Perfectly competitive market, 64
Quantity demanded, 65
Quantity supplied, 68
Substitutes, 73
Substitution effect, 66
Supply schedule, 68

Problems and Discussion Questions

1. Figure 4.A shows the supply and demand curves for CD players. Complete the following statements.

a. At the market equilibrium (shown by point _____), the price of CD players is _____ and the quantity of CD players is _____.

b. At a price of $100, there would be excess _____, so we would expect the price to _____ (fill in with increase or decrease).

c. At a price exceeding the equilibrium price, there would be excess _____, so we would expect the price to _____ (fill in with increase or decrease).

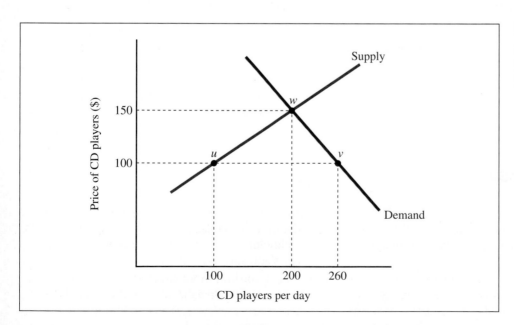

Figure 4.A
Supply and Demand for CD Players

2. The following table shows the quantities of corn supplied and demanded at different prices:

Price per Ton	Quantity Supplied	Quantity Demanded	Excess Demand or Excess Supply
$ 80	600	1,200	_____
$ 90	800	1,100	_____
$100	1,000	1,000	_____
$110	1,200	900	_____

   a. Complete the table.

   b. Draw the demand curve and the supply curve.

   c. What is the equilibrium price of corn?

3. Consider the market for personal computers. Suppose that the demand is stable: The demand curve doesn't change. Predict the effects of the following changes on the equilibrium price of computers. Illustrate your answer with a supply and demand diagram.

   a. The cost of memory chips (one component of a computer) decreases.

   b. The government imposes a $100 tax on personal computers.

4. Draw a supply-demand diagram to illustrate the effect of an increase in income on the market for restaurant meals.

5. Suppose that the tuition charged by public universities increases. Draw a supply-demand diagram to illustrate the effects of the tuition hike on the market for private college education.

6. Suppose that the government imposes a tax of $1 per pound of fish and collects the tax from fish producers. Draw a supply-demand diagram to illustrate the market effects of the tax.

7. As summer approaches, the equilibrium price of rental cabins increases and the equilibrium quantity of cabins rented increases. Draw a supply-demand diagram that explains these changes.

8. Suppose that the initial price of a pocket phone is $100 and that the initial quantity demanded is 500 phones per day. Depict graphically the effects of a technological innovation that decreases the cost of producing pocket phones. Label the starting point with an *i* and the new equilibrium with an *n*.

9. You've been hired as an economic consultant to evaluate the nation's airport security systems (metal detectors and machines that allow security people to see what's inside carry-on luggage). Suppose these security systems add $5 to the typical airplane ticket and require 10 minutes of extra time for each passenger. List the questions you will answer in your evaluation.

10. Suppose a freeze in Florida wipes out 20% of the orange crop. How will this affect the equilibrium price of California oranges? Defend your answer with a graph.

11. The Multifiber Agreement sets import quotas for various apparel products—including shirts—coming into the United States. Use a supply-demand graph to show the effects of the shirt quota on the equilibrium price of shirts in the United States.

12. Web Exercise: Visit the Web site of the National Association of Realtors [*http://www.realtor.com*]. Follow the "Find a Home" instructions and check housing prices for a three-bedroom, two-bath house in several cities, for example, San Francisco, California; Topeka, Kansas; Dallas, Texas; Concord, Massachusetts; and Seattle, Washington. Use supply and demand diagrams to explain why housing prices vary from city to city.

13. Web Exercise: Visit the Web site of eBay, a company that provides on-line auctions [*http://www.ebay.com*]. Suppose you want to buy a traditional 35mm camera. Access the listing of cameras being auctioned and check the most recent bids. Suppose someone develops a digital camera that takes better pictures than the traditional 35mm camera at half the cost. Predict the effects of the new camera on the supply of traditional 35mm cameras and the prices for cameras auctioned on the ebay site.

Take It to the Net

We invite you to visit the O'Sullivan/Sheffrin page on the Prentice Hall Web site at: **http://www.prenhall.com/osullivan/** for additional World Wide Web exercises for this chapter.

Chapter-Opening Questions

1. As is explained in A Closer Look on page 85, fewer infants would die in airplane crashes, but more people would die in automobile crashes as many parents responded to the higher cost of airline travel by switching to the alternative travel mode.

2. As is explained in one of the Economic Detective exercises, a lower price doesn't necessarily mean that supply has increased. The equilibrium quantity decreased at the same time, so the price drop was caused by a decrease in demand.

3. As is explained in one of the "Using the Tools" exercises, we can't draw a demand curve from a table of price and quantity data unless we know that the other determinants of demand (income, population, prices of substitutes and complementary goods, tastes, advertising) are fixed over the period covered by the data.

4. Innovations in poultry processing decreased the cost of producing poultry products. The resulting increase in supply decreased the equilibrium price, causing consumers to buy more poultry products.

Test Your Understanding

1. decrease, increase

2. Consumer income, the prices of substitute goods, the prices of complementary goods, consumer tastes, advertising, the number of consumers, and price expectations.

3. Input costs, technology, price expectations, number of producers, taxes and subsidies.

4. supply, demand

5. less, greater

6. demand, supply

7. One group is a, e, and f; another group is b, c, and d.

8. The statement is incorrect because it confuses the direction of causality. The correct statement is: "The demand curve shifted because demand increased." When something other than the price of the product changes, the relationship between price and quantity changes, causing the demand curve to shift.

9. right, left

10. Circle quantity of pencils demanded and price of pencils. Cross out number of consumers, price of pens, and consumer income.

11. One group is a, c, and e; another group is b, d, and f.

12. True. An increase in the wage increases production cost, so fewer computers will be supplied at each price.

13. Circle quantity of housing supplied and price of houses. Cross out number of consumers, price of wood, and consumer income.

14. demand, supply

15. The supply of oranges decreases, shifting the supply curve to the left. The equilibrium price will increase.

16. The demand decreases, shifting the demand curve to the left (an end to the Jurassic Park fad buying?), decreasing both the price and the quantity.

Using the Tools

2. Using Data to Draw a Demand Curve. It's tempting to use the data in the table to plot three combinations of price and quantity, connect the points with a curve, and call it a demand curve. That is not appropriate because we don't know what happened to the other determinants of the demand for gasoline over this period (consumer income, prices of substitutes and complements, tastes, advertising, price expectations). To draw a demand curve with these data, we must have additional data showing that these other variables did not change. If any of these other variables changed, we cannot draw a demand curve.

3. Foreign Farm Workers and the Price of Berries. The higher wage caused by the elimination of foreign farm workers will increase the production costs of berry farmers. The resulting decrease in supply of berries will shift the supply curve to the left. In Figure 4.B, the equilibrium price of berries increases from $0.60 to $0.73.

4. Market Effects of an Import Ban. An import ban has the same effect as a decrease in the number of firms in the market: supply decreases, shifting the market supply curve to the left. In Figure 4.C, the free-trade equilibrium is shown by point *f*, and the equilibrium with an import ban is shown by point *b*.

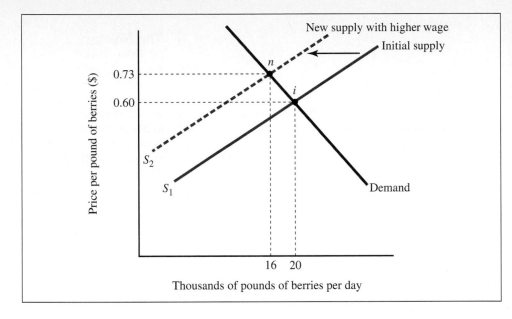

Figure 4.B
Market Effects of Higher Farm Wages
Reducing the number of foreign farm workers will increase the wage of farm workers, increasing the production costs of berry producers. The supply curve shifts to the left: At each price, a smaller quantity is supplied. Equilibrium is restored at point *n*, with a higher price ($0.73, up from $0.60) and a smaller quantity (16,000 pounds, down from 20,000 pounds).

The ban on imported shoes increases the price of shoes from $25 to $34.

5. The Mystery of Free Used Newspapers. Between 1987 and 1992 the price and quantity moved in opposite directions, meaning that the decrease in price was caused by an increase in supply. Over this five-year period, hundreds of communities adopted curbside recycling programs. These programs increased the supply of used newspapers, generating an excess supply of used newspapers that decreased the equilibrium price. In Figure 4.D, the increase in supply was so large that the equilibrium price fell to zero.

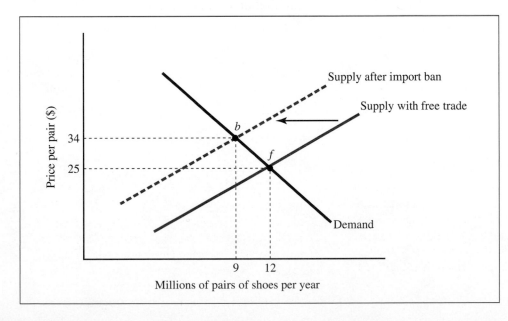

Figure 4.C
The Market Effects of an Import Ban
A ban on shoe imports decreases the supply of shoes, shifting the supply curve to the left. The free-trade equilibrium is shown by point *f*, and the equilibrium under the import ban is shown by point *b*. The import ban increases the price from $25 to $34 and decreases the quantity from 12 million to 9 million pairs of shoes.

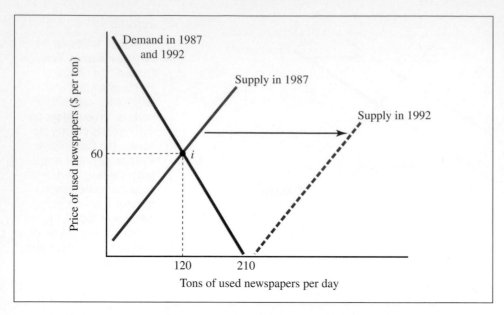

Figure 4.D

The Mystery of Free Used Newspapers

Between 1987 and 1992 the price of used newspapers decreased from $60 per ton to zero, a result of increases in supply caused by the expansion of curbside recycling programs.

Notes

1. *The News and Observer*, "Raleigh, N.C.-Based Companies Tap Growing Market for Wind Power," January 26, 2001; *Associated Press Online,* "Wind Farm to Power 70,000 Homes," January 10, 2001.

2. Mark R. Weimar and Richard Stillman, "Market Trends Driving Broiler Consumption," Livestock and Poultry Situation and Outlook Report LPS-44 (Washington, DC: U.S. Department of Agriculture, Economic Research Service, November 1990).

3. Kenneth R. Clark, "Legalize Drugs. A Case for Koppel," *Chicago Tribune*, August 30, 1988, sec. 5, p. 8.

4. U.S. Department of Justice, *Drugs, Crime, and the Justice System* (Washington, DC: U.S. Government Printing Office, 1992), p. 30.

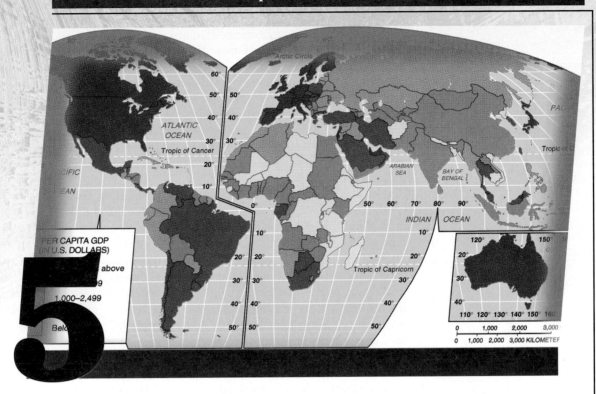

PER CAPITA GDP
(IN U.S. DOLLARS)

above

1,000–2,499

Below

Measuring a Nation's Production and Income

On December 7, 1999, the United States Department of Commerce announced its "achievement of the century." What could be a highlight of a century that could rival other great U.S. accomplishments such as providing electricity to homes and businesses throughout the country, completing the interstate highway system, and landing a man on the moon? The Department of Commerce chose, as its great achievement, the development of the National Income and Product Accounts.

How can a mere system of accounting compare to the other great feats of the century? The Department of Commerce noted the role of the National Income and Product Accounts in winning World War II, providing a basis to understand the development of our economy, and allowing policymakers to stabilize the economy and promote economic growth. An accounting system can indeed be powerful.

Production, Income, and the Circular Flow
Measuring Gross Domestic Product

Who Purchases GDP?
Consumption Expenditures
Private Investment Expenditures
Government Purchases
Net Exports

Who Gets the Income?

Real Versus Nominal GDP

GDP as a Measure of Welfare

Using the Tools

Macroeconomics: The branch of economics that looks at the economy as a whole.

his chapter begins your study of **macroeconomics:** the branch of economics that deals with any nation's economy as a whole. Macroeconomics focuses on the economic issues—unemployment, inflation, growth, trade, and the gross domestic product—that are most often discussed in newspapers, on the radio, and on television.

Macroeconomic issues are at the heart of political debates. All presidential candidates must learn a quick lesson in macroeconomics. Once elected, a President learns that the prospects for reelection will depend on how well the economy performs during his or her term of office. If the voters believe that the economy has performed well, the President will be reelected: otherwise, the President will not likely be reelected. Democrats such as Jimmy Carter, as well as Republicans such as George H. W. Bush, have failed in their bids for reelection because of the voters' economic concerns. Bill Clinton survived a personal scandal in part because of the superb performance of the U.S. economy while he was President.

Macroeconomic events profoundly affect our everyday lives. For example, if the economy fails to create enough jobs, workers will become unemployed throughout the country, and millions of lives will be disrupted. Similarly, slow economic growth will mean that living standards will not increase rapidly in the future. By contrast, if prices for all goods start increasing rapidly, some people will find it difficult to maintain their lifestyles.

This chapter and the next will introduce you to the concepts you need to understand macroeconomics. In this chapter, we will explain how economists and government statisticians measure the income and production for an entire country. The next chapter will discuss unemployment and inflation. Both chapters will explain the terms that are often used when economics is reported in the media.

Macroeconomics focuses on two basic issues. One focus is on long-run economic growth. We need to understand what happens during the long run to understand what factors are behind the rise in living standards in modern economies. Today, in the United States, living standards are much higher than they were for our grandparents; and our living standards are much higher than those of millions of people throughout the globe.

The other focus of macroeconomics is fluctuations in economic performance. Although living standards have improved over time, the economy has not grown smoothly. There are periods when the economy appears to malfunction and no longer grows as rapidly. A recession is a period when the economy fails to grow for at least six consecutive months. During these periods, not enough jobs are created, and large numbers of workers become unemployed. At other times, unemployment may not be a problem, but we become concerned that the prices of everything that we buy seem to increase rapidly. In later chapters, we will study these fluctuations in detail.

Before we can study growth and fluctuations, we need to have a basic vocabulary and understanding of some key concepts. We begin with production and income because these are the most fundamental concepts. Every day, men and women go off to work, where they produce or sell merchandise or provide services, then return home with paychecks at the end of the week or month. The income that they earn allows them to purchase the goods and services necessary to conduct modern life. This chapter steps back from these individual details and looks at the economy as a whole. From the perspective that looks at the entire economy, we will be able to construct measures that can tell us how quickly the entire economy is growing or whether it has failed to grow. We will also be able to measure the total income generated in the economy and how this income flows back to workers and investors. These measures are critical for understanding how many people find jobs and whether their living standards are rising or falling.

After reading this chapter, you will be able to answer the following questions:

1. How are production and income related?

2. What is the gross domestic product?

3. When prices change, how do we measure real income?

4. Do increases in gross domestic product necessarily translate into improvements in the welfare of citizens?

As we learn the answers to these questions, we will build the necessary foundation for studying macroeconomics.

Production, Income, and the Circular Flow

Let's begin with the circular flow introduced in Chapter 3. We use the circular flow to make a very simple but fundamental point: Production generates income.

In the simple economy depicted in Figure 5.1, there are only households and firms, which make transactions in both factor markets and product markets. In the factor markets, the households supply inputs to production. The primary inputs are labor and capital—what economists call *factors of production*. Households supply labor by working for firms, and households supply capital—buildings, machines, and equipment—to the firms. In the factor markets, households are paid by the firms for supplying these factors: wages for their work and interest, dividends, and rents for supplying capital. The households then take their income and purchase the goods and services produced by the firms in the product markets. The payments the firm receives from the sale of its products are used to pay for the factors of production. The important part of this diagram is that production generates income; corresponding to the production of goods and services in the economy are flows of income to households.

For example, consider a manufacturer of computers. At the same time the computer manufacturer produces and sells new computers, it also generates income through its production. The computer manufacturer pays wages to workers, perhaps pays rent on office and factory buildings, and pays interest on borrowed money. Whatever is left over after paying for the cost of production is the firm's profit, which is

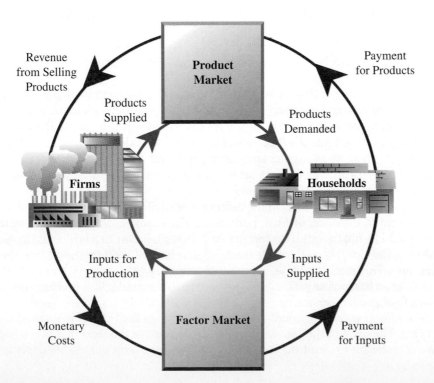

Figure 5.1

Circular Flow
The circular flow diagram shows how production of goods and services generates income for households and how households purchase goods and services produced by firms.

income to the owners of the firm. Wages, rents, interest, and profits are all different forms of income.

In another example, your taxes pay for a school district to hire principals, teachers, and other staff to provide educational services to the students in your community. These educational services are considered production in the modern economy. At the same time, the principals, teachers, and staff all earn income through their employment with the school district. The school district may also rent buildings where classes are held and pay interest on borrowed funds.

Our goal is to understand both sides: the production in the economy and the generation of income in the economy. In the United States, the National Income and Product Accounts, published by the Department of Commerce, are the source for the key data on production and income in the economy. In this chapter, we will study how these accounts work in practice. Let's begin by understanding how to measure the production for the entire economy.

Measuring Gross Domestic Product

To measure the production of the entire economy, we need to combine an enormous array of goods and services, from new computers to professional basketball games. We can add computers to basketball games, much as we can really add apples and oranges if we are interested in the total monetary value of an apple harvest and an orange harvest. Our goal is to summarize the total production of an entire economy into a single number, which we call the gross domestic product.

Gross domestic product [GDP]: The total market value of all the final goods and services produced in an economy in a given year.

The most common measure of the total output of an economy is **gross domestic product [GDP]**, the total market value of all the final goods and services produced within an economy in a given year. All the words in this definition are important. Let's analyze each part of this definition.

"Total market value" means that we take the quantity of goods produced and multiply them by their respective prices and then add up the totals. If an economy produced 2 cars at $15,000 per car and 3 computers at $3,000 per computer, the total value of these goods and services would be

$$(2 \text{ cars} \times \$15,000/\text{car}) + (3 \text{ computers} \times \$3,000/\text{computer}) = \$39,000$$

The reason we multiply the goods by their prices is that we cannot simply add together the number of cars and the number of computers. Using prices allows us to express the value of everything in a common unit of measurement—in this case dollars. (In countries other than the United States, we would express the value in terms of the local currency.) This is how we add apples and oranges together: by finding out what is the value of both the apples and the oranges (as measured by what you would pay for them) and adding them up in terms of their prices.

"Final goods and services" in the definition of GDP means those goods and services that are sold to ultimate, or final, purchasers. For example, the 2 cars that were produced would be final goods if they were sold to households or to a business. However, in producing the cars, the automobile manufacturer bought steel that went into the body of the cars. This steel would not be counted as a final good or service in GDP. It is an example of an **intermediate good**, a good that is used in the production process; therefore it is not a final good or service.

Intermediate goods: Goods used in the production process that are not final goods or services.

The reason we do not count intermediate goods as final goods is to avoid double-counting. The price of the car already reflects the price of the steel that is contained in it. We do not want to count the steel twice. Similarly, the large volumes of paper used by an accounting firm are also intermediate goods because they become part of the final product delivered by the accounting firm to its clients.

The final words in our definition of GDP are "in a given year." GDP is expressed as a rate of production, that is, as so many dollars per year. In 2000, for example, GDP in the United States was $9,962 billion. Goods produced in prior years, such as used cars, are not included in GDP this year.

Because we measure GDP using the current prices for goods and services, GDP will increase if prices increase, even if the physical amount of goods that are produced remains the same. Suppose that next year the economy again produces 2 cars and 3 computers, but in the following year, all the prices in the economy have doubled: The price of cars is $30,000, and the price of computers is $6,000. GDP in the following year will also be twice as high, or $78,000—(2 cars × $30,000/car) + (3 computers × $6,000/computer)—even though quantity produced is the same as during the prior year.

Let's apply the reality principle, one of our five basic principles of economics:

Reality **PRINCIPLE**

What matters to people is the real value of money or income— its purchasing power—not the face value of money or income.

We would like to have another measure of total output in the economy that does not increase just because prices increase. For this reason, economists have developed the concept of **real GDP**, a measure of GDP that takes into account price changes.

Later in this chapter, we explain how real GDP is calculated. The basic idea is simple. When we use current prices to measure GDP, that is what we call **nominal GDP**. Nominal GDP can increase for one of two reasons: Either the production of goods and services has increased or the prices of those goods and services has increased.

To explain real GDP, we need first to look at a simple example. Suppose an economy produced a single good: computers. In year 1, 10 computers were produced, and each sold for $1,000. In year 2, 12 computers were produced, and each sold for $1,100. Nominal GDP would be $10,000 in year 1 and $13,200 in year 2. Nominal GDP would have increased by a factor of 1.32.

We can measure real GDP by calculating GDP using year 1 prices as a measure of what was produced in year 1 *and* also what was produced in year 2. In year 1, real GDP would be 10 computers × $1,000/computer = $10,000; and in year 2, it would be 12 computers × $1,000/computer = $12,000. Real GDP in year 2 is greater than real GDP in year 1 by a factor of 1.2. The key idea is that we construct a measure using the same prices for both years and thereby take price changes into account.

Figure 5.2 plots real GDP for the U.S. economy for the years 1930–2000. The data for real GDP are constructed so that nominal GDP and real GDP are set equal for a single year, in this case 1992. For both earlier and later years, the data for real GDP take into account changes in prices and thus measure movements in real output only.

The graph shows that real GDP has grown substantially over this period. This is what economists call **economic growth**: sustained increases in the real production of an economy over a long time. Later, in Chapter 8, we will study economic growth in detail. We will also look carefully at the behavior of real GDP over shorter periods, during which real GDP can rise and fall. Decreases in real GDP cause great disruption and lead to a loss of jobs and unemployment.

Real GDP: A measure of GDP that adjusts for changes in prices.

Nominal GDP: The value of GDP in current dollars.

Economic growth: Sustained increases in the real production of an economy over a period of time.

Figure 5.2
**U.S. Real GDP,
1930–2000**

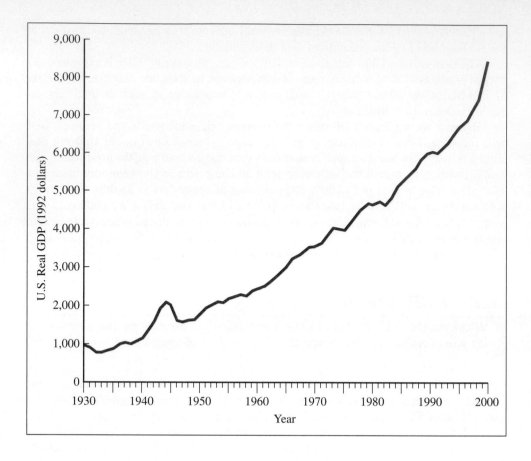

Who Purchases GDP?

To gain further insight into gross domestic product, let's look at its components. Economists divide GDP into four broad categories, each corresponding to different types of purchasers represented in GDP:

1. Consumption expenditures: purchases by consumers.
2. Private investment expenditures: purchases by firms.
3. Government purchases: purchases by federal, state, and local governments.
4. Net exports: net purchases by the foreign sector, or domestic exports minus domestic imports.

Before discussing these categories, let's look at some data for the U.S. economy to get a sense of the size of each of these four components. Table 5.1 shows the figures for GDP

Table 5.1 Composition of U.S. GDP, Second Quarter 2000
(billions of dollars expressed at annual rates)

GDP	Consumption Expenditures	Private Investment Expenditures	Government Purchases	Net Exports
9,945	6,706	1,852	1,742	−355

Source: U.S. Department of Commerce.

for the second quarter of 2000. (A quarter is a three-month period; the second quarter runs from April through June.) In the second quarter of 2000, GDP was $9,945 billion, or approximately $9.9 trillion. To get a sense of the magnitude, consider that the U.S. population is approximately 281 million people, making GDP per person approximately $35,392.

Consumption Expenditures

Consumption expenditures are purchases by consumers of currently produced goods and services, either domestic or foreign. These purchases include TV sets, VCRs, automobiles, clothing, hair-styling services, jewelry, movie tickets, food, and all other consumer items. We can break down consumption into durable goods, nondurable goods, and services. **Durable goods** last for a long time, such as automobiles or refrigerators. **Nondurable goods**, such as food, last for a short time. **Services** reflect work done in which people play a prominent role in delivery (such as a dentist filling a cavity); they range from haircutting to health care. Services are the fastest-growing component of consumption. Overall, consumption spending is the most important component of GDP, constituting about 67% of total purchases.

Private Investment Expenditures

Private investment expenditures in GDP consist of three components:

1. First, there is spending on new plants and equipment during the year. If a firm builds a new factory or purchases a new machine, that is included in GDP. Purchasing an existing building or buying a used machine does not count in GDP because the goods were not produced during the current year.
2. Second, newly produced housing is included in investment spending. The sale of an existing home to a new owner is not counted because the house was not built in the current year.
3. Finally, if firms add to their stock of inventories, the increase in inventories during the current year is included in GDP. If a hardware store had $1,000 worth of nuts and bolts on its shelves at the beginning of the year and $1,100 at the year's end, its inventory investment would be $100 ($1,100 − $1,000). The $100 increase in inventory investment is included in GDP.

We call the total of new investment expenditures **gross investment**. During the year, some of the existing plant, equipment, and housing will deteriorate or wear out. This wear and tear is called **depreciation**. If we subtract depreciation from gross investment, we obtain **net investment**. Net investment is the true addition to the stock of plant, equipment, and housing in a given year.

Make sure you understand this distinction between gross investment and net investment. Consider the $1,852 billion in total investment spending for the second quarter of 2000, a period in which there was $1,244 billion in depreciation. That means that there was only ($1,852 − $1,244) = $608 billion, in net investment by firms in that year. 67% of gross investment went to make up for depreciation of existing capital.

Warning: When we discuss measuring production in the GDP accounts, we use *investment* in a different way than when we use *investment* in the sense we have come to understand it. For an economist, investment in the GDP accounts means purchases of new final goods and services by firms. In everyday conversation, we may talk about investing in the stock market or investing in gold. Buying stock for $1,800 on the stock market is a purchase of an existing financial asset; it is not the purchase of new goods and services by firms. So that $1,800 does not appear anywhere in GDP. The same is true of purchasing a gold bar. In GDP accounting, *investment* denotes the purchase of new

Consumption expenditures: Purchases of newly produced goods and services by households.

Durable goods: Goods that last for a long period of time, such as appliances.

Nondurable goods: Goods that last for shorter periods of time, such as food.

Services: Work done in which people play a prominent role in delivery, ranging from haircutting to health care.

Private investment expenditures: Purchases of newly produced goods and services by firms.

Gross investment: Actual investment purchases.

Depreciation: The wear and tear of capital as it is used in production.

Net investment: Gross investment minus depreciation.

capital. Be careful not to confuse the common usage of *investment* with the definition of *investment* as we use it in the GDP accounts.

Government Purchases

Government purchases are the purchases of newly produced goods and services by federal, state, and local governments. They include any goods that the government purchases plus the wages and benefits of all government workers (paid when the government purchases their services as employees). The majority of spending in this category actually comes from state and local governments: $1,137 billion of the total $1,742 billion in 2000.

This category does not include all the spending by governments. It excludes **transfer payments**; these are funds paid to individuals but are not associated with the production of goods and services. For example, payments for Social Security, welfare, and interest on government debt are all considered transfer payments and are not included in government purchases in GDP. The reason they are excluded is that nothing is being produced in return for the payment. But wage payments to the police, postal workers, and the staff of the Internal Revenue Service are all included because they do correspond to services that are currently being produced.

Because transfer payments are excluded from GDP, a vast portion of the budget of the federal government is not part of GDP. In 2000, the federal government spent approximately $1,956 billion, of which only $604 billion (about one-third) was counted as federal government purchases. Transfer payments are important, however. They affect both the income of individuals and their consumption and savings behavior. They also affect the size of the federal budget deficit, which we will study in a later chapter. At this point, keep in mind the distinction between government purchases—which are included in GDP—and total government spending or expenditure—which may not be included.

Net Exports

The United States has an open economy; that means that the United States trades with other economies. Recall from Chapter 3 that imports are goods we buy from other countries and exports are goods made here and sold to other countries. **Net exports** are total exports minus total imports. In Table 5.1, we see that net exports in the second quarter of 2000 were –$355 billion. Net exports were negative because our imports exceeded our exports.

The services of a city police force are included in GDP under government purchases.

In creating a measure of GDP, we try to measure the goods produced in the United States. Consumption, investment, and government purchases include all purchases by consumers, firms, and the government, whether or not the goods were produced in the United States. But purchases of foreign goods by consumers, firms, or the government should be subtracted when we calculate GDP because these goods were not produced in the United States. At the same time, we must add to GDP any goods produced here and sold abroad. For example, supercomputers made in the United States and sold in Europe should be added to GDP. By including net exports as a component of GDP, we correctly measure U.S. production by adding exports and subtracting imports.

For example, suppose someone in the United States buys a $25,000 Toyota made in Japan. If we look at final purchases, we will see that consumption spending rose by $25,000 because a consumer made a purchase of a consumption good. Net exports fell by $25,000, however, because the value of the import was subtracted from total exports. Notice that total GDP did not change with the purchase of the Toyota. This is exactly what we want in this case, because there was no U.S. production.

Now suppose that the United States sells a car for $18,000 to a resident of Spain. In this case, net exports would increase by $18,000 because the car was a U.S. export. GDP would also be a corresponding $18,000 higher because this sale represents U.S. production.

For the United States in the second quarter of 2000, net exports were –$355 billion dollars. In other words, in that quarter, the United States bought $355 billion more goods from abroad than it sold abroad. When we buy more goods from abroad than we sell, we have a **trade deficit**. A **trade surplus** occurs when our exports exceed our imports.

Trade deficit: An excess of imports over exports.

Trade surplus: An excess of exports over imports.

Figure 5.3 shows the U.S. trade surplus as a share of GDP from 1960 to 2000. While at times the United States had a trade surplus, in the 1980s and the late 1990s the United States ran a trade deficit that often exceeded 3% of GDP. What are the consequences of such large trade deficits?

When the United States runs a trade deficit, U.S. residents are spending more on goods and services than they are currently producing. Although the United States does sell many goods abroad (e.g., supercomputers, movies, records, and CDs), it buys even more goods and services from abroad (e.g., Toyotas, VCRs, German machine tools).

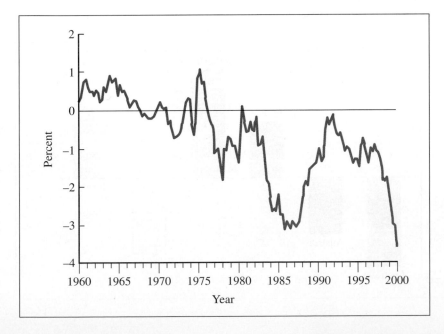

Figure 5.3
U.S. Trade Balance as a Share of GDP, 1960–2000

The result is that the United States is forced to sell some of its assets to individuals or governments in foreign countries. Here is how it works: When U.S. residents buy more goods abroad than they sell, they give up more dollars for imports than they receive in dollars from the sale of exports. These dollars given up to purchase imports end up in the hands of foreigners, who can use them to purchase U.S. assets such as stocks, bonds, or real estate. In the early 1990s, Japanese investors bought many assets in the United States. This should not have been terribly surprising because we had been running large trade deficits with the Japanese. They were willing to sell us more goods than we were selling to them, and therefore, they accumulated U.S. dollars with which they could purchase U.S. assets.

It is the total trade surplus with all the other countries that determines the amount of foreign assets that a single country will acquire. If a country ran a trade surplus with one country and an equally large trade deficit with another, it would not add to its stock of foreign assets. Figure 5.4 shows the trade surplus as a percent of GDP for a variety of other countries. For these countries, the Netherlands had the largest trade surplus as a share of GDP, followed by Sweden. As you can see, the United States was not alone in running a trade deficit. In later chapters, we study how trade deficits can affect a country's economy.

TEST Your Understanding

1. What are the four components of GDP?

2. The circular flow describes the process by which GDP generates _____, which is spent on goods.

3. What part of government spending is excluded from GDP because it does not correspond to goods or services being produced currently?

4. What is the difference between gross investment and net investment?

5. Define net exports.

Figure 5.4
Trade Balance as a Percent of GDP, 2000

Source: *The Economist*, January 5, 2001.

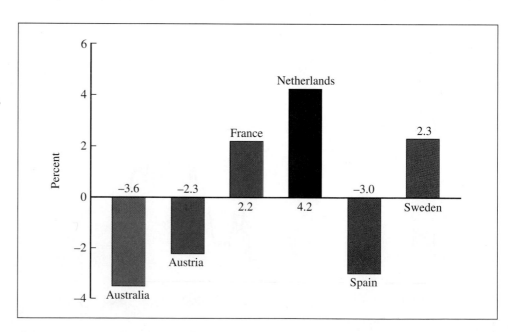

Who Gets the Income?

Recall from the circular flow that when GDP is produced, income is created. The income that flows to the private sector is called **national income**. To measure national income, economists first make three adjustments to GDP.

First, we add to GDP the net income earned by U.S. firms and residents abroad. To make this calculation, we add to GDP any income earned abroad by U.S. firms or residents and subtract any income earned in the United States by foreign firms or residents. For example, we add the profits earned by U.S. multinational corporations that are sent back to the United States but subtract the profits from multinational corporations operating in the United States that are sent back to their home countries. The result of these adjustments is the total income earned worldwide by U.S. firms and residents. This is called the **gross national product [GNP]**.

For most countries, the distinction between what they produce within their borders, GDP, and what their citizens earn, GNP, is not that important. For the United States, the difference between GDP and GNP is typically just 0.2%. In some countries, however, the differences are much larger. The country of Kuwait, for example, earned vast amounts of income from its oil riches, which it invested abroad. Earnings from these investments are included in Kuwait's GNP; in 1999, those earnings comprised approximately 15% of the total income of Kuwait. Australia has traditionally borrowed from foreign countries to finance its investments. Consequently, its net income from abroad was negative in 1999 and Australian GDP in that year exceeded Australian GNP by 3%.

The second adjustment that we make on the way to calculating national income is to subtract depreciation from GNP. Recall that depreciation is the wear and tear on plant and equipment that occurred during the year. In a sense, our income is reduced because our buildings and machines are wearing out. When we subtract depreciation from GNP, we reach **net national product [NNP]**, where "net" means after depreciation.

The third and last adjustment we make to reach national income is to subtract **indirect taxes**, which are sales taxes or excise taxes on products. If a store sells you a product for $1.00 and the sales tax is $0.08, your total bill is $1.08. However, only $1.00 of that purchase goes to the store to pay wages, rent, interest, and maybe even some profit to the owners. The remainder, $0.08, goes to the government; it is not part of private-sector income.

After making all three adjustments, we reach national income. Table 5.2 shows these adjustments (ignoring a few minor items) for the second quarter of 2000.

National income is divided among five basic categories: compensation of employees (wages and benefits), corporate profits, rental income, proprietor's income (income of unincorporated business), and net interest (interest payments received by households

National income: Net national product less indirect taxes.

Gross national product [GNP]: GDP plus net income earned abroad.

Net national product [NNP]: GNP minus depreciation.

Indirect taxes: Sales and excise taxes.

Table 5.2   From GDP to National Income, Second Quarter 2000 (billions of dollars)

Gross domestic product plus net income from abroad =	9,945
Gross national product minus depreciation =	9,937
Net national product minus indirect taxes (and other adjustments) =	8,693
National income	7,983

Source: U.S. Department of Commerce.

Table 5.3 Composition of U.S. National Income, Second Quarter of 2000 (billions of dollars)

National income	7,983
Compensation of employees	5,603
Corporate profits	964
Rental income	141
Proprietor's income	709
Net interest	566

Source: U.S. Department of Commerce.

from business and from abroad). Table 5.3 presents U.S. data for the second quarter of 2000. Approximately 70% of all national income goes to workers in the form of wages and benefits. For most of the countries in the world, wages and benefits are the largest part of national income.

Value added: The sum of all the income (wages, interest, profits, and rent) generated by an organization.

One way to measure national income is to look at the **value added** of each firm in the economy. Economists define the value added of a firm as the sum of all the income—wages, profits, rents, and interest—that it generates. By adding up the value added for all the firms in the economy (plus nonprofit and governmental organizations), we can calculate national income. Consider a simple example.

Suppose an economy consists of two firms: an automobile firm that sells its cars to consumers and a steel firm that sells only to the automobile firm. If the automobile company sells a car for $16,000 to consumers and purchases $6,000 worth of steel from the steel firm, the auto firm has $10,000 remaining—its value added—which can then be distributed as wages, rents, interest, and profits. If the steel firm sells $6,000 worth of steel but does not purchase any inputs from other firms, its value added is $6,000, which is paid out in the form of wages, rents, interest, and profits. Total value added in the economy from both firms is $16,000 ($10,000 + $6,000), which is the sum of wages, rents, interest, and profits for the entire economy, because there are only these two firms in the entire economy.

As this example illustrates, we measure the value added for a typical firm by starting with the value of its total sales and subtracting the value of any inputs it purchases from other firms. The amount of income that remains is the firm's value added, which is then distributed as wages, rents, interest, and profits. In calculating national income, it is important to include all the firms in the economy, even the firms that produce intermediate goods.

Personal income: Income (including transfer payments) received by households.

In addition to national income, which measures the income earned in a given year by the entire private sector, we are sometimes interested in determining the total payments that flow directly into households, a concept known as **personal income**. To calculate personal income, we begin with national income and subtract any corporate profits that are retained by the corporation and not paid out as dividends to households. We also subtract all social insurance taxes, which are payments for Social Security and Medicare. We then add any personal interest income received from the government and consumers and all transfer payments. The result is the total income available to households or personal income. The amount of personal income that households keep after paying income taxes is called **personal disposable income.**

Personal disposable income: Personal income after income taxes.

In summary, we can look at GDP from two sides: We can ask who buys the output that is produced, or we can ask who gets the income that is created through the production process. From the spending side, we see that nearly 67% of GDP consists of consumer expenditures. From the income side, we see that nearly 70% of national income is paid in wages and benefits.

KEEPING UP WITH A CHANGING ECONOMY

The United States Department of Commerce spends considerable effort trying to ensure that its methods accurately track the U.S. economy. Decades ago, they developed "hedonic methods" to take into account quality differences in products. For example, computers differ in speed and memory and it is important to distinguish between differences in the quality of the new computers that are sold.

Most recently, the Department of Commerce recognized that business and government expenditures on software should be counted as investment in the National Income and Product Account, since they produce a flow of services that last longer than one year. Including software expenditures as investment led to an increase of GDP of $152 billion in 1998.

The Commerce Department is currently working on a number of other projects to keep pace with changes in the economy. The measurement of services has traditionally been a difficult area. More research is needed on how to measure insurance and other financial services, as well as services provided by the health sector. Finally, the Department of Commerce is also pursuing an initiative to identify e-business (electronic business), to measure its scope and how it is distributed across industries. This project will be invaluable as we attempt to measure the effects of new technology on the growth of the economy.

Source: Brent R. Moulton, "Getting the 21st-Century GDP Right: What's Underway," American Economic Association Papers and Proceedings, May 2000, pp. 253–258.

Over time, the economy changes in many ways. New goods, such as personal computers, are introduced while others, such as long playing (LP) records, disappear. As "A Closer Look: Keeping Up With a Changing Economy" shows, the Department of Commerce must take into account these changes.

TEST Your Understanding

6. What do we add to GDP to reach GNP?

7. What is the largest component of national income?

8. Complete the statement with *households* or *firms*: Personal income and personal disposable income refer to payments ultimately flowing to _____.

Real Versus Nominal GDP

Output in the economy can increase from one year to the next. And prices can rise from one year to the next. Realizing that, we need a measure of output that reflects actual increases in production, separate and apart from any price changes that may have occurred in the economy during the year. Recall that we defined nominal GDP as GDP measured in current prices, and we defined real GDP as GDP adjusted for price changes. Now we take a closer look at how real GDP is measured in modern economies.

Let's start with a simple economy in which there are only two goods, cars and computers, produced in the years 2004 and 2005. The data for this economy, the prices and quantities produced for each year, are shown in Table 5.4. The production of cars and the production of computers increased, but the production of computers increased more rapidly. The price of cars rose, while the price of computers remained the same.

Table 5.4   GDP Data for a Simple Economy

Year	Quantity Produced		Price	
	Cars	Computers	Cars	Computers
2004	4	1	$10,000	$5,000
2005	5	3	12,000	5,000

Let's first calculate nominal GDP for this economy in each year. Nominal GDP is the total value of goods and services produced in each year. Using the data in the table, we can see that nominal GDP for the year 2004 is:

$$(4 \text{ cars} \times \$10,00/\text{car}) + (1 \text{ computer} \times \$5,000/\text{computer}) = \$45,000$$

Similarly, nominal GDP for 2005 is $75,000.

Now we'll find real GDP. To compute real GDP, we calculate GDP using constant prices. What prices should we use? For the moment, let's use the prices for the year 2004. Because we are using 2004 prices, real GDP and nominal GDP for 2004 are both equal to $45,000. For 2005, real GDP is

$$(5 \text{ cars} \times \$10,000/\text{car}) + (3 \text{ computers} \times \$5,000/\text{computer}) = \$65,000$$

Note that real GDP for 2005, which is $65,000, is less than nominal GDP for 2005, which is equal to $75,000. The reason real GDP is less than nominal GDP here is because prices of cars rose between 2004 and 2005, and we are measuring GDP using 2004 prices. We can measure real GDP for any other year simply by calculating GDP using constant prices.

We now calculate the growth in real GDP for this economy between 2004 and 2005. Because real GDP was $45,000 in 2004 and $65,000 in 2005, real GDP grew by

$$(\$65,000 - \$45,000)/\$45,000 = .444$$

which equals 44.4%. This is an average of the growth rates for both goods, cars and computers.

We can also use the data in Table 5.4 to measure the changes in prices for this economy. The basic idea is that the differences between nominal GDP and real GDP for any year arise only because of changes in prices. Thus, by comparing real GDP and nominal GDP, we can measure the changes in prices for the economy. In practice, we do this by creating an index, called the **GDP deflator**, which measures how prices change over time. Because we are calculating real GDP using year 2004 prices, we will set the value of this index equal to 100 in the year 2004, which we call the base year. To find the value of the GDP deflator for the year 2005 (or other years), we use the following formula:

GDP deflator: An index that measures how the prices of goods included in GDP change over time.

value of GDP deflator in 2005 = 100 × [(nominal GDP in 2005)/(real GDP in 2005)]

Using this formula, we find that the value of the GDP deflator for 2005 is

$$100 \times (\$75,000/\$65,000) = 100 \times 1.15 = 115$$

Since the value of the GDP deflator is 115 in 2005 and was 100 in the base year of 2004, this means that prices rose by 15% ([(115 − 100)/100] = .15 or 15%) between the two years. Note that this 15% is an average of the price changes for the two goods, cars and computers.

Up until 1996, the Commerce Department, which produces the GDP figures, used these methods to calculate real GDP and measure changes in prices. It chose a base year and measured real GDP by using the prices in that base year and also calculated the GDP deflator, just as we did, by taking the ratio of nominal GDP to real GDP. Today, the Commerce Department calculates real GDP and the price index for real GDP using a more complicated method. In our example, we measured real GDP using 2004 prices. But we could have also measured real GDP using prices from 2005. If we did, we would have come up with slightly different numbers both for the increase in prices between the two years and for the increase in real GDP. To avoid this problem, the Commerce Department today uses a **chain index**, a method for calculating price changes based on taking an average of price changes using base years from neighboring years (that is, 2004 and 2005 in our example). If you look in the newspapers today or at the data produced by the Commerce Department, you will see real GDP measured in *chained-dollars* and a *chain-type price index* for GDP.

Chain index: A method for calculating changes in prices that includes an average of price changes using base years from neighboring years.

GDP as a Measure of Welfare

GDP is our best measure of the value of output produced by an economy. But it is not a perfect measure. There are several recognized flaws in the construction of GDP of which you need to be aware. Because of these flaws, we should be cautious if we want to interpret GDP as a measure of our economic well being. First, GDP ignores transactions that do not take place in organized markets. The most important example is services, such as cleaning, cooking, and providing free child care, that are performed in the home. Because these services are not transferred through markets, GDP statisticians cannot measure them. This has probably led us to overestimate the growth in GDP. In the last three decades, there has been a big increase in the percentage of women in the labor force. Since more women are now working outside the home, there is naturally a demand for more meals in restaurants, more cleaning services, and more paid child care. All this new demand shows up in GDP, but the services that were provided earlier—when they were provided free—did not show up in earlier GDP. This naturally overstates the true growth in GDP.

Second, leisure time is not included in GDP, since GDP is designed to be a measure of the production that occurs in the economy. Leisure time, along with other non-market activities, is ignored in GDP accounting. To the extent that leisure is valued by households, increases in leisure time will lead to higher social welfare, but not higher GDP.

Third, GDP ignores the underground economy, where transactions are not reported to official authorities. These transactions can be legal, but people don't report the income they have generated, because they want to evade paying taxes on that income. For example, waiters and waitresses may not report all their tips, and owners of flea markets may make under-the-table cash transactions with their customers. There are also illegal transactions that result in unreported income, such as profits from the illegal drug trade.

In the United States, the Internal Revenue Service estimated in the early 1990s that about $100 billion in federal income taxes from the underground economy were not collected each year. If the average federal income tax rate in the country is about 20%, this means approximately $500 billion ($100/0.20) in income escapes the GDP accountants from the underground economy every year, about 7% of GDP at the time.

Fourth, GDP does not value changes in the environment that arise through the production of output. Suppose a factory produces $1,000 of output but pollutes a river and lowers the river's value by $2,000. Instead of recording a loss to society of $1,000, GDP will show a $1,000 increase. This is an important limitation of GDP accounting as a measure of our economic well-being because changes in the environment are important. In principle, we can make adjustments to try to correct for this deficiency.

The U.S. Department of Commerce, which collects the GDP data, had a project to try to account for environmental changes. In 1994, it released a report on the first phase

The growth in GDP is exaggerated because the cost of restaurant meals includes cooking services that were previously performed at home and not counted in GDP.

of the study, in which it focused on the value of mineral resources (oil, gas, coal, etc.) in the United States. The government first measured proven reserves of minerals from 1958 to 1991: those reserves of minerals that can be extracted, given current technology and current economic conditions. They decrease when minerals are extracted and increase when new investments (such as oil wells or mines) are made.

The question the Commerce Department asked was whether the stock of proven reserves had been depleted—that is, depreciated—over time. If it had been depreciated, the reduction in the value of the stock of minerals should be subtracted from GDP to measure national income correctly. It is important to note that this calculation focuses only on proven reserves, not the total stock of minerals in the earth. The reason the Commerce Department counts only proven reserves is that some mineral deposits are simply too expensive to extract under current economic conditions. Changes in proven reserves alone correspond most closely to changes in our current economic well-being.

A CLOSER LOOK DOES MONEY BUY HAPPINESS?

Two economists, David G. Blanchflower of Dartmouth College and Andrew J. Oswald of Warwick University in the United Kingdom, have systematically analyzed surveys over nearly a 30-year period that ask individuals to describe themselves as "happy, pretty happy, or not too happy." The results of their work is provocative. Over the last 30 years, reported levels of happiness have actually declined in the United States and remained relatively flat in the United Kingdom, despite very large increases in per capita income in both countries. Could it be the increased stress of everyday life has taken its toll on our happiness despite the increase in income?

At any point in time, however, money does appear to buy happiness. Holding other factors constant, individuals with higher incomes do report higher levels of personal satisfaction. But these "other factors" are quite important. Unemployment and divorce lead to sharply lower levels of satisfaction. Blanchflower and Oswald calculate that a stable marriage is worth $100,000 in terms of equivalent reported satisfaction.

Perhaps most interesting is their findings about trends in the relative happiness of different groups in our society. While whites report higher levels of happiness than blacks, the gap has decreased over the last 30 years as the happiness of blacks has risen faster than whites. Men's happiness has risen relative to that of women over the last 30 years. Finally, reported happiness appears to peak at age 40. What economic and social factors do you think account for these trends?

Source: David G. Blanchflower and Andrew J. Oswald, National Bureau of Economic Research Working Paper 7847, January 2000.

It turned out that the Commerce Department found that these adjustments had very little affect on measures of national income. But mineral stocks are only part of our environment. These methods can be extended to include renewable resources, such as forests and fish, although the data may not be as accurate as the data for minerals. A much more challenging task would be to value changes in clean air and clean water. Has our environment improved or deteriorated as we experienced economic growth? Finding the answer to this question will pose a real challenge for the next generation of economic statisticians.

Finally, most of us would prefer to live in a country with a high standard of living and few of us would want to experience poverty up close. But does a higher level of GDP really lead to more satisfaction? As "A Closer Look: Does Money Buy Happiness?" explores, higher income does not necessarily lead to higher levels of perceived happiness.

Using the **TOOLS**

In this chapter, we looked closely at how we measure a nation's production and how we measure its income. Here's an opportunity to test your understanding of the key concepts.

APPLICATIONS

1. Nominal GDP Versus Real GDP
Economists observed that in one country nominal GDP increased two years in a row, but real GDP fell over the same two years. How can this have occurred? Construct a numerical example to illustrate this possibility.

2. Fish and National Income
Suppose you were worried that national income did not adequately take into account the depletion of the stock of fish in the economy. Describe how you would advise the Commerce Department to take this into account in their calculations.

3. Transfer Payments Versus Government Employment
In Economy A, the government puts on the payroll as government employees workers who cannot find jobs for long periods, but these "employees" do no work. In Economy B, the government does not hire any long-term unemployed workers; instead it just gives them cash grants. How do the GDP statistics compare between the two otherwise identical economies?

Summary

In this chapter, we explored how economists and government statisticians measure our national income and production. Developing meaningful statistics for an entire economy is difficult. As we have seen, statistics can convey useful information—if they are used with care. Here are some of the main points to remember in this chapter:

1. The circular flow helps represent the idea that the production of GDP also generates income.

2. GDP is the market value of all final goods and services produced in a given year.

3. GDP is divided into consumption, investment, government purchases, and net exports.

4. National income is obtained from GDP by adding net income from abroad, then subtracting depreciation and indirect taxes.

5. Real GDP is calculated by using constant prices. The Commerce Department now uses methods that take an average using base years from neighboring years.

6. GDP does not include nonmarket transactions, leisure time, the underground economy, or changes to the environment.

Key Terms

chain index, 109
consumption expenditures, 101
depreciation, 101
durable goods, 101
economic growth, 99
GDP deflator, 108
government purchases, 102
gross domestic product [GDP], 98
gross investment, 101
gross national product [GNP], 101

indirect taxes, 105
intermediate goods, 98
macroeconomics, 96
national income, 105
net exports, 102
net investment, 101
net national product [NNP], 105
nominal GDP, 99
nondurable goods, 101

personal income, 106
personal disposable income, 106
private investment expenditures, 101
real GDP, 99
services, 101
trade deficit, 103
trade surplus, 103
transfer payments, 102
value added, 106

Problems and Discussion Questions

1. Should we care more about the growth of nominal GDP or real GDP?

For Problems 2–4, use the following data:

| | Quantities Produced | | Prices | |
	CDs	Tennis Rackets	$/CD	$/Tennis Rackets
Year 2004	100	200	20	110
Year 2005	120	210	22	120

2. Calculate real GDP using prices from 2004. By what percent did real GDP grow?

3. Calculate the value of the price index for GDP for 2005 using 2004 as the base year. By what percent did prices increase?

4. Repeat Problem 2 but use prices from 2005.

5. Suppose someone told you that the value of a price index in a country was 115. Is this information, by itself, useful?

6. A student once said, "Trade deficits are good because we are buying more goods than we are producing." What is the downside to trade deficits?

7. Consumer durables depreciate over time. In your household, which consumer goods have substantial depreciation? Can you estimate the value of depreciation in a given year for consumer goods in your household?

8. A publisher buys paper, ink, and computers to produce textbooks. Which of these purchases is included in investment spending?

9. Air quality in Los Angeles deteriorated in the 1950s through 1970s and then improved in the 1980s and 1990s. How could a change in air quality like this be incorporated into our measures of national income?

10. When we calculate value added, we add up the value created in all organizations, even those producing intermediate goods. Can you explain why this does not cause double-counting?

11. In the 1980s and 1990s, computers were rapidly introduced into the economy. The prices of computers fell rapidly over time during this period. Suppose that in calculating real GDP, the Commerce Department used a single base year, one in which computer prices were still at their earlier, high levels. What distortions would using this base year cause to measures of real GDP and to changes in prices?

12. Web Exercise. Go to the Web site for the Federal Reserve Bank of St. Louis [*http://www.stls.frb.org/fred/*]. Find the data for nominal GDP, real GDP in chained dollars, and the chain price index for GDP.

   a. Calculate the percentage growth for nominal GDP since 1990 until the most recent year.

   b. Calculate the percentage growth in real GDP since 1990 until the most recent year.

   c. Finally, calculate the percentage growth in the chain price index for GDP over this same period and compare it to the difference between your answers to (a) and (b).

13. Web Exercise. Search the Web for articles on the underground economy. You might want to start with the topic "IRS and Underground Economy" on yahoo.com. What are some of the different ways in which economists try to measure the size of the underground economy?

Model Answers to Questions

Chapter-Opening Questions

1. Production also generates income in an economy.
2. GDP is the market value of all final goods and services produced in an economy.
3. We use constant prices to measure real GDP.
4. GDP is not a perfect measure of true economic welfare.

Test Your Understanding

1. The four components of GDP are consumption, investment, government spending, and net exports.
2. Income.
3. Transfer payments are excluded.
4. The difference is depreciation.
5. Net exports are exports minus imports.
6. We add net income earned abroad.
7. The largest component is compensation of employees.
8. Households.

Using the Tools

1. Nominal GDP Versus Real GDP. Real GDP can fall, but prices rise sufficiently to make nominal GDP increase. Any example with very large increases in prices will work.

2. Fish and National Income. Follow the same procedure for mineral wealth. First, estimate (at appropriate prices) the value of all the fish in the sea at the beginning of the year and the end of the year. Then calculate the change in the value of the stock of fish. If the value of the stock of fish has decreased, this is similar to depreciation, and the decrease in value should be subtracted from GDP to obtain national income. If the value of the stock of fish has increased, the increase in value should be added to national income. Note that there may be problems with national boundaries. Whose GDP is affected if the stock of fish declines in the middle of the Atlantic or Pacific oceans?

3. Transfer Payments Versus Government Employment. In Economy A, GDP would be higher because the wages of government employees would count as government purchases of goods and services. The cash grants would not be part of GDP in Economy B because they are just transfer payments.

Unemployment and Inflation

Chances are that, when a graduating college student begins to look for a job, he or she will be more likely to surf the Internet in search of employment than to look in the help wanted ads in the local papers. Large Internet firms now specialize in posting job vacancies and collecting resumes for prospective employees. Information about jobs all over the country are available online. The Internet has certainly reduced the costs associated with seeking employment.

But could the Internet solve all our unemployment problems? Let's suppose the following: Every employer posted every job vacancy on the Internet, and everyone seeking a job posted his or qualifications on the Internet. Private firms, or perhaps a government agency, organized these postings by geographical area and the type of job. Would information made available in this way reduce unemployment to zero? Would this really work?

I n this chapter, we look at unemployment and inflation, two key concepts in macroeconomics. Unemployment and inflation are at the heart of all macroeconomic policy. Losing a job is one of the most stressful experiences a person can suffer. For the elderly, the fear that the purchasing power of their wealth will evaporate with inflation is also a source of deep concern.

In this chapter, we examine how economists define unemployment and inflation and the problems in measuring them. Once we have a basic understanding of what unemployment is and what inflation is, we will be able to investigate further their causes and consequences.

After studying this chapter, you will be able to answer the following questions:

1. What is unemployment? Why can't it be driven down to zero?

2. What demographic groups suffer the most unemployment? Can the unemployment statistics tell us the answer?

3. What is the Consumer Price Index and how is it related to the cost of living?

4. How accurately can we measure inflation in the economy? If we don't do a good job, what impact does our inaccuracy have?

What Is Unemployment?

One of the reasons we want to avoid poor economic performance is that it imposes costs on individuals and society. If the economy fails to create enough jobs, many individuals will not find work, causing hardship for them and their families. Recall from Chapter 5 that one of the key issues for macroeconomics is understanding economic fluctuations—the ups and downs of the economy. During periods of poor economic performance, such as economic recessions when real GDP declines, unemployment rises sharply and becomes a cause of public concern. During times of good economic performance and rapid economic growth, unemployment is reduced but does not disappear. Our first task is to understand how economists and government statisticians measure unemployment and then learn to interpret what they measure.

Definitions

Unemployed: People who are looking for work but do not have jobs.

Employed: People who have jobs.

Labor force: The employed plus the unemployed.

Let's begin with some definitions.

The **unemployed** are those individuals who do not currently have a job but who are actively looking for work. The phrase *actively looking* is critical. Individuals who looked for work in the past but are not looking currently are not counted as unemployed. The **employed** are individuals who currently have jobs. Together, the unemployed and employed comprise the **labor force.**

$$\text{labor force} = \text{employed} + \text{unemployed}$$

The unemployment rate is the number of unemployed divided by the total labor force; it represents the percentage of the labor force unemployed and looking for work:

$$\text{unemployment rate} = \text{unemployed/labor force}$$

Labor force participation rate: The fraction of the population that is over 16 years of age that is in the labor force.

Finally, we need to understand what is meant by the **labor force participation rate**, defined as the labor force divided by the population 16 years and older. It represents the fraction of the population 16 years and older that is in the labor force:

$$\text{labor force participation rate} = \text{labor force/population 16 and over.}$$

To illustrate these concepts, suppose that an economy consists of 200,000 individuals 16 years and older, of whom 122,000 are employed and 8,000 are unemployed. In this exam-

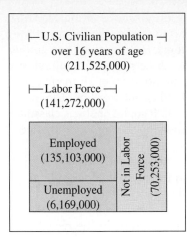

Figure 6.1
Unemployment Data, 2001

Source: Bureau of Labor Statistics, U.S. Department of Labor, 2001.

ple, the labor force is 130,000 (122,000 + 8,000) people. The labor force participation rate is 0.65, or 65% (130,000/200,000). The unemployment rate is 0.0615, or 6.15% (8,000/130,000).

Figure 6.1 helps to put these definitions into perspective for the U.S. economy. The large box is the total population 16 years and older, which in 2001 was comprised of 211,525,000 individuals. This population is divided into two groups: those in the labor force and those outside the labor force. For this year, the labor force participation rate was 67%. Within the labor force, there were 135,103,000 employed and 6,169,000 unemployed.

Table 6.1 contains some international data on unemployment for 2001. Notice the sharp differences between countries; for example, the Netherlands had a 1.9% unemployment rate, while Spain had an unemployment rate of 13.1%.

Issues in Measuring Unemployment

Recall that we defined the unemployed as those people who are looking for work but do not currently have jobs. With that in mind, let's take a closer look at our measures of unemployment.

Table 6.1 Unemployment Rates Around the World, 2001

Country	Unemployment Rate (%)
United States	4.4
Belgium	10.0
Sweden	3.5
France	8.7
Italy	9.9
Spain	13.1
United Kingdom	5.0
Netherlands	1.9
Japan	4.8
Australia	6.9

Source: The Economist, June 23, 2001.

It is relatively straightforward in principle to determine who is employed: Just count the people who are working. What is more difficult is to distinguish between those who are unemployed and those who are not in the labor force. How are these two groups distinguished? Each month, the Bureau of Labor Statistics directs its staff to interview a large sample of households. It asks about the employment situation of all members of households 16 years and older. If someone in a household is not working, the interviewer asks whether the person is actively looking for work. If so, he or she is classified as unemployed; but if the unemployed person is not actively looking for work, that person is classified as not being in the labor force.

Obviously, it is difficult for an interviewer to determine whether someone is truly looking for work. Without knowing whether someone in the household actually made any effort to look for a job during the time before the interview, the interviewer must rely on good-faith responses to the questions.

What about those people who were looking for work sometime in the recent past but did not find any opportunities and have stopped looking? These people are considered **discouraged workers**. They are not included in the official count of the unemployed.

The Bureau of Labor Statistics (BLS) has long recognized that it is difficult to distinguish between people who are unemployed, and people who are unemployed and not in the labor force. In 1994, the BLS interviewers changed the way they asked questions to avoid biasing responses in the direction of not being in the labor force. Studies revealed these changes did not have much effect on the overall unemployment rate but did raise the unemployment rate somewhat for older workers.

To add to difficulties in measurement and interpreting what is measured, some workers may hold a part-time job but prefer to work full time. Other workers may hold jobs far below their capabilities. Workers in either of these situations are called **underemployed**. It is very difficult for the government to distinguish between employed and underemployed workers.

Another fact about unemployment that we have to understand is that different groups of people suffer more unemployment than other groups. Table 6.2 contains some unemployment statistics for selected groups for May 2001. Adults have substantially lower unemployment rates than teenagers. Minorities have higher unemployment rates;

Discouraged workers: Workers who left the labor force because they could not find jobs.

Underemployed: Workers who hold a part-time job but prefer to work full time or hold jobs that are far below their capabilities.

Table 6.2 Selected U.S. Unemployment Statistics, Unemployment Rates for May 2001 (in percent)

Total	4.4
Males 20 years and older	3.9
Females 20 years and older	3.8
Both sexes, 16–19 years	13.6
White	3.8
African American	8.0
White, 16–19 years	11.8
African American, 16-19 years	25.1
Married men	2.6
Married women	2.9
Women maintaining families	6.2

Source: Bureau of Labor Statistics, U.S. Department of Labor, 2001.

African-American teenagers having extremely high unemployment rates. On average, men and women have roughly the same unemployment rates, but the unemployment rates for married men and married women are lower than unemployment rates of women who maintain families alone.

These relative differentials among unemployment rates do vary somewhat as GDP rises and falls. Teenage and minority unemployment rates often rise very sharply during poor economic times. In better times, there is typically a reduction of unemployment for all groups. Nonetheless, teenage and minority unemployment remains high at all times.

Most of the employment and unemployment statistics reported in the newspapers are *seasonally adjusted*. Many economic time series, including employment and unemployment, are substantially influenced by seasonal factors. These are recurring calendar-related effects caused by, for example, the weather, holidays, the opening and closing of schools, and related factors. The Bureau of Labor Statistics uses statistical procedures to remove these seasonal factors—that is, they seasonally adjust the series—so that users of the data can more accurately interpret underlying trends in the economy. As an example, actual unemployment rates for teenagers increase in the early summer as teenagers seek summer jobs. The seasonally adjusted unemployment data take this recurring pattern into account. The seasonally adjusted unemployment rates do not have the predictable summer increase in the unemployment rate for teenagers.

Types of Unemployment

We can divide unemployment into three basic types. By studying each type separately, we can gain insight into some of the causes of each type of unemployment.

The unemployment rate is closely tied to the overall fortunes of the economy. Unemployment rises sharply during periods when real GDP falls and decreases when real GDP grows rapidly. During periods of falling GDP, firms will not want to employ as many workers as they do in good times because they are not producing as many goods and services. Firms will lay off or fire some current workers and will be more reluctant to add new workers to their payrolls. The result will be fewer workers with jobs and rising unemployment. Economists call the unemployment that accompanies fluctuations in real GDP **cyclical unemployment**. Cyclical unemployment rises during periods when real GDP falls or grows at a slower than normal rate and decreases when the economy improves.

Cyclical unemployment: The component of unemployment that accompanies fluctuations in real GDP.

Unemployment occurs even during periods when the economy is growing. Since 1970, for example, the unemployment rate in the United States has not fallen below 3.9% of the labor force. Unemployment that is not associated with economic fluctuations is either frictional unemployment or structural unemployment.

Frictional unemployment is the unemployment that occurs naturally during the normal workings of an economy. It can occur for a variety of reasons. People change jobs, move across the country, get laid off from their current jobs and search for new opportunities, or take their time after they enter the labor force to find an appropriate job. Suppose that when you graduate from college, you take six months to find a job that you like. During the six months in which you are looking for a good job, you are among those unemployed who make up frictional unemployment. Searching for a job, however, makes good sense. It would not be wise to take the first job you were offered if it had low wages, poor benefits, and no future.

Frictional unemployment: The part of unemployment associated with the normal workings of the economy, such as searching for jobs.

The chapter opening story raised the possibility that the Internet could help to reduce unemployment down to zero, as firms could post help-wanted advertisements and workers could indicate interest in seeking employment. As we think about the nature of search and frictional unemployment, we can see that mere exchanges of information would not reduce frictional unemployment down to zero. Some workers, for example, would prefer to continue searching for jobs in their own area rather than moving across country to seek another job. Firms would also want to scrutinize employees very carefully because hiring and training a worker is costly. Improving information flows could even have a perverse effect of informing workers of other opportunities in the economy and thereby lead to more workers quitting their current jobs and seeking other employment.

Structural unemployment: The part of unemployment that results from the mismatch of skills and jobs.

Structural unemployment occurs because of a mismatch between the jobs that are available and the skills of workers who are seeking jobs. Workers with low skills may not find opportunities for employment. If the government requires employers to pay wages, taxes, and benefits that exceed the contribution of these workers, firms will not be likely to hire them. Similarly, workers whose skills do not match the employment opportunities in their area may be unemployed. Aerospace engineers in California will not find jobs in their area if the aerospace industry relocates to Alabama.

The line between frictional unemployment and structural unemployment is sometimes hard to draw. Suppose a highly skilled steelworker is laid off because his company shuts down its plant in his area and moves to a new plant overseas. The worker would like to find a comparable job, but only low-wage, unskilled work is available in his town. Jobs are available but not his kind of job, and the steel company will never return. Is this person's unemployment frictional or structural? There really is no correct answer. You might think of the steelworker as experiencing either frictional or structural unemployment. In practice, it does not matter, either to the steelworker or to the economist, whether this episode of unemployment is frictional or structural.

Economic Detective

Suspicious Unemployment Statistics

Suppose that after a long period of high unemployment, government statisticians noticed that the labor force was smaller than it was before the spell of unemployment. Is there any reason you might be suspicious of these numbers? As an economic detective, you may have good reasons to be suspicious of these numbers. During the period of high unemployment, some workers may have become discouraged and dropped out of the labor force. They may return to the labor force when economic conditions improve.

Natural rate of unemployment: The level of unemployment at which there is no cyclical unemployment.

Full employment: The level of employment that occurs when the unemployment rate is at the natural rate.

Total unemployment in an economy is composed of cyclical, frictional, and structural unemployment. The level of unemployment at which there is no cyclical unemployment is called the **natural rate of unemployment**. The natural rate of unemployment consists of only frictional unemployment and structural unemployment. The natural rate of unemployment is the economist's notion of the rate unemployment should be, when there is **full employment**. It may seem strange to think that workers can be unemployed when the economy is at full employment. But economists choose to consider the economy to be at full employment when there is no cyclical unemployment, although there is frictional and structural unemployment. The economy needs some frictional unemployment to operate efficiently: it is the unemployment that exists so that workers and firms find the right matches.

In the United States today, economists estimate that the natural rate of unemployment is between 4.0% and 5.5%. The natural rate of unemployment can vary over time and will differ across countries. In Europe, for example, estimates of the natural rate of unemployment place it between 7% and 10%. In a later chapter, we explore why the natural rate of unemployment is higher in Europe than in the United States and why the natural rate of unemployment can vary over time in the same country.

The actual unemployment rate can be higher or lower than the natural rate of unemployment. During a period in which the real GDP fails to grow at its normal rate, there will be positive cyclical unemployment, and actual unemployment can far exceed the natural rate of unemployment. For example, in the United States in 1983, unem-

Specialized journals provide important information about job opportunities in the economy.

ployment exceeded 10% of the labor force. A more extreme example occurred in 1933 during the Great Depression, when the unemployment rate reached 25%. On the other hand, when the economy grows very rapidly for a long period, actual unemployment can fall below the natural rate of unemployment. With sustained rapid economic growth, employers will be aggressive in hiring workers. During the late 1960s, unemployment rates fell below 4%; the natural rate of unemployment was estimated to be over 5% at that time. In this case, cyclical unemployment was negative.

Just as a car will overheat if the engine is overworked, so the economy will overheat if economic growth is too rapid. At low unemployment rates, firms will find it difficult to recruit workers, and competition among firms will lead to increases in wages. As wages increase, increases in prices soon follow. The sign of this overheating will be a general rise in prices for the entire economy, which we commonly call inflation. As we discuss in later chapters, when the actual unemployment rate falls below the natural rate of unemployment, inflation will increase.

TEST Your Understanding

1. How do economists measure the unemployed?
2. Previously unemployed individuals who have stopped looking for work are called _____ workers.
3. The three types of unemployment are cyclical, frictional, and _____
4. The natural rate of unemployment consists solely of _____ and _____ unemployment.

The Consumer Price Index and the Cost of Living

Suppose you moved to France and began to work. You received your first paycheck, which was in Euros, the European currency. The actual number of Euros written on the check would not mean much to you initially. What you would like to know is what goods and services your paycheck could buy. Was this a fat paycheck or a thin one? Should you celebrate your first paycheck with a 5-course gourmet dinner or head for the nearest inexpensive café?

Even in our own country, where we feel we have a reasonable sense of what a dollar can buy, we do know that the value of a dollar—what it purchases—varies over time. In

1976, a new starting professor of economics was paid $15,000. In 2001, a new starting professor at the same university was paid $55,000. Prices, of course, had risen in those 25 years. Which starting professor had the best deal?

These examples are illustrations of one of our five principles of economics, the reality principle:

Reality **PRINCIPLE**

> **What matters to people is the real value of money or income—its purchasing power—not the face value of money or income.**

Consumer Price Index [CPI]: A price index that measures the cost of a fixed basket of goods chosen to represent the consumption pattern of individuals.

Economists have developed a number of different measures to track the cost of living over time. The best known of these measures is the **Consumer Price Index [CPI]**.

The CPI is widely used by both government and the private sector to measure changes in prices facing consumers. The CPI is an index that measures changes in a fixed *basket of goods*—a collection of items chosen to represent the purchasing pattern of a typical consumer. We first find out how much this basket of goods costs in a given year, called the base year. We then ask how much it costs in other years and measure changes in the cost of living relative to this base year. The CPI index for a given year, say year K, is defined as

$$\text{CPI in year } K = (\text{cost of basket in year } K / \text{cost of basket in base year} \times 100$$

Suppose a basket of goods costs $200 in the base year of 1992 and $250 in 1997. First, the value for the CPI in 1992 (the base year) is

$$\text{CPI in 1992} = (200/200) \times 100 = 100$$

The CPI in 1992 is 100. The way that the CPI is constructed its value in a base year will always be 100. Now let's calculate the value of the CPI for 1997:

$$\text{CPI in 1997} = (250/200) \times 100 = 125$$

The CPI in 1997 is 125. The CPI rose from 100 in 1992 to 125 in 1997 in this example, a 25% increase in average prices over this 5-year period.

Here is how you would use this information. Suppose you had $300 in 1992. How much would you need to be able to have the same standard of living in 1997? The answer is given by multiplying the $300 by the ratio of the CPI in 1997 to the CPI in 1992:

$$\$300 \times (125/100) = \$375$$

You need $375 in 1997 just to maintain what was your standard of living in 1992. This is the type of calculation that economists do to evaluate changes in living standards over time.

How do we actually calculate the CPI in practice? Each month, the Bureau of Labor Statistics sends its employees out to sample prices for over 90,000 specific items around the entire country. Figure 6.2 shows the broad categories that are used in the CPI and the importance of each category in household budgets. Rent and food and beverages account for 44% of total spending by households.

The CPI Versus the Chain Index for GDP

In Chapter 5, we discussed measuring nominal GDP and real GDP. We also mentioned that since 1996, the Commerce Department has used a chain index (replacing the GDP deflator) to measure changes in prices for goods and services included in GDP. The chain index for GDP and the CPI are both measures of average prices for the economy, yet they differ in several ways.

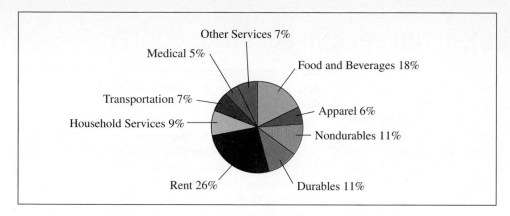

Figure 6.2
**Components
of the CPI**
Source: Bureau of Labor Statistics Handbook (Washington, DC: U.S. Government Printing Office, 1992).

First, the CPI measures the costs of a typical basket of goods for consumers. It includes goods produced in prior years (such as older cars) as well as imported goods. The chain price index for GDP does not measure price changes from either used goods or imports. The reason that the chain index for GDP does not include used or imported goods is that it is based on the calculation of GDP, which measures only goods and services produced currently in the United States.

Second, unlike the chain price index for GDP, the CPI asks how much a fixed basket of goods costs in the current year compared to the cost of those same goods in a base year. Because consumers will tend to buy less of goods whose prices have risen, the CPI will tend to overstate true changes in the cost of living. For example, if the price of steak rises, consumers may switch to chicken and spend less on steak. But if the current basket of goods and services in the CPI includes steak, the CPI thinks the share of higher-priced steak in the basket is the same as the share of steak before its price increase; the CPI does not allow the share of steak in the index to decrease.

Problems in Measuring Changes in Prices

Most economists believe that in reality all the indexes—the chain index for GDP and the CPI—overstate actual changes in prices. In other words, the increase in prices is probably less than the reported indexes tell us. The principal reason for this overstatement is that we have a difficult time measuring quality improvements. Suppose that the new computers sold to consumers become more powerful and more efficient each year. Further, suppose that the dollar price of a new computer remains the same each year. Even though the prices remain the same, the computers in later years are of much higher quality. If we looked simply at the prices of computers and did not take into account the change in quality, we would say there was no price change for computers. But in later years we are getting more computer power for the same price. If we failed to take the quality change into account, we would not see that the price of computer power has fallen.

Government statisticians do try to adjust for quality when they can. But quality changes are so common in our economy and products evolve so rapidly that it is impossible to keep up with all that is occurring. As a result, most economists believe that we overestimate the inflation rate by between 0.5% and 1.5% each year. This overstatement has important consequences. Some government programs, such as Social Security, automatically increase payments when the CPI goes up. Some union contracts also have **cost-of-living adjustments** or automatic wage changes based on the CPI. If the CPI overstates increases in the cost of living, the government and employers might be overpaying Social Security recipients and workers for changes in the cost of living, as "A Closer Look: The CPI and Social Security" explains.

Cost-of-living adjustments:
Automatic increases in wages or other payments that are tied to a price index.

Inflation

We have now looked at two different price indexes: the chain price index used for calculating real GDP and the Consumer Price Index. Using either price index, we can calculate the percentage rate of change of the index. The percentage rate of change of a price index is the **inflation rate:**

Inflation rate: The percentage rate of change of the price level in the economy.

$$\text{inflation rate } = \text{ percentage rate of change of a price index}$$

Here is an example. Suppose that a price index in a country was 200 in 1998 and 210 in 1999. Then the inflation rate between 1998 and 1999 was

$$\text{inflation rate} = (210 - 200)/200 = .05 = 5\%$$

The country experienced a 5% inflation rate.

It is important to distinguish between the price level and the inflation rate. In everyday language, people sometimes confuse the *level of prices* with inflation. You might hear someone say that inflation is high in San Francisco because rents on apartments are high, but this is not a correct use of the term *inflation*. Inflation refers not to the level of prices, whether they are high or low, but to their percentage change. If rents were high in San Francisco but remained constant between 2 years, there would be no inflation in rents there during that time.

To gain some historical perspective, Figure 6.3 plots a price index for GDP from 1875 to 2000 for the United States. As you can see from the figure, from 1875 to the period just before World War I, there was virtually no change in the price level. The price level rose during World War I, fell after the war ended, and also fell sharply during the early 1930s. However, the most pronounced feature of the figure is the sustained rise in prices beginning around the 1940s. Unlike the earlier periods, in which the price level did not have a trend, after 1940 the price level increased sharply. By 1995, the price level had increased by a factor of 12 over its value in 1940.

Taking a closer look at the period following World War II, Figure 6.4 plots the inflation rate, the percentage change in the price index, for 1950–2000 for the United States. In the 1950s and 1960s, the inflation rate was frequently less than 2% a year. The

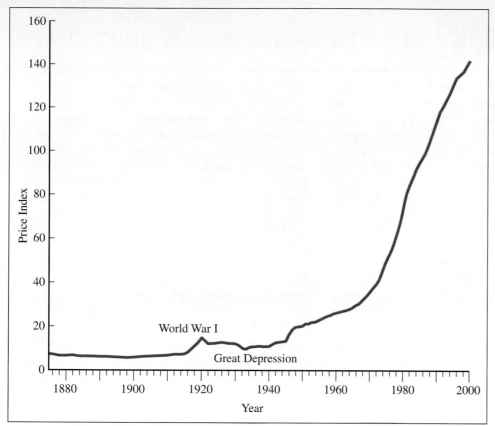

Figure 6.3
Price Index of U.S. GDP, 1875–2000

Source: R.J. Gordon, *Macro-economics* (N.Y.: Harper Collins 1993), U.S. Department of Commerce.

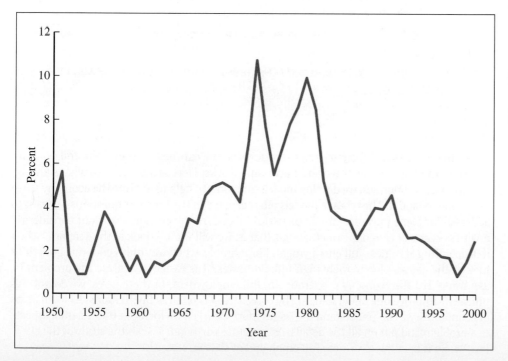

Figure 6.4
U.S. Inflation Rate, 1950–2000, Based on Chain Price Index

Source: U.S. Department of Commerce.

If you were born after 1952 and lived in the United States, you have never experienced a year without the price level rising. You might think it would be great if prices fell and we had what economists term a deflation. It may surprise you that we think you should hope that this never occurs.

During the Great Depression, the United States underwent a severe deflation, with the average level of prices falling 33% between 1929 and 1933. Wages fell along with prices during this period. The biggest problem caused by a deflation is that people cannot repay their debts. Imagine that you owe $40,000 for your education and expect to be able to pay it off over several years if you earn $27,000 a year. If a massive deflation caused your wages to fall to $18,000, you might not be able to pay your $40,000 debt, which does not fall with deflation. You would be forced to default on your loan, as millions of people did during the Great Depression.

Today, Japan is experiencing a deflation, although much milder than the Great Depression in the United States. Prices fell nearly 1% in 2001 and forecasters anticipate future declines in prices for the next several years. Banks in Japan have faced rocky economic times as borrowers, including large corporations, have defaulted on loans or missed payments. With their banks in difficult shape, Japan's economy has suffered. Japan's experience today mirrors the experience of other countries throughout the world in the 1930s during the period of deflation.

inflation rate was a lot higher in the 1970s, reaching nearly 12% per year. In recent years, the inflation rate has subsided, and has been near 2% in recent years. Prices rarely fall today but as "A Closer Look: Deflations, Yesterday and Today" shows, prices have actually fallen at times in world history.

TEST Your Understanding

5. The value of a price index in the base year is _____.

6. Economists believe that the CPI tends to underestimate the increase in the cost of living over time. True or false? Explain.

7. Unlike the CPI, the chain price index for GDP does not include used goods or _____ goods.

8. If a price index is 50 in 1998 and 60 in 1999, the rate of inflation between the two years is _____.

Looking Ahead

With this basic vocabulary of macroeconomics, we can begin to explain and you can begin to understand how the overall economy works. Here is a preview of what's ahead.

In macroeconomics, we develop models and tools to help us analyze the economy as we try to understand it. The types of models often depend on the topics or questions we want to address. For some purposes, it will be useful to analyze the economy without considering business cycles or economic fluctuations; that is, we will want to look at the economy when it is operating at or near full employment. For example, when we study economic growth or look at the causes of extremely high inflation rates, it is easier to analyze the problem by assuming that the economy is operating at full employment. In these cases, we do not significantly improve our understanding by considering economic fluctuations. As in all areas of economics, we can understand the issues more clearly if we focus on the essential aspects of a problem and not on all the details. As a useful shorthand, we call the study of the economy when it operates at or near full employment **classical economics**.

Classical economics: A school of economic thought that provides insights into the economy when it operates at or near full employment.

At other times, we will be concerned with business cycles, economic fluctuations, and sharp changes in unemployment rates. For these issues, we want to understand how the economy can deviate from full employment. As another useful shorthand, we will call the study of business cycles and economic fluctuations that we develop **Keynesian economics** (after John Maynard Keynes, who made fundamental contributions to macroeconomics). Our understanding of economic fluctuations today has progressed substantially since Keynes's initial writings and incorporates many different perspectives, including those of economists who were highly critical of Keynes. Our use of the term *Keynesian economics* is therefore just convenient shorthand for our study of economic fluctuations.

Keynesian economics: A school of economic thought that provides insights into the economy when it operates away from full employment.

In this book, we use insights from both classical economics and Keynesian economics and integrate them into our story of how the macroeconomy works. In particular, we will see that the factors stressed by Keynes and the tradition that followed him are useful for understanding the behavior of the economy in the short run, when the economy can be far away from full employment. However, in the long run, there are forces pushing the economy back to full employment. When the economy reaches full employment, the insights from classical economics become valuable.

Sometimes the words *classical* and *Keynesian* are used to refer to two different schools of economic thought. Classical economists, though recognizing that economic fluctuations do occur (and often developing their own theories of fluctuations), believe that the economy has a strong tendency to return to full employment. They therefore place great importance on studying the behavior of the economy at or near full employment.

Keynesian economists believe that the economy returns to full employment only slowly, if at all, and emphasize the role of economic fluctuations. In this book, we draw freely on the ideas of both schools because both have important perspectives that we need to understand the full range of macroeconomic phenomena. As we will see, one of the principal disagreements among macroeconomists is about precisely how strong the forces are that push the economy back to full employment.

Using the **TOOLS**

APPLICATIONS

1. Government Employment and the Unemployment Rate
Suppose the government hires workers who are currently unemployed but does not give them any work to do. What will happen to the measured unemployment rate? Is this an accurate reflection of the underlying economic situation?

2. Starting Salaries for Young Professors
The starting salary for a new assistant professor was $15,000 in 1976 and $55,000 in 2001. The value of the CPI for 2001 was 177.5 compared to 56.4 in 1976. In which year did a newly hired professor earn more in real terms?

3. Interpreting World Unemployment Statistics
A student looking a Table 6.1 argues that Spain must have very high cyclical unemployment compared to Japan because Spain's unemployment rate is so high. Explain why the student may not be correct.

4. Apartment Vacancies and Unemployment
In a major city, the vacancy rate for apartments was approximately 5%, yet substantial numbers of individuals were searching for new apartments. Can you explain why this occurs and relate it to unemployment?

Summary

In this chapter, we continued our introduction to the basic concepts of economics and explored the definition and nature of both unemployment and inflation. We also looked at the complex issues involved in measuring unemployment and inflation. Here are some of the key points to remember:

1. The unemployed are individuals who do not have jobs but are actively seeking employment.

2. The three types of unemployment are cyclical, frictional, and structural.

3. Unemployment rates vary across groups. It is often difficult to distinguish between the unemployed and discouraged workers who were once unemployed but stopped looking for work.

4. Economists measure changes in the cost of living through the Consumer Price Index, which is based on the cost of purchasing a standard basket of goods and services.

5. We measure inflation as the percentage change in the price level.

6. Economists believe that most price indices overstate true inflation because they fail to capture quality improvements.

7. Sometimes, we want to study the behavior of the economy when it operates at or near full employment. The study of the economy at full employment is known as classical economics. At other times, we want to study economic fluctuations, which are the subject of what we call Keynesian economics. In this book, we draw freely on the insights of both approaches to macroeconomic problems.

Key Terms

classical economics, 126
consumer price index [CPI], 122
cost-of-living adjustments, 123
cyclical unemployment, 119
discouraged workers, 118
employed, 116

frictional unemployment, 119
full employment, 120
inflation rate, 124
Keynesian economics, 127
labor force, 116
labor force participation rate, 116

natural rate of unemployment, 120
structural unemployment, 120
underemployed, 118
unemployed, 116

Problems and Discussion Questions

1. Here are some data for an economy:
   - 10 million individuals 16 years and older
   - 5.5 million employed
   - 0.5 million unemployed

   Calculate the labor force, the labor force participation rate, and the unemployment rate for this economy.

2. Sometimes at the beginning of an economic boom, total employment increases sharply but the unemployment rate does not fall. Why might this occur?

3. In inner cities, minority youths have high unemployment rates. Many economists believe that the unemployment picture is worse than the statistics portray. What could be the basis for this belief?

4. Suppose the government decided that housewives and househusbands should be counted as employed because they perform important services. How do

   you think this change would affect our measure of the labor force, the labor force participation rate, and the unemployment rate? (You may want to construct a numerical example.)

5. Why is the natural rate of unemployment always positive?

6. When oil prices increased sharply in the 1970s, some businesses were affected more adversely than others. Explain why some economists believe that the oil price increase led to higher frictional unemployment.

7. A country reports a price index of 55 in 1990 and 60 in 1991. What is the inflation rate between 1990 and 1991?

8. A job paid $3,000 in 1960. The CPI in 1960 was 29.3 compared to 164 in 1999. In 1999, what salary would be comparable to 1960's $3,000 in real terms?

9. An economy has 100,000,000 people employed, 8,000,000 unemployed, and 4,000,000 discouraged workers. What is the conventional measure of the unemployment rate? What would be the best alternative measure that takes into account discouraged workers?

10. Critically evaluate the following statement: "Tokyo is an expensive place to live. They must have a high inflation rate in Japan."

11. Web Exercise. Go to the data section of the Web site for the Bureau of Labor Statistics [*http://stats.bls.gov*]. Contrast the change in the price indexes

from 1960 to the present for the overall CPI with the change in some of its components such as food and beverage and medical care services. What are some of your findings?

12. Web Exercise. Use the Web to find articles about the difficulties in precisely measuring changes in prices in the economy. You might want to start with the Boskin report which can be found on the history page of the Social Security Administration [*http://www.ssa/gov/history/repstud.html*]. On the basis of your reading, what do you consider to be the most important problem?

Take It to the Net

We invite you to visit the O'Sullivan/Sheffrin page on the Prentice Hall Web site at: **http://www.prenhall.com/osullivan/** for additional World Wide Web exercises for this chapter.

Model Answers to Questions

Chapter-Opening Questions

1. The unemployed are individuals without jobs and actively seeking work. The unemployment rate cannot be driven down to zero because of natural frictions in the labor market.

2. Teenagers and minorities have the highest unemployment rates.

3. The Consumer Price Index is a price index that is used to measure changes in the cost of living.

4. Because of changes in the quality of goods and other factors, we cannot measure inflation perfectly and probably tend to overestimate the true inflation rate. This will have financial implications if payments are linked to changes in measured prices.

Test Your Understanding

1. The unemployed are individuals who are not employed but are actively looking for work.

2. Discouraged.

3. Structural.

4. Frictional and structural.

5. 100.

6. False. The CPI overestimates the increase in the cost of living over time for two reasons. It does not fully take into account technological change and assumes that the quantities of goods consumed do not decrease as prices increase.

7. Imported.

8. 20%.

Using the Tools

1. Government Employment and the Unemployment Rate. If the government hires an individual, that individual is an employee and no longer unemployed. The unemployment rate would fall. But the underlying economic reality has not changed: The individual is not producing any goods or services.

2. Starting Salaries for Young Professors. Starting salaries were higher in 2001. The 2001 equivalent of the 1976 salary of $15,000 is $15,000 × (177.5/56.4) = $47,887, which is less than the actual salary of $55,000 for 1999.

3. Interpreting World Unemployment Statistics. Spain could have higher frictional unemployment or structural unemployment than Japan. Without detailed knowledge of an economy, we cannot tell how much of unemployment is cyclical, frictional, or structural.

4. Apartment Vacancies and Unemployment. Owners of apartments naturally want to choose reliable renters, while at the same time, prospective tenants want to find the best apartments. This results in a process of search, just like in the labor market. Apartment vacancies are analogous to job vacancies and apartment seekers are analogous to the unemployed.

Classical Economics: The Economy at Full Employment

The Statue of Liberty is an enduring symbol in the United States. Throughout its history, immigrants have ventured to this country. In the late nineteenth and early twentieth century, they came primarily from Europe and Eastern Europe, arriving in boats and often viewing the famous statue in the New York harbor. In the last 20 years, immigrants to the United States now frequently come from Mexico, Latin America, and many parts of Asia. Most U.S. history books stress how the character of our country has been influenced and enriched by immigration.

Yet today, immigration is a hotly contested political issue. Employers, ranging from owners of large farms who seek farm workers, to entrepreneurs in the Silicon Valley in California who want computer programmers and technicians, support programs that bring foreign workers into the country. They contend that without these workers their industries could not profit. Union representatives, on the other hand, contend that bringing in foreign workers displaces existing U.S. workers and lowers wages. How does increased immigration affect output and wages in the economy?

Classical economics: A school of economic thought that provides insights into the economy when it operates at or near full employment.

e will explain how the amount of capital and labor determine GDP when an economy is producing at full employment. The study of how the economy operates at full employment is commonly known as **classical economics**. As you will see, classical economics is based on the principle that prices adjust in a natural way to bring the markets for goods and labor into equilibrium.

The classical economists believed that there are strong forces pushing the economy back to full employment after shocks that caused excessive unemployment. Although they did not deny that the economy could experience booms or busts, classical economists believed that booms and busts were temporary and that the economy would return naturally to full employment.

There are several reasons for studying classical economics. First, there are issues in macroeconomics concerning the long run that we should know about. Here are a few examples: Suppose the government increases spending for several years to fight a war or to rehabilitate our cities. What effects will this have on the level of consumption or investment in the economy? Or suppose we are concerned about low wages in the economy. What public policy actions can we take to raise the level of wages in the economy in the long run? The classical model that we develop in this chapter provides the tools to answer these questions.

Second, many of today's debates in economics can best be analyzed with the tools of classical economics. For example, economists and politicians debate the effects of taxes on the level of work effort and output in the economy. One school of economists, known as **supply-siders**, made this the basis of their analysis of the economy. The tools of classical economics can help us to understand some of these debates.

Supply-siders: Economists who emphasize the role of taxation for influencing economic activity.

Third, the tools of classical economics are used by a new school of economic thought—real business cycle theory—to explain why there are economic booms and recessions.

When the economy is at full employment, that does not mean there are no unemployed workers. Recall the distinction between frictional, structural, and cyclical unemployment. Frictional unemployment occurs naturally in the labor market as workers search for jobs. Structural unemployment arises from a mismatch of skills and jobs. Cyclical unemployment is the part of unemployment that rises and falls with economic fluctuations. Cyclical unemployment can be positive, when unemployment exceeds the natural rate during a recession, or negative, when unemployment is less than the natural rate during a boom. Full employment corresponds to zero cyclical unemployment; that means that when the economy is at full employment, the only unemployment is frictional and structural.

Here are issues that we can address with the tools we develop in this chapter:

1. How does increased immigration affect wages and the level of output in the economy?
2. What are the benefits of increased investment?
3. What happens to wages, employment, and GDP if employers must pay higher taxes for hiring labor?
4. If our governments spend more, does this mean we must have a lower level of consumption or investment in our economy?

In the classical model, wages and prices are assumed to adjust freely and quickly to all changes in demand and supply. It is precisely this flexibility in wages and prices that distinguishes the classical model from the Keynesian models that we examine in later chapters. You must keep this assumption and this distinction in mind as we develop the classical model in this chapter.

The Aggregate Production Function for the Economy

One of the most extremely simplified assumptions in macroeconomics is the aggregate production function. As a reminder, a function is just a convenient way to describe the relationship between variables. The **aggregate production function** explains the relationship of the total inputs used throughout the economy to the total level of production in the economy or GDP. We assume that there are only two factors of production: capital and labor. The **stock of capital** comprises all the machines, equipment, and buildings in the entire economy. **Labor** consists of the efforts of all the workers in the economy. We write the aggregate production function as

$$Y = F(K, L)$$

where Y is total output, or GDP, K is the stock of capital, and L is the labor force.

What the math says in words is that total output is produced from both capital and labor. The aggregate production function $F(K,L)$ tells us how much output is produced from the inputs to production, K and L. More inputs of either capital or labor lead to increased output.

The stock of capital that a society has at any point in time is given to us by its past investments in new plants and equipment. Investments taken today will have no or little immediate effect on the total stock of machines, equipment, and buildings in existence today. It takes time for investment to change the stock of capital. In this chapter, most of our discussion will assume that the stock of capital is fixed at a constant level, which we call K^*. But there will be a few places where we will stray from that assumption to consider what happens when there are changes in the stock of capital. We promise to let you know where we are straying from the assumption of fixed capital.

With the stock of capital fixed at the constant level K^*, only variations in the amount of labor can change the level of output in the economy. Figure 7.1 plots the relationship between the amount of labor used in an economy and the total level of output with a

Aggregate production function: Shows how much output is produced from capital and labor.

Stock of capital: The total of all the machines, equipment, and buildings in the entire economy.

Labor: The total effort of all employed workers in an economy.

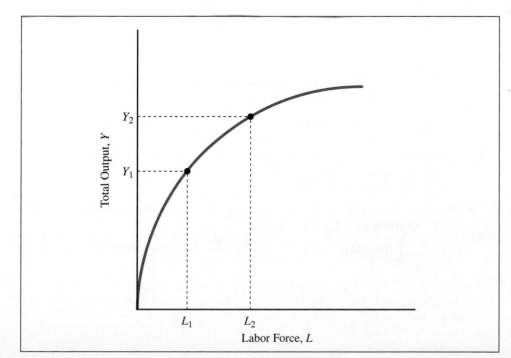

Figure 7.1

Relationship Between Labor and Output with Fixed Capital
With capital fixed, output increases with labor input but at a decreasing rate.

Short-run production function: Shows how much output is produced from varying amounts of labor when the capital stock is held constant.

fixed stock of capital. Because the amount of labor can be changed over a short period, resulting in a corresponding change in output, also within a short time, this diagram is called the **short-run production function**.

Figure 7.1 shows that as labor inputs are increased from L_1 to L_2, output increases from Y_1 to Y_2. The relationship between output and labor shown here reflects the principle of diminishing returns.

PRINCIPLE of Diminishing Returns

Suppose that output is produced with two or more inputs and that we increase one input while holding the other inputs fixed. Beyond some point—called the point of diminishing returns—output will increase at a decreasing rate.

To explain what diminishing marginal returns means, look at the data in Table 7.1 from a typical production function. The table shows the amount of output that can be produced from different amounts of labor inputs while the stock of capital is held constant at some amount. (We don't care what amount, as long as it is constant.) First, notice that as the amount of labor increases, so does the amount of output produced. Second, as output increases, it increases at a diminishing rate. For example, as labor input increases from 3 to 4 labor units, output increases by 5 output units, from 10 to 15 output units. But as labor input increases from 4 to 5 labor units, output only increases by 4 output units, from 15 to 19 output units. The rate of output dropped from 5 output units per additional unit of labor input to 4 output units per additional unit of labor input, and that's diminishing returns.

What happens if the stock of capital increases, say, from K^* to K^{**}? Figure 7.2 shows that when the stock of capital increases, the entire short-run production function shifts upward. At any level of labor input, more output can be produced than before the stock of capital was increased. As we add more capital, workers become more productive and can produce more output. That's why the production function curve is higher for more capital. For example, an office has five staff members who must share one copier. They will inevitably waste some time waiting to use it. Adding a copier will enable the staff to be more productive. The benefit of additional capital is a higher level of output from any level of labor input.

TEST Your Understanding

1. What is an aggregate production function?
2. Complete the statement with *increases* or *decreases*. With the stock of capital fixed, output increases with labor input but at a rate that _____.
3. Complete the statement with *upward* or *downward*. An increase in the stock of capital shifts the production function _____.

Table 7.1 Output and Labor Output

Y (Output)	L (Labor Input)
10	3
15	4
19	5
22	6

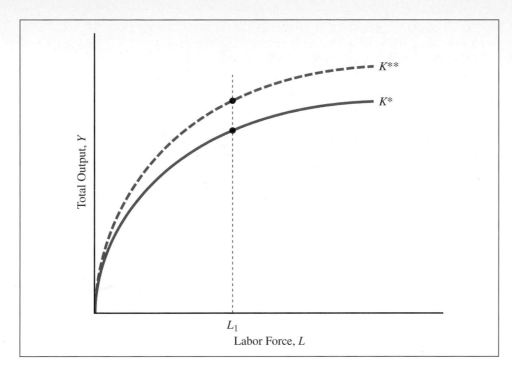

Figure 7.2

Increase in the Stock of Capital
When capital increases from K^* to K^{**} the production function shifts up. At any level of labor input, the level of output increases.

The Demand and Supply for Labor

We've just seen that with the amount of capital fixed, the level of output in the economy will be determined exclusively by the amount of labor employed. Now we'll see how the amount of employment in an economy is determined by the demand and supply for labor.

On the basis of what you already know about supply and demand from Chapter 4, you should be able to see what Figure 7.3 represents with respect to the demand and supply for labor for the entire economy. Firms hire labor to produce output and make profits. The amount of labor they will hire depends on the **real wage**: the wage rate paid to employees adjusted for changes in prices. To understand the demand for labor, we use the marginal principle:

Real wage: The wage paid to workers adjusted for changes in prices.

Marginal **PRINCIPLE**

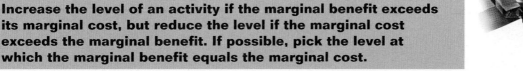

Increase the level of an activity if the marginal benefit exceeds its marginal cost, but reduce the level if the marginal cost exceeds the marginal benefit. If possible, pick the level at which the marginal benefit equals the marginal cost.

The marginal benefit that a firm receives from hiring an additional worker is the value of the extra output that results when that additional worker is hired. The marginal cost of the worker is the real wage a firm pays to hire the additional worker. The firm will continue to hire additional workers as long as the marginal benefit from an additional worker exceeds the marginal cost of the additional worker. For example, if the real wage is $20 per hour, a firm will continue to hire additional workers as long as the marginal benefit from an additional hour of work exceeds $20 and will continue hiring only until the marginal benefit from an additional hour equals $20.

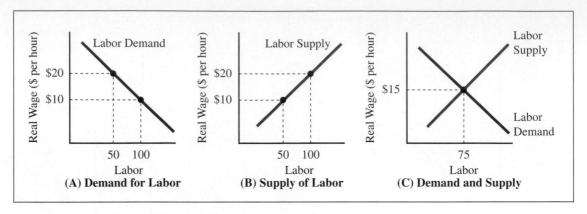

Figure 7.3 **Demand for and Supply of Labor**

If the real wage falls, the marginal cost of labor falls. As the cost falls, the firm will again hire additional labor—again, only until the marginal benefit again equals marginal cost. For example, suppose the real wage is $20 per hour and the marginal benefit from an extra hour of work is $20. Let's say the wage falls $10 per hour. Then, the marginal benefit to the firm will exceed the wage. The firm will respond by hiring more labor until the marginal benefit from hiring an additional worker equals $10.

As the real wage falls, firms will hire more labor. The labor demand curve in Figure 7.3 is therefore downward sloping. In panel A, we see that as the real wage falls from $20 to $10 per hour, the firm will increase the amount of its labor from 50 to 100 workers.

The labor supply curve is based on the decisions of workers. They must decide how many hours they want to work and how much leisure they want to enjoy. Changes in wages have two different effects on workers' decisions about those wants.

First, an increase in the real wage will make working more attractive and raise the opportunity cost of not working. Called the **substitution effect**, this increase leads workers to supply more hours of labor. This is called the substitution effect because workers want to substitute work for leisure. Second, a higher wage raises a worker's income for the amount of hours that he or she is currently working. As income rises, a worker may choose to enjoy more leisure hours and work fewer hours. This is known as the **income effect** because as workers have more income, they can afford to have more leisure time.

The substitution effect and the income effect work in opposite directions. In principle, a higher wage could lead workers to supply either more or fewer hours of work. In our analysis, we assume that the substitution effect dominates, so a higher wage rate will lead to increases in the supply of labor. In panel B of Figure 7.3 we see that 50 people would like to work at $10 per hour, but $20 per hour motivates 100 people to want to work.

Panel C puts the demand and supply curves together. At a wage of $15 per hour, the amount of labor that firms want to hire—75 workers—will be equal to the number who want to work—75 workers. This is the labor market equilibrium: The quantity demanded for labor equals the quantity supplied. Together, the demand and supply curves determine the level of employment in the economy and the level of real wages.

When firms increase their capital stock, they find that the marginal benefit from hiring workers increases because each worker becomes more productive with the additional capital. For example, suppose that the marginal benefit of an additional hour of work is initially $15, and an increase in the supply of capital raises it to $20. Firms will

Substitution effect: An increase in the wage rate increases the opportunity cost of leisure and leads workers to supply more labor.

Income effect: An increase in the wage rate raises a worker's income at the current levels of hours of work and may lead to more leisure and a decreased supply of labor.

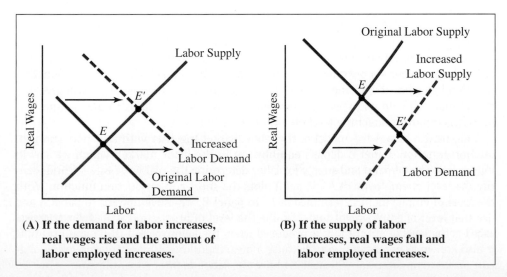

The capital equipment in this modern plant allows workers to produce high levels of output.

want to hire additional workers at the existing wage until the marginal benefit again equals the marginal cost.

Because the demand for labor increases at any real wage, the labor demand curve shifts to the right. Panel A of Figure 7.4 shows the effects of an increase in labor demand. The new market equilibrium moves from E to E'. Real wages increase, and the amount of labor employed in the economy increases as well. Having more capital in the economy is beneficial for workers.

We also can analyze the effect of an increase in the supply of labor that might come, for example, from immigration. If the population increases, we would expect that more people would want to work at any given wage. This means that the labor supply curve would shift to the right. Panel B of Figure 7.4 shows that with an increase in the supply

Figure 7.4
Shifts in Demand and Supply

(A) If the demand for labor increases, real wages rise and the amount of labor employed increases.

(B) If the supply of labor increases, real wages fall and labor employed increases.

of labor, the labor market equilibrium moves from E to E'. Real wages have fallen, and the amount of labor employed has increased. Workers who were employed before the increase in labor supply suffer because real wages have fallen—all wages, including theirs.

We can now see why currently employed workers might be reluctant to favor increased immigration. The additional supply of labor will tend to decrease real wages. Our model also explains why workers would like to see increases in the supply of machines and equipment as long as full employment can be maintained. The increased supply of capital increases labor demand and leads to higher real wages.

Economic Detective

The Case of Asian Wages and Employment

Suppose you were told that in one Asian country, both wages and employment increased. As an economic detective, would you start looking for factors that increased labor demand or factors that increased the supply of labor? To solve this mystery, you want to look for factors that increased the demand for labor. Increases in the demand for labor will increase both real wages and employment.

TEST Your Understanding

4. Labor market equilibrium occurs at a real wage at which the quantity demanded for labor equals the quantity _____ of labor.

5. Explain why the demand curve for labor is negatively sloped and the supply curve for labor is positively sloped.

6. Complete the statement with *right* or *left*. An increase in the amount of capital in the economy will shift the demand for labor curve to the _____ leading to higher real wages and employment.

7. Complete the statement with *right* or *left*. Increased immigration is likely to lead to a shift in the labor supply curve to the _____ .

8. If wages and employment both fall, this is likely caused by a decrease in the demand for labor. True or false? Explain.

Labor Market Equilibrium and Full Employment

We now show exactly how much output the economy can produce when it is operating at full employment—a big objective of this chapter. We'll put the short-run production function in a context with the demand and supply for labor. Together, they will give us a model that will help us to achieve our objective as well as help us to understand how taxes on employers affect the level of output.

Figure 7.5 brings the model of the labor market together with the short-run production function. Panel B depicts equilibrium in the labor market, which we saw in Figure 7.3. The demand and supply for labor determine the real wage rate W^* and identify the level of employment L^*. Panel A plots the short-run production function. With the level of employment determined at L^* in panel B, we move upward to panel A and use that level of employment to determine the level of production is Y^*. **Full-employment output** is the level of output that is produced when the labor market is in equilibrium. It is also known as *potential output* because a meaningful measure of an economy's long-run productive potential will need to have the labor market in equilibrium. How do

Full-employment output: The level of output that results when the labor market is in equilibrium. (Also known as potential output.)

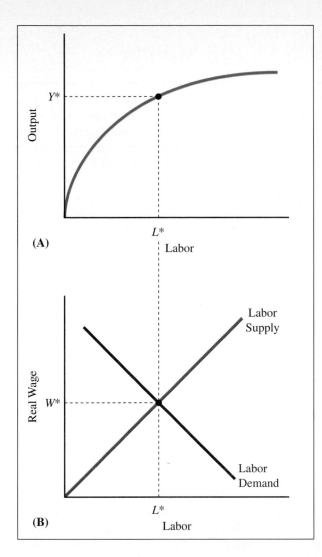

Figure 7.5
Determining Full Employment Output
Panel B determines the equilibrium level of employment at L^* and the real wage rate at W^*. Full employment output in panel A is Y^*.

economists typically measure the level of full employment output, or potential output? They start with an estimate of what the unemployment rate would be if cyclical unemployment were zero—that is, if the only unemployment were due to frictional or structural factors. In the United States, estimates of the natural rate in recent years have varied between 4.0% to 5.5%. Economists then estimate how many workers will be employed and use the short-run production function to determine potential output.

The level of potential output in an economy increases as the supply of labor increases or the stock of capital increases. An increase in the supply of labor, perhaps from more liberal immigration, would shift the labor supply curve to the right and lead to a higher level of employment in the economy. With a higher level of employment, the level of full employment output will increase. An increase in the stock of capital will increase the demand for labor. As labor demand increases, the result will be higher wages and increased employment. Higher employment will again raise the level of full employment output.

Potential output depends on both capital and labor. Consequently, differences in the quantity of labor supplied to the market will affect the level of potential output in a country. As "A Closer Look: Variations in Labor Supply" shows, the supply of labor by workers does vary over time and across countries.

The Classical Model in Historical Perspective

The term "classical model" was actually first used by John Maynard Keynes in the 1930s to contrast his theory with the received wisdom of the time. Classical economics refers to the body of work developed over time starting with Adam Smith. Other classical economists—Jean Baptiste Say, David Ricardo, John Stuart Mill, Thomas Malthus, and others—developed their work from approximately the late eighteenth and nineteenth century.

Say's Law

Say's Law: The doctrine that states that supply creates its own demand.

Classical economics is often associated with **Say's Law**, the doctrine that "supply creates its own demand." To understand Say's Law, recall from our discussion of GDP accounting in Chapter 5 that production in an economy creates an equivalent amount of income. For example, if GDP is $9 trillion, then production is $9 trillion and generates $9 trillion in income. The classical economists argued that the $9 trillion of production also created $9 trillion in demand for current goods and services. This meant that there could never be a shortage of demand for total goods and services in the economy. Demand would always be sufficient to purchase the goods and services produced—thus, there never could be an excess supply of output in the economy.

But suppose that consumers, who earned income, decided to save their income rather than spend it. Wouldn't this increase in savings lead to a shortfall in the total demand for goods and services? Classical economists argued that the increase in savings would eventually find its way to an equivalent increase in investment spending by firms. Savings by households gets channeled to investments by firms. The result would be that spending on consumption and investment together would be sufficient to purchase the goods and services produced in the economy.

Keynes argued that there could be situations in which total demand fell short of total production in the economy—at least for extended periods of time. In particular, if consumers increased their savings, there was no guarantee that there would be a rise in investment spending to offset the decrease in consumption. And, if total spending did fall short of total demand, the result could be a recession or depression. Producers would find that they could not sell their goods and cut back on production, and output in the economy would consequently fall.

Keynesian and Classical Debates

The debates between Keynesian and classical economists continued for several decades after Keynes developed his theories. Professors Don Patinkin and Franco Modigliani clarified the conditions for which the classical model would be true. In particular, they studied the conditions under which there would be sufficient demand for goods and services when the economy was at full employment. Both emphasized that one of the necessary conditions for the classical model to be true was that wages and prices were fully flexible—that is, they adjust rapidly to changes in demand and supply.

If wages and prices are not fully flexible, then Keynes's view that demand could fall short of production is more likely to be true. As we discuss in more detail in later chapters, over short periods of time, wages and prices are not fully flexible, so the insights of Keynes are important. Over longer periods of time, wages and prices do adjust and the insights of the classical model are restored.

Later in this chapter we discuss a current economic theory—real business cycle theory—that is based on the classical model. Proponents of real business cycle theory and related theories are proud to call themselves "classical economists" today.

Applications of the Classical Model

The classical model is used extensively in macroeconomics to analyze a wide range of issues.

Many politicians and economists have argued that high tax rates have hurt the U.S. economy and reduce the level of output and production. We will use the classical model to explore the logic of these claims.

We will also see how the classical model can be used to explain booms and recessions—fluctuations in output. This will allow us to understand the fundamental idea of an influential school of economic thought: real business cycle theory.

Taxes and Potential Output

We use the classical model in Figure 7.6 to study the effects of a tax paid by employers for hiring labor, such as the taxes they pay for workers' Social Security. Economists use similar arguments to study a variety of taxes, including personal and corporate income taxes. A tax on labor will make labor more expensive and raise the marginal cost of hiring workers. For example, let's say that there is no tax on labor, and suddenly a 10% tax is imposed. An employer who had been paying $10 an hour for workers will now find that labor costs $11 an hour. Since the marginal cost of hiring workers has gone up but the marginal benefit has not changed, employers will respond by hiring fewer workers at any given wage. In panel A of Figure 7.6, the labor demand curve shifts to the left, reflecting the tax as the increased cost of labor. As the demand curve shifts to the left, the market equilibrium moves from E to E_1. The result is lower real wages and lower employment.

As we have just seen, higher taxes lead to less employment. With reduced employment, potential output in the economy will be reduced as the economy moves to a lower level of output on the short-run production function. Higher taxes therefore lead to lower output. The size of the reduction in output depends critically on the slope of the labor supply curve. The slope of the labor supply curve indicates how sensitive labor supply is to changes in real wages. Panel B in Figure 7.6 shows the effect of the same tax with a vertical labor supply curve. A vertical labor supply curve means that workers will supply the same amount of labor regardless of the wage. For example, a single parent might work a full 40 hours a week regardless of the wage. His or her supply curve will be vertical. If other workers in the economy put in the same hours regardless of the wage,

Figure 7.6

**Effects of
Employment Taxes**

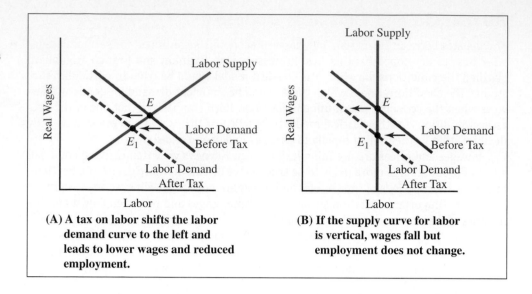

**(A) A tax on labor shifts the labor
demand curve to the left and
leads to lower wages and reduced
employment.**

**(B) If the supply curve for labor
is vertical, wages fall but
employment does not change.**

the supply curve for labor in the economy will be vertical. In panel B, we see that with a vertical supply curve, the tax will reduce wages but have no effect on employment and therefore no effect on output.

This example illustrates that taxes can affect wages and output. In both cases, either output or wages were lowered when the tax was imposed. However, the extent of the decline in output depends on the slope of the labor supply curve. To understand the effects of taxes on output, we need information about the slope of the labor supply curve.

There have been many studies of labor supply. Most show that full-time workers do not change their hours worked very much when wages change. There is some evidence that part-time workers or second earners in a family are more sensitive to changes in wages and do vary their labor supply when wages change. But the bulk of the evidence suggests that the supply curve for the economy as a whole is close to vertical. This implies that it is more likely higher taxes will reduce wages and not have pronounced effects on output.

The entire area of taxation and economics is an active branch of economics research. Economists such as Martin Feldstein of Harvard University have studied how many different types of taxes affect employment, savings, and production. Economists use models to try to measure these effects, just as we did for the employment tax. "A Closer Look: The Laffer Curve and Capital Gains" highlights one controversial policy debate about taxation.

Real Business Cycle Theory

Fluctuations in economic activity can result from a variety of causes. Here are some examples: A developing country that is highly dependent on agriculture can lose its cash crop to a prolonged drought. According to economic historian Stanley Lebergott, the nineteenth century U.S. agricultural-based economy was devastated by grasshopper invasions in North Dakota in 1874 to 1876 and by the boll weevil migration from Mexico to Texas in 1892. Sharp increases in the price of oil can hurt economies that use oil in production, as was the case throughout the world in both 1973 and 1979. Wars can devastate entire regions of the world, and natural disasters, such as earthquakes or floods, can cause sharp reductions in GDP.

Major shifts in technology can also cause economic fluctuations. Consider some economic developments, starting with the early nineteenth century. There were large

THE LAFFER CURVE AND CAPITAL GAINS

Is it possible for a government to cut tax rates yet still raise more revenue? That's a politician's dream People would face lower tax rates yet there would be more money for politicians to spend. Economist Arthur Laffer argued in the late 1970s that there was a strong possibility that we could do this in the U.S. economy, and his views influenced many politicians at that time.

Here is an example of what is called the **Laffer curve**. Suppose a government imposed extremely high tariffs (taxes) on imported goods, tariff rates so high that no one could afford to import any goods whatsoever. If this were the case, the government would not collect any revenue from the tariffs. But, if the government cut the rates and individuals began to buy imported goods, the government would start to collect some tariff revenue. This is the Laffer curve in action: lower taxes (tariffs) leading to higher government revenues.

Virtually all economists today believe this argument does *not* apply to broad-based income taxes or payroll taxes. For these taxes, cutting rates will simply reduce the revenues that the government collects. But there are some taxes for which this claim is plausible.

Let's say that you buy a share of stock which then rises in price. Then you sell it. You will pay a tax known as the *capital gains tax* on the difference between your original purchase price and your selling price. Many economists believe that cutting the tax rate for capital gains will actually lead to more total tax revenue. They argue that the individual does not have to sell a stock that has increased in value. If the capital gains tax burden is too large, the individual could simply hold onto the stock. If the capital gains tax rate is cut, more individuals will be induced to sell their stocks, and total revenues will increase.

Many economists do believe that in the short run, cutting capital gains tax rates will increase revenue as enough individuals will sell their stocks. But there is more dispute about the longer-run consequences. Tax revenues may increase now as individuals sell their stocks but only at the expense of fewer sales of stocks (and revenue) in the future. This remains a very active area of economics research.

---

investments in textile mills and steam power. The birth of the steel industry and railroads dominated the last half of the century. At the end of the nineteenth century, new industries arose that were based on chemical manufacturing, electricity, and the automobile. It is inconceivable that the vast change in technology that led to the creation of these new industries would not have profound effects on the economy, particularly because these changes in technology often came in short bursts.

Economic fluctuations can also occur because a number of small shocks all hit the economy at the same time. For example, a country that primarily produces tea might face a sudden shift of consumer preferences throughout the world to coffee. Or a series of small improvements to technology could cause output to rise among worldwide producers of tea.

One school of economic thought, known as **real business cycle theory**, emphasizes that shocks to technology can have a big part in causing economic fluctuations. Led by Edward Prescott of the University of Minnesota, real business cycle economists have developed new models that integrate shocks to technology into the classical model we have been discussing.

The idea behind real business cycle theory is simple: Changes in technology will usually change the level of full employment or potential output. For example, if there is a significant technological improvement, it will enable the economy to increase the level of both actual and potential output. Similarly, if there are adverse technological developments (such as would occur if the Internet were to crash, for example) or adverse shocks to the economy, output and potential output will fall.

Laffer curve: A relationship between tax rates and tax revenues that illustrates that high tax rates may not always lead to high tax revenues if high tax rates discourage economic activity.

Real business cycle theory: An economic theory that emphasizes how shocks to technology can cause fluctuations in economic activity.

Figure 7.7

Effects of an Adverse Technology Shock
An adverse shock to the economy shifts the labor demand curve to the left and leads to lower wages, reduced employment, and reduced output.

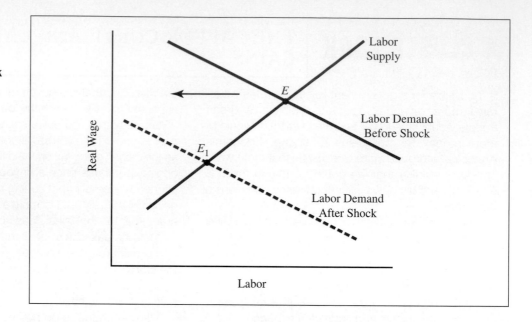

Figure 7.7 gives a simple example of how the real business cycle theory works. Suppose an adverse technological shock occurred, decreasing the demand for labor. The demand curve for labor would shift to the left, and the labor market equilibrium would move from E to E_1. The result would be a lower level of employment and lower real wages. Total GDP would fall both because employment would be low and because the economy would be less productive than before from the adverse technological shock.

The real business cycle school of thought has been influential with some academic economists but is generally viewed as controversial. Critics of the real business cycle theory find it difficult to understand how many of the post-World War II recessions could be explained by adverse changes in technology. In addition, it does not provide an explanation of unemployment. In the real business cycle model, the labor market is in equilibrium and the quantity demanded for labor equals the quantity supplied. At the equilibrium wage, the quantity of labor demanded equals the quantity of labor supplied, and everyone who seeks employment finds employment. Proponents of the real business cycle model counter that other types of economic models can be used to explain unemployment, but the real business cycle can still explain fluctuations in employment. So far, real business cycle theory has not had an impact on current macroeconomic policy. However, real business cycle theory is an active area of research, and its methods and approach, grounded in classical economics, influence professional research today.

The Division of Output Among Competing Demands

Our model of full employment is based entirely on the supply of factors of production. The demand for and supply of labor determine the real wage and total employment in the economy. Together, labor and the supply of capital determine the level of output through the production function. And that means that in a full-employment economy, total GDP is determined by the supply of factors of production.

Full-employment GDP must be divided among competing demands in the economy. From the previous two chapters, you know that economists think of GDP as being composed of consumption, investment, government purchases, and net exports, which we denote as $C + I + G + NX$. In this section, we first discuss how different societies' total GDP is composed. Because governments, for many different reasons, increase their level of spending, we would like to know how increased government spending would affect other types of spending. We will see how increases in government spending must reduce other types of expenditures when the economy is operating at full employment. This phenomenon is called **crowding out**.

Crowding out: Reductions in consumption, investment, or net exports caused by an increase in government purchases.

Some Comparative Data

Countries divide GDP among its competing demands in very different ways. Table 7.2 presents data on the percent of GDP in alternative uses for five countries in 1998. Recall that consumption (C), investment (I), and government purchases (G) refer to total spending by residents of that country. Net exports (NX) is the difference between exports (sales of goods to foreign residents) and imports (purchases of goods abroad). If a country has positive net exports (Japan, France, Singapore, and Germany), it is selling more goods in other countries than it is buying from other countries. If a country has negative net exports (United States), it is buying more goods than it is selling to other countries.

Let's make one more point: These data are from the *World Development Indicators*, which is published by the World Bank. In these statistics, government purchases include only government consumption (such as military spending or wages for government employees). Government investment (such as spending on bridges or roads) is included in the investment category (I).

Table 7.2 reveals considerable diversity among countries. The United States consumes 67% of its GDP, a higher fraction than all the other countries. The United States and France also invest a smaller share of GDP than other countries. Japan and Singapore have the greatest investment rates at 27% and 33%, respectively. Countries also differ greatly in government consumption. Germany and France have the highest rates of government consumption, while Japan and Singapore have the lowest. Finally, the countries differ sharply in the size of net exports relative to GDP.

This wide diversity challenges economists to explain these differences. Some economists have suggested that Japan has a high savings rate, that is, a relatively low percent of GDP devoted to consumption, because it has a relatively fast-growing population, and young adults tend to be a high-saving part of the population. Other economists have suggested that high payroll taxes in Singapore reduce workers' incomes and their ability to consume. But not all economists accept these explanations, and there are no obvious, purely economic reasons why the United States, France, and Germany should exhibit such different behavior.

Table 7.2 Alternative Uses of GDP for 1998 (percent of total GDP)

	C	I	G	NX
Japan	61	27	10	2
United States	67	20	14	−1
France	55	19	23	3
Singapore	37	33	10	20
Germany	58	22	19	1

Source: World Bank, *World Development Indicators*, 2001.

Crowding Out in a Closed Economy

We know that government spending is part of GDP. Let's say that GDP is given and government increases its spending. What happens in a country that increases its government purchases within a fixed GDP? Because the level of full employment output is given by the supply of factors in the economy, an increase in government spending must come at the expense of other uses of GDP. Another way of looking at this: Increased government spending crowds out other demands for GDP. This is an example of the principle of opportunity cost:

PRINCIPLE of Opportunity Cost

The opportunity cost of something is what you sacrifice to get it.

At full employment, the opportunity cost of increased government spending is some other component of GDP.

To understand crowding out, let's first consider what will happen when government spending increases in an economy without international trade. An economy without international trade is called a **closed economy**. In a closed economy, full employment output is divided among just 3 different demands: consumption, investment, and government purchases. We can write this as

$$\text{output} = \text{consumption} + \text{investment} + \text{government purchases}$$
$$Y = C + I + G$$

Closed economy: An economy without international trade.

Because we are considering an economy at full employment, the supply of output (Y) is fixed. Increases in government spending must reduce—that is, crowd out—either consumption or investment; in general, both are affected.

For example, crowding out occurred in the United States during World War II as the share of government spending in GDP rose sharply. Figure 7.8 and Figure 7.9 show that at the same time the share of government spending increased, the shares of consumption and investment spending in GDP decreased.

Crowding Out in an Open Economy

Open economy: An economy with international trade.

In an **open economy**, an economy with international trade, full-employment output is divided among 4 uses: consumption, investment, government purchases, and net exports (exports – imports):

$$Y = C + I + G + NX$$

In an open economy, increases in government spending need not crowd out either consumption or investment. Increased government spending could lead to reduced exports and increased imports. Therefore, what could instead get crowded out is net exports.

Here is how this might happen: Suppose the U.S. government began buying domestic goods to use for some governmental purpose. Let's say these are goods that consumers would have purchased but now cannot. If consumers want to maintain their consumption level despite the goods no longer being available because the government's got them, they could purchase goods previously sold abroad (exports) and purchase goods sold by foreign countries (imports). The result would be a decrease in the amount of goods exported and an increase in imports, that is, a decrease in net exports. In practice, increases in government spending in an open economy would crowd out consumption, investment, and net exports.

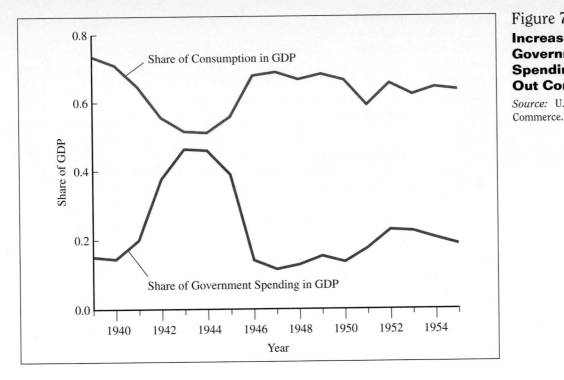

Crowding In

Governments do not always increase spending. Sometimes, they decrease it. When the government cuts spending and the level of output is fixed, some other type of spending will be crowded in, or increase. In a closed economy, consumption or investment or both could increase. In an open economy, net exports could increase as well. As an example,

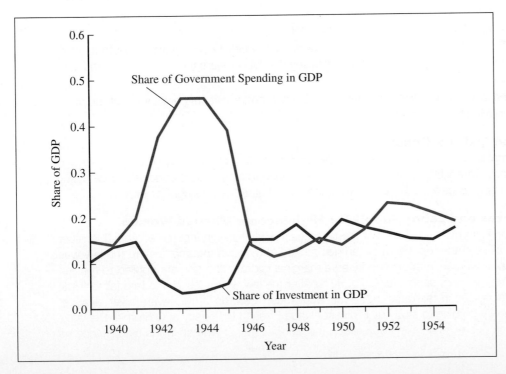

Figure 7.9
Increased Government Spending Also Crowds Out Investment
Source: U.S. Department of Commerce.

after a war, we might see increases in consumption, investment spending, or net exports as they replace military spending.

The nature of changes in government spending will have some effect on the type of spending that is crowded out (or crowded in). If the government built more public swimming pools, households would most likely cut back on their own spending on backyard pools. If the government spent less on mail service, businesses and households would most likely spend more.

TEST Your Understanding

9. When the economy operates at full employment, an increase in government spending must crowd out consumption. True or false? Explain.

10. In an open economy, increases in government spending can crowd out consumption, investment, or _____.

11. Compared to other countries, does the United States have a relatively high or low share of consumption spending in GDP?

Using the TOOLS

In this chapter, we developed several tools, including labor demand, labor supply, and the short-run production function. Using these tools, we developed a model of potential output. Here are four problems that test and extend your understanding of the tools developed in this chapter.

APPLICATIONS

1. Payroll Tax for a Health Program
To finance a health care program, the government places a 10% payroll tax on all labor that is hired.

a. Show how this shifts the demand for labor.

b. If the labor supply function is vertical, what are the effects on real wages, output, and employment? Explain why economists say that labor bears the full burden of the tax in this case.

c. If the labor supply were horizontal, what would be the effects on wages, output, and employment?

2. Too Quick a Conclusion?
A journalist noticed that wages had fallen and wrote that the quantity of labor demanded must have fallen. Do you think he may have jumped to a premature conclusion? What key piece of evidence would help you to determine whether he was right or wrong?

3. Taxes and Labor Supply for High-Income Married Women
The Tax Reform Act of 1986 cut the tax rates sharply for high-income earners. Consider the families in the top 1% of all families ranked in terms of income. Before the law was passed, a woman in this group faced a marginal tax rate (the tax rate applied to the first dollar she earned) of an average of 52%. After the law was passed, the rate fell to 38%. The decreases in tax rates, however, were much less for families with lower levels of income. According to study by Professor Nada Eissa of University of California, Berkeley, after the decrease in taxes took effect, the labor supply of women in the highest income group increased more than for the other income groups.

Use a labor demand and supply model to illustrate the differences between the high-income group and other groups.

4. Would a Subsidy for Wages Necessarily Increase Employment?
Suppose the government paid a subsidy to firms for hiring workers, that is, it paid them an amount for every worker they hired. Using supply and demand diagrams, show how this could possibly lead to higher wages but no increase in employment. Under what circumstances would employment increase the most?

Summary

In this chapter, we analyzed the classical model of full employment. In this model, the level of GDP is determined by the supply of factors of production, labor, and capital. We focused on how the economy operates when it is at full employment; in later chapters, we consider economic fluctuations. Here are the main points from this chapter:

1. Full employment or potential output is the level of GDP produced from a given supply of capital when the labor market is in equilibrium. Potential output is fully determined by the supply of factors of production in the economy.

2. Increases in the stock of capital raise the level of full-employment output and real wages.

3. Increases in the supply of labor will raise the level of full-employment output but lower the level of real wages.

4. The classical model depends on the flexibility of wages and prices.

5. The classical model has many applications. Many economists use it to study the effects of taxes on potential output. Others have found it useful in understanding economic fluctuations.

6. At full employment, increases in government spending must come at the expense of other components of GDP. In a closed economy, either consumption or investment must be crowded out. In an open economy, net exports can be crowded out as well. Decreases in government spending will crowd in other types of spending.

Key Terms

Aggregate production function, 133
classical economics, 132
A closed economy, 146
crowding out, 145
full-employment output, 138
income effect, 136

labor, 133
Laffer curve, 143
open economy, 146
real business cycle theory, 143
real wage, 135

Say's Law, 140
short-run production function, 134
stock of capital, 133
substitution effect, 136
supply-siders, 132

Problems and Discussion Questions

1. Economists who are interested in the damage that taxation can do to the economy often discuss the labor market in Europe, where there are high payroll taxes and employment growth has been low. Why are they interested in this case?

2. Suppose economist A claims that the natural rate of unemployment is 4%, while economist B claims

that it's 5%. Which economist will estimate a higher value for potential output?

3. Explain why labor unions might be interested in limiting the employment of young workers.

4. Some economists have argued that while immigration does not have a major impact on the overall level of wages, it does increase the wage gap

between high school graduates and college graduates. Can you explain the wage gap?

5. Studies have shown that U.S. towns near the border with Mexico have lower wages than towns farther away. Can you explain why?

6. Let's say the labor supply curve is close to vertical. Explain why cutting payroll tax rates will not increase the total revenue the government receives from the payroll tax.

7. Draw a graph to show how a real business cycle economist would explain an economic boom. According to real business cycle theory, how do real wages behave during recessions and booms?

8. Some Japanese economists have argued that we should limit the use of our credit cards in the United States to increase our rate of investment. Explain why they say this.

9. At one time, labor economists found that married women had relatively flat labor supply curves, which are very sensitive to real wages. Do you believe that married women still have relatively flat labor curves today?

10. In some societies, it is a custom for the bride's family to give a gift having very large monetary value to the family of the groom. How might this affect the savings rate in those societies?

11. Suppose that a country has very limited opportunities for successful investment projects but that the population has a high savings rate. Explain why this country is likely to have a large trade surplus.

12. **Web Exercise.** Go to the Web site for the Congressional Budget Office [*http://www.cbo.gov*] and find a study that explores the effects of taxation on economic behavior and on total tax revenue.

13. **Web Exercise.** Edward Prescott is one of the leaders of the real business cycle school. Several of his influential papers are on the Web site of The Federal Reserve Bank of Minneapolis [*http://research.mpls.frb.fed.us/research/economists/ecp.html*]. Read his article "Theory Ahead of Business Cycle Measurement." What is the key message he is trying to convey?

Take It to the Net

We invite you to visit the O'Sullivan/Sheffrin page on the Prentice Hall Web site at: **http://www.prenhall.com/osullivan/** for additional World Wide Web exercises for this chapter.

Model Answers for This Chapter

Chapter-Opening Questions

1. Increased immigration will typically lower real wages while increasing the level of output in the economy.

2. Increased investment will mean a higher capital stock in the future. The higher stock of capital will allow a higher standard of living.

3. If employers are required to pay higher taxes for hiring labor, wages will fall; typically, employment and GDP will fall as well. As the chapter explains, the amount that employment and GDP fall depends on how sensitive labor supply is to real wages.

4. In a closed economy (not open to trade) operating at full employment, increased government spending must lead to reduced spending on either consumption or investment. In an open economy (which allows for trade), higher government spending could lead to a reduction in net exports.

Test Your Understanding

1. An aggregate production function shows the relationships between inputs and outputs in the economy.

2. Decreases.

3. Upward.

4. Supplied.

5. The demand curve slopes downward because when wages are lower, the firm will want to hire more labor. The supply curve slopes upward because at higher wages, more people will seek employment.

6. Right.

7. Right.

8. True. The demand curve shifts to the left, lowering both wages and employment.

9. False. Investment could also be crowded out.

10. Net exports.

11. It is high.

Using the Tools

1. Payroll Tax for a Health Program

   a. The tax will shift the labor demand curve to the left. At any wage, the employer's cost is 10% greater. The employer will hire less labor at any wage, since labor has become more expensive.

   b. The demand for labor shifts to the left, lowering the real wage. Since the labor supply curve is vertical, the amount of labor supplied does not change, nor does total output. Labor bears the full burden of the tax because wages fall by the total amount of the tax.

   c. If the supply of labor were horizontal, the decrease in labor demand would not reduce real wages but would reduce employment. Full-employment output would fall as well.

2. Too Quick a Conclusion? The piece of evidence you would like to have is the change in the quantity of employment. If the quantity of employment fell along with wages, the demand curve shifted to the left and the demand of labor fell. But if the quantity of employment increased along with the fall in wages, this is best explained by an increase in the supply of labor, that is, a rightward shift in the labor supply curve.

3. Taxes and Labor Supply for High-Income Married Women. With the sharp decrease in tax rates, the supply of labor for high-income married women shifted sharply to the right. For other women, who experienced a smaller tax cut, the shift in labor supply was smaller.

4. Would a Subsidy for Wages Necessarily Increase Employment? A subsidy is the reverse of a tax. A subsidy for hiring labor would shift the firm's demand curve to the right. If the supply of labor were vertical (that is, not sensitive to the real wage), the subsidy would raise wages but not employment. The subsidy would be most effective in raising employment if the supply curve for labor were relatively flat.

Why Do Economies Grow?

To understand what economic growth means, consider how the typical American lived in 1783, seven years after the Declaration of Independence was written. According to economic historian Stanley Lebergott, an average U.S. home at that time had no central heat, one fireplace, no plumbing, no hot water, and toilets that were outdoor shacks surrounding a hole in the ground. The lack of plumbing meant that hygiene was not like it is today: Well into the nineteenth century, a typical farmer took a bath once a week. Houses had no electricity or gas; a solitary candle provided light at night. There were no refrigerators, no toasters, or any appliances. Bedrooms contained no furniture other than a bed (with no springs); two people slept in what we now consider a single bed. For women, things were particularly hard. They were expected to bake over half a ton of bread a year, kill chickens, and butcher hogs, as well as prepare all vegetables. Canned foods were not readily available until a century later. And you really don't want to hear about medical "science" in those days.[1]

Our living standards are dramatically different today because there has been a remarkable growth in GDP per person. Growth in GDP is perhaps the most critical aspect of a country's economic performance. Over long periods, there is no other way to raise the standard of living in an economy.

With the tools developed in this chapter, here are some questions we can answer:

1. What countries have the highest living standards today?

2. Do countries with high savings rates have faster rates of GDP growth?

3. Do trade deficits help or hinder economic growth?

4. What factors determine technological progress?

The chapter begins by looking at some data from both rich and poor countries over the last 30 years. We will see how GDP per capita (meaning per person—every man, woman, and child) compare over this period.

Capital deepening: Increase in the stock of capital per worker.

Technological progress: An increase in output without increasing inputs.

We then look at how growth occurs. Economists believe that there are two basic mechanisms that increase GDP per capita over the long term. One is **capital deepening**, increases in an economy's stock of capital—its total stock of plant and equipment—relative to its workforce. **Technological progress** is the other mechanism by which economies can grow. To economists technological progress specifically means that an economy operates more efficiently, producing more output, but without using any more inputs. In other words, the economy gets more output without any more capital or labor. Technological progress does occur and is a key element of economic growth. We examine different theories of the origins of technological progress and discuss how to measure its overall importance for the economy.

Finally, we discuss in detail the role of education and investments in human beings in fostering economic development.

The appendix to this chapter contains a simple model of capital deepening known as the Solow model. It shows how increases in capital per worker lead to economic growth. It will also allow us to better understand the role of technological progress in sustaining economic growth.

The Diversity of Economic Experience

Throughout the world, there are vast differences in standards of living and in rates of economic growth. To understand these differences, we first need to look at the concepts and the tools economists use to study economic growth. With these concepts and tools, we will be equipped to understand the data that measures economic growth.

Measuring Economic Growth

From earlier chapters, we know that real GDP measures in constant prices the total value of final goods and services in a country. Since countries differ in the size of their populations, we want to know what is a country's real GDP per person, or its **real GDP per capita**.

Real GDP per capita: Gross domestic product per person adjusted for changes in prices. It is the usual measure of living standards across time and between countries.

Real GDP per capita typically grows over time. A convenient way to describe the changes in real GDP per capita is growth rates. The **growth rate** of a variable is the percentage change in that variable from one period to another. For example, calculate the growth rate of real GDP from year 1 to year 2. Suppose real GDP was 100 in year 1 and 104 in year 2. The growth rate of real GDP is

Growth rate: The percentage change of a variable.

$$\text{growth rate, in percent} = [(\text{GDP in year 2} - \text{GDP in year 1})/\text{GDP in year 1}] \times 100$$

$$= [(104 - 100)/100] \times 100$$

$$= [4/100] \times 100$$

$$= [0.04] \times 100 = 4\% \text{ per year}$$

Real GDP grew by 4% per year.

Economies can grow at different rates from one year to the next. But it often is useful to consider what happens when an economy grows at a constant rate, say g, for a number of years. Suppose that real GDP for an economy was 100 and that the economy grew at a rate g for n years. How large would the real GDP be after n years? The answer is given by a simple formula:

$$\text{GDP } [n \text{ years later}] = (1 + g)^n (100)$$

Example: The economy starts at 100 and grows at a rate of 4% a year for 10 years. Output after 10 years will be

$$\text{GDP } [10 \text{ years later}] = (1 + 0.04)^{10}(100) = (1.04)^{10}(100) = (1.48)(100)$$

$$= 148$$

which is nearly 50% higher than in the first year.

Here's a rule of thumb to help you understand the power of growth rates. Suppose you know the growth rate of real GDP and it is constant, but you want to know how many years it will take until the level of real GDP doubled. The answer is given by the **rule of 70**:

$$\text{years to double} = 70/(\text{percentage growth rate})$$

Example: For an economy that grew at 5% a year, it would take

$$70/5 = 14 \text{ years}$$

for real GDP to double. (In case you were curious, the rule of 70 is derived by using the mathematics of logarithms.)

Making comparisons of real GDP across countries is difficult. Every country has its own currency and its own price system. In the United States, we quote prices in dollars, the Swiss use francs, the British use pounds, and the Israelis use shekels. The simplest way to compare the GDPs across countries would be to convert the GDP into a common currency, using current **exchange rates**. Recall from Chapter 3 that the exchange rate is the rate at which one currency trades for another. Using current exchange rates, all countries' GDPs could be converted, for example, into U.S. dollars.

However, this simple method fails to take into account one important fact: Relative prices differ sharply across countries. For example, land is scarce in Japan so that the price of housing is higher (relative to other goods) than in the United States. As a rule of thumb, goods that are not traded, such as services or land, are typically relatively cheaper than traded goods in developing countries, as compared to developed countries. In other words, while all residents of the world may pay the same for gold jewelry, hiring a cook or a household helper is considerably less expensive in India than in the United States. Using market exchange rates, without recognizing that nontraded goods are cheaper in developing countries, tends to understate the true standard of living in developing countries.

In making accurate comparisons of GDP across countries, it is important to take differences in relative prices into account. Fortunately, a team of economists led by Robert Summers and Alan Heston of the University of Pennsylvania has devoted decades to developing methods for measuring real GDP across countries. Their procedures are based on gathering extensive data on prices of comparable goods in each country and using this data to make adjustments for differences in relative prices and consumption patterns. These methods are now officially used by the World Bank and the International

Rule of 70: If an economy grows at x percent per year, output will double in 70/x years.

Exchange rate: The rate at which one currency trades for another.

Monetary Fund in making cross-country comparisons of GDP. Most economists view this approach as the best way to make an accurate comparison of living standards across countries.

According to these methods, the country with the highest level of income in 1999 was Luxembourg; its real income per capita was $41,230. The United States was second at $31,910 and Switzerland was third at $28,760. If we simply converted per capita GDP at current exchange rates, Switzerland would have shown a higher level of income than the United States.

Growth Rates and Patterns of Growth

Table 8.1 lists real GNP per capita for 1999 and average annual growth rate of GNP per capita between 1960 and 1999 for 11 countries. Japan, with a GNP per capita of $25,170, follows the United States. Not far behind are France, the United Kingdom, and Italy. More representative of typical countries were Mexico and Costa Rica, with GNPs per capita in 1999 of $8,070 and $7,880, respectively. This is less than 30% of per capita GNP in the United States. The very poor countries have extremely low GNP per capita. Pakistan, for example, had a GNP per capita of $1,860—6% of the GNP per capita of the United States.

In the third column of Table 8.1, notice the differences in growth rates. Consider Japan. In 1960 Japan had a GDP per capita that was one-half France's and one-fourth the United States' GDP per capita. But Japan's GDP per capita grew at 4.43% per year, compared to 2.13% for the United States and 2.76% for France. To place Japan's growth rate for this period into perspective, recall the rule of 70. If an economy grows at an average annual rate of x percent a year, it takes $70/x$ years for output to double. In Japan's case, per capita output was doubling every 70/4.43 years, or approximately every 16 years. At this rate, from the time someone is born to the time that person reaches the age of 32, living standards have increased by a factor of four—an extraordinary rate of growth.

Table 8.1 GNP per Capita and Economic Growth

Country	GNP per Capita in 1999 Dollars	Average per Capita Growth Rate, 1960–1999 (%)
United States	$31,910	2.13
Japan	25,170	4.43
France	23,020	2.76
United Kingdom	22,200	2.07
Italy	22,000	3.00
Mexico	8,070	2.36
Costa Rica	7,880	2.23
Zimbabwe	2,610	1.28
India	2,230	1.98
Pakistan	1,860	1.04
Zambia	720	−1.31

Source: World Bank Development Indicators, 2001 and the Penn World Tables.

One question economists ask is whether poorer countries can close the gap between their level of GDP per capita and the GDP per capita of richer countries. Closing this gap is called **convergence**. To converge, poorer countries have to grow at more rapid rates than richer countries are growing. Since 1960 Japan, Italy, and France all have grown more rapidly than the United States and have narrowed the gap in per capita incomes.

Convergence: The process by which poorer countries catch up with richer countries in terms of real GDP per capita.

For a more extensive look at the evidence, Figure 8.1 plots for 16 currently developed countries the average growth rate from 1870 to 1979 versus the level of GDP in 1870. The line through the points slopes downward, which means that countries with higher levels of GDP in 1870 grew more slowly than countries with lower levels of GDP; in other words, there was a tendency for countries with lower levels of initial income to grow faster and thus catch up. Depending on which countries we look at, there seems to have been convergence among the currently developed countries.

If we compare the less developed countries to the advanced industrial countries, the picture is not so clear. While Mexico grew at a faster rate than the United States, Pakistan grew only 1.04% per year and fell farther behind advanced economies. In Africa GDP per capita fell substantially in Zambia, while in Zimbabwe GDP per capita grew at a slower rate than the U.S. rate.

Economists who have studied the process of economic growth in detail find weak evidence that poorer countries are closing the gap in per capita income with richer countries. On average, it does not appear that poorer countries grow at substantially higher rates than richer countries are growing. Although there are some success stories, such as Japan and other Asian economies, including Hong Kong and Singapore, there are also economies such as Zambia's that have regressed.

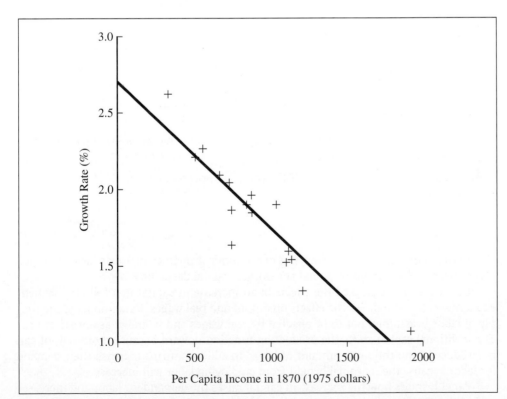

Figure 8.1
Countries with Lower Income in 1870 Grew Faster

Source: M. Obstfeld and K. Rogoff, *Foundation of International Macroeconomics* (Cambridge, MA: MIT Press, 1996), Table 7.1.

Cell phones are a sign of economic growth throughout the entire world.

The rule of 70 reinforces how important are small differences in economic growth rates. A per capita GDP growth rate of 5% a year means that the living standard doubles in 14 years. With only 1% growth, doubling would take 70 years.

TEST Your Understanding

1. What measure of output do we use to measure living standards across countries with populations of different sizes?

2. How do relative prices for nontraded goods compare between poor countries and rich countries?

3. Economists who have studied economic growth find only weak evidence for convergence. True or false? Explain.

4. At a 2% annual growth rate in GDP per capita, how many years would it take for GDP per capita to double?

Capital Deepening

One of the most important mechanisms of economic growth economists have identified is increases in the amount of capital per worker: capital deepening.

In Chapter 7, we studied the effects of an increase in capital in a full-employment economy. Figure 8.2 shows the effects on output and real wages. For simplicity, the supply of labor is assumed not to be affected by real wages and is drawn as a vertical line. The additional capital shifts the production function upward because more output can be produced from the same amount of labor. In addition, firms increase their demand for labor because the marginal benefit from employing labor will increase.

Panel B shows how the increase in capital raises the demand for labor and increases real wages. As firms increase their demand and compete for the fixed supply of labor, they will bid up real wages in the economy. In panel A, we show how the increase in the

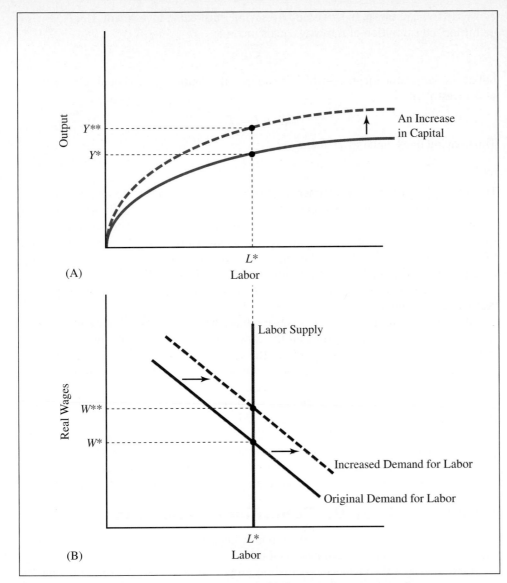

Figure 8.2
Increase in the Supply of Capital
An increase in the supply of capital will shift the production function upward and increase the demand for labor. Real wages will increase from W^* to W^{**}, and potential output will increase from Y^* to Y^{**}.

amount of capital in the economy shifts the production function upward and allows more output to be produced for any level of labor input. With a given supply of labor, increases in the stock of capital both raise real wages and lead to increases in output.

An economy is better off with an increase in the stock of capital. With additions to the stock of capital, workers will enjoy higher wages, and total GDP in the economy will increase. Workers are more productive because each worker has more capital at his or her disposal.

But how does an economy increase its stock of capital per worker?

Saving and Investment

Let's begin with the simplest case: an economy with a constant population, producing at full employment, that has no government or foreign sector. In this simple economy, output can be purchased only by consumers or by firms. In other words, output consists solely of consumption and investment. At the same time, this output generates an amount of income that is equivalent to the amount of output. Any income that is not

Saving: Total income minus consumption.

consumed we call **saving**. In this economy, saving must equal investment. Here's why: By definition, consumption plus saving equals income:

$$C + S = Y$$

but at the same time income—which is equivalent to output—also equals consumption plus investment:

$$C + I = Y$$

Thus, saving must equal investment:

$$S = I$$

This means that whatever consumers decide to save goes directly into investment.

Next, we need to link the level of investment in the economy to the stock of capital in the economy. The stock of capital depends on two factors. The stock of capital increases with any gross investment spending but decreases with any depreciation. (Recall that *gross* means "before taking depreciation into account.") For example, suppose the stock of capital at the beginning of the year is $100. During the year, if there were $10 in gross investment and $4 in depreciation, the capital stock at the end of the year would be $106 (= $100 + $10 − $4).

It may be helpful to picture this as being like a bathtub. The level of water in a bathtub (the stock of capital) depends on the flow of water into the bathtub through the input faucet (gross investment) minus the flow of water out of the bathtub down the drain (depreciation). As long as the flow in exceeds the flow out, the water level in the bathtub (the stock of capital) will increase.

Higher saving, which leads to higher gross investment, will therefore tend to increase the stock of capital available for production. As the stock of capital grows, however, there typically will be more depreciation, because there is more capital to depreciate. It is the difference between gross investment and depreciation, which is net investment, that ultimately determines the change in the stock of capital for the economy and therefore the level of real wages and real output. In our example net investment is $10 − $4 = $6.

Population Growth, Government, and Trade

So far we've considered the simplest economy. Let's consider a more realistic economy with population growth, government, and trade.

First, consider the effects of population growth. A larger labor force will allow the economy to produce more total output. However, with a fixed amount of capital and an increasing labor force, the amount of capital per worker will be less. With less capital per worker, output per worker will also tend to be less because each worker has fewer machines to use. This is an illustration of the principle of diminishing returns.

PRINCIPLE of Diminishing Returns

> **Suppose that output is produced with two or more inputs and that we increase one input while holding the other inputs fixed. Beyond some point—called the point of diminishing returns—output will increase at a decreasing rate.**

Consider India, which has the world's second largest population, with over one billion people. Although India has a large labor force, the amount of capital per worker is low. With sharp diminishing returns to labor, per capita output in India will tend to be low.

The government can affect the process of capital deepening in several ways through its policies of spending and taxation. Suppose the government taxed its citizens so that it could fight a war, pay its legislators higher salaries, or give foreign aid to needy countries. The higher taxes will reduce total income. If consumers save a fixed fraction of their income, total private saving (savings from the nongovernmental sector) will fall. In these cases the government is not investing the funds it collects, putting those funds into capital formation. Instead, it is draining from the private sector saving that would have been used for capital deepening. The overall result is a reduction of total investment in the economy and less capital deepening. In these examples the government is taxing the private sector to engage in consumption spending, not investment.

Now suppose the government took all the tax revenues and invested them in valuable infrastructure such as roads, buildings, and airports. Suppose consumers were saving 20% of their incomes. If the government took a dollar in taxes, private saving would fall by 20 cents, but government investment would increase by $1. The net result is an increase in total social saving (private plus government) of 80 cents. This would promote capital deepening: In this case the government is taxing its citizens to provide investment.

Finally, the foreign sector can affect capital deepening. An economy can run a trade deficit and import investment goods to aid capital deepening. The United States, Canada, and Australia built their vast railroad systems in the nineteenth century by running trade deficits (selling less goods and services to the rest of the world than they were buying, financing this gap by borrowing) to enable them to purchase the large amount of capital needed to build their rail networks. In these cases, the large trade deficits were valuable for the economy. They enabled growth to occur at more rapid rates through the process of capital deepening. Eventually, these economies had to pay back the funds that were borrowed from abroad by running trade surpluses, selling more goods and services to the rest of the world than they would buy. But since economic growth raised GDP and the wealth of the economy, they could afford to pay back the borrowed funds. Therefore, this was a reasonable strategy for these countries to follow.

Not all trade deficits promote capital deepening, however. Suppose a country ran a trade deficit because it wanted to buy more consumer goods. The country would be borrowing from abroad, but there would be no additional capital deepening, just additional consumption spending. When the country was forced to pay back the funds, there would be no additional GDP to help foot the bill. Society will be poorer in the future when it must pay the bill for what it consumes now—its current consumption.

Limits to Capital Deepening

There are inherent limits to growth through capital deepening. To understand these limits, let's recall that the stock of capital increases only when there is positive net investment. Remember that net investment equals gross investment minus depreciation. Gross investment depends on the rate of saving in the economy. Depreciation depends on the total stock of capital that the economy has in place.

As the economy accumulates capital and the stock of capital increases, there will be an increase in the total amount of depreciation of capital in the economy. We show, in the appendix to this chapter, that as the stock of capital increases, the economy eventually reaches a point where gross investment equals depreciation. At this point, net investment becomes zero and the stock of capital will no longer increase.

Therefore, there is a limit to growth through capital deepening as depreciation eventually catches up to the level of gross investment. While a higher rate of saving can increase the level of real GDP, eventually the process of growth through capital deepening comes to a halt. However, it takes time—decades—for this point to be reached. Capital deepening can be an important source of economic growth for a long time.

5. Explain why saving must equal investment if we are not taking into account the government sector or the foreign sector.

6. If everything else is held equal, how does an increase in the size of the population affect total and per capita output?

7. If the private sector saves 10% of its income and the government raises taxes by $200 to finance public investments, by how much will total investment—private and public—increase?

8. If a country runs a trade deficit to finance increased current consumption, it will have to reduce consumption in the future to pay back its borrowings. True or false? Explain.

The Key Role of Technological Progress

The other mechanism affecting economic growth is technological progress. Economists use the term technological progress in a very specific way: It means that an economy operates more efficiently by producing more output without using any more inputs.

In practice, technological progress can take many forms. The invention of the light bulb made it possible to read and work indoors at night; the invention of the thermometer assisted doctors and nurses in their diagnoses; and the invention of disposable diapers made life easier at home. All these examples—and you could provide many more—enable society to produce more output without more labor or more capital. With higher output per person, we enjoy a higher standard of living.

Technological progress can be thought of as the birth of new ideas. These new ideas enable us to rearrange our economic affairs and make us more productive. Not all technological innovations are necessarily major scientific breakthroughs; some are much more mundane. Good commonsense ideas from the workers or managers of a business allow it to make more effective use of its capital and labor and to deliver a better product to its consumers at the current price—this is also technological progress. As long as there are new ideas, inventions, and new ways of doing things, the economy can become more productive and per capita output can increase.

How Do We Measure Technological Progress?

If someone asked you how much of the increase in your standard of living were due to technological progress, how would you answer?

Robert Solow, a Nobel laureate in economics from the Massachusetts Institute of Technology, developed a method for measuring technological progress in an economy. As is usual with good ideas, his theory was simple. It was based on the idea of a production function.

You know from Chapter 7 that the production function links inputs to outputs:

$$Y = F(K, L)$$

where output (Y) is produced from capital (K) and labor (L), which are linked through the production function F. What Solow did was include in the production function some measure of technological progress, A:

$$Y = F(K, L, A)$$

Table 8.2 Sources of Real GDP Growth, 1929–1982 (average annual percentage rates)

Due to capital growth	0.56
Due to labor growth	1.34
+ technological progress	1.02
Output growth	2.92

Source: Edward F. Denison, *Trends in Economic Growth 1929–82* (Washington, DC: The Brookings Institution, 1985).

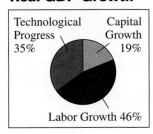

Figure 8.3
Percentage Contributions to Real GDP Growth

Source: Data from Edward F. Denison, *Trends in Economic Growth 1929–82* (Washington, DC: The Brookings Institution, 1985).

Increases in *A* represent technological progress. Higher values of *A* mean that more output is produced from the same level of inputs *K* and *L*. If we could find some way to measure *A*, we could estimate how much technological progress affected output.

Solow noted that over any period, we can observe increases in capital, labor, and output. Using these, we can measure technological progress indirectly. We first ask how much of the change in output can be explained by contributions from the changes in the amount of inputs—capital and labor—that are used. Whatever growth we cannot explain must have been caused by increases in technological progress. The method that Solow developed for determining the contributions to economic growth from increased capital, labor, and technological progress is called **growth accounting**.

Following this basic approach, Table 8.2 contains a breakdown of the sources of growth for the U.S. economy for 1929 to 1982. Figure 8.3 shows the relative contributions of the sources of growth based on these data. Over 1929 to 1982 total output grew at a rate of nearly 3%. Because capital and labor growth are measured at 0.56% and 1.34%, respectively, the remaining portion of output growth, 1.02%, must be due to technological progress. That means that approximately 35% of output growth comes directly from technological progress.

Growth accounting: A method to determine the contribution to economic growth from increased capital, labor, and technological progress.

Growth Accounting: Three Examples

Growth accounting is a useful tool for understanding different aspects of economic growth. Here are three examples of how economists use growth accounting.

Singapore and Hong Kong

Singapore and Hong Kong have both had phenomenal post-World War II economic growth. From 1980 to 1985 each grew at a rate of approximately 6% a year. But a closer examination, by Alwyn Young of the University of Chicago, revealed that the sources of growth in each were very different.[2] In Singapore nearly all the growth was accounted for by increases in labor and capital. In particular, the ratio of investment to GDP reached as high as 43% in 1983.

Hong Kong had a much lower investment rate—approximately 20% of GDP—and technological progress made an important contribution. This meant that the residents of Hong Kong could enjoy the same level of GDP but consume, not save, a higher fraction of GDP. Residents of Hong Kong were enjoying higher consumption than residents of Singapore were, despite the similarity in growth rates.

The difference in the sources of economic growth between Singapore and Hong Kong may also have important implications for future growth. As we explained a moment ago, there are natural limits to growth through capital deepening. Singapore increased its GDP by increasing its labor inputs and increasing its stock of capital. Eventually, Singapore will find it difficult to keep increasing inputs to production.

Economic leaders became concerned that unless they managed to increase their rate of technological progress, their long-term growth prospects would not be strong.

In Hong Kong, there is a different concern. Now that Hong Kong is part of China, residents hope the Chinese will allow them to continue to maintain their free and open economy in which technological progress has flourished. Technological progress has been the driving force for growth in Hong Kong, where there is a strong desire to maintain the system that produced technological innovation.

Understanding Labor Productivity

Labor productivity: Output per hour of work.

One of the common statistics reported about the U.S. economy is **labor productivity**. Defined as output per hour of work, labor productivity is a simple measure of how much a typical worker can produce given the amount of capital in the economy and the state of technological progress. Since 1973, there has been a slowdown in the growth of labor productivity in the United States and other countries in the world. Table 8.3 shows U.S. productivity growth for different periods since 1959.

The table shows that productivity growth was extremely high during the 1960s. It slowed a bit in the late 1960s and then slowed dramatically after the oil shocks in the 1970s. In recent years there has been a resurgence in productivity growth, which reached 2.5% from 1994–2000. Nonetheless, the rate of productivity growth was very low from the late 1960s to the mid-1990s.

Similar patterns have been observed in other countries. Zvi Grilliches, a Harvard economist and expert on productivity, compared the growth of output per hour in the manufacturing for 12 countries over different periods.[3] If we use his data and compare the periods 1960 to 1973 and 1979 to 1986, we find that productivity growth slowed in 11 of 12 countries. In Japan, it fell from 10.3% to 5.6%; in Canada, it fell from 4.5% to 1.4%. Only the United Kingdom exhibited any increase in productivity growth over those periods, and that increase was only from 4.3% to 4.4%.

The slowdown in productivity growth has also meant slower growth in real wages and in GDP in the United States since 1973. Figure 8.4 plots real hourly earnings for U.S. workers; it shows that real hourly earnings have fallen since 1973. Total compensation, which includes employee benefits such as health insurance, did continue to rise through the 1980s and 1990s as employees received lower wages but higher benefits. But the rate of growth of total compensation was less than the growth of real hourly earnings in the pre-1973 period.

The decrease in the growth of labor productivity was the primary factor behind this pattern of real wages, because wages can rise with a growing labor force only if output per worker continues to increase. What can explain this decrease in the growth rate?

Table 8.3   U.S. Annual Productivity Growth, 1959–2000

Years	Annual Growth Rate (%)
1959–1968	3.5
1968–1973	2.5
1973–1980	1.2
1980–1986	2.1
1986–1994	1.4
1994–2000	2.5

Source: Economic Report of the President (Washington, DC: U.S. Government Printing Office, 2000) and Bureau of Labor Statistics.

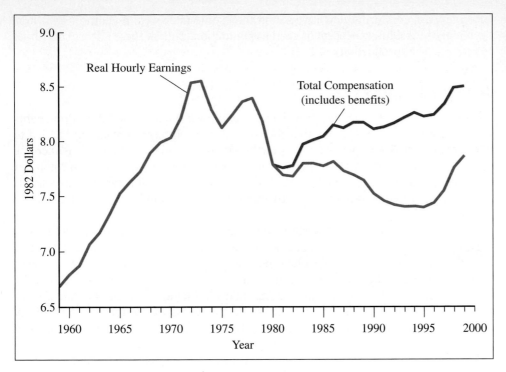

Figure 8.4
Real Hourly Earnings and Total Compensation in the United States

Source: Economic Report of the President (Washington, DC: U.S. Government Printing Office, 2000).

Economists are not short of possible answers. The factors, they say, are declines in the education and skills of the workforce, lower levels of investment and thus a lower level of capital, less spending on infrastructure (such as highways and bridges), and the belief that managers of companies are more concerned with producing short-term profits than long-term profits, among lots of other economic and sociological factors as well.

Growth accounting has been used to narrow the range of plausible explanations. Using growth accounting methods, economists typically find that the slowdown in labor productivity, in the United States and abroad, cannot be explained by reduced rates of capital deepening. Nor can they be explained by changes in the quality or experience of the labor force. Either a slowdown in technological progress or other factors that are not directly included in the analysis, such as higher worldwide energy prices, must be responsible for the slowdown. Moreover, since the slowdown has been worldwide, it's possible that factors that affect all countries (such as higher energy prices) are responsible rather than factors specific to a single country. Dale Jorgenson, a Harvard economist, has conducted extensive research attempting to link higher energy prices to the slowdown in productivity growth. Not all economists accept this view, however, and the productivity slowdown remains a bit of a mystery.

Recessions and Labor Productivity

Economic Detective

Economists have long observed that labor productivity falls sharply during recessions. Suppose that a recession is caused by factors unrelated to changes in technical progress. As an economic detective can you uncover a reason why labor productivity might fall during a recession? [*Hint*: Think of how capital is utilized during a recession.]

During a recession, firms cut back on production. Typically, this means that the existing capital stock, which was built for a robust economy, is not fully utilized. Some equipment and parts of plants may be idle. In addition, in many industries it is difficult to lay off workers during downturns, and thus some firms retain additional workers beyond those absolutely needed for current production. Both of these factors contribute to reduced labor productivity.

A New Economy?

As Table 8.3 shows, productivity growth climbed in the last half of the 1990s. Proponents of a "new economy" proclaimed that the computer and Internet revolution had led to permanent increases in productivity growth. Skeptics wondered whether this increase in productivity growth was truly permanent or just temporary. Investment in computer technology had proceeded rapidly since the mid-1980s, but until recently there was little sign of increased productivity growth. Had the investment in information technology finally paid off?

Robert J. Gordon of Northwestern University used growth accounting methods to shed light on this issue. After making adjustments for the low unemployment rate and high GDP growth rate in the late 1990s, he found that there had been increases in technological progress. But he found that these increases were confined to just 12% of the economy, the durable goods manufacturing industry, including the production of computers itself. Since the increase in technological progress was confined to a relatively small portion of the economy, Gordon was skeptical that we were now operating in a "new economy" with permanently higher productivity growth.

Other economists, also using growth accounting methods, came to different conclusions as they analyzed the data. A study by the President's Council of Economic Advisors found that the increase in technological progress was more widespread throughout the economy, suggesting that more of the increase was likely to be permanent. Unfortunately, economic growth slowed sharply in the United States in 2000 and 2001. Productivity growth also fell during this slowdown, as customary during slowdowns. With this temporary decline in growth, economists will have to wait several years to determine if the long run rate of productivity growth has permanently increased.

While capital deepening and technological progress are key to growth, other factors are important as well. As "A Closer Look: Tropics and Democracy" illustrates, noneconomic factors can be important determinants of growth.

A CLOSER LOOK   TROPICS AND DEMOCRACY

As economists intensively studied economic growth, they have uncovered a number of interesting noneconomic factors that influence growth. Jeffrey Sachs of Harvard University has emphasized the role of geography. Virtually all the tropical countries remain undeveloped. There are two prominent exceptions, Hong Kong and Singapore. All the other developed countries lie in more temperate zones. Sachs also found that access to oceans or navigable rivers is important. Land-locked countries have some of the lowest levels of economic growth.

Dani Rodrick, also of Harvard University, has explored the role of democratic versus authoritarian governments. He argued that authoritarian countries typically have more extreme outcomes—either very high growth rates or very low growth rates. Democracy, in this sense, is "safer" in terms of economic performance. Other economists have noted that authoritarian governments tend to invest more in physical equipment than democracies. On the other hand, democracies tend to invest more in education.[4] Which strategy will work best in the long run?

What Causes Technological Progress?

Because technological progress is an important source of growth, we want to know how it occurs and what government policies can do to promote it. Economists have identified a variety of factors that may influence the pace of technological progress in an economy.

Research and Development in Fundamental Science

One way to induce more technological progress in an economy is to pay for it. If the government or large firms employ workers and scientists to advance the frontiers in physics, chemistry, and biology, their work can lead to technological progress in the long run. Figure 8.5 presents data on the spending on research and development as a percent of GDP for each of seven major countries for 1998. Although the United States spends the most in total on research and development, as a percent of GDP it spends less than Japan. Moreover, a big part of U.S. spending on research and development is in defense-related areas, unlike in Japan. The United States has the highest percentage of scientists and engineers in the labor force in the world.

But not all technological progress is "high tech." An employee of a soft-drink company who discovers a new and popular flavor for a soft drink is engaged in technological progress, just as scientists and engineers are.

Monopolies That Spur Innovation

The radical notion that monopolies spur innovation was put forth by economist Joseph Schumpeter. In his view a firm will try to come up with new products and more efficient ways to produce products only if it reaps a reward. The reward a firm seeks is high profit from its innovations. And high profit can be obtained only if the firm is the sole seller or monopolist for the product. Other firms will try to break its

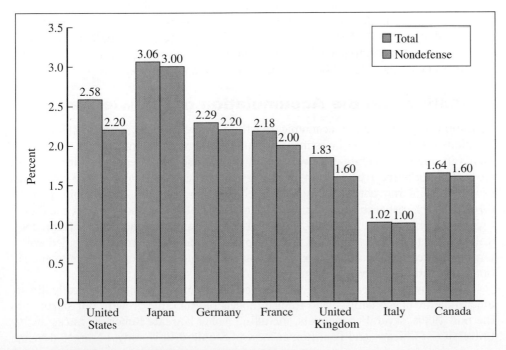

Figure 8.5

Research and Development as a Percent of GDP, 1998

Source: National Patterns of R&D Resources, 2001, Washington, D.C.

monopoly through more innovation, a process Schumpeter called **creative destruction**. By allowing firms to compete to be monopolies, society benefits from increased innovation.

Governments do allow temporary monopolies for new ideas by issuing patents. A patent allows the inventor of a product to have a monopoly until the term of the patent expires, which in the United States is now 20 years. With a patent, we tolerate some monopoly power (the power to raise prices that comes with limited competition) in the hope of spurring innovation.

A related idea, which is becoming increasingly important in modern society, is the need to protect intellectual property rights. Publishers of both books and computer software face problems of unauthorized copying, particularly in some developing countries. While the residents of those countries clearly benefit from inexpensive copied software or books, the producers of the software and books in the developed countries will face reduced incentives to enter the market. Large and profitable firms with secure domestic markets may continue to produce despite unauthorized copying, but other firms may be discouraged. The United States has put piracy and unauthorized reproduction among its top agenda items in recent trade talks with several countries.

The Scale of the Market

Adam Smith stressed that the size of a market was important for economic development. In larger markets there are more incentives for firms to come up with new products and new methods of production. Just as Schumpeter suggested, the lure of profits guides the activities of firms, and larger markets enable firms the opportunity to make larger profits. This provides another rationale for free trade. With free trade, markets are larger, and there is more incentive to engage in technological progress.

Induced Innovations

Some economists have emphasized that innovations come about through inventive activity designed specifically to reduce costs. This is known as induced innovation. For example, during the nineteenth century in the United States, the largest single cost in agriculture was wages. Ingenious farmers and inventors came up with many different machines and methods to cut back on the amount of labor required.

Education and the Accumulation of Knowledge

Education can contribute to economic growth in two ways. First, increased knowledge and skills can be a form of investment in human beings that complements our investments in physical capital, as we will see in the next section. Second, education can enable the workforce in an economy to use its skills to develop new ideas or to copy ideas or import them from abroad. Consider a developing country today. In principle, it has at its disposal the vast accumulated knowledge of the developed economies. If it could find a way to tap into this knowledge, it could more quickly and easily adapt their technological progress to its own economies. But this probably requires a broad and skilled workforce—one reason why many developing countries send their best students to educational institutions in developed countries.

For many years, economists who studied technological progress typically did so independently of economists who studied models of economic growth. But starting in the mid 1980s, several economists, including Nobel laureate Robert E. Lucas of the University of Chicago and Paul Romer, now of Stanford University, began to develop

The rate of return to elementary school education in Africa probably exceeds the rate of return to investment in machines and buildings.

models of growth that contained technological progress as essential features. Their work helped to initiate what is known as **new growth theory**, which accounts for technological progress within a model of economic growth. In this field, economists study, for example, how incentives for research and development, new product development, or international trade interact with the accumulation of physical capital. It enables economists to address policy issues, such as whether subsidies for research and development are socially justified and whether policies that place fewer taxes on income earned from investment will spur economic growth or increase economic welfare. Current research in economic growth now takes place within a broad framework that includes explanation of technological progress.

All growth theory today is "new growth theory."

New growth theory: Modern theories of growth that try to explain the origins of technological progress.

Human Capital

Increasing knowledge and skills can be considered a form of **human capital**—an investment in human beings. Many economists, including Nobel laureate Gary Becker of the University of Chicago have studied this in detail.

Human capital: Investment in education and skills.

A classic example of human capital is the investment a student makes to attend college. The costs of attending college consist of the direct out-of-pocket costs (tuition and fees) plus the opportunity costs of forgone earnings. The benefits of attending college are the higher wages and more interesting jobs offered to college graduates as compared to high school graduates. Individuals decide to attend college because these benefits exceed the costs, and it is a rational economic decision. A similar calculation faces a newly graduated doctor who must decide whether to pursue a specialty. Will the forgone earnings of a general physician (which are quite substantial) be worth the time spent learning a specialty that will eventually result in extra income? Investments in health and nutrition can be analyzed within the same framework.

Human capital theory has two implications for understanding economic growth.

First, not all labor is equal. When economists measure the labor input in a country, they must adjust for differing levels of education. These levels of education reflect past investments in education and skills; individuals with higher educational levels will, on average, be more productive.

Second, health and fitness also affect productivity. In developing countries, economists have found that there is a strong correlation between the height of individuals and the wages that they can earn in the farming sector. At the same time, increases in income through economic growth have led to sharp increases in height and weight as "A Closer Look: Our Tiny Ancestors," explains.

As you may have seen in a museum, men and women have grown taller and heavier in the last 300 years. As an example, an average American male adult today stands at approximately 5′10″, nearly 4.5 inches taller than the typical Englishman in the late eighteenth century. Body weights are also substantially higher today. According to Nobel laureate Robert Fogel of the University of Chicago, the average weight of English males in their thirties was about 134 pounds in 1790—20% below today's average. A typical Frenchman in his thirties at that time weighed only 110 pounds!

Fogel has argued that these lower weights and heights reflected inadequate food supplies and chronic malnutrition. Not only did lower food supplies lead to smaller physical stature, they also led to a higher incidence of chronic disease. Fogel estimated that the chronic malnutrition caused by limited food supplies at those times limited labor productivity. In France, 20% of the labor force lacked enough physical energy to put in more than 3 hours of light work a day. A high percentage of workers in the society were too frail and ill to contribute much to national output.

Economic growth produced a "virtuous" circle. It increased food supplies, enabling workers to become more productive and increase GDP even more.

Human capital theory can also serve as a basis for important public policy decisions. Should a developing country invest in capital (either public or private) or in education? The poorest developing countries lack many things: good sanitation systems, effective transportation systems, and capital investment for agriculture and industry. However, the best use of investment funds may not be for bridges, sewer systems, and roads but for human capital and education. Studies demonstrate that the returns from investing in education are extremely high in developing countries. The gains from elementary and secondary education, in particular, often exceed the gains from more conventional investments. In developing countries, a person having an extra year in school can often raise his or her wages by 15% to 20% a year.

The returns to investing in the education of females in developing countries are often higher than those for men. This is particularly true in the poorest countries, where female literacy rates are often less than 10%. Women's health in developing countries is closely tied to their education. Education promotes not only productivity but basic social development as well. For these reasons, the World Bank has focused attention on the crucial role that increased female education can play in promoting economic development.

As you see, human capital analysis is a valuable tool for understanding economic growth.

TEST Your Understanding

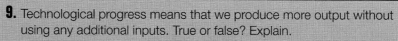

9. Technological progress means that we produce more output without using any additional inputs. True or false? Explain.

10. Explain how economists estimate the contribution of technological change to the growth of output.

11. Who invented the theory of creative destruction?

12. Define *human capital*.

Using the TOOLS

In this chapter, we studied what affects economic growth. Here are some opportunities to do your own economic analysis.

APPLICATIONS

1. Shorten the Length of Patents?

A group of consumer activists claim that drug companies earn excessive profits because of the patents they have on drugs. The activists advocate cutting to five years the length of time that a drug company can hold a patent. They argue this will lead to lower prices for drugs because competitors will enter the market after the five-year period. Do you see any drawbacks to this proposal?

2. Capital Deepening

Which of the following will promote economic growth through capital deepening?

a. Higher taxes used to finance universal health care

b. Increased imports to purchase new VCRs for consumers

c. Increased imports to purchase supercomputers for industry

3. Future Generations

Some economists say that economic growth involves a trade-off between current generations and future generations. If a current generation raises its saving rate, what does it sacrifice? What will be gained for future generations?

4. Will the Poorer Country Catch Up?

Suppose one country has a GDP that is one-eighth the GDP of its richer neighbor. But the poorer country grows at 10% a year, while the richer country grows at 2% a year. In 35 years, which country will have a higher GDP? (*Hint*: Use the rule of 70.)

Summary

In this chapter, we explored the mechanisms of economic growth. Although economists do not have a complete understanding of what leads to growth, they regard increases in capital per worker, technological progress, and human capital as key factors. In this chapter we discussed these factors in detail. Here are the main points to remember:

1. There are vast differences in per capita GDP throughout the world. There is debate about whether poorer countries in the world are converging in per capita incomes to richer countries.

2. Economies grow through two basic mechanisms: capital deepening and technological progress. Capital deepening is an increase in capital per worker. Technological progress is an increase in output with no additional increases in inputs.

3. Ongoing technological progress will lead to sustained economic growth.

4. A variety of theories try to explain the origins of technological progress and determine how we can promote it. They include spending on research and development, creative destruction, the scale of the market, induced inventions, and education and the accumulation of knowledge.

5. Investments in human capital are an important component of economic growth.

Key Terms

capital deepening, 154
convergence, 157
creative destruction, 168
exchange rate, 155
growth accounting, 163

growth rate, 154
human capital, 169
labor productivity, 164
new growth theory, 169
real GDP per capita, 154

rule of 70, 155
saving, 160
technological progress, 154

Problems and Discussion Questions

1. If a country's GDP grows at 3% per year, how many years will it take for GDP to increase by a factor of four?

2. The growth rate of real GDP per capita equals the growth rate of real GDP minus the growth rate of the population. If the growth rate of population is 1% per year, how fast must real GDP grow for real GDP per capita to double in 14 years?

3. Describe briefly how we can compare GDP per capita in the United Kingdom with GDP per capita in the United States even though the British measure GDP using their own currency, pounds.

4. Explain why the expansion of markets from free trade can lead to increased technological innovation.

5. If we cannot measure every invention or new idea, how can we possibly measure the contribution to growth of technological progress?

6. Even with a high savings rate, there is a natural limit to capital deepening. Why is there a limit?

7. Suppose a government places a 10% tax on incomes and spends half of the money from taxes on investment and half on a public consumption good such as military parades. Individuals save 20% of their income and consume the rest. Does total investment (public and private) increase or decrease in this case?

8. The United States ran large trade deficits during the 1980s and 1990s. How would you determine whether these trade deficits led to increased or decreased capital deepening?

9. Economic historians have found that the average height of individuals in both the United States and the United Kingdom fell during the mid-nineteenth century before rising again. This was a period of rapid industrialization as well as migration into urban areas and foreign immigration. Incomes appeared to continue to rise. What factors do you think might account for this fall in height and how would it affect your evaluation of economic welfare during the period?

10. Most law students tend to be in their twenties and thirties, rather than in their forties. Explain this phenomenon, using the idea of investment in human capital.

11. Web Exercise. The Web site for the National Bureau of Economic Research [*http://www.nber.org*] contains links to online data, including the Penn World Tables. Using these links, compare the relative growth performance for real GDP of Italy, Great Britain, and France (or other countries) over a period of your choice.

12. Web Exercise. Using the Web site for the World Bank (*http://www.worldbank.org*), prepare a short paper on prospects and barriers for economic growth in Africa.

Take It to the Net

We invite you to visit the O'Sullivan/Sheffrin page on the Prentice Hall Web site at: **http://www.prenhall.com/osullivan/** for additional World Wide Web exercises for this chapter.

Model Answers for This Chapter

Chapter-Opening Questions

1. Countries with the highest standard of living today include the United States, Luxembourg, Japan, and Germany.

2. Countries with higher savings rates can grow faster for some period of time, although the growth of per capita income in the long run is determined by the rate of technical progress.

3. A trade deficit that is used to finance investment can lead to higher growth; however, a trade deficit that is used to finance consumption will allow higher consumption now but will reduce consumption in the future.

4. Technological progress depends on a number of factors, including research and development, the process of creative destruction, the scale of the market, induced innovations, and education and the accumulation of knowledge.

Test Your Understanding

1. We use per capita real GDP.

2. Nontraded goods are relatively cheaper in poor countries.

3. True. Developing countries have not caught up to developed countries.

4. It would take 35 years (70/2).

5. Output is divided into consumption and investment. Output also equals income. Income is either consumed or saved. Therefore, saving must equal investment.

6. Total output increases, while per capita output falls.

7. $180. Government investment is $200; but with a saving rate of 10%, the $200 in taxes reduces private saving (and private investment) by $20.

8. True. Without using the trade deficit to increase investment, consumption must fall in the future.

9. True. Technological progress means more output without additional inputs.

10. The contribution from technological progress is estimated by determining how much of the growth in output cannot be explained by the growth in inputs.

11. Joseph Schumpeter.

12. Human capital includes investments in education and skills.

Using the Tools

1. Shorten the Length of Patents? The drawback to the proposal is that the shorter patent life will reduce the incentive of drug companies to invest in the discovery of new drugs. As Schumpeter emphasized, firms need incentives in the form of monopoly profits to engage in long-term research. However, prices are clearly higher as long as a single firm has a patent.

2. Capital Deepening. Only c, increased imports to purchase supercomputers for industry, adds to capital deepening. The others will not increase the stock of capital.

3. Future Generations. A country that increases its saving rate must cut back on its consumption. The long-run benefit will be a higher stock of capital for future generations. The current generation, however, will have to make a sacrifice, in terms of reduced consumption, to provide the additional capital. Therefore, there will be a trade-off in consumption between the present generation and future generations.

4. Will the Poorer Country Catch Up? After 35 years, GDP in the initially poorer country will exceed the GDP of its slower growing neighbor. Because the poorer country grows at 10% a year, the rule of 70 implies that its GDP doubles every seven years. In 35 years, its GDP will have doubled five times. This means that its GDP will have grown by a factor of 32 over the 35-year period. According to the rule of 70, the richer country, growing at 2% a year, will only double its GDP in 35 years. This implies that the country that was poorer initially will have a higher level of GDP after 35 years, even though it started at one-eighth the level of the richer country. To see this, suppose that the poorer country had a GDP of 1 and the richer country had a GDP of 8. After 35 years, the initially poorer country would now have a GDP of 32, while the initially richer country would have a GDP of 16.

Notes

1. Stanley Lebergott, *The Americans* (New York: W.W. Norton, 1984), pp. 65–68.

2. Alwyn Young, "A Tale of Two Cities: Factor Accumulation and Technical Change in Hong Kong and

Singapore," in *NBER Macroeconomic Annual 1992*, edited by Olivier Blanchard and Stanley Fischer (Cambridge, MA: MIT Press 1992); pp. 1–53.

3. Zvi Grilliches, "Productivity Puzzles and R&D: Another Nonexplanation," *Journal of Economic Perspectives,* vol. 2, Fall 1988, pp. 9–21.

4. Jeff Madrick, "Economic Science: Democracy has the Edge When It Comes to Advancing Growth" The *New York Times,* April 13, 2000, C2.

APPENDIX

A Model of Capital Deepening

Here's simple model showing the links among saving, depreciation, and capital deepening. Developed by Nobel laureate Robert Solow of the Massachusetts Institute of Technology, the Solow model, will help us understand more fully the critical role technological progress must play in economic growth. In using it, we rely on one of our basic principles of economics to help explain the model as well as make a few simplifying assumptions. We assume constant population and no government or foreign sector. In the chapter we discussed the qualitative effects of population growth, government, and the foreign sector on capital deepening. Here we focus solely on the relationships among saving, depreciation, and capital deepening.

Figure 8A.1 plots the relationship in the economy between output and the stock of capital, holding the labor force constant. Notice that output increases as the stock of capital increases but at a decreasing rate. This is an illustration of the principle of diminishing returns.

PRINCIPLE of Diminishing Returns

> **Suppose output is produced with two or more inputs and we increase one input while holding the other inputs fixed. Beyond some point—called the point of diminishing returns—output will increase at a decreasing rate.**

Figure 8A.1
Diminishing Returns to Capital
Holding labor constant, increases in the stock of capital increases output but at a decreasing rate.

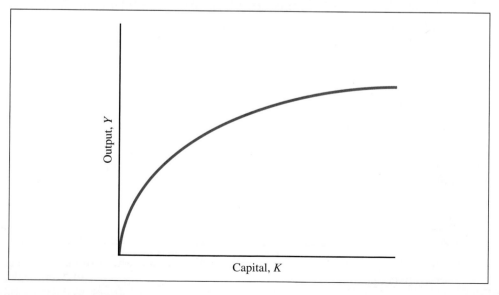

Increasing the stock of capital while holding the labor force constant will increase output, but at a decreasing rate.

As Figure 8A.1 indicates, output increases with the stock of capital. But what causes the stock of capital to increase? The capital stock will increase as long as gross investment exceeds depreciation. Therefore, we need to determine the level of gross investment and the level of depreciation to see how the capital stock changes over time.

Recall that without government or a foreign sector, saving equals gross investment. Thus, to determine the level of investment, we need to specify how much of output is saved and how much is consumed. We will assume that a fraction s of total output (Y) is saved. For example, if $s = 0.20$, then 20% of GDP would be saved and 80% would be consumed. Total saving will be sY, the product of the saving rate and total output.

In panel A of Figure 8A.2, the top curve is total output as a function of the stock of capital. The curve below it represents saving as a function of the stock of capital. Because saving is a fixed fraction of total output, the saving curve is a constant fraction of the output curve. If the saving rate is 0.2, saving will always be 20% of output for any level of the capital stock. Total saving increases in the economy with the stock of capital, but at a decreasing rate.

To complete our model, we need to determine depreciation. Let's say the capital stock depreciates at a constant rate of d per year. If $d = 0.03$, the capital stock would depreciate at 3% a year. If the capital stock were 100 at the beginning of the year, depreciation would equal 3. Total depreciation can be written as dK, where K is the stock of capital.

Panel B of Figure 8A.2 plots total depreciation as a function of the stock of capital. The larger the stock of capital, the more total depreciation there will be. Because the depreciation rate is assumed to be constant, total depreciation as a function of the stock of capital will be a straight line through the origin. Then if there is no capital, there will be no depreciation, no matter what the depreciation rate.

If the depreciation rate is 3% and the stock of capital is 100, depreciation will be 3; if the stock of capital is 200, the depreciation rate will be 6. Plotting these points will give a straight line through the origin.

We are now ready to see how the stock of capital changes:

$$\text{change in the stock of capital} = \text{savings} - \text{depreciation}$$

$$= sY - dK$$

The stock of capital will increase—the change will be positive—as long as total saving in the economy exceeds depreciation.

Figure 8A.3 shows how the Solow model works by plotting output, saving, and depreciation all on one graph. Suppose the economy starts with a capital stock K_0. Then total sav-

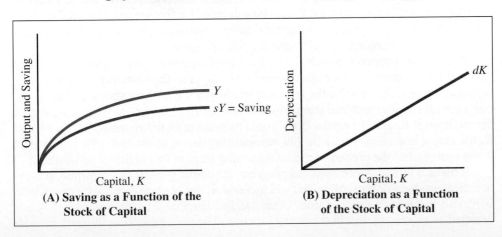

Figure 8A.2

Saving and Depreciation as Functions of the Stock of Capital

(A) Saving as a Function of the Stock of Capital

(B) Depreciation as a Function of the Stock of Capital

Figure 8A.3

Basic Growth Model

Starting at K_0, saving exceeds depreciation. The stock of capital increases. This process continues until the stock of capital reaches its long-run equilibrium at K^*.

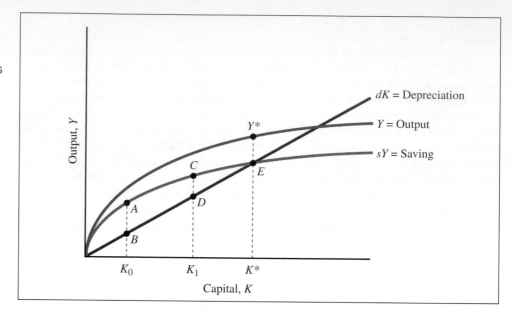

ing will be given by point A on the saving schedule. Depreciation at the capital stock K_0 is given by point B. Because A lies above B, total saving exceeds depreciation and the capital stock will increase. As the capital stock increases, there will be economic growth through capital deepening. With more capital per worker in the economy, output is higher and real wages increase. The economy benefits from the additional stock of capital.

Using the diagram, we can trace the future for this economy. As the stock of capital increases, we move to the right. When the economy reaches K_1, total saving is at point C and total depreciation is at point D. Because C is still higher than D, saving exceeds depreciation and the capital stock continues to increase. Economic growth continues. Eventually, after many years, the economy reaches capital stock K^*. The level of output in the economy now is Y^*, and the saving and depreciation schedules intersect at point E. Because total saving equals depreciation, the stock of capital no longer increases. The process of economic growth through capital deepening has stopped.

In this simple model, the process of capital deepening must eventually come to an end. As the stock of capital increases, output increases but at a decreasing rate because of diminishing returns. Because saving is a fixed fraction of output, it will also increase but also at a diminishing rate. On the other hand, total depreciation is proportional to the stock of capital. As the stock of capital increases, depreciation will always catch up with total saving in the economy. It may take decades for the process of capital deepening to come to an end. But as long as total saving exceeds depreciation, the process of economic growth through capital deepening will continue.

What would happen if a society saved a higher fraction of its output? Figure 8A.4 shows the consequences of a higher saving rate. Suppose the economy were originally saving at a rate s_1. Eventually, the economy would reach E_1, where saving and depreciation meet. If the economy had started to save at the higher rate s_2, saving would exceed depreciation at K_1 and the capital stock would increase until the economy reached K_2. At K_2 the saving line again crosses the line representing depreciation. Output is higher than it was initially, but the process of capital deepening stops at this higher level of output.

If there is ongoing technological progress, economic growth can continue. If technological progress raises GDP, saving will increase as well, because saving increases with GDP. This will lead to a higher stock of capital. In Figure 8A.5 technological progress is depicted as an upward shift of the saving function. The saving function shifts up because

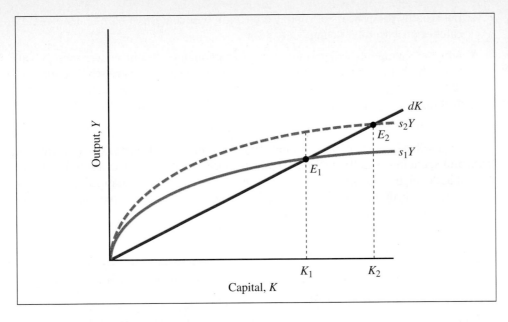

Figure 8A.4

Increase in the Saving Rate
A higher saving rate will lead to a higher stock of capital in the long run. Starting from an initial capital stock of K_1, the increase in the saving rate leads the economy to K_2.

saving is a fixed fraction of output and we have assumed that technological progress has raised the level of output.

With a higher level of saving, the stock of capital will increase. If the stock of capital were originally at K_0, the upward shift in the saving schedule will lead to increases in the stock of capital to K_1. If there are further gains in technological process, capital deepening will continue.

Technological progress conveys a double benefit to a society. Not only does the increased efficiency directly raise per capita output, it also leads to additional capital deepening. Therefore, output increases for two reasons.

Let's summarize the basic points of the Solow model:

1. Capital deepening, an increase in the stock of capital per worker, will occur as long as total saving exceeds depreciation. As capital deepening occurs, there will be economic growth and increased real wages.

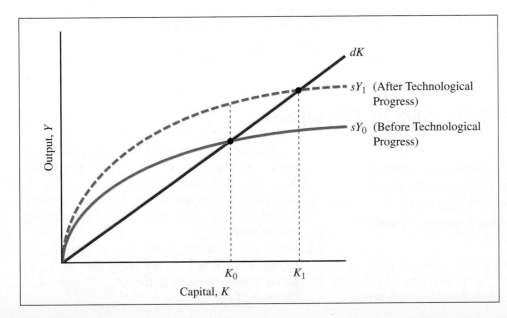

Figure 8A.5

Technological Progress and Growth
Technological progress shifts up the saving schedule and promotes capital deepening.

2. Eventually, the process of capital deepening will come to a halt as depreciation catches up with total saving.

3. A higher saving rate will promote capital deepening. If a country saves more, it will have a higher output. But eventually, the process of economic growth through capital deepening alone comes to an end, even though this may take decades to occur.

4. Technological progress not only directly raises output but allows capital deepening to continue.

It is possible to relax our assumptions and allow for population growth, government taxes and spending, and the foreign sector. In more advanced courses these issues are treated in detail, but the underlying message is the same. There is a natural limit to economic growth through capital deepening. Technological progress is required to ensure that per capita incomes grow over time.

TEST Your Understanding

1. What two factors determine how the stock of capital changes over time?

2. Why does capital deepening come to an end?

3. Does a higher saving rate lead to a permanently higher rate of growth?

Using the **TOOLS**

APPLICATIONS

1. Germany and Japan After World War II
Much of the stock of capital in the economies of Japan and Germany was destroyed during World War II. Both economies had high saving rates after the war ended. Use the Solow model to explain why after the war growth in the economies was higher than that in the United States.

2. Faster Depreciation
Suppose a society switches to equipment that depreciates rapidly. Use the Solow model to show what will happen to the stock of capital and output if the rate of depreciation increases.

Model Answers for the Appendix

Test Your Understanding
1. The factors are gross investment and depreciation.
2. Depreciation eventually catches up with saving.
3. No. A higher saving rate will raise the level of output, but eventually, capital deepening and economic growth comes to an end.

Using the Tools
1. Germany and Japan after World War II. Both Germany and Japan started after World War II with a low capital stock and a high saving rate. Both would be expected to have high rates of capital deepening. The United States, however, would be closer to the long-run position, in which capital deepening would cease in the absence of technological progress.

2. Faster Depreciation. If the rate of depreciation increases, the line from the origin that gives total depreciation will rotate to the left. This will reduce the stock of capital.

Aggregate Demand and Aggregate Supply

Economic times were good in the 1990s in the United States. But the 1930s were a different story. During the Great Depression, nearly one-fourth of the labor force was unemployed. Unemployed workers could not buy goods and services. Factories were shut down because there was little or no demand for their products. As factories shut down, more workers became unemployed. How could this destructive chain of cause and effect be stopped and turned around? Why were the 1930s so different from the 1990s?

Economic fluctuations: Movements of real GDP above or below normal trends.

Business cycles: Another name for economic fluctuations.

conomies do not always operate at full employment, nor do they always grow smoothly. At times, real GDP grows below its potential or falls steeply, as it did in the Great Depression. Recessions and excess unemployment occur when real GDP falls. At other times, GDP grows too rapidly, and unemployment falls below the natural rate of unemployment. When real GDP grows too fast, the result is an increase in the rate of inflation. Real GDP growth that is too slow and real GDP growth that is too fast are examples of **economic fluctuations**, movements of GDP away from potential output. Economic fluctuations, also called **business cycles**, are the subject of this part of the book.

After studying this chapter, you will be able to answer the following questions:

1. How do we define a recession?

2. Why doesn't the economy always operate at full employment?

3. Why can a sharp decrease in government spending cause a recession?

4. How do changes in the demand for goods and services affect prices and output in the short run and in the long run?

Let's begin by getting familiar with the terms we use when we talk about economic fluctuations.

During the Great Depression, there was a failure in coordination. Factories would have produced more output and hired more workers if there had been more demand for their products. If that had happened, the additionally employed workers would have been able to demand and afford to buy the additional goods that the factories produced.

Insufficient demand for goods and services was a key problem, identified by John Maynard Keynes, during the Great Depression. Since then, economists have viewed real GDP as determined by demand in the short run, when these coordination problems are most pronounced. We will make clear that the short run in macroeconomics is the time when prices do not fully adjust to changes in demand. In the next several chapters, we examine **Keynesian economics;** we will be analyzing models based on the idea that demand determines output in the short run.

Keynesian economics: A school of economic thought that provides insights into the economy when it operates away from full employment.

In this chapter, we develop tools for analyzing economic fluctuations in both the short run and the long run. We introduce the aggregate demand and aggregate supply curves, which will assist us in understanding some aspects of business cycles. The aggregate demand and aggregate supply curves will set the stage for our investigations of economic fluctuations in later chapters.

Business Cycles and Economic Fluctuations

To begin our study of economic fluctuations, let's look at data on real GDP at the end of the 1980s and the early 1990s. Figure 9.1 plots real GDP for the United States from 1988 to 1992. Notice that in mid-1990, real GDP begins to fall. A **recession** is a period when real GDP falls for six or more consecutive months. Economists talk more in terms of quarters of the year—consecutive three-month periods—than in terms of months. So they would say that when real GDP falls for two consecutive quarters, that's a recession. The date at which the recession starts, when output starts to decline, is called the **peak**; and the date at which the recession is considered to have begun to end, when output starts to increase again, is called the **trough**. In Figure 9.1 we see the peak and trough of the recession. After a trough, the economy enters a recovery period or period of **expansion**.

Recession: Six consecutive months of negative economic growth.

Peak: The time at which a recession begins.

Trough: The time at which output stops falling in a recession.

Expansion: The period from a trough to the next peak of a business cycle.

From World War II through 2001, the United States experienced ten recessions. Table 9.1 contains the dates of the peaks and troughs of each recession as well as the percent decline in real GDP from each peak to each trough. The sharpest decline in output occurred during the recession from 1973 to 1975, which started as a result of a sharp rise in world oil prices. In the last two decades of the twentieth century, there were two recessions—one starting in 1981 and the other in 1990.

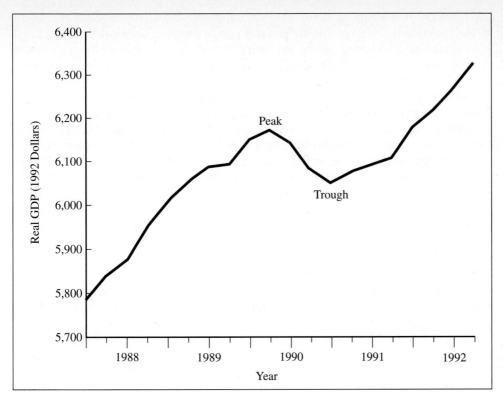

Figure 9.1
The 1990 Recession
Source: U.S. Department of Commerce.

The twenty-first century started off with a recession. Economic growth slowed considerably in 2001 and employment began to fall in March. With the economy already in a weakened state, the terrorist attack on September 11, 2001 disrupted economic activity, damaged producer and consumer confidence, and plunged the economy into a recession.

Throughout the broader sweep of U.S. history, there have been other periods of downturns—20 of them from 1860 up to World War II. Not all of these were particularly severe, and in some, unemployment hardly changed. However, there were economic downturns, such as those in 1893 and 1929, that were severe.

Depression is the common term for a severe recession. In the United States, the Great Depression refers to 1929–1933, the period when real GDP fell by over 33%. It created

Depression: The common name for a severe recession.

Table 9.1   Ten Postwar Recessions

Peak	Trough	Percent Decline in Real GDP
November 1948	October 1949	1.5
July 1953	May 1954	3.2
August 1957	April 1958	3.3
April 1960	February 1961	1.2
December 1969	November 1970	1.0
November 1973	March 1975	4.9
January 1980	July 1980	2.5
July 1981	November 1982	3.0
July 1990	March 1991	1.4
March 2001	—	—

the most severe disruptions to ordinary economic life in the United States during the twentieth century. Throughout the country and in much of the world, banks closed, businesses failed, and many people lost their jobs and their life savings. Unemployment rose sharply. In 1933, over 25% of people who were looking for work failed to find jobs.

Although the United States has not experienced a depression since that time, other countries have. During the late 1980s and 1990s, several Asian countries and several Latin American countries suffered severe economic disruptions that were true depressions.

Although the definition of recessions focuses on the behavior of real GDP, other important economic measures follow the behavior of output. In particular, unemployment rises sharply during recessions. Figure 9.2 plots the unemployment rate for 1965 to 2000. The periods of recessions are marked on the graph with shaded bars. As you can see in the graph, unemployment rises sharply during recessions. For example, during the 1990 recession, the unemployment rate rose from 5.5% to 7.5% before beginning to turn downward.

Okun's law: A relationship between changes in real GDP and the unemployment rate.

The relationship between changes in real GDP and corresponding changes in unemployment is called **Okun's law**. To understand Okun's law, we first need to remember that potential GDP typically grows over time. We call the average rate of potential GDP growth the *trend* rate of growth. Here is Okun's law: For every percentage point that real GDP grows faster than the normal rate of increase in potential output, the unemployment rate falls by 1/2 of a percentage point. For example, suppose the trend rate of growth of real GDP is 3% per year and the current unemployment rate is 5% of the total labor force. If real GDP then grows at 4% for a year (1 percentage point above trend), the unemployment rate will fall by 1/2 of a percentage point, to 4.5%. If real GDP grew at only 2% per year (1 percentage point below trend), the unemployment rate would rise to 5.5%. Okun's law provides a link between real GDP growth and the unemployment rate.

Other economic measures also rise and fall along with real GDP. Both investment spending and consumption spending rise and fall along with increases and decreases in

Figure 9.2
The Unemployment Rate During Recessions
Shaded areas are recessions according to NBER Business Cycle reference dates.

Source: Bureau of Labor Statistics, Department of Labor.

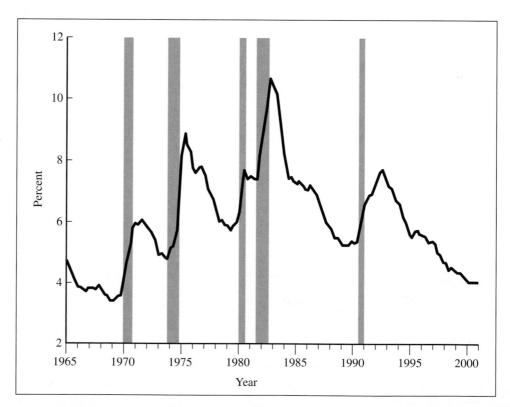

real GDP. The prices of shares of stocks also tend to rise and fall as real GDP goes up and down. We use the term **procyclical** to describe economic measures that move in conjunction with real GDP. Thus, investment spending, consumption spending, and prices of stocks are all procyclical. Economic measures that fall as real GDP rises are known as **countercyclical**. Unemployment, for example, is countercyclical.

Be sure you understand that when economists say "business cycle," they are not referring to a regularly recurring cycle, such as phases of the moon, the rotation of the seasons, or the appearance of the 17-year locusts. There are no fixed time intervals between recessions, as you can see in Table 9.1. During the 1960s and the 1990s, there were long periods without economic downturns. Yet there were two back-to-back recessions in the early 1980s.

Moreover, recessions tend to be unpredictable. After a recession has occurred, we can sometimes pinpoint its possible causes: either external shocks to the economy (such as sharp increases in the world price of oil) or changes in economic policy (such as sharp decreases in government spending). And the stock market always plunges sharply during recessions. But the wise men and women of Wall Street never anticipate the precise timing of an economic downturn.

Although we have focused on recessions, don't forget that a sustained period during which economic growth is too rapid can also damage the economy. Although an economy can operate for a time beyond its level of potential output, if output stays above potential output for too long a time, it will also be disruptive to the economy. When real GDP grows faster than its trend rate of growth, unemployment will fall. When the unemployment rate falls sufficiently below the natural rate of unemployment, the result will be an increase in the inflation rate for the economy.

This is why good economic policy tries to avoid both unnecessary downturns and recessions as well as prolonged booms that reduce unemployment below the natural rate. Whether we have become more successful in recent years in reducing economic fluctuations is a subject of current debate as we discuss in "A Closer Look: Is the Economy More Stable Today?"

A CLOSER LOOK — IS THE ECONOMY MORE STABLE TODAY?

From the mid-1980s through 2000, there has been only one recession in the early 1990s and that was relatively mild compared to other postwar recessions. Economists Margaret M. McConnel and Gabriel Perez Quiros have suggested that economic fluctuations may have become less severe in recent years, compared to the rest of the postwar period.

In particular, these economists find that since 1984, virtually all components of GDP have become less volatile. The largest decreases in volatility, however, occurred in the durable goods industry. The main cause of this change in volatility appears to be the behavior of inventory investment. Borrowing methods of managing inventories from Japan, firms in the durable goods industry have kept better track of their inventories since 1984. They were able to avoid wild swings in inventory investment that characterized early periods.

Of course, factors other than changes in inventory strategy could have contributed to decreased fluctuations in output. Economic policy could have been better than earlier periods or the country simply could have had the good fortune to avoid major shocks. But the fact that inventory behavior seems to have changed may suggest that the decrease in volatility was a structural change in the economy.

The recession starting in 2001 will provide additional data to test these theories. After the economy recovers from the downturn, economists will be able to explore the behavior of the components of GDP and determine whether the previous patterns that were uncovered continue to hold.

Source: Virginia Postrel, "Economic Scene: The Roots of Stable Expansion Extend Well Beyond the Greenspan Era," *The New York Times,* January 25, 2001, p. C2.

TEST Your Understanding

Sticky Prices and Demand-Side Economics

Why do recessions occur? In Chapter 7, we discussed how real, adverse shocks to the economy could cause economic downturns. We also outlined the theory of real business cycles, which focuses on how shocks to technology cause economic fluctuations. Now we examine another approach to understanding economic fluctuations.

John Maynard Keynes and many economists since have identified difficulties in coordinating economic affairs as providing the starting point for understanding fluctuations in economic activity.

Normally, the price system is the mechanism that coordinates what goes on in an economy, even in a complex economy. In microeconomics, we learn that the price system helps to coordinate who does what, what resources to use, how much to make, from whom to buy, and so on, so that the economy produces as efficiently as possible. Prices give the correct signals to all producers in the economy so that resources are used efficiently and without waste. If consumers decide to consume fresh fruit rather than chocolate, the price of fresh fruit will rise and the price of chocolate will fall. The economy will produce more fresh fruit and less chocolate on the basis of these price signals. On a day-to-day basis, the price system works silently in the background, matching the desires of consumers with the output from producers.

But the price system does not always work instantaneously. If prices are slow to adjust, then the proper signals are not given quickly enough to producers and consumers. Demands and supplies will not be brought immediately into equilibrium, and coordination can break down.

In modern economies, some prices are very flexible, while others are not. Arthur Okun, the economist who came up with Okun's law, distinguished between *auction prices*, prices that adjust on a nearly daily basis, and *custom prices*, prices that adjust slowly. Prices for fresh fish, vegetables, and other food products are examples of auction prices—they typically are very flexible and adjust rapidly. Prices for industrial commodities such as steel rods or machine tools are custom prices and tend to adjust slowly to changes in demand. As shorthand, economists often refer to slowly adjusting prices as *sticky prices* (just like a door that won't open immediately but sometimes gets stuck).

Wages, the price of labor, adjust very slowly. Workers often have long-term contracts that do not allow employers to change workers' wages at all during a given year. Union workers, university professors, high-school teachers, and employees of state and local governments are all groups whose wages adjust very slowly. As a general rule, there are very few workers in the economy whose wages change quickly. Perhaps movie stars, athletes, and rock stars are the exceptions; their wages rise and fall with their popularity. But they are far from the typical worker in the economy. Even unskilled, low-wage workers are often protected from decreases in their wages by minimum wage laws.

For most firms, the most important cost of doing business is wages. If wages are sticky, firms' overall costs will be sticky as well. This means that firms' product prices will remain sticky. Sticky wages causing sticky prices get in the way of the economy's ability to coordinate economic activity, and bring demand and supply into balance.

Because prices and wages are sticky over short periods, prices do not fully do the job of bringing demands and supplies into balance over short periods of time.

Typically, firms such as automobile manufacturers and steel firms let demand determine the level of output in the short run. To understand this idea, consider an automobile firm that buys material from a steelmaker on a regular basis. Because the auto firm and the steel producer have been in business with one another for a long time and have an ongoing relationship, they have negotiated a contract that keeps steel prices fixed in the short run.

Suppose that the automobile company's cars suddenly become very popular. The firm needs to expand production, so it needs more steel. Under their agreement, the steel company would meet this higher demand for its product and sell more steel—without raising its price—to the automobile company. So the production of steel is totally determined in the short run by the demand from automobile producers, not by price.

But, what if the firm discovered that it had produced an unpopular car and needed to cut back on its planned production? The firm would require less steel. Under the agreement, the steelmaker would supply less steel but not reduce its price. Again, demand, not price, determines steel production in the short run.

Similar agreements between firms, both formal and informal, exist throughout the economy. Typically, in the short run, firms will meet changes in the demand for their products by adjusting production with only small changes in the prices they charge their customers.

Prices for industrial commodities adjust slowly to changes in demand.

What we have just illustrated for an input such as steel applies in the same way to workers as inputs to production. Suppose that the automobile firm hires union workers under a contract that fixes their wages for a specific period. If the economy suddenly thrives at some point during that period, the automobile company will employ all the workers and perhaps require some to work overtime. If the economy stagnates at some point during that period, the firm will lay off some workers, using only part of the union labor force. In either case, wages will not change during the period of the contract.

Over longer time, prices do change. Suppose the automobile company's car remains popular for a long time. The steel company and the automobile company will adjust the price of steel on their contract to reflect this increased demand. These price adjustments only occur over long periods; in the short run, demand, not prices, determines output, and prices are slow to adjust. The **short run in macroeconomics** is the period when prices do not change or don't change very much. In the macroeconomic short run, demand determines output.

In the long run, prices adjust fully to changes in demand. But over short periods, both formal and informal contracts between firms mean that changes in demand will be reflected primarily in changes in output, not prices. We will use the term *Keynesian economics* to mean that demand determines output in the short run.

Aggregate Demand and Aggregate Supply

We now develop the graphical tool known as the aggregate demand and aggregate supply model. We consider aggregate demand and aggregate supply to understand how output and prices are determined in both the short run and in the long run. We will be able to do that because we will consider two types of aggregate supply curves: one for the long run and one for the short run.

Aggregate Demand

The **aggregate demand curve** plots the total demand for GDP as a function of price level. (Recall that the price level is the average level of prices in the economy, as measured by a price index.) For each price level, we ask what the total quantity demanded will be for all goods and services in the economy. In Figure 9.3, the aggregate demand curve is

Short run in macroeconomics: The period of time in which prices do not change very much.

Aggregate demand curve: The relationship between the level of prices and the quantity of real GDP demanded.

Figure 9.3

Aggregate Demand
The aggregate demand curve plots the total demand for real GDP as a function of the price level. The aggregate demand curve slopes downward, indicating that aggregate demand increases as the price level falls.

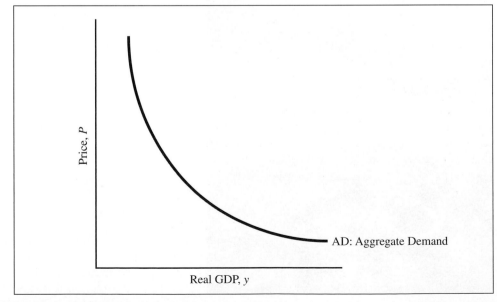

downward sloping. As the price level falls, the total quantity demanded for goods and services increases. To understand what the aggregate demand curve represents, we must first learn why it is downward sloping, and then we must learn what factors shift it.

The Slope of the Aggregate Demand Curve

Let's consider the supply of money in the economy. We discuss the supply of money in detail in later chapters, but for now, just think of the supply of money as being the total amount of currency (cash plus coins) held by the public and the value of all deposits in checking accounts in the economy. If you have $100 in cash and $900 in your checking account, you have $1,000 of money.

As the price level or average level of prices in the economy changes, so does the purchasing power of your money. This is an example of the reality principle:

Reality **PRINCIPLE**

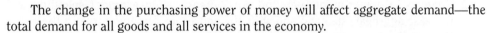

What matters to people is the real value or purchasing power of money or income, not the face value of money or income.

The change in the purchasing power of money will affect aggregate demand—the total demand for all goods and all services in the economy.

As the price level falls, the purchasing power of money will increase, and your $1,000 can purchase more goods and services. As the price level falls, increasing the purchasing power of money, people find that they are wealthier. With increased wealth, people want to increase their spending on goods and services. And so the quantity demanded for goods and services will increase as the price level falls. This means that the aggregate demand curve is downward sloping.

When the price level increases, the real value of money decreases, reducing wealth and thus reducing the total demand for goods and services. And so as the price level increases, total demand for goods and services in the economy decreases.

The increase in spending that occurs because the real value of money increases when the price level falls is known as the **wealth effect**. This is one reason the aggregate demand curve slopes downward. Lower prices lead to higher levels of wealth. Higher levels of wealth increase spending on total goods and services.

Wealth effect: The increase in spending because the real value of money increases when the price level falls.

There are two other reasons why the aggregate demand curve is downward sloping: one has to do with interest rates, and the other has to do with international trade.

First, consider the interest rate effect. With a given supply of money in the economy, a lower price level will lead to lower interest rates. As interest rates fall, the demand for investment goods in the economy (both investment by firms and consumer durables by households) will increase. We'll explain this in detail in later chapters.

Second, consider the effects from international trade. In an open economy, a lower price level will mean that domestic goods become cheaper relative to foreign goods, so the demand for domestic goods will increase. Moreover, as we will see, lower interest rates will affect the exchange rate to make domestic goods become relatively cheaper than foreign goods. The wealth effect, the interest rate effect, and the effects from international trade reinforce one another, leading to the downward sloping aggregate demand curve in Figure 9.3.

Factors That Shift the Aggregate Demand Curve

Different factors can shift the aggregate demand curve. At any price level, an increase in aggregate demand means that total demand by all sectors of the economy for all the goods and services contained in real GDP has increased, and the curve shifts to the right. Factors that decrease aggregate demand will shift the aggregate demand curve to the left. At any price level, a decrease in aggregate demand means that total demand for the goods and services contained in real GDP has decreased.

Let's look at the key factors that shift the aggregate demand curve:

1. Changes in the supply of money. An increase in the supply of money in the economy will increase aggregate demand and shift the aggregate demand curve to the right. We know that an increase in the supply of money will lead to higher demand by both consumers and firms. At any given price level, a higher supply of money will mean more consumer wealth and an increased demand for goods and services. A decrease in the supply of money will decrease aggregate demand and shift the aggregate demand curve to the left. (We will discuss the money supply and aggregate demand further in later chapters.)

2. Changes in taxes. A decrease in taxes will increase aggregate demand and shift the aggregate demand curve to the right. Lower taxes will increase income available to households and increase their spending on goods and services. Aggregate demand will increase as taxes are decreased. For opposite reasons, increases in taxes will decrease aggregate demand and shift the aggregate demand curve to the left. (We will discuss taxes and aggregate demand further in the next chapter.)

3. Changes in government spending. An increase in government spending will increase aggregate demand and shift the aggregate demand curve to the right. Because the government is a source of demand for goods and services, higher government spending naturally leads to an increase in total demand for goods and services. Similarly, decreases in government spending will decrease aggregate demand and shift the curve to the left. (We will discuss government spending and aggregate demand further in the next chapter.)

4. Other factors. Any change in demand from households, firms, or the foreign sector will also change aggregate demand. For example, if the Japanese economy expands very rapidly and the Japanese buy more U.S. goods, our aggregate demand will increase. Similarly, if firms become optimistic about the future and increase their investment spending, aggregate demand will also increase.

When we discuss factors that shift aggregate demand, we must not include any changes in the demand for goods and services that arise from movements in the price level. Changes in aggregate demand that accompany changes in the price level are already included in the curve and do not shift the curve. The increase in consumer spending that occurs from the wealth effect when the price level falls is included in the curve and does not shift the curve.

Both Figure 9.4 and Table 9.2 summarize our discussion. Decreases in taxes, increases in government spending, and increases in the supply of money all shift the aggregate demand curve to the right. Increases in taxes, decreases in government spending, and decreases in the supply of money shift it to the left. In general, any increase in demand (not brought about by a change in the price level) will shift the curve to the right. Decreases in demand shift it to the left.

Aggregate Supply

Aggregate supply curve: The relationship between the level of prices and the quantity of output supplied.

The **aggregate supply curve** depicts the relationship between the level of prices and real GDP. We will develop two different aggregate supply curves: one corresponding to the long run and one to the short run.

The Classical Aggregate Supply Curve

Classical aggregate supply curve: A vertical aggregate supply curve. It reflects the idea that in the long run, output is determined solely by the factors of production.

First we'll consider the aggregate supply curve for the long run, that is, when the economy is at full employment; it is also called the **classical aggregate supply curve**. In previous chapters, we saw that the level of full-employment output y^* depends solely on the sup-

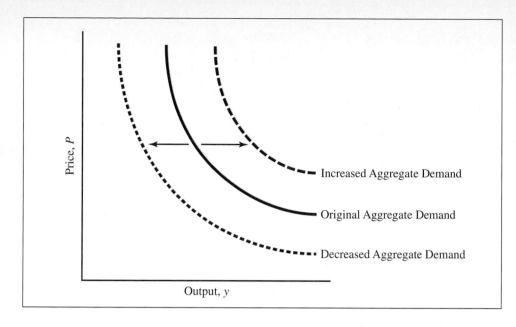

Figure 9.4
Shifting Aggregate Demand
Decreases in taxes, increases in government spending, and an increase in the supply of money all shift the aggregate demand curve to the right. Higher taxes, lower government spending, and a lower supply of money shift the curve to the left.

ply factors—capital and labor—and the state of technology. These are the fundamental factors that determine output in the long run, that is, when the economy operates at full employment.

The level of full-employment output does not depend on the level of prices in the economy. Because the level of full-employment output does not depend on the price level, we can plot the classical aggregate supply curve as a vertical line (unaffected by the price level), as in Figure 9.5.

We combine the aggregate demand curve and the classical aggregate supply curve in Figure 9.6. Given an aggregate demand curve and an aggregate supply curve, their intersection determines the price level and level of output. At that intersection point, the total amount demanded will just equal the total amount supplied. The position of the aggregate demand curve will depend on the level of taxes, government spending, and the supply of money. The level of full-employment output determines the classical aggregate supply curve.

An increase in aggregate demand (perhaps brought about by a tax cut or an increase in the supply of money) will shift the aggregate demand curve to the right as in Figure 9.6. With a classical aggregate supply curve, the increase in aggregate demand will raise prices but leave the level of output unchanged. In general, shifts in the aggregate demand curve when we have a classical supply curve do not change the level of output in the economy but only change the level of prices. That is, an increase in demand when we

Table 9.2 Factors That Shift Demand

Factors That Increase Aggregate Demand	Factors That Decrease Aggregate Demand
Decrease in taxes	Increase in taxes
Increase in government spending	Decrease in government spending
Increase in money supply	Decrease in money supply

Figure 9.5
Classical Aggregate Supply
In the long run, the level of output y^* is independent of the price level.

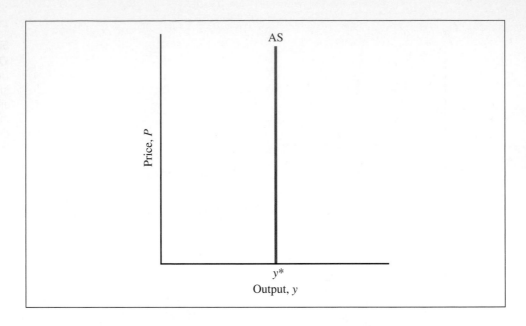

have a classical supply curve will only raise the average level of prices in the economy but not change the level of real output.

This is the main long-run result from the classical model. In the long run, output is determined solely by the supply of capital and the supply of labor. As our model of the aggregate demand curve with the classical aggregate supply curve indicates, changes in demand will affect only prices, not the level of output.

The Keynesian Aggregate Supply Curve

In the short run, prices are sticky (slow to adjust), and output is determined primarily by demand. We can use the aggregate demand curve combined with a **Keynesian aggregate supply curve** to illustrate this idea. Figure 9.7 shows a relatively flat Keynesian aggregate supply curve (AS). The Keynesian aggregate supply curve is relatively flat because in the short run, firms are assumed to supply all the output demanded, with small changes in

Keynesian aggregate supply curve: A relatively flat supply curve. It reflects the idea that prices do not change very much in the short run and that firms adjust production to meet demand.

Figure 9.6
Aggregate Demand and Classical Aggregate Supply
Output and prices are determined at the intersection of AD and AS. An increase in aggregate demand leads to a higher price level.

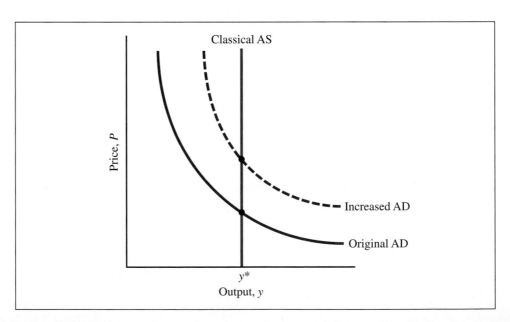

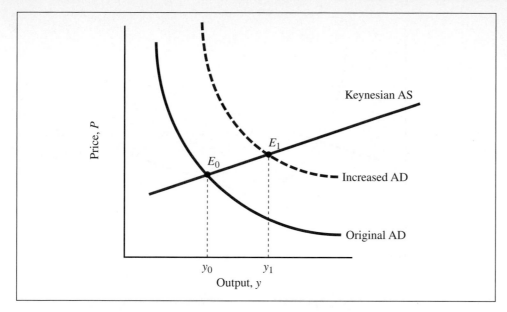

prices. We previously discussed that with formal and informal contracts, firms will supply all the output that is demanded with only relatively small changes in prices. The Keynesian aggregate supply curve has a small upward slope. As they supply more output, firms may have to increase prices somewhat if, for example, they have to pay higher wages to obtain more overtime from workers or pay a premium to obtain some raw materials.

As we just explained, the Keynesian supply curve is relatively flat because at any point in time, firms are assumed to supply all the output demanded with relatively small changes in prices. However, the entire Keynesian supply curve can shift upward or downward as prices adjust to their long-run levels, as we shall see later in this chapter. Our description of the aggregate supply curve is consistent with evidence about the behavior of prices in the economy. Most studies find that changes in demand have relatively little effect on prices within a few quarters. Thus, the aggregate supply curve can be viewed as relatively flat within a limited time. However, changes in aggregate demand will ultimately have an effect on prices.

The intersection of the AD and AS curves at point E_0 determines the price level and the level of output. Because the aggregate supply curve is flat, aggregate demand primarily determines the level of output. In Figure 9.7, as aggregate demand increases, the new equilibrium will be at a slightly higher price, and output will increase from y_0 to y_1.

It is important to realize and understand that the level of output where the aggregate demand curve intersects the Keynesian aggregate supply curve need not correspond to full-employment output. Firms will produce whatever is demanded. If demand is very high, output may exceed full-employment output; if demand is very low, output will fall short of full-employment output. Because prices do not adjust fully over short periods of time, the economy need not always remain at full employment or potential output. Changes in demand will lead to economic fluctuations with sticky prices and a Keynesian aggregate supply curve. Only in the long run, when prices fully adjust, will the economy operate at full employment.

Supply Shocks

Up to this point, we have been exploring how changes in aggregate demand affect output and prices in the short run and in the long run. However, even in the short run, it is possible for external disturbances to hit the economy and cause the Keynesian aggregate

Figure 9.8
Supply Shock
An adverse supply shock, such as an increase in the price of oil, will shift up the AS curve. The result will be higher prices and a lower level of output.

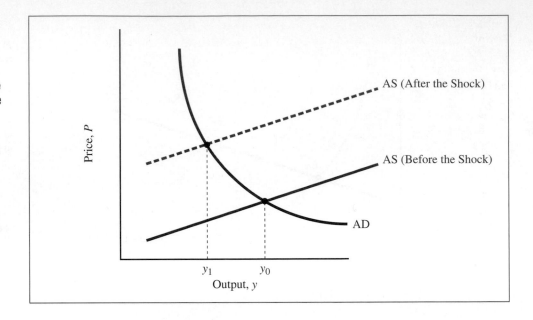

supply curve to move. **Supply shocks** are external events that shift the aggregate supply curve.

The most important illustrations of supply shocks for the world economy are the sharp increases in the price of oil that occurred in 1973 and again in 1979. When oil prices increased sharply, firms no longer sold all the goods and services that were demanded at the current price—meaning the price before the increases in oil prices. Because oil was a key input to production for many firms in the economy, the additional costs of oil reduced the profits of firms. To maintain their profit levels, firms raised the prices of their products.

Figure 9.8 illustrates a supply shock that raises prices. The Keynesian aggregate supply curve shifts up with the supply shock because firms will supply their output only at a higher price. The shift of the AS curve raises the price level and lowers the level of output from y_0 to y_1. Adverse supply shocks can therefore cause a recession (a fall in output) with increasing prices. This situation corresponds closely to the events of 1973, when higher oil prices led to both a recession and rising prices for the economy.

Favorable supply shocks, such as falling prices, are also possible. In this case the Keynesian aggregate supply curve will shift down. As "A Closer Look: Favorable Supply Shocks" indicates, this happened to the United States in the 1990s.

Economic Detective

Did Higher Taxes Cause the Recession?

The economy went into a recession. The political party that was in power blamed an increase in the price of world oil and food. Opposing politicians blamed a tax increase that the party in power had enacted. On the basis of aggregate demand and aggregate supply analysis, what evidence should you look at to try to determine what caused the recession?

To determine whether increases in world prices for oil and food or tax increases caused the recession, you need to look at what happened to domestic prices in the economy. If prices rose sharply while output fell, then supply shocks (increases in world oil and food prices) caused the recession. However, if prices fell while output fell, tax increases probably were the culprit.

FAVORABLE SUPPLY SHOCKS

During the 1970s, the world economy was hit with a series of unfavorable supply shocks, raising prices and lowering output. These shocks included a spike (a sudden steep increase) in the price of oil in 1973, another in 1979 when producers of oil reduced their supplies to the market, and increases in the prices of many agricultural commodities.

In the 1990s, things were different—pleasantly different. Between 1997 and 1998, the price of oil on the world market fell from $22 a barrel to less than $13 a barrel. The result was that gasoline prices, adjusted for inflation, were lower than they had ever been in our lifetimes. This not only meant cheaper vacations and commuting, it also had positive macroeconomic effects. Favorable supply shocks allowed output to rise and prices to fall simultaneously—the best of all worlds. These favorable shocks allowed the U.S. economy to grow rapidly and reduced unemployment without incurring risks of increased inflation.

Output and Prices in the Short Run and in the Long Run

Up to this point, we have examined how aggregate demand and aggregate supply determine output and prices both in the short run and in the long run. You may be wondering how long is the short run and how short is the long run. Here is a preview of how the short run and the long run are connected.

In Figure 9.9, we show the aggregate demand curve intersecting the Keynesian aggregate supply curve at E_0 at an output level y_0. We also depict the classical aggregate supply curve in this figure. The level of output in the economy, y_0, exceeds the level of potential output y_p. In other words, this is a boom economy: Output exceeds potential. Because the economy is producing at a level beyond its long-run potential, the level of unemployment will be very low. This will make it difficult for firms to recruit and retain workers. They will also find it more difficult to purchase needed raw materials and other

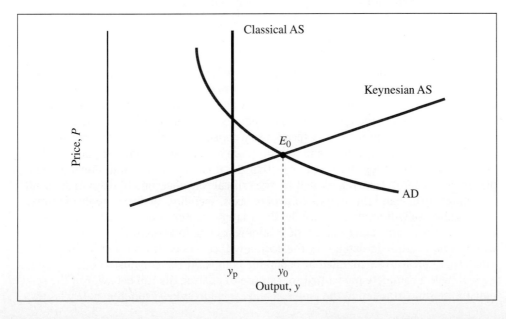

Figure 9.9

The Economy in the Short Run
In the short run, the economy produces at y_0, which exceeds potential output y_p.

Figure 9.10
Adjusting to the Long Run
With output exceeding potential, the AS curve shifts upwards as depicted by the dotted lines. The economy adjusts to the long-run equilibrium at E_1.

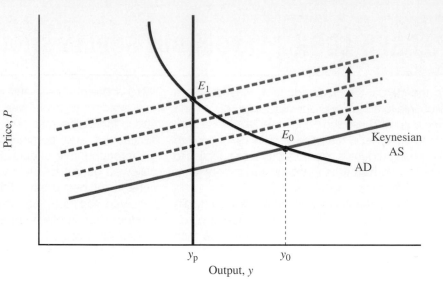

inputs for production. As firms compete for labor and raw materials, there will be a tendency for both wages and prices to increase over time.

Increasing wages and prices will shift the Keynesian aggregate supply curve upward. Figure 9.10 illustrates this graphically; the dashed lines indicating how the Keynesian aggregate supply curve shifts upward over time. As long as the economy is producing at a level of output that exceeds potential output, there will be continuing competition for labor and raw materials that will lead to continuing increases in wages and prices. In the long run, the Keynesian aggregate supply curve will keep rising until it intersects the aggregate demand curve at E_1. At this point, the economy reaches the long-run equilibrium—precisely the point where the aggregate demand curve intersects the classical aggregate supply curve.

The lesson here is that adjustments in wages and prices take the economy from the short-run Keynesian equilibrium to the long-run classical equilibrium. In later chapters, we will explain in detail how this adjustment occurs, and we will show how changes in wages and prices can steer the economy back to full employment in the long run.

Looking Ahead

The aggregate demand and aggregate supply models in this chapter provide an overview of how demand affects output and prices in both the short run and the long run. The next several chapters explore more closely how aggregate demand determines output in the short run. We expand our discussion of aggregate demand to see in detail how such realistic and important factors as spending by consumers and firms, government policies on taxation and spending, and foreign trade affect the demand for goods and services. We will also study the critical role that the financial system and monetary policy play in determining demand. We will see the critical role government plays in determining aggregate demand through its control of taxes, spending, and the supply of money.

Finally, we will study in more depth in later chapters how the aggregate supply curve shifts over time and can lead the economy back to full employment. From this, we will be able to study in detail how the economy recovers both from recessions and the inflationary pressures generated by economic booms. At the conclusion of our studies, we will have a complete model that we can use to analyze the full behavior of the economy in the short run and in the long run and can address key economic policy issues.

TEST Your Understanding

Using the **TOOLS**

In this chapter we explored the nature of economic fluctuations and developed the tools of aggregate demand and aggregate supply. Take this opportunity to test your skills using the tools we developed in this chapter.

APPLICATIONS

1. Counting Recessions

Consider the data for the fictitious economy of Euroclive.

Year and Quarter	2000:1	2000:2	2000:3	2000:4	2001:1	2001:2	2001:3
Real GDP	195	193	195	196	195	194	198

How many recessions occurred in the economy over the time indicated?

2. The Internet and Sticky Prices

The Internet enables us to search for the lowest prices for goods such as books, music CDs, and airline tickets. Prices for these goods are likely to become more flexible as consumers shop around quickly and easily on the Internet. What types of goods and services do you think may not become more flexible because of the Internet?

3. Frugal Consumers

Suppose households become nervous about the future and decide to increase their saving and decrease their consumption spending. How will this shift the aggregate demand curve? Use the Keynesian aggregate supply curve to figure out what will happen to prices and output in the short run. Use the classical aggregate supply curve to determine what will happen to prices and output in the long run.

4. Stagflation

Suppose oil prices suddenly increase and the economy is hit by an adverse supply shock. What will happen to the price level and real GDP? Why is this sometimes called stagflation?

Summary

We examined the nature of business cycles and economic fluctuations and provided the foundation for studying short-run, demand-side economics. We also developed aggregate demand and aggregate supply as tools to help us analyze what is happening or has happened in the economy. Here are the main points to remember in this chapter:

1. Recessions occur when real output falls for two quarters.

2. Unemployment rises during recessions; other economic measures rise and fall with real GDP.

3. Economists think of GDP as being determined primarily by demand factors in the short run.

4. The aggregate demand curve depicts the relationship between the price level and total demand for real output in the economy. The aggregate demand curve is downward sloping because of the wealth effect, an interest rate effect, and an international trade effect.

5. Decreases in taxes, increases in government spending, and increases in the supply of money all increase aggregate demand and shift the aggregate demand curve to the right. Increases in taxes, decreases in government spending, and decreases in the supply of money all decrease aggregate demand and shift the aggregate demand curve to the left. In general, anything (other than price movements) that increases the demand for total goods and services will increase aggregate demand.

6. The aggregate supply curve depicts the relationship between the price level and the level of output firms supply in the economy. Output and prices are determined at the intersection of the aggregate demand and aggregate supply curves.

7. The classical aggregate supply curve is vertical because, in the long run, output is determined by the supply of factors of production. The Keynesian aggregate supply curve is fairly flat because, in the short run, prices are largely fixed and output is determined by demand.

8. Supply shocks can shift the Keynesian aggregate supply curve even in the short run.

9. The Keynesian aggregate supply curve shifts in the long run, restoring the economy to the full employment equilibrium.

Key Terms

aggregate demand curve, 186	**economic fluctuations**, 180	**procyclical**, 183
aggregate supply curve, 188	**expansion**, 180	**recession**, 180
business cycles, 180	**Keynesian aggregate supply curve**, 190	**short run in macroeconomics**, 186
classical aggregate supply curve, 188	**Keynesian economics**, 180	**supply shocks**, 192
countercyclical, 183	**Okun's law**, 182	**trough**, 180
depression, 181	**peak**, 180	**wealth effect**, 187

Problems and Discussion Questions

1. What can be misleading about the term *business cycle?*

2. Explain intuitively why the unemployment rate is countercyclical.

3. To compare how deeply recessions affected the economies of two different countries, we might use the following measures:

  a. The number of recessions

  b. The proportion of time each economy was in a recession

  c. The magnitude of the worst recession

  Draw several diagrams that show economies experiencing recessions. Use these diagrams to illustrate how these measures convey different features of recessions.

4. Explain why the aggregate demand curve is downward sloping.

5. Give an example of a good or service whose prices are sticky. What factors tend to make its price sticky?

6. Explain why the classical aggregate supply curve is vertical and why the Keynesian supply curve is horizontal.

7. Suppose that in the classical model, there was a new higher level of full-employment output. What would happen to the level of prices in the economy?

8. In the short run, what happens to the unemployment rate if aggregate demand suddenly falls?

9. Suppose the economy is at full employment and aggregate demand falls. Show the effects on output and prices in the short run. Also show how the Keynesian aggregate supply curve adjusts over time to bring the economy to the long-run equilibrium.

10. Use aggregate demand and aggregate supply diagrams to show the effects of "favorable" supply shocks.

11. **Web Exercise.** Is the U.S. trade balance (export minus imports) procyclical or countercyclical? Use the World Wide Web to find data of the trade balance and GDP to explore this answer. A good place to start might be the Web site of the Federal Reserve Bank of St. Louis [*http://www.stls.frb.org/fred/*]. You might also want to explore this issue for other countries.

12. **Web Exercise.** How are movements in the stock market related to business cycles? Use the Web site in question 11 or your own source to answer this question.

Take It to the Net

We invite you to visit the O'Sullivan/Sheffrin page on the Prentice Hall Web site at: **http://www.prenhall.com/osullivan/** for additional World Wide Web exercises for this chapter.

Model Answers to Questions

Chapter-Opening Questions

1. A recession occurs when real GDP declines for two consecutive quarters.

2. Because wages and prices are slow to adjust, the economy may not always operate at full employment.

3. In the short run, output is largely determined by demand. Therefore, a sharp decrease in government spending could cause a recession.

4. In the short run, changes in the demand for goods and services primarily affect output. In the long run, changes in demand for goods and services primarily affect prices.

Test Your Understanding

1. Six.

2. Countercyclical.

3. Peak.

4. Recovery.

5. Increases in government spending, decreases in taxes, and increases in the supply of money.

6. False. Changes in prices are movements along the aggregate demand curve, not shifts of the curve.

7. Vertical.

8. In the classical model, an increase in the money supply will raise prices but not change output. In the Keynesian model, an increase in the supply of money will increase output but not change prices very much.

Using the Tools

1. Counting Recessions. There was only one recession in Euroclive, the peak of which was in 2000:4. Although output did fall in 2000:2, the decline was only for one quarter. The decline beginning in 2001:1 lasted for two quarters.

2. The Internet and Sticky Prices. Books, music CDs, and airline tickets are all standardized commodities. Consumers can shop for them on the Internet with confidence that the product will be what they desire. Products that are not standardized require more research and negotiation and the flexibility of their prices will not likely be changed by the Internet. Examples of these include consumer or business services (e.g., legal and accounting services) or goods that are made special to order or require long-term contracts.

3. Frugal Consumers. The decrease in consumption spending is a decrease in the demand for total goods and services—therefore, a decrease in aggregate demand. The aggregate demand curve shifts to the left. In the short run, output falls and prices decrease slightly. In the long run, prices fall and output returns to full employment.

4. Stagflation. If the Keynesian aggregate supply curve shifts upward, the result will be a lower level of output and higher prices. This is sometimes called stagflation because the falling output means that the economy is stagnating and the rising prices mean that the inflation rate will rise.

Keynesian Economics and Fiscal Policy

During the decade of the 1990s, the Japanese economy was in a prolonged recession. Economists and journalists put forward many different ideas to try to jump start the economy. One suggestion was that the government would issue everyone in the economy a certificate entitling each person to the equivalent, in yen, of $200. However, these yen certificates would only be valid for purchases for one month; after that time, the certificates would be worthless.

The logic behind issuing these time-dated certificates was straightforward. Individuals would feel compelled to rush out and use the certificates within the month. They would therefore immediately purchase goods and services and stimulate demand. Firms would increase production to meet the increased demand, thereby creating more jobs and lifting the economy out of the recession. The economic theory underlying these time-dated certificates came straight from the writings of John Maynard Keynes.

ewspaper and television stories about the economy tend to focus on what causes the changes in short term real GDP. For example, it is common to read about how changes in economic conditions in Europe or Asia or changes in government spending or taxation will affect near-term economic growth. To understand these stories, we need to understand the behavior of the economy in the short run. To do that, we will get help from John Maynard Keynes.

In this chapter, we explore Keynes's idea that spending determines output or GDP, at least over short periods. In macroeconomics, the short run is the period during which prices do not change or change very little. Until prices adjust in the long run, the demand for goods and services determines the level of GDP. Producers will supply, in the short run, all the output that is demanded. This was Keynes's point: In the short run, the level of GDP is determined primarily by demand.

We start this chapter with the simplest case: a model of the behavior of the economy in the short run that ignores the role of the government and the foreign sector. We then bring government and the foreign sector into our model and illustrate how it works with examples of what really happens.

We also introduce the Keynesian cross, a graph that we will use as an analytical tool. The Keynesian cross enables us to understand how demand determines output in the short run and how changes in demand change output. We also use simple formulas that help to reinforce the ideas behind the demand-side models. The appendix to the chapter shows how these formulas are derived.

With the tools in this chapter, you will be able to answer the following questions:

1. Why do governments cut taxes to increase economic output?
2. Why is the U.S. economy more stable today than it was prior to World War II?
3. If consumers become more confident about the future of the economy, can that confidence lead to faster economic growth?
4. If a government increases spending by $10 billion, could total GDP increase by more than $10 billion?
5. If a country stops buying our exports, could that drop in exports lead to a recession?

The Simplest Keynesian Cross

Let's begin with the simplest model of how demand determines output in the short run. The simplest model is a graph with the demand for goods and services represented on the vertical axis, output (y) represented on the horizontal axis, and a 45° diagonal line, as shown in Figure 10.1, representing a key relationship between demand and output. From any point on that 45° diagonal line, the distance leftward over to the vertical axis is equal to the distance downward to the horizontal axis. That's simple graphical math: From any point on the diagonal, the vertical distance and horizontal distance measured to the axes are equal—a key fact that you must understand and remember as we proceed.

Understanding what the diagonal represents, we can start to build a simple demand-side model. Let's start by assuming that neither the government nor the foreign sectors exist. Only consumers and firms can demand output: Consumers demand consumption goods, and firms demand investment goods. We make things even simpler, assuming that consumers and firms each demand a fixed amount of goods. Let consumption demand be an amount C and let investment demand be an amount I. Total demand will be $C + I$.

In the short run, demand determines output:

$$\text{output} = \text{demand}$$

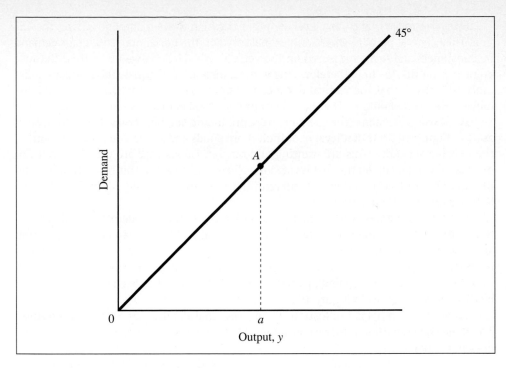

Figure 10.1
The 45° Line
Any point on the 45° line corresponds to the same vertical and horizontal distances. The distance 0a equals the distance Aa.

In this case,

$$\text{output} = \text{demand} = C + I$$

Figure 10.2 can help us to understand how output—the level of real GDP—is determined. On the demand-output diagram, we superimpose the line representing demand, $C + I$, which is a horizontal line, because both C and I are fixed amounts. Because total demand is fixed at $C + I$, it does not depend on output.

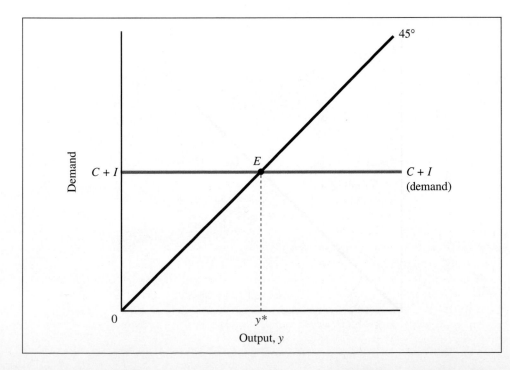

Figure 10.2
The Keynesian Cross
At equilibrium output y^*, total demand Ey^* equals output $0y^*$.

Equilibrium output: The level of GDP at which the amount of demand for output equals the amount that is produced.

Equilibrium output is at y^*, the level of output at which the demand line crosses the 45° line. They cross at point E, where output measured on the horizontal axis equals demand by consumers and firms measured on the vertical axis. How do we know this? Because point E is on the 45° line; therefore, the vertical distance Ey^* equals the horizontal distance $0y^*$. Recall that the vertical distance is total demand and that the horizontal distance is the level of output. Therefore, at output y^*, total demand equals output.

What would happen if the economy were producing at a higher level of output, such as y_1 in Figure 10.3? At that level of output, more goods and services are being produced than consumers and firms are wanting and buying. Goods that are produced but not purchased will pile up on the shelves of stores. Firms will react to this by cutting back on production. The level of output will fall until the economy reaches y^*, as indicated by the leftward arrow in Figure 10.3.

If the economy were producing at a lower level of output, y_2, demand would exceed total output. When demand exceeds output, firms find that the demand for consumption and investment goods is greater than their current production. Inventories disappear from the shelves of stores, and firms face increasing backlogs of orders for their products. Firms respond by stepping up production, so GDP increases back to y^*, as indicated by the rightward arrow in Figure 10.3.

Table 10.1 also helps to illustrate the process that determines equilibrium output. The table shows, with a numerical example, what happens to production when demand does not equal output.

Demand (consumption plus investment) equals 100 billion dollars. In the first row, we see that if current production is only 80 billion, stocks of inventories will be depleted by 20 billion, so firms will increase output to restore their inventory levels. In the second row, production is at 120 billion, creating an excess of inventories of 20 billion, and firms will cut back production. In the last row, demand equals output: Neither inventories nor production changes.

Be sure you remember that in the short run, the equilibrium level of output occurs where total demand equals production. If the economy were not producing at that level,

Figure 10.3
Equilibrium Output
Equilibrium output (y^*) is determined at E, where demand intersects the 45° line. If output were higher (y_1), it would exceed demand and production would fall. If output were lower (y_2), it would fall short of demand and production would rise.

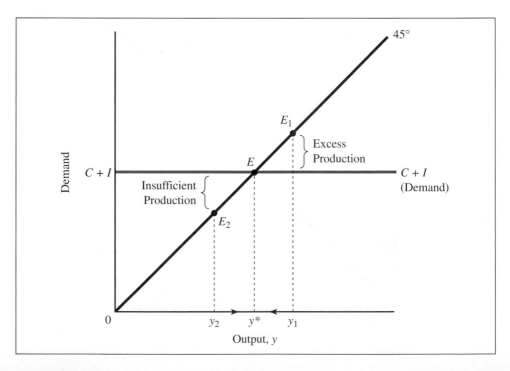

Table 10.1 Adjustments to Equilibrium Output

$C + I$	Production	Inventories	Direction of Output
100	80	Depletion of inventories of 20	Output increases
100	120	Excess of inventories of 20	Output decreases
100	100	No change	Output stays constant

we would find either that the demand for goods was too great relative to production or that there was insufficient demand relative to production. In either case, the economy would rapidly adjust to reach the equilibrium level of output.

The Consumption Function and the Multiplier

Consumer Spending and Income

We now start to make our model more realistic. Economists have found that consumer spending depends on the level of income in the economy. When consumers have more income, they want to purchase more goods and services. The relationship between consumer spending and income is known as the **consumption function:**

$$C = C_a + by$$

where consumption spending C has two parts. The first part, C_a, is a constant and is independent of income. This means that much of consumption spending does not depend on the level of income. For example, all consumers, regardless of their current income, will have to purchase some food. Economists call this **autonomous consumption spending.** The second part, by, represents the part of consumption that is dependent on income. It is the product of a fraction b, called the **marginal propensity to consume [MPC]**, and the level of income y in the economy. The MPC (or b in our formula) tells us how much consumption spending will increase for every dollar that income increases. For example, if $b = 0.6$, then for every \$1 that income increases, consumption increases by \$0.60.

In our simple economy, output (or real GDP) is also equal to the income that flows to the households. As firms produce output, it is paid to the households as income (wages, interest, profits, and rents). We can therefore use the symbol y to represent both output and income.

We plot a consumption function in Figure 10.4. The consumption function is a line that intersects the vertical axis at C_a, the level of autonomous consumption spending; autonomous consumption must be greater than zero, so the line does not pass through the zero point on the origin. Its slope equals b, the marginal propensity to consume. Although output is plotted on the horizontal axis, remember that it is also equal to income, so income rises dollar for dollar with output. That is why we can plot the consumption function (which depends on income) on the same graph that determines output.

The marginal propensity to consume (the slope of the line) is always less than one. A consumer who receives a dollar of income will spend part of it and save the rest. The fraction that the consumer spends is given by his or her MPC. The fraction that the consumer saves is determined by his or her **marginal propensity to save [MPS].** The sum of the marginal propensity to consume and the marginal propensity to save is always equal to one. For example, if the MPC is 0.8, then the MPS must be 0.2. When a consumer receives an additional dollar, he or she spends \$0.80 and saves the remaining \$0.20.

Consumption function: The relationship between the level of income and consumption spending.

Autonomous consumption spending: The part of consumption that does not depend on income.

Marginal propensity to consume [MPC]: The fraction of additional income that is spent.

Marginal propensity to save [MPS]: The fraction of additional income that is saved.

Figure 10.4
**Consumption
Function**
The consumption function
relates desired consumer
spending to the level of
income.

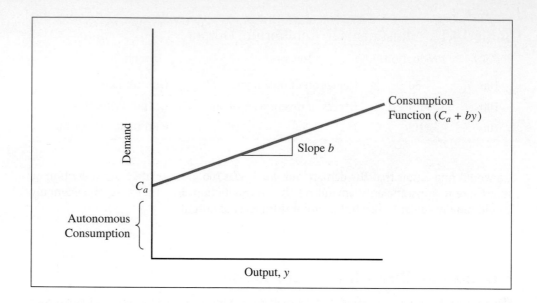

Changes in the Consumption Function

The consumption function is determined by the level of autonomous consumption and by the MPC. The level of autonomous consumption can change, and so can the MPC. Changes in either shift the consumption function to another position on the graph. A higher level of autonomous consumption but no change in MPC will shift the entire consumption function upward and parallel to its original position. Why it shifts upward should be clear: because increased autonomous consumption is represented as a higher intercept on the vertical axis. We show an increase in autonomous consumption in panel A of Figure 10.5.

A number of factors can cause autonomous consumption to change. Here are two:

- Increases in consumer wealth will cause an increase in autonomous consumption. (Wealth consists of the value of stocks, bonds, and consumer durables—consumer goods that last a long time, such as automobiles and refrigerators. Wealth is not the same as income; income is the amount of money earned during a period, such as in a given year.) Nobel laureate Franco Modigliani has emphasized that increases in

Figure 10.5

**Movements of the
Consumption
Function**

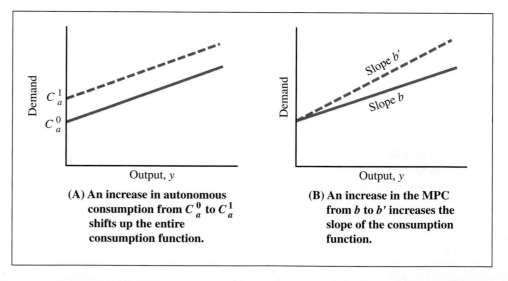

(A) An increase in autonomous
consumption from C_a^0 to C_a^1
shifts up the entire
consumption function.

(B) An increase in the MPC
from b to b' increases the
slope of the consumption
function.

stock prices, which raise consumer wealth, will lead to increases in autonomous consumption. Conversely, a sharp fall in stock prices would lead to a decrease in autonomous consumption.

- Changes in consumer confidence will shift the consumption function. Increases in consumer confidence will increase autonomous consumption. Forecasters pay attention to consumer confidence, based on household surveys; consumer confidence is reported regularly in the financial press.

A change in the marginal propensity to consume will cause a change in the slope of the consumption function. We show an increase in the MPC in panel B of Figure 10.5, where we assume that autonomous consumption is fixed. As the MPC increases, the consumption function rotates upward, counterclockwise; that means that the consumption function line gets steeper.

Several factors can change the MPC. Here are two:

- Consumers' perceptions of changes in their income affect their MPC. If consumers believe that an increase in their income is permanent, they will consume a higher proportion of the increased income than they would if they believed the increase was temporary. As an example, consumers will spend a higher proportion of a permanent salary increase than they would spend of a one-time bonus. Similarly, studies have shown that consumers save—not spend—a high proportion of one-time windfall gains, such as lottery winnings.

- Changes in tax rates change the slope of the consumption function, as we will see later in this chapter.

Determining GDP

Using the consumption function, we are now ready to show how real GDP is determined. We assume that GDP is ultimately determined by demand (as before). We continue to assume that investment spending, I, is a constant with respect to changes in income. The only difference between what we did in the preceding section and what we are about to do here is that we now recognize that consumption increases with the level of income.

Figure 10.6 shows how GDP is determined. We first plot the consumption function, C, as before: a sloping line graphically representing that consumption spending is a function of income. Because we are assuming that investment is constant at all levels of income, to graphically get the $C + I$ line, we can simply add vertically the constant level of investment I to the consumption function. Doing this gives us the $C + I$ line, representing total spending in the economy. This line is upward sloping because consumption spending increases with income. At any level of income, we now know the level of total spending, $C + I$.

The level of equilibrium output, y^*, occurs where the spending line $C + I$ crosses the 45° diagonal line. At this level of output, total spending equals output. At any other level of production, spending will not equal output and the economy will adjust back to y^*, for the same reasons and in the same way as in the corresponding example in the preceding section.

In the appendix to this chapter, we show that the equilibrium output in this simple economy is

equilibrium output = (autonomous consumption + investment)/(1 − MPC)

or, in the mathematical terms representing those words,

$$y^* = (C_a + I)/(1 - b)$$

Figure 10.6
Determining GDP
GDP is determined where the $C + I$ line intersects the 45°
line. At that level of output,
y^*, desired spending equals
output.

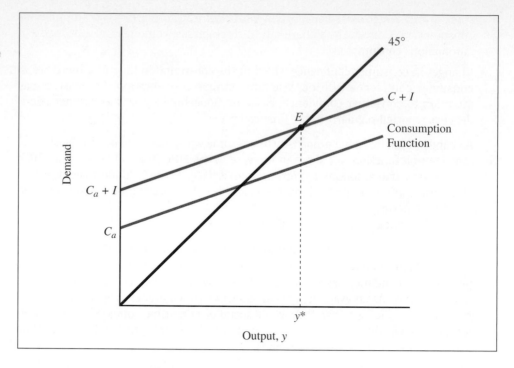

From this relationship and the numerical values for C_a, b, and I, we can calculate
equilibrium output. Suppose that

$$C_a = 100$$
$$b = 0.6$$
$$I = 40$$

(This means that the consumption function is $C = 100 + 0.6y$.) Then, using our formula
for equilibrium output, we have

$$y^* = (100 + 40)/(1 - 0.6)$$
$$= 140/0.4$$
$$= 350$$

Savings and Investment

Equilibrium output can be determined in another way, which highlights the relationship between savings and investment. To understand this relationship, recall that in an
economy without taxation or government, the value of output, or production (y), equals
the value of income. Households receive this income and either consume it (C), save it
(S), or some of both. Realizing that, we can say that savings equals output minus consumption or, in mathematical terms,

$$S = y - C$$

In our simple economy, output is determined by demand, $C + I$, or

$$y = C + I$$

If we subtract consumption from both sides of this equation, we have

$$y - C = I$$

But we just saw that the left side, $y - C$, equals savings, S, so we have

$$S = I$$

Thus, equilibrium output is determined at the level of income where savings equal investment.

The level of savings in the economy is not fixed; it changes, and how it changes depends on the real GDP. To illustrate this, let's return to the previous example in which the consumption function is $C = 100 + 0.6y$. Because $S = y - C$, savings is

$$S = y - (100 + 0.6y)$$
$$S = -100 + 0.4y$$

This is the savings function for this example. A **savings function** describes the relationship between savings and income. In this example's savings function, the marginal propensity to save is 0.4. That means that for every dollar y increases, savings increase by $0.40.

In our previous example, investment $I = 40$, and equilibrium income was 350. Let's check that savings does equal that level of investment. Plugging in the value of equilibrium output (or income) into the savings function, we get

$$S = -100 + 0.4(350)$$
$$S = -100 + 140$$
$$S = 40$$

So savings equals investment at the level of equilibrium output.

Savings function: The relationship between the level of income and the level of savings.

TEST Your Understanding

1. Explain why equilibrium output occurs where the demand line crosses the 45° line.

2. What happens if the level of output exceeds demand?

3. What is the slope of the consumption function called?

4. Complete the statement with *upward* or *downward*. An increase in autonomous consumption will shift the consumption function _____.

5. In our simple model, if $C = 100 + 0.8y$ and $I = 50$, equilibrium output will be

_____.

6. If the MPC is 0.7, the marginal propensity to save must be _____.

The Multiplier

In all economies, investment spending fluctuates. We can use the model we developed that determines output in the short run to see what happens if there are changes in investment spending. Suppose investment spending originally was I_0 and increased to I_1, an increase that we will call ΔI (the symbol Δ, the Greek capital letter delta, is universally used to represent change). What happens to equilibrium output?

Figure 10.7 shows how equilibrium output is determined at the original level of investment and at the new level of investment. The increase in investment spending shifts the $C + I$ curve upward by ΔI. The intersection of the $C + I$ curve with the 45° line shifts from E_0 to E_1. GDP increases from y_0 to y_1 by the amount Δy.

The figure shows that the increase in GDP—that is, the amount Δy—is greater than the increase in investment—the amount ΔI—or $\Delta y > \Delta I$.

This is a general result; the increase in output always exceeds the increase in investment. The increase in output divided by the increase in investment is called the **multiplier**

Multiplier: The ratio of changes in output to changes in spending. It measures the degree to which changes in spending are "multiplied" into changes in output.

Figure 10.7

Multiplier

When investment increases by ΔI from I_0 to I_1, equilibrium output increases by Δy from y_0 to y_1. The change in output (Δy) is greater than the change in investment (ΔI).

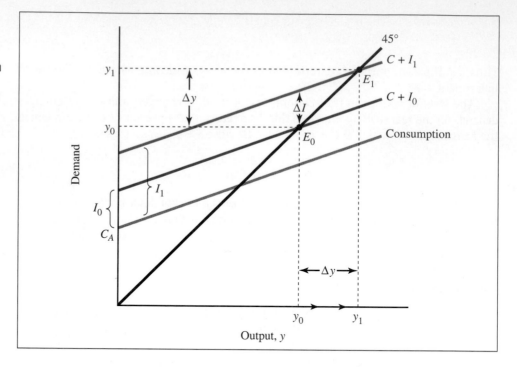

for investment. Because output increases more than the initial increase in investment, the multiplier is greater than 1.

The basic idea of how the multiplier works in an economy is simple. Let's say that a computer firm invests $10 million in building a new plant. Initially, total spending in the economy increases by this $10 million paid to a construction firm. The construction workers and owners of the construction firm then spend part of the income they are paid. Suppose the owners and workers spend $8 million on new automobiles. Producers of these automobiles will expand their production because of the increase indicated by this demand. In turn, workers and owners in the automobile industry will earn an additional $8 million in wages and profits. They, in turn, will spend part of this additional income, let's say $6.4 million, on televisions and other goods and services. And the workers in the production of the televisions and those other goods and services will earn additional income, and so on, and so on.

Table 10.2 shows how the multiplier works in detail. In the first round, there is an initial increase of investment spending of $10 million. This additional demand leads to an initial increase in GDP and income of $10 million. Assuming that the MPC is 0.8, the $10 million of additional income will increase consumer spending by $8 million. Round 2 begins with this $8 million increase in consumer spending. Because of this increase in demand, GDP and income increase by $8 million. At the end of round 2, consumers will have an additional $8 million; with a MPC of 0.8, consumer spending will therefore increase by 0.8 × $8 million, or $6.4 million. The process continues in round 3 with an increase in consumer spending of $6.4 million. It continues, in diminishing amounts, through subsequent rounds. If we add up the spending in all the (infinite) rounds, we will find that the initial $10 million of spending leads to a $50 million increase in GDP and income. In this case, the multiplier is 5.

The multiplier also works in reverse. Suppose that consumers become pessimistic, cutting back on autonomous consumption by $10 million. Demand for GDP falls by $10 million, which means that output and income fall by $10 million. Consumers then cut back their spending further because their incomes have fallen. What happens is the

Table 10.2   The Multiplier in Action

Round of Spending	Increase in Demand	Increase in GDP and Income	Increase in Consumption
1	$10	$10	$8
2	8	8	6.4
3	6.4	6.4	5.12
4	5.12	5.12	4.096
5	4.096	4.096	3.277
$\vdots$	$\vdots$	$\vdots$	$\vdots$
Total	50 million	50 million	40 million

Note: All figures for increases indicate millions of dollars.

reverse of what we just described for the multiplier working in the positive direction. If the MPC were 0.8, total spending would fall by $50 million.

We show how to derive the formula for a simple multiplier in the appendix to this chapter:

$$\text{multiplier} = 1/(1 - \text{MPC})$$

Suppose the MPC = 0.8; then the multiplier would be $1/(1 - 0.8)$, or 5.

Notice that the multiplier increases as the MPC increases. If MPC = 0.4, the multiplier = 1.67; if the MPC = 0.6, the multiplier = 2.5. To see why the multiplier increases as the marginal propensity to consume MPC increases, think back to our examples of the multiplier. The multiplier occurs because the initial increase in investment spending increases income, which leads to higher consumer spending. With a higher MPC, the increase in consumer spending will be greater, since consumers will spend a higher fraction of the additional income they receive as the multiplier increases. With this extra spending, the eventual increase in output will be greater, and therefore so will the multiplier.

Government Spending and Taxation

Keynesian Fiscal Policy

We now make our model more realistic, bringing in government spending and taxation, therefore making the model useful for understanding economic policy debates. In those debates, we often hear recommendations for increasing government spending to increase GDP or cutting taxes to increase GDP. As we will explain, both the level of government spending and the level of taxation, through their influence on the demand for goods and services, affect the level of GDP in the short run.

Using taxes and spending to influence the level of GDP in the short run is known as **Keynesian fiscal policy**. As we discussed in Chapter 7, changes in taxes can also affect the supply of output in the long run through the way taxes can change incentives to work or invest. However, in this chapter, we concentrate on the role of taxes and spending in determining demand for goods and services and, hence, output, in the short run.

Keynesian fiscal policy: The use of taxes and government spending to affect the level of GDP in the short run.

Let's look first at the role government spending plays in determining GDP. Government purchases of goods and services are a component of spending:

Total spending including government = $C + I + G$

Increases in government purchases, G, shift the $C + I + G$ line upward, just as increases in investment I or autonomous consumption do. If government spending increases by $1, the $C + I + G$ line will shift upward by $1.

Panel A of Figure 10.8 shows how increases in government spending affect GDP. The increase in government spending from G_0 to G_1 shifts the $C + I + G$ line upward and increases the level of GDP from y_0 to y_1.

As you can see, changes in government purchases have exactly the same effects as changes in investment or changes in autonomous consumption. The multiplier for government spending is also the same as for changes in investment or autonomous consumption:

multiplier for government spending = $1/(1 - \text{MPC})$

For example, if the MPC were 0.6 and the multiplier were 2.5, a $10 billion increase in government spending would increase GDP by $25 billion. The multiplier for government spending works just like the multiplier for investment or consumption. An initial increase in government spending raises GDP and income. The increase in income, however, generates further increases in demand as consumers increase their spending.

Now let's consider taxes. We need to take into account that government programs affect households' **disposable personal income**—income that ultimately flows back to households and to consumers after subtraction from their income of any taxes paid and after addition to their income of any transfer payments they receive (such as Social Security, unemployment insurance, or welfare). If the government takes $10 net out of every $100 you make, your income after taxes and transfer payments is only $90.

Here's how we include taxes and transfers into the model: We make consumption spending depend on income after taxes and transfers, or $y - T$, where T is net taxes (taxes paid to government minus transfers received by households). For simplicity, we'll just refer to T as taxes, but remember that it is taxes less transfer payments. The consumption function with taxes is

$$C = C_a + b(y - T)$$

Disposable personal income:
The income that flows back to households, taking into account transfers and taxes.

Figure 10.8
Keynesian Fiscal Policy

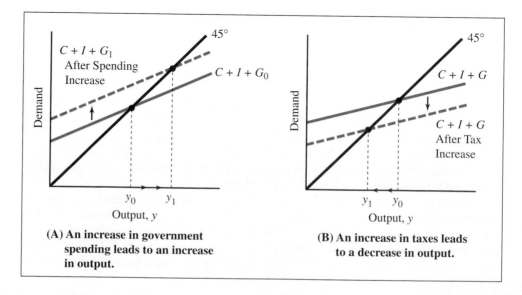

(A) An increase in government spending leads to an increase in output.

(B) An increase in taxes leads to a decrease in output.

If taxes increase by $1, after-tax income will decrease by $1. Since the marginal propensity to consume is b, this means that consumption will fall by $b \times \$1$, and the $C + I + G$ line will shift downward by $b \times \$1$. For example, if b is 0.6, a $1 increase in taxes will mean that consumers will have a dollar less of income and will therefore decrease consumption spending by $0.60.

Panel B of Figure 10.8 shows how an increase in taxes will decrease the level of GDP. As the level of taxes increases, the demand line will shift downward by b (the increase in taxes). Equilibrium income will fall from y_0 to y_1.

The multiplier for taxes is slightly different than the multiplier for government spending. If we cut government spending by $1, the $C + I + G$ will shift downward by $1. However, if we increase taxes by $1, consumers will cut back their consumption by only $b \times \$1$. Thus, the $C + I + G$ line will shift downward by slightly less than $1, or $b \times \$1$. For example, if $b = 0.6$, the demand line would shift down vertically only by $0.60.

Since the demand line does not shift by the same amount with taxes as it does with government spending, the formula for the tax multiplier is slightly different. Here's the formula for the tax multiplier; in the appendix, we show how to derive it:

$$\text{tax multiplier} = -b/(1 - b)$$

The tax multiplier is negative because increases in taxes decrease disposable personal income and lead to a reduction in consumption spending. If the MPC = 0.6, the tax multiplier will be $-0.6/(1 - 0.6) = -1.5$.

Notice that the tax multiplier is smaller (in absolute value) than the government-spending multiplier, which for the same MPC is 2.5. The reason the tax multiplier is smaller is that an increase in taxes first reduces income of households by the amount of the tax. However, because the MPC is less than 1, the decrease in consumer spending is less than the increase in taxes.

Finally, you may wonder what would happen if we increased both government spending and taxes by an equal amount at the same time. Because the multiplier for government spending is larger than the multiplier for taxes, equal increases in both government spending and taxes will increase GDP. Economists call the multiplier for equal increases in government spending and taxes *the balanced budget multiplier* because equal changes in government spending and taxes will not unbalance the budget. In the appendix, we show that the balanced budget multiplier in our simple model is always equal to 1. For example, if spending and taxes are both increased by $10 billion, then GDP will also increase by $10 billion.

Let's look at several examples of how we can use fiscal policy, altering taxes and government spending to affect GDP. In all these examples, suppose that GDP is $6,000 billion, the marginal propensity to consume is 0.6, the government-spending multiplier is $1/(1 - 0.6) = 2.5$, and the tax multiplier is $-0.6/(1 - 0.6) = -1.5$.

1. Suppose policymakers want to increase GDP by 1%, or $60 billion. By how much do policymakers have to increase government spending to meet this target? Since the multiplier for government spending is 2.5, we need to increase government spending by only $24 billion. With a multiplier of 2.5, the $24 billion increase in government spending leads to an increase in GDP of $60 billion ($24 billion $\times$ 2.5 = $60 billion).

2. Suppose policymakers wanted to use tax cuts rather than government spending increases to increase GDP by $60 billion. How large a tax cut would be necessary? Since the tax multiplier is -1.5, we need to cut taxes by $40 billion. The $40 billion tax cut times the multiplier will lead to the objective, a $60 billion increase in GDP ($-\$40$ billion $\times -1.5 = \$60$ billion).

3. Finally, if policymakers wanted to change taxes and government spending by equal amounts, so as to not affect the federal budget, how large a change would be needed to increase GDP by $60 billion? Since the balanced budget multiplier is 1, both government spending and taxes must be increased by $60 billion.

The models that we are using are very simple and leave out important factors. Nonetheless, the same basic principles apply in real situations. Here are five examples of real Keynesian fiscal policy from recent times.

1. In 1993, the three members of the President's Council of Economic Advisers wrote a letter to President Clinton stating that they thought the cuts in government spending being proposed at the time were $20 billion too large. The economic model the council members used had a multiplier for government spending of approximately 1.5. With this multiplier, the decrease in GDP from the $20 billion spending cut would be ($20 billion × 1.5) = $30 billion. This was approximately 0.5% of GDP. If, in the absence of these cuts, GDP was expected to grow at 3% a year, the President's advisers estimated that with these cuts, GDP would grow at only 2.5% a year. However, the advice of the council members came too late to influence the policy decisions.

2. During 1994, the U.S. government urged the Japanese to increase Japanese public spending and cut taxes to stimulate their economy. The Japanese came up with a plan and presented it to U.S. policymakers. U.S. policymakers evaluated the effects of this plan by using multiplier analysis. The United States thought that this plan did not provide enough fiscal stimulus and urged the Japanese to take more aggressive actions. Several years later, the Japanese did adopt a more aggressive plan.

3. During the late 1990s, the Chinese economy came under pressure from the economic downturn in Asia and its own attempts to reform and restructure the economy. To prevent a severe economic slowdown, the Chinese engaged in active Keynesian fiscal policy. The government decided to increase its spending on domestic infrastructure, including roads, rails, and urban facilities.

4. In 2001, President George W. Bush led the effort for a tax cut that would be phased in over 10 years. In the first year, however, all taxpayers would receive a onetime cut of up to a maximum of $600. This was designed to provide direct stimulus to a sluggish economy.

5. After the September 11, 2001 terrorist attack, the government increased spending for disaster relief in New York and provided subsidies and loan guarantees to the airlines. In addition, President George W. Bush and the Congress immediately began to work on additional spending programs and tax relief programs to stimulate the economy.

Not all fiscal policy experiments are successful, as "A Closer Look: The Chinese Vacation Experiment" explains.

We use special terminology to describe government actions taken to effect changes in the economy. Government policies that increase total demand and GDP are called **expansionary policies.** Government policies that decrease total demand and GDP are **contractionary policies.** Tax cuts and government spending increases are examples of expansionary policies. Tax increases and government spending cuts are examples of contractionary policies.

When a government increases its spending or cuts taxes to stimulate the economy, it will increase the government's **budget deficit;** the difference between its spending and its tax collections. For example, suppose the budget were initially balanced (government spending equaled taxes received) and the government increased its spending. The government would then be running a budget deficit—government spending exceeding tax-

Expansionary policies:
Government policy actions that lead to increases in output.

Contractionary policies:
Government policy actions that lead to decreases in output.

Budget deficit: The difference between a government's spending and its revenues from taxation.

THE CHINESE VACATION EXPERIMENT

In order to stimulate consumer spending, the Chinese government embarked on an unusual strategy in 2000. Historically, the Chinese had one week of annual vacation. The Chinese government decided to encourage consumer spending by mandating three, one-week holidays throughout the year. Their idea was that these long and extended vacations would induce Chinese consumers to spend more of their earnings as they fled their jobs and went on vacations.

Did this policy work? Chinese consumers did increase their spending during the long vacations.

However, consumption fell before and after the vacations so that it appears that there were no long-lasting effects. It appears that the increase in consumer spending was just temporary and displaced spending at other times of the year. This is consistent with a Keynesian consumption function: Total consumption did not change because income did not change.

Source: Peter Wonacott, "A Nice Long Vacation May Not Cure What Ails China," *Wall Street Journal*, January 25, 2001, p. A16.

ation. To pay for its additional spending, the government would have to borrow money by selling government bonds, which are government IOUs, to the public. Traditional Keynesian models assume that this borrowing has no significant effects on the economy.

Although Keynesian models are very simple and leave out many factors, like all models, they illustrate some important lessons:

- An increase in government spending will increase the total demand for goods and services.

- Cutting taxes will increase the after-tax income of consumers and will also lead to an increase in the total demand for goods and services.

In the short run, the level of GDP is determined primarily by the demand for goods and services.

TEST Your Understanding

7. If the MPC is 0.4, what is the government spending multiplier?

8. Using taxes and government spending to control the level of GDP in the short run is known as Keynesian _____ policy.

9. An increase in government spending of $10 billion will shift the $C + I + G$ line upward by _____ and increase GDP by this amount times the government spending multiplier.

10. If the MPC is 0.8, by how much will GDP decrease if taxes are increased by $10 billion?

11. If economic advisers fear that the economy is growing too rapidly, what fiscal policies should they recommend?

Keynesian Fiscal Policy in U.S. History

The elements of Keynes theory were developed in the 1930s, but it took a long time before economic policy decisions were based on Keynesian principles. Many people associate Keynesian fiscal policy in the United States with actions taken by President Franklin Roosevelt during the 1930s. But this is a misleading view. During the 1930s, politicians did not believe in Keynesian fiscal policy, largely because they feared the consequences of government budget deficits. According to E. Cary Brown, an economist from M.I.T., fiscal policy was only mildly expansionary during the 1930s, only during two years, and only because of bonus payments made to veterans. On balance, active fiscal policy was not tried during the Great Depression.

Although Keynesian fiscal policy was not deliberately used during the 1930s, the growth in military spending at the onset of World War II increased total demand in the economy and helped to pull the economy out of its long decade of poor performance. But to see Keynesian fiscal policy in action, we need to turn to the 1960s. It was not until the presidency of John F. Kennedy during the early 1960s that Keynesian fiscal policy came to be accepted.

Walter Heller, the chairman of the President's Council of Economic Advisors under John F. Kennedy, was a forceful advocate of Keynesian economics. From his perspective, the economy was operating far below its potential, and a tax cut was the perfect medicine to bring the economy back to full employment. When Kennedy entered office, the unemployment rate was 6.7%. Heller believed that the unemployment rate at full employment was approximately 4%. He convinced Kennedy of the need for a tax program to stimulate the economy, and Kennedy put forth an economic program that was based largely on Keynesian principles.

Two other factors led the Kennedy administration to support the tax cut: First, tax rates were extremely high at the time. The top individual tax rate was 91%, compared to about 40% today. The corporate tax rate was 52%, compared to 35% today. Second, Heller convinced Kennedy that even if a tax cut led to a federal budget deficit (the gap between federal spending and taxes), it was not a problem. In 1961, the federal deficit was less than 1% of GDP, and future projections indicated that the deficit would disappear as the economy grew because of higher tax revenues.

The tax cuts were enacted into law in February 1964, after Lyndon Johnson became President following Kennedy's assassination. The tax cuts included permanent cuts in tax rates for both individuals and corporations. Estimating the actual effects that the tax cuts had on the economy is difficult; to have a valid comparison, we need to estimate how the economy would have behaved without the tax cuts. However, the economy grew at a rapid rate following the tax cuts. From 1963 to 1966, both real GDP and consumption grew at rates exceeding 4%. We cannot rule out the possibility that the economy could have grown this rapidly without the tax cuts. Nonetheless, the rapid growth during this period suggests that the tax cuts had the effect, predicted by Keynesian theory, of stimulating economic growth. (Some economists would argue that supply-side factors, such as lower marginal tax rates, could also have stimulated growth.)

The next major use of Keynesian theory in economic policy occurred in 1968. As the Vietnam War began and military spending increased, unemployment fell to very low levels. From 1966 to 1969, the overall unemployment rate fell below 4%. Policymakers became concerned that the economy was overheating and that this would lead to a higher inflation rate for the economy. In 1968, a temporary tax surcharge of 10% was enacted to reduce total demand for goods and services. The 10% surcharge was a tax on a tax, so it raised the taxes paid by households by 10%. The surcharge was specifically designed to be temporary and was scheduled to expire within a year.

The surcharge did not decrease consumer spending as much as economists had initially estimated. Part of the reason was that the tax increase was temporary. Economists who have studied consumption behavior have noticed that consumers often base their spending on an estimate of their long-run average income or **permanent income**, not on their current income.

Permanent income: An estimate of a household's long-run average level of income.

For example, consider a salesman who usually earns $50,000 a year, although his income in any single year might be higher or lower than $50,000. On the basis of his

President George W. Bush signed a major tax cut into law in 2001.

permanent income, he consumes $45,000, for an MPC of 0.9 of his permanent income. If his income in one year is higher than average, say $55,000, he may still consume $45,000, as if he earned his normal $50,000, and save the rest.

The temporary, one-year tax surcharge did not have a major effect on the permanent income of households. Because their permanent income was not decreased very much by the tax surcharge, households that based their consumption decisions on their permanent income would be expected to maintain their prior level of consumption. Instead of reducing consumption, they would simply reduce their saving for the period that the surcharge was in effect. It appears that this is what consumers did, resulting in a smaller decrease in demand for goods and services than economists anticipated.

During the 1970s, there were many changes in taxes and spending but no major changes in overall fiscal policy. There was a tax rebate and other tax incentives in 1975 following the recession in 1973. However, these tax changes were mild.

The tax cuts enacted during 1981 at the beginning of the first term of President Ronald Reagan were significant. However, they were not proposed on Keynesian grounds, to increase aggregate demand. Instead, the tax cuts were justified on the basis of improving economic incentives and increasing the supply of output. As we discussed in Chapter 7, taxes can have important effects on the supply of labor, saving, and economic growth. Proponents of the 1981 tax cuts emphasized these effects and not increases in aggregate demand. Nonetheless, the tax cuts did appear to increase consumer demand and helped the economy recover from the back-to-back recessions in the early 1980s.

By the mid-1980s, large government budget deficits began to emerge. Policymakers became concerned with those growing budget deficits. As deficits grew and became the focus of attention, there was no longer interest in using Keynesian fiscal policy to manage the economy. While there were government spending and tax changes in the 1980s and the early 1990s, few of them were justified solely by Keynesian thinking.

At the beginning of his administration, President Bill Clinton proposed a "stimulus package," but it was defeated in Congress. He later successfully passed a major tax increase to bring the budget into balance. By the year 2000, the federal budget began to show surpluses rather than deficits, setting the stage for tax cuts. During his first year in office, President George W. Bush passed a 10-year tax cut plan that decreased marginal tax rates. Although the justification for his plan was largely based on improved incentives from lower tax rates, the first year of the tax cut featured tax refunds of up to $600 per married couple. The justification for the refunds was purely Keynesian—they were designed to give a slowing economy a boost.

After the September 11, 2001 terrorist attack, the focus of fiscal policy began to change again. The President and the Congress became less concerned with balancing the federal budget in a period of economic distress and immediately authorized new spending programs to provide relief to victims of the economy, to ensure the solvency of the airlines, and to stimulate the economy. Most of the subsequent discussions about proposed increases in spending and decreases in taxes were framed in Keynesian terms: Which policies and actions would be the most effective in providing the needed stimulus to the economy?

Automatic Stabilizers

With a slight addition to our basic model, we can explain one of the important facts in U.S. economic history. Figure 10.9 plots the rate of growth of U.S. real GDP from 1871 to 2000. It is apparent from the graph that the U.S. economy has been much more stable after World War II than before. The reason is that government taxes and transfer payments (such as unemployment insurance and welfare payments) grew sharply after the war. These taxes and transfer payments can automatically reduce fluctuations in real GDP and thereby stabilize the economy. We say that taxes and transfers act as **automatic stabilizers** for the economy.

Automatic stabilizers: Taxes and transfer payments that stabilize GDP without requiring policymakers to take explicit actions.

Here is how the automatic stabilizers work. When income is high, the government collects more taxes and pays out less in transfer payments. Because the government is taking funds out of the hands of consumers, there will be reduced consumer spending. On the other hand, when output is low (such as during recessions), the government collects less taxes and pays out more in transfer payments, increasing consumer spending because the government is putting funds into the hands of consumers. The automatic stabilizers prevent consumption from falling as much in bad times and from rising as much in good times. This stabilizes the economy without any need for decisions from Congress or the White House.

Figure 10.9
Growth Rate of U.S. GDP, 1871–2000

Source: Angus Maddison, *Dynamic Forces in Capitalist Development* (New York: Oxford University Press, 1991); Bureau of Economic Analysis, Department of Commerce.

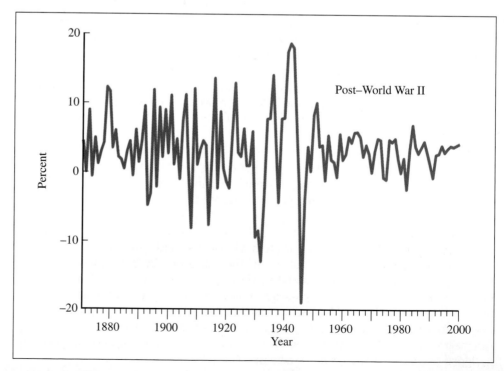

This Internal Revenue Service worker in Austin, Texas is an integral part of a process to stabilize the U.S. economy.

To see how automatic stabilizers work in our model, we must take into account that the government levies income taxes by applying a tax rate to the level of income. To simplify, suppose there were a single tax rate of 0.2 (in percent, 20%) and income were $100. The government would then collect $0.2 \times \$100 = \$20$ in taxes.

In general, we can view the total taxes collected by the government, T, as a product of the tax rate, t, and output, y:

$$T = ty$$

Consumer's after-tax income will be

$$(y - ty) = y(1 - t) = (1 - t)y$$

If consumption depends on after-tax income, we have the following consumption function:

$$C = C_a + b(1 - t)y$$

This is the consumption function with income taxes. The only difference between the consumption function with income taxes and the consumption function without income taxes is that the marginal propensity to consume is adjusted for taxes, and so

$$\text{Adjusted MPC} = b(1 - t)$$

The reason for this adjustment is that consumers keep only a fraction $(1 - t)$ of their income; the rest, t, goes to the government. When income increases by $1, consumers' after-tax incomes increase by only $\$1 \times (1 - t)$, and of that $\$(1 - t)$, they spend a fraction b.

Raising the tax rate therefore lowers the MPC adjusted for taxes. Figure 10.10 shows the consequences of raising tax rates. With a higher tax rate, the government takes a higher fraction of income, and less is left over for consumers. Recall that the slope of the $C + I + G$ line is the marginal propensity to consume. Raising the tax rate lowers the adjusted MPC and reduces the slope of this line. The $C + I + G$ line with taxes intersects the 45° line at a lower level of income. Output falls from y_0 to y_1.

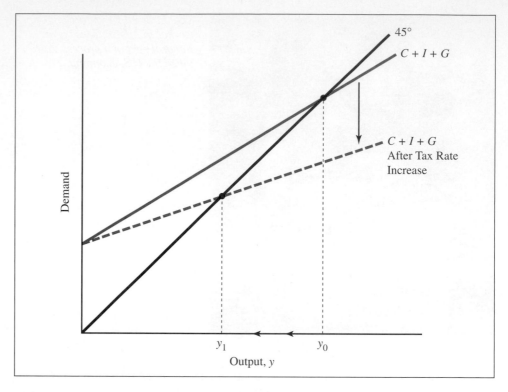

Remember that a smaller marginal propensity to consume also leads to a lower value for the multiplier. As tax rates increase and the adjusted MPC falls, the multiplier will decrease. A smaller multiplier means that any shocks, such as shocks to investment, will have less of an impact on the economy.

Now that we have introduced income taxes into our model, we can see how automatic stabilizers work. Since World War II, taxes and transfer payments in the United States have increased sharply. As we have seen, higher tax rates will lower the multiplier and make the economy less susceptible to shocks. With higher taxes and transfer payments, there is a much looser link between fluctuations in disposable personal income and fluctuations in GDP. Because disposable personal income is more stable, consumption spending is also more stable. Thus, there is a smaller multiplier, and the economy is more stable.

It is important to emphasize that automatic stabilizers work silently in the background, doing their job without requiring explicit action by policymakers. Total tax collections rise and fall with GDP without requiring that policymakers change tax rates. The fact that the automatic stabilizers work without any laws being enacted is particularly important at times when it is difficult to obtain a political consensus for taking any action and policymakers are reluctant to use Keynesian fiscal policy as a deliberate policy tool.

Other factors contribute to the stability of the economy. We explained how consumers base their spending decisions in part on their permanent income, not just on their current level of income. If households base their consumption decisions partly on their permanent or long-run income, they will not be very sensitive to changes in their current income. If their consumption does not change very much with current income, the marginal propensity to consume out of current income will be small, which will make the multiplier for investment or autonomous consumption spending small as well. When consumers base their decisions on long-run factors, not just on their current level of income, the economy tends to be stabilized.

Exports and Imports

With international trade becoming an increasingly important economic and political issue, it is critical to understand how exports and imports affect the level of GDP. Two simple modifications of our model will allow us to understand how exports and imports affect GDP in the short run.

Exports and imports affect GDP through their influence on how the world beyond the United States demands goods and services produced in the United States. An increase in exports means that there's an increase in the demand for goods produced in the United States. An increase in imports means that there's an increase in foreign goods purchased by U.S. residents. Importing goods rather than purchasing them from our domestic producers reduces the demand for U.S. goods. For example, if we in the United States spend a total of $10 billion on all automobiles but we imported $3 billion in automobiles, then only $7 billion is spent on U.S. automobiles.

To get a clearer picture of the effects on GDP from exports and imports, let's for the moment ignore government spending and taxes. In the appendix, we present a complete model with both government and foreign countries to whom we sell our exports and from whom we buy our imports. To modify our model to include the effects of exports and imports, we need to take two steps:

1. Add exports, X, to other sources of spending as another source of demand for U.S. goods and services. We assume that the level of exports (foreign demand for U.S. products) is given.

2. Subtract imports, M, from total spending by U.S. residents. We will assume that imports, like consumption, increase with the level of income.

Consumers will import more goods as income rises. We can write this as

$$\text{imports} = M = my$$

where m is a fraction known as the **marginal propensity to import**. We subtract this fraction from b, the overall marginal propensity to consume, to obtain the MPC for spending on domestic goods, $b - m$. For example, if $b = 0.8$ and $m = 0.2$, then for every $1 that GDP increases, total consumption increases by $0.80 but spending on domestic goods increases only by $0.60 because $0.20 is spent on imports. The MPC in this example, adjusted for imports is $(0.8 - 0.2) = 0.6$.

Figure 10.11 shows how equilibrium output is determined in an open economy, that is, an economy that engages in trade with the rest of the world. We plot total demand for U.S. goods and services on our graph and find the level of equilibrium income where it intersects the 45° line. The total demand line has an intercept on the vertical axis of $C_a + I + X$, which is the sum of autonomous consumption, investment, and exports. The slope of the line is $b - m$, which is the MPC adjusted for imports. Equilibrium output is the value of output where the demand line for U.S. goods crosses the 45° line.

Let's examine an application of the model that we just developed. Suppose the Japanese decide to buy another $5 billion worth of goods from the United States. What will happen to U.S. domestic output? Panel A of Figure 10.12 shows the effect of an increase in exports. The demand line will shift vertically upward by the increase in exports (ΔX). This will increase equilibrium income from y_0 to y_1.

The increase in income will be larger than the increase in exports because of the multiplier effect. This multiplier is based on the MPC adjusted for trade. For example, if $b = 0.8$ and $m = 0.2$, the adjusted MPC $(b - m)$ is 0.6 and the multiplier will be $1/(1 - 0.6) = 2.5$. Therefore, a $5 billion increase in exports will lead to a $12.5 billion increase in GDP.

Now, suppose that U.S. residents become more attracted to foreign goods, and as a result, our marginal propensity to import increases. What happens to GDP? Panel B of

Marginal propensity to import:
The fraction of additional income that is spent on imports.

Figure 10.11
**Determining Output
in an Open
Economy**
Output is determined where
the demand for domestic
goods equals output.

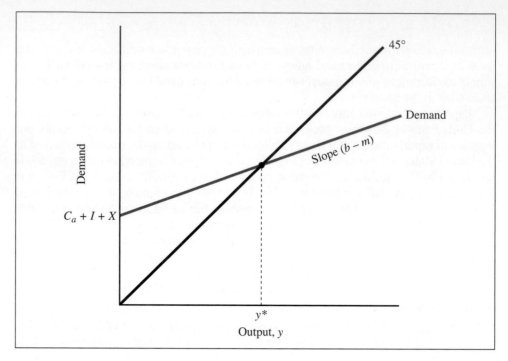

Figure 10.12 depicts the effect of an increase in imported foreign goods. The adjusted MPC $(b - m)$ will fall as the marginal propensity to import increases. This reduces the slope of the demand line, and output will fall from y_0 to y_1.

We can now understand why our domestic political leaders are eager to sell our goods abroad. Whether it is electronics or weapons, increased U.S. exports will increase U.S. GDP and reduce unemployment in the short run. At the same time, we can also understand why politicians will find "buy American" policies attractive in the short run. To the extent that U.S. residents buy U.S. goods rather than imports, output will be higher.

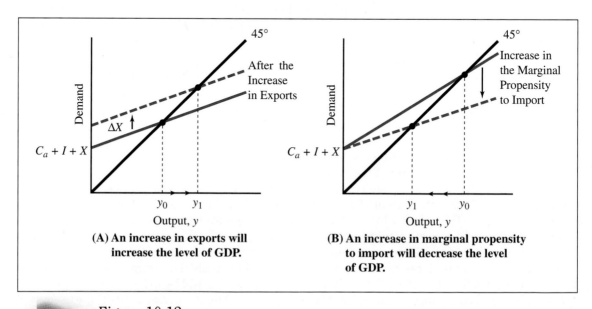

**(A) An increase in exports will
increase the level of GDP.**

**(B) An increase in marginal propensity
to import will decrease the level
of GDP.**

Figure 10.12
Increase in Exports and Imports

The Netherlands's Multiplier

Some economists have argued that the multiplier for government spending in the Netherlands is smaller than the multiplier for government spending in the United States. As an economic detective, can you explain this difference? (Hint: Imports and exports are a higher fraction of GDP in the Netherlands.)

The Netherlands is a small country and highly dependent on foreign trade. It has a high marginal propensity to import, which makes its adjusted MPC $(b - m)$ low. A low adjusted MPC will make the multiplier low as well. Thus, the multiplier for fiscal policy in the Netherlands is less than the fiscal policy multiplier for the United States because the Netherlands has a higher marginal propensity to import.

A Final Reminder

It is important to emphasize that all the models in this chapter are based on short-run considerations. Policies appropriate for the short run are not necessarily appropriate for the long run. In this chapter, we have seen that an increase in desired consumption spending will raise equilibrium output in the short run. But in our chapter on long-run growth, we saw that higher saving (lower consumption) would increase output in the long run. The models in this chapter are designed only to analyze short-run fluctuations in output. They are not designed for advising what should be long-run policy. In the next several chapters, we continue our study of short-run models by including interest rates and monetary policy as determinants of demand. Later, we will see how changes in wages and prices lead the economy from the short run to the long run.

Using the **TOOLS**

In this chapter, we developed the graphical tools and the mathematical formulas to analyze Keynesian economics. Here is an opportunity to do your own economic analysis.

1. ECONOMIC EXPERIMENT: Estimating the Marginal Propensity to Consume

For this experiment, each class member is asked to fill out the following table. Given a certain monthly income, how would you spend it and how much would you save? The top row of each column gives you the monthly disposable income. How would you allocate it each month among the various categories of spending in the table and savings? Complete each column in the table. The sum of your entries should equal your disposable income at the top of each column.

Monthly Disposable Income	$1,250	$1,500	$1,750	$2,000
Expenditures and Savings				
Food				
Housing				
Transportation				
Medical				
Entertainment				
Other expenses				
Savings				

After you have filled out the chart, compute the changes in your savings and total consumption as your income goes up. What is your marginal propensity to save (MPS)? What is your marginal propensity to consume (MPC) over your total expenditures? Graph your consumption function.

APPLICATIONS

2. Estimating Changes to Output

a. Suppose $C = C_a + 0.6y$; a shock decreases C_a by $10 billion. By how much will GDP decrease?

b. An economy has a MPC = 0.6. By how much will a $10 billion increase in government purchases increase GDP? By how much will a $10 billion increase in taxes decrease GDP?

3. The Paradox of Thrift

One implication of Keynesian models is that an increase in the desire of consumers to save more will not necessarily lead to higher savings. In fact, total savings will either remain the same or perhaps fall. Let's see why this is true with an example.

a. Suppose that $I = 40$ and the savings function is $S = -100 + 0.4y$. Equilibrium output, y, in the economy is 350. Now suppose consumers wish to increase their savings; the new savings function becomes $S = -80 + 0.4y$. Calculate the new level of equilibrium output and savings after the change in the savings function.

b. Explain why equilibrium output is unchanged.

c. Now suppose that with a decline in GDP, investment also falls. What would be the effect on equilibrium output and total savings if households now wished to increase their desired savings?

4. Tax Refunds and Consumer Spending

In 1999, the Internal Revenue Service began to mail out refund checks because of changes in the tax law in 1998. Economic forecasters predicted that consumption and GDP would increase because of higher refunds on income taxes. Evaluate the reasoning of these forecasters under the following different assumptions:

a. Taxpayers were not aware that they would receive refunds until they had completed their income tax statements.

b. Taxpayers did know that they would receive refunds but, as consumers, based their spending decisions solely on their current level of income.

c. Taxpayers did know that they would receive refunds and, as consumers, based their consumption decisions on their long-run permanent income.

 **Summary**

In this chapter, we explained the logic of Keynesian economics: The demand for goods and services determines GDP in the short run. We also discussed the role that government spending and taxes play in determining output. Finally, we showed how the level of exports and imports can affect the economy in the short run. Here are this chapter's main points:

1. The level of GDP in the short run is determined by the total demand for goods and services.

2. Consumption spending consists of two parts: One part is independent of income (autonomous consumption); the other part depends on the level of income.

3. An increase in spending will typically lead to a larger increase in GDP. This effect is called the multiplier.

4. In the short run, increases in government spending lead to increases in GDP; increases in taxes lead to decreases in GDP.

5. Keynesian fiscal policies were used aggressively in the 1960s to manage the economy. Concerns about budget deficits limit the use of these policies.

6. Higher tax rates reduce fluctuations in GDP caused by shocks to spending.

7. Increases in exports lead to increases in GDP; increases in imports lead to lower GDP.

Key Terms

automatic stabilizers, 216
autonomous consumption spending, 203
budget deficit, 212
consumption function, 203
contractionary policies, 212

disposable personal income, 210
equilibrium output, 202
expansionary policies, 212
Keynesian fiscal policy, 209
marginal propensity to consume [MPC], 203

marginal propensity to import, 219
marginal propensity to save [MPS], 203
multiplier, 207
permanent income, 214
savings function, 207

Problems and Discussion Questions

1. Consider an economy in which $C = 200 + 0.5y$ and $I = 200$.
   a. Find equilibrium income.
   b. What is the multiplier for investment spending for this economy?
   c. What is the savings function?
   d. What is the level of savings at the level of equilibrium income?

2. A country wishes to increase its GDP by 100. The marginal propensity to consume is 0.8.
   a. Using the government spending multiplier, by how much should government spending be increased?
   b. Using the tax multiplier, by how much should taxes be decreased?

3. A country has a marginal propensity to consume of 0.6 and a tax rate of 0.15. How much of an increase in investment would be needed to raise GDP by 150?

4. In an open economy, the marginal propensity to consume is 0.9, and the marginal propensity to import is 0.3. How much of an increase in exports would be necessary to raise GDP by 200?

5. Explain why in the model in this chapter, a higher tax rate leads to a lower multiplier for the economy. Does that mean that raising the tax rate is good for the economy in the model in this chapter?

6. John Maynard Keynes once suggested that the reason the economy of ancient Egypt prospered was because the government had a systematic project of building pyramids.
   a. Explain the logic of Keynes' argument.
   b. What are the modern equivalent of pyramids?
   c. How would a classical economist respond to Keynes' argument?

7. a. Suppose clothing stores anticipate a good season and add substantially to inventories in their stores? What will happen to GDP?
   b. Suppose economists see inventories suddenly increasing. Does this necessarily mean that there are increases in demand?

8. Sometimes the newspapers state that if the economies of Europe and Japan grow rapidly, this will increase the growth of real GDP in the United States. Using our model with exports and imports, explain the logic of this argument.

9. During the 1970s, President Gerald Ford proposed that taxes be decreased but, to avoid increasing the government budget deficit, government spending should be decreased by the same amount. What happens to GDP if taxes and government spending are both decreased by the same amount?

10. Why could a collapse of the stock market lead to reduced consumer spending?

11. Using the idea of automatic stabilizers, explain why states with more generous unemployment insurance programs will experience smaller fluctuations in output.

12. **Web Exercise.** As we have seen in this chapter, changes in consumer spending can have powerful effects on the economy. While many factors, including income and wealth, affect consumer spending, general consumer confidence may also be a factor. For many years, the University of Michigan has published an index of consumer sentiment. Using the business/fiscal data on the Web site for the Federal Reserve Bank of St. Louis [*http://www.stls.frb.org/fred*], explore the relation-ships between changes in consumer sentiment and consumer spending for the periods preceding several postwar recessions.

13. **Web Exercise.** Although John Maynard Keynes is best known today for his book *The General Theory of Employment, Interest and Money*, he wrote several other books as well. Use the Web to find information about some of Keynes's other well-known books. You may want to start with the Web sites for "The London School" [*http://www.thefirmament.com/London*] or from *Time Magazine's* list of the most important people in the twentieth century [*http://www.pathfinder.com/time/time100*]. What were his other writings about?

Take It to the Net

We invite you to visit the O'Sullivan/Sheffrin page on the Prentice Hall Web site at: **http://www.prenhall.com/osullivan/** for additional World Wide Web exercises for this chapter.

Model Answers to Questions

Chapter-Opening Questions

1. Cutting taxes that consumers pay leads to higher consumer spending, which increases demand and, in the short run, increases output.

2. The U.S. economy is more stable today because of automatic stabilizers.

3. Increased consumer confidence can lead to higher consumer spending, which will lead to higher GDP in the short run.

4. An increase in government spending of $10 billion will lead to an increase of GDP of more than $10 billion because of the multiplier.

5. Because exports are a component of the demand for an economy's goods and services, a reduction in exports could cause a recession.

Test Your Understanding

1. At the point where the demand line crosses the 45° line, demand equals output.

2. If production exceeds demand, inventories will pile up and firms will cut production.

3. It is the MPC.

4. Upward.

5. 750.

6. 0.3.

7. The multiplier is 1.67.

8. Fiscal.

9. $10 billion.

10. GDP will decrease by $40 billion. (The tax multiplier is −4.)

11. Increase taxes or cut government spending.

Using the TOOLS

2. Estimating Changes to Output

   a. In this case, the multiplier is $1/(1 − 0.6) = 2.5$. Therefore, output will fall by $25 billion.

   b. With an MPC = 0.6, the multiplier is 2.5 $[1/(1 − 0.6)]$. An increase in government spending of $10 billion will lead to an increase in GDP of $25 billion. With an MPC = 0.6, the tax multiplier is −1.5. Thus GDP will fall by $15 billion from a $10 billion increase in taxes.

3. The Paradox of Thrift

   a. To find equilibrium output, set the savings function equal to investment or $−80 + 0.4y = 40$. Solving for equilibrium output, we find that $y = 300$. With $y = 300$, total savings will be $−80 + .4(300) = 40$.

b. The reason that total savings did not change is because the increase in desired savings (or decreased desired consumption) caused output and income to fall. Moreover, since investment did not change, ultimately total savings must equal investment.

c. If investment falls with a decline in GDP, then the decrease in GDP caused by an increase in the desire to save would also decrease investment. Since in equilibrium savings must equal investment, then total savings will fall—despite the increased desire of households to save more. The increase in desired savings now causes even a larger fall in GDP (because of the additional effect on investment) than in the previous case. As a result, total savings falls.

4. Tax Refunds and Consumer Spending

a. If the tax refunds were not expected and consumers base their spending on current income, then consumer spending should increase, increasing GDP.

b. The same would be true if they anticipated the refund but still based their spending on the current value of income (which was increased by the refund).

c. If they had anticipated the refund and also based their spending on their long-run income, there would be no change in consumption spending. In this case, the tax refund would not change their long-run income and thus would not change their spending decisions.

Formulas for Equilibrium Income and the Multiplier

In this appendix, we do three things:

- Derive a simple formula for calculating equilibrium output for the simplest economy in which there is no government spending nor taxes.

- Derive the multipliers for the economy without government.

- Derive equilibrium output with both government and the foreign sector.

To derive the formula for equilibrium output, we use simple algebra in the following steps:

1. We know that equilibrium output occurs where output equals demand, and we know that demand $= C + I$, therefore,

$$\text{output} = \text{demand, and demand} = C + I$$
$$\text{output} = C + I$$

2. Next, we substitute the symbol y for output; more important, we substitute for the consumption function, $C = (C_a + by)$:

$$y = (C_a + by) + I$$

3. Collect all terms in y on the left side of the equation:

$$y - by = C_a + I$$

4. Factor the left side:

$$y(1 - b) = C_b + I$$

5. Divide both sides by $(1 - b)$:

$$y^* = (C_a + I)/(1 - b)$$

where y^* means the equilibrium level of output.

This is the formula for equilibrium output in the text.

Now let's find the multiplier for investment in this simple economy. To do that, we use the formula we just derived and calculate the equilibrium income at one level of investment, which we call the original level, and then calculate the equilibrium income at some other level of investment, which we call the new level. (We will "calculate" in general terms, not in specific numerical quantities.) What we will get is a formula for the change in output that results from the changes in investment.

For the original level of investment at I_0, we have

$$y_0 = (C_a + I_0)/(1 - b)$$

For a new level of investment at I_1, we have

$$y_1 = (C_a + I_1)/(1 - b)$$

The change in output Δy is the difference between the two levels of output that occur at each level of investment:

$$\Delta y = y_1 - y_0$$

Substituting for the levels of output, we have

$$\Delta y = (C_a + I_1)/(1 - b) - (C_a + I_0)/(1 - b)$$

Because the denominator in both expressions is the same $(1 - b)$, we can put the numerators over that common denominator:

$$\Delta y = [(C_a + I_1) - (C_a + I_0)]/(1 - b)$$
$$\Delta y = (I_1 - I_0)/(1 - b)$$

Finally, because $(I_1 - I_0)$ is the change in investment, ΔI, we can write

$$\Delta y = \Delta I/(1 - b)$$

or

$$\Delta y/\Delta I = 1/(1 - b)$$

Therefore, because the multiplier is the ratio of the change in income to the change in investment spending, we have

$$\text{the multiplier} = \Delta y/\Delta I = I/(1 - b)$$

Here is another way to derive the formula for the multiplier. This way helps to illustrate its underlying logic. Suppose investment spending increases by $1. Because spending determines output, output will rise by $1. However, because consumption depends on income, consumption will increase by the marginal propensity to consume times the change in income. This means that as output rises by $1, consumption will increase by $(b \times \$1)$. Because spending determines output, this additional increase in consumer demand will cause output to rise further $(b \times \$1)$. But again, as output and income increase, consumption will increase by MPC times the change in income, which in this case will be $b \times (b \times \$1)$ or $b^2 \times \$1$. As we allow this process to continue, the total change in output will be

$$\Delta y = \$1 \times (\$1 \times b) \times (\$1 \times b^2) \times (\$1 \times b^3)\dots$$

or

$$\Delta y = \$1 \times (1 + b + b^2 + b^3 + \dots)$$

The term in parentheses is an infinite series whose value is equal to $1/(1 - b)$. Substituting this value for the infinite series, we have the expression for the multiplier:

$$\Delta y = \$1 \times 1/(1 - b)$$

Now we introduce government spending and taxes. Government spending is another determinant of demand, and consumption spending depends on after-tax income, so consumption equals $C_a + b(y - T)$. Following the same steps we used for equilibrium output without government, we do the same, but now with government:

$$\text{output} = \text{demand} = (C + I + G)$$
$$y = C_a + b(y - T) + I + G$$

We first collect all terms in y on the left and leave the other terms on the right:

$$y = by = C_a - bT + I + G$$

We then factor the left side:

$$y(1 - b) = C_a - bT + I + G$$

We then divide both sides by $(1 - b)$:

$$y^* = (C_a - bT + I + G)/(1 - b)$$

Using this formula and the method outlined above, we can find the multiplier for changes in government spending, taxes, and the multiplier for changes in taxes:

$$\text{government spending multiplier} = 1/1(1 - b)$$
$$\text{tax multiplier} = -b/(1 - b)$$

The multiplier for an increase in government spending is larger than the tax multiplier for a reduction in taxes in the same amount as an increase in government spending. Government spending increases total demand directly. Reductions in taxes first affect consumers' incomes. Because consumers will save a part of their income increase from the tax cut, not all of the tax cut is spent. Therefore, the tax multiplier is smaller (in absolute value) than the government spending multiplier.

As we explained in the text, because government spending has a larger multiplier than taxes, equal increases in government spending and taxes, called balanced budget increases, will increase total output. For equal dollar increases in both taxes and government spending, the positive effects from the spending increase will outweigh the negative effects from the tax increase. To find the balanced budget multiplier, just add the government spending and tax multipliers:

$$\text{balanced budget multiplier} = \text{government spending multiplier} + \text{tax multiplier}$$
$$= 1/(1 - b) + -b/(1 - b)$$
$$= (1 - b)/(1 - b)$$
$$= 1$$

The balanced budget multiplier equals 1; a $10 billion increase in both taxes and government spending will increase GDP by $10 billion.

Finally, we derive equilibrium output with both government spending, and taxes, and the foreign sector. First, recall that equilibrium output occurs where output equals demand. We now must include demand from both the government sector and the foreign sector. Demand from the foreign sector is exports minus imports:

$$\text{output} = \text{demand} = (C + I + G + X - M)$$

Consumption depends on disposable income:

$$C = C_a + b(y - T)$$

and imports depend on the level of output:

$$M = my$$

Substitute the equations for consumption and imports into the equation where output equals demand:

$$y = C_a + b(y - T) + I + G + X - my$$

Collect all terms in y on the left and leave the other terms on the right:

$$y - (b - m)y = C_a - bT + I + G + X$$

Factor the left side:

$$y[1 - (b - m)] = C_a - bT + I + G + X$$

Divide both sides by $[1 - (b - m)]$:

$$y^* = (C_a - bT + I + G + X)/[1 - (b - m)]$$

This is the expression for equilibrium income with government in an open economy. It can be used, following the method we outlined, to calculate multipliers in the open economy.

Using the **TOOLS**

APPLICATIONS

1. Find the Multiplier
An economy has a marginal propensity to consume $b = 0.6$ and a marginal propensity to import $m = 0.2$. What is the multiplier for government spending for this economy?

2. The Effects of Taxes and Spending
Suppose the economy has a marginal propensity to consume $b = 0.4$. The government increases its spending by $2 billion and raises taxes by $1 billion. What happens to equilibrium income?

3. Savings and Taxes
When there are taxes, savings is defined as disposable income minus consumption or $S = (y - T) - C$. In an economy with government but no foreign sector—a closed economy—equilibrium income is determined where output equals demand or $y = C + I + G$. Show that we can also determine equilibrium income using the relationship $S + T = I + G$.

4. Working with a Model
An economy has

$$C = 100 + 0.5(y - T)$$
$$I = 50$$
$$G = 50$$
$$T = 20$$

a. Find equilibrium income.

b. What is the multiplier for government spending?

c. Find the savings function.

d. What are the level of savings when the economy is in equilibrium?

e. Show that at equilibrium, $S + T = G + I$

Model Answers to Questions

Using the Tools

1. Find the Multiplier. Since $b = 0.6$ and $m = 0.2$, the marginal propensity to consume adjusted for taxes is 0.4. The multiplier is $1/(1 - 0.4)$, or 1.67. Alternatively, you could use the last formula in the appendix to derive the multiplier explicitly.

2. The Effects of Taxes and Spending. The government spending multiplier in this case is $1/(1 - 0.4)$, or 1.67. The tax multiplier is $-0.4/(1 - 0.4)$, or -0.67. Thus, equilibrium income will increase by (\$2 billion × 1.67) − (\$1 billion × 0.67) = \$2.67 billion.

3. Savings and Taxes. First, $y - T - C = S$ or $y - C = S + T$. Second, $y = C + I + G$ or $y - C = I + G$. Thus, $S + T = I + G$.

4. Working with a Model

a. $y = 100 + 0.5 (y - 20) + 50 + 50$, which yields $y = 380$.

b. The multiplier is $1/0.5 = 2$.

c. The savings function is $S = (y - T) - [100 + 0.5 (y - T)]$, or $S = -100 + 0.5(y - T)$.

d. At the equilibrium income of 380 and with $T = 20$, $S = 80$.

e. In this case, substituting in $S + T = I + G$ yields 80 + 20 = 50 + 50 or 100 = 100.

Investment
and Financial
Intermediation

In 1983, the prospects for gaining financial success by building commercial office buildings looked very promising. The economy was beginning to recover from a severe recession, inflation was on the decline, and it appeared that the economy was about to embark on a period of sustained growth. In addition, in 1981 Congress had passed a tax bill that provided valuable incentives to invest in real estate. Taking advantage of these incentives and the economic climate, firms built new office buildings throughout the country. Investment in commercial buildings grew at a much more rapid rate than overall investment.

But, unfortunately, several factors intervened to cloud the picture. In 1986, Congress passed another bill, which reduced the tax incentives to invest in commercial buildings. In addition, the building boom that started in 1983 had led to more office space being built than was truly needed. As a consequence, office rents fell and many buildings were not fully occupied. As a result, investment in commercial real estate proved to be unprofitable and the rate of investment was sharply curtailed. Investing is a risky business.

n this chapter, we study the role of investment in the economy and the part that institutions such as banks and savings and loans (often called S&Ls) play in facilitating that investment. In the previous chapter, we assumed that the level of investment was constant. You are about to see the factors that govern investment decisions and how financial markets make it easier for an economy to invest.

In this chapter, you will develop some insight into investment and finance. For example, you will discover how to answer these kinds of questions:

1. Why does investment spending depend on interest rates? Does it depend also on other factors?
2. Why do businesses and homeowners want to borrow in inflationary times, when interest rates are high?
3. How can banks and other financial institutions make risk seem to vanish?
4. Why would most investments in the economy not occur if there were no financial institutions?
5. Why do runs on healthy and profitable banks, which occur when depositors all try to get their money out of banks at the same time, rarely happen today?

An investment, broadly defined, is an action today that has costs today and provides benefits in the future. A firm that builds a new plant today incurs costs today and will earn revenues in the future. College students incur costs to attend school now to earn higher income in the future. A government spends money for a few years to build a dam to have a source of hydroelectric power for many years into the future. These are examples of investments. Notice that we're using the term *investment* in a broader sense than we did in Chapter 5 when we discussed private domestic investment in the GDP accounts. Here an investment is an action taken by any party, such as a college student, that has costs today and provides benefits in the future.

To understand how investment decisions are made, we need to learn about interest rates. To understand how interest rates influence those decisions you need to learn the distinction between nominal interest rates and real interest rates:

Nominal interest rates: Interest rates quoted in the financial markets.

Real interest rate: The nominal interest rate minus the inflation rate.

Financial intermediaries: Organizations that receive funds from savers and channel those funds to investors.

- **Nominal interest rates** are the rates actually charged in the market.
- **Real interest rates** are nominal rates that are adjusted for inflation by subtracting the inflation rate—a concept that we will explain later in this chapter.

Financial institutions such as banks, savings and loans, and insurance companies play a role in making it easier for an economy to invest. These organizations receive funds from savers and channel savers' funds to investors. You will see that these institutions—called **financial intermediaries**—help to reduce the risks and costs associated with investment and allow a greater volume of investment to occur in the economy.

Investment: A Plunge into the Unknown

Let's look again at the definition of investment: actions today that have costs today and provide benefits in the future. Looking at it again, we can see that investments are trade-offs that occur over time: Firms or individuals incur costs today in the hope of future gain. The phrase "hope of" is an important aspect of investment decisions. That simply means that payoffs occurring in the future cannot be known with certainty. Investments are a plunge into the unknown.

Consider a few examples: When an automobile firm builds a new plant because it anticipates increased future demand for its cars, it is taking a gamble. Suppose the model in the future proves to be unpopular or the economy goes into a recession and consumers cut back their purchases of all cars. By building a new plant when it was not needed, the firm will have made an investment decision that didn't pay off in the future. Suppose a government builds nuclear plants, then citizens decide that they are unsafe and force the plants to be closed. The government would have wasted resources on this investment.

Firms and individuals are regularly revising their estimates of the future—because it is uncertain. Sometimes, they're optimistic, deciding to increase their investment spending; other times, they're pessimistic, cutting back on investment spending. These changes in outlook can occur suddenly and may lead to sharp swings in investment spending. John Maynard Keynes said these sharp swings were often irrational, reflecting, perhaps, our most basic, primal instincts. He often referred to what he called the animal spirits of investors.

To estimate future events, firms will look carefully at current developments. If economic growth is currently sluggish, firms may project that it will be sluggish in the future as well. If there is an upsurge in economic growth, firms may become optimistic, increasing their investment spending. Investment spending tends to be closely related to the current pace of economic growth. One theory of investment spending, known as the **accelerator theory,** emphasizes the role of expected growth in real GDP on investment spending. When real GDP growth is expected to be high, firms anticipate that their investments in plant and equipment will be profitable and therefore increase their total investment spending.

Accelerator theory: The theory of investment that says that current investment spending depends positively on the expected future growth of real GDP.

Projections for the future and investors' current animal spirits are both likely to move in conjunction with real GDP growth. For these reasons, we would expect that investment spending would be a volatile component of GDP. As Figure 11.1 indicates, this is the case.

A high-rise building is a risky venture for its investors who are betting that the office space will be needed in the future.

Figure 11.1

Investment Spending as a Share of U.S. GDP, 1970–2000
Shaded areas indicate recessions.

Source: U.S. Department of Commerce.

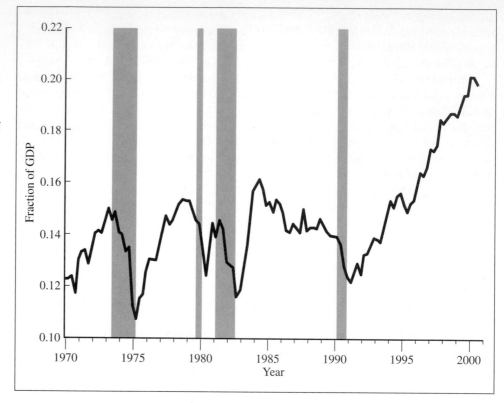

Figure 11.1 plots total investment spending as a share of U.S. GDP from 1970 to 2000. There are two things we need to be sure you see in this figure:

- Over this period, the share of investment in GDP ranged from a low of nearly 11% to a high of nearly 20%—a dramatic difference of nine percentage points of GDP.

- These swings in investment spending often occur over short periods. During periods of recessions, investment spending falls sharply. Investment spending is highly **procyclical,** meaning that investment spending increases during booms and falls during recessions.

Procyclical: A component of GDP is procyclical if it rises and falls with the overall level of GDP.

Figure 11.1 also shows that after the recession in the early 1990s, the investment rate in the United States continued to climb. By 2000, the share of investment in GDP was approximately 20%. This is very high by historical standards in the United States. It reflects the rapid economic growth in the 1990s as well as the confidence that firms (both domestic and foreign) have in the long-run prospects for the U.S. economy. The pace of investment spending dropped off sharply in 2001 as the economy began to enter a new contractionary period.

Although investment spending is a much smaller component of GDP than consumption, it is much more volatile than consumption. It is therefore important for understanding fluctuations in real GDP. Recall that changes in investment are amplified by the multiplier. If the multiplier is 1.5 and investment spending initially falls by 1% of GDP, then GDP will fall by 1.5%. If the fall in GDP makes firms more pessimistic, they may cut investment even further. This further cut in investment will lead to still further reductions in GDP. A small initial fall in investment can trigger a much larger fall in GDP. Nobel laureate Paul Samuelson expressed these interactions with his **multiplier-accelerator model.** In this model, a downturn in real GDP leads to a sharp fall in investment, which further reduces GDP through the multiplier for investment spending.

Multiplier-accelerator model: A model in which a downturn in real GDP leads to a sharp fall in investment, which triggers further reductions in GDP through the multiplier.

Investment spending is not affected only by psychology or expectations about real GDP growth in the future. Because investments are really trade-offs—something in the present traded for something in the future—the terms affecting what is the trade-off between the present and the future are also important. The terms affecting trade-offs between the present and the future are interest rates, as we shall see next.

Nominal Interest Rates and Real Interest Rates

If you deposit $100 in a bank and the interest rate the bank pays is 6% a year, at the end of one year you will have $106 ($100 × 1.06). Here are some other familiar examples of interest rates: If you borrow money for college tuition from a bank, the bank will require you to pay the funds back with interest. If a hardware store borrows money from a bank to purchase its inventory, the store will have to pay the funds back to the bank with interest. If you buy from the government or a corporation a $1,000 bond for one year at a 6% annual interest rate, you will receive $1,060 ($1000 × 1.06) next year from the issuer. Remember that a **bond** is a promise to pay money in the future. In buying the bond, you have loaned your $1,000 to the issuer, who has promised to repay it with interest.

Bond: A promise or IOU to pay money in the future in exchange for money now.

The interest rates quoted in the market—that is, at savings and loans, or banks for bonds—are called nominal interest rates. These are the actual rates that individuals and firms pay or receive when they borrow money or lend money. There are many different interest rates in the economy, as "A Closer Look: A Variety of Interest Rates" illustrates.

When there is inflation, the dollar costs of borrowing or lending will not reflect the true costs. To provide an accurate measure of the costs of borrowing or lending, we need to apply the reality principle and make adjustments for changes in prices.

Reality **PRINCIPLE**

> **What matters to people is the real value of money or income—its purchasing power—not the face value of money or income.**

Distinguishing between nominal interest rates and real interest rates is how economists account for inflation in their measurements of the costs of borrowing and lending. The real rate of interest is defined as the nominal interest rate minus the inflation rate:

$$\text{real rate} = \text{nominal rate} - \text{inflation rate}$$

If the nominal rate of interest is 6% per year and the inflation rate is 4% during the year, the real rate of interest is 2% (6% − 4% = 2%) over that year.

To understand what the real rate of interest means, consider this example. You have $100, and there is 4% annual inflation. It's not hard to figure out that next year you will need $104 to have the same purchasing power that you have today. Let's say you deposit today $100 in a bank that pays 6% annual interest. At the end of the year, you have $106 ($100 × 1.06).

Let's calculate your real gain. After 1 year, you have increased your holdings by $6, starting with $100 and ending with $106. But taking into account the $4 you need to keep up with inflation, your gain is only $2 ($6 − $4). The real rate of interest you earned, the nominal rate adjusted for inflation, is 2% or $2, on the original $100 deposit.

A similar calculation applies to firms or individuals who borrow money. Suppose a firm borrows $100 at a 10% annual interest rate when there is 6% inflation during the year. The firm must pay back $110 at the end of the year ($100 × 1.10). But the borrower will be paying back the funds with dollars whose value has been reduced because of inflation. Since there was 6% inflation during the year, the lender would have to receive $106

A CLOSER LOOK   A VARIETY OF INTEREST RATES

There are many different interest rates in the economy. Loans vary by their riskiness and by their maturity (the length of the loan). Riskier loans and loans for longer maturities typically have higher interest rates.

Figure 11.2 depicts movements in three interest rates during 2000: a 30-year fixed-rate mortgage (30-year loans to homeowners with a constant rate), corporate AAA bonds (loans to corporations that are good

credit risks), and 6-month Treasuries (loans to the U.S. government for 6 months).

Notice that rates for the 30-year mortgages are higher than U.S treasuries and corporate bonds. That's because homeowners are less likely to pay back their loans than large corporations or the U.S. government. The U.S. government pays the lowest rates because it is borrowing for a short period (6 months) and has little risk of not paying its debt.

(or 6 extra dollars) just to keep up with inflation over the year. There is only a $4 gain ($10 – $6). Thus, the real rate of interest to the borrower is just 4%, or $4 on the original $100 loan, correcting for the effects of inflation.

We defined the real interest rate as the nominal interest rate minus the actual inflation rate. When firms or individuals borrow or lend, they do not know what the rate of inflation will actually be. Instead, they must form an expectation—an estimate—of what they believe the inflation rate will be in the future. For a given nominal interest rate, we can define the **expected real interest rate** as the nominal rate minus the expected inflation rate. The expected real interest rate is the rate at which borrowers or lenders expect to make transactions.

Expected real interest rate:
The nominal interest rate minus the expected inflation rate.

Figure 11.2

Mortgage, Corporate, and Government Interest Rates

Source: Federal Reserve Bank of St. Louis.

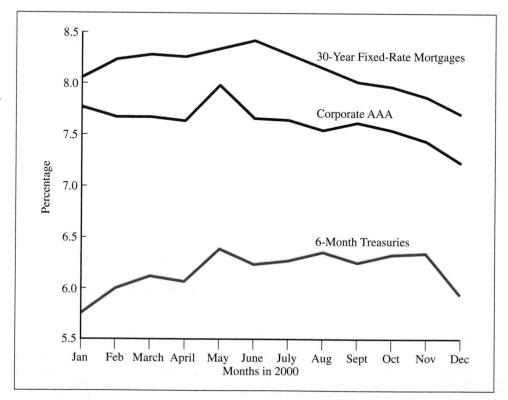

Table 11.1 Expected Real Rates of Interest (percent per year)

Country	3-Month Interest Rate	Inflation Rate Forecast for 2001	Expected Real Rate of Interest
Australia	4.94	3.60	1.34
Canada	4.26	2.40	1.86
Denmark	4.80	2.30	2.50
Switzerland	3.25	1.20	2.05
United States	3.52	2.90	0.62

Source: The Economist, June 28, 2001.

It is difficult to determine expected real rates of interest that are precise because we never know exactly what inflation rates people anticipate. One approach is to use the judgments of professional forecasters. In Table 11.1, we present estimates of the expected real rates of interest based on this idea using data and forecasts for a few developed countries from *The Economist* magazine. In the second column, we show interest rates on 3-month loans; in the third column, the inflation forecasts for 2001. The last column shows estimates of the expected real rate of interest in each country by subtracting the inflation forecast from the interest rate. As you can see, both nominal and real interest rates differ among the developed countries.

TEST Your Understanding

1. Investment is a smaller component of GDP than consumption, but it is a more stable component. True or false? Explain.

2. Investment spending is very procyclical, moving in conjunction with GDP. True or false? Explain.

3. Complete the statement with *real* or *nominal:* The rate of interest that you earn in the bank is known as a _____ or dollar rate of interest.

4. With 6% annual inflation, a nominal rate of interest of 10% per year means a real rate of interest of _____ % per year.

Investment Spending and Interest Rates

To understand the link between investment spending and interest rates, here's a simple example. A firm can invest $100 today in a project and receive $104 one year from today. There is no inflation: A dollar today and a dollar next year have the same purchasing power. Figure 11.3 depicts this investment. A cost is incurred today and the return occurs one year later. Should the firm make this investment?

To decide whether to invest the $100, the firm should take into account the principle of opportunity cost.

PRINCIPLE of Opportunity Cost

The opportunity cost of something is what you sacrifice to get it.

We have to look at the $100 the firm would give up today to get $104 one year from today. What we look at is how that $100 could have been used for other purposes.

Figure 11.3

Typical Investments
A typical investment, in which a cost of $100 incurred today yields a return of $104 next year.

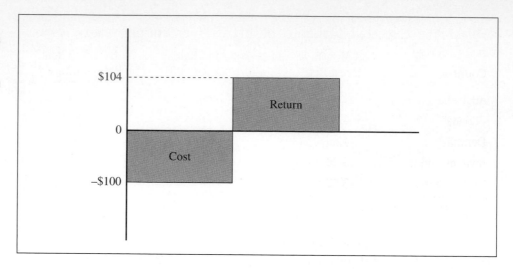

Suppose the annual interest rate in the economy were 3%. The firm could lend the $100 at 3% and receive $103 in one year. The interest rate prevailing in the economy provides a measure of the opportunity cost of the investment.

In this case, the firm would not be too smart lending the $100 at 3% annual interest return. The investment is the smart thing to do. The firm will earn a net return of $4 ($104 – $100) from the investment project, whereas the return from lending the $100 would have been only $3. Because the net return from the investment exceeds the opportunity cost of the funds, the firm is better off investing.

What if the annual interest rate in the economy were 6%? Lending the $100 would return $6—the opportunity cost that could be earned by lending instead of investing in the project. The return on the investment of $4 would be less than the opportunity cost of $6. The firm would be better off making a loan of the $100, not investing it. The higher lending interest rate makes the difference as to which is the more profitable use of the $100.

There are millions of investment projects that can be undertaken, nearly all providing different returns from any other. Consider the array of investments A through E in Table 11.2. At a market interest rate of 2% per year, only investment A is unprofitable. All the other investments have a return greater than the opportunity cost of the funds. If the interest rate in the market increased to 4%, both A and B would be unprofitable. Investment C would join A and B as being unprofitable at an interest rate of 6%; D would become unprofitable if the market interest rate increased to 8%. If interest rates exceeded 9%, all the investments would become unprofitable.

Table 11.2   Returns on Investment

Investment	Cost	Return
A	$100	$101
B	$100	$103
C	$100	$105
D	$100	$107
E	$100	$109

Firms will compare the net return on an investment with the opportunity cost of that investment, and they will invest as long as the net return exceeds the opportunity cost. As market interest rates rise, there will be fewer profitable investments. The total level of investment spending in the economy will decline as market interest rates increase. Figure 11.4 depicts the negative relationship—graphically represented as the downward-sloping line—between interest rates and investment.

Real investment spending is inversely related to the real interest rate. To understand why, let's return to our example in which a $100 investment today would yield a $104 return in one year, the interest rate was 3%, and there was no inflation. Because there was no inflation, nominal interest rates and real interest rates were the same. In this case, the firm looked at the real net return on the investment of $4 which is a real return of 4% from the investment, compared it to the real rate of interest of 3%, and decided that the investment was profitable.

Now suppose that the return from the investment project and the real interest rate in the economy are the same—3% per year—but there is 2% annual inflation. Also suppose that the nominal interest rate increases to 5%: the real rate of interest of 3% plus the inflation rate of 2%. The investment project will still cost $100, but it will pay a return of $100 plus $6 = $106 in one year. The extra $2 arises because of the 2% inflation: When the firm sells its product on the market, it will earn 2% more because of the rise in prices in the economy.

The firm will compare its nominal or dollar net return of 6% to the opportunity cost of 5% and find that the investment will be more profitable than making the loan. Because both the nominal net return and nominal interest rates in the economy increase by the rate of inflation of 2%, the firm faces the identical situation as if there were no inflation.

You can see now that investment spending is negatively related to real interest rates. That's why nominal interest rates are not a good indicator of the true cost of investing. If nominal interest rates are 10% but inflation is 9%, the real rate of interest is 1%. If a firm had a project that paid a real net return greater than 1%, it would want to undertake this investment. Inflation would increase the nominal net return and the nominal interest rate equally. The firm makes its investment decisions by comparing its expected real net return from investment projects to the real rate of interest.

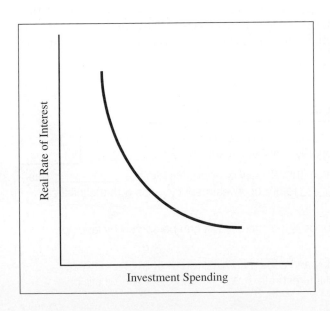

Figure 11.4

Interest Rates and Investment

As the real interest rate declines, investment spending in the economy increases.

During the 1970s, homeowners in California understood this logic. They bought homes even though they had to borrow from the bank at interest rates exceeding 10%. They were willing to borrow at such high rates because they had seen housing prices rise by more than 10% and were projecting this rise in prices to continue in the future. For example, if they expected housing prices to rise by 12% a year, they could earn a 2% annual return just by borrowing at 10% and watching their homes appreciate in value at 12%. (They would earn this return only when they sold their home.) They calculated that their real interest rate was –2%. This caused a housing boom in California that lasted until housing prices stopped rising at such high rates.

Economic Detective

The Case of High Interest Rates and Investment

Some journalists were puzzled that a country with high inflation had high interest rates but also had high levels of investment spending. As an economic detective, can you explain this phenomenon?

To resolve the mystery, you need to distinguish between real and nominal interest rates. Investment spending depends negatively on real interest rates. However, if there are high levels of inflation, real interest rates could be low, while nominal interest rates remain high.

Economists have incorporated these insights about interest rates and investment into theories of aggregate investment spending. In addition to interest rates, they have also considered other factors, including taxes and the stock market.

Here are two of the key theories: In the **neoclassical theory of investment**, pioneered by Dale Jorgenson of Harvard University, real interest rates and taxes play a key role in determining investment spending. Jorgenson used his theory to analyze the responsiveness of investment to a variety of tax incentives, including investment tax credits that are subsidies to investment. The **Q-theory of investment**, originally developed by Nobel laureate James Tobin of Yale University, looks a bit different from the neoclassical theory on its surface. The Q-theory states that investment spending increases when stock prices are high. If a firm's stock price is high, it can issue new shares of its stock at an advantageous price and use the proceeds to undertake new investment. Recent research has shown a close connection between the Q-theory and neoclassical theory and has highlighted the key role that real interest rates and taxes play in the Q-theory as well.

Neoclassical theory of investment: A theory of investment that says that both real interest rates and taxes are important determinants of investment.

Q-theory of investment: The theory of investment that links investment spending to stock prices.

TEST Your Understanding

5. Complete the statement with *increases* or *decreases*: As real rates of interest increase in the economy, real investment spending _____.

6. Complete the following statement with *real* or *nominal*: Both the _____ rate of interest and the _____ return on investment increase with the inflation rate.

7. The _____ cost of funds is the interest that can be earned by lending the funds.

8. If a project costs $100 today and pays a nominal return of $107 next year, what is the nominal annual interest rate at which the project should still be undertaken?

How Financial Intermediation Facilitates Investment

Investment spending in an economy comes from savings. When households earn income, they consume part of it and save the rest. These savings are the source of funds for investment.

Why Financial Intermediaries Emerge

Households save for different reasons than the ones firms have for investing. A typical household might be saving for the children's education or for financial security in later life. Such households do not want their savings, usually considered "life savings," to be subject to risk. And they want their savings to be readily accessible—what economists call **liquid**—in case of financial emergencies. Funds deposited in a bank account, for example, provide a source of liquidity for households; these funds can be obtained at any time.

Liquid: Easily convertible to money on short notice.

Firms and business managers who make investments in the economy are typically risk-takers. They are gambling that their vision of the future will come true and make them vast profits. They need funds that must be tied up for a long time. For example, an entrepreneur who wants to build skyscrapers or large casinos may need financing for several years before they can start building their projects, and years after that before those projects begin to produce profits.

Suppose individual entrepreneurs had to obtain funds directly from individual savers. First, the entrepreneur would have to negotiate with thousands of savers to obtain sufficient funds for a large-scale project. These negotiations would be costly. Second, the savers would face extraordinary risks if they loaned all their funds to a single entrepreneur who had a risky project to undertake. Not only would all their funds be tied up in a single project, they would also have difficulty monitoring investor's decisions. How would they know that the entrepreneur would not run off with the money? Finally, this investment would not be liquid. If the funds were tied up in a major project, households would not be able to get access to them in case of emergencies.

In these circumstances, households would demand extraordinarily high interest rates to compensate them for the costs of negotiation, risk, and lack of liquidity. High interest rates would make it impossible for an entrepreneur to make a profit; no profit from a project means no investors in the project. Society would not be able to turn its savings to profitable investment projects. Figure 11.5 depicts this dilemma. How can society solve it?

Society needs institutions that can reduce costs, monitor investments, reduce risks, and provide liquidity. Fortunately, there are such institutions—the financial intermediaries.

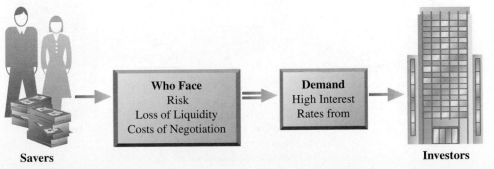

Figure 11.5
Savers and Investors

Savers

| Who Face |
| Risk |
| Loss of Liquidity |
| Costs of Negotiation |

| Demand |
| High Interest |
| Rates from |

Investors

Financial intermediaries are banks, savings and loans, insurance companies, money market mutual funds, and many other types of financial institutions. These institutions accept funds from savers and make loans to businesses and individuals. For example, a local bank accepts deposits from savers and uses the funds to make loans to local businesses. Savings and loan institutions will accept deposits in savings accounts and use these funds to make loans, often for housing. Insurance companies accept premium payments from individuals in exchange for the protection provided by the insurance payments. Then insurance companies lend the premiums received to earn returns from investments so that they can pay off the insurance claims of individuals. Figure 11.6 shows how financial intermediaries create a valuable link between savers and investors.

These institutions pool the funds of savers. By pooling funds and making loans to individual businesses, financial intermediaries reduce the costs of negotiation, such as businesses trying to negotiate terms with each individual investor. They also acquire expertise in both evaluating and monitoring investments. Some financial intermediaries, such as banks, provide liquidity to households. In normal circumstances, not all households converge on a bank to take out their money at the same time. Because that doesn't happen and is not expected to happen, the bank can lend most of its funds to businesses and still have funds on hand to meet emergency withdrawals by depositors.

By pooling funds and gaining expertise, financial intermediaries can reduce costs and provide liquidity. But how do they reduce risk? Financial intermediaries reduce risk by diversification, that is, by not putting all their eggs in one basket.

Risk can be reduced by investing in a large number of projects whose returns, although uncertain, are independent of one another. By independence, we mean that the return from one investment is unrelated to the return on another investment. Consider a bank investing in a large number of projects that altogether produce an average return of 8% annually. Each project alone is risky and could pay either a higher or a lower return than 8%. As long as the returns on these projects are independent, the number of projects with higher returns will be matched by an equal number of projects with lower returns. Some of those projects will have good fortune; others will have bad luck. By investing in a large number of projects, the bank can be confident that it will earn an 8% return on all of them as a group.

Financial intermediaries reduce risk in this way. Using the funds that they receive from households' savings, financial intermediaries invest in a large number of projects. Every household has a small stake in many projects. No one household would be able to do this. But if many households deposit their funds in financial intermediaries, the

Figure 11.6
Financial Intermediaries

Financial Intermediaries

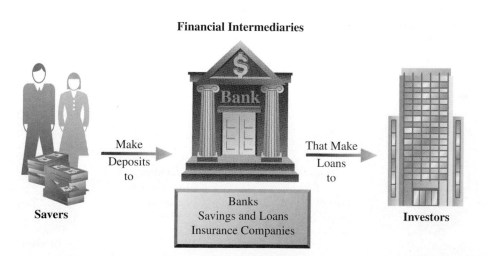

Make Deposits to

That Make Loans to

Savers

Banks
Savings and Loans
Insurance Companies

Investors

financial intermediaries can invest in a wide range of projects and reduce risk for the households.

Other financial intermediaries reduce risks in related ways. A fire insurance company accepts premiums from many individuals and uses the funds to make investments. Since not all houses will burn down in the same year, the insurance company knows that it will have a stable source of funds for its investments. Banks also benefit from risk reduction when they accept deposits. While some individual depositors may want to withdraw funds on a given day, banks can be confident that not all depositors will come in to withdraw on the same day.

Diversification in insurance works well only when companies insure events that are independent. Some events are not independent and therefore cannot easily be insured. For example, an insurance company would be unwise to provide earthquake insurance for just the Los Angeles area. If an earthquake did occur, the firm would be faced with making many payments to its clients who suffered loss. In somewhat the same way, even bank loans are not fully independent. During a recession, many firms will be operating unprofitably all at the same time, and they will have difficulties meeting their loan obligations to their banks.

Diversification can also reduce the risks of investing in the stock market. But it cannot eliminate them, as "A Closer Look: Diversification and the Stock Market" explains.

When Financial Intermediation Malfunctions

Financial intermediation can sometimes go wrong. When it does, the economy suffers. Important examples of the failure of financial intermediation include commercial bank failures during the Great Depression, the savings and loans crisis of the 1980s in the United States, and a similar crisis in Japan in the 1990s.

During the 1930s in the early days of the Great Depression, many banks in the United States, particularly in rural areas, provided farmers or local businesses loans that turned out not to be profitable. This worried depositors, and rumors started that banks would soon be closing their doors and depositors would lose all their funds. This triggered runs on the banks—all depositors panicking to withdraw their deposits simultaneously.

A CLOSER LOOK   DIVERSIFICATION AND THE STOCK MARKET

Buying shares in an individual company is extremely risky. Special factors can always hurt the fortunes of an individual company. However, by purchasing a *mutual fund*, an investor can reduce some of his or her risk. A mutual fund is a financial intermediary that invests in a broad range of stocks. By diversifying across a wide range of stocks, overall risk can be reduced by eliminating the influence of company-specific factors. But the risk of investing in the stock market cannot be eliminated. First, the overall market itself is risky. For example, from 1972 to 2000, the average annual real return from investing in the total U.S. stock market was approximately 9%. However, in seven of those years, the return was negative and, in one year the return was −28%. The overall risk of the U.S. stock market cannot be diversified away.

Second, not all mutual funds invest in the full range of the U.S. market. This can also be an additional source of risk. For example, from March 2000 to March 2001, the index for the NASDAQ stock exchange (which trades many high-tech stocks) fell from 5000 to 2000—a much steeper fall than for the broader indexes for the entire market. If your mutual fund was heavily invested in NASDAQ stocks, you would have suffered extremely large losses.

Depositors gathered anxiously outside as banks closed during the Great Depression.

No bank, profitable or unprofitable, can survive a run. As financial intermediaries, banks make profits by lending out their deposits. They never keep 100% of these deposits on hand. That's how the runs on banks closed thousands of healthy banks and destroyed the entire banking system in large parts of the United States. Many farmers and businesses could no longer find a source of loans. This failure in the financial system worsened the severity of the Great Depression.

To prevent this from happening again, the U.S. government began to provide deposit insurance for banks and savings and loans. This insurance guarantees that the government will provide you with funds up to $100,000 even if your bank fails. Since everyone knows their deposits are secure, runs on banks no longer occur.

During the Great Depression, bank failures occurred throughout the world. In 1931, a panic broke out after the collapse of Creditanstalt, Austria's largest bank. Banking panics occurred throughout other countries in Europe, including Belgium, France, Germany, Italy, and Poland. Studies have shown that the countries with the most severe banking panics were hardest hit by the Depression. Today, most countries have some form of deposit insurance intended to prevent panics.

Ironically, deposit insurance indirectly helped to create the savings and loan crisis in the United States during the 1980s. In the early 1970s, savings and loan institutions made mortgage loans to households at low interest rates. In the late 1970s, nominal interest rates rose sharply as inflation increased. The savings and loans were in trouble: They had to pay high interest rates to attract deposits, but they were earning interest at low rates from their past investments. Many S&Ls went bankrupt.

The government tried to assist the saving and loan industry by reducing the regulations that restricted the range of their investments and allowing them to make investments other than housing in the hope that they would gain more profits. Depositors were not concerned because their savings were insured. Savings and loans soon became aggressive investors in speculative real estate and other risky projects. Unfortunately, many investment projects collapsed, and the government was forced to provide funds to the many savings and loans at a cost of nearly $100 billion to taxpayers. Depositors' savings, don't forget, were protected through deposit insurance up to a certain amount. So most depositors did not suffer directly from the collapse of their savings and loan institutions, but taxpayers did.

Japan suffered from similar problems in the 1990s. By 1995, seven of the eight largest mortgage lenders in Japan went bankrupt during falling real estate markets. The Japanese government chose to use taxpayer funds, equivalent to nearly 13 billion U.S. dollars, to rescue these companies and prevent further disruptions in the financial market.

From these examples, you can see that there are reasons why financial intermediation does not always work. There is a continual debate on the role government should play in investment decisions for the economy, and its role in regulating financial intermediaries.

Using the **TOOLS**

In this chapter, we studied investment and financial intermediation and examined the factors that affect firms' investment decisions. Here's an opportunity to do your own economic analysis.

1. ECONOMIC EXPERIMENT: Diversification

This classroom exercise illustrates the power of diversification. Your instructor will describe the game and how to participate. To take part in this exercise, you need to recall a simple lesson from basic statistics: If you flip a coin many times, the fraction of heads that results approaches 1/2 as you increase the number of flips.

You are offered a chance to play this game in which you receive a payoff according to the following formula.

$$\text{payoff} = \$10 + \$100(\text{number of heads/number of tosses} - 0.5)$$

In this game, you first get $10, but you either win or lose additional funds, depending on whether the fraction of heads that comes up exceeds 1/2.

To help you understand what's going on in this game, suppose you toss the coin only once. Here, the outcome depends only on whether the coin comes up either heads or tails:

$$\text{Heads} \quad \$10 + \$100(1/1 - 0.5) = \$60$$
$$\text{Tails:} \quad \$10 + \$100(0/1 - 0.5) = -\$40$$

If the one coin toss comes up heads, you win $60; if it comes up tails, you lose $40 dollars.

The game does have a positive expected payoff or return. The expected or average payoff for this game is the probability of getting a head (1/2) times $60 if a head results plus the probability of getting a tail (1/2) times –$40 if a tail results. This is

$$\text{expected payoff} = (0.5)\$60 + (0.5)(-\$40) = \$10$$

On average, if you toss the coin many times, this game would pay $10. But this game is risky if you are allowed to toss the coin only once. Now that you understand the game, answer the following question:

• Would you play this game if limited to only one toss?

Now suppose you were free to toss the coin 1,000 times and received 450 heads. If that happened, your payoff would be

$$\$10 + \$100 (450/1000 - 0.5) = \$5$$

• Would you play if you could toss the coin 1,000 times?

a. Did a higher percentage of the class agree to play the game with 1,000 tosses? How does this illustrate the principle of diversification?

b. If you toss the coin 1,000 times, what is the expected payoff?

c. If you toss the coin 1,000 times and receive heads fewer than 400 times, you will lose money. What do you think is the probability of this occurring?

2. Animal Spirits
Use the $C + I + G$ diagram from Chapter 25 to show the effects of increased "animal spirits" that leads to higher investment in the economy.

3. Brazilian Economics
During the early 1990s, interest rates in Brazil were typically at double-digit levels, but firms were investing in a large number of projects. Does this make economic sense? If so, in what way?

4. Understanding Banks
How can a bank invest in illiquid loans (say, lend depositors' savings to home buyers over 25 years) and still provide liquid deposits (provide depositors with their savings when they ask for it)?

Summary

We discussed investment spending, interest rates, and financial intermediation. You saw that investment spending is volatile, rising and falling sharply with real GDP, and depends on expectations about the future. We also explained why investment spending also depends inversely on real interest rates. Finally, we examined how financial intermediaries channel funds from savers to investors, reduce interest rates and promote investment. Here are the main points of this chapter to keep in mind:

1. Investments incur costs today, to provide benefits in the future.

2. Investment spending is a volatile component of GDP because expectations of the future can be volatile and investment decisions are made with an eye to the ever-changing future.

3. Investment spending depends inversely on real interest rates.

4. Financial intermediaries reduce risk and costs of making investments through their expertise and through pooling the funds of savers.

Key Terms

accelerator theory, 233
bond, 235
expected real interest rate, 236
financial intermediaries, 232

liquid, 241
multiplier-accelerator model, 234
neoclassical theory of investment, 240

nominal interest rates, 232
procyclical, 234
Q-theory of investment, 240
real interest rate, 232

Problems and Discussion Questions

1. The components of investment spending in the national income accounts include plant and equipment, housing, and inventories. Give a reason why spending in each of these categories is likely to be volatile.

2. "When real interest rates are high, so is the opportunity cost of funds." What does this statement mean?

3. "If the real interest rate were zero, it would be a financially sound decision to level the Rocky Mountains so that automobiles and cars would save on gas mileage." Putting aside ecological concerns, why is this statement true?

4. Traditionally, savings and loan institutions made loans only for housing. At one point, this was viewed as a safe way of doing business. Explain

why making loans only for housing may be very risky.

5. If the inflation rate is 10% over the year and annual interest rates are 9%, would you invest in a project that only paid an annual real return of 1%?

6. Explain why some insurance companies have been interested in national programs for insurance for floods, earthquakes, and hurricanes.

7. A business borrows at a 10% annual interest rate from a bank and expects 8% annual inflation. What is the real interest rate and the nominal interest rate facing this borrower?

8. Why does it make sense for individual investors to invest in mutual funds (which invest in a wide range of stocks), rather than in just a few individual companies?

9. Why do many investors put their funds in investments in countries throughout the world, not just investments in the United States?

10. While deposit insurance protects depositors, savings and prevents runs on banks, it can motivate banks to take excessive risks in the loans they make. Explain why.

11. **Web Exercise.** Search the Web to find the current values for interest rates on short-term and long-term government bonds, the prime rate, and long-term corporate bonds. You may want to start with the data Web site for the Federal Reserve Bank of St. Louis [*http://www.stls.frb.org/fred*]. Try to account for the differences in these rates.

12. **Web Exercise.** Use the Federal Reserve Bank of St. Louis Web site [*http://www.stls.frb.org/fred*] to find out how investment in residential housing behaved over the 1990–91 recession. Compare it to other types of investment.

Take It to the Net

We invite you to visit the O'Sullivan/Sheffrin page on the Prentice Hall Web site at: **http://www.prenhall.com/osullivan/** for additional World Wide Web exercises for this chapter.

Model Answers to Questions

Chapter-Opening Questions

1. Interest rates represent the opportunity cost of an investment. The higher the opportunity cost, the less the investment. Investment also depends on other factors such as expectations, taxes, and the expected growth of the economy.

2. Borrowing depends on the real interest rate, which is the nominal interest rate adjusted for inflation. In inflationary periods, there may be a high nominal interest rate but a low real interest rate.

3. Diversification of independent risks makes it possible for financial intermediaries to reduce risk.

4. Without financial institutions, it would be too costly for individuals to make loans directly to firms.

5. Federal deposit insurance prevents the runs on banks that occurred during the Great Depression.

Test Your Understanding

1. False. Investment is more volatile than consumption.

2. True. Investment rises and falls with GDP.

3. Nominal.

4. 4%.

5. Decreases.

6. Nominal, nominal.

7. Opportunity.

8. The highest rate is 7%.

Using the Tools

1. Economic Experiment: Diversification

   a. A higher percentage of the class should agree to play the game if students could toss the coin 1,000 times rather than a single time. That's because the expected payoff of 1,000 tosses is the same $10 as the expected payoff of a single toss, but the risk is much less.

b. If a coin is tossed 1,000 times, the probability of fewer than 400 heads is less than 1 in a million.

2. Animal Spirits. The increase in investment will lead to a vertical shift in the $C + I + G$ demand line. This will lead to higher output.

3. Brazilian Economics. While nominal interest rates were at double-digit levels in Brazil during that period, inflation was also at double-digit levels. Real interest rates were substantially lower, which is why firms still wanted to undertake investment projects.

4. Understanding Banks. Using basic statistics, a bank can estimate that only a fraction of its depositors will ask for withdrawals on any given day. Therefore, the bank can allocate a large fraction of the deposits to illiquid loans.

12

Money, the Banking System, and the Federal Reserve

As long as there has been paper money, there have been counterfeiters. In 1023, China formed a government agency to print paper money; by 1107, they had begun to print money in three colors to thwart counterfeiters. In 1998, the U.S. Treasury introduced a new $20 bill, using modern technology to make life difficult for counterfeiters. The portrait of Andrew Jackson is slightly off-center, and imbedded in the paper is a plastic thread, invisible to the unaided human eye, that glows green under ultraviolet light. The new $20 bills are also printed with a special ink that looks green when viewed directly but changes to black when viewed from side to side. These are ingenious technological marvels. But the institution of money is even a greater marvel.

What Is Money?
Definition of Money
Three Properties of Money

Measuring Money in the U.S. Economy

Banks as Financial Intermediaries

The Process of Money Creation

The Role of the Federal Reserve in the Money Creation Process
Open Market Operations
Other Tools

The Structure of the Federal Reserve

Using the Tools

Appendix: Formula for Deposit Creation

he term *money* has a special meaning for economists, so we'll look carefully at how they define money and the role that it plays in the economy.

The supply of money in the economy is determined primarily by the banking system and the actions of the Federal Reserve, our nation's central bank. We will see how the Federal Reserve, operating through the banking system, can create and destroy money. We will also study how the Federal Reserve operates and who controls it.

The supply of money is very important for the economy's performance. In our discussion of aggregate demand, we indicated how increases in the supply of money increase aggregate demand. In the short run, when prices are largely fixed, increases in the money supply will raise total demand and output. In the long run, continuing money growth leads to inflation. Therefore, changes in the supply of money have important effects on both output and prices: how much is produced, the cost of producing output, and what will be the prices of what is produced. In this chapter, we explain in detail how the supply of money in the economy is determined.

After reading this chapter, you should be able to answer the following questions:

1. Why do all societies have some form of money?
2. Why do banks play a special role in our economy?
3. Can banks really create money through computer entries?
4. When the Federal Reserve uses its special powers to buy and sell government bonds, how do buying and selling government bonds affect the supply of money in the economy?
5. Why is the chairman of the Federal Reserve one of the most powerful people in the country?

What Is Money?

Let's first discuss the definition and role of money and then see how it is measured in the U.S. economy.

Definition of Money

Money: Anything that is regularly used in exchange.

Economists define **money** as anything that is regularly used in economic transactions or exchanges. Let's consider some examples of money used in that way.

We use money regularly, every day. In an ice-cream store, we hand the person behind the counter some dollar bills and coins, and we receive an ice-cream cone. This is an example of an economic exchange: One party hands over currency—the dollar bills and the coins—and the other party hands over goods and services (the ice-cream cone). Why do the owners of ice-cream stores accept the dollar bills and coins in payment for the ice cream? The reason is that they will be making other economic exchanges with the dollar bills and coins they accept. Suppose they take the currency they receive from selling the ice cream and pay their supplier with it. The ice-cream cones cost $1.50 each, and 100 ice-cream cones are sold in a day. The seller then has $150 in currency. If the ice cream costs the seller $100, the seller pays $100 of the currency received and keeps $50 for other expenses and profits.

In the real world, transactions are somewhat more complicated. The ice-cream store will take the currency it receives each day and deposit it into an account at its local bank. It will typically pay its suppliers with a check drawn on its account at that local bank. This is another example of an economic exchange: The ice-cream supplier sells ice cream to the store in exchange for a check.

Why does the supplier accept a check? The supplier can use the check to make further transactions. The supplier can deposit the check in his or her own bank account and then either withdraw currency from this account or write checks on it.

In these examples, what is money? Recall the definition of money: anything that is regularly used in economic transactions or exchanges. Clearly, currency is money because it was used to purchase ice cream. Checks are also money because they are used to pay the supplier.

At other times and in other societies, different items have been used as money. In some ancient cultures, precious stones were used in exchanges; therefore, those stones constituted money. In more recent times, gold bars have served as money. During World War II, prisoners of war did not have currency, but they did have rations of cigarettes. The cigarettes began to be used for exchanges among the prisoners and played the role of money in the prison camps.

Three Properties of Money

Regardless of what money is in a particular society, it serves several functions, all related to making economic exchanges easier. Here we discuss three key properties of money.

1. Money Serves as a Medium of Exchange

As our examples illustrate, money is accepted in economic exchanges; that is, it serves as a **medium of exchange**. Suppose money did not exist and you had a car you wanted to sell to buy a boat. You could look for a person who had a boat and wanted to buy a car and then trade your car directly for a boat. This would be an example of **barter**: trading goods directly for goods.

But there are obvious problems with barter. Suppose local boatbuilders were interested in selling boats but not interested in buying your car. Unless there were a **double coincidence of wants**—that is, unless you wanted to trade a car for a boat and the boat owner wanted to trade a boat for your car—this economic exchange could not occur. The probability of a double coincidence of wants occurring is very, very tiny. Even if a boat owner wanted a car, he or she might want a different type of car than yours.

By serving as a medium of exchange, money solves this problem. A car owner can sell the car to anyone who wants it and receive money in return. With that money, the car owner can then find someone who owns a boat and purchase the boat for money. The boat owner can use the money in any way he or she pleases. With money, there is no need for a double coincidence of wants. This is why money exists in all societies: It makes economic transactions much easier.

Medium of exchange: The property of money that exchanges are made through the use of money.

Barter: Trading goods directly for goods.

Double coincidence of wants: The problem in a system of barter that one person may not have what the other desires.

2. Money Serves as a Unit of Account

Money also provides a convenient measuring rod when prices for all goods are quoted in money terms. A boat may be listed for sale at $5,000, a car at $10,000, and a movie ticket at $5.00. All these prices are quoted in money. We could in principle quote everything in terms of movie tickets. The boat would be worth 1,000 tickets, and the car would be worth 2,000 tickets. But since we are using money (and not movie tickets) as a medium of exchange, it is much easier if all prices are expressed in terms of money. We say that money is used as a **unit of account**, and all we mean by that is that prices are quoted in terms of money. This also makes it easier to conduct economic transactions, since there is a standard unit—whether that unit is movie tickets or the more convenient unit of dollars—in which to do so.

Unit of account: The property of money that prices are quoted in terms of money.

3. Money Serves as a Store of Value

If you sell your car to purchase a boat, you may not be able to purchase the boat immediately. In the meantime, you will be holding the money you received from the sale of the car. Ideally, during that period, the value of the money should not change. What we are referring to here is the function of money to be a **store of value**.

Store of value: The property of money that it preserves value until it is used in an exchange.

Money is actually a somewhat imperfect store of value because of inflation. Suppose inflation is 10% a year, which means that all prices rise 10% each year. Let's say you sold a tennis racket for $100 to buy 10 CDs worth $100 but that you waited a year to buy them. Unfortunately, at the end of the year, during which there was 10% inflation, the 10 CDs now cost $110 ($100 × 1.10), or $11 each. With your $100, you can now buy only 9 CDs and get $1 in change. Money has lost some of its stored value.

As long as inflation is low and you do not hold money for a long time, the loss in the purchasing power of money will not be a major problem. But as inflation rates increase, money becomes less useful as a store of value.

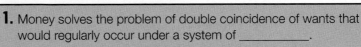

TEST Your Understanding

1. Money solves the problem of double coincidence of wants that would regularly occur under a system of _____.

2. Why is money only an imperfect store of value?

3. What is the problem associated with the double coincidence of wants?

4. Because we measure all prices in monetary units, money serves as a unit of account. True or false? Explain.

5. Why are checks included in the definition of money?

Measuring Money in the U.S. Economy

In the United States and other modern economies, there are typically several different ways in which economic transactions can be carried out. In practice, this leads to different definitions of money.

M1: The sum of currency in the hands of the public plus demand deposits plus other checkable deposits.

The most basic measure of money in the United States is called **M1**. Table 12.1 contains the components of M1 and their size for January 2001, and Figure 12.1 shows their relative percentages.

The first part of M1 is currency that is held by the public, that is, all currency held outside of bank vaults. The next two components are deposits in checking accounts, called *demand deposits*. Until the 1980s, checking accounts did not pay interest, and a new category, entitled *other checkable deposits*, was introduced in the early 1980s to describe checking accounts that did pay interest. Today, this distinction is not as meaningful because many checking accounts pay interest if the account balance is sufficiently high. Finally, travelers' checks are included in M1 because they are regularly used in economic exchanges.

Let's take a closer look at the amount of currency in the economy. Since there are approximately 280 million people in the United States, the $534 billion of currency

Table 12.1 Components of M1, January 2001

Currency held by the public	$ 534 billion
Demand deposits	$ 316 billion
Other checkable deposits	$ 242 billion
Travelers' checks	$ 8 billion
Total of M1	$1100 billion

Source: Federal Reserve Bank of St. Louis.

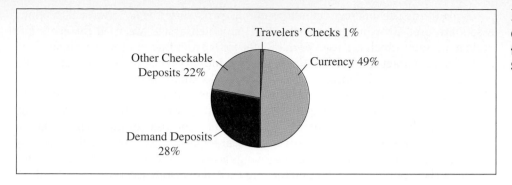

Figure 12.1
Components of M1 for the United States

Travelers' Checks 1%

Other Checkable Deposits 22%

Currency 49%

Demand Deposits 28%

amounts to over $1,907 in currency for every man, woman, and child in the United States. Do you and your friends each have $1,907 of currency?

Most of the currency in the official statistics is not used in ordinary commerce in the United States. Much of it is held abroad by wealthy people who want U.S. currency in case of emergencies or who use it to keep their wealth out of sight of their own governments and tax authorities. Some of it circulates in other countries along with their local currencies. Currency is also used in illegal transactions such as the drug trade. Few dealers of illegal drugs open bank accounts that could be inspected by international law authorities.

M1 does not include all the assets that are used to make economic exchanges. Economists also use a somewhat broader definition of money known as **M2**, which includes assets that are sometimes used in economic exchanges or can be readily turned into M1. M2 consists of all the assets in M1 plus several other assets such as deposits in money market mutual funds. These are funds in which individuals can invest; they earn interest and can be used to write checks over some minimum amount. Deposits in savings accounts are also included in M2. While deposits in savings accounts cannot generally be used directly in exchanges, they can be converted to M1 and then used in exchanges. In January 2001, M2 totaled $4,995 billion.

M2: M1 plus other assets, including deposits in savings and loans and money market mutual funds.

Currency held by the public is part of the official money supply.

Economists use different definitions of money because it is not always clear which assets are used primarily as money—that is, which assets are used for economic exchanges—and which are used primarily for saving and investing. For example, consider money market mutual funds, which came into existence only in the late 1970s. Although people can use these funds to write checks and engage in economic transactions, many people use them in other ways. Some may have their wealth temporarily invested in these funds in anticipation of moving their wealth into the stock market. Others may use them to earn interest while avoiding the risks of the stock market or bond market. Sometimes, money market mutual funds are used like regular checking accounts; other times, they are used like savings accounts. If they are used like checking accounts, they should be in M1; but if they are used like savings accounts, they should be part of M2. Economists keep an eye on both M1 and M2 because they often do not know precisely how money market accounts are used.

While credit cards are commonly used in our economy to make transactions, they are not part of the money supply. Here is why: Suppose you have a credit card from the First Union Bank and purchase a new television set from an electronics store. As you use your credit card, you are effectively borrowing the amount for the purchase of the television set from the First Union Bank, who, in turn, will pay the electronics store. When you receive your credit card bill, you must begin to pay off the loan from the bank. Credit cards enable you to purchase goods now, but use money to pay for them at a later date. The credit card is—unlike money—not a medium of exchange, a unit of account, or a store of value. Credit cards do make it easier to conduct business, but they are not an official part of the money supply.

TEST Your Understanding

6. About one-third of M1 consists of _____.

7. Complete the statement with *M1* or *M2*: Economists use _____ to measure the amount of money that is regularly used in transactions.

8. Which is greater: M1 or M2?

9. How do you explain the fact that the total amount of currency divided by the U.S. population is approximately $1,907?

10. Why are money market mutual funds hard to classify?

Banks as Financial Intermediaries

Now let's see what part banks play in the creation of the supply of money. In Chapter 26, we discussed how financial intermediaries help to bring savers and investors together. By using their expertise and the powers of diversification, financial intermediaries reduce risk to savers and allow investors to obtain funds on better terms. Commercial banks operate precisely in this manner.

A typical commercial bank will accept funds from savers in the form of deposits, for example, in a checking account. The bank does not leave all these funds idle; if it did, it could never make a profit. Instead, the bank turns the money around and makes loans to businesses. A local hardware store might need a $100,000 loan to purchase its inventory. To make this loan, the bank would pool deposits from many savers. It will make other loans as well, reducing its risk through diversification.

Balance sheet: An account for a bank which shows the sources of its funds (liabilities) as well as the uses for the funds (assets).

It will be easier to understand how banks work if we examined a simplified **balance sheet** for a commercial bank. A balance sheet shows how banks raise money and where the money goes.

Assets		Liabilities	
$ 200 Reserves		$2,000 Deposits	
$2,000 Loans		$ 200 Net Worth	
Total: $2,200		Total: $2,200	

Figure 12.2

Balance Sheet for a Bank

Balance sheets have two sides: one for assets and one for liabilities. **Liabilities** are the source of funds for the bank. If you open a checking account and deposit your funds in that account, the bank is liable for returning these funds to you. Your deposits are liabilities to the bank.

Assets are the uses of these funds. Assets generate income for the bank. Loans are examples of a bank's assets because a borrower must pay interest to the bank.

The difference between a bank's assets and its liabilities is its **net worth:**

$$\text{net worth} = \text{assets} - \text{liabilities}$$

If a bank has $1,000 of assets and $900 of liabilities, it has a net worth of $100. When a bank is started, its owners must place their own funds into the bank. These funds are the bank's initial net worth. If a bank makes profits, its net worth increases; if it loses money, its net worth decreases.

In Figure 12.2, we show the assets and liabilities of a hypothetical bank. On the liability side, the bank has $2,000 of deposits. The net worth of the bank is $200. This is entered on the liability side of the balance sheet because it is also a source of funds. The total source of funds is therefore $2,200—the deposits in the bank plus its net worth.

On the asset side, the bank holds $200 in **reserves**; these are assets that are not lent out. Banks are required by law to hold a specific fraction of their deposits as reserves and not make loans with it; this fraction of deposits is called **required reserves.** Banks may choose to hold additional reserves beyond what is required; these are called **excess reserves.** A bank's reserves are the sum of its required and excess reserves. Reserves can be either cash kept in a bank's vaults or deposits with the Federal Reserve. Banks do not earn any interest on these reserves.

In our example, the bank is holding 10% of its deposits, or $200, as reserves. The remainder of the bank's assets consists of loans. In this case the bank makes $2,000 in loans.

By definition, total assets will always equal liabilities plus net worth. Balance sheets must always balance.

The Process of Money Creation

To understand the role that banks play in determining the supply of money, let's suppose that someone walks into the First Bank of Hollywood and deposits $1,000 in cash to open a checking account. Because currency held by the public and checking deposits are both included in the supply of money, the total money supply has not changed. The money supply did not change because the cash deposit of currency into the checking account reduced the currency held by the public by precisely the amount that the deposit in the checking account increased.

However, banks do not keep in their vaults all the cash they receive. For a bank to make a profit, it must make loans. Let's assume that banks are required to keep 10% of

Liabilities: The sources of funds for a bank, including deposits.

Assets: The uses of the funds of a bank, including loans and reserves.

Net worth: The difference between assets and liabilities.

Reserves: The fraction of banks' deposits that are set aside in either vault cash or as deposits at the Federal Reserve.

Required reserves: The fraction of banks' deposits that banks are legally required to hold in their vaults or as deposits at the Fed.

Excess reserves: Any additional reserves that a bank holds above its required reserves.

Figure 12.3

Process of Deposit Creation: Changes in Balance Sheets

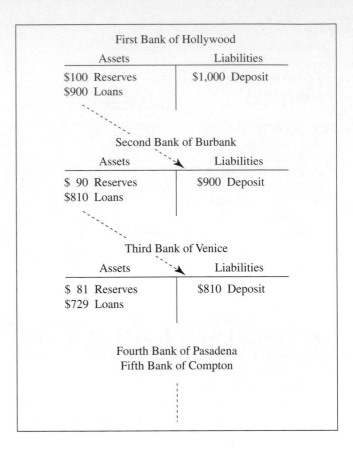

First Bank of Hollywood

Assets	Liabilities
$100 Reserves	$1,000 Deposit
$900 Loans	

Second Bank of Burbank

Assets	Liabilities
$ 90 Reserves	$900 Deposit
$810 Loans	

Third Bank of Venice

Assets	Liabilities
$ 81 Reserves	$810 Deposit
$729 Loans	

Fourth Bank of Pasadena
Fifth Bank of Compton

Reserve ratio: The ratio of reserves to deposits.

deposits as reserves and hold no excess reserves. That means that the **reserve ratio**—the ratio of reserves to deposits—will be 0.1 The First Bank of Hollywood will keep $100 in reserves and make loans totaling $900. The top panel in Figure 12.3 shows the change in the bank's balance sheet after it has made its loan.

Suppose the First Bank of Hollywood loaned the funds to an aspiring movie producer. The bank opens a checking account, with a balance of $900, for the producer, who needs the funds to buy equipment. The producer buys the equipment from a supplier who accepts payment in the form of a $900 check, and deposits the check in the Second Bank of Burbank. The next panel in Figure 12.3 shows what happens to the balance sheet of the Second Bank of Burbank. Liabilities increase by the deposit of $900. The bank must hold $90 in reserves (10% of the $900 deposit) and can lend out $810. Suppose that it lends the $810 to an owner of a coffeehouse and opens a checking account with a balance of $810 for her. She then purchases coffee costing $810, paying with a check to the supplier, who deposits the $810 check into the Third Bank of Venice.

The Third Bank of Venice receives a deposit of $810. It must keep $81 in reserves and can lend out $729. This process continues throughout the Los Angeles area with new loans and deposits. The Fourth Bank of Pasadena will receive a deposit of $729, hold $72.90 in reserves, and lend out $656.10. The Fifth Bank of Compton will receive a deposit of $656.10 as the process goes on.

The original $1,000 cash deposit has created checking account balances throughout Los Angeles. What total amount of checking account balances has been created? Adding up the new accounts in all the banks (even the ones we have not named), we have

$$\$1,000 + \$900 + \$810 + \$729 + \$656.10 + \ldots = \$10,000$$

How did we come up with this sum? It's from the following simple formula, which we derive in the appendix to this chapter:

total increase in checking account balance throughout all banks
= (initial cash deposit) × (1/reserve ratio)

In our example, the reserve ratio is 0.1, so the increase in checking account balances is 1/0.1, or 10 times the initial cash deposit. The initial $1,000 deposit led to a total increase in checking account balances throughout all banks of $10,000.

Recall that the money supply, M1, is the sum of deposits at commercial banks plus currency held by the public. Therefore, the change in the money supply, M1, will be the change in deposits in checking accounts plus the change in currency held by the public. Notice that we referred to "change," meaning increase or decrease. Here's why: In our example, deposits increased by $10,000, but the public (as represented by the person who made that first deposit at the First Bank of Hollywood) holds $1,000 less of currency because the person deposited the currency in the bank. Therefore, the money supply, M1, increased by $9,000 ($10,000 – $1,000). No single bank lent out more than it had in deposits. Yet for the banking system as a whole, the money supply expanded by a multiple of the initial cash deposit.

The term *1/reserve ratio* in the formula is called the **money multiplier**. It tells us what the total increase in checking account deposits would be for any initial cash deposit. Recall the multiplier for government spending in our demand-side models: An increase in government spending led to larger increases in output through the multiplier. The government spending multiplier arose because additional rounds of consumption spending were triggered by an initial increase in government spending. In the banking system, an initial cash deposit triggers additional rounds of deposits and lending by banks. This leads to a multiple expansion of deposits.

As of 2001 in the United States, banks were required to hold 3% reserves against checkable deposits up to $42.8 million and 10% on all checkable deposits exceeding $42.8 million. Since large banks would face a 10% reserve requirement on any new deposits, you might think, on the basis of our formula, that the money multiplier would be approximately 10.

However, the money multiplier for the United States is between 2 and 3, much smaller than the value of 10 implied by our simple formula. The primary reason is that our formula assumed that all loans made their way directly into checking accounts. In reality, people hold part of their loans as cash. The cash that people hold is not available for the banking system to lend out. The more money people hold in cash, the lower the amount of money they deposit, creating fewer deposits, thus decreasing the money multiplier. The money multiplier would also be less if banks held excess reserves. We can represent these factors in a money multiplier ratio, but it will not be as simple as the one we introduced here.

The money creation process also works in reverse. Suppose you go to your bank and ask for $1,000 in cash from your checking account. The bank must pay you the $1,000. Its liabilities fall by $1,000, but its assets must also fall by $1,000. Withdrawing your $1,000 means two things at the bank: First, if the reserve ratio is 0.1, the bank will reduce its reserves by $100. Second, your $1,000 withdrawal minus the $100 reduction in reserves means that the bank has $900 less to lend out; hence, it will reduce its loans by $900. With fewer loans, there will be fewer deposits in other banks. The money multiplier working in reverse decreases the money supply.

You may wonder how a bank goes about reducing its outstanding loans. If you had borrowed from a bank to invest in a project for your business, you would not want the bank phoning you, asking for its funds, which are not lying idle but are invested in your

Money multiplier: An initial deposit leads to a multiple expansion of deposits. In the simplified case, increase in deposits = (initial deposit) × (1/reserve ratio).

business. Banks do not typically call in loans from outstanding borrowers. Instead, if banks cannot tap into their excess reserves when their customers want to withdraw cash, they have to make fewer new loans. In these circumstances, a new potential borrower would find it harder to obtain a loan from the bank.

Up to this point, our examples have always started with an initial cash deposit. However, suppose that Paul receives a check from Freda and Paul deposits it into his bank. Paul's bank will eventually receive payment from Freda's bank. When Paul's bank does receive payment, the bank will initially have an increase in both deposits and reserves, just as if a cash deposit were made. Because Paul's bank has to hold only a fraction of the deposits as reserves, it will be able to make loans with the remainder.

However, there is one crucial difference between this example in which one individual writes a check to another and our earlier example in which an individual makes a cash deposit: When Paul receives the check from Freda, the money supply will not be changed. Here's why it won't: When Freda's check is deposited in Paul's bank, the money supply will begin to expand, but when Freda's bank loses its deposit, the money supply will start to contract. The expansions and contractions offset each other when private citizens and firms write checks to one another.

TEST Your Understanding

11. Banks are required by law to keep a fraction of their deposits as _____.

12. Define net worth.

13. Why does a bank prefer to make loans rather than keep reserves?

14. If the reserve ratio is 0.2 and a deposit of $100 is made into a bank, the bank will lend out _____.

15. If the reserve ratio is 0.2, the simplified money multiplier will be _____.

16. Why is the actual money multiplier much smaller than in our simple formula?

The Role of the Federal Reserve in the Money Creation Process

Banks can expand the money supply only if new reserves come into the banking system. When private citizens and firms write checks to one another, there will be no net change in the supply of money in the system. Because the total amount of reserves in the system is unchanged, the money supply cannot expand. There is one organization, however, that has the power to change the total amount of reserves in the banking system: the Federal Reserve.

Open Market Operations

Open market purchases: The Fed's purchase of government bonds, which increases the money supply.

Open market sales: The Fed's sales of government bonds to the public, which decreases the money supply.

The Federal Reserve (the Fed) can increase or decrease the total amount of reserves in the banking system through either of the following operations:

- In **open market purchases,** the Federal Reserve buys government bonds from the private sector.

- In **open market sales,** the Fed sells government bonds to the private sector.

To understand how the Fed can increase the supply of money, let's trace what happens after an open market purchase. Suppose the Federal Reserve purchases $1 million worth of government bonds from the private sector. The Fed writes a check for $1 million and presents it to the party who sold the bonds. The Federal Reserve now owns those bonds.

The party who sold the bonds has a check written on the Federal Reserve for $1 million. He deposits this check in his bank. The bank credits his account in the amount of $1 million because it has the check for $1 million written against the Federal Reserve.

Here is the key to how that increases the supply of money: Checks written against the Federal Reserve count as reserves for banks. As soon as the bank presents the check to the Federal Reserve, the bank will have $1 million in new reserves. If the reserve requirement is 10%, the bank must keep $100,000 in reserves, but it can make loans for $900,000. And so the process of money creation begins. Open market purchases increase the money supply.

The Federal Reserve has powers that ordinary citizens and even banks do not have. The Fed can write checks against itself to purchase government bonds without having any explicit "funds" in its account for the purchase. Banks accept these checks because they count as reserves for the bank.

As you might expect, open market sales will decrease the supply of money. Suppose the Federal Reserve sells $1 million worth of bonds to a Wall Street firm. The firm will pay for the bonds with a check for $1 million drawn on its bank and give this check to the Federal Reserve. The firm now owns the bonds.

The Federal Reserve presents this check to the Wall Street firm's bank. The bank must either hand over $1 million in cash or, more likely, reduce its reserve holding with the Federal Reserve by $1 million. (Banks keep accounts with the Fed, and in this case, the Fed would reduce the bank's account balance by $1 million.) Because the bank's reserves have fallen, it must decrease its loans to increase reserves to their required levels. And so, the process of money destruction begins. Open market sales decrease the money supply.

In summary, if the Federal Reserve wishes to increase the money supply, it buys government bonds from the private sector—called open market purchases. If the Fed wishes to decrease the money supply, it sells government bonds to the private sector—called open market sales.

Other Tools

Open market operations are by far the most important way in which the Federal Reserve changes the supply of money. There are two other ways in which the Fed can change the supply of money:

- Change the reserve requirement.
- Change the discount rate.

If the Fed wishes to increase the supply of money, it can reduce banks' reserve requirements. Banks would then only need to hold a smaller fraction of their deposits as reserves and could make more loans, expanding the money supply. To decrease the supply of money, the Federal Reserve could raise reserve requirements.

Although changing reserve requirements can be a strong tool, the Federal Reserve does not use it very often because it is disruptive to the banking system. Suppose a major bank whose clients were multinational corporations held exactly 10% of its deposits as reserves and the remainder as loans. If the Federal Reserve suddenly increased its reserve requirement to 20%, the bank would be forced to call in or cancel many of its loans. Its multinational clients would not like this! For these reasons, the Fed today does not make sharp changes in reserve requirements. In the past, the Fed did change reserve requirements sharply; when it did, the results were extremely disruptive to banks and their customers.

Discount rate: The interest rate at which banks can borrow from the Fed.

Federal funds market: The market in which banks borrow and lend reserves to one another.

The Fed will lend banks reserves at an interest rate called the **discount rate**. Suppose a major customer comes to the bank and asks for a loan. Unless the bank could find an additional source of funds, it would have to refuse to make the loan. Banks are reluctant to turn away major customers. They first try to borrow reserves from other banks through the **federal funds market**, a market in which banks borrow or lend reserves to each other. If the federal funds rate seemed too high to the bank, it could borrow directly from the Federal Reserve at the discount rate.

By changing the discount rate, the Federal Reserve can influence the amount of borrowing by banks. If the Fed raised the discount rate, banks would be discouraged from borrowing reserves because it has become more costly to borrow. Lowering the discount rate will induce banks to borrow additional reserves.

In principle, the Federal Reserve could use the discount rate as a tool independent of monetary policy: lowering the discount rate to expand the money supply and raising the discount rate to reduce the money supply. In practice, the Fed keeps the discount rate close to the federal funds rate to avoid large swings in borrowed reserves by banks. Changes in the discount rate, however, are quite visible to financial markets. Participants in the financial markets often interpret these changes as revealing clues about the Fed's intentions for future monetary policy.

The media typically describes the Federal Reserve as setting the federal funds rate. In fact, the Fed does conduct monetary policy by setting targets for the federal funds rate. Once it has set those targets, it uses open market operations to keep the actual funds rate on target.

TEST Your Understanding

17. Complete the statement with *increases* or *decreases*: When the Federal Reserve buys bonds, it _____ the money supply.

18. Complete the statement with *sale* or *purchase*: An open market _____ will lead to a reduction of reserves in banks.

19. Who borrows and lends in the federal funds market?

20. What is the discount rate?

The Structure of the Federal Reserve

The Federal Reserve System was created in 1913 after a series of financial panics in the United States. Financial panics can occur when there is bad news about the economy or about the health and vitality of financial institutions that causes concern among individuals doing business in the financial markets. During these panics, depositors became fearful that they would not be able to withdraw their account balances if they delayed, so they started to withdraw their funds immediately. This meant that banks could no longer make loans to businesses, resulting in severe economic downturns. Congress created the Federal Reserve System to be a **central bank**, serving as a banker's bank. One of the Fed's primary jobs was to serve as a **lender of last resort**. If there was a panic in which depositors wanted to withdraw their funds, the Federal Reserve would be there to lend funds to banks, thereby reducing some of the adverse consequences of the panic.

Central bank: A banker's bank; an official bank that controls the supply of money in a country.

Lender of last resort: A central bank is the lender of last resort, the last place, having failed all others, that banks in emergency situations can obtain loans.

The Federal Reserve's important role as a lender of last resort came into play immediately following the September 11, 2001 tragedy. "A Closer Look: The Fed Responds to the Terrorist Attack" outlines the key steps that the Federal Reserve took to ensure the continuing operation of the financial system.

All countries have central banks. The Indian central bank is known as the Reserve Bank of India. In the United Kingdom, the central bank is the Bank of England. Central

A CLOSER LOOK

THE FED RESPONDS TO THE TERRORIST ATTACK

When the financial markets closed after September 11, many firms who borrowed funds regularly in the markets did not have sufficient cash on hand to meet their ongoing bills and obligations. Unless some actions were taken quickly, these firms would default on their debts, leading to payment problems for other firms and further defaults. To prevent this avalanche of defaults, the Federal Reserve immediately took a number of steps to provide additional funds to the financial system. These steps have been recounted by William Poole, president of the Federal Reserve Bank of St. Louis.

The first tool that the Federal Reserve used was to allow banks to borrow more from the Federal Reserve itself at the discount rate. In regular times, the volume of these direct loans from the Federal Reserve is not very large. On Wednesday, September 12, total lending to banks rose to $45.5 billion, up from just $99 million the week before.

In normal times, the Federal Reserve System serves as a clearinghouse for checks. A bank will bring checks it receives from customers to the Federal Reserve and receive immediate credit on its accounts.

The Federal Reserve then debits the account of the bank upon which the check was written. The difference between the credits and the debits extended by the Federal Reserve is called the "Federal Reserve Float." Immediately following September 11, the Federal Reserve allowed this float to increase sharply from $2.9 billion to $22.9 billion. These actions effectively put an additional $20 billion into the banking system.

The Federal Reserve also increased its open market purchases of government securities in the market by nearly $30 billion. They also arranged to provide dollars to foreign central banks who needed them to meet their own needs and the needs of their banks in this crisis. Taken together, all these actions increased the credit extended by the Federal Reserve by over $90 billion. This massive response by the Federal Reserve prevented a financial panic that could have had devastating effects on the world economy.

Source: William Poole, "The Role of the Government in the U.S. Capital Markets," paper delivered at UC Davis, October 18, 2001.

---

banks serve as lenders of last resort to the banks in their countries and provide the levers through which they change their money supply.

Congress was aware that it was creating an institution with vast powers, so it deliberately created a structure in which, at least on paper, it attempted to disperse power away from the financial centers (e.g., New York) to the rest of the country. To understand the structure of the Federal Reserve today, keep in mind it has three distinct subgroups: Federal Reserve Banks, the Board of Governors, and the Federal Open Market Committee.

The United States was divided into 12 Federal Reserve districts, each of which has a **Federal Reserve Bank.** These district banks provide advice on monetary policy, take part in decision-making on monetary policy, and provide a liaison between the Fed and the banks in their districts.

Federal Reserve Banks: One of 12 regional banks that are an official part of the Federal Reserve System.

Figure 12.4 is a map of the United States, identifying geographically each of the 12 Federal Reserve Banks. At the time the Fed was created, economic and financial power in this country was concentrated in the East and the Midwest. This is no longer true. What major Western city does not have a Federal Reserve Bank?

The **Board of Governors of the Federal Reserve** is the true seat of power over the monetary system. Headquartered in Washington, D.C., the seven members of the board are appointed for staggered 14-year terms by the President and must be confirmed by the Senate. The chairperson of the Board of Governors serves a four-year term. As the principal spokesperson for monetary policy in the United States, what the chairperson says, or might say, is carefully observed or anticipated by financial markets throughout the world.

Board of Governors of the Federal Reserve: The seven-person governing body of the Federal Reserve system in Washington, D.C.

Figure 12.4
Federal Reserve Banks of the United States

Federal Open Market Committee [FOMC]: The group that decides on monetary policy; it consists of the seven members of the Board of Governors plus five of 12 regional bank presidents on a rotating basis.

Decisions on monetary policy are made by the **Federal Open Market Committee [FOMC]**. The FOMC is a 12-person board consisting of the seven members of the Board of Governors, the president of the New York Federal Reserve bank plus the presidents of four other regional Federal Reserve Banks. (Presidents of the regional banks other than New York serve on a rotating basis; the seven nonvoting bank presidents attend the meetings and provide their views). The chairperson of the Board of Governors also serves as the chairperson of the FOMC. The FOMC makes the actual decisions on changes in the money supply. Its members are assisted by vast teams of professionals at the Board of Governors and at the regional Federal Reserve Banks. The structure of the Federal Reserve System is depicted in Figure 12.5.

The chairperson of the Board of Governors is also required to report to Congress on a regular basis. Although the Federal Reserve operates with independence from the U.S. Treasury, it is a creation of Congress. The U.S. Constitution gives Congress the power to "coin money and regulate the value thereof." In practice, the Fed takes its actions first

Figure 12.5
Structure of the Federal Reserve

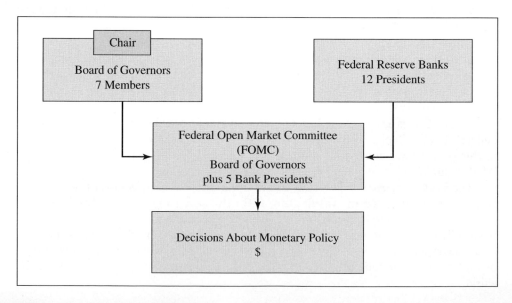

and later reports its actions to Congress. The chairperson of the Federal Reserve often meets with members of the executive branch to discuss economic affairs.

On paper, the powers of monetary policy appear to be spread throughout the government and the country. In practice, however, the Board of Governors and especially the chairperson have the real control. The Board of Governors operates with considerable independence. Presidents and members of Congress can bring political pressures on the Board of Governors, but 14-year terms provide some insulation from external pressures.

In recent years, the Federal Reserve has had two strong and effective chairmen who led the debate of monetary policy. "A Closer Look: Two Decades, Two Chairmen" briefly introduces the personalities of each chairman.

Countries differ in the degree to which the central bank is independent of political authorities. In both the United States and the United Kingdom, the central banks operate with considerable independence of elected officials. In other countries, the central bank is part of the treasury department of the government and potentially subject to more direct political control.

There is a lively debate among economists and political scientists as to whether more independent central banks (with less external political pressure) have less inflation. Even if there is an advantage to an independent central bank, there still is an important issue: In a democratic society, why should we allow there to be an important and powerful institution that is not directly subject to control by the people or our elected officials?

Why should we care about the Fed and the supply of money? In this chapter, we have discussed the role that money plays in the economy, how commercial banks play a key role in the creation of money, and how the Fed exercises ultimate control of the money supply. In the next chapter, we will see that the Fed can also determine short-term interest rates and thereby influence the level of economic activity. It is precisely this power over the economy that makes the Fed such a subject of public interest.

A CLOSER LOOK   TWO DECADES, TWO CHAIRMEN

Since 1979, the Federal Reserve Board has only had two chairmen: Paul Volcker, who served from 1979 to 1987, and Alan Greenspan, who served from 1987, until the present time. In their day, each was the country's major figure in monetary policy.

Paul Volcker was appointed by President Jimmy Carter, who sought an established banker to help combat inflation. Volcker, who served as the President of the New York Federal Reserve Bank, took a pay cut to come to Washington to fight inflation. A tall, imposing figure, who smoked cigars, Volcker was relentless in his fight against inflation. Under his regime, the Federal Reserve drove interest rates up to 18% and precipitated a recession in order to bring down inflation. By the time Volcker left office, inflation was fully under control.

Alan Greenspan was appointed by President Ronald Reagan. One week after assuming office, he faced a major crisis with the stock market crash of 1987. Stock prices fell 23% on October 19, 1987, wiping out nearly a $1 trillion of wealth. Greenspan handled the crisis adeptly, making it clear the Federal Reserve would provide loans to banks and firms to weather the financial storm. This was precisely the right medicine.

Over the next fourteen years, Greenspan presided over a successful period for monetary policy. Except for the recessions in the early 1990s and in 2001, the economy grew smoothly and inflation remained under control. During the mid-1990s, the Federal Reserve allowed the economy to grow at a faster rate than most economists believed possible, but the gamble paid off and there was no resurgence of inflation. In 1999 and 2000, the Federal Reserve may have tightened monetary policy prematurely, contributing to the subsequent contraction. Nonetheless, Greenspan's performance has earned universal praise and one author deemed him the "maestro."

Using the TOOLS

In this chapter, we studied the money creation process as it works through the banking system. Take this opportunity to do your own economic analysis.

1. ECONOMIC EXPERIMENT: Money and the Store of Value

This experiment demonstrates that goods that are more effective stores of value can become the medium of exchange. There are three types of individuals (A, B, C) and three types of goods in the economy (1, 2, 3). Type A consumes good 1; Type B consumes good 2; and Type C consumes good 3. No type produces the good it consumes: Type A produces Good 2; Type B produces Good 3; and Type C produces Good 1. Here is how the game works: In the first period, individuals start with 1 unit of the good they produce and are randomly paired with other individuals. They can either engage in trade or not. If they successfully trade for the good they are allowed to consume, they consume it immediately and earn 100 points. At that time they also costlessly produce 1 unit of their good for the next round of play. If individuals do not trade, they must store their goods. They lose 10 points for storing good 1, lose 20 points for storing good 2, and lose 30 points for storing good 3. The game proceeds for several periods, and the individual with the most points wins. What good do you think emerges as the medium of exchange?

APPLICATIONS

2. Bad Loans to South America

During the 1980s, U.S. banks made loans to South American countries. Many of these loans turned out to be worthless. How did this affect the assets, liabilities, and net worth of these banks?

3. Reserve Requirements as a Tax

Left on their own, most banks would reduce their reserve requirements far below 10%. Consequently, banks view reserve requirements as a "tax" on their holdings of deposits. Explain how a 10% reserve requirement could be viewed as a 10% tax.

4. High-Powered Money

Economists define high-powered money as the reserves at banks plus the currency held by the public. The Federal Reserve is often said to control the stock of high-powered money. Does the stock of high-powered money change when:

a. Currency is deposited into a bank?

b. A bank makes a loan?

c. The Federal Reserve buys government bonds?

Summary

We began this chapter examining the role money plays in the economy and how economists define *money*. We then took a closer look at banks as financial intermediaries. We saw how banks can create money through deposit creation. And we learned how the Federal Reserve can control the supply of money through open market purchases and sales and other policies. Here are the main points you should remember from this chapter:

1. Money consists of anything that is regularly used in making exchanges, that is, buying and selling goods and services. In modern economies, money consists primarily of currency and deposits in checking accounts.

2. Banks are financial intermediaries that earn profits by accepting deposits and making loans. Deposits, which are liabilities of banks, are included in the money supply.

3. Banks are required by law to hold a fraction of their deposits as reserves, either in cash or in deposits with the Federal Reserve. Total reserves consist of required reserves plus excess reserves.

4. If there is an increase in reserves in the banking system, the supply of money will expand by a multiple of the initial deposit. This multiple is known as the money multiplier.

5. The Federal Reserve's primary tool for increasing or decreasing the total amount of reserves in the banking system is through open market purchases of government bonds (which increase reserves) or open market sales (which decrease reserves).

6. The Federal Reserve can also change the supply of money by changing reserve requirements or changing the discount rate.

7. Decisions about the supply of money are made at the Federal Open Market Committee (FOMC), which includes the seven members on the Board of Governors and the president of the New York Federal Reserve Bank, as well as four of the 11 other regional bank presidents, who serve on a rotating basis.

 ## Key Terms

assets, 255
balance sheet, 254
barter, 251
Board of Governors of the Federal Reserve, 261
central bank, 260
discount rate, 260
double coincidence of wants, 251
excess reserves, 255
federal funds market, 260

Federal Open Market Committee [FOMC], 262
Federal Reserve Banks, 261
lender of last resort, 260
liabilities, 255
M1, 252
M2, 253
medium of exchange, 251
money, 250

money multiplier, 257
net worth, 255
open market purchases, 258
open market sales, 258
required reserves, 255
reserve ratio, 256
reserves, 255
store of value, 251
unit of account, 251

 ## Problems and Discussion Questions

1. Why are travelers' checks classified as money?

2. Both insurance companies and banks are financial intermediaries. Why do macroeconomists study banks more intensively than insurance companies?

3. What is the opportunity cost to a bank of holding excess reserves?

4. If a customer took $2,000 in cash from a bank and the reserve ratio was 0.2, by how much would the supply of money be eventually reduced?

5. If the Federal Reserve undertakes an open market sale of $2 million and the reserve ratio is 0.15, by how much will the money supply decrease?

6. If banks hold excess reserves, how will this affect the money multiplier?

7. Explain the mechanism through which an increase in the discount rate affects the money supply.

8. Occasionally, some economists or politicians suggest that the Secretary of Treasury become a member of the Federal Open Market Committee. How do you think this would affect the independence of the Federal Reserve?

9. Suppose the Federal Reserve purchased gold or foreign currency. How would this purchase affect the domestic money supply? (Hint: Think about open market purchases of government bonds.)

10. The Federal Reserve has traditionally conducted its open market operations through the purchase and sale of government bonds. In principle, could the Federal Reserve conduct monetary policy through the purchase and sale of stocks on the New York Stock Exchange? Do you see any potential drawbacks to such a policy?

11. In 1992, the state of California ran out of funds and could not pay its bills. It issued IOUs, called warrants, to its workers and suppliers. Only large banks and credit unions accepted the warrants. Should these warrants be viewed as money?

12. Web Exercise. Go to the Web site of the Federal Reserve [*http://www.federalreserve.gov*] and read the minutes from the last Open Market Committee meeting. What decisions did they make with regard to open market operations? What other items of business were on their agenda that day?

13. Web Exercise. Go to the data Web site of the Federal Reserve Bank of St. Louis [*http://www.stls.frb.orgl fred*]. Look carefully at the components of M1 and M2 over the last 10 years. What trends do you see?

Take It to the Net

We invite you to visit the O'Sullivan/Sheffrin page on the Prentice Hall Web site at: **http://www.prenhall.com/osullivan/** for additional World Wide Web exercises for this chapter.

Model Answers to Questions

Chapter-Opening Questions

1. All societies have money because it makes it much easier to conduct trade.

2. Banks play a special role in our economy because the liabilities of banks are part of the supply of money.

3. The banking system as a whole can create money through the process of multiple expansion. However, this depends on the actions of the Federal Reserve.

4. When the Federal Reserve purchases bonds from the public, it increases reserves in banks and leads to an increase in the supply of deposits and loans. When the Federal Reserve sells bonds to the public, the supply of loans and deposits decreases.

5. The chairman of the Federal Reserve is the most powerful person in the Federal Reserve System, which determines the supply of money in the economy.

Test Your Understanding

1. Barter.

2. Inflation makes money an imperfect store of value.

3. Without money, you would need to find someone who had the good that you wanted to buy and also wants to trade for the good that you have.

4. True. Money serves as a unit of account because prices are quoted in terms of money.

5. Checks are counted as money because they are regularly used in economic exchanges.

6. Currency held by the public.

7. M1.

8. M2 is greater.

9. A "typical" person in the United States does not hold this amount of currency. Some currency is held abroad, and some is held for illegal purposes.

10. Money market mutual funds are used both for making transactions and savings.

11. Reserves.

12. Net worth is assets minus liabilities.

13. Banks do not earn interest on reserves, but they do on loans.

14. $80.

15. 5.

16. The simplified formula does not take into account that individuals hold some cash from their loans.

17. Increases.

18. Sale.

19. Banks borrow and lend.

20. The discount rate is the interest rate at which banks can borrow from the Fed.

Using the Tools

1. Economic Experiment: Money and the Store of Value. As the experiment should reveal, good 1 should emerge as the most likely medium of exchange.

2. Bad Loans to South America. Bad loans will reduce the assets of a bank. Because they do not change the liabilities of a bank (its deposits), the net worth of the bank must also fall along with the value of its assets. If the net worth of a bank falls too far, the bank can be closed.

3. Reserve Requirements as a Tax. Because a bank earns no interest on reserves, the reserve requirement acts as a tax. Suppose the bank held no

reserves at all and could earn 20% interest on loans. A 10% reserve requirement means that the bank could only earn 20% interest on 90% of its deposits. This is equivalent to a tax of 10%.

4. High-Powered Money. The stock of high-powered money changes only when the Federal Reserve buys a government bond. In this case, the total of reserves plus currency increases. If the public deposits currency in the bank, currency held by the public falls but the currency held by the bank (which counts as reserves) increases. When a bank makes a loan, the total reserves in the banking system do not change.

Formula for Deposit Creation

To show how to derive the formula for deposit creation, let's use the example in the text. We showed that with 10% held as reserves, a $1,000 deposit led to total deposits of

$$\$1,000 + \$900 + \$810 + \$729 + \$656.10 + \ldots$$

Let's find the total sum of all these deposits. Because each bank successively had to hold 10% in its reserves, that means that each successive bank received only 0.9 of the deposits of the prior bank. Therefore, we can write the total for the deposits in all the banks as

$$\$1,000 \times (1 + 0.9 + 0.9^2 + 0.9^3 + 0.9^4 + \ldots)$$

We need to find the sum of the terms in parentheses. Using a formula for an infinite sum,

$$1 + b + b^2 + b^3 + b^4 + \ldots = 1/(1-b)$$

the expression becomes

$$1 + 0.9 + 0.9^2 + 0.9^3 + 0.9^4 + \ldots = 1/(1-0.9) = 1/0.1 = 10$$

Therefore, the total increase in deposits will be

$$\$1,000 \times 10 = \$10,000$$

To derive the general formula, note that if the reserve ratio is r, the bank will lend out $(1 - r)$ per dollar of deposits. Following the steps we just outlined, we find the infinite sum will be $1/[1 - (1 - r)] = 1/r$ or 1/reserve ratio. Therefore, in general, we have the formula

increase in checking account balances = (initial deposit) $\times$ (1/reserve ratio)

Monetary Policy in the Short Run

On January 3, 2001, the Federal Reserve took the financial markets by total surprise. And, for the markets, it was a pleasant surprise.

The chairman of the Federal Reserve, Alan Greenspan, had become disturbed by recent economic news. In May 2000, the Fed had raised the federal funds rate from 6.00% to 6.50% as they worried about inflationary pressures. Shortly after this rate increase, evidence began to accumulate that the economy was slowing. Nonetheless, the Fed did not lower the rate at the Open Market Committee meeting in December. The next meeting was not until late January.

Alan Greenspan did not feel he could wait that long. On January 3, he arranged a conference call in the morning, and by afternoon, lowered the federal funds rate back to 6.00%. This turned out to be the beginning of an aggressive policy of cutting interest rates during 2001.

Cutting the funds rate between scheduled meetings was an unusual and bold step for the Fed. It was discussed throughout the world—from taxi drivers to brokers on Wall Street. But did it mean that the Fed would now take action to try to prevent a recession or was it an admission that the Fed had underestimated the weakness of the economy?

n this chapter, we will learn why everyone is so interested in what the Federal Reserve is about to do. In the short run, when prices don't have enough time to change, so we consider them temporarily fixed, the Federal Reserve can influence the level of interest rates in the economy. When the Federal Reserve lowers interest rates, investment spending and GDP increase. When the Fed increases interest rates, that will reduce investment spending and GDP. It is this power of the Fed to affect interest rates in the short run that will influence firms' decisions to invest. It also explains why everyone wants to know what the Fed will do about interest rates in the near future.

After reading this chapter, you will be able to answer the following questions:

1. Why do short-term interest rates rise after the Federal Reserve makes open market sales?

2. Why do the prices of bonds usually fall when the Federal Reserve raises interest rates?

3. How does the housing and the construction industry respond after the Federal Reserve decides to increase the money supply?

4. Why might the Fed refuse to lower interest rates even if everyone agrees the economy is in a slump?

The Federal Reserve influences the level of interest rates in the short run by changing the supply of money through open market operations: selling or buying bonds in the open market. We will explain in this chapter how interest rates are determined in the short run by the supply and demand for money:

- The supply of money is determined largely by the Federal Reserve.

- The demand for money comes from the private sector. Using two principles of economics, *opportunity cost* and the *reality principle*, we will explain the factors that determine the demand for money.

- Putting demand for money and supply of money together, we will see how interest rates are determined in the short run.

Changes in interest rates affect total spending and output in the economy. For example, an open market purchase of bonds increases the money supply, which leads to lower interest rates and increased investment spending. A higher level of investment spending will ultimately lead to a higher level of GDP. Here is the sequence of events to keep in mind as you read this chapter:

| open market purchases | $\rightarrow$ | increase in money supply | $\rightarrow$ | fall in interest rates | $\rightarrow$ | rise in investment spending | $\rightarrow$ | increase in GDP |

We have already seen that the Fed's open market purchases of bonds increase the money supply, increases in the money supply decrease interest rates, decreased interest rates increase investment spending, and higher investment spending leads to higher levels of GDP. From the preceding chapters, all but the link between the money supply increase and falling interest rates should be familiar to you. In this chapter, we add that link to the sequence.

This sequence also works in reverse: The Fed's open market sales of bonds will reduce the money supply, raise interest rates, and lower investment and GDP.

In this chapter, we also discuss how monetary policy works in an open economy: an economy with international trade.

The Fed has immense power, but there are limits to the extent it can effectively control the economy. As we have discussed, in the long run, increases in the money supply affect only prices, not the level of output. In this chapter, we explore the limits of the Fed's monetary policy and fiscal policy in the short run.

Model of the Money Market

We begin by learning the factors that determine the public's demand for money. Once we understand what affects the demand for money, we can see how actions taken by the Federal Reserve determine interest rates in the short run.

The Demand for Money

Let's think of money as simply one part of wealth. Suppose your total wealth is valued at $1,000. In what form will you hold your wealth? Should you put all your wealth into the stock market? Or perhaps into the bond market? Or should you hold some of your wealth in money, that is, currency and checking accounts?

If you invest your wealth in assets such as stocks or bonds, you earn income on your investment. Stocks pay dividends and increase in value; bonds pay interest. If you hold your wealth in currency or a checking account, you receive either no interest or very low interest. Holding your wealth in the form of money means that you sacrifice some potential income.

Money does, however, provide valuable services. It facilitates transactions. If you go to a grocery store to purchase some cereal, the store will accept currency or a check, but you won't be able to pay for your cereal with your stocks and bonds. People hold money primarily for this basic reason: Money makes it easier to conduct transactions. Economists call this reason for holding money the **transactions demand for money**.

To understand the demand for money, we rely on the principle of opportunity cost.

Transactions demand for money: The demand for money based on the desire to facilitate transactions.

PRINCIPLE of Opportunity Cost

> **The opportunity cost of something is what you sacrifice to get it.**

If you hold more of your wealth in terms of money, it makes it easier to conduct everyday business. But when you hold money, you sacrifice income by not investing that amount in assets (such as stocks and bonds) that earn returns.

The opportunity cost of holding money is the return that you could have earned by holding your wealth in other assets. We measure the opportunity cost of holding money by the interest rate. Suppose that the interest rate available to you on a long-term bond is 6% per year. If you hold $100 of your wealth in the form of this bond, you earn $6 a year. If you hold currency instead, you earn no interest. So the opportunity cost of holding $100 in currency is $6 per year or 6% per year.

As interest rates increase in the economy, the opportunity cost of holding money also increases. Economists have found that as the opportunity cost of holding money increases, the public demands less money. The quantity demanded of money will decrease with an increase in interest rates.

In Figure 13.1, we draw a demand for money curve, M^d, as a function of the interest rate. At higher interest rates, individuals will want to hold less money than they will at lower interest rates because the opportunity cost of holding money is higher. As interest rates rise from r_0 to r_1, the quantity demanded of money falls from M_0 to M_1.

Figure 13.1
Demand for Money
As Interest rates Increase from r_0 to r_1, the quantity of money demanded falls from M_0 to M_1.

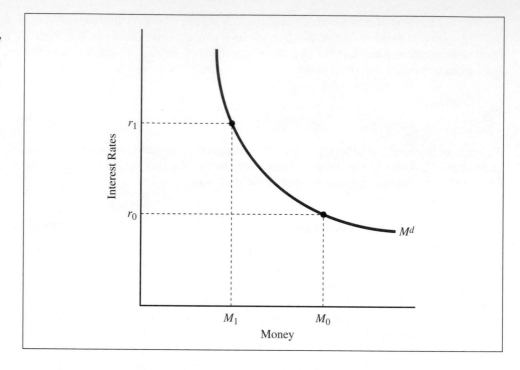

The demand for money also depends on two other factors. One is the overall price level in the economy. The demand for money will increase as the level of prices increases. If prices for your groceries are twice as high, you will need twice as much money to purchase them. The amount of money people typically hold during any time period will be closely related to the dollar value of the transactions that they make. This is an example of the reality principle in action.

Reality **PRINCIPLE**

What matters to people is the real value of money or income—its purchasing power—not the face value of money or income.

The other factor that influences the demand for money is the level of real GDP or real income. It seems obvious that as income increases, individuals and businesses will make more purchases. As real GDP increases, individuals and businesses will be making more transactions. To facilitate these transactions, they will want to hold more money.

Figure 13.2 shows how changes in prices and income affect the demand for money. Increases in money demand will shift the money demand curve to the right. Panel A shows how the demand for money shifts to the right as the price level increases. At any interest rate, people will want to hold more money as prices increase. Panel B shows how the demand for money shifts to the right as real GDP increases. At any interest rate, people will want to hold more money as real GDP increases. These graphs both show the same result. An increase in prices or an increase in real GDP will increase money demand.

Traditionally, economists have identified other motives besides transactions for individuals or firms to hold money. If you hold your wealth in the form of property, such as a house or a boat, it is costly to sell the house or boat on short notice if you need to obtain funds. These forms of wealth are *illiquid*, meaning that they are not easily transferable into money. If you hold your wealth in currency or checking accounts, you do

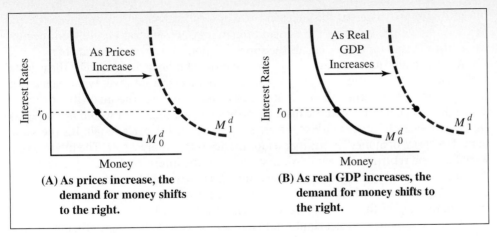

Figure 13.2

Shifting the Demand for Money

Changes in prices and real GDP shift the demand for money.

(A) As prices increase, the demand for money shifts to the right.

(B) As real GDP increases, the demand for money shifts to the right.

not have this problem. Economists recognize that individuals have a **liquidity demand for money**: People want to hold money to be able to make transactions on quick notice.

Individuals may also wish to hold some types of money—particularly savings accounts and assets contained in M2—that pay interest but are less risky than holding stocks or bonds. Over short periods, individuals may not wish to hold stocks or bonds because prices of stocks and bonds might fall. Holding your wealth in a savings account avoids the risk of falling stock or bond prices. The demand for money that arises because it is safer than other assets is called the **speculative demand for money**.

The demand for money, in practice, will be the sum of transactions, liquidity, and speculative demands. As we continue, keep in mind that the demand for money will depend positively on the level of income and prices and negatively on interest rates.

Liquidity demand for money: The demand for money that represents the needs or desires of individuals or firms to make purchases on short notice without incurring excessive costs.

Speculative demand for money: The demand for money that reflects holding money over short periods is less risky than holding stocks or bonds.

Interest Rate Determination

Combining the supply of money, determined by the Fed, with the demand for money, determined by the public, we can see how interest rates are determined in the short run in a demand and supply model of the money market.

Figure 13.3 depicts a model of the money market. The supply of money is determined by the Federal Reserve, and we assume for simplicity that it is independent of

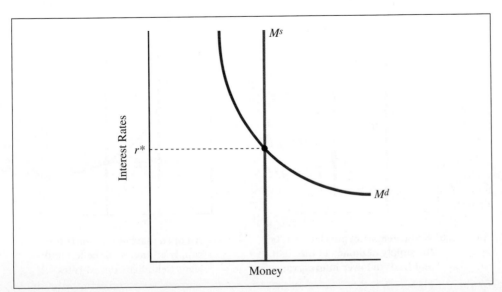

Figure 13.3

Equilibrium in the Money Market

Equilibrium in the money market occurs at an interest rate of r^* at which the quantity of money demanded equals the quantity of money supplied.

interest rates. We represent this independence by a vertical supply curve for money, M^s. In the same graph, we draw the demand for money M^d. Market equilibrium occurs where the demand for money equals the supply of money, at an interest rate of r^*.

At this equilibrium interest rate, r^*, the quantity of money demanded by the private sector equals the quantity of money supplied by the Federal Reserve. What happens if the interest rate is higher than r^*? At a higher interest rate, the quantity of money demanded would be less than the fixed quantity supplied; the result would be an excess supply of money. In other markets, excess supplies cause the price to fall. It's the same here. The "price of money" in the market for money is the interest rate. The interest rate would fall and return to the equilibrium value, r^*. If the interest rate were below r^*, the demand for money would exceed the fixed supply: There would be an excess demand for money. As in other markets when there are excess demands, the price rises. Here, the "price of money," or the interest rate, would rise until it reached r^*.

As you see, money market equilibrium follows the same logic as any other economic equilibrium.

We can use this simple model of the money market to understand the power of the Federal Reserve. Suppose the Federal Reserve increased the money supply through an open market purchase of bonds. In panel A of Figure 13.4, an increase in the supply of money shifts the money supply curve to the right, leading to lower interest rates. A decrease in the money supply through the Fed's open market sale of bonds, as depicted in panel B of Figure 13.4, will decrease the supply of money, shifting the money supply curve to the left, increasing interest rates.

We can also think of the process from the perspective of banks. Recall our discussion of money creation through the banking system. After the Fed's open market purchase of bonds, banks will find that they have additional reserves and will want to make loans. To entice businesses to borrow, banks will lower the interest rates they charge on their loans. After an open market purchase of bonds by the Fed, interest rates will fall throughout the entire economy.

Now we understand why potential new homeowners—as well as businesspeople and politicians—want to know what the Federal Reserve is likely to do in the near future. The Fed exerts direct control over interest rates in the short run. If the Fed decides interest rates should be lower, it buys bonds in the open market to increase the supply of money. If it wants higher interest rates, it sells bonds in the open market to decrease the money supply.

Figure 13.4
Federal Reserve and Interest Rates
Changes in the supply of money will change interest rates.

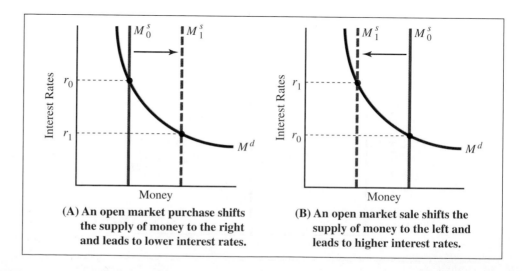

(A) An open market purchase shifts the supply of money to the right and leads to lower interest rates.

(B) An open market sale shifts the supply of money to the left and leads to higher interest rates.

In the short run, the Federal Reserve determines interest rates. The Fed affects interest rates to influence the level of GDP and inflation in the economy.

The Mystery of Increasing Interest Rates and Economic Recovery

Economic Detective

Economists have often noticed that as an economy recovers from a recession, interest rates start to rise. Some observers have felt that this was mysterious because they believed that higher interest rates were associated with lower output. Using the demand and supply for money diagram, explain why interest rates can rise during an economic recovery.

The key to understanding the mystery is that the increase in income that occurs during the recovery will increase the demand for money. As the demand for money increases while the supply of money remains fixed, interest rates will rise. Thus, we expect to see rising interest rates during a period of economic recovery.

Bond Prices and Interest Rates

When interest rates rise in the economy, bond prices fall. To see why, you first must recall that bonds are promises to pay money in the future. If you own a bond, you are entitled to receive payments from it in the future. Why do the prices of bonds move in the opposite direction from interest rates?

For a bond that promises to pay money one period in the future, there is a simple formula that mathematically represents the relationship between interest rates and bond prices:

$$\text{price of bonds} = \text{promised payment}/(1 + \text{interest rate})$$

The price of a bond is the promised payment divided by 1 plus the interest rate. Suppose the promised payment next year were $106 and the interest rate were 6% per year. The price of the bond would be

$$\text{price of bond} = \$106/1.06 = \$100$$

In this case, the bond would cost $100.

There is an easy way to understand this formula. If you had $100 today and invested it at a 6% annual interest rate, you would have $106 at the end of next year. Therefore, a bond that promises to pay you $106 dollars next year is worth exactly $100 today if you can invest at 6% per year. So it makes sense that the price of the bond will be the $100 amount you would be willing to pay today for the $106 promised payment next year. The formula shows that bond prices change in the opposite direction from changes in interest rates: Bond prices rise when interest rates fall, and bond prices fall when interest rates rise.

To really understand that, let's consider two examples:

- Suppose that the promised payment is still $106 but the interest rate falls from 6% to 4% per year. Using the formula, the price of the bond is $106/1.04, or $101.92. The price of the bond rose because, at the lower interest rate, you would need $101.92 today to invest at 4% per year to have $106 next year.

- Suppose that interest rates rose from 6% to 8% per year. The price of the bond would fall to $106/1.08, or $98.15. The reason the price of the bond fell is that you need only $98.15 to invest at 8% per year to have $106 next year. As interest rates rose, the price of the bond fell.

In financial markets, there are many types of complex bonds that pay different sums of money at different times in the future. However, all bonds, no matter how complex or simple, promise to pay money in the future. As interest rates rise, investors need less money for the promised payments in the future, so the price of bonds falls. As interest rates fall, investors need more money for the promised payments. Therefore, prices of bonds will rise as interest rates fall. The same logic that applied to simple one-period bonds applies to more complex bonds.

There is another way to understand why when bond prices change in one direction, interest rates will change in opposite directions. We know that when the Federal Reserve buys bonds in the open market, interest rates fall. But think about what the Federal Reserve is doing when it conducts the open market purchase. The Federal Reserve is buying bonds from the public. As it buys bonds, it increases the demand for bonds and raises their price. Thus, prices of bonds rise as interest rates fall.

Similarly, interest rates rise following an open market sale of bonds by the Fed. When the Fed conducts an open market sale, it is selling bonds, increasing the supply of bonds in the market. With an increase in the supply of bonds, the price of bonds will fall. Thus, prices of bonds fall as interest rates increase.

Because the Federal Reserve can change interest rates and bond prices in the short run, you can now see why Wall Street firms typically hire Fed watchers (often former officials of the Federal Reserve) to try to predict what the Fed will do. If a Wall Street firm had an inside scoop that the Fed would surprise the market and lower interest rates, the firm could buy millions of dollars of bonds for itself or its clients and make a vast profit as bond prices subsequently rose.

The Federal Reserve is aware of the importance of its deliberations and strives for secrecy. Sometimes it even calls on the law for help. In September 1996, some newspapers reported that they had learned that eight regional bank presidents favored interest rate increases at the next meeting. The Federal Reserve called in the Federal Bureau of Investigation to explore whether there were leaks to the press. (As it turned out, the Fed did not raise interest rates that month.)

We can use our understanding of the relationship between bond prices and interest rates to explain a puzzling phenomenon about the bond market. "A Closer Look: Why Is Good News for the Economy Bad News for the Bond Market?" explains this phenomenon using the tools we have developed.

TEST Your Understanding

1. How do we measure the opportunity cost of holding money?
2. Complete the statement with *increase* or *decrease*. The quantity of money demanded will _____ as interest rates increase.
3. Complete the statement with *increase* or *decrease*: Both increases in the price level and increases in real GDP will _____ the demand for money.
4. What will happen to interest rates if the Fed sells bonds on the open market?
5. If interest rates are 3% per year, what will be the price of a bond that promises to pay $109 next year?

Interest Rates, Investment, and Output

To show how the Fed's actions affect the economy, we expand our short-run, demand model of the economy to include money and interest rates. Our model will have three related graphs representing the following relationships:

WHY IS GOOD NEWS FOR THE ECONOMY BAD NEWS FOR THE BOND MARKET?

You may have heard on television or read in the newspaper that prices in the bond market often fall in the face of good economic news, such as an increase in real output. Are the markets perverse? Why is good news for the economy bad news for the bond market?

We can understand the behavior of the bond market by thinking about the demand for money. When real GDP increases, the demand for money will increase. As the demand for money increases, the money demand curve will shift to the right. From our model of the money market, we know that increased money demand will increase interest rates. Bond prices move in the opposite direction from interest rates. Therefore, good news for the economy is bad for the bond market.

High GDP growth may also lead to expectations of higher inflation in the future. These expectations will tend to push up nominal interest rates as investors try to protect themselves against future inflation. Higher interest rates will mean lower bond prices, which is bad news for the bond market.

Finally, despite the good news in the economy, stock prices still can fall as well. As interest rates on bonds rise, it becomes more attractive to own bonds rather than stocks, so the demand for stocks falls. The result may be lower stock prices. Sometimes, however, stock prices increase in the face of good news if the good news leads investors to think that profits (and thus future dividends from holding the stock) will be very high in the future.

1. The supply and demand for money, which determines interest rates in the economy.
2. An investment function, which shows that investment spending decreases when interest rates increase, and vice versa.
3. A model in which the demand-side $C + I + G + NX$ line and the 45° line intersect at the level of output where total demand equals total production.

In this expanded short-run demand model, here's what happens:

- The rate of interest is determined in the money market.
- The rate of interest, in turn, determines the level of investment in the economy.
- Knowing the level of investment, we can find the level of output at which total demand for goods and services equals total output.

Figure 13.5 shows how the model works. In panel A we have the demand and supply for money, which determines the rate of interest, r_0. In panel B, we plot investment as a decreasing function of the interest rate. At the interest rate r_0, we find that investment spending will be I_0. In panel C, we show how the level of demand $C + I_0 + G + NX$ determines equilibrium output at y_0 using our familiar 45° line graph. The level of investment spending that we use in the 45° line graph is the same level of investment that we find from the two other panels.

Before illustrating how monetary policy works in this model, we should note that consumption as well as investment can depend on interest rates. Spending on consumer durables, such as automobiles or refrigerators, will also depend negatively on the rate of interest. Consumer durables are really investment goods for the household: If you buy an automobile, you incur the cost today and receive benefits (the ability to use the car) in the future. As interest rates rise, the opportunity costs of investing in the automobile will rise. Consumers will respond to the increase in the opportunity cost by purchasing fewer cars. In the rest of this chapter, we discuss how changes in interest rates affect investment, but keep in mind that purchases of consumer durables will be affected as well.

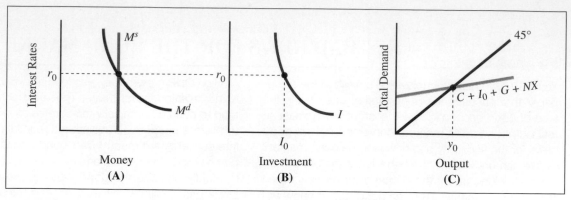

Figure 13.5   **Demand-Side Model with Money**
In panel A, the demand and supply for money determines the interest rate r_0. At this interest rate, panel B shows investment spending at I_0. Finally, in panel C, output is determined where the total demand line, with investment at I_0, intersects the 45° line.

Monetary Policy

Through its actions, the Federal Reserve can change the level of output in the short run. How does it? Consider an open market purchase. The Fed buys government bonds from the public, increasing the supply of money. With an increase in the supply of money, interest rates fall. As we explained in Chapter 11, lower interest rates stimulate additional investment spending. Output, or GDP, increases by the multiplier.

Figure 13.6 shows how an open market purchase of bonds by the Fed works. In panel A, the supply of money increases from M_0^s to M_1^s and interest rates fall from r_0 to r_1. In panel B, investment spending increases from I_0 to I_1 by the increment ΔI. In panel C, the increase in investment spending shifts the total demand line upward by the same incremental amount ΔI. GDP increases from y_0 to y_1, increasing by the increment Δy.

An open market sale of bonds by the Fed works precisely in reverse. In an open market sale, the Fed sells bonds to the private sector, reducing the money supply. Interest rates increase in the money market. With higher interest rates, firms reduce their

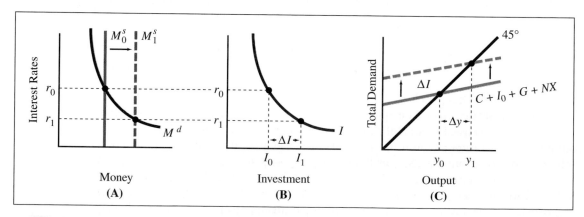

Figure 13.6   **Open Market Purchase**
An open market purchase increases the supply of money, decreases interest rates, and increases the level of output.

investment spending. The decrease in investment spending decreases the total demand for goods and services in the economy. The reduced demand for goods and services leads to a reduction in GDP. We can represent this entire sequence of events:

$$\text{open market sale} \rightarrow \text{decrease in money supply} \rightarrow \text{rise in interest rates} \rightarrow \text{fall in investment spending} \rightarrow \text{decrease in GDP}$$

Stop here for a moment, and think of the sequence of events by which the Federal Reserve can affect the level of GDP in the short run. It all starts in the financial markets. By buying and selling government bonds, the Federal Reserve can change the supply of money and the level of interest rates. In making their investment decisions, firms and individuals are influenced by the level of interest rates. Finally, changes in the demand for goods and services will affect the level of GDP in the short run. The sequence of events may be a bit indirect, but it is powerful.

The Federal Reserve can also influence the level of output through other tools, such as changes in reserve requirements or changes in the discount rate, discussed in Chapter 12. Actions that the Federal Reserve takes to influence the level of GDP are known as **monetary policy**.

This expanded short-run demand model can be used to understand why bank failures are harmful to the economy. During the Great Depression, there were severe bank failures throughout the world. How did these affect the level of GDP? Because deposits are part of the money supply, bank failures reduce the supply of money. As banks closed, they could no longer make loans; and as loans decreased, so did the amount of deposits into other banks. Bank failures therefore led to a contraction of the money supply. The effects of bank failures are similar to the effects of an open market sale of bonds by the Fed. This decrease in the supply of money will reduce the level of output in the economy. And when banks fail, there is less financial intermediation in the economy. Less financial intermediation makes the economy less efficient, which further reduces investment spending. Some economists believe that bank failures were the reason why the Great Depression was so severe in the United States.

> **Monetary policy:** The range of actions taken by the Federal Reserve to influence the level of GDP or the rate of inflation.

Monetary Policy in an Open Economy

We have been discussing monetary policy without taking into account international trade or international movements of financial funds across countries. Once we bring in these considerations, we will see that monetary policy operates through an additional route.

Suppose the Federal Reserve conducts an open market purchase of bonds, lowering U.S. interest rates. As a result, investors in the United States will be earning lower interest rates and will seek to invest some of their funds abroad. To invest abroad, they will need to sell dollars and buy foreign currency of the country where they intend to invest. This will affect the **exchange rate**: the rate at which one currency trades for another currency. As investors sell their dollars to buy foreign currency, the exchange rate, which is the value of the dollar from the perspective of the U.S. investor, will fall. A fall in the exchange rate or a decrease in the value of a currency is called **depreciation**. Lower U.S. interest rates will cause the dollar to depreciate, which means that it declines in value.

The lower value of the dollar will mean that U.S. goods become cheaper on world markets. Suppose that the exchange rate were 2 Swiss francs to the dollar, meaning you received 2 Swiss francs for every dollar. If a U.S. machine tool sold for $100,000, the machine tool would cost the Swiss 200,000 francs. Suppose the value of the dollar fell, so you received only 1 franc for each dollar. The same machine tool would cost the Swiss only 100,000 francs. The lower value of the dollar makes U.S. goods cheaper to foreigners.

> **Exchange rate:** The rate at which one currency trades for another in the market.
>
> **Depreciation:** A fall in the exchange rate or a decrease in the value of a currency.

Foreign residents will want to buy more U.S. goods as they become less expensive to foreign residents. So the U.S. exports more to foreign countries.

That's the good news about the lower value of the U.S. dollar. The bad news is that the lower value of the dollar will make it more expensive for U.S. residents to buy foreign goods. If the exchange rate were 2 Swiss francs to the dollar and Swiss chemicals cost 60,000 francs, the chemicals would cost a U.S. resident $30,000. If the exchange depreciates to 1 franc per dollar, the same chemicals will cost $60,000. As the U.S. exchange rate falls, imports become more expensive, and U.S. residents tend to import fewer goods.

As we have seen, as the U.S. dollar exchange rate falls, U.S. goods become cheaper and foreign goods become more expensive. The United States will export more goods and import fewer goods. Because exports increase and imports decrease, net exports will increase. The increase in net exports increases the demand for U.S. goods and increases GDP in the short run. We can represent this sequence of events:

$$\text{open market purchase} \rightarrow \text{increase in money supply} \rightarrow \text{fall in interest rates} \rightarrow \text{fall in exchange rate} \rightarrow \text{increase in net exports} \rightarrow \text{increase in GDP}$$

The three new links in the sequence are from interest rates to exchange rates, from exchange rates to net exports, and from net exports to GDP.

This sequence also works in reverse. If the Fed raises interest rates, investors from around the world will want to invest in the United States. As they buy dollars, the U.S. dollar exchange rate will increase, and the dollar will increase in value. An increase in the value of a currency is called **appreciation**. The appreciation of the dollar will make U.S. goods more expensive to foreigners and make imports cheaper for U.S. residents. Suppose the exchange rate appreciates to 3 francs to the dollar. That machine tool will increase in price to the Swiss to 300,000 francs, while the Swiss chemicals will fall in price to U.S. residents to $20,000.

When U.S. interest rates increase, we expect exports to decrease and imports to increase, decreasing net exports. The decrease in net exports will decrease the demand for U.S. goods and lead to a fall in output in the short run.

Appreciation: A rise in the exchange rate or an increase in the value of a currency.

Here is the expanded sequence of events:

open market sale	→	decrease in money supply	→	rise in interest rates	→	rise in exchange rate	→	decrease in net exports	→	decrease in GDP

To summarize, an increase in interest rates will reduce both investment spending (including consumer durables) and net exports. A decrease in interest rates will increase investment spending and net exports. Monetary policy is even more powerful in an open economy than in a closed economy.

TEST Your Understanding

6. Complete the statement with *higher* or *lower*: When the Federal Reserve sells bonds on the open market, it leads to _____ levels of investment and output in the economy.

7. Complete the statement with *sale* or *purchase*: To increase the level of output, the Fed should conduct an open market _____ of bonds.

8. What are all the events in the sequence from an open market purchase to a change in output in a closed economy?

9. Complete the statement with *appreciate* or *depreciate*: An increase in the supply of money will _____ a country's currency.

10. Explain how monetary policy works in an economy that is open to trade.

Stabilization Policy and Its Limitations

Now that we have brought money into our expanded short-run demand model, we can see that the government has two different types of tools to change the level of GDP in the short run: The government can use either fiscal policy—changes in the level of taxes or government spending—or monetary policy—changes in the supply of money and interest rates—to alter the level of GDP.

If the current level of GDP is below full employment or potential output, the government can use **expansionary policies** such as tax cuts, increased spending, or increases in the money supply to raise the level of GDP and reduce unemployment.

If the current level of GDP exceeds full employment or potential output, the economy will overheat, and the rate of inflation will increase. To avoid this, the government can use **contractionary policies** to reduce the level of GDP back to full employment or potential output.

Both expansionary policies and contractionary policies are examples of **stabilization policies**, actions to move the economy closer to full employment or potential output.

On paper, this sounds simple. In practice, it is difficult—very difficult—for two big reasons. First, there are lags, or delays, in stabilization policy. Lags arise because decision-makers are often slow to recognize and respond to changes in the economy, and monetary policies and fiscal policies take time to operate. The other reason, alas, is that economists simply do not know enough about the economy to be accurate in all their forecasts.

Lags

Poorly timed policies can magnify economic fluctuations. Suppose that (1) GDP was currently below full employment but would return to full employment on its own within one year and (2) stabilization policies took a full year to become effective. If policymakers tried to expand the economy today, their actions would not take effect until a year

Expansionary policies: Policies that aim to increase the level of GDP.

Contractionary policies: Policies that aim to decrease the level of GDP.

Stabilization policy: Policy actions taken to bring the economy closer to full employment or potential output.

from now. One year from now, the economy would normally, by itself, be back at full employment. But one year from now, if stabilization policies were enacted, the economy would be stimulated unnecessarily, and output would exceed full employment.

Figure 13.7 illustrates the problem caused by lags. Panel A shows an example of successful stabilization policy. The solid line represents the behavior of GDP in the absence of policies. Successful stabilization policies can dampen (reduce in magnitude) economic fluctuations, lowering output when it exceeds full employment and raising output when it falls below full employment. This would be easy to accomplish if there were no lags in policy. The dashed curve shows how successful policies can reduce economic fluctuations.

Panel B shows the consequences of ill-timed policies. Again, assume that policies take a year before they are effective. At the start of Year 1, the economy is below potential. If policymakers engaged in expansionary policies at the start of Year 1, the change would not take effect until the end of Year 1. This would raise output even higher above full employment. Ill-timed stabilization policies can magnify economic fluctuations.

Where do the lags in policy come from? Economists recognize two broad classes of lags: inside lags and outside lags. **Inside lags** are the lags in implementing policy; **outside lags** refer to the time it takes for policies to actually work. To help you understand them, imagine that you are steering a large ocean liner and you are looking out for possible collisions with hidden icebergs. The time it takes you to spot an iceberg, communicate this information to the crew, and initiate the process of changing course is the inside lag. Because ocean liners are large and have lots of momentum, it will take a long time before your ocean liner begins to turn; this is the outside lag.

Inside lags: Lags in implementing policy.

Outside lags: The time it takes for policies to work.

Inside Lags

Inside lags occur for two basic reasons. One reason is that it takes time to identify and recognize a problem. For example, the data available to policymakers may be poor and conflicting. Some indicators of the economy may look fine; others may appear worri-

Figure 13.7
Possible Pitfalls in Stabilization Policy

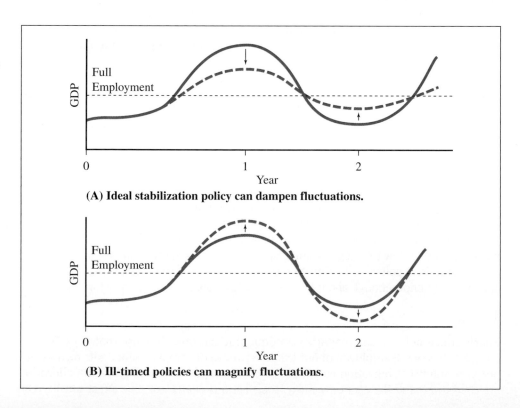

(A) Ideal stabilization policy can dampen fluctuations.

(B) Ill-timed policies can magnify fluctuations.

some. It often takes from several months to a year before it is clear that there is a serious problem with the economy.

A good example of this problem occurred during the 1990 recession. Today, we date the beginning of the recession from July 1990, a month before Iraq invaded Kuwait. After the invasion, there was some concern that higher oil prices and the uncertainty of the political situation would trigger a recession. However, Alan Greenspan, the chairman of the Federal Reserve, testified before Congress as late as October 1990 that the economy had not yet slipped into a recession. Not until that December did Greenspan declare that the economy had entered into a recession. Yet, looking back, we now know that a recession had started five months earlier.

A second example of an inside lag was described in the story that opened the chapter. The Fed, fearing inflation, raised interest rates by one-half of a percentage point in May but cut rates by precisely the same amount in early January—seven months later—as they now worried, correctly in hindsight, about a slowing economy. The Fed tries to avoid policy reversals like these but is limited by accurate data about the trends in the economy.

A third example of an inside lag occurred at the beginning of the Great Depression. Although the stock market crashed in October 1929, we know through newspaper and magazine accounts that business leaders were not particularly worried about the economy for some time. Not until late in 1930 did the public begin to recognize the severity of the depression.

The other reason for inside lags is that once a problem has been diagnosed, it still takes time before any actions can be taken. This problem is most severe for fiscal policy in the United States. Any changes in taxes or spending must be approved by both houses of Congress and by the President. In recent years, the political system has been preoccupied with fights about the size and role of government. In this environment, it is difficult to obtain a consensus for tax or spending changes in a timely manner.

For example, soon after he was elected, President Bill Clinton proposed a stimulus package as part of his overall budget plan. This stimulus package contained a variety of spending programs and was designed to increase the level of GDP and avoid the risks of a recession. However, his plan was attacked as wasteful and unnecessary government spending, and it did not survive. As it turned out, the stimulus package was not necessary, as the economy grew rapidly in the next several years. Nonetheless, this episode illustrates how difficult it is to conduct an active fiscal policy. Monetary policy is not subject to the same long inside lags. Smaller groups such as the Federal Open Market Committee (FOMC) can more easily reach consensus. The FOMC meets eight times a year and can decide on major policy changes at any time. It can even give the chairperson of the Board of Governors some discretion between meetings.

Decisions about monetary policy are made by a committee. From your own experience, you may wonder whether committees are efficient decision-makers. The results of experiments described in "A Closer Look: Do Committees Make Better or Worse Decisions?" may surprise you.

Outside Lags

Both monetary policy and fiscal policy are subject to outside lags, the time it takes for policy to be effective. Consider monetary policy: The Federal Reserve can increase the money supply to rapidly lower interest rates, but firms must change their investment plans before monetary policy can be effective.

Economists use **econometric models** to estimate the length of outside lags. Econometric models are mathematical versions of the models that we have studied that use data to attempt to replicate the behavior of the economy. For example, one part of an

Econometric models:
Mathematical computer-based models that economists build to capture the actual dynamics of the economy.

DO COMMITTEES MAKE BETTER OR WORSE DECISIONS?

When Professor Alan Blinder returned to teaching after serving as vice-chairman of the Federal Reserve from 1994 to 1996, he was convinced that committees were not effective for making decisions about monetary policy. However, there was no research on this topic in the literature. With another researcher, Blinder developed several experiments to test whether individuals or groups made decisions more rapidly and to explore who was more accurate.

The type of experiment they developed was designed to explore how quickly individuals or groups could distinguish changes in underlying trends from random events. For example, if unemployment rises in one month, it could be a temporary aberration, which will soon be reversed, or the beginning of recession. Changing monetary policy would be a mistake if the increase was temporary, but waiting too long to change policy would be costly if the change were permanent. Who was better at making these sorts of determinations?

The results showed that committees performed better than individuals. They made decisions as quickly and were more accurate than individuals by themselves. Moreover, committee decisions were not simply related to the average performance of the individuals who composed the committee—the actual process of having meetings and discussions appears to have improved overall performance.

Source: Alan Krueger, "Economic Scene: A Study Shows Committees Can Be More Than the Sum of Their Members," *The New York Times*, December 7, 2000, p. C2.

econometric model of the economy could consist of a consumption function with numerical values for autonomous consumption and the marginal propensity to consume. Economists use economic theory and statistical methods to build an econometric model. Most econometric models predict that an interest rate cut will take at least two years for most of its effects to occur. However, some models predict shorter lags, while others predict longer lags.

Fiscal policy is also subject to outside lags. If taxes are cut, individuals and businesses must change their spending plans to take advantage of the cuts; it will take some time before any effects of the tax cuts will be felt in the economy. It will also take some time before increases in spending will raise GDP. Although fiscal policy has a much longer inside lag than monetary policy, its outside lag is shorter. For example, one model predicts that an increase in government spending will increase GDP by its maximum effect after just six months.

Congress may debate and pass a tax cut, but it will take time to affect the economy.

Forecasting Uncertainties

What makes the problem of lags even worse is that economists are not very accurate in forecasting what will happen in the economy. For example, a classic problem that policymakers face when the economy appears to be slowing down is knowing whether the slowdown is temporary or will persist. Unfortunately, stabilization policy cannot be effective without accurate forecasting. If economic forecasters predict an overheated economy and the Federal Reserve adopts a contractionary policy, the result could be disastrous if the economy weakened before the policy took effect. Today, most economic policymakers understand these limitations and are cautious in using activist policies.

Looking Ahead

The demand-side models that we developed in this chapter can be used to understand the behavior of the economy *only in the short run*, when prices do not change. Monetary policy can affect output in the short run when prices are largely fixed, but in the long run, changes in the money supply only affect inflation. The Federal Reserve cannot control real interest rates in the long run. In the next part of the book, we explain how prices change over time and how the economy makes the transition by itself from the short run to the long run.

Using the **TOOLS**

In this chapter, we developed the money demand curve, which enabled us to understand how interest rates are determined. We integrated money demand, money supply, and investment spending into a complete demand-side model of the economy. Here is an opportunity to use the tools developed in this chapter.

APPLICATIONS

1. Interest Rates on Checking Accounts
During the 1980s, banks started to pay interest (at low rates) on checking accounts for the first time. Given what you know about opportunity costs, how would interest paid on checking affect the demand for money?

2. Pegging Interest Rates
Suppose the Federal Reserve wanted to fix, or "peg," the level of interest rates at 6% per year. Using a simple supply and demand diagram, show how increases in money demand would change the supply of money if the Federal Reserve pursued the policy of this fixed interest rate. Use your answer to explain this statement, "If the Federal Reserve pegs interest rates, it loses control of the money supply."

3. Nominal Interest Rates and the Demand for Money
We know that investment spending depends on real interest rates. Yet the demand for money will depend on nominal interest rates, not on real interest rates. Can you explain why money demand should depend on nominal rates?

4. The Presidential Praise and Blame Game
Presidents like to take credit for good economic performance. If there are lags in policies, explain why Presidents may not deserve all the credit (or blame) for economic policies.

Summary

This chapter brought money and monetary policy into a demand-side model of the economy for the short run. The Fed can control the level of interest rates by open market purchases or sales of bonds. Changes in interest rates will in turn affect investment and output. In an open economy, exchange rates and net exports are also affected by interest rates. We also discussed that there are limits to how successful the results of stabilization policy can be. Here are the main points of the chapter:

1. The demand for money depends negatively on the interest rate and positively on the level of prices and real GDP.

2. The level of interest rates is determined in the money market by the demand for money and the supply of money.

3. To increase the level of GDP, the Federal Reserve buys bonds on the open market. To decrease the level of GDP, the Federal Reserve sells bonds on the open market.

4. An increase in the money supply will decrease interest rates, increase investment spending, and increase output. A decrease in the money supply will increase interest rates, decrease investment spending, and decrease output.

5. In an open economy, a decrease in interest rates will depreciate the exchange rate and lead to an increase in net exports. An increase in interest rates will appreciate the exchange rate and lead to a decrease in net exports.

6. Both lags in economic policies and economists' uncertainties about the economy make successful stabilization policy extremely difficult in practice.

Key Terms

appreciation, 280
contractionary policies, 281
depreciation, 279
econometric models, 283
exchange rate, 279

expansionary policies, 281
inside lags, 282
liquidity demand for money, 273
monetary policy, 279

outside lags, 282
speculative demand for money, 273
stabilization policy, 281
transactions demand for money, 271

Problems and Discussion Questions

1. Give another example from your own experience of the liquidity demand for money.

2. If a bond promised to pay $110 next year and the interest rate was 5% per year, what would be the price of the bond?

3. If you strongly believed that the Federal Reserve was going to surprise the markets and raise interest rates, would you want to buy bonds or sell bonds?

4. Explain why interest rates are sometimes called the price of holding money.

5. If investment spending became less sensitive to interest rates, how would this reduced sensitivity affect the strength of monetary policy?

6. Refrigerators and clothing are to some extent, durable. Explain why the decision to purchase a refrigerator is likely to be more sensitive to interest rates than the decision to buy clothing.

7. In an open economy, changes in monetary policy affect both interest rates and exchange rates. Comparing the United States and the Netherlands, in which country would monetary policy have a more significant effect on GDP through changes in exchange rates?

8. Explain why interest rates usually fall in a recession.

9. It has been suggested that the President of the United States be given the authority to temporarily increase or decrease taxes. How would this affect the inside lag for fiscal policy? Do you think it is a wise policy?

10. Some members of the Board of Governors have looked at changes in prices of commodities such as gold or copper for early warning signs of inflation. What policies would they recommend if they saw

the price of gold beginning to rise? Can you think of any reasons not related to the general inflation rate why the price of gold might start to increase?

11. **Web Exercise.** The Federal Reserve uses both econometric models as well as other more general information about the economy to make decisions about monetary policy. To see what some of this general information looks like, go to the Web site for the Federal Reserve Open Market Committee [*http://www.federalreserve.gov/fomc*] and read the report of the Beige Book (a briefing book named for

the color of its cover). What type of information is provided in the Beige Book?

12. **Web Exercise.** As international trade becomes more important, monetary policy becomes more heavily influenced by developments in the foreign exchange markets. Go to the Web page of the Federal Reserve [*http://www.federalreserve.gov*] and read some recent speeches given by Fed officials. Do international considerations seem to affect policymakers in the United States today?

Take It to the Net

We invite you to visit the O'Sullivan/Sheffrin page on the Prentice Hall Web site at: **http://www.prenhall.com/osullivan/** for additional World Wide Web exercises for this chapter.

Model Answers to Questions

Chapter-Opening Questions

1. When the Federal Reserve sells bonds on the open market, the money supply decreases. Given the demand for money, this raises interest rates.

2. The price of bonds is inversely related to interest rates. Because bonds are promises to pay money in the future, these promises are worth less today when interest rates rise.

3. If the Fed increases the supply of money, interest rates will fall. Lower interest rates will lead to more production of housing and increased construction.

4. It takes time for lowered interest rates to stimulate the economy. If the Federal Reserve believed that a slump was only temporary, it would be reluctant to reduce interest rates for fear of creating too much demand at the time when the economy recovered.

Test Your Understanding

1. We use the interest rates to measure the opportunity cost of holding money because the alternative to holding money is holding assets that pay interest.

2. Decrease.

3. Increase.

4. Interest rates will increase.

5. The price will be $109/1.03 = $105.83.

6. Lower.

7. Purchase.

8. An increase in the money supply will lower interest rates, raise investment, and raise output.

9. Depreciate.

10. An increase in the money supply will lower interest rates, depreciate the exchange rate, raise net exports, and raise output.

Using the Tools

1. **Interest Rates on Checking Accounts.** When interest is paid on checking accounts, it lowers the opportunity costs of holding wealth in these accounts, since you earn interest on the checking account. With a lower opportunity cost, the demand for money will increase.

2. **Pegging Interest Rates.** Start with a graph showing the demand for money and the supply of money, where the equilibrium interest rate is 6% per year. An increase in the demand for money will shift the demand curve to the right and raise interest rates above 6%. To prevent this from occurring, the Federal Reserve must increase the supply of money. Similarly, a decrease in the demand for money will lower interest rates below 6% unless the Federal Reserve decreases the demand for money. In either case the Federal Reserve will lose control of the supply of money. If there are shifts in the demand for money, the Federal Reserve cannot control interest rates and control the supply of money at the same time.

3. **Nominal Interest Rates and the Demand for Money.** The nominal interest rate measures the opportunity cost of holding money. If you hold money you earn no interest. If you invest in a bond you earn the nominal rate of interest.

4. **The Presidential Praise and Blame Game.** Lags make it difficult to tell whether a President is truly responsible for economic developments. If there is a two-year lag in the effects of policies, the performance of the economy for a new President during the first half of his or her term is largely determined by his or her predecessor.

From the Short Run to the Long Run

They could not have had sharper differences on economic theory and policy.

Milton Friedman believed that, left to its own devices, an economy was very resilient and could quickly restore itself to full employment after any shocks or disturbances. His greatest fear was that the government would actually make things worse, through its attempts to stabilize the economy. His prime example was the Great Depression, in which he believed that a disastrous monetary policy turned a routine recession into a great depression.

John Maynard Keynes was skeptical that an economy in a deep slump would ever return to full employment. Even if it did eventually return to full employment, the process could be extremely slow. Moreover, Keynes did not believe that it was necessary to endure the pain. Swift and sensible action by the government could bring an economy out of a slump.

How can we understand the differences between Friedman and Keynes?

One of the great debates in macroeconomics centers on short-run versus long-run considerations for macroeconomic policy. Up to here, we have discussed separately the economics of the long run—classical economics—and the economics of the short run—Keynesian economics. Now we'll explain how the economy evolves from the short run to the long run. The relationship between the short run and the long run is one of the most important concepts in modern macroeconomics.

These are some of the questions we answer in this chapter:

1. When do wages in all sectors of the economy rise or fall together?
2. Why does expanding the money supply raise output in the short run but only lead to higher prices in the long run?
3. Why does the Federal Reserve "remove the punch bowl from the party" and what does this mean?
4. Why might tax cuts have beneficial effects for the economy now but have harmful effects in the future?

Definitions

To begin to understand how the short run and the long run are related, let's return to what we mean by the long run and short run in macroeconomics.

Long Run

In the long run, when prices are flexible, the level of GDP is determined by the demand and supply for labor, the stock of capital, and technological progress. In the long run, the economy operates at full employment. With the supply of output fixed at what can be produced at full employment, any increases in government spending must come at the sacrifice of some other use of the output. We also saw in Chapter 9 that increases in the supply of money (or any other increase in aggregate demand) increase only the level of prices and not the level of output in the long run.

Short Run

In the short run, when prices are primarily fixed, the level of GDP is determined by the total level of demand for goods and services. Increases in the supply of money lower interest rates, stimulate investment, and increase GDP. Increases in government spending or cuts in taxes will also lead to increases in GDP.

Should economic policy be guided by what is expected to happen in the short run or what is expected to happen in the long run? To answer this question, we need to know two things:

1. How does what happens in the short run determine what happens in the long run?
2. How long is the short run?

In Chapter 9, we explained how in the short run, wages and prices are sticky and do not change immediately in response to changes in demand. Over time, wages and prices adjust, and the economy reaches its long-run equilibrium. Short-run, Keynesian economics applies to the period when wages and prices do not change—at least not substantially. Long-run, full-employment economics applies after wages and prices have largely adjusted to changes in demand.

Wage and Price Adjustments

Wages and prices change every day. If the demand for roller blades rises at the same time as there's a fall in the demand for tennis rackets, we would expect to see a rise in the price of roller blades and a fall in the price of tennis rackets. Wages in the roller blade industry would tend to increase; wages in the tennis racket industry would tend to fall.

Sometimes, we see wages and prices in all industries rising or falling together. For example, prices for steel, automobiles, food, and fuel may all rise together. Why? Wages and prices will all tend to increase together during booms when GDP exceeds its full-employment level or potential output. Wages and prices will fall together during periods of recessions when GDP falls below full employment or potential output.

If the economy is producing at a level above full employment, firms will find it increasingly difficult to hire and retain workers. Unemployment will be below its natural rate. Workers will find it easy to obtain a job and easy to change jobs. To attract workers to their firms and to prevent their own workers from quitting, firms will have to raise wages to try to outbid firms looking to hire workers. As one firm raises its wage, other firms will have to raise their wages even higher to attract workers.

For most firms, wages are the largest cost of production. As their labor costs increase, they have no choice but to increase the prices of their products. As prices rise, workers know that they need higher dollar or nominal wages to maintain their real wage. This is an illustration of the reality principle:

Reality **PRINCIPLE**

> **What matters to people is the real value of money or income—its purchasing power—not the face value of money or income.**

This process by which rising wages cause higher prices and higher prices feed higher wages is known as a **wage-price spiral**. It occurs when the economy is producing at a level of output that exceeds the potential output of the economy.

Wage-price spiral: Changes in wages and prices causing more changes in wages and prices.

When the economy is producing below full employment or potential output, the process works in reverse. Unemployment will exceed the natural rate, and there will be excess unemployment. Firms will find that it is easy to hire and retain workers and that they can offer less than other firms to hire skilled workers. As all firms cut wages, the average level of wages in the economy falls. Because wages are the largest component of costs, prices start to fall as well. In this case, the wage-price spiral works in reverse.

Table 14.1 summarizes our discussion of unemployment, output, and changes in wages. It is important, however, to emphasize one point. The changes in wages and prices that occur when the economy is not producing at full employment are typically changes away from a trend in inflation. Suppose the economy had been experiencing 6% annual inflation. If output exceeds full employment, prices will rise at a faster rate than 6% per year. If output is less than full employment, prices will rise at a slower annual

---

Table 14.1 Unemployment, Output, and Wage and Price Changes

When unemployment is below the natural rate...	When unemployment is above the natural rate...
Output is above potential Wages and prices rise	Output is below potential Wages and prices fall

rate than 6%. For the rest of this chapter, we ignore ongoing inflation. We return to the topic of ongoing inflation in the next chapter.

In summary, when output exceeds potential output, wages and prices throughout the economy will rise above previous inflation rates. If output is less than potential output, wages and prices will fall relative to previous inflation rates.

Aggregate Demand, Aggregate Supply, and Adjustment

The transition between the short run and the long run is easy to understand. If GDP is higher than potential output, the economy starts to overheat, and wages and prices increase. This increase in wages and prices will push the economy back to full employment.

Using aggregate demand and aggregate supply, we can illustrate graphically how the economy moves from a short-run equilibrium to the long run. First, let's review the graphical representations of aggregate demand and aggregate supply.

Aggregate demand curve: The relationship between the price level and the quantity of real GDP demanded.

Classical aggregate supply curve: The vertical aggregate supply curve at full employment.

Keynesian aggregate supply curve: A relatively flat supply curve. It reflects the idea that prices do not change very much in the short run and that firms adjust production to meet demand.

1. Aggregate demand. The **aggregate demand curve** represents real output—the total demand for all goods and services—on the horizontal axis for any level of prices on the vertical axis.

2. Aggregate supply. There are two aggregate supply curves. The **classical aggregate supply curve**—showing the long-run aggregate supply—is represented as a vertical line at the full-employment level of output. The **Keynesian aggregate supply curve**—showing the short-run aggregate supply—is represented as a relatively flat curve. It reflects the idea that prices do not change very much in the short run and that firms adjust production to meet demand.

Figure 14.1 shows an aggregate demand curve and the two aggregate supply curves. In the short run, output and prices are determined where the aggregate demand curve intersects the Keynesian aggregate supply curve—the short-run aggregate supply curve—at point A. This corresponds to a level of real output y_0 and a price level P_0.

In the long run, the level of prices and output is given by the intersection of the aggregate demand curve and the classical aggregate supply curve—the long-run aggre-

Figure 14.1

Aggregate Demand and Aggregate Supply

The aggregate demand curve *AD* intersects the Keynesian aggregate supply curve at point *A* and the classical aggregate supply curve at point *D*.

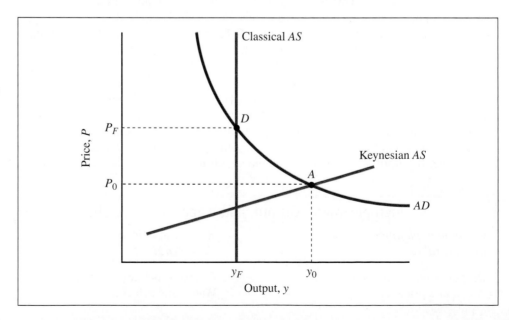

gate supply curve—at point D in the diagram. Output is at full employment y_F, while prices are at P_F. How does the economy move from point A in the short run to point D in the long run?

At point A, the current level of output y_0 exceeds the full employment level of output y_F. With output exceeding full employment, the unemployment rate is below the natural rate. Firms find it difficult to hire and retain workers, and the wage-price spiral begins. As the level of prices increases, the Keynesian aggregate supply curve shifts upward over time. The Keynesian aggregate supply curve shifts upward because increases in wages raise costs for firms. Firms paying higher costs must charge higher prices for their products or they would lose money, become unprofitable, and go out of business.

This shift in the Keynesian aggregate supply curve will bring the economy to long-run equilibrium, as shown in Figure 14.2. The economy initially starts at point A, where output exceeds full employment. As prices rise, the aggregate supply curve shifts upward from AS_0 to AS_1. The aggregate demand curve and the new aggregate supply curve intersect at point B. This corresponds to a higher level of prices and a lower level of real output. But that lower level of output still exceeds full employment. Wages and prices will continue to rise, shifting the Keynesian aggregate supply curve upwards. At point C, the aggregate supply curve AS_2 intersects the aggregate demand curve at a higher level of price and lower level of output than where AS_1 intersected the aggregate demand curve. As the aggregate supply curve continues to shift upward, it will intersect the aggregate demand curve at higher levels of prices and lower levels of output.

Eventually, the aggregate supply curve will shift to AS_3, and the economy will reach point D, the intersection of the aggregate demand curve and the classical aggregate supply curve—the long-run aggregate supply curve. At this point, the adjustment stops; the economy is at full employment, and the unemployment rate is at the natural rate. With unemployment at the natural rate, the wage-price spiral ends. The economy has made the transition to the long run. Note that the result is predicted by the classical model: Prices are higher, and output returns to full employment.

If the current level of output is below full employment, wages and prices will fall to return the economy to its long-run equilibrium at full employment, shown graphically in Figure 14.3. The economy starts at point A, a level of output below full employment.

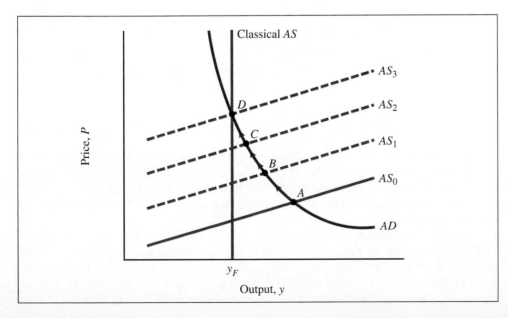

Figure 14.2

Shifts in the Keynesian Aggregate Supply
As prices rise in the economy, the Keynesian aggregate supply curve shifts upwards. The economy moves from point A to point B. The process continues until the economy reaches the long-run equilibrium point at D.

Figure 14.3

Returning to Full Employment

If the initial level of output is less than full employment, wages and prices will fall. As the aggregate supply curve shifts downwards, the economy returns to full employment at point *D*.

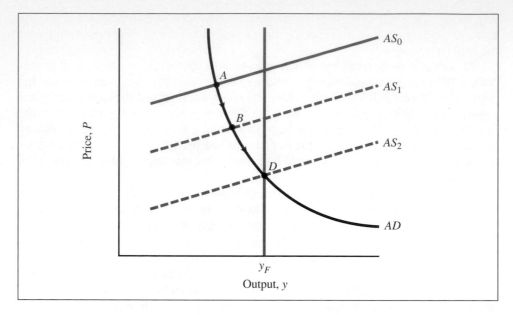

With unemployment above the natural rate and excess unemployment, the level of wages and prices will fall. As the aggregate supply curve shifts from AS_0 to AS_1, the economy moves from point *A* to point *B*, closer to full employment. The process ends when the aggregate supply curve shifts to AS_2 and the economy returns to full employment at point *D*. This is how an economy recovers from a recession or a downturn.

In summary, the economy will eventually return to full employment:

- If output exceeds full employment, prices will rise and output will fall back to full employment.

- If output is less than full employment, prices will fall as the economy returns to full employment.

TEST Your Understanding

1. Wages and prices will increase when unemployment exceeds the natural rate. True or false? Explain.

2. In what direction does the Keynesian aggregate supply curve move if the economy's actual output is below full-employment output?

The Speed of Adjustment and Economic Policy

How long does it take to move from the short run to the long run? Economists disagree on the answer. Some estimate that it takes the U.S. economy two years, some say six years, and others say somewhere in between. Because the adjustment process is slow, there is room, in principle, for policymakers to step in and guide the economy back to full employment.

Suppose the economy were operating below full employment at point *A* in Figure 14.4. One alternative for policymakers would be to do nothing, allowing the economy to adjust itself, with falling wages and prices, until it returns by itself to full employment, point *D*. This may take several years. During that time, the economy will experience excess unemployment and a level of real output below potential.

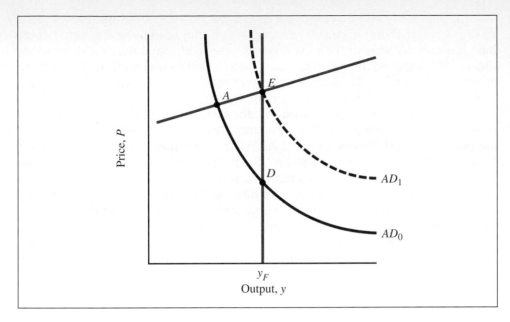

Figure 14.4
Using Economic Policy to Fight a Recession
Rather than letting the economy naturally return to full employment at point *D*, we can increase aggregate demand from AD_0 to AD_1 to bring the economy to full employment at point *E*.

Another alternative would be to use expansionary policies (open market purchases, increases in government spending, or tax cuts) to shift the aggregate demand curve to the right. In Figure 14.4, we show how expansionary policies could shift the aggregate demand curve from AD_0 to AD_1 and move the economy to full employment, point *E*. Notice here that the price level is higher at point *E* than it would be at point *D*.

Demand policies can also be used to prevent a wage-price spiral from emerging if the economy is producing at a level of output above full employment. Rather than letting an increase in wages and prices bring the economy back to full employment, we can reduce aggregate demand. Either contractionary monetary policy (open market sales) or contractionary fiscal policy (cuts in government spending or tax increases) can be used to reduce aggregate demand and the level of GDP until it reaches potential output.

Expansionary policies and demand policies are stabilization policies, which look simple on paper or on graphs. In practice, the lags and uncertainties that we discussed in Chapter 13 make the task difficult. For example, suppose we are in a recession and decide to increase aggregate demand through expansionary monetary policy. With the lags in monetary policy, it takes time for the aggregate demand curve to shift to the right. In the meantime, the adjustment that occurs during a recession (falling wages and prices) has begun to shift the Keynesian aggregate supply curve downward. It is conceivable that if the adjustment were fast enough, the economy would be restored to full employment before the effects of the expansionary monetary policy were actually felt. When the expansionary monetary policy actually kicks in and the aggregate demand curve finally shifts to the right, the additional aggregate demand would increase the level of output so that it exceeded the full employment level, leading to a wage-price spiral. In this case, our economic policy would have destabilized the economy.

Active economic policies are more likely to destabilize the economy if the adjustment is quick enough. Economists who believe that the economy adjusts rapidly to full employment generally oppose using monetary or fiscal policy to try to stabilize the economy. Economists who believe that the economy adjusts slowly are more sympathetic to using monetary or fiscal policy to stabilize the economy.

It is possible that the speed of adjustment can vary over time, making decisions about policy even more difficult. As an example, economic advisers for President George Bush had to decide whether the economy needed any additional stimulus after the recession of 1990. Based on the view that the economy would recover on its own, only some minor steps were taken. The economy recovered completely at the very end of the Bush administration but too late for his reelection prospects.

Up to this point, we have assumed that the economy could always recover from a recession without active policy, although it may take a long time. As our chapter opening story mentioned, Keynes expressed doubts about whether a country could recover from a major recession without active policy. He had two distinct reasons. First, as we will discuss later in the chapter, the adjustment process requires interest rates to fall and thereby increase investment spending. But suppose that nominal interest rates become so low that they cannot fall any further. Keynes called this situation a **liquidity trap**. When the economy is experiencing a liquidity trap, the adjustment process no longer operates. Second, Keynes also feared that falling prices could hurt business. Japan seems to have suffered from both of these problems in recent years, as "A Closer Look: Japan's Lost Decade" explains.

Liquidity trap: A situation in which interest rates are so low, they can no longer fall.

A Closer Look at the Adjustment Process

We have explained that changes in wages and prices restore the economy to full employment in the long run. But exactly how does this happen? We can explain using the short-run model from Chapter 13.

A CLOSER LOOK   JAPAN'S LOST DECADE

Japan's rapid post–World War II economic growth came to a halt around 1992, and by 1993–1994, the country was suffering from a recession. Inflation started to fall as the economy entered the recession. By 1995, inflation had nearly disappeared from the economy, and wholesale prices had fallen for several years.

Yet the reduction in inflation caused problems for the economy. Real estate prices fell nearly 50% starting in 1990. Large banks that were major investors in real estate lost vast sums of money, and became reluctant to make loans for other investments. Inflation rates were lower than business and household borrowers had anticipated. This raised the burden of debt for both businesses and households and made them more reluctant to purchase goods and services. With fewer loans from banks for new investment and reluctant households and firms, aggregate demand for goods and services was weak.

For a number of years, the United States urged Japan to increase public spending to end its recession. Eventually Japan did try this approach, but by 2001 the economy was still in a slump and government budget deficits were very large. Nominal interest rates were also very close to zero, making it difficult to use monetary policy to stimulate the economy. Some observers claimed that Japan was suffering from a Keynesian liquidity trap. Faced with these difficulties, restoring the health of the banking system became a major priority for economic policy.

While the lights may have been bright in Tokyo, Japan experienced difficult times in the 1990s.

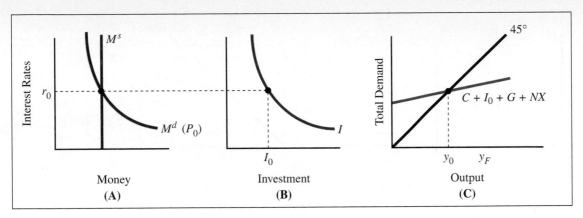

Figure 14.5 Model of Demand with Money
At the current price level P_0, the economy is producing at a level of output y_0 that is below full employment y_F.

In Figure 14.5, we show the three graphs that make up the model: the money market, the investment schedule, and the 45° line demand diagram. From these diagrams, we know the following:

• The demand and supply for money determine interest rates.

• Interest rates determine the level of investment spending in the economy.

• Investment spending—along with consumption, government spending, and net exports—determines the level of GDP.

The part of this diagram that we want to focus on here is money demand. Recall the reality principle:

Reality **PRINCIPLE**

> **What matters to people is the real value of money or income—its purchasing power—not the face value of money or income.**

According to this principle, the amount of money that people want to hold depends on the price level. If prices are cut in half, you need to hold only half as much money to purchase the same goods and services. Decreases in the price level will cause the money demand curve to shift to the left.

In Figure 14.5, the price level is P_0. At that price level, interest rates are at r_0, investment spending is at I_0, and the economy is producing at y_0. At y_0, output is below full employment. With output below full employment, actual unemployment will exceed the natural rate of unemployment, so there will be excess unemployment. Wages and prices will start to fall.

The fall in the price level will decrease the demand for holding money. In Figure 14.6, as the price level decreases from P_0 to P_1, the demand for money shifts to the left. Interest rates fall from r_0 to r_1, and the falling interest rates increase investment spending from I_0 to I_1. As the level of investment spending in the economy increases, the total demand line shifts upward, raising the level of output in the economy.

What we have just described continues until the economy reaches full employment. As long as actual output is below the economy's full employment level, prices will continue to fall. A fall in the price level reduces money demand and interest rates. Lower

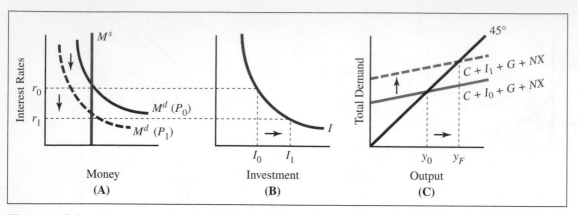

Figure 14.6 **Returning to Full Employment**
When output is below full employment, the price level falls. This reduces the demand for money and lowers interest rates. Lower interest rates increase investment and stimulate spending. The economy returns to full employment.

interest rates stimulate investment spending and push the economy back toward full employment.

All of this works in reverse if current actual output exceeds the economy's potential output. In this case, the economy is overheating and wages and prices rise. A higher price level will increase the demand for money and raise interest rates. Higher interest rates will decrease investment spending and reduce the level of output. All this continues until the economy returns to full employment.

Can you now see why changes in wages and prices restore the economy to full employment? The key to seeing why is that (1) changes in wages and prices will change the demand for money and interest rates and (2) changes in interest rates affect investment and the level of GDP in the economy.

We can also use the graphical model that we just developed to understand the liquidity trap. If an economy is in a recession, interest rates will fall, restoring the economy to full employment. But it's not impossible that at some point, interest rates may become so low that they become zero. Nominal interest rates cannot go far below zero, because investors would rather hold money (which pays a zero rate) than hold a bond that promises a negative return. Suppose, however, that as interest rates approach zero, the economy is still in a slump. The adjustment process then has nowhere to go.

As we mentioned previously, this appears to be what happened in Japan in the 1990s. Interest rates on government bonds were zero. Prices continued to fall. But the fall in prices, by itself, could not restore the economy to full employment. Policymakers have limited options in this case. Normal monetary policy will not work because nominal interest rates cannot fall any further. In principle, fiscal policy can still be effective in restoring the economy to full employment.

Long-Run Neutrality of Money

An increase in the money supply has a different effect on the economy in the short run than it does in the long run. In Figure 14.7, we show the effects of expansionary monetary policy in both the short run and the long run. In the short run, as the supply of money increases, the economy moves from the original equilibrium at point E to point A, with output above potential. But in the long run, the economy returns to point B at

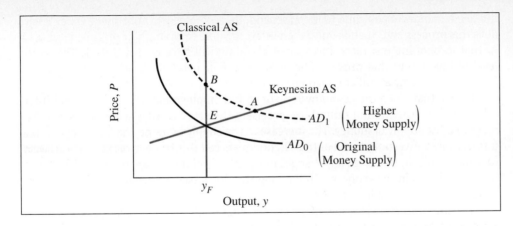

Figure 14.7
Monetary Policy in the Short Run and the Long Run
As the Fed increases the supply of money, the aggregate demand curve shifts from AD_0 to AD_1. The economy moves to point A. In the long run, the economy moves to point B.

full employment but at a higher price level than at E. How is it that the Federal Reserve can change the level of output in the short run but affect prices only in the long run? Why is the short run different from the long run? We can use the model of demand with money to understand this issue.

Figure 14.8 can help us to understand some answers to these questions. The economy starts at full employment y_F. Interest rates are at r_F, and investment spending is at I_F. Suppose the Federal Reserve increases the money supply from M_0^s to M_1^s. In the short run, the increase in the supply of money will reduce interest rates to r_0. The level of investment spending will increase to I_0. The increased demand for output will raise output above full employment to y_0. All this occurs in the short run. The single-headed arrows in Figure 14.8 show these movements.

However, now output exceeds full employment, and wages and prices will start to increase. As the price level increases, the demand for money will increase. This will start to increase interest rates. Investment will start to fall as interest rates increase, leading to a fall in output. The double-headed arrows in Figure 14.8 show the transition as prices increase. As long as output exceeds full employment, prices will continue to rise,

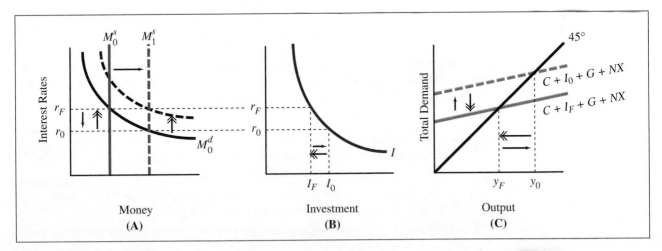

Figure 14.8
Neutrality of Money
Starting at full employment, an increase in the supply of money will initially reduce interest rates from r_F to r_0, raise investment spending from I_F to I_0, and increase output above full employment from y_F to y_0 (single-headed arrows). As wages and prices increase, the demand for money increases, restoring interest rates, investment, and output to full employment (double-headed arrows).

money demand will continue to increase, and interest rates will continue to rise. Where does this process end? It ends only when interest rates return to their original level of r_F. At that level of interest rates, investment spending will have returned to I_F. This is the level of investment that provides the total level of demand for goods and services that keeps the economy at full employment.

Notice that when the economy returns to full employment, the levels of real interest rates, investment, and output are precisely the same as they were before the Fed increased the supply of money. The increase in the supply of money had no effect on real interest rates, investment, and output. Economists call this the **long-run neutrality of money**. In other words, in the long run, changes in the supply of money are neutral with respect to real variables in the economy. In the long run, increases in the supply of money have no effect on real variables, only on prices.

Long-run neutrality of money: An increase in the supply of money has no effect on real interest rates, investment, or output in the long run.

To better understand the idea of the long-run neutrality of money, consider this thought experiment: Suppose one morning the government announced that we would replace all our normal green currency with blue currency. Every green dollar bill would be replaced by 2 blue dollars. What would happen to prices that are now quoted in blue currency? You should easily be able to see that if all wages and prices in blue dollars doubled, everything would essentially be the same as before. Although everyone has twice as many blue dollars as they formerly had of green dollars, blue dollar prices are twice as high as green dollar prices were, so the purchasing power of blue money is the same as it was for green money. Moreover, because wages and prices have doubled, real wage rates will be the same as before. This currency conversion will have no effect on the real economy and will be neutral.

This example points out how, in the long run, it really does not matter how much money is in circulation because prices will adjust to the amount of nominal money available. Whether additional money comes from an open market purchase or a currency conversion, such as from green to blue money, it will be neutral in the long run.

Money is not neutral in the short run, however. In the short run, changes in the supply of money do affect interest rates, investment spending, and output. The Fed does have strong powers over real GDP, but those powers are ultimately temporary. In the long run, all the Fed can do is to determine the level of prices in the economy.

Now we can understand why the job of the Federal Reserve has been described by William McChesney Martin, Jr., a former Federal Reserve chairman, as "taking the punch bowl away at the party." The punch bowl at the party is monetary policy: It can increase output or give the economy a brief high. But if the Federal Reserve is worried about increases in prices in the long run, it must take the punch bowl away. If the Federal Reserve continues to increase the supply of money in the economy, the result will be continuing increases in prices, or inflation.

TEST Your Understanding

3. What happens to the demand for money and interest rates as the price level increases in the economy?

4. If output is below full employment, we expect wages and prices to fall, money demand to decrease, and interest rates to fall. True or false? Explain.

5. An increase in the money supply will have no effect on the interest rate in the long run. True or false? Explain.

Crowding Out in the Long Run

Keynesian economists often advocate increased government spending to stimulate the economy. Critics of Keynesian economics say increases in spending provide only temporary relief and ultimately harm the economy because government spending will "crowd out" investment spending. In Chapter 7 on classical economics, we discussed the idea of **crowding out**. We can use the model now to understand it in more detail.

In Figure 14.9, the economy starts at full employment, and government spending is increased from G_0 to G_1, say, to stimulate the economy. In panel C, we see that the total demand line ($C + I + G_0 + NX$) shifts upward (the single-headed arrow), and output increases in the short run, just as the Keynesian demand models claim. However, now the economy is operating above full employment, and wages and prices begin to increase. The increase in the price level raises both the demand for money and the level of interest rates. Higher interest rates reduce the level of investment. As investment spending falls, the level of output returns to the economy's full employment output level. The double-headed arrows in Figure 14.9 show the final adjustment of the economy following the increase in government spending. Interest rates increase to r_1, and investment spending falls to I_1 in the long run.

The increase in government spending had no long-run effect on the level of output. Instead, the increase in government spending displaced, or crowded out, investment spending. The increase in government spending led to a higher level of interest rates, which reduced the incentives for investment in the economy. As we have discussed, the economy adjusts in the long run to the equilibrium predicted by the classical model. In this case, higher government spending crowds out investment spending. This reduction in investment will have further effects on the economy. As we saw in earlier chapters, a reduction in investment spending will reduce capital deepening and lead to lower levels of real income and wages in the future.

A similar argument applies to tax cuts. Tax cuts initially will increase consumer spending and lead to a higher level of GDP. In the long run, however, adjustments in wages and prices restore the economy to full employment. Interest rates will rise during the adjustment process. The increase in interest rates will crowd out investment. In the long run, the increase in consumption spending will come at the expense of lower investment spending, less capital deepening, and lower levels of real income and wages in the future. That is why tax cuts have different effects on income in the long run than they do in the short run.

Crowding out: The reduction of investment (or other component of GDP) in the long run caused by an increase in government spending.

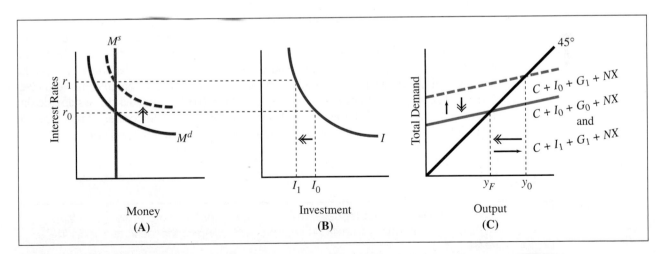

Figure 14.9
Crowding Out in the Long Run
Starting at full employment, an increase in government spending from G_0 to G_1 shifts up the total demand line and raises output above full employment (single-headed arrows). As wages and prices increase, the demand for money increases, raising interest rates from r_0 to r_1 and reducing investment from I_0 to I_1. The economy returns to full employment but with a higher level of interest rates and a lower level of investment spending (double-headed arrows).

The idea of crowding out should not be difficult to understand. Because the economy ultimately returns to full employment in the long run, a higher level of government spending must come at the expense of some other component of spending. In Figure 14.9, we showed how investment spending would be crowded out. In other situations, it is possible for consumption or net exports to be crowded out along with investment spending. Keynesian demand policy will increase GDP but only in the short run.

Crowding in: The increase of investment (or other component of GDP) in the long run caused by a decrease in government spending.

Decreases in government spending (such as a cut in military spending) will lead to increases in investment in the long run, which we call **crowding in**. Initially, a decrease in government spending will cause a decrease in real GDP. But as prices fall, the demand for money will decrease, and interest rates will fall. Lower interest rates will crowd in investment as the economy returns to full employment. In the longer run, the higher investment spending will raise living standards through capital deepening.

Crowding out and crowding in provide examples of this chapter's theme: The short-run effects of policy will generally differ from the long-run effects. Just as an increase in the money supply will increase output only in the short run, changes in government spending have different effects in the short run than they do in the long run.

Political Business Cycles

Political business cycle: The effects on the economy of using monetary or fiscal policy to stimulate the economy before an election to improve reelection prospects.

Using monetary policy and fiscal policy in the short run to improve a politician's reelection prospects may generate what is known as a **political business cycle**.

Here is how a political business cycle might work. About a year or so before an election, a politician might use expansionary monetary policy or fiscal policy to stimulate the economy and lower unemployment. If voters respond favorably to lower unemployment, the incumbent politician may be reelected. After reelection, the politician faces the prospect of higher prices or crowding out. To avoid this, the politician may engage in contractionary policies. The result is a classic political business cycle: Because of actions taken by politicians for reelection, the economy booms before an election but then contracts after the election. Good news comes before the election, and bad news comes later.

The evidence is not clear that the classic political business cycle always occurs. There are episodes that fit what we just described, such as President Nixon's reelection campaign in 1972. However, there are also counterexamples, such as President Carter's deliberate attempt to reduce inflation at the end of his term. According to the theory, Carter would not have adopted policies with adverse consequences just before the election. Although the evidence on the classic political business cycle is mixed, there may be links between elections and economic outcomes. More recent research has investigated the systematic differences that may exist between political parties and economic outcomes. All this research takes into account both the short- and long-run effects of economic policies.

Using the **TOOLS**

In this chapter, we developed a model showing the transition from the short run to the long run. Take this opportunity to deepen your understanding of the ideas and tools in this chapter.

APPLICATIONS
1. Economic Policies and Supply Shocks

a. In Chapter 24, we discussed supply shocks, sudden increases in the prices of commodities such as oil or food. These shocks shift the Keynesian aggregate supply curve. For example, an increase in oil prices will shift the Keynesian aggregate supply curve upward because firms' costs have risen and firms must charge higher prices to avoid losing money. Suppose that the economy is operating at full employment and foreign countries raised the world price of oil. Assuming that policymakers do not take any action, describe what will happen to prices and output in the short run and in the long run.

b. Suppose the Federal Reserve decided that it wanted to offset any adverse effects on output. What actions could it take? What would happen to the price level if the Fed used monetary policy to fight unemployment?

c. Economists say that supply shocks create a dilemma for the Federal Reserve that shocks to demand (for example, from investment) do not create. Explain why economists say this, using your answer to part (b) and the aggregate demand and supply diagram.

2. Understanding Japanese Fiscal Policy

During the early 1990s, the Japanese were suffering from a recession. Some economists prescribed expansionary fiscal policy. The finance ministry agreed to income tax cuts— but only if national sales taxes were increased several years later. Explain the logic of the finance ministry, using your understanding of the short-run effects and the long-run effects of fiscal policy. What was the finance ministry trying to prevent?

3. Optimistic Firms in the Long Run

Suppose the economy was operating at full employment and firms became increasingly optimistic about the future. They increase their investment spending; graphically, that means that their investment schedule shifts to the right. What happens to real GDP in the short run? Describe what happens to interest rates, investment, and real GDP in the long run. How is the investment boom self-correcting?

Summary

This chapter explained how the economy makes the transition from the short run to the long run. It also highlighted why monetary and fiscal policies have different effects in the short run than the effects they have in the long run. Understanding the distinction between the short run and the long run is critical to evaluating economic policy. Here are the main points to remember from this chapter:

1. When output exceeds full employment, wages and prices rise faster than their past trends. If output is less than full employment, wages and prices fall relative to past trends.

2. The price changes that occur when the economy is away from full employment push the economy back to full employment. Economists disagree on the length that this adjustment process takes; estimates range from two years to six years.

3. If the economy is operating below full employment, falling wages and prices will reduce money demand and lower interest rates. The fall in interest rates

will stimulate investment and lead the economy back to full employment.

4. The reverse occurs when output exceeds full employment. Increases in wages and prices will increase money demand and interest rates. As investment spending falls, the economy returns to full employment.

5. In the long run, increases in the supply of money are neutral; that is, increases in the money supply do not affect real interest rates, investment, nor output.

6. Increases in government spending will raise real interest rates and crowd out investment in the long run. Decreases in government spending will lower real interest rates and crowd in investment in the long run.

7. To improve their chances of being reelected, politicians can potentially take advantage of the difference between the short-run effects and the long-run effects of economic policies.

Key Terms

aggregate demand curve, 292
classical aggregate supply curve, 292
crowding in, 302

crowding out, 301
Keynesian aggregate supply curve, 292
liquidity trap, 296

long-run neutrality of money, 300
political business cycle, 302
wage-price spiral, 291

Problems and Discussion Questions

1. When the unemployment rate fell to 4% in 1998, some economists became concerned that inflation would increase. Explain their concern.

2. Economists who believe that the transition from the short run to the long run occurs rapidly do not generally favor using active stabilization policy. Use the aggregate demand and aggregate supply graphs to illustrate how active policy, with a rapid adjustment process, could destabilize the economy.

3. During an economic boom, interest rates rise. Investment spending typically increases in the beginning of the boom and then declines. Can you explain why this pattern of economic activity occurs?

4. Suppose households decide to increase their desired savings. What will be the effect on GDP in the short run, the intermediate run, and the very long run?

5. Countries that have high money growth for long periods do not grow more rapidly than countries with low money growth. Why?

6. Explain why advocates for the housing industry (an industry very sensitive to interest rates) might want to advocate lower government spending for the long term.

7. Use the model in this chapter to explain how tax cuts for consumers will eventually lead to higher interest rates and crowd out investment spending in the long run.

8. The adjustment process can run into problems during a liquidity trap when interest rates are driven close to zero and the economy remains below full employment. Draw a money demand curve and an investment schedule to illustrate this possibility.

9. At one time in 1998, nominal interest rates on short-term Japanese government debt were slightly negative. Some foreign-owned banks also paid negative rates on yen deposits. Daniel L. Thornton, an economist at the St. Louis Federal Reserve Bank, argued that even though cash paid a zero rate of interest, banks could still attract funds with negative rates because there were costs to holding cash. What are some of these costs? How negative do you think interest rates could actually go?

10. Some economists estimate that the adjustment process takes up to six years to restore an economy back to full employment. What do you think makes the process so slow? (Hint: Think of the factors that cause lags in monetary policy.)

11. **Web Exercise.** During the Great Depression in the United States, some interest rates became close to zero. Search the historical database at the Web site of the National Bureau of Economic Research [*http://www.nber.org*] to find out how low interest rates actually became and when they were at their lowest.

12. **Web Exercise.** Use the Web site for the Federal Reserve Bank of St. Louis [*http://www.stls.frb.org/ fred*] to find historical data on unemployment rates. Use these data to explore whether unemployment behaves differently in the first two years of a presidential term compared to the final two years. Are there any systematic differences in unemployment between Democratic and Republican presidencies?

Take It to the Net

We invite you to visit the O'Sullivan/Sheffrin page on the Prentice Hall Web site at:
http://www.prenhall.com/osullivan/ for additional World Wide Web exercises for this chapter.

Chapter-Opening Questions

1. Wages and prices will rise together when the economy is operating at a level of output that exceeds full employment. Conversely, they will fall (relative to trend) when the output level of the economy is below full employment.

2. In the short run, the higher demand from lower interest rates will raise output. But because prices rise when output exceeds full employment, the only long-run effect is higher prices.

3. The Federal Reserve is responsible for preventing inflation from emerging or increasing. This may require high interest rates to reduce output at a time when the economy is producing at too high a level.

4. Tax cuts stimulate consumer demand and lead to higher output in the short run. In the long run, increased consumer spending will crowd out investment spending. Lower investment means a lower capital stock in the future and reduced future output.

Test Your Understanding

1. False. Wages and prices decrease when unemployment exceeds the natural rate.

2. The curve moves downward.

3. Money demand increases, interest rates increase.

4. True. This sequence of events occurs when output is below full employment.

5. True. Money is neutral in the long run.

Using the Tools

1. Economic Policies and Supply Shocks

   a. A supply shock shifts the Keynesian aggregate supply curve upward. Prices will rise and output will fall in the short run. With output below full employment, prices will fall. The economy will return to full employment at the initial price level.

   b. The Federal Reserve could increase the supply of money (such as through open market purchases) and shift the aggregate demand curve. The price level would remain at the higher level.

   c. Unlike shocks to aggregate demand, if the Fed tries to offset the effects of an adverse supply shock on output or on unemployment, the price level will remain permanently higher.

2. Understanding Japanese Fiscal Policy. The Japanese finance ministry was worried about crowding out of investment in the long run. They hoped that the income tax cut would stimulate spending in the short run and pull the economy out of a recession. Later, however, they wanted to reduce consumer spending so that it would not displace investment spending.

3. Optimistic Firms in the Long Run. With an investment boom, real GDP would increase with the additional investment spending. However, as output exceeds full employment, prices would rise, leading to increased money demand and interest rates. The higher interest rates would cut back on investment, lowering real GDP.

15

The Dynamics of Inflation and Unemployment

Monetary affairs were truly a mess in Russia during the 1990s. Inflation was so severe that the central bank tried many attempts at monetary reform. As a result of these reforms, the central bank issued three different sets of bank notes. But that posed a problem: what to do with all the old Russian rubles?

The emerging private sector found a solution for this problem. It turned out that old Russian rubles could be converted into roofing material. After soaking them in water and mixing them with paper scraps and shredded cloth, the rubles became part of a roofing material called ruberoid that prevents roofs from leaking.

Certainly this is a clever use for useless rubles, but the purpose of the central bank is not to provide inexpensive roofing material. How did Russia find itself in this odd predicament to begin with?

Source: Andrew Higgins, "Worthless Rubles Have Their Uses in Keeping Roofs From Leaking," *Wall Street Journal*, July 26, 2000, p. A1.

Money Growth, Inflation, and Interest Rates
Expectations and the Phillips Curve
U.S. Inflation and Unemployment in the 1980s
Shifts in the Natural Rate in the 1990s

Credibility and Inflation

Inflation and the Velocity of Money

Budget Deficits and Hyperinflations

The Costs of Unemployment and Inflation
Costs of Unemployment
Costs of Inflation

Using the Tools

wo themes that we've been stressing separately will now be integrated:

- In the short run, changes in money growth affect real output and real GDP.
- In the long run, the rate of money growth determines the rate of inflation and not real GDP.

This chapter brings these two themes together.

Our economic policy debates often concern inflation and unemployment. We will look at the relationships between inflation and unemployment, examining macroeconomic developments in the United States in the 1980s and 1990s. We also explore why heads of central banks typically appear to be strong enemies of inflation.

Although the United States had serious difficulties fighting inflation in the 1970s and 1980s, other countries have, at times, had much more severe problems with inflation. We study the origins of extremely high inflationary periods and their links to government budget deficits. And we'll take a close look at how unemployment and inflation impose costs on a society.

In this chapter, we address these questions:

1. Why do countries with lower rates of money growth have lower interest-rate levels than countries with higher rates of money growth?

2. Why is the relationship between lower unemployment and higher inflation only temporary?

3. Why are the heads of central banks (such as the Chairman of the Board of Governors of the Federal Reserve) typically very conservative, in that they prefer to risk increasing unemployment rather than risk increasing the inflation rate?

4. Why do countries with large budget deficits often suffer from massive inflation?

5. Why do societies deliberately increase unemployment to reduce the rate of inflation? Is the pain of increased unemployment worth the benefit of reduced inflation?

Money Growth, Inflation, and Interest Rates

An economy can, in principle, produce at full employment with any inflation rate. There is no "magic" inflation rate that is necessary to sustain full employment. To understand this point, consider the long run when the economy operates at full employment. As we have seen, in the long run, money is neutral. If the Federal Reserve increases the money supply at 5% a year, there will be 5% annual inflation; that is, prices in the economy will rise by 5% a year.

Nominal wages: Wages in dollars.

Real wages: Nominal or dollar wages adjusted for changes in purchasing power.

Let's think about how this economy looks. The **nominal wages**—wages in dollars—of workers are all rising at 5% a year. However, because prices are also rising at 5% a year, **real wages**—wages adjusted for changes in purchasing power—remain constant.

Some workers may feel cheated by the 5% inflation. They might believe that without the inflation they would experience real wage increases, because their nominal wages are rising by 5% a year. Unfortunately, they are wrong. They suffer from what economists call **money illusion**, a confusion of real and nominal magnitudes. Here's the source of the illusion: The only reason their nominal wages are rising by 5% a year is the general 5% inflation. If there were no inflation, their nominal wages would not increase at all.

Money illusion: Confusion of real and nominal magnitudes.

Expectations of inflation: The beliefs held by the public about the likely path of inflation for the future.

After a time, everyone in the economy would begin to expect that the 5% annual inflation would continue. Economists say that in this situation, individuals hold **expectations of inflation**. These expectations affect all aspects of economic life. For example, automobile producers will on average expect their prices to be 5% higher next year. They will also expect their costs—labor and steel, for example—to increase by 5% a year. Workers would begin to understand that their 5% increases in wages would be matched by a 5% increase in the prices of the goods they buy. Continued inflation becomes the normal state of affairs. Expectations of inflation become ingrained in decisions made in all aspects of life.

When the public holds expectations of inflation, real and nominal rates of interest will differ. Recall that the nominal interest rate—the rate quoted in the market—is equal to the real rate of interest plus the expected inflation rate. So if inflation is 5% a year, nominal rates will exceed real rates by 5%.

In Chapter 14, you saw that in the long run, the real rate of interest does not depend on monetary policy because money is neutral; that is, changes in the supply of money do not affect real variables in the long run. However, nominal rates of interest depend on the rate of inflation, which in the long run is determined by the growth of the money supply. Monetary policy therefore does affect the nominal interest rate in the long run. If Country A and Country B had the same real rate of interest but Country A had a higher inflation rate, then Country A would also have a higher nominal interest rate. As Nobel laureate Milton Friedman pointed out, countries with higher money growth typically have higher nominal interest rates than the nominal interest rates in countries with lower money growth rates—and that's because of the differences in inflation across the countries.

Money demand will also be affected by expectations of inflation. If the public expects 5% inflation a year, then the public's demand for money will also increase by 5% a year. Recall the reality principle:

Reality **PRINCIPLE**

> **What matters to people is the real value of money or income— its purchasing power—not the face value of money or income.**

Using this principle, we can say that the public cares about the real value of its transactions. When prices rise at 5% a year, so does the value of transactions, such as your purchases at the grocery store. The public will need to hold 5% more money each year for these transactions. As long as the Fed allows the supply of money to increase by 5%, the demand for money and supply of money will grow at the same rate. With money's demand and supply both growing at the same rate, real interest rates and nominal interest rates will remain constant.

In the short run, however, changes in the growth rate of money will affect real interest rates. To continue with our example, suppose the public expects 5% annual inflation and both the money supply and money demand grow at 5% a year. Now let the Fed suddenly decrease the annual growth rate of money to 4% while the public continues to expect 5% annual inflation. Because money demand grows at 5% but the money supply grows at only 4%, the growth in the demand for money will exceed the growth in the supply of money. Because demand grows faster than supply, the result will be an increase in both real interest rates and nominal interest rates. Higher real rates of interest will reduce investment spending by firms and reduce consumer durable spending by households. With reduced demand for goods and services, real GDP will fall and unemployment will rise. The reduction in the growth rate of the money supply is contractionary.

In the long run, however, the economy will eventually adjust to the lower rate of money growth. Output will return to full employment through the adjustment process described in Chapter 14. Because money is neutral in the long run, the real rate of interest will return to its previous value. In the long run, inflation will fall to 4% per year, the rate of growth of the money supply. Because the real rate of interest has returned to its original value and inflation has fallen, nominal interest rates will also fall.

This basic pattern fits U.S. history in the late 1970s and early 1980s. At that time, the Federal Reserve sharply decreased the rate of growth of the money supply, and interest rates rose. By 1981, interest rates on three-month Treasury bills rose to over 14% from 7% in 1978. The economy went into a severe recession, with unemployment exceeding 10%. By the mid-1980s, however, the economy returned to full employment with lower interest rates and lower inflation rates. By 1986, Treasury bill rates were below 6%.

This is an example in which the long-run effects of policy actions differ from their short-run effects. In the short run, a policy of tight money, meaning slower money growth, raised interest rates. But in the long run, reduced money growth led to reduced inflation and lower interest rates.

TEST Your Understanding

1. The expected real rate of interest is the nominal interest rate minus the expected inflation rate. True or false? Explain.

2. Explain why, in the long run, an inflation rate of 10% per year will lead to an increase in the demand for money of 10% per year.

Expectations and the Phillips Curve

One of the key regularities in U.S. economic data is that inflation increases when economic activity booms and unemployment falls below its natural rate. Similarly, the rate of inflation falls when the economy is in a recession and unemployment exceeds the natural rate. This relationship between unemployment and inflation is known as the **expectations Phillips curve**.

Expectations Phillips curve:
The relationship that describes the links between inflation and unemployment, taking into account expectations of inflation.

The expectations Phillips curve is a refined version of the adjustment mechanism for the economy that we described in Chapter 14. There, we discussed how prices and wages rise if output is above potential output and unemployment is below the natural rate. Wages tend to rise during boom periods as firms compete for workers, and prices rise along with wages. Similarly, prices fall when output is below potential, and unemployment exceeds the natural rate. During recessions, high levels of unemployment lead to falling wages and prices.

However, once we take ongoing inflation into account, we need to modify this story slightly: Wages and prices can change, for two reasons: First, just as before, wages and prices will tend to rise during booms and fall during recessions. Second, workers and firms will have expectations of ongoing inflation. Both workers and firms will raise their nominal wages and prices to the extent that they expect ongoing inflation, to maintain the same level of real wages and real prices.

If the economy is operating at full employment, wages and prices will rise at the rate of inflation expected by workers and firms. If unemployment exceeds the natural rate, the high level of unemployment will put downward pressure on wages and prices, and inflation will fall relative to what was expected. Similarly, if unemployment were below the natural rate, employers would bid aggressively for workers, and wages and prices would rise faster than what was expected previously.

According to the expectations Phillips curve, unemployment varies with *unanticipated inflation*. When unemployment is below the natural rate, the actual inflation rate is higher than what was expected. Similarly, when unemployment is above the natural rate, actual inflation is lower than what was anticipated. When the unemployment rate is at the natural rate, the actual inflation rate equals the expected or anticipated inflation rate. Table 15.1 provides a summary of the key points about the expectations Phillips curve.

The expectations Phillips curve was introduced into the economics profession in the late 1960s by Edmund Phelps of Columbia University and Nobel laureate Milton Friedman, then at the University of Chicago. Friedman argued that when the inflation rate suddenly increases, it is likely that some of this sudden increase was not fully anticipated. Actual inflation will then exceed expected inflation. Workers will see their *nominal wages* increase with the inflation, but because they do not fully expect this sudden inflation, they will think that their *real wages* have increased. With higher perceived real wages, potential workers will accept more jobs, and consequently, unemployment will fall below the natural rate. That's why we will often see an association between increases in the inflation rate and a decrease in the unemployment rate.

After workers recognize that the inflation rate is higher, they will incorporate this higher inflation rate into their expectations of inflation. They will no longer confuse a higher nominal wage with a higher real wage. Unemployment will then return to its natural rate. Thus, there is no permanent relationship between the level of unemployment and the level of inflation.

Similarly, if the inflation rate falls, at least part of this fall may be unexpected. If inflation is less than expected, workers will believe that their real wages have fallen because their nominal wage will not be increasing as fast as their expectations of inflation. With lower perceived real wages, potential workers will accept fewer jobs and the unemployment rate will increase. Once they recognize that inflation is lower than expected, they will no longer be confused. Unemployment will again return to the natural rate. Thus, a decrease in the inflation rate is likely to be associated with temporary increases in unemployment.

Friedman's work forced the economics profession to pay careful attention to the process by which the public forms expectations of inflation. Although it has been over 30 years since Friedman first outlined his theory, there are still many different approaches to analyzing how expectations are formed. As we discuss later in the chapter, some economists believe that workers and firms form expectations taking into account the full array of information available in the economy. Other economists, however, believe workers and firms rely more on simple rules of thumb to form their expectations. Since predictions from economic models will depend on how workers and firms form expectations, this has been an important area of economic research.

The expectations Phillips curve differs from initial attempts to explain the relationship between inflation and unemployment. In the late 1950s, an engineer named A.W. Phillips noticed that there seemed to be a negative relationship between the level of inflation and unemployment in British data. He found lower unemployment to be associated with higher inflation. This relationship became known as the Phillips curve. In the early 1960s, Nobel laureates Paul Samuelson and Robert Solow found a similar relationship between unemployment and the level of the inflation rate in the United States. However, these original studies examined periods of history when there was no significant underlying inflation and did not take into account expectations of inflation. As we

Table 15.1 Expectations and Business Fluctuations

	Unemployment	Inflation
Boom	Unemployment below the natural rate	Inflation higher than expected
Recession	Unemployment above the natural rate	Inflation lower than expected

have seen, once we take expectations of ongoing inflation into account, the expectations Phillips curve, the relationship between inflation and unemployment, becomes a bit more complex.

U.S. Inflation and Unemployment in the 1980s

We can use the expectations Phillips curve to help describe the patterns of inflation and unemployment in the 1980s. For the sake of this discussion, we will rely on Friedman's generalization that sudden increases in inflation are partly unanticipated and thus are accompanied by lower unemployment. Conversely, temporarily higher unemployment is associated with decreases in inflation.

When President Jimmy Carter took office at the beginning of 1977, the inflation rate was approximately 6.5% per year, and unemployment exceeded 7% of the labor force. By 1980, however, annual inflation had risen to 9.4%. There were two reasons for this increase: One, unemployment had been steadily reduced during the Carter administration, falling below 6% by 1979. Because the natural rate of unemployment was close to 6% of the labor force, this led to an increase in the annual inflation rate. The other reason: There was an oil shock in 1979 that also contributed to higher inflation.

Fears of even higher inflation led President Carter to appoint a well-known inflation fighter, Paul Volcker, as the chair of the Federal Reserve. Volcker immediately began to institute a tight money policy, and interest rates rose sharply by 1980. When President Ronald Reagan took office, he supported Volcker's policy. Eventually, high real interest rates took their toll, and unemployment rose to over 10% by 1983. As actual unemployment exceeded the natural rate of unemployment, the inflation rate fell, just as was predicted by the expectations Phillips curve. By 1986, the inflation rate fell to approximately 2.7% per year with unemployment at 7% of the labor force. The severe recession had done its job in reducing the inflation rate.

However, as we can see in Figure 15.1, after 1986 the unemployment rate began to fall again. As actual unemployment fell below the natural rate of unemployment, inflation began to increase again. By 1989, annual inflation had risen to 4.5%. This led the Fed to

Figure 15.1
Dynamics of Inflation and Unemployment, 1986–1993

Source: Data from *Economic Report of the President* (Washington, DC: U.S. Government Printing Office, yearly).

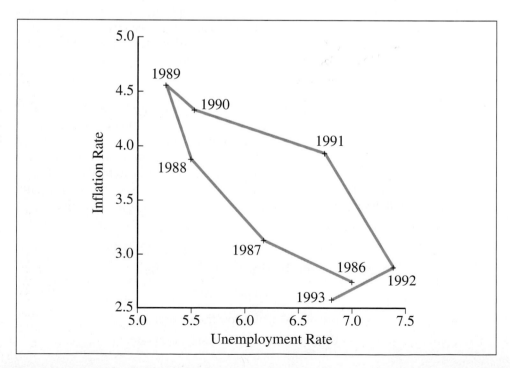

raise interest rates, thereby reducing output and increasing unemployment, to bring down the inflation rate. By 1992, the actual unemployment rate had increased to 7.4% of the labor force, and by 1993, annual inflation had again been brought down below 3%.

President George Bush suffered the consequences of this episode of fighting inflation. By the time he took office in 1989, actual unemployment was below the natural rate of unemployment, inflation had been rising, and the Fed was about to start slowing the economy. Although the rate of inflation was eventually reduced, the recovery back to full employment came too late in his term to be fully appreciated by the voters, and he lost his bid for reelection.

Shifts in the Natural Rate in the 1990s

Up to this point, we have assumed that the natural rate of unemployment is a constant, say, for example, 5% of the labor force. If actual unemployment falls below this constant rate, then inflation will tend to increase. Similarly, if the actual unemployment exceeds 5%, inflation will then fall.

But as you will see next, the natural rate of unemployment can shift over time. At the beginning of the 1990s in the United States, most economists believed that the natural rate of unemployment was in the 5% to 6% range. By the late 1990s, the actual unemployment rate had fallen to almost 4% of the labor force. If the natural rate of unemployment had been in the 5% to 6% range, we would have expected to see an increase in the inflation rate. But, in fact, the inflation rate continued to fall during the late 1990s. This continued drop in inflation suggests that the natural rate of unemployment had fallen. Of course, it is possible that special one-time factors, such as lower world oil prices, may have contributed to the decrease in the inflation rate over this period. But by the late 1990s, many economists had begun to believe that the natural rate of unemployment had decreased.

What factors can shift the natural rate of unemployment? Economists have identified three basic factors that can shift the natural rate of unemployment:

- Demographics. The composition of the work force can change to decrease the natural rate. For example, we know teenagers have higher unemployment rates than adults. If changes in population lead to a lower percentage of teenagers in the labor force, we would expect the natural rate of unemployment to decrease. Demographic factors appeared to have lowered the natural rate in the United States in the 1990s.

- Institutional changes. Changes in laws, regulations, and economic institutions can influence the natural rate of unemployment. Suppose the government decreased the length of time during which it made payments to workers who were unemployed. We would then expect that the unemployed would return to work more rapidly and the natural rate of unemployment would decrease. Some economists have argued that the rise of temporary employment agencies in the United States during the 1990s made the labor market more efficient and contributed to the decline of the natural rate. In Europe, institutional factors worked in the opposite direction, raising the natural rate of unemployment. In addition to generous benefits for the unemployed, restrictions on employers that made it more difficult to fire workers, also led them to hire fewer of them in the first place.

- The state of the economy. Some economists believe the economic performance of the economy itself may influence the natural rate of unemployment. Suppose the economy goes into a long recession. During that time, many young people may not be able to find jobs and fail to develop a strong work ethic. Other workers may lose some of their skills during a prolonged period of unemployment. Both factors could lead to longer-term unemployment and an increase in the natural rate of unemployment.

TEST Your Understanding

3. If inflation increases faster than expected, will the actual unemployment rate be above or below the natural rate of unemployment?

4. Will a sustained boom tend to increase or decrease the natural rate of unemployment?

Credibility and Inflation

Why are the heads of central banks (such as the chair of the Board of Governors) typically very conservative and constantly warning about the dangers of inflation? The basic reason is that these monetary policymakers can influence expectations of inflation. Expectations of inflation will influence actual behavior. For example, workers will want higher nominal wages if they anticipate inflation. If policymakers are not careful, they can actually make it difficult to fight inflation in a society.

Consider an example. A large union is negotiating wages for workers in the auto and steel industries. If the union negotiates a very high nominal wage, other unions will follow, negotiating for and winning high wages. Prices will inevitably rise. Because of these wage settlements, the Fed will begin to see inflation emerge. The Fed had been keeping the money supply constant. What are the Fed's options?

We depict the Fed's dilemma in Figure 15.2. By setting a higher nominal wage, the union shifts the aggregate supply curve from AS_0 to AS_1. The Fed then has a choice:

- Keep the money supply and aggregate demand at AD_0. The economy will initially fall into a recession.

- Increase the money supply and raise aggregate demand from AD_0 to AD_1. This will keep the economy at full employment but lead to higher prices.

Figure 15.2

Choices for the Fed

If workers push up their nominal wages, the aggregate supply curve will shift from AS_0 to AS_1. If the Fed keeps aggregate demand constant at AD_0, a recession will occur at A, and the economy will eventually return to full employment at E. If the Fed increases aggregate demand, the economy remains at full employment at F but with a higher price level.

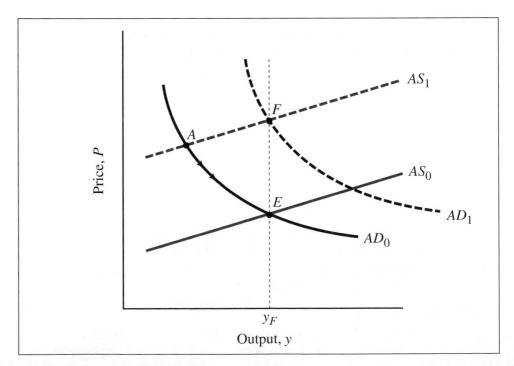

The actions of the union will depend on what its leaders expect the Fed to do. If they believe that the Fed will not increase aggregate demand, their actions will trigger a recession, and the union leaders are aware their actions will trigger a recession. They may be reluctant to negotiate a high wage. If they do not increase nominal wages, the economy will remain at full employment and there will be no increase in prices. But if union leaders believe that the Fed will increase aggregate demand, the union has nothing to lose and will increase the nominal wage. The result will be higher prices in the economy.

As this example illustrates, expectations about the Fed's determination to fight inflation will affect behavior in the private sector. If the Fed is credible or believable in its desire to fight inflation, it can deter the private sector from taking aggressive actions that drive up prices. This is the reason the heads of central banks are conservative, preferring to take the risks of increasing unemployment rather than risking an increase in inflation. For example, having a conservative chair of the Fed, someone who strongly detests inflation, sends a signal to everyone in the economy that the Fed will be unlikely to increase the money supply, regardless of what actions are taken in the private sector.

New Zealand took a different approach to ensure the credibility of its central bank. Since 1989, the central bank has been operating under a law that specifies that its only goal is to attempt to maintain stable prices, which, in practice, requires it to keep inflation between zero and 2% a year. This policy sharply limits the central bank's ability to stabilize real GDP, but it does signal to the private sector that the central bank will not be increasing the money supply, regardless of the actions taken by wage setters or unions.

Our example suggests that with a credible central bank, a country can have lower inflation without experiencing extra unemployment. Some political scientists and economists have suggested that central banks that have true independence from the rest of the government, and are therefore less subject to political influence, will be more credible in their commitment to fighting inflation.

There is evidence to support this conjecture. Figure 15.3 plots an index of independence against average inflation rates from 1955 to 1988 for 16 countries. The points appear to lie along a downward-sloping line, meaning that more independence is associ-

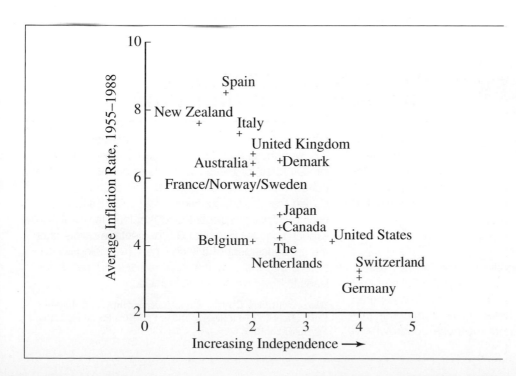

Figure 15.3

Inflation Versus Central Bank Independence

Source: Data from Alesina and Summers, "Central Bank Independence and Macroeconomic Performance," *Journal of Money, Credit, and Banking,* May 1993.

ated with lower inflation. Germany and Switzerland, the countries which had the most independent central banks, had the lowest inflation rates.

Another piece of evidence is provided by the changes in the United Kingdom as "A Closer Look: Inflation Expectations and the Bank of England" explains.

As our discussion illustrates, it's necessary to understand how central bank behavior affects expectations to be able to understand the behavior of output and prices for the economy. As we have noted, economists have paid increasing attention to the role of expectations in many different areas of economics. They have recognized that people develop their expectations in complex ways that take into account the information they have available.

Rational expectations: The economic theory that analyzes how people form expectations in such a manner that, on average, they forecast the future correctly.

In the 1970s, a group of economists led by Nobel laureate Robert E. Lucas, Jr., from the University of Chicago developed the theory of **rational expectations**, which analyzes how firms and individuals may base their expectations on all the information available to them. According to the theory of rational expectations, individuals form their expectations such that, on average, they anticipate the future correctly. Although they may make mistakes in specific instances, on average their expectations are rational or correct. The theory of rational expectations has been used extensively in many areas of economics, including the example with the union and the Fed that we just discussed. In that example, the theory of rational expectations implies that the union will, on average, anticipate whether the Fed will adopt a policy of expanding the money supply in the face of wage increases. A credible Fed, therefore, will tend to deter wage increases. Although not all economists believe that the public is fully rational in economic affairs, insights from this theory have heavily influenced economic research in many different areas.

Expectations play a significant role in almost all areas of economics. For example, as we have seen, both lenders and borrowers must form expectations about future inflation rates in setting nominal interest rates. There are many other examples as well. Prices of stocks of firms will depend on investors' expectations about future dividends that the firm will pay. Even your decision to buy a home or rent will depend on your expectation about the future prices of homes. If you believe that home prices will rise sharply in the future, you will be more likely to buy a home and earn a profit from the investment. Economists study how expectations are formed in all these markets, whether they are rational or not, and how expectations influence actual market outcomes.

A CLOSER LOOK — INFLATION EXPECTATIONS AND THE BANK OF ENGLAND

On May 6, 1997, the Chancellor of Exchequer in Great Britain, Gordon Brown, announced a major change in monetary policy. From that time forward, the Bank of England would be more independent from the government. While the government would still retain the authority to set the overall goals for policy, the Bank of England would be free to pursue its policy goals without direct political control.

Mark Spiegel, an economist with the Federal Reserve Bank of San Francisco, studied how the British bond market reacted to the change in policy. He compared the interest rates on two types of long-term bonds that existed in the United Kingdom: those bonds whose prices are automatically adjusted (or indexed) for inflation, and those that are not. Based on the changes in interest rates for these two types of bonds during the period that the announcement was made, he concluded that the announcement did influence expectations of inflation. Spiegel found that long-term inflation expectations fell by about 0.5 percentage points after the announcement of this change. This finding is consistent with the view that central bank independence leads to lower expectations of inflation.

Source: "British Central Bank Independence and Inflation Expectations," Federal Reserve of San Francisco Economic Letter, November 28, 1997.

Inflation and the Velocity of Money

Countries sometimes experience stunning inflation rates. For example, in a period of 15 months from August 1922 to November 1923, the price level in Germany rose by a factor of 10 billion! To explain these extremely high inflation rates and to provide more insight into the links between money growth and inflation, we now introduce a concept that is closely related to money demand: the velocity of money.

The **velocity of money** is defined as the ratio of nominal GDP to the money supply:

$$\text{velocity of money} = \text{nominal GDP/money supply}$$

One useful way to think of velocity is that it is the number of times that money must change hands, or turn over, in economic transactions during a given year to purchase nominal GDP.

To understand this, consider a simple example. Suppose that nominal GDP in a country is $5 trillion per year and the money supply is $1 trillion. Then the velocity of money in this economy will be

$$\begin{aligned}\text{velocity} &= \text{\$5 trillion per year/\$1 trillion} \\ &= \text{5 per year}\end{aligned}$$

In this economy, the $1 trillion money supply has to change hands or turn over an average of 5 times a year to purchase the $5 trillion of nominal GDP.

If the money supply turns over 5 times in one year, this means that people are holding each dollar of money for 365 days/5 = 73 days a year. If velocity is very high, individuals turn over money very quickly and do not hold money for a very long time on average. If velocity is low, they turn over money slowly and hold onto money for a longer period of time.

To further understand the role of money and velocity, let's rewrite the definition of velocity as

$$\text{money supply} \times \text{velocity} = \text{nominal GDP}$$
$$\text{or}$$
$$M \times V = P \times y$$

where M is the money supply, V is the velocity of money, P is a price index for GDP, and y is real GDP. This equation is known as the equation of exchange or the **quantity equation**. On the right side, $P \times y$ is nominal GDP, the product of price index and real GDP. This is the total value of spending. On the left side, the money supply, M, is multiplied by V, the velocity of money.

The quantity equation links the money supply and velocity to nominal GDP. If velocity is predictable, we can use the quantity equation and the supply of money to predict nominal GDP. But it's not that easy; the velocity of money does vary over time. For example, in the United States between 1959 and 2001, the velocity of M2 (the measure of the money supply that includes currency, demand deposits, saving accounts, and deposits in money market mutual funds) varied between 1.4 and 2.0. In other words, the total amount of M2 held by the public turned over between 1.4 and 2.0 times a year to purchase nominal GDP for each year during this period.

The basic quantity equation can be used to derive a closely related formula for understanding inflation in the long run:

$$\text{Growth rate of money} + \text{growth rate of velocity}$$
$$= \text{growth rate of prices} + \text{growth rate of real output}$$

Velocity of money: Nominal GDP divided by the money supply. It is also the rate at which money changes hands or turns over during the year.

Quantity equation: The equation that links money, velocity, prices, and real output. In symbols, we have M × V = P × y.

Growth version of the quantity equation: An equation that links the growth rates of money, velocity, prices, and real output.

We will call this the **growth version of the quantity equation**. Here is how to use this formula: Suppose that money growth is 10% a year, the growth of real output is 3% a year, and velocity has zero growth (it is constant). Then the rate of growth of prices, which is the inflation rate, is

$$10\% + 0\% = \text{growth rate of prices} + 3\%$$
$$7\% = \text{growth rate of prices} = \text{inflation}$$

Inflation will be 7% a year. This formula allows for real economic growth and for growth in velocity. For example, if velocity grew during this period at the rate of 1% a year, the inflation rate will be 1% higher, or 8% $(10 + 1 - 3)$ a year.

There is a definite link between increases in the growth of money and the rate of inflation. Inflation was lowest in the 1950s, when money growth was lowest. It was also highest in the 1970s, when money growth was highest. The link is not perfect because real GDP and velocity grew at different rates during the decades. But years of economic research have revealed that sustained increases in money growth will lead to inflation.

The links between money growth and inflation are particularly dramatic when money growth is extremely high. But what leads countries to vast increases in their money supply?

TEST Your Understanding

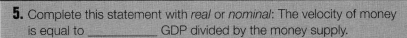

5. Complete this statement with *real* or *nominal*: The velocity of money is equal to _____ GDP divided by the money supply.

6. If the growth of the money supply is 6% a year, velocity decreases by 1%, and there is no growth in real GDP, what is the inflation rate?

Budget Deficits and Hyperinflations

The inflation rates observed in the United States in the last 40 years are insignificant compared to some of the inflation rates around the world throughout history. Economists call very high inflation rates—over 50% per month, which is approximately 13,000% per year—**hyperinflation**. One of the first studies of hyperinflations was conducted by Phillip Cagan of Columbia University. Table 15.2 presents selected data from his study.

Hyperinflation: An inflation rate exceeding 50% per month.

Table 15.2 Some Classic Hyperinflations

Country	Dates	Monthly Rate of Inflation	Monthly Rate of Money Growth	Approximate Increase in Velocity
Greece	November 1943 to November 1944	365%	220%	14.00
Hungary	August 1945 to July 1946	19,800%	12,200%	333.00
Russia	December 1921 to January 1924	57%	49%	3.70

Source: Adapted from Phillip Cagan, "The Monetary Dynamics of Hyperinflation," in *Studies in the Quantity Theory of Money*, edited by Milton Friedman (Chicago: University of Chicago Press, 1956), p. 26.

Greece, Hungary, and Russia are three countries that have had hyperinflation. According to the data in Table 15.2, for a period of one year, Greece had a monthly inflation rate of 365%. A monthly inflation rate of 365% per month means the price level rises by a factor of 4.65 each month. (If the price level rises by 4.65, its percent increase is $(4.65 - 1)/1 = 3.65$, or 365%.) To get a sense of what this means, suppose that we had inflation of this magnitude in the United States. At the beginning of the month, $1 could buy a large order of French fries. Because prices are rising by a factor of 4.65 each month, by the end of the month it would take $4.65 to buy the same order of French fries, and one dollar by the end of the month would be worth only $1/4.65 = 0.215$, or 21.5 cents.

After two months, a dollar would be worth only $(0.215) \times (0.215) = 0.046$ of its original value, or 4.6 cents. Suppose this continues month after month. After one year, a dollar bill would be worth only 1 millionth of 1 cent! In hyperinflations, money does not hold its value very long.

In Hungary after World War II, prices rose by 19,800% each month. The hyperinflation in Russia in the early 1920s seems moderate by comparison: prices rose by 57% per month.

On the basis of the quantity theory, we suspect that these hyperinflations must have all been caused by money growth. We can see this in the data. For example, in Greece, the monthly inflation of 365% was accompanied by 220% money growth. In Hungary, the monthly inflation of 19,800% was caused by 12,200% money growth.

The value of money deteriorates sharply during hyperinflations. Money no longer serves as a good store of value. In these extreme circumstances, we expect that people will not want to hold money very long but will immediately try to spend it. In other words, we expect the velocity of money to increase sharply during hyperinflations. This is precisely what happens.

The last column of Table 15.2 shows how velocity increases during hyperinflations. In the hyperinflation in Greece, velocity increased by a factor of 14. In the hyperinflation in Hungary, velocity increased by over 333 times.

Hyperinflations have also occurred in recent times. The chapter opening story highlights Russia in the 1990s. Table 15.3 presents data on three hyperinflations during the 1980s—in Bolivia, Argentina, and Nicaragua, all averaging about 100% per month.

During hyperinflations, money no longer works very well in facilitating exchange. Because prices are changing so fast and unpredictably, there is typically massive confusion about the true value of commodities. Different stores may be raising prices at different rates, and the same commodities may sell for radically different prices. Everyone spends all their time hunting for bargains and finding the lowest prices, a process that becomes very costly in human terms. No country can easily live very long with hyperin-

Table 15.3 High Inflations in the 1980s

| Country | Year | Rate of Inflation | | Monthly Money Growth Rate |
		Yearly	Monthly	
Bolivia	1985	1,152,200%	118%	91%
Argentina	1989	302,200%	95%	93%
Nicaragua	1988	975,500%	115%	66%

Source: International Financial Statistics Yearbook, 1992. (Washington, DC: International Monetary Fund).

flations. Governments are forced to put an end to hyperinflation before it totally destroys their economies.

The cause of all hyperinflations is excessive money growth. But why do governments allow the money supply to grow so fast and cause these economic catastrophes? The answer lies in understanding how some governments finance their deficits—the gap between government spending and revenues.

A government deficit must be covered in some way. If a government wants to spend $1,000 but is collecting only $800 in taxes, where can it get the needed $200? One option is to borrow the $200 from the public. The government will then issue government bonds—IOUs—to the public for $200. In the future, the government will have to pay back the $200 plus interest on the bonds.

An alternative to borrowing from the public is to print $200 worth of new money. All governments have the ability to run the printing presses and come up with $200 in new currency.

In principle, governments could use a mix of borrowing funds from public and printing money as long as the deficit is covered:

$$\text{government deficit} = \text{new borrowing from the public} + \text{new money created}$$

Now we are in a position to understand how hyperinflations originate. Consider Hungary after World War II. Its economy was destroyed by the war, and its citizens were demanding government services. The government had limited ability to collect taxes because of the poor state of the economy, but it gave in to the demands from its citizens for spending at levels that far exceeded what it could collect. The result was a large deficit. Then the government faced a problem: How would this large deficit be financed?

During Germany's hyper-inflation in the 1920s, it was cheaper to start a fire with currency than it was to purchase wood for kindling.

No individuals or governments wanted to buy bonds or IOUs from Hungary (that is, lend Hungary money) because its economy was in such poor shape that it would be unlikely to pay off any debts in the near future. Without an option to borrow, Hungary resorted to printing money at a massive rate. The result was hyperinflation.

Hyperinflations always occur in countries that have large deficits but cannot borrow and are forced to print new money. For example, Argentina in the 1980s had large state-run firms that consistently lost vast sums of money. Because Argentina had a history of past inflations, it could not borrow easily and resorted to printing money. Large, money-losing state enterprises and limited ability to borrow combined to bring money creation and hyperinflation.

To stop hyperinflations, it is necessary to eliminate the government deficit, which is the fundamental cause. Either taxes must be increased or spending must be cut, both of which cause some economic pain. There is no other remedy. Once the deficit has been cut and the government stops printing money, the hyperinflation will end. Without money growth to feed it, hyperinflation will quickly die of starvation.

Economists who traditionally emphasized the role that the supply of money played in determining nominal income and inflation were often called **monetarists**. The most famous monetarist is Nobel laureate Milton Friedman, who studied complex versions of the quantity equation and explored the role of money in all aspects of economic life. Friedman had many influential students, such as Philip Cagan, who is best known for his work on hyperinflations. They, along with other monetarist economists, did pioneering research on the link between money, nominal income, and inflation. Today, most economists agree with the monetarists that, in the long run, inflation is caused by growth in the money supply.

Monetarists: Economists who emphasize the role of money in determining nominal income and inflation.

The Costs of Unemployment and Inflation

While we can understand why societies cannot tolerate hyperinflations, it is less clear what problems occur with what may be considered more ordinary inflation rates. Why do societies deliberately create recessions and unemployment for the purpose of lowering the rate of inflation? In this section, we take a closer look at the costs of unemployment and inflation to better understand the options facing policymakers.

Costs of Unemployment

When there is excess unemployment—actual unemployment above the natural rate of unemployment—both society and individuals suffer economic loss. From a social point of view, excess unemployment means that the economy is no longer producing at its potential. The resulting loss of resources can be very large. For example, in 1983, when the unemployment rate averaged 9.6%, typical estimates of the shortfall of GDP from potential were near 6%. Simply put, this meant that society was wasting 6% of the total resources at its disposal.

That social loss translates into reduced income and lower employment for individuals. When unemployment increases, more workers are fired or laid off from their existing jobs, and individuals seeking employment find fewer opportunities available. To families with fixed obligations such as mortgage payments, the loss in income can bring immediate hardships. **Unemployment insurance**, payments received from the government upon becoming unemployed, can cushion the blow to some degree, but unemployment insurance is typically only temporary and does not replace a worker's full earnings.

The effects of unemployment can also linger into the future. As we noted, workers who suffer from a prolonged period of unemployment are likely to lose some of their

Unemployment insurance: Payments received from the government upon becoming unemployed.

skills. For example, an unemployed stockbroker might be unaware of the latest developments and trends in financial markets. This will make it more difficult for him or her to find a job in the future. Economists who have studied the high rates of unemployment among young people in Europe point to the loss of both skills and good work habits (such as coming to work on time) as key factors leading to long-term unemployment.

The costs of unemployment are not simply financial. In our society, a person's status and position are largely associated with the type of job the person holds. Losing a job can impose severe psychological costs. Some studies, for example, have found that increased crime, divorce, and suicide rates are associated with increased unemployment.

Costs of Inflation

Anticipated inflation: Inflation that is expected.

Unanticipated inflation: Inflation that is not expected.

Economists typically separate the costs of inflation into two categories. One includes costs associated with fully expected or **anticipated inflation**. The other includes the costs associated with unexpected or **unanticipated inflation**. Although inflation causes both types of costs, it is convenient to discuss each case separately.

Anticipated Inflation

Let's consider the costs of anticipated inflation first. Suppose the economy had been experiencing 4% annual inflation for many years and everyone was fully adjusted to it. Workers knew that nominal wage increases of 4% each year were not real wage increases because prices will rise by 4% over the year. Investors earning a 7% annual rate of interest on their bonds knew that their real return would be only 3% after adjusting for inflation.

Menu costs: Costs of inflation that arise from actually changing prices.

Even in this case, inflation still has some costs. First, there are the actual physical costs of changing prices, which economists call **menu costs**. Restaurant owners, catalog producers, and any other business that must post prices will have to incur costs to change their prices because of inflation. Economists believe that these costs are relatively small for the economy.

Second, people will hold less real cash balances when there is inflation. The cost of holding money is its opportunity cost, which is best measured by the nominal rate of interest. Because an increase in inflation will raise the nominal rate of interest, it will raise the cost of holding cash or checking accounts that do not pay interest. People will respond by holding less cash at any one time. If they hold less cash, they must visit the bank or their ATM more frequently because they will run out of cash sooner. Economists use the term **shoe-leather costs** to refer to the additional wear and tear necessary to hold less cash. Economists who have estimated these costs find that they can be large, as much as 1% of GDP.

Shoe-leather costs: Costs of inflation that arise from trying to reduce holdings of cash.

In practice, our tax system and financial system do not fully adjust even to fully anticipated inflation. It is difficult for the government and businesses to change their normal rules of operation when inflation changes. As an example, consider the tax system. Our tax system is based on nominal income, not real income. Suppose the yearly inflation rate is 3%, nominal interest rates are 7% per year, and you have $100 in a savings account. At the end of the year, you will have earned $7. Your income taxes will be based on the full $7, not on $4, which is your earnings adjusted for inflation. This can make a considerable difference. If your tax rate is 50%, you pay $3.50 in taxes, giving you a nominal return after taxes of 3.5% on your original $100 [($7 − $3.50)/$100]. Taking into account the 3% inflation, your real return is only 0.5% (3.5 − 3).

Now suppose that there is no inflation, there is a 4% real rate of return, and the tax rate is 50%. Your taxes will be $2, which, in the absence of inflation, will give you a higher real return after taxes of 2% [($4 − 2)/$100]. Inflation lowered your real after-tax return because the tax system is based on nominal income, not real income. This increase in taxes was not a deliberate action of the legislature; it is solely a creature of inflation.

There are other examples of how inflation interacts with taxation. In the United States before 1986, inflation could have pushed you into a higher tax bracket—for example, from 15% to 28%—with the result that the government took a higher fraction of your income. Since 1986, tax brackets have been adjusted for inflation, eliminating this particular problem. Even today, however, you pay taxes when you sell a stock whose price has increased solely because of inflation even if the real value of the stock did not increase. The government can also lose from inflation as well. Homeowners can deduct from their taxes their nominal interest payments on their mortgages, not their real interest payments. Higher inflation gives homeowners more deductions and lowers their income tax bills.

Many financial markets are also not fully adjusted for inflation. For example, some states have **usury laws**, or ceilings on interest rates. These ceilings are on nominal rates, not real rates. At times of high inflation, some lenders may require nominal rates above the usury ceilings to provide them with an adequate real return. If they cannot lend at rates above the ceiling, the market may actually disappear.

Usury laws: Laws that do not allow interest rates to exceed specified ceilings.

The column in Table 15.4 on anticipated inflation summarizes our discussion. If the economy can adjust fully to inflation, the only costs of fully anticipated inflation are the small menu costs and shoe-leather costs. But if institutions such as the tax system do not adjust, there will be other costs, such as distortions in the tax system, as well.

Unanticipated Inflation

The last column in Table 15.4 shows the costs of unexpected or unanticipated inflation. The first cost of unanticipated inflation is arbitrary redistributions of income. Suppose the public had been accustomed to 4% annual inflation but inflation reaches 6%. Who would gain and who would lose? Lenders would lose, and borrowers would gain. If lenders and borrowers agreed to a real rate of interest of 3% and expected 4% inflation, the nominal rate would have been 7%. However, with 6% inflation, the real rate actually paid would fall to 1%. Borrowers would rejoice, and lenders would despair.

Anyone making a nominal contract to sell a product would lose. For example, workers who set nominal wages based on expected inflation would earn a lower real wage. Buyers with nominal contracts, such as firms setting nominal wages, would gain. These are unfair redistributions of income, or transfers, caused by unanticipated inflation.

These redistributions eventually impose real costs on the economy. Consider an analogy. Suppose you live in a very safe neighborhood where no one locks their doors. If a rash of burglaries (transfers between you and the crooks) starts to occur, people will invest in locks, alarms, and more police. You and your community will incur real costs to prevent these arbitrary redistributions.

The same is true for unanticipated inflation. If a society experiences unanticipated inflation, individuals and institutions will change their behavior. For example, potential

Table 15.4 Costs of Inflation

	Anticipated Inflation	Unanticipated Inflation
Institutions do not adjust	Distortions in the tax system, problems in financial markets	Unfair redistributions
Institutions adjust	Cost of changing prices, shoe-leather costs	Institutional disintegration

homeowners will not be able to borrow for long periods at fixed rates of interest but will be required to accept loans whose rates can be adjusted as inflation rates change. This imposes more risk on homeowners. If unanticipated inflation becomes extreme, individuals will spend more of their time trying to profit from inflation rather than working at productive jobs. As inflation became more volatile in the late 1970s in the United States, many people devoted their time to speculation in real estate and commodity markets to try to beat inflation. The economy becomes less efficient when people take actions based on beating inflation. Latin American countries that have experienced high and variable inflation rates know all too well these costs from inflation.

When inflation becomes a problem, some societies have tried to index nominal contracts, that is, adjust the nominal amounts for inflation. For example, if you had an indexed wage of $10.00 an hour and there was 15% inflation, your wage would rise to $11.50 to compensate you for the inflation ($10.00 × 1.15 = $11.50). The U.S. government has now joined other countries in providing indexed bonds to protect investors from inflation.

In practice, countries find that indexing is not a perfect solution to the problems caused by inflation. There are three reasons:

1. Some policymakers worry that indexing lowers the resolve to fight inflation and therefore could lead to higher inflation.
2. We know that price indices are far from perfect and are extremely difficult to construct when prices are increasing rapidly.
3. Some economists believe that indexing builds inflation into the economic system and makes it difficult to reduce inflation. If price increases automatically lead to wage increases, it becomes difficult to stop wage-price spirals. In 1995, for example, Brazil began to dismantle its very extensive system of indexing precisely for this reason.

Although Table 15.4 is useful for discussing the different costs of inflation, it is important to note that it is not easy to distinguish anticipated inflation from unanticipated inflation. Most inflations are a mixture of the two. Moreover, in all countries, institutions can adjust to inflation only partially. Thus, all the costs outlined in Table 15.4 may apply to any episode of inflation.

These costs are compounded as inflation rises. Studies have shown that as inflation rises, both anticipated inflation and unanticipated inflation increase. At high inflation rates, these costs grow rapidly, and at some point, policymakers are forced to engineer a recession to reduce the inflation rate. Although unemployment and recessions are quite costly to society, they sometimes become necessary in the face of high inflation.

Using the **TOOLS**

In this chapter we examined how inflation becomes embedded into expectations and the problems in taming inflation. Take the opportunity to do your own economic analysis.

1. ECONOMIC EXPERIMENT: Money Illusion

Economists say that people suffer from money illusion if their behavior is influenced by nominal changes that are also not real changes. Consider the following scenarios and be prepared to discuss them in class.

a. Erin bought an antique clock for $100. Two years later, Betsy bought an identical clock for $121. Meanwhile, there had been inflation each year at 10%. Both Erin and Betsy sell their clocks to other collectors. Erin sold hers for $130; Betsy sold hers for $133. Who profited more in their transactions?

b. Bob and Pete are classic comic book traders. A year ago, Bob and Pete each bought the same comic book for $10. Bob sold his a couple of days later for $20. Pete waited a year and sold his for $21. If inflation last year was 6%, who made the better deal?

APPLICATIONS

2. Inflation: A Recipe for Japan?

In the late 1990s, Japan's economy was still in a prolonged slump. Nominal interest rates were approximately zero, which many economists believed limited the scope for monetary policy. Professor Paul Krugman of Princeton University disagreed. He argued that Japan's central bank should increase the money supply rapidly with an intention to cause inflation. Moreover, they should credibly promise to continue this inflation policy into the future. The result, he predicted, would be increased investment and higher GDP growth.

Krugman's recommendation was based on the distinction between real and nominal interest rates. Can you explain the logic of his recommendation?

3. Tax Indexation

An economy has two income tax brackets for individuals: a tax rate of 10% for the first $30,000 of income and a tax rate of 20% for any income exceeding $30,000.

a. A family earns $40,000. How much tax does it pay?

b. Suppose prices double and the family earns $80,000. How much tax does the family pay?

c. How does the tax as a percentage of income change with the increase in prices? How could the tax system be fixed to ensure that the percentage of income that goes to the tax collector does not change with the level of prices?

4. Public Pronouncements and Fed Officials

When Alan Blinder, a Princeton University professor of economics, was appointed vice-chair of the Federal Reserve in 1994, he gave a speech to a group of central bankers and monetary policy specialists. In that speech, he repeated one of the lessons in this chapter: In the long run, the rate of inflation is independent of unemployment and depends only on money growth; in the short run, lower unemployment can raise the inflation rate. Blinder's speech created an uproar in the financial press. He was attacked by some commentators as not being sufficiently vigilant against inflation. Use the idea of credibility to explain why an apparently innocent speech would cause such an uproar in the financial community.

 **Summary**

In this chapter, we explored the role expectations of inflation plays in the economy and how societies deal with inflation. Interest rates, as well as changes in wages and prices, both reflect expectations of inflation. These expectations depend on the past history of inflation and on expectations about central bank behavior. To reduce inflation, policymakers must increase actual unemployment above the natural rate of unemployment. We also looked at the ultimate causes of hyperinflations. Finally, we discussed the costs of unemployment and inflation and why policymakers sometimes deliberately cause recessions to reduce the rate of inflation. Here are main points to remember from this chapter:

1. In the long run, higher money growth leads to higher inflation and higher nominal interest rates.

2. A decrease in the growth rate of money will initially lead to higher real interest rates and higher nominal interest rates. Real interest rates will eventually return to their prior levels. Nominal interest rates

will be permanently decreased with the decrease in inflation.

3. The rate of inflation increases when actual unemployment falls below the natural rate of unemployment; the rate of inflation decreases when actual unemployment exceeds the natural rate of unemployment. Economists explain this relationship by the expectations Phillips curve.

4. Monetary policymakers need to be cautious in their statements and pronouncements because what they say can influence expectations of inflation. Conservative central bankers can dampen expectations of inflation.

5. The quantity equation and the growth version of the quantity equation show the relationship between money, velocity, and nominal income.

6. Governments sometimes print new money to finance large portions of their budget deficits. When they do, the result is rapid inflation.

7. The costs of unemployment include the loss of output for society and economic and psychological hardships for individuals.

8. The costs of inflation arise from both anticipated and unanticipated inflation. In practice, both types of costs rise with the inflation rate.

Key Terms

anticipated inflation, 322
expectations of inflation, 308
expectations Phillips curve, 310
growth version of the quantity
   equation, 318
hyperinflation, 318

menu costs, 322
monetarists, 321
money illusion, 308
nominal wages, 308
quantity equation, 317
rational expectations, 316

real wages, 308
shoe-leather costs, 322
unanticipated inflation, 322
unemployment insurance, 321
usury laws, 323
velocity of money, 317

Problems and Discussions Questions

1. Interpret the following statement: "High interest rates are the evidence of loose monetary policy, not tight monetary policy."

2. If a business borrows funds at 10% per year, the business has a 40% tax rate, and the annual inflation rate is 5%, what are the real after-tax costs of funds to the business?

3. Are workers or firms more likely to have more accurate information about the future course of inflation?

4. Some economists argue that the natural rate of unemployment did not really decrease in the United States in the late 1990s, but there were temporary factors that kept the inflation from rising. How would you go about determining whether the natural rate of unemployment decreased in the late 1990s in the United States?

5. If the government increases the rate at which it injects money into the economy, individuals and firms will hold onto money for shorter periods. Can you explain this?

6. If the growth rate of money is 10% per year, annual inflation is 7%, and the growth rate of velocity is 1% per year, what is the growth rate of real output?

7. Some economists argue that foreign aid can reduce both the likelihood and the severity of hyperinflations. Explain this argument.

8. How do you think the Internet and on-line shopping would affect the menu costs from inflation?

9. Discuss this quote: "Most businesses are debtors. They will therefore benefit from inflation."

10. Many people find owning their home an attractive investment during times of inflation. Interest payments for the house can be deducted from income before calculating income taxes. When a house is sold at a price that has risen through inflation, most of the profit from owning it is free of tax. Why does an increase in inflation increase the attractiveness of owning a house? Why do people often buy larger houses during periods of high inflation than they normally would?

11. **Web Exercise.** In the 1990s, the U.S. Treasury introduced bonds that were indexed to inflation. Go to the Web site for the Bureau of the Public Debt [*http://www.publicdebt.treas.gov/sec/seciis.htm*] and read about these bonds. Search the Web (or other sources) and compare the interest rates on 30-year Treasury bonds that are indexed for infla-

tion with those that are not. What factors can explain the difference in interest rates?

12. **Web Exercise.** Since teenagers and younger workers tend to have higher unemployment rates than older workers, some economists have argued that changes in the age composition of the labor force can partly explain shifts in the natural rate. Using the Web site for the Bureau of Labor Statistics [*http://www.bls.gov*], find information on the age composition of the labor force today and compare it to ten years ago.

Take It to the Net

We invite you to visit the O'Sullivan/Sheffrin page on the Prentice Hall Web site at: **http://www.prenhall.com/osullivan/** for additional World Wide Web exercises for this chapter.

Model Answers to Questions

Chapter-Opening Questions

1. Countries with lower rates of money growth will have lower inflation rates than countries with higher money growth. Nominal interest rates (which reflect inflation) will also be lower.

2. In the long run, actual unemployment returns to the natural rate of unemployment, and inflation is largely determined by money growth. Therefore, lower unemployment will lead to higher inflation, but actual unemployment will return to the natural rate of unemployment.

3. It is prudent to have conservative heads of central banks because the private sector will then be less tempted to aggressively raise wages and prices.

4. Budget deficits must be financed by either issuing debt or creating money. When deficits are very large, it is difficult to issue debt, so money is created, causing massive inflation.

5. Inflation imposes real costs on the economy, which is why societies sometimes cause recessions to reduce inflation. However, there are costs to unemployment as well, and these costs need to be balanced against the costs of inflation.

Test Your Understanding

1. True. To find the expected real interest rate, subtract the expected inflation rate from the nominal rate of interest.

2. This is an application of the reality principle. If prices rise, people will want to hold more money to make transactions.

3. When inflation is higher than expected, actual unemployment will be below the natural rate of unemployment.

4. A sustained boom will tend to lower the natural rate of unemployment.

5. Nominal.

6. Use the growth version of the quantity equation: $6 - 1 = $ inflation $+ 0$. Inflation is thus 5% per year.

Using the Tools

1. Economic Experiment: Money Illusion

   a. As you discuss this in class, first recognize that with 10% inflation, the $100 dollars that Erin paid for the clock was the same as the $121 Betsy paid for the clock two years later. Since Betsy then sold her clock for more than Erin, she made the best deal on the transaction in real terms.

   b. While Pete sold his comic book for $21 and Bob sold his for $20, Pete sold his a year later. With 6% inflation, Bob made the better deal in real terms.

2. Inflation: A Recipe for Japan. Krugman believed that rapid growth in the money supply would cause inflation. If the public believed that the Japanese bank would continue with this policy, then expectations of inflation would rise. The real rate of interest is the nominal rate minus the expected inflation rate. With the nominal rate at zero, increased expectations of inflation would lower the real rate of interest. The fall in the real rate of interest would stimulate investment spending and lead to higher GDP.

3. Tax Indexation

   a. The family pays $5,000 in taxes ($3,000 on the first $30,000 plus $2,000 on the next $10,000).

   b. Now the family pays $13,000 in taxes ($3,000 on the first $30,000 plus $10,000 on the next $50,000).

c. In the first case, the family pays 12.5% of its income in taxes. In the second case, the family pays 16.3%, although their real income before taxes was the same in both cases. To prevent inflation from leading to higher tax burdens, the level at which the higher rate takes effect should be adjusted, or indexed, for the price level. If the level of income at which the 20% rate took effect was raised to $60,000, then the family will pay $10,000 in taxes or 12.5% of their income.

4. Public Pronouncements and Fed Officials. The financial markets reacted negatively to Blinder's comments because they perceived that it signaled he was soft on inflation. A conservative central banker will typically not even mention that lower unemployment could increase inflation because that might leave the impression that they might not be aggressive in fighting inflation.

16

Current Issues in Macroeconomic Policy

Your elderly uncle draws you aside at a family gathering. "So, I hear you're studying economics," he says. "You know, this country has been going downhill ever since President Roosevelt started deficit spending. We're governed by incompetents. Inflation nearly wiped me out in the 1970s. But that recession in the 1980s really did me in. All these politicians—they just want to get reelected. They have totally abandoned good policies. And the taxes I pay are eating me alive. Do they teach you that in college these days?"

You start to respond, but you are saved by the bell—the dinner bell.

As a student and citizen you are inevitably drawn into economic debates. Sometimes, debates revolve around simple factual issues. For example, when was the last time inflation was below 3%? But in most cases, the debates are complex. They are a mixture of facts, theories, and opinions. Value judgements play a large role in economic debates. Your views on the proper role of tax policy, for example, will depend on whether you believe that low-income earners should receive a higher share of national income. And your views on the size of government will depend on whether you believe that individuals or the government should play a larger role in economic affairs.

In previous chapters, you learned the basic vocabulary of economics and studied different theories of the economy. Now we can address some of the key policy issues in macroeconomics. We will focus on three issues in macroeconomics, which are at the center of many other related economic debates. After reading this chapter, you should have an informed opinion on these three issues:

1. Should the government balance its budget?
2. Should the Federal Reserve aim for zero inflation?
3. Should fiscal policies be designed solely to promote economic growth?

Unlike the chapter opening questions in other chapters, there are no simple answers to these questions. But these questions do trigger fundamental economic debates.

Should We Balance the Federal Budget?

Some Background

Deficit: The excess of total expenditures over total revenues.

Surplus: The excess of total revenues over total expenditures.

Government expenditure: Spending on goods and services plus transfer payments.

Government debt: The total of all past deficits.

Before we begin to consider the answers to that question, let's define some terms: Governments run a **deficit** when they spend more than they currently receive in revenues from either taxes or fees. A **surplus** occurs when revenues exceed spending. Governments run a balanced budget when revenues equal spending—purchases of goods and services or transfer payments. Recall that purchases of goods and services are included in GDP, but transfer payments—such as Social Security, welfare payments, and interest on the federal debt—are not included in GDP. To measure total spending by the government, we must include transfer payments and spending on goods and services. We use **government expenditure** to include transfer payments and purchases of goods and services. The **government debt** is the total of all its deficits. For example, if a government initially had a debt of $100 billion and then ran deficits of $20 billion next year, $30 billion the year after that, and $50 billion during the third year, the government's total debt at the end of the third year would be $200 billion (the initial $100 debt plus the successive yearly deficits of $20 + $30 + $50 = $200, all numbers in billions). If a government ran a surplus, it would decrease its total debt. For example, suppose the debt were $100 billion and the government ran a surplus of $10 billion. With the surplus of $10 billion, the government would buy back $10 billion of debt from the private sector, thereby reducing the remaining debt to $90 billion.

The fiscal picture for the United States has changed substantially over the last 20 years. Beginning in the 1980s and through most of the 1990s, the federal budget ran large deficits—"deficits as far as the eye can see," according to David Stockman, the director of the Office of Management and Budget in President Reagan's administration. Stockman's eyes, however, did not accurately see developments in the late 1990s. In fiscal year 1998 (which began on October 1, 1997 and ended September 30, 1998), the federal government ran a surplus of $69 billion, the first time there had been a surplus for 30 years. The federal government continued to run surpluses for the next three fiscal years as well.

When President George W. Bush took office in January 2001, the prospect of extremely large surpluses for the next decade was one of the important factors leading to his proposal for substantial tax cuts. The president and Congress passed a 10-year tax cut totaling $1.35 billion over the 10-year period. Although the tax cut was large, the Congressional Budget Office (CBO) nonetheless estimated that the federal government would continue to run surpluses throughout the next decade.

The CBO noted that, as a result of these federal government surpluses, the outstanding stock of federal debt held by the public would be reduced. Since GDP would be growing over this period, the stock of debt relative to GDP, which is the standard way to measure the effect of debt in an economy, would also decline. They estimated that in 2011, the ratio of debt to GDP would fall to 5.2% from its value of 32% in 2000. This would be low by historical standards. Figure 16.1 depicts the debt to GDP ratio from 1791 to 2000. As you can see, except for the period in the 1980s, the ratio rises sharply during wars and falls during peacetime. By historical standards, the CBO predicted a relatively low GDP ratio by the end of the decade.

The September 11, 2001 terrorist attack changed the federal budget picture considerably, at least for the short term. Budget analysts recognized that the predicted surpluses would shrink because of policy changes made in response to the attack, including increased government spending and lower federal taxes. Moreover, since the attack led to a deterioration in economic conditions, tax revenues would decrease as well, further reducing the predicted surpluses. Whether surpluses will re-emerge for the rest of the decade will depend on the future state of the economy as well as future actions taken by politicians.

Federal budget surplus figures include revenue and expenditure from the Social Security system. Over the next decade, the Social Security system is expected to run a surplus, because taxes from Social Security exceed spending. Indeed, a very high proportion of the federal surpluses that the CBO had predicted for the next decade arose from the surpluses in the Social Security system. Some economists have argued that

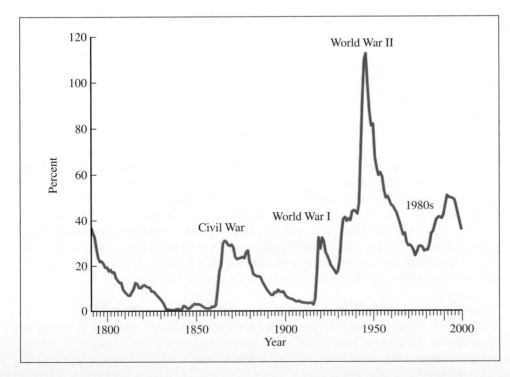

Figure 16.1

Debt as a Percent of GDP, 1791–2000

Sources: Congressional Budget Office; Economic Report of the President; Historical Statistics of the United States; Berry Senior (1988), Production and Population Since 1789

Social Security should not be included in federal surplus figures because the taxes will ultimately be necessary to pay Social Security recipients in the future.

Over a longer horizon, the surpluses in Social Security will disappear and turn to deficits. As our society grows older, expenditure on the elderly for both Social Security and medical care will increase. It's those increasing expenditures that are causing the CBO to predict emerging federal deficits and increases in the debt-to-GDP ratio to over 50% by 2050 and 129% by 2060. These long-term estimates are highly speculative, but they do indicate that deficits will be a long-term concern for this country.

As we have seen, federal budgets are heavily affected by a wide range of factors including wars, demographic pressures, recessions, as well as the choices made by our politicians on spending and taxes. But what principles should guide our policymakers? Should they cut spending and raise taxes to reduce the national debt over time? Or does the level of the national debt really matter? Let's take a look at the debates over the national debt.

The Debates

1. Do Deficits Lead to Inflation?

If a government runs a deficit, it is spending more money than it is taking in, and the gap must be covered in some way. If a government is spending $2,000 but is collecting only $1,600 in taxes, where can it get the $400 needed to fill the gap? One option would be to borrow the $400 from the public in return for government bonds (in effect IOUs). In the future, the government would have to pay back the $400 plus any interest on the bonds. Another way to cover the gap is simply to print $400 worth of new money.

In principle, governments could use a mix of borrowing money and printing money, as long as the total covers its deficits:

$$\text{government deficit} = \text{new borrowing from the public} + \text{new money created}$$

In the United States, the Treasury Department always issues government bonds to finance the deficit. The Federal Reserve, however, has the option of buying existing government debt (including the new issues). If the Federal Reserve does purchase the government's bonds, it takes the government debt out of the hands of the public and creates money through its purchase. Economists call the purchase by a central bank of newly created government debt **monetizing the deficit**. If governments finance deficits by creating new money, the result will be inflation. In the United States, we finance only a very small portion of our deficits by creating money. For example, between 1992 and 1993, the Federal Reserve purchased only $15 billion of a government deficit of approximately $270 billion for that period. The remainder of the debt was financed by issuing new government bonds to the public.

If a country has no options other than creating money to finance its deficits, those deficits will inevitably cause inflation. As we discussed in Chapter 15, hyperinflations occur when economies run large deficits and monetize them. Germany and Russia after World War I, Bolivia and Argentina in the 1980s, and the Ukraine in the 1990s are just some of the countries that have had massive inflations through monetizing their deficits. However, large, stable countries that can borrow from the public, such as the United Kingdom, the United States, and Japan, do not have to monetize their deficits. For these countries, deficits do not have to lead inevitably to inflation.

2. Is Government Debt a Burden on Future Generations?

The national debt (another commonly used term for total government debt) can pose two different burdens for society, both of which fall on future generations. First, a large debt can reduce the amount of capital in the economy and thereby reduce future

Monetizing the deficit:
Purchases by a central bank of newly issued government bonds.

incomes and real wages. Second, a large national debt will mean that future generations will have to pay higher taxes to finance the interest on the debt.

An economy increases its capital stock through the savings of individuals and institutions. These savings flow into capital formation. For example, savers who purchase new stock issued by a company provide the funds that allow the company to invest in plants and equipment. Savers hold the shares of stock as assets.

When governments run deficits and increase their national debt, they finance their deficits by selling bonds to the public. These bonds must be bought by the same individuals and the same institutions that are saving in the economy. This means that the savers will be saving both by buying stock in companies and by buying government bonds. Savers will hold both shares of stock and government bonds as assets, let's say, for their retirement. Further, let's say that all savers' total level of savings in the economy is given, that is, desired savings are $1,000. Now the government needs to finance a $200 deficit, so it sells $200 in new bonds. That means that only $800 is available for savings in new shares. The $200 in government bonds to finance the deficit crowds out $200 in new shares.

The result of government deficits is that less savings are available to firms for investment. As we discussed in earlier chapters, reduced saving will ultimately reduce the stock of private capital, such as new factories and equipment, in society. There will be less capital deepening. With lower capital per worker, real incomes and real wages will be lower.

The second burden of the national debt on future generations is the additional taxes they must pay toward servicing the debt; that is, future generations will be paying interest on the national debt. These interest payments arise because we borrowed in the past and ran up a large debt. Just like your college loans, the bill eventually comes due—even for the national debt.

Some economists say that these interest payments are not a real burden because we owe the national debt to ourselves. Let's first imagine a circumstance in which this would really be true. Today, the national debt is just over $14,000 per person in the United States. Suppose we all owned this debt equally, that is, all taxpayers actually had in their possession $14,000 in government bonds. In this case, the taxes we pay to service the debt would come right back to us as interest payments. It would go out of one pocket into the other and not pose any burden.

In reality, we do not equally share in owning the national debt. Some of it is held by foreigners. A high proportion of it is held by older, wealthy individuals or institutions, which at one point loaned money to the government and now want to be paid back. All working people must pay taxes to service the debt, but they do not earn all the interest. This is a price we pay for running deficits in the past.

Moreover, even if we shared equally in owning the national debt, it would still pose a burden if we held the debt at the expense of holding capital. Here's what we mean by that burden: From an individual point of view, a saver earns a return from holding either government bonds or private capital. But from a social point of view, if society holds bonds rather than capital, the stock of capital available for use in production will be smaller and our living standards will be reduced correspondingly.

Some economists do not believe that government deficits, resulting in government debt, impose a burden on a society. These economists believe in **Ricardian equivalence**, the proposition that it does not matter whether government expenditure is financed by taxes or financed by issuing debt. To understand the case for Ricardian equivalence, consider this example. A government initially has a balanced budget. It then cuts taxes and issues new debt to finance the deficit left by the reduction in taxes. Everyone understands that the government will have to raise taxes in the future to service the debt, so everyone increases his and her savings to pay for the taxes that will be increased in the future. If

Ricardian equivalence: The proposition that it does not matter whether government expenditure is financed by taxes or debt.

saving rises sufficiently, the public—everyone—would be able to purchase the new debt without reducing funds for investment. Since investment does not decline, there will be no burden of the debt.

As you can see, Ricardian equivalence requires that savings by the private sector increase when the deficit increases. Do savers behave this way? It is actually difficult to provide a definite answer because many other factors must be taken into account in any empirical study of saving. However, it appears that during the early 1980s, savings decreased somewhat when government deficits increased. This is precisely opposite to what Ricardian equivalence predicts. Nonetheless, the evidence on this topic is mixed, and it is an area of active research today.

A recent, alternative approach to analyzing deficits, highlights the role of transfers between generations, as "A Closer Look: Generational Accounting" explains.

3. How Do Deficits Affect the Size of Government?

Generational accounting:
Methods that assign the tax burden of debt and other programs to different generations.

Nobel laureate James Buchanan has argued that because people are less aware of deficits than they are aware of taxes, financing government expenditure through deficits, rather than through taxes, will inevitably lead to higher government spending. While this argument may seem plausible, it faces two difficulties. First, throughout recent U.S. history, spending by state and local governments grew much faster than federal spending. State and local governments face many more restrictions in borrowing than the federal gov-

---

A CLOSER LOOK   GENERATIONAL ACCOUNTING

An increased government debt means that future generations must pay higher interest payments to service the increased debt. But interest is not the only financial burden that governments can impose on future generations. Consider an example. Suppose the government invents a new program that promises everyone over the age of 65 a retirement pension (largely free of tax) and subsidized medical care. These benefits are to be paid through payroll taxes on workers. It does not show up as an official government deficit, but it's not hard to see that this program would pose a burden on future generations who must pay for it.

This is precisely the situation we face today. Social Security and Medicare, programs that promise retirement and health benefits to retirees in the United States, are financed through payroll taxes on current workers, not the past contributions of the retirees.

Laurence Kotlikoff, an economist at Boston University, has developed a new way to measure the full burden on future generations from all government programs, not just government deficits. His approach, called **generational accounting,** provides estimates of the burdens on future generations from all the past actions taken by the government. His study indicates bad news for future generations: In the era

since World War II, we have promised large benefits for future retirees that will have to be paid by future generations. According to Kotlikoff's recent estimates, future Americans will face net tax rates (taxes less benefits received) more than 50% higher than those facing current young Americans. In other countries, the picture is even more grim. For example, in Japan and Italy, future generations face burdens that are more than twice those facing current generations.

If the government raised the retirement age or cut back on its promises of future medical care, this would reduce the burden on future generations of workers without showing up in the official deficit statistics. Kotlikoff's main point is that we should not become obsessed by one single number called the deficit. Other government programs can have profound effects on the burden of future generations.

All of these projections are based on the premise that future benefits will not be changed and the burden of financing these programs will fall entirely on future generations. Neither of these outcomes will necessarily occur. However, generational accounting demonstrates the powerful budgetary forces that are currently in place and frame all future decisions.

ernment faces when it borrows. Second, why would the federal government start running surpluses, as we did in the late 1990s, if deficits were so favored by the politicians?

More recent thinking suggests that deficits can be used strategically to reduce the growth of government. During the 1980s, there were large deficits caused by a combination of a deep recession and major tax cuts. These deficits made it difficult for politicians to propose new spending programs. Proponents of smaller government, therefore, may wish to cut taxes to reduce surpluses or increase deficits in order to make it more difficult for other politicians to increase government spending. They want to create deficits to avoid "putting sand in Congress's sandbox." Some politicians supported President Bush's tax cut in 2001, which reduced the surplus over a 10-year period, precisely for this reason.

4. Can Deficits Be Good for an Economy?

At times, deficits can be good for a country. They can provide cushion for the economy during economic downturns by stimulating private-sector spending in bad times. Governments may also deliberately create deficits to pull the economy out of a recession.

We encountered both of these ideas in Chapter 10, on Keynesian economics. The increase in the deficit during economic downturns shows the automatic stabilizers of the economy in action, putting additional income into the hands of the public during bad economic times. This additional income allows people to avoid drastic cuts in their consumption spending. Because total spending does not fall as much, the severity of recessions is decreased.

How do automatic stabilizers work? As incomes fall during a recession, so do tax payments. Moreover, transfer payments such as welfare and food stamps rise. Because government spending increases while tax revenues fall, the deficit must rise. Figure 16.2 plots the deficit as a percent of GDP and the unemployment rate for the period 1970 to

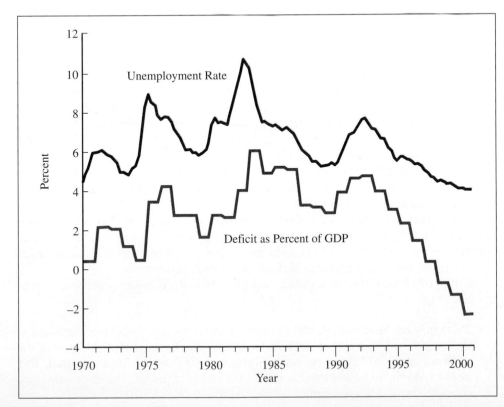

Figure 16.2

U.S. Deficits and Unemployment Rates, 1970–2000

Source: Bureau of Labor Statistics and Congressional Budget Office.

2000. Because increases in the unemployment rate signal bad economic times, we expect the deficit to rise and fall along with the unemployment rate. This is precisely what Figure 16.2 shows.

The deficit can also change if the government tries to stabilize the economy through fiscal policy. For example, if a government engages in expansionary fiscal policy, by cutting taxes or increasing spending to pull the economy out of a recession, the result will be to increase the deficit. However, during a recession, this may be the appropriate means to steer the economy back to full employment.

The existence of automatic stabilizers and the use of expansionary fiscal policy during recessions suggest that we should not worry about short-run government deficits. Over short time periods, deficits can help the economy to cope with shocks, such as oil price increases or a collapse in the stock market, that may hit the economy. They give the government some room to maneuver out of a recession. Most economists believe that automatic stabilizers have reduced economic fluctuations during the twentieth century.

Professor Robert Barro of Harvard University has also pointed out that deficits can play a role in tax smoothing. Suppose that there is a large, temporary increase in government spending, such as might occur during a war. The government could either finance the war by running a deficit and issuing debt or raise taxes to keep the budget in balance. Barro has argued that it is more efficient to keep tax rates relatively constant than to raise them sharply and then lower them later. Temporarily raising tax rates to very high levels could cause distortions in economic behavior that we would like to avoid. Thus, by running deficits and only gradually raising taxes later to service the debt, we avoid creating excess distortions in the economy.

5. How Would a Balanced Budget Amendment Really Work?

For many years, there were strong efforts to enact a constitutional amendment to balance the federal budget. The budget surpluses in the late 1990s have dampened (at least for now) interest in this constitutional reform. In early 1995, Congress came very close to passing a balanced budget amendment, sending it back to the states for ratification. It passed in the House of Representatives but failed by a single vote in the Senate. How would a balanced budget amendment actually work?

Many different budgetary constitutional amendments have been proposed. They all require that after a phase-in period, Congress propose in each fiscal year a budget in which total revenues (excluding borrowing) cover total expenditures. The amendments also have various escape clauses—for example, to allow borrowing during wartime. Some amendments also allow Congress to suspend the requirement to propose a balanced budget for other reasons, such as during a recession when deficits naturally emerge. Finally, some versions of the amendment would limit the rate of spending increases to the growth rate of GDP.

Proponents of the balanced budget amendment say that it will finally exert discipline on the federal government, preventing large deficits in peacetime, such as occurred in the 1980s. We can thus avoid the adverse effects of deficits: reduced capital formation and a shift in the burden of taxation to future generations.

Critics of a balanced budget amendment point to many different problems, such as the following:

- There may not be enough flexibility to deal with recessions. Under some versions of the amendment, unless three-fifths of Congress votes to suspend requirements, the government would have to cut expenditures or raise taxes during a recession. This would make the recession worse and limit the ability of the government to use fiscal policy to stabilize the economy.

- The Constitution is not the right mechanism to try to enforce complicated budget rules. As various interested parties challenge the actions of Congress, the courts would become heavily involved in federal budget matters.

- Congress could devise special budgets to get around the requirement, for example, by taking some types of spending "off budget," which means simply not counting it as part of the official budget.

- Congress could also find nonbudgetary ways to carry out the policies that it desires. For example, it could issue more regulations or impose mandates or requirements on business or other governments to carry out its will.

TEST Your Understanding

1. If a government runs a surplus, will it increase or decrease the outstanding stock of debt?

2. Proponents of Ricardian equivalence are primarily concerned about deficits crowding out the stock of capital. True or false? Explain.

3. Explain how deficits can lead to inflation.

Should the Federal Reserve Aim for Zero Inflation?

Some Background

In Chapter 15, we examined some of the costs of inflation, including the following:

- Menu costs, the costs firms had to incur to change posted prices

- Shoe-leather costs, the costs individuals and firms must pay as they try to find ways to economize on holding money

- Distortions in our tax system and financial system from not adjusting our accounts for inflation

- Arbitrary redistributions between debtors and creditors from unanticipated inflation

By the late 1990s, the rate of inflation had fallen to roughly between 2% and 3%. This suggested to some economists that the time was right to avoid all the costs of inflation and bring the inflation rate down to zero and keep it there. A zero inflation rate would mean complete price stability. To achieve zero inflation, the Fed would have to take two actions: First, it would have to use monetary policy to bring the inflation rate to zero from a positive level. Second, it would need to commit to a policy of keeping inflation at zero and not have any other goals.

The Debates

1. How Costly Is It to Reduce Inflation?

You saw in Chapter 15 that to reduce inflation usually requires actual unemployment to rise above the natural rate of unemployment. That means reducing inflation will have a temporary cost in terms of higher unemployment. How large is this cost?

In the United States, economists who study this problem have developed a rough rule of thumb: When actual unemployment exceeds the natural rate of unemployment by 1 percentage point for one year, the inflation rate falls by 0.5 percentage points per year. The following example illustrates this simple rule of thumb. The natural rate of unemployment is 5% of the labor force and the inflation rate is 3% per year. To bring the inflation rate down to zero would require that the unemployment rate exceed the natural rate by 6 percentage points. If this is spread over a three-year period, the unemployment rate for those three years would have to be 7%. Those numbers mean that we would need to create a mild recession to bring the inflation rate down to zero.

Some economists would argue that unemployment would not have to increase as much if the Federal Reserve was credible in its commitment to reducing inflation. As we discussed in Chapter 15, if workers can adjust their expectations (and the contracts that they made in the past based on their expectations), it might be possible to reduce inflation with a smaller increase in unemployment. However, on the basis of past U.S. experience, our rule of thumb works reasonably well.

One complicating factor in measuring the costs of reducing inflation is that the burden of increased unemployment would not be evenly spread across the economy. The increased unemployment will be concentrated among a small fraction of the labor force, who will experience true hardship. In many cases, these workers will be young, unskilled, and from minority populations that already experience high unemployment rates.

The costs of this unemployment need to be measured against the permanent gains from reducing the inflation rate. There is not a consensus, however, on the actual benefits of reduced inflation. For example, there are no precise measures of the increased menu costs that arise at higher inflation rates.

Some economists argue that with zero inflation, the economy will be less able to adjust to adverse aggregate demand shocks, because workers do not want to see their wages cut in absolute terms. For example, if investment spending suddenly falls, the adjustment process requires that nominal wages fall as well to restore the economy to full employment. When there is ongoing inflation, there is no need for wages literally to fall; all wages need to do is to increase less rapidly than the ongoing inflation rate. But with zero inflation, wages actually have to fall. If workers resist this fall in wages, the adjustment mechanism that restores the economy back to full employment may not function efficiently. If we take this argument seriously, we should never try to reduce inflation below 2% to 3% to have sufficient wage flexibility.

Even if we were determined to commit to price stability, there are legitimate questions about what the term *stable prices* really means. As we have discussed, it is very difficult to measure changes in prices accurately when there is significant technological change in the economy. If, as many economists believe, our price indexes overstate the true inflation rate, 2% annual inflation may in reality be true price stability. If so, it would seem particularly foolish to engineer a recession to bring inflation to zero.

2. Should Monetary Policy Target Only Inflation?

Suppose we do reduce the inflation rate to zero. Should monetary policy then focus exclusively on maintaining price stability?

Some economists argue quite strongly that the Fed should have only one goal: price stability. We have learned that in the long run, monetary policy can influence only the level of prices, not the level of employment. Having the Fed worry about other factors—unemployment or the exchange rate—will distract the Fed from its mission. Preoccupation with other goals can easily lead the Fed astray and lead to long-run inflationary pressures building in the economy.

Moreover, if the Fed were committed to the single goal of price stability, it would have enhanced credibility. As we have seen, if the Fed is credible, the private sector will become more responsive to changes in economic policy. Credible policies decrease the need for active monetary policies.

Having a single goal would also help to keep the Fed free from political pressures. Such political pressures might include attempts to stimulate the economy to favor the reelection prospects of incumbents or to give a temporary boost to financial markets.

However, other economists would strongly object to having the Fed concentrate solely on price stability. In the United States, the President and the Congress have not used active fiscal policy as a stabilization tool for decades. While there are automatic fiscal stabilizers, they are often not sufficient to cushion the economy in the face of shocks. In practice, only monetary policy is available as a tool to stabilize output and prevent deep recessions from emerging. If monetary policy is geared solely to price stability and fiscal policy is not used, how can we stabilize the economy? Critics of stabilization policy, of course, believe that not using monetary policy to try to stabilize the economy would actually improve our economic performance. In their view, attempts to stabilize the economy have done more harm than good over the years. In previous chapters, we discussed the difficulties in conducting stabilization policy. These include lags, uncertainties about the strength and timing of policies, and difficulties in estimating the natural rate of unemployment. Whether or not you believe that these difficulties are insurmountable will affect your beliefs about the desirability of using monetary policy to stabilize output and not just maintain price stability.

One recent view is that the Fed should not deliberately set out to bring inflation to zero but should take advantage of favorable shocks. In 1996, a new phrase about monetary policy hit the financial pages: *opportunistic disinflation*. Several economists at the Federal Reserve put forth the idea that the Fed should not deliberately create excess unemployment to reduce inflation. Rather, it should wait for favorable opportunities, such as favorable supply shocks or unforeseen recessions, and use its monetary tools to ensure that these outcomes lead to permanently lower inflation. If the Fed followed this policy for a long period, it would eventually reduce inflation.

Although this seems like a sensible policy, its mere appearance in the newspapers worried some inflation hawks in the financial markets. They wondered whether this policy would mean that the Fed would no longer be as committed to fighting inflation as in the past. If not, the Fed could lose much of the credibility it had gained in recent years, which would make its job even more difficult in the future. To reassure financial markets, officials at the Fed noted that this was just a study, and their views on fighting inflation had not changed.

TEST Your Understanding

4. Why are the costs of reducing inflation temporary but the benefits permanent?

5. Explain why zero inflation implies stable prices.

6. Give two arguments in favor of the Fed solely targeting price stability.

Should Tax Policy Be Designed Solely for Growth?

Some Background

As we discussed in earlier chapters, the United States is a country with a low savings rate. This hurts our long-run growth prospects because our investment spending is limited by our own savings and savings from abroad that arise through current account deficits. Many factors—not purely economic—contribute to our low saving rate. For example, colleges will reduce the financial aid for students whose families have saved for college, thereby reducing the incentive of families to save for themselves. Many of our welfare programs also provide disincentives for individuals to save, as they reduce benefits for families that have saved in the past. The U.S. tax system also discourages savings.

In the United States, we tax income as people earn it and also tax the returns from any savings as those returns are earned. Suppose that you earn $100 and face a tax rate of 20%; you keep $80 after taxes. Now suppose that you save $50 and invest it at a 10% rate for a year. At the end of the year, you will earn an additional $5 (10% × $50) but will get to keep only $4 because the government will take $1 in taxes (20% × $5). You will have paid the government $21 in total: $20 on the $100 you earned plus $1 on your $50 savings. If you did not save at all, you would pay only $20 in taxes, not $21.

Not all tax systems work this way. Tax systems that are based on consumption do not penalize individuals who save. Sales taxes in the U.S. and value-added taxes abroad are familiar examples of **consumption taxes**. It is also possible to create a consumption tax from an income tax by exempting the returns from savings from taxes, just as we do with tax-exempt bonds issued by state and municipal governments. The key feature of consumption taxation is that you do not face any additional taxes if you decide to save more of your income.

In the United States, there are some other methods to save that have reduced taxes on savings. In addition to tax-exempt bonds, they include IRAs (individual retirement accounts) as well as other saving vehicles, such as 401K, 403B, and Keogh plans. However, all of these plans come with restrictions and limitations on their use.

Consumption taxes: Taxes which are based on the consumption, not the income, of individuals.

The Debates

Proponents claim that taxes based on consumption will increase total savings and be more equitable. Let's explore these claims.

1. Will Consumption Taxes Lead to More Savings?

There is no question that consumption taxes provide more incentives to save because the return from savings increases. However, there is no guarantee that these extra incentives will produce more savings. As we discussed with respect to taxes and supply of labor, taxes have both *substitution* effects and an *income* effect. Reducing the tax rate on savings provides direct incentives for increased savings, through the substitution effect. On the other hand, with lower tax rates on savings, individuals have more wealth, and the income effect will lead them to consume more, which means that they save less. Whether savings increase or decrease when tax rates are cut ultimately must be settled by careful research.

Although there has been much research on the effects of taxation on saving, it is far from conclusive. It is true that individuals will allocate their savings to tax-favored investments over investments that are not favored. For example, individuals will put their funds into IRAs. What is not clear is whether the funds that flow into IRAs are literally new savings—meaning reduced consumption—or merely transfers from other accounts, such as conventional savings accounts, which do not have the same tax advantages. Disentangling these effects is a difficult issue, and it remains an active area of ongoing research.

The corporate tax system also creates other disincentives for savings and investment. Suppose you purchase a share of stock in a corporation. When the corporation earns a profit, it pays taxes at the corporate tax rate. When the corporation pays you a dividend for holding the stock, you must pay taxes on the dividend income that you receive. Corporate income is taxed twice: once when it is earned and again when it is paid out. Some economists have argued that the corporation tax leads to less efficient investment because it forces capital into other sectors of the economy, such as real estate, that do not suffer from this double-taxation.

2. Are Consumption Taxes Fair?

The basic idea behind a consumption tax seems fair. Individuals should be taxed on what they take from the economy's total production—that is, what they consume—not on what they actually produce. If an individual produces a lot but does not consume the proceeds from what he or she produced, and instead plows it back into the economy for investment, that individual is contributing to the growth of total output and should be rewarded, not punished. Individual A earns $50 and consumes it all; individual B earns $100 but consumes only $40. Who should pay more?

In practice, moving to a consumption tax system, for example by exempting the return from savings from the income tax, would have a major impact on the distribution of income in the economy. It is the wealthy and high-income individuals who save the most and earn income through interest, dividend, rents, and capital gains. Table 16.1 provides some data from the Congressional Budget Office over a 10-year period to illustrate this point for one type of income: capital gains, the profits earned from the sale of stocks, bonds, real estate, or other assets. As you can see from Table 16.1, taxpayers with annual income exceeding $200,000 earned over half of the capital gains over this period. Capital assets are highly concentrated among the wealthy in the economy.

If capital gains and other types of capital income were not included for calculating taxes, total tax revenue would fall, and the government would have to raise tax rates—on everyone—to maintain the same level of spending. Excluding capital income from taxation does have its costs.

Another complication is inherited wealth. Suppose someone inherits $100 million dollars from his or her parents, invests it at 5% per year, and lives comfortably on $5 million a year. Should that individual be exempt from tax on the inheritance income?

Should taxes be based on consumption?

Table 16.1   Share of Capital Gains by Income

Income Class	Share of Capital Gains
$10,000–20,000	2.6%
$20,000–30,000	2.9%
$30,000–40,000	4.4%
$40,000–50,000	3.4%
$50,000–75,000	9.0%
$75,000–100,000	8.5%
$100,000–200,000	15.7%
$200,000 and over	56.8%

Source: Congressional Budget Office, *Perspective on the Ownership of Capital Assets and the Realization of Capital Gains*, May 1997. (Based on a 10-year average. Excludes category reporting negative income.)

3. Are There Other Means to Increase Savings?

Even if tax incentives did increase private savings, that is no guarantee that total savings—public savings plus private savings—would increase. Suppose that expanding an existing IRA program cost the taxpayers $5 billion in lost revenue but led to $4 billion in increased private saving. Total savings, public plus private, would fall by $1 billion because of the loss of revenue.

This suggests that we should think more broadly about the sources of saving for the economy. Any policies that reduce the federal deficit or increase the surplus will lead to increases in total savings unless they adversely affect private savings. Cuts in government spending or increases in taxes (that do not hurt private savings) will lead to an increase in total savings for the economy.

TEST Your Understanding

7. Give an example of savings that you can make, completely free of tax.

8. Why would switching to a consumption tax not necessarily increase total savings?

9. Explain why dividends from stock are taxed twice.

Using the **TOOLS**

In this chapter, we explored several policy issues using a variety of different tools. Take this opportunity to do your own economic analysis.

APPLICATIONS

1. Debt and Deficits in Belgium

Here are some data for Belgium in 1989:

GDP	6160 billion Belgian francs
Debt	6500 billion Belgian francs
Deficit	380 billion Belgian francs
Interest rate on bonds	8.5 percent

Use these data to answer the following questions:

a. What are the deficit/GDP ratio and debt/GDP ratio? How do these ratios compare to the same ratios in the United States today? To what period in U.S. history does the debt/GDP ratio in Belgium correspond?

b. Approximately how much of the budget in Belgium is devoted to interest payments on the debt? If Belgium could wipe out its debt overnight, what would happen to its current budget deficit?

2. Unemployment and Reducing Inflation to Zero

A country that has a natural rate of 4% unemployment is currently at the natural rate of unemployment. Annual inflation rate is 4%.

a. Using the simple rule of thumb that inflation falls by 0.5% when the unemployment rate exceeds the natural rate by 1 percentage point for the year, describe a path for the unemployment rate that will bring the inflation rate to zero.

b. Suppose the country had a more favorable rule of thumb. Inflation fell by 1 percentage point when the actual unemployment rate exceeded the natural rate of unemployment by 1 percentage point for one year. Describe a path for unemployment that would result in zero inflation in this case.

3. IRAs and Zero Tax Rate

With an IRA, you get to deduct the amount you contribute from your current taxable income, invest the funds free from tax, but then pay taxes on the full amount you withdraw. Suppose your tax rate is 50% and you initially deposit $2000 in an IRA. The proceeds double in seven years to $4000; in seven years when you retire, you pay taxes on the $4000 at your 50% rate.

Show that this is the same outcome if you were free from all taxes (a zero tax rate), invested $1000 for seven years, and doubled your initial investment.

Summary

In this chapter, we explored three topics that are the center of macroeconomic policy debates today. Here are the key points to remember:

1. A deficit is the difference between expenditures and revenue. The government debt is the sum of all past deficits.

2. Deficits can be financed through either borrowing or money creation. Money creation leads to inflation.

3. Deficits can be good for the country. Automatic stabilizers and expansionary fiscal policy both work through the creation of deficits.

4. The national debt involves two burdens: The national debt can reduce the amount of capital in an economy, leading to lower levels of income. And the national debt can raise taxes on future generations.

5. Reducing inflation down to zero would require that actual unemployment exceed the natural rate of unemployment for some period.

6. If the Fed's only goal was to maintain price stability, there would be few tools left for active stabilization policy.

7. A consumption tax would increase the incentives for private savings. However, it is not clear that total savings would necessarily increase, and there would be concerns about the fairness of this form of taxation.

Key Terms

consumption taxes, 340
deficit, 330
generational accounting, 334

government debt, 330
government expenditure, 330
monetizing the deficit, 332

Ricardian equivalence, 333
surplus, 330

Problems and Discussion Questions

1. A country has outstanding debt of $10 million. The interest rate on the debt is 10% per year. Expenditures (other than interest payments) are $1 billion, and taxes are $1 billion. What is the debt at the end of next year?

2. In the previous example, suppose that the inflation rate was 5% per year. By how much did the real burden of the debt increase?

3. Why are government deficits more serious in countries with limited abilities to borrow from the private sector?

4. How is a decrease in the age at which workers are eligible for Social Security similar to an increase in the government deficit?

5. In what ways could a balanced budget requirement limit the ability of the government to conduct fiscal policy? Do you think this is a serious loss?

6. With near-term surpluses and very large long-term deficits, one economist argued that "tax smoothing" required increases in current taxes, which would mean increasing current surpluses even further. Another economist, fearful of the consequences in Congress of budget surpluses, advocated cutting taxes to reduce the surplus. Explain the logic of both positions.

7. An economist suggests that what matters for financial markets is a stable inflation rate, not a zero inflation rate. As long as inflation is stable, all individuals can take this into account in their actions. What are the costs associated with a stable 2% inflation rate? Do you believe that it is easier or more difficult to stabilize inflation at 2% rather than at zero?

8. Some economists believe that the Federal Reserve should follow strict rules for the conduct of monetary policy. These rules would require the Fed to make adjustments to interest rates based on information that is fully available to the public, information such as the current unemployment rate and the current inflation rate. What do you see as the pros and cons of such an approach?

9. Suppose the government launches a new program that allows individuals to place funds up to $2000 into a tax-free account. Do you believe that this will have a significant effect on national savings?

10. Evaluate this quote: "Since high-income individuals save more, any tax policies that favor savings will also help the wealthy at the expense of the poor."

11. **Web Exercise.** The Web site for the Congressional Budget Office [*http://www.cbo.gov*] contains their projections for future budget surpluses and deficits as well as options for increasing the surplus. Using this site, find some options that you think are desirable that would have a significant effect on increasing the budget surplus.

12. **Web Exercise.** Have you ever thought that it would be easy to cut government spending or raise taxes to improve the surplus? Now is your chance to find out. Play the National Budget Simulation game hosted on the Web site of the Graduate School of Public Policy at UC Berkeley [*http://garnet.berkeley.edu:3333/budget/budget.html*]. What changes can you make to really improve the deficit without disrupting the functions of government?

Take It to the Net

We invite you to visit the O'Sullivan/Sheffrin page on the Prentice Hall Web site at:
http://www.prenhall.com/osullivan/ for additional World Wide Web exercises for this chapter.

Model Answers to Questions

Test Your Understanding

1. Decrease.
2. False. Proponents of Ricardian equivalence do not believe that deficits crowd out capital.
3. Inflation arises when deficits are monetized by the central bank.
4. The increase in unemployment to bring down the inflation rate is the cost, and it is only temporary. However, the temporary increase in unemployment does lead to a permanent reduction in the inflation rate.
5. Because inflation is the rate of change of prices, zero inflation means no change in prices, which means price stability.
6. The Fed can only control inflation in the long run, and it is not effective in stabilizing output.
7. Individual retirement accounts.
8. There are both income effects and substitution effects.
9. The income is taxed at the corporate level and then again at the individual level.

Using the Tools

1. Debt and Deficits in Belgium
   a. The deficit/GDP ratio is 6.2%, and the debt/GDP ratio is 106%. The debt/GDP ratio resembles what the debt/GDP ratio was in the United States during World War II.
   b. With a debt of $6,500 and an interest rate of 0.085, interest payments are approximately $6,500 × 0.085 = $552. Because the budget deficit is $380, if the debt disappeared, the budget would have a surplus of $172.

2. Unemployment and Reducing Inflation to Zero
   a. Actual unemployment must rise by 8 percentage points above the natural rate of unemployment. If this occurs over four years, unemployment will be 6% for four years.
   b. In this case, actual unemployment must rise by only four percentage points above the natural rate of unemployment. If this occurs over four years, unemployment will be 5% for four years.

3. IRAs and Zero Tax Rate. With the IRA, you deposit $2,000 and get a reduction of taxes of $1,000, so your initial investment is only $1,000. You withdraw $4,000 from the IRA after seven years, but pay a 50% tax, so your net proceeds are $2,000. This is the identical outcome to investing $1,000 tax-free for seven years and doubling your initial investment.

17

International Trade and Public Policy

In November 1999, large numbers of colorful protestors gathered in Seattle, Washington, at a meeting of world leaders, to express their indignation about recent developments in international trade, multinational corporations, and international organizations. Protestors carried signs denouncing the WTO, or World Trade Organization, a recently created and relatively obscure international agency.

The protest at times turned violent and protestors smashed windows in downtown Seattle. Protestors returned to their homes fondly remembering the "spirit of Seattle." The intensity of the protest took many observers by surprise. Since World War II, trade has grown steadily and the world has become more interdependent. Were the protestors just expressing discontent about modern life or were there fundamental problems with our system of international trade?

A s the world economy grows, our policies toward international trade become ever more important. Many people view trade as a "zero-sum game." They believe that if one country gains from international trade, another must lose. Based on this belief, they advocate restricting trade with other countries. Indeed, the United States does restrict trade in many areas, for example, protecting jobs in apparel and steel. One lesson from this chapter is that free trade could, in principle, make everyone better off. The challenge for policymakers is to develop a set of principles that accomplish this goal—or come as close as possible to accomplishing it.

In this chapter, we discuss the rationale for international trade, and we explore the effects of policies that restrict trade. Here are some of the practical questions that we answer:

1. What are the trade-offs associated with free trade? Who wins? Who loses?
2. Why is a tariff (a tax on an imported good) superior to an import quota?
3. Why might a firm's export price be less than its domestic price? (The domestic price is the price in the domestic market.)
4. Do trade laws inhibit environmental protection?
5. Does trade increase income inequality?

Benefits from Specialization and Trade

If your nation produced everything it consumed, it would not be dependent on any other nation for its economic livelihood. If you were put in charge of your nation, would you pursue such a policy of national self-sufficiency? Although self-sufficiency may sound appealing, it would be better to specialize in some products and trade some of those products with other nations for products that your nation doesn't produce. You saw in Chapter 3 that specialization and exchange can make both parties better off. In this chapter, we use a simple example to explain the benefits of specialization and international trade between two nations.

Let's say there are two nations, each produces computer chips and shirts, and each nation consumes computer chips and shirts. Table 17.1 shows the daily output of the two goods for the two nations, Shirtland and Chipland. In a single day, Shirtland can produce a maximum of either 108 shirts or 36 computer chips, while Chipland can produce a maximum of either 120 shirts or 120 computer chips. The last two rows of the table show the opportunity costs of the two goods. Recall the principle of opportunity cost:

PRINCIPLE of Opportunity Cost

The opportunity cost of something is what you sacrifice to get it.

In Chipland, there is a one-for-one trade-off of shirts and chips: The opportunity cost of one shirt is one chip, and the opportunity cost of one chip is one shirt. In Shirtland, people can produce three times as many shirts as chips in a given amount of time: The opportunity cost of one chip is three shirts; that is, by producing one chip, we sacrifice three shirts; conversely, the opportunity cost of one shirt is one-third of a chip.

Production possibilities curve:
A curve showing the combinations of two goods that can be produced by an economy, assuming that all resources are fully employed.

Production Possibilities Curve

Let's start by seeing what happens if each nation is self-sufficient. Each nation can use its resources (labor, land, buildings, machinery, equipment) to produce its own shirts and its own chips. The **production possibilities curve** shows all the feasible combinations of

Table 17.1 Output and Opportunity Cost

	Shirtland	Chipland
Shirts produced per day	108	120
Chips produced per day	36	120
Opportunity cost of shirts	1/3 chip	1 chip
Opportunity cost of chips	3 shirts	1 shirt

the two goods, assuming that the nation's resources are fully employed. This curve, which we discussed in earlier chapters, provides a sort of menu of production options. To keep things simple, we assume that the curve is a straight line, indicating a constant trade-off between the two goods. As shown by Shirtland's production possibilities curve in Figure 17.1, the following combinations of chips and shirts are possible.

1. **All shirts and no chips: point *r*.** If Shirtland uses all its resources to produce shirts, it will produce 108 shirts per day.
2. **All chips and no shirts: point *t*.** If Shirtland uses all its resources to produce chips, it will produce 36 chips per day.
3. **Equal division of resources: point *h*.** Shirtland could divide its resources between shirts and chips to produce daily 54 shirts and 18 chips.

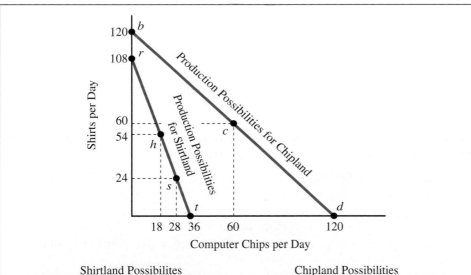

Shirtland Possibilities

Point	Shirts	Chips
r	108	0
h	54	18
s	24	28
t	0	36

Chipland Possibilities

Point	Shirts	Chips
b	120	0
c	60	60
d	0	120

Figure 17.1

Production Possibilities Curve
The production possibilities curve shows the combinations of two goods that can be produced with a nation's resources. For Chipland, there is a one-for-one trade-off is between the two goods. For Shirtland, the trade-off is three shirts for every computer chip. In the absence of trade, Shirtland picks point *s* (28 chips and 24 shirts), and Chipland picks point *c* (60 chips and 60 shirts).

All the other points on the line connecting points *r* and *t* are also feasible. One option is point *s*, with 28 chips and 24 shirts. The slope of the curve is the opportunity cost of computer chips: one chip per three shirts. Figure 17.1 also shows the production possibilities curve for Chipland. This nation can produce daily 120 shirts and no chips (point *b*), 120 chips and no shirts (point *d*), or any combination of chips and shirts between these two points. In Chipland, the trade-off is one shirt per computer chip: The opportunity cost of a chip is one shirt, so the slope of the production possibilities curve is 1.0.

Each nation could decide to be self-sufficient in chips and shirts. In other words, each nation could pick a point on its production possibilities curve and produce everything it wants to consume. For example, Shirtland could pick point *s*, producing daily 28 chips and 24 shirts, and Chipland could pick point *c*, producing daily 60 chips and 60 shirts. In the language of international trade, this is a case of **autarky**, or self-sufficiency (in Greek, *aut* means "self" and *arke* means "to suffice").

Comparative Advantage and the Terms of Trade

Would the two nations be better off if each nation specialized in the production of one good and traded with the other nation? To decide which nation should produce a particular good, we need to figure out which nation has a lower opportunity cost for that good. As you saw in Chapter 3, the nation with the lower opportunity cost has a **comparative advantage** in producing that good.

1. Chips produced in Chipland. The opportunity cost of one chip is one shirt in Chipland, and the opportunity cost of one chip is three shirts in Shirtland. Chipland has a comparative advantage in the production of chips. Because Chipland sacrifices fewer shirts to produce one chip, Chipland should produce chips.

2. Shirts produced in Shirtland. The opportunity cost of one shirt is one chip in Chipland, and the opportunity cost of one shirt is 1/3 of a chip in Shirtland. Shirtland has a comparative advantage in the production of shirts. Shirtland sacrifices fewer chips to produce one shirt, so Shirtland should produce shirts.

Trade will make it possible for people in each specialized nation to consume both goods. At what rate will the two nations exchange shirts and chips? To determine the **terms of trade**, let's look at how much Shirtland is willing to pay to get one chip and how much Chipland is willing to accept to give up one chip.

1. To get one chip, Shirtland is willing to pay up to three shirts. That's how many shirts it would sacrifice if it produced its own chip: Shirtland's opportunity cost of one chip is three shirts. For example, if the nations agree to exchange two shirts per chip, Shirtland could rearrange its production, producing one less chip but three more shirts. After exchanging two of the newly produced shirts for one chip, Shirtland will have the same number of chips but one additional shirt.

2. To give up one chip, Chipland is willing to accept any amount greater than one shirt: Chipland's opportunity cost of one chip is one shirt. For example, if the nations agree to exchange two shirts per chip, Chipland could rearrange its production, producing one more chip and one less shirt. After it exchanges the newly produced chip for two shirts, Chipland will have the same number of chips but one additional shirt.

There is an opportunity for mutually beneficial trade because the willingness to pay—three shirts by Shirtland—exceeds the willingness to accept—one shirt by Chipland. It's possible the two countries will split the difference between the willingness to pay and the willingness to accept, exchanging two shirts per chip.

The Consumption Possibilities Curve

A nation that decides to specialize and trade will not be limited to the options shown by its own production possibilities curve. The **consumption possibilities curve** shows the combinations of two goods (computer chips and shirts in our example) that a nation can consume when it specializes in one good and trades with another nation.

Figure 17.2 shows the consumption possibilities curve for our two nations, assuming that they exchange two shirts per chip.

- In panel A, Chipland will specialize in chips, the good for which it has a comparative advantage, so it produces 120 chips (point *d*). Given the terms of trade, Chipland can exchange 40 chips for 80 shirts, leading to point *x* on the consumption possibilities curve.

- In panel B, Shirtland specializes in shirts (point *r*) and can exchange 80 shirts for 40 chips, leading to point *y* on its consumption possibilities frontier.

How do the outcomes with specialization and trade compare to the autarky outcomes? Chipland moves from point *c* (autarky) to point *x*, so trade increases the consumption of each good by 20 units. Shirtland moves from point *s* to point *y*, so this nation consumes 12 additional chips and 4 additional shirts.

In Figure 17.2, each consumption possibilities curve lies above the nation's production possibilities curves, meaning that each nation has more options about how much to consume under specialization and trade. In most cases, a nation picks a point on the consumption possibilities curve that provides more of each good.

The Employment Effects of Free Trade

You've now seen that trade allows each nation to consume more of each good. But we haven't yet discussed the effects of trade on employment. Under free trade, each nation will begin to specialize in a single good, causing considerable changes in the country's employment in different industries. In Chipland, the chip industry doubles in size—output increases from 60 to 120 chips per day—while the shirt industry disappears.

> **Consumption possibilities curve:** A curve showing the combinations of two goods that can be consumed in a nation when that nation specializes in producing a particular good and trades with another nation.

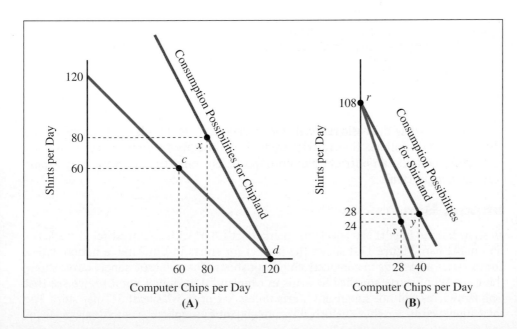

Figure 17.2
Consumption Possibilities Curve
The consumption possibilities curve shows the combinations of computer chips and shirts that can be consumed if each country specializes and trades. In panel A, Chipland produces 120 chips and trades 40 of these chips to Shirtland for 80 shirts. In panel B, Shirtland produces 108 shirts and trades 80 of these shirts to Chipland for 40 chips.

Workers and other resources will leave the shirt industry and move to the chip industry. In Shirtland, the flow is in the opposite direction: Workers and other resources move from the chip industry to the shirt industry.

Is free trade good for everyone? Switching from self-sufficiency to specialization and trade increases consumption in both nations, so on average, people in each nation will benefit from free trade. Some people will be harmed by free trade. In Chipland, people in the shirt industry will lose their jobs when the shirt industry disappears. Some workers can easily move into the expanding computer-chip industry; for these workers, free trade is likely to be beneficial. Other shirt workers will be unable to make the move to the chip industry; they will be forced to accept lower-paying jobs or face unemployment. Free trade is likely to make these displaced workers worse off.

There is a saying, "Where you stand on an issue depends on where you sit." In our example, a worker sitting at a sewing machine in Chipland is likely to oppose free trade because that worker is likely to lose his or her job. A worker sitting at a workstation in a computer-chip fabrication facility is likely to support free trade because the resulting increase in computer-chip exports will generate more employment opportunities in the industry.

TEST Your Understanding

1. Use Figure 17.1 to complete the following statements with numbers: If Chipland starts at point *c* and decides to produce 10 more chips, it will produce _____ shirts. If Shirtland produces only 10 chips, it will produce _____ shirts.

2. In nation H, the opportunity cost of tables is five chairs, while in nation B, the opportunity cost of tables is only one chair. Which country should produce tables, and which should produce chairs?

3. Nations H and B split the difference between the willingness to pay for tables and the willingness to accept. What are the terms of trade?

4. List the two bits of information you need to draw the consumption possibilities curve for a particular nation.

5. In Figure 17.2, suppose the nations agree to exchange one shirt for each chip. Will the consumption possibilities curve for Chipland still be above its production possibilities curve?

Protectionist Policies

Now that you know the basic rationale for specialization and trade, we can explore the effects of public policies that restrict trade. We will consider four common import-restriction policies: an outright ban on imports, an import quota, voluntary export restraints, and a tariff.

Import Ban

To show how an import ban affects the market, let's start with an unrestricted market—no import ban. Figure 17.3 shows the market for shirts in Chipland, a nation with a comparative advantage in computer chips, not shirts. The domestic supply curve shows the quantity of shirts supplied by firms in Chipland. Looking at point *m*, we see that Chipland firms will not supply any shirts unless the price is at least $17 per shirt. The total supply curve for shirts, which shows the quantity supplied by both domestic firms and foreign firms (in Shirtland), lies to the right of the domestic supply curve. At each

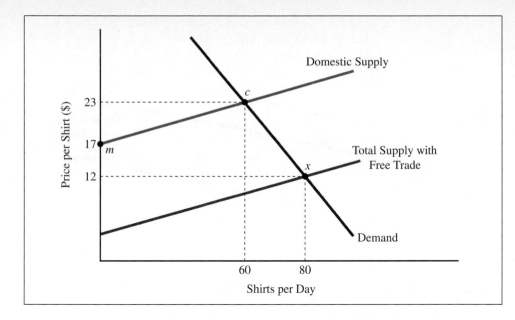

Figure 17.3
**Effects of an
Import Ban**
In the free-trade equilibrium,
demand intersects the total
supply curve at point *x*, with
a price of $12 and a quantity
of 80 shirts. If shirt imports
are banned, the equilibrium
is shown by the intersection
of the demand curve and the
domestic supply curve (point
c). The price increase to $23.

price, the total supply of shirts exceeds the domestic supply because foreign firms supply shirts too. Point *x* shows the free-trade equilibrium: The demand curve from domestic residents intersects the total supply curve at a price of $12 per shirt and a quantity of 80 shirts. Because this price is below the minimum price for domestic firms, domestic firms produce no shirts, and all the shirts in Chipland are imported from Shirtland.

What will happen if Chipland bans imported shirts? Foreign suppliers will disappear from the shirt market, so the total supply of shirts will be the domestic supply. In Figure 17.3, point *c* shows the equilibrium when Chipland bans imported shirts: The domestic demand curve intersects the domestic supply curve at a price of $23 per shirt and a quantity of 60 shirts. In other words, the decrease in supply resulting from the import ban increases the price and decreases the quantity of shirts.

Quotas and Voluntary Export Restraints

An alternative to an import ban is an **import quota**, defined as a limit on the amount of a good that can be imported. An import quota is a restrictive policy that falls between free trade and an import ban: Imports are decreased but not eliminated. Price falls between the price with free trade ($12 per shirt, as in our example) and the price with an import ban ($23 per shirt).

Figure 17.4 shows the effect of an import quota. Starting from the free-trade equilibrium at point *x*, an import quota will shift the total supply curve to the left: At each price there will be a smaller quantity of shirts because foreign suppliers cannot supply as many owing to the import limitation. The total supply curve when there is an import quota will lie between the domestic supply curve and the total supply curve under free trade. In the case of an import quota, the equilibrium occurs at point *q*, where the demand curve intersects the total supply curve, reflecting the import limitation. The $20 price per shirt with the import quota exceeds the $17 minimum price of domestic firms, so domestic firms supply 22 shirts (point *e*). Under a **voluntary export restraint [VER]**, an exporting nation voluntarily decreases its exports in an attempt to avoid more restrictive trade policies. A VER has the same effect as an import quota, which is illegal under the rules of the World Trade Organization (WTO), an organization with over 130 member nations that oversees the General Agreement on Tariffs and Trade and other international agreements. Although VERs are legal under WTO rules, they violate the spirit of

Import quota: A limit on the amount of a good that can be imported.

Voluntary export restraint [VER]: A scheme under which an exporting country voluntarily decreases its exports.

Figure 17.4
Market Effects of a Quota, a VER, or a Tariff

An import quota shifts the supply curve to the left. The market moves upward along the demand curve to point *q*, which is between point *x* (free trade) and *c* (an import ban). We can reach the same point with a tariff that shifts the total supply curve to the same position.

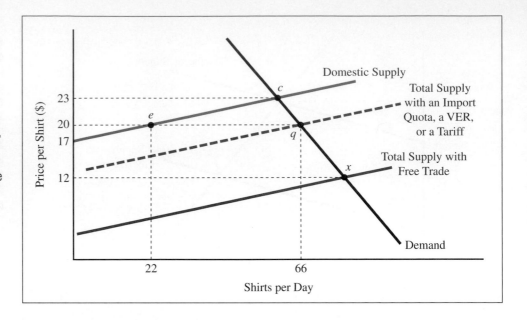

international trade agreements. Like a quota, a VER increases the price of the restricted good, allowing domestic firms to participate in the market.

A quota or a VER produces winners and losers. The winners include foreign and domestic shirt producers. In our example, foreign firms can sell shirts at a price of $20 instead of $12 each. In some cases, the government issues import licenses to some citizens, who can then buy shirts from foreign firms at a low price, such as $12, and sell the shirts at the higher domestic price, $20. In addition, the import restrictions allow domestic shirt firms to participate in the market, generating benefits for the firms and their workers. The losers are consumers, who pay a higher price for shirts.

Price Effects of Quotas and VERs

We know that consumers pay higher prices for goods that are subject to protectionist policies, but how much more? In the United States, voluntary export restraints for Japanese automobiles in effect in 1984 increased the price of a Japanese car by about $1,300 and increased the price of a domestic car by about $660.[1] In 1990, U.S. consumers incurred a total cost of $70 billion as a result of the nation's protectionist policies, about $270 per person per year.[2] The largest costs resulted from protectionist policies for apparel (about $84 per person) and textiles (about $13 per person).

Many European nations used VERs to limit their domestic market shares of Japanese automobiles. Figure 17.5 shows the cost of these policies in terms of their effects on the price of Japanese automobiles in several nations. For example, in France, the VERs increased the price of Japanese automobiles by 35%, compared to a 1% increase in price in Germany and a 55% higher price in Italy.

Tariffs

Tariff: A tax on an imported good.

An alternative to a quota or a VER is an import **tariff**, which is a tax on an imported good. We know from our earlier discussion of the market effects of taxes that a tax shifts the supply curve to the left and increases the equilibrium price. In Figure 17.4, suppose the tariff shifts the total supply curve, so it intersects the domestic demand curve at point *q*. In other words, we reach the same point we reached with the quota: Consumers pay the same $20 price per shirt, and domestic firms produce the same quantity: 22 shirts.

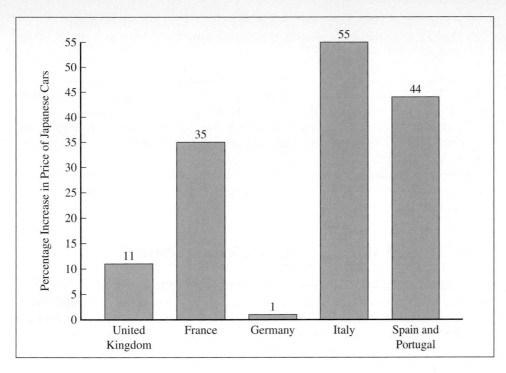

Figure 17.5
Price Effects of VERs for Japanese Cars
Many European nations use VERs to limit the number of Japanese cars imported. The VERs increase the price of Japanese cars.

Source: Alasdair Smith and Anthony J. Venables, "Cost of Voluntary Export Restraints in the European Car Market," Chapter 10 in *International Trade and Trade Policy*, edited by Ethanan Helpman and Asaaf Razin (Cambridge, MA: MIT Press, 1991).

There is one fundamental difference between a quota and a tariff. An import quota allows importers to buy shirts from foreign suppliers at a low price, say, $12 per shirt, and sell them for $20 each, the artificially high price. In other words, importers make money from the quota. Under a tariff, the government gets the money, collecting $8 per shirt from foreign suppliers. Citizens in Chipland will prefer the tariff to the quota because the government can use the revenue from the tariff to cut other taxes or expand public programs.

Responses to Protectionist Policies

A restriction on imports is likely to cause further restrictions on trade. For example, if Chipland bans shirt imports, the shirt industry in Shirtland may call for retaliation in the form of a ban on computer chips from Chipland. A trade war of this sort could escalate to the point at which the two nations return to self-sufficiency. If that happened, we could see the result by looking back at Figure 17.2: Chipland would move from point *x* to point *c*, and Shirtland would move from point *y* to point *s*. This sort of retaliatory response is common. Because it is, we know that the protection of one industry in a nation is likely to harm that nation's export industries. Chipland's shirt industry, if protected from imports, may grow, but at the expense of its computer-chip industry.

There are many examples of import restrictions that led to retaliatory policies that decreased trade substantially. Here are a few:

1. Smoot-Hawley tariff of 1930. When the United States increased its average tariff to 59%, its trading partners retaliated with higher tariffs. The trade war decreased international trade and deepened the worldwide depression of the 1930s.[3]
2. Chicken tariff of 1963. The European Economic Community (EEC, the predecessor of the European Union) imposed a large tariff on frozen chickens from the United States, cutting U.S. imports in half. The United States retaliated by increasing its tariffs on expensive brandies (from France), potato starch (from Holland), and light trucks (from Germany).[4]

3. Pasta tariff of 1985. The United States imposed tariffs on pasta from the EEC, and the EEC retaliated by increasing its tariffs on lemons and walnuts from the United States.[5]

The threat of retaliatory policies may persuade a nation to loosen its protectionist policies. In 1995, the United States announced that it would impose 100% tariffs on Japanese luxury cars (with total sales of $6 billion per year) if Japan didn't ease its restrictions on imported auto parts. Just hours before the tariffs were to take effect, the two nations reached an agreement that was expected to increase the sales of U.S. auto parts to Japanese firms by about $9 billion per year.[6]

Import restrictions also create an incentive to smuggle goods. The restrictions create a gap between the cost of purchasing the restricted goods abroad and the price of goods in the protected economy, so there is a profit to be made from smuggling.

Economic Detective

NAFTA and the Giant Sucking Sound

The North American Free Trade Agreement (NAFTA), which took effect in January 1994, will gradually phase out tariffs and other trade barriers between the United States, Canada, and Mexico. In the debates over the effects of NAFTA on trade between the United States and Mexico, economists predicted that NAFTA would increase both imports from Mexico and exports to Mexico. This is sensible because NAFTA decreases the tariffs and trade barriers of both nations. Because the pre-NAFTA tariffs between the United States and Mexico were low—about 4%—no one expected any dramatic changes in trade patterns. Instead, the expectation was for moderate growth in both imports and exports.

Table 17.2 provides some trade data for the United States and Mexico for the years surrounding the NAFTA agreement. Several observers, including two presidential candidates, used the figures for 1993 and 1995 to claim that NAFTA was responsible for turning the small $2 billion trade surplus in 1993 into the huge $16 billion trade deficit in 1995. One candidate suggested that NAFTA caused a "giant sucking sound" as jobs moved from the United States to Mexico.

Who is right? The economists who predicted that NAFTA would cause moderate growth in both imports and exports, or the presidential candidates?

The clues that we need to solve this puzzle are shown in the fourth column of Table 17.2. The exchange rate in 1994 was about the same as it was in 1993, so in the first year of NAFTA, imports and exports grew at nearly the same rate, about 22%, as predicted by economists. The following year was different: The exchange rate of the dollar for the peso rose from 3.11 to 5.33 pesos per dollar. An increase in the exchange rate—more

Table 17.2 Trade Data for the United States and Mexico

Year	U.S. Imports from Mexico (billions)	U.S. Exports to Mexico (billions)	Exchange Rate: Pesos per Dollar	U.S. Trade Surplus (+) or Deficit (−) with Mexico (billions)
1993	$40	$42	3.12	$+2
1994	$49	$51	3.11	$+2
1995	$62	$46	5.33	$−16

Source: U.S. Department of Commerce, *Statistical Abstract of the United States, 1996* (Washington, DC: U.S. Government Printing Office, 1996).

NAFTA helps promote the growth of foreign investment in Mexico.

pesos per dollar—will make U.S. goods more expensive for Mexican consumers, so U.S. exports to Mexico will drop. At the same time, Mexican goods will become less expensive for U.S. consumers, so U.S. imports from Mexico will rise. According to Table 17.2, that's exactly what happened: Imports increased by $13 billion, and exports dropped by $5 billion. This suggests that the U.S. trade deficit with Mexico was caused by the fall in the value of the peso, not by NAFTA.

TEST Your Understanding

6. Complete the following statement: If a country bans the importation of a particular good, the market equilibrium is shown by the intersection of the _____ curve and the _____ curve.

7. Complete the statement with *above* or *below*. The equilibrium price under an import quota is _____ the price that occurs with an import ban and _____ the price that occurs with free trade.

8. From the perspective of consumers, which is better: a tariff or a quota?

9. Under the quota system underlying Figure 17.4, what fraction of the shirt market is supplied by domestic firms?

Rationales for Protectionist Policies

What are the rationales for protectionist policies such as an import ban, an import quota, a voluntary restraint, or a tariff? We will discuss three possible motivations for policies that restrict trade:

1. To shield workers from foreign competition
2. To nurture infant industries until they mature
3. To help domestic firms establish monopolies in world markets

To Shield Workers from Foreign Competition

One of the most basic arguments for protectionism is that it protects workers in industries that would be hurt by trade. Suppose that relative to the United States, nations in the Far East have a comparative advantage in producing textiles. If the United States reduced existing tariffs for the textile industry, domestic manufacturers could not compete. They would have to close their factories and lay off workers. In an ideal world, the laid-off workers would take new jobs in other sectors of the economy. In practice, this is difficult. Many workers don't have the skills to work in other sectors, and obtaining these skills takes time. Moreover, the textile industry is heavily concentrated in the southeastern part of the United States. Politicians from that region will try to keep tariffs in place to prevent the temporary unemployment and changes in employment patterns that free trade would cause. The result of this protection is less efficient production, higher prices, and lower consumption for the United States. For a discussion of the trade-offs between job protection and consumer prices, read "A Closer Look: The Cost of Protecting Jobs."

To Nurture Infant Industries

Learning by doing: Knowledge gained during production, resulting in increases in productivity.

Infant industry: A new industry that is protected from foreign competitors.

During World War II, the United States built hundreds of boats, called Liberty Ships, for the Navy. As more and more of these ships were built, each required fewer hours to complete because workers learned from their experiences, acquiring knowledge during the production process. Engineers and economists call this phenomenon **learning by doing**. To learn a new game, such as Ping-Pong, you learn by doing. At first, you may find it difficult to play, but your skills improve as you go along.

Tariffs and other protectionist policies are often defended on the grounds that they protect new industries, or **infant industries**, that are in the early stages of learning by doing. A tariff shields a young industry from the competition of its more mature rivals.

A CLOSER LOOK   THE COST OF PROTECTING JOBS

What is the trade-off between protecting domestic jobs and higher prices for consumers? As shown in the table, protectionist policies for textiles and apparel imposed an annual cost of over $10 billion and saved 126,050 jobs—at a cost of $82,316 per job. To protect 300 jobs in the footwear industry, we spent over $1 million dollars per worker!

Industry Protected	Annual Cost (millions)	Jobs Protected	Cost per Job
Textiles and apparel	$10,376	126,050	$ 82,316
Maritime transport	$ 1,324	4,860	$ 272,427
Sugar	$ 986	1,990	$ 495,477
Footwear	$ 501	300	$1,670,000
Dairy	$ 152	160	$ 950,000

Source: Update of *The Economic Effects of Significant U.S. Import Restraints* (Washington, D.C., U.S. International Trade Commission, second update 1999).

After the infant industry grows up, the tariff can be eliminated because the industry is able to compete.

In practice, infant industries rarely become competitive with their foreign rivals. During the 1950s and 1960s, many Latin American countries used tariffs and other policies to protect their young manufacturing industries from foreign competition. Unfortunately, the domestic industries never became as efficient as foreign suppliers, and the Latin American countries that tried this policy suffered.

Another problem with protecting an infant industry is that once an industry is given tariff protection, it is difficult to take such protection away. For an interesting discussion of the merits of protecting an industry from "unfair" competition, read "A Closer Look: Protection for Candle Makers."

To Help Domestic Firms Establish Monopolies in World Markets

If the production of a particular good has very large-scale economies, the world market will support only a few firms. A nation might be tempted to adopt policies to capture the monopoly profits for itself. Suppose the commercial aircraft industry can support only one large firm; if two firms enter the industry, both will lose money. A nation that decides to get into this industry could agree to provide financial support to a domestic firm to guarantee that the firm will make a profit. With such a guarantee, the domestic firm will enter the industry. Knowing this, a foreign firm will be reluctant to enter, so the domestic firm will capture the monopoly profit.

One example of this is the Airbus, an airplane that is produced in Europe. Several European countries provided large subsidies for firms producing the Airbus. These subsidies allowed the Airbus firms to underprice some of their rivals in the United States, and at least one U.S. manufacturer of commercial airplanes was forced out of business. What could go wrong with these monopoly-creation policies? If both nations subsidize

---

A CLOSER LOOK PROTECTION FOR CANDLE MAKERS

In response to the spread of protectionism, the French economist Frédéric Bastiat (1801–1851) wrote the following fictitious petition, in which French candle makers ask for protection from "unfair" competition:

We are suffering from the intolerable competition of a foreign rival, placed, it would seem, in a condition so far superior to ours for the production of light, that he absolutely inundates our national market at a price fabulously reduced. The moment he shows himself, our trade leaves us— all of our customers apply to him; and a branch of native industry, having countless ramifications, is all at once rendered completely stagnant. This rival . . . is none other than the sun.

What we pray for is, that it may please you to pass a law ordering the shutting up of all windows, sky-lights, dormerwindows, curtains, blinds, bull's eyes; in a word all openings, holes, chinks, clefts, and fissures, by or through which the light of the sun has been in use to enter houses, to the prejudice of the meritorious manufactures with which we . . . have accommodated our country—a country which, in gratitude, ought not to abandon us now.

Does it not argue to the greatest inconsistency to check as you do the importation of coal, iron, cheese, and goods of foreign manufacture, merely because . . . their price approaches zero, while at the same time you freely admit, and without limitation, the light of the sun, whose price is during the whole day at zero?

Source: Frédéric Bastiat, *Economics Sophisms* (Edinburgh: Oliver & Boyd, 1873), pp. 49–53.

their domestic firms, both firms will enter the market and lose money. The taxpayers in both countries will then have to pay for the subsidies. And there is the possibility a nation may pick the wrong industry to subsidize. Together, the British and French subsidized an airplane known as the Concorde to provide supersonic travel between Europe and the United States. Although the Concorde captured the market, the market was not worth capturing. The Concorde lost money because it was very costly to develop, and people are not willing to pay a very large premium for supersonic travel.

TEST Your Understanding

10. Comment on the following statement: If we eliminated our textile tariffs, the dislocated workers could easily switch to other jobs.

11. Explain the infant-industry argument.

12. List the two problems associated with subsidizing an industry in the hope of establishing a worldwide monopoly.

Recent Policy Debates and Trade Agreements

We're now ready to discuss three recent policy debates concerning international trade:

1. Are foreign producers dumping their products?
2. Do trade laws inhibit environmental protection?
3. Does trade cause income inequality?

We also discuss some recent trade agreements that have lowered trade barriers and increased international trade.

Are Foreign Producers Dumping Their Products?

Dumping: A situation in which the price a firm charges for a product in a foreign market is lower than either the price it charges for that product in its home market or the product's production cost.

While tariff rates have been reduced in recent years, a number of trade controversies remain. One of these is the rules for dumping. A firm is **dumping** when the price it charges in a foreign market is either lower than the price it charges in its home market or lower than its production cost. Dumping is illegal under international trade agreements; hundreds of cases of alleged dumping are presented to WTO authorities each year. Here are some recent cases in which the WTO concluded that dumping had occurred: Hong Kong VCRs sold in Europe; Chinese bicycles sold in the United States; Asian TV sets sold in Europe; steel from Brazil, India, Japan, and Spain sold in the United States; U.S. beef sold in Mexico; and Chinese computer disks sold in Japan and the United States. Under the current provisions of the WTO, a nation can impose antidumping duties on products that are being dumped.

Why would a firm dump—charge a low price in the foreign market? The first reason is price discrimination. If a firm has a monopoly in its home market but faces strong competition in a foreign market, the firm will naturally charge a higher price in the home market. The foreign price looks low, but only because we compare it to a very high monopoly price in the home market. The firm uses its monopoly power to discriminate against consumers in its home market, so the problem is in the home market, not the foreign market.

To illustrate how international price discrimination works, let's look at the case of Korean VCRs.[7] In the 1980s there were only three firms, all Korean, selling VCRs in Korea, but there were dozens of firms selling VCRs in Europe. The lack of competition in Korea generated very high prices for Korean consumers: They paid much more than European consumers for identical Korean VCRs. Korean firms used their market power to discriminate against Korean consumers. When international trade authorities concluded that Korean firms were dumping VCRs in Europe, the Korean firms responded by cutting prices in their home market. They did not increase their prices in Europe—much to the dismay of European producers and the delight of European consumers.

The second reason for dumping is predatory pricing: cutting prices in an attempt to drive rival firms out of business. The predatory firm sets its price below its production cost. The price is low enough that both the predator and its prey (a firm in the foreign market) lose money. After the prey goes out of business, the predator increases its price to earn monopoly profit. This is also known as *predatory dumping*.

Although the rationale for antidumping laws is to prevent predatory dumping, it is difficult to determine whether low prices are the result of predatory pricing or price discrimination. Many economists are skeptical about how frequently predatory pricing actually occurs; they suspect that many nations use their antidumping laws as protectionist policies in disguise. Because WTO rules limit tariffs and quotas, some nations may be tempted to substitute antidumping duties for these protectionist policies.

Until the 1990s, antidumping cases were brought almost exclusively by Australia, New Zealand, Europe, Canada, and the United States. However, starting in the 1990s, the developing countries began to emulate the developed countries and now bring approximately one-half of the cases. Professor Thomas Prusa of Rutgers University has studied antidumping and found that it is a potent weapon for domestic industries. If a case is settled or a tariff is imposed, imports typically fall by 50 to 70% over the first three years of protection. Even if a country loses a claim, imports still fall by 15 to 20%.[8]

Do Trade Laws Inhibit Environmental Protection?

In recent trade negotiations, a new player—environmental groups—appeared on the scene. Starting in the early 1990s, environmentalists began to question whether policies that liberalized trade could harm the environment. The issue that attracted their attention was the killing of dolphins by tuna fishers.

Anyone who catches tuna with a large net will also catch the dolphins that swim with the tuna, and most of the captured dolphins will die. In 1972, the United States outlawed the use of tuna nets by U.S. ships. A short time later, ships from other nations, including Mexico, began netting tuna and killing dolphins. The United States responded with a boycott of Mexican tuna caught with nets, and the Mexican government complained to an international trade authority that the tuna boycott was an unfair trade barrier. The trade authority agreed with Mexico and forced the United States to remove the boycott.

Under current WTO rules, a country can adopt any environmental standard it chooses, as long as it does not discriminate against foreign producers. For example, the United States can limit the exhaust emissions of all cars that operate in the United States. As long as emissions rules apply equally to all cars, domestic and imports, the rules are legal according to the WTO. An international panel upheld U.S. fuel efficiency rules for automobiles on this principle.[9]

The tuna boycott was a violation of WTO rules because killing dolphins does not harm the U.S. environment directly. For the same reason, the United States could not ban imported goods that are produced in factories that generate air or water pollution in other countries. It is easy to understand why WTO rules do not allow countries to restrict trade on the basis of the methods that are used to produce goods and services. Countries differ in the value they place on the environment. For example, a poor nation may be willing to tolerate more pollution if it means attaining a higher standard of living.

If trade restrictions cannot be used to protect the dolphins and deal with other global environmental problems, what else can we do? International agreements have been used for a variety of different environmental goals, from limiting the harvest of whales to eliminating the chemicals that deplete the ozone layer. These agreements are difficult to reach, and some nations will be tempted to use trade restrictions to pursue environmental goals. If they do, they will encounter resistance because WTO rules mean that a nation can pursue its environmental goals only within its own borders.

Trade disputes about environmental issues are part of a larger phenomenon of trade issues intersecting with national regulations. At one time, most trade disputes were simply matters of protecting domestic industries from foreign competition. Agriculture, textile, and steel were frequently beneficiaries of protection in many different countries throughout the world. But in recent years, there has been a new breed of trade disputes that revolve around social issues and the role of government regulation.

As an example, the European Union and the United States became embroiled in a trade dispute over hormone-treated beef. After the European Union banned imports of hormone-treated beef, the United States and Canada successfully challenged this ban with the WTO because they argued that there was no scientific evidence that suggested any adverse health impacts from hormone-treated beef. The European Union refused to rescind the ban and, as a consequence, the United States and Canada were permitted to impose tariffs on a range of European products.

The European Union ban on hormone-treated beef was intended to protect European farmers from imports but also reflected the nervousness of European citizens about technology. After all, Europe banned all hormone-treated beef, not just imports. Shouldn't a country have a right to pursue this policy, even if it is not based on the best science of the day? While the costs of the policy are straightforward in terms of higher beef prices, the benefits, in terms of potential safety and peace of mind, are much more difficult to assess. Similar issues will arise as genetically modified crops become more commonplace. As a world trading community, we will have to decide at what point we allow national policy concerns to override principles of free trade.

Does Trade Cause Inequality?

Inequality in wages has been growing in the United States since 1973. Wages of skilled workers have risen faster than the wages of unskilled workers. World trade has also boomed since 1973. Could there be a connection between increased world trade and income inequality?

Trade theory suggests a link between increased trade and increased wage inequality. Here is how they might be linked: Suppose the United States produces two types of goods: one using skilled labor (say, airplanes) and one using unskilled labor (say, textiles). The United States is likely to have a comparative advantage in products that use skilled labor; developing countries are likely to have a comparative advantage in products that use unskilled labor. An increase in world trade will increase both exports and imports. An increase in U.S. exports means that we'll produce more goods requiring skilled labor, so the domestic demand for skilled labor will increase, pulling up the wage of skilled labor in the United States. At the same time, an increase in U.S. imports means that we'll import more goods produced by unskilled labor, so the domestic demand for unskilled labor will decrease, pulling down the wage of unskilled labor in the United States. As a result, the gap between the wages of the two types of workers will increase.

Economists have tried to determine how much trade has contributed to growing wage inequality. As usual, there are other factors that make such a determination difficult. It is difficult, for example, to distinguish between the effects of trade and the effects of technical progress. Technical change, such as the rapid introduction and use of computers, will also tend to increase the demand for skilled workers and decrease the demand for unskilled workers. Economists have noted, however, that the exports of goods using skilled labor and the imports of goods using unskilled labor have both increased, just as the theory predicts. At least some of the increased wage inequality is caused by international trade.

One response to this undesirable side effect of trade is to use trade restrictions to protect industries that use unskilled workers. Another approach is to ease the transition to an economy with a larger fraction of skilled jobs. In the long run, workers will move to industries that use skilled workers, so they will eventually earn higher wages. The government could facilitate this change by providing assistance for education and training.

Recent Trade Agreements

In the last few decades, there has been considerable progress in lowering the barriers to international trade. Here are some examples of international trade agreements:

1. North American Free Trade Agreement (NAFTA). Took effect in 1994 and is being implemented over the following 15 years. The agreement will eventually eliminate all tariffs and other trade barriers among Canada, Mexico, and the United States. NAFTA may soon be extended to other nations in the Western Hemisphere.

2. World Trade Organization (WTO). Has more than 130 member nations and oversees the General Agreement on Tariffs and Trade and other international trade agreements. There have been eight rounds of tariff negotiations, lowering tariffs among the member nations. For example, between 1930 and 1995, the average tariff in the United States has dropped from about 59% to about 5%. The last full set of negotiations, the so-called Uruguay Round, completed in 1994, decreased tariffs by about one-third their prior levels. WTO promotes trade in other ways: It has eliminated many import quotas, reduced agricultural subsidies, and outlawed restrictions on international trade in services such as banking, insurance, and accounting.

3. European Union (EU). Designed to remove all trade barriers within Europe and create a single market. Fifteen nations have joined.

4. Asian Pacific Economic Cooperation (APEC). In 1994, the leaders of 18 Asian nations signed a nonbinding agreement to reduce trade barriers among their nations.

These agreements have reduced trade barriers and increased international trade. For example, the Uruguay Round was expected to increase the volume of world trade by at least 9% and perhaps as much as 24%.[10]

TEST Your Understanding

13. What is dumping?

14. What restrictions do WTO rules place on a nation's environmental policies?

15. Consider a nation having a comparative advantage in the production of goods using unskilled labor. What types of workers will benefit from increased trade, and what types of workers will lose?

Using the **TOOLS**

In this chapter, we've discussed the trade-offs associated with protectionist policies and have used supply and demand curves to show the market effects of protectionist policies. Here are some opportunities to do your own economic analysis.

1. ECONOMIC EXPERIMENT: Protectionist Policies
Recall the market equilibrium experiment from Chapter 4. We can modify the experiment to show the effects of protectionist policies on equilibrium prices and quantities. On the supply side of the market, there are domestic apple producers and foreign apple produc-

ers; the domestic producers have higher unit costs. After several trading periods without any government intervention, you can change the rules as follows:

a. Apple imports are banned: Foreign producers cannot participate in the market.

b. There is a tariff (a tax on imports) of $5 per bushel.

APPLICATIONS

2. Incentives for Smuggling

If a country bans imports, smugglers may try to penetrate its markets. Suppose Chipland bans shirt imports, causing some importers to bribe customs officials, who "look the other way" as smugglers bring shirts into Chipland. Your job is to combat shirt smuggling. Use the information in Figure 17.3 in this chapter to answer the following questions:

a. Suppose importers can sell their shirts on the world market at a price of $12 per shirt. How much is an importer willing to pay to get customs officials to look the other way?

b. What sort of change in trade policy would make your job easier?

3. Trade in Genetically Modified Crops

Suppose the residents of a country become fearful of using genetically modified crops in their food supply. Consider the following two possible scenarios:

a. Aware of consumer sentiment, the largest supermarket chains in the country adopt a policy that they will not purchase food products that use genetically modified crops.

b. The government, aware of voter sentiment during an election year, bans the import of the food products that use genetically modified crops.

In both cases, no genetically modified crops enter the country. Do either of these cases run afoul of WTO policies?

4. Ban on Shoe Imports

Consider a country that initially consumes 100 pairs of shoes per hour, all of which are imported. The price of shoes is $40 per pair before a ban on importing them. Depict graphically the market effects of a ban on shoe imports.

Summary

In this chapter, we discussed the benefits of specialization and trade, and we explored the trade-offs associated with protectionist policies. There is a basic conflict between consumers, who prefer free trade because free trade decreases prices, and workers in the protected industries, who want to keep their jobs. Here are the main points of the chapter:

1. If one country has a comparative advantage vis-à-vis another country in producing a particular good (a lower opportunity cost), specialization and trade will benefit both countries.

2. An import ban or an import quota increases the prices of the restricted good and shifts resources from a domestic export industry into the protected domestic industries.

3. Because the victims of protectionist policies often retaliate, the protection of a domestic industry may harm an exporting industry.

4. A tariff (a tax on imports) generates revenue for the government, while an import quota—a limit on imports—generates revenue for foreigners or importers.

5. In principle, the laws against dumping are designed to prevent predatory pricing. In practice, it is difficult to prove predatory pricing, and the laws are often used to shield a domestic industry from competition.

6. Under WTO rules, each country may pursue its environmental goals only within its own borders.

7. International trade has contributed to the widening gap between the wages of low-skilled and high-skilled labor.

autarky, 350
comparative advantage, 350
consumption possibilities curve, 351
dumping, 360

import quota, 353
infant industry, 358
learning by doing, 358
production possibilities curve, 348

tariff, 354
terms of trade, 350
voluntary export restraint [VER], 353

Problems and Discussion Questions

1. In one minute, Country B can produce either 1,000 TVs and no computers or 500 computers and no TVs. Similarly, in one minute, country C can produce either 2,400 TVs or 600 computers.

   a. Compute the opportunity costs of TVs and computers for each country. Which country has a comparative advantage in producing TVs? In producing computers?

   b. Draw the production possibilities curves for the two countries.

2. In country U, the opportunity cost of a computer is 10 pairs of shoes. In Country C, the opportunity cost of a computer is 100 pairs of shoes.

   a. Suppose the two countries split the difference between the willingness to pay for computers and the willingness to accept computers. Compute the terms of trade, that is, the rate at which the two countries will exchange computers and shoes.

   b. Suppose the two countries exchange one computer for the number of shoes dictated by the terms of trade you computed in part (a). Compute the net benefit from trade for each country.

3. In Figure 17.2, suppose the two countries trade 35 computer chips for 70 shirts. For each country, compute the amounts of chips and shirts consumed.

4. Consider two countries, Tableland and Chairland, each capable of producing tables and chairs. Chairland can produce the following combinations of chairs and tables:

   • All chairs and no tables: 36 chairs per day

   • All tables and no chairs: 18 tables per day

   Tableland can produce the following combinations of chairs and tables:

   • All chairs and no tables: 40 chairs per day

   • All tables and no chairs: 40 tables per day

   In each country, there is a fixed trade-off of tables for chairs.

   a. Draw the two production possibilities curves, with chairs on the vertical axis and tables on the horizontal axis.

   b. Suppose that each country is initially self-sufficient and each country divides its resources equally between the two goods. How much does each country produce and consume?

   c. Which country has a comparative advantage in tables? Which has a comparative advantage in chairs?

   d. If the two countries split the difference between the buyer's willingness to pay for chairs and the seller's willingness to accept, in terms of chairs per table, what are the terms of trade?

   e. Draw the consumption possibilities curves.

   f. Suppose each country specializes in the good for which it has a comparative advantage, and they exchange 14 tables for some quantity of chairs. Compute the consumption bundles—bundles means the consumption of tables and chairs—for each country.

5. The current approach to restricting automobile imports is to use voluntary export restraints. Evaluate the wisdom of this approach and propose an alternative policy.

6. Evaluate this comment: "If a country bans imports, smuggling is inevitable. We should welcome smuggling because it improves consumer welfare."

7. The European Union is committed to eliminating most of the trade barriers among its 15 member nations. What types of people will benefit? Which types will lose?

8. What is the cost to consumers for each motor-vehicle job protected by import restrictions? In your opinion, is protecting these jobs worthwhile at this cost? If not, how much should we as a society be willing to pay for each job that is protected?

9. Suppose the president of a nation proposes to switch from a system of import quotas to a system

of tariffs, with the idea that the switch would not affect the quantity of goods imported. Who will be in favor of the switch? Who will oppose it? Would you expect the proponents and the opponents to have the same political influence on the president?

10. Suppose residents of one nation are very fearful of biotechnology and they pass a law prohibiting the sale of all genetically altered foods in their country. Another nation, which produces these foods, claims that this law is an unfair trade barrier. In your view, should the first nation be allowed to prevent these imports, even if there is no scientific basis for their claim?

11. **Web Exercise.** Go to the Web site for the World Trade Organization [*http://www.wto.org*] and explore some of the ongoing trade disputes. Pick one or two of these disputes and find additional background information, such as newspaper stories, on the Web. Use this information to understand the nature of the controversy.

12. **Web Exercise.** Go to the Web site for the U.S. Trade Representative [*http://www.ustr.gov*], which is an office within the executive branch of the government. From the Web site, what are some of the key trade issues for the U.S. government today?

Take It to the Net

We invite you to visit the O'Sullivan/Sheffrin page on the Prentice Hall Web site at: **http://www.prenhall.com/osullivan/** for additional World Wide Web exercises for this chapter.

Model Answers to Questions

Chapter-Opening Questions

1. The winners are the domestic nation's consumers, who pay lower prices, and the domestic nation's workers in export industries. The losers are people in the domestic nation who lose their jobs as imports replace domestically produced goods.

2. A tariff generates revenue for the government; a quota generates profits for importers.

3. First, if a firm has a monopoly in its home market but faces strong competition in a foreign market, the firm will naturally charge a higher price in the home market (price discrimination). Second, a firm may be engaging in predatory pricing, the practice of cutting prices in an attempt to drive rivals out of business.

4. Under current WTO rules, a country cannot adopt any environmental standard that discriminates against foreign producers. For example, the United States cannot impose an import ban on goods that are produced in polluting factories in other nations. This rule means that global environmental issues must be resolved with international agreements, not trade restrictions.

5. Although trade increases income inequality, it is unclear just how much of the recent increase in inequality can be attributed to the expansion of trade.

Test Your Understanding

1. 50, 78 (108 – 30).

2. Nation B should produce tables, and nation H should produce chairs.

3. Three chairs per table: Nation H is willing to pay five chairs, and nation B is willing to accept one chair.

4. We need to know the maximum output of the good for which the nation has a comparative advantage and the terms of trade.

5. No. The consumption curve will be the same as the production curve.

6. Demand, domestic supply.

7. Below, above.

8. If a quota and a tariff led to the same price for a good, consumers would be indifferent between them. However, as citizens, they should prefer the tariff which provides revenue to the government, allowing the government to either increase expenditure or reduce taxation.

9. Domestic firms supply 22 units, which is one-third of the total quantity (66).

10. This is false. Some workers do not have the skills to work in other sectors, and it takes time to obtain new skills.

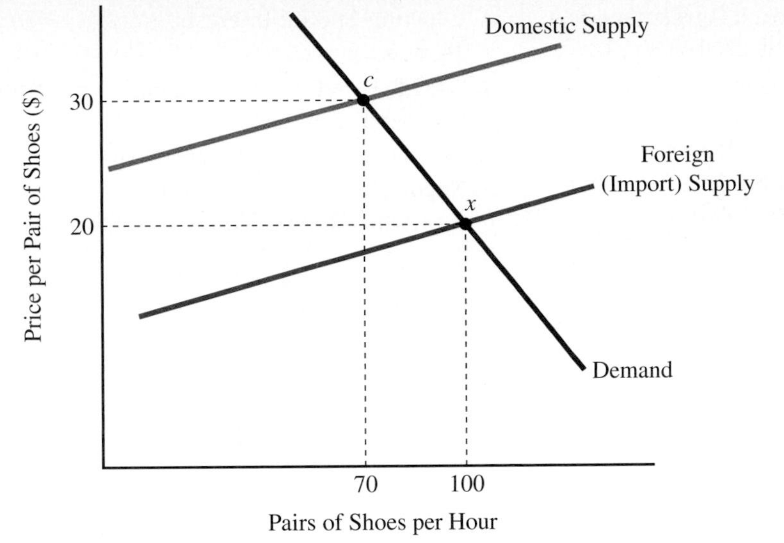

Figure 17.A
Ban on Shoe Imports

Using the Tools

11. It takes some time for a new industry to learn by doing, so it may be sensible to protect a young industry when it is vulnerable to competition from foreign firms.

12. If two nations subsidize firms in the same industry, each nation could lose money. In addition, a nation might pick the wrong industry to subsidize.

13. A foreign firm is dumping when it sells a product in another country at a price below the price it charges in its own market. It is difficult to determine whether dumping is occurring, and many countries used dumping laws as a disguised form of protectionism.

14. A nation's environmental laws must not discriminate against imported goods. The laws must apply equally to imports and domestic goods.

15. The wage of unskilled labor will increase; the wage of skilled labor will decrease.

Using the Tools

2. Incentives for Smuggling
   a. Importers are willing to pay a bribe up to $11 per shirt (the difference between the equilibrium price with the import ban and the world price).
   b. If the import ban were replaced by a tariff of $11 per shirt, the smuggling problem might diminish, although there would still be an incentive to smuggle shirts to avoid the tariff.

3. Trade in Genetically Modified Crops. The WTO cannot prevent the large supermarket chains from not purchasing food that contains genetically modified crops. In the absence of scientific evidence, the government, however, could not ban the crops without violating WTO rules.

4. Ban on Shoe Imports. In Figure 17.A we move from point *x* (price = $20 per pair; quantity = 100 pairs) to point *c* (price = $30 per pair; quantity = 70 pairs).

Notes

1. *A Review of Recent Developments in the U.S. Automobile Industry Including an Assessment of the Japanese Voluntary Restraint Agreements* (Washington, DC: U.S. International Trade Commission, February 1985).

2. Gary C. Hufbauer, Diane T. Berliner, and Kimberly A. Elliot, *Measuring the Cost of Protectionism in the United States* (Washington, DC: Institute for International Economics, 1994).

3. Charles Kindleberger, *The World in Depression, 1929-1939* (London: Allen Lane, 1973).

4. John A. C. Conybeare, *Trade Wars* (New York: Columbia University Press, 1987).

5. Conybeare, *Trade Wars*.

6. Helene Cooper and Valerie Reitman, "Averting a Trade War, U.S. and Japan Reach Agreement on Autos," *Wall Street Journal*, June 29, 1995, p. 1.

7. Taeho Bark, "The Korean Consumer Electronics Industry: Reaction to Antidumping Actions," Chapter 7 in *Antidumping: How It Works and Who Gets Hurt*, edited by J. Michael Finger (Ann Arbor, MI: University of Michigan Press, 1993).

8. Virgina Postrel, "Curb Demonstrates Faults of Courting Special Interests," *New York Times*, June 14, 2001, p. C1.

9. "GATT Panel Supports U.S.," *New York Times*, October 1, 1994, p. A49.

10. Norman S. Fieleke, "The Uruguay Round of Trade Negotiation: An Overview," *New England Economic Review*, May/June 1995.

The World of International Finance

Today, the world currency markets are always open. When foreign exchange traders in New York City are sound asleep at 3:00 A.M., their counterparts in London are already on their phones and computers at 8:00 A.M. In Tokyo, it's 6:00 P.M., and the day is just ending. By the time Tokyo traders return home after their long commutes, the New York traders are back at work. The currency markets keep working even when mere human beings rest.

On any given day, trillions of dollars of value are exchanged in these markets. The fortunes of industries and sometimes countries are determined by the ups and downs of currencies. Do these markets work efficiently and effectively?

n this world market, all currencies are traded 24 hours a day. The value of every currency depends on news and late-breaking developments throughout the world. News from Singapore, South Africa, or Sweden can easily affect the price at which currencies trade, for example, the price of U.S. dollars in terms of Japanese yen. The U.S. Secretary of the Treasury utters a casual remark that might or might not have something to do with currency exchange, and it reverberates instantly throughout the world. Modern communications—fax, e-mail, cell phones, video-conferencing, and satellite transmissions—accelerate the process.

How do changes in the value of currencies affect the U.S. economy? In this chapter, we explain the links between exchange rates and the performance of the economy. Understanding this will help you to interpret the often complex news from abroad. For example, if the value of the dollar starts to fall against the Japanese yen, what does it mean? Is this good news or bad news?

After reading this chapter, you should be able to answer the following questions:

1. If U.S. interest rates increase, how will this affect the exchange rate between U.S. dollars and Swiss francs? What will increasing interest rates in the United States do to the cost of a summer trip to Europe?

2. If the dollar increases in value against the Japanese yen, how will the increase affect the balance of trade between the United States and Japan?

3. Why do governments intervene in the foreign exchange market by buying and selling currencies?

4. Why have a group of European countries adopted a common currency?

5. How do international financial crises emerge?

How Exchange Rates Are Determined

In this section, we examine how the value of a currency is determined in world markets. We then look at the factors that can change the value of a currency.

What Are Exchange Rates?

Exchange rate: The rate at which one currency can be exchanged for another.

Let's start by reviewing a key concept introduced in Chapter 3. To conduct international transactions between countries with different currencies, it is necessary to exchange one currency for another. The **exchange rate** is defined as the rate at which we can exchange one currency for another. Suppose a U.S. songwriter sells the rights of a hit song to a Japanese producer. The U.S. songwriter agrees to accept $50,000. If the exchange rate between U.S. dollars and Japanese yen is 100 yen per dollar, it will cost the Japanese producer 5,000,000 yen to purchase the rights to the song. Because international trade occurs between nations with different currencies, the exchange rate—the price at which one currency trades for another currency—is a crucial determinant of the trade in goods and assets.

Appreciation: An increase in the value of a currency.

An increase in the value of a currency is called an **appreciation**. If the exchange rate between the dollar and the yen increases from 100 yen per dollar to 110 yen per dollar, one dollar will purchase more yen. Because the dollar has increased in value, we say that the dollar has appreciated against the yen.

Depreciation: A decrease in the value of a currency.

A **depreciation** is a reduction in the value of a currency. If the exchange rate falls to 90 yen per dollar, we get fewer yen for each dollar, so we say that the dollar has depreciated against the yen.

Throughout this chapter, we measure the exchange rate in units of foreign currency per dollar, that is, as 100 yen per dollar or 2 francs per dollar. We can think of the exchange rate as the price of dollars in terms of foreign currency. If the dollar appreciates from 100 yen per dollar to 110 yen per dollar, the price of dollars in terms of yen has increased, that is, the dollar has become more expensive in terms of yen. An appreciation of the dollar, therefore, is an increase in the price of dollars in terms of yen. Similarly, a depreciation of the dollar against the yen is a decrease in the price of dollars in terms of yen.

Be sure you understand that if the dollar appreciates against the yen, the yen must depreciate against the dollar. If we get more yen in exchange for the dollar, each yen will trade for fewer dollars. If the dollar appreciates from 100 to 110 yen per dollar, 100 yen will exchange for $0.91 rather than $1.00. Similarly, if the dollar depreciates against the yen, the yen must appreciate against the dollar. If we get less yen per dollar, each yen will exchange for more dollars. If the dollar depreciates from 100 yen to 90 yen per dollar, 100 yen will exchange for $1.11 rather than $1.00.

The exchange rate enables us to convert prices in one country to values in another country. A simple example illustrates how an exchange rate works. If you want to buy a watch from Switzerland, you need to know what a watch would cost. You call the store in Switzerland; you are told that the watch sells for 300 Swiss francs. The store owners live in Switzerland and want to be paid in Swiss francs. To figure out what it will cost you in dollars, you need to know the exchange rate between francs and dollars. If the exchange rate is 2 francs per dollar, the watch would cost you $150:

$$300 \text{ francs}/2 \text{ francs per dollar} = \$150$$

If the exchange rate is 3 francs per dollar, the watch would cost only $100. The exchange rate allows you to convert the value of the watch (or any other good or service) from francs (or any other currency) to dollars.

Supply and Demand

How are exchange rates determined? The exchange rate between U.S. dollars and Swiss francs is determined in the foreign exchange market, the market in which dollars trade for Swiss francs. To understand this market, we can use simple supply and demand analysis.

In Figure 18.1, we plot the demand and supply curves for dollars in exchange for Swiss francs. On the vertical axis, we have the exchange rate, e, in francs per dollar: e

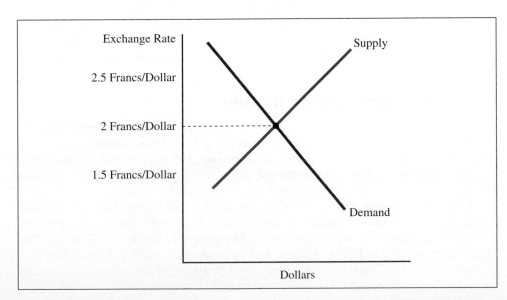

Figure 18.1

Demand for and Supply of Dollars
Market equilibrium occurs where demand equals supply.

will measure how many francs trade for one dollar. For example, if you receive 2 francs per dollar, then e = 2 francs/dollar. If e increases, 1 dollar buys more francs, and the price of dollars in terms of francs has increased. For example, if e increases from 2 francs/dollar to 2.5 francs/dollar, the dollar has become more valuable—meaning that it has appreciated—against the franc. Similarly, if the exchange rate falls to 1.5 francs/dollar, the dollar has depreciated in value against the franc, and the price of dollars in terms of francs has decreased.

Be sure you see both sides of the same exchange coin: If the dollar appreciates against the franc, then the franc depreciates against the dollar. If the exchange rate increases from 2 to 2.5 francs/dollar, a single franc falls in value from \$0.50/franc to \$0.40/franc:

$$(2.5 \text{ francs/dollar} = 1/(2.5) \text{ dollars/francs} = 0.4 \text{ dollars/franc} = \$0.40/\text{franc})$$

Figure 18.1 shows the supply and demand curves for dollars in exchange for francs. The supply curve is the quantity supplied of dollars in exchange for francs. Individuals or firms that want to buy Swiss goods or assets will need to exchange dollars for francs. For example, to invest in the Swiss stock market, a U.S. investor must first trade dollars for francs because Swiss sellers of stocks or bonds want to be paid in their own currency. We have defined the exchange rate as francs per dollar, so an increase in the exchange rate means that each dollar exchanges for more francs and francs become cheaper relative to dollars. The supply curve is drawn under the assumption that as francs become cheaper, total spending on Swiss goods and assets will increase. Therefore, the supply curve is upward sloping: As the value of the dollar increases, more dollars will be supplied to the currency market in exchange for francs.

The demand curve represents the quantity demanded of dollars in exchange for francs. Individuals or firms in Switzerland that want to buy U.S. goods or assets must trade francs for dollars. For example, to visit Disneyland, a Swiss family must exchange francs for dollars. As the exchange rate falls, dollars become cheaper in terms of francs. This makes U.S. goods and assets less expensive for Swiss residents because each Swiss franc buys more U.S. dollars. As U.S. goods and assets become cheaper, we assume that more Swiss residents will want to trade francs for dollars. Therefore, the demand curve is downward sloping: Total demand for dollars will increase as the price of the dollar falls, or depreciates, against the franc.

Equilibrium in the market for foreign exchange occurs where the demand curve intersects the supply curve. In Figure 18.1, this occurs at an exchange rate of 2 francs/dollar. At this price, the willingness to trade dollars for francs just matches the willingness to trade francs for dollars. The foreign exchange market is in balance.

Changes in Demand or Supply

Changes in demand or changes in supply will change equilibrium exchange rates. In Figure 18.2, we show how an increase in demand, a shift of the demand curve to the right, will increase, or appreciate, the exchange rate. U.S. dollars will become more expensive relative to Swiss francs as the price of U.S. dollars in terms of francs increases.

Two factors will shift the demand curve for dollars: First, higher U.S. interest rates will lead to an increased demand for dollars. With higher returns in U.S. markets, investors throughout the world will want to buy dollars to invest in U.S. assets. The other factor, lower U.S. prices, will also lead to an increased demand for dollars. For example, if prices at Disneyland fell, there would be an overall increase in the demand for dollars because more tourists would want to visit Disneyland.

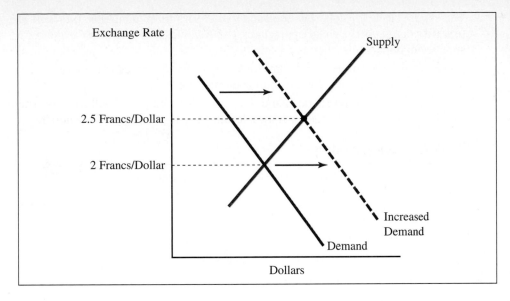

Figure 18.2

Shifts in Demand for Dollars
An increase in the demand for dollars will increase (appreciate) the exchange rate. Higher U.S. interest rates or lower U.S. prices will increase the demand for dollars.

Figure 18.3 shows the effects of an increase in the supply of dollars, a shift in the supply curve to the right. An increase in the supply of dollars will lead to a fall, or depreciation, of the value of the dollar against the franc. What will cause the supply of dollars to increase? Again, the same two factors: interest rates and prices. Higher Swiss interest rates will lead U.S. investors to purchase Swiss bonds or other interest-paying assets. Purchasing Swiss bonds will require U.S. investors to supply dollars for francs, which will drive down the exchange rate for dollars. Lower Swiss prices will also lead to an increase in the supply of dollars for francs.

Let's summarize the key facts about the foreign exchange market, using Swiss francs as our example:

1. The demand curve for dollars represents the demand for dollars in exchange for francs. It is downward sloping. As the dollar depreciates, there will be an increase in the quantity demanded of dollars in exchange for francs.

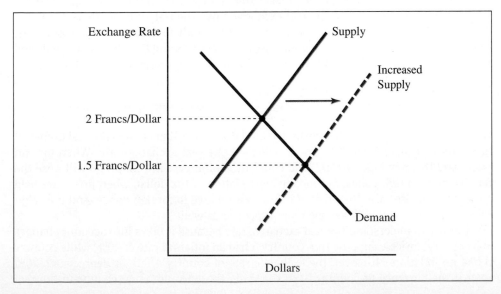

Figure 18.3

Shifts in the Supply of Dollars
An increase in the supply of dollars will decrease (depreciate) the exchange rate. Higher Swiss interest rates or lower Swiss prices will increase the supply of dollars.

2. The supply curve for dollars is the supply of dollars in exchange for francs. It is upward sloping. As the dollar appreciates, there will be an increase in the quantity supplied of dollars in exchange for francs.

3. Increases in U.S. interest rates and decreases in U.S. prices will increase the demand for dollars, leading to an appreciation of the dollar.

4. Increases in Swiss interest rates and decreases in Swiss prices will increase the supply of dollars in exchange for francs, leading to a depreciation of the dollar.

TEST Your Understanding

Use demand and supply analysis to determine whether the dollar will appreciate or depreciate against the franc in each of these cases.

1. Banks cut interest rates in Switzerland.

2. Interest rates fall in the United States.

3. Annual inflation increases from 4% to 6% in the United States.

4. The Swiss inflation rate falls from 5% to 3% per year.

Real Exchange Rates and Purchasing Power Parity

As our examples of Swiss watches and Disneyland indicate, changes in market exchange rates can affect the demand for a country's goods and services. However, we have been assuming that the prices of watches and trips to Disneyland do not change. In general, prices change over time, and we need to adjust the exchange rate determined in the foreign exchange market to take into account changes in prices. This is an application of the reality principle.

Reality **PRINCIPLE**

What matters to people is the real value of money or income—its purchasing power—not the face value of money or income.

Real exchange rate: The market exchange rate adjusted for prices.

Economists have developed a concept that adjusts the market exchange rates for changes in prices. It is called the real exchange rate. The **real exchange rate** is defined as the price of all U.S. goods and services relative to all foreign goods and services, expressed in a common currency. We measure it by expressing U.S. prices for goods and services in foreign currency and comparing them to foreign prices. Here is the formula for the real exchange rate:

real exchange rate = (exchange rate × U.S. price index)/foreign price index

We can use this formula to help us understand the factors that change the real exchange rate. First, an increase in U.S. prices will raise the real exchange rate. When foreign prices and the exchange rate are held constant, an increase in U.S. prices will raise the relative price of U.S. goods. Second, an appreciation of the dollar, when prices are held constant, will also raise the price of U.S. goods relative to foreign goods. And if foreign prices fall, U.S. goods will become more expensive as well.

Be sure to understand the real exchange rate because it takes into account changes in a country's prices. Suppose that country A had an inflation rate of 20%, while country B had no inflation. Moreover, the exchange rate of country A fell, or depreciated, 20% against the currency of country B. In this case, there would be no change in the real exchange rate between the two countries. Although prices in country A would have increased by 20%, its currency would be 20% cheaper. From the point of view of residents of country B, nothing has changed at all; it would still cost them the same price in their currency to buy goods in country A.

Economists have found that a country's net exports (exports minus its imports) will decrease when its real exchange rate increases. For example, if the U.S. real exchange rate increases, the prices of U.S. goods will increase relative to foreign goods. This will reduce U.S. exports because our goods will have become more expensive; it will also increase imports to the United States because foreign goods will have become cheaper. As a result of the decrease in U.S. exports and the increase in U.S. imports, net exports will decline.

Figure 18.4 plots an index of the real exchange rate for the United States against net exports as a share of GDP for 1980 to 2000, a period in which there were large changes in net exports and in the real exchange rate. The index is based on an average of real exchange rates with all U.S. trading partners; it's called a **multilateral real exchange rate**. Notice that when the multilateral real exchange rate increased, U.S. net exports fell. As you can see in the figure, both in 1984 and 1996 the real exchange rate increased sharply. Subsequently, net exports as a share of GDP fell. The relationship between the real exchange rate and net exports is not perfect—other factors also affect net exports.

Multilateral real exchange rate: An index of the real exchange rate with a country's trading partners.

Real exchange rates vary over time, as shown in Figure 18.4. But for goods traded easily across countries (such as gold bars), we would expect the price to be the same when expressed in a common currency. For example, the price of gold bars sold in France should be nearly identical to the price of gold bars sold in New York. If the price were higher in France, demand would shift to New York, raising the price in New York and lowering the price in France until the prices were equal.

The tendency for easily tradable goods to sell at the same price when expressed in a common currency is known as the **law of one price**. Metals, agricultural commodities, computer chips, and other tradable goods follow the law of one price.

Law of one price: The theory that goods that are easily tradable across countries should sell at the same price, expressed in a common currency.

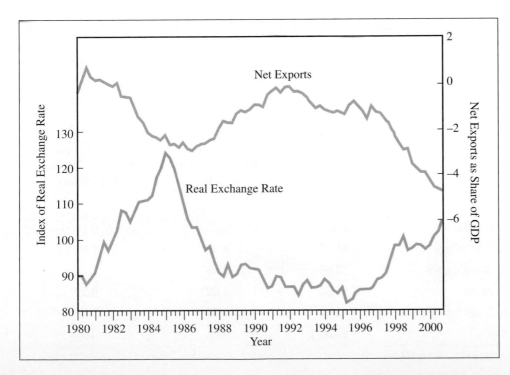

Figure 18.4
Real Exchange Rate and Net Exports as Share of GDP, 1980–2000

Source: Department of Commerce and Federal Reserve.

If all goods were easily tradable and the law of one price held exactly, exchange rates would reflect no more than the differences in the way the price levels are expressed in the two countries. For example, if a basket of goods in Switzerland costs 3,000 francs and the identical basket costs $1,000 in the United States, an exchange rate of 3 francs/dollar would make the costs the same in either currency.

According to one theory of how market exchange rates are determined, market exchange rates simply reflect differences in the overall price levels between countries. This theory is known as **purchasing power parity**. In our Switzerland-United States example, the theory of purchasing power parity predicts a market exchange rate of 3 francs/dollar. At that exchange rate, Swiss and U.S. goods would sell for the same price if their products were expressed in a common currency.

Purchasing power parity: A theory of exchange rates stating that the exchange rate between two currencies is determined by the price levels in those two countries.

Research has shown that purchasing power parity does not hold precisely. An example of this has been created by *The Economist* magazine, which measured the price of a Big Mac throughout the world and checked to see whether the law of one price held. Table 18.1 contains the results for selected countries.

Big Macs sell for widely different prices around the globe compared to the $2.54 they go for in the United States. They are a bargain in Hong Kong at $1.37 but expensive in Switzerland at $3.65. The price in Japan of $2.38 is nearly the same as the price in the United States.

Table 18.1 also contains the market exchange rate predicted by the theory of purchasing power parity. To obtain this exchange rate, divide the price of Big Macs in the foreign country by the dollar price. For example, in Hong Kong the purchasing power exchange rate is

4.21 HK dollars/U.S. dollars (10.7 HK dollars/$2.54 = 4.21 HK dollars/U.S. dollars)

At this exchange rate, the Big Mac in Hong Kong would cost the same as in the United States. The actual exchange rate for the HK dollar in April 2001 when these prices were computed was 7.80 HK dollars/U.S. dollar, so the Big Mac was cheaper in Hong Kong.

Clearly, purchasing power parity does not give accurate predictions for exchange rates. The reason is that many goods are not traded across countries. For example, housing and services (such as haircuts) are not traded across countries. The law of one price

Table 18.1 The Big Mac Around the World

Country	Price of a Big Mac in Local Currency	Price of a Big Mac in Dollars	Predicted Purchasing Power Exchange Rate (Foreign Currency per Dollar)	Actual Exchange Rate (Foreign Currency per Dollar)
United States	2.54 dollars	$2.54		
United Kingdom	1.99 pounds	$2.85	0.78	0.70
Hong Kong	10.7 HK dollars	$1.37	4.21	7.80
Switzerland	6.30 Swiss francs	$3.65	2.48	1.73
Mexico	21.9 pesos	$2.36	8.62	9.29
Singapore	3.30 Singapore dollars	$1.82	1.30	1.81
Japan	294 yen	$2.38	116	124

Source: Data from *The Economist*, April 21, 2001, p. 74.

does not hold for nontraded goods, which make up approximately 50% of the value of production in an economy. There is some truth to purchasing power parity because exchange rates do reflect differences in the price level between countries. But as the Big Mac example shows, purchasing power parity is not a reliable guide to exchange rate levels when nontraded goods must be considered.

Economists have successfully used purchasing power parity theory in other settings. Countries that had been experiencing hyperinflation but then brought the inflation to a halt often need assistance in setting an appropriate exchange rate. Purchasing power parity provides a reasonable guide in such cases. Problems associated with nontraded goods are negligible compared to the vast increases in the price level caused by the hyperinflation.

TEST Your Understanding

5. What is the key difference between the real exchange rate and the market exchange rate? Why should we care?

6. Explain why gold bars sell for the same price around the world but Big Macs do not.

The Current Account and the Capital Account

Economists find it useful to divide international transactions into two types: One is called the current account, and the other is called the capital account. A country's **current account** is the sum of its

- net exports (exports minus imports),
- net income received from investments abroad, and
- net transfer payments from abroad (such as foreign aid).

If a country has a positive current account, we say that its current account is in surplus; if it has a negative current account, we say that its current account is in deficit. If the income from investments abroad and net transfer payments is negligible, the current account becomes equivalent to a country's net exports.

We measure a country's transactions in existing assets on its capital account. The **capital account** is defined as the value of the country's net sales (sales less purchases) of assets. If the United States sold $100 billion net in assets, its capital account would be $100 billion. If the value on the capital account is positive, we say that the country has a surplus on the capital account. Similarly, if the value on the capital account is negative, we say that it has a deficit on the capital account.

Here is a simple rule for understanding transactions on both the current account and on the capital account: Any action that gives rise to a demand for foreign currency is a deficit item on the current account or on the capital account. Any action that gives rise to a supply of foreign currency is a surplus item on the current account or on the capital account.

Let's apply this rule to the current account and the capital account, taking the point of view of the United States.

1. Current account. A U.S. import is a deficit (negative) item on the current account because we need to demand foreign currency to acquire the import. On the other hand, with a U.S. export, foreign currency is supplied to the United States in exchange for dollars, so it gives rise to a surplus (positive item) on the current account. Income from

Current account: The sum of net exports (exports minus imports) plus net income received from investments abroad plus net transfers from abroad.

Capital account: The value of a country's sales less purchases of assets. A sale of a domestic asset is a surplus item on the capital account, while a purchase of a foreign asset is a deficit item on the capital account.

investments abroad and net transfers received are treated like exports because they result in a supply of foreign currency for dollars. Summarizing, we have

$$\text{U.S. current account surplus} = \text{U.S. exports} - \text{U.S. imports}$$
$$+ \text{ net income from foreign investments}$$
$$+ \text{ net transfers from abroad}$$

2. Capital account. The purchase of a foreign asset by a U.S. resident gives rise to a deficit (negative) item on the capital account because it requires a demand for foreign currency. (You can think of the purchase of a foreign asset as importing assets.) On the other hand, a purchase of a U.S. asset by a foreign resident leads to a supply of foreign currency and a surplus (positive) item on the current account. (This can be thought of as exporting assets.) Summarizing, we have

$$\text{U.S. capital account surplus} = \text{ foreign purchases of U.S. assets}$$
$$- \text{ U.S. purchases of foreign assets}$$

The current account and the capital account of a country are linked by a very important identity:

$$\text{current account } + \text{ capital account } = 0$$

The current account plus the capital account must sum to zero.

The current account and the capital account must sum to zero because any excess demand for foreign currency that arises from transactions in goods and services—that means we're looking at the current account—must be met by an excess supply of foreign currency arising from asset transactions—the capital account. For example, if the United States had a current account deficit of $50 billion, it would have an excess demand of foreign exchange of $50 billion. This excess demand could be met only by a supply of foreign exchange from $50 billion of net purchases of U.S. assets. The $50 billion net purchase of U.S. assets is a $50 billion surplus on the U.S. capital account. So the current account deficit is offset by the capital account surplus.

Let's look at this from a slightly different angle. Consider again the case in which the United States is running a current account deficit because imports from abroad exceed exports. (For simplicity, transfers and income earned from investments abroad are both zero.) The current account deficit means that, on net, foreign residents and their governments are the recipients of dollars because they have sold more goods to the United States than they have purchased.

What do they do with these dollars? They can either hold them or use them to purchase U.S. assets. In either case, foreign residents and their governments have acquired U.S. assets, either dollars or other U.S. assets. The value of these assets is the U.S. current account deficit. Because a sale of a U.S. asset to a foreign resident is a surplus item on the U.S. capital account, the value of the capital account will be equal to the negative of the value of the current account. So from this perspective also, the current account and the capital account must sum to zero.

If a country runs a current account surplus, it acquires foreign exchange. It can either keep the foreign exchange or use it to buy foreign assets. In either case, its purchases of net foreign assets will equal its current account surplus. Because the capital account is the negative of the purchases of net foreign assets, the current account and capital account will again sum to zero.

Since 1982, the United States has run a current account deficit every year. This means that the United States has run a capital account surplus of equal value for these years as well. Because a capital account surplus means that foreign nations acquire a

Table 18.2   U.S. Current Account and Capital Account, 1999 (billions)

Current account	
Goods	–345
Services	80
Net investment income	–18
Net transfers	–48
Total on current account	–331
Capital account	
Increases in U.S. holdings abroad	–434
Increases in foreign holdings in U.S.	754
Total on capital account	320
Statistical discrepancy	11
Sum of current account, capital account, and statistical discrepancy	0

Source: Economic Report of the President (Washington, DC: U.S. Government Printing Office, 2001).

country's assets, the United States has reduced its net holding of foreign assets. In 1986, the U.S. Department of Commerce estimated that the United States had a **net international investment position** of $136 billion, meaning that U.S. holdings of foreign assets exceeded foreign holdings of U.S. assets by $136 billion. Because of its current account deficits, the U.S. net international investment position fell every year. By 1999, it was –$1,474 billion, meaning that foreign residents owned $1,474 billion more U.S. assets than U.S. residents owned foreign assets. You may have heard the United States referred to as a net debtor; this is just another way of saying that the U.S. net international investment position is negative.

Net International Investment position: Domestic holdings of foreign assets minus foreign holdings of domestic assets.

Table 18.2 shows the current account and capital account for the United States for 1999. The current account is made up of the balance in goods, services, net investment income, and net transfers. In 1999, all elements of the current account but the service component were negative. The capital account includes net increases in U.S. holdings abroad (negative entries in the capital account) and foreign holdings of U.S. assets (positive entries in the capital account). Because the current account and capital account data are collected separately, there is a statistical discrepancy. Once we include this statistical discrepancy, the current account and the capital account sum to zero.

The capital account is defined to include purchases and sales of assets by governments as well as private individuals. As you will see next, governments often buy or sell foreign exchange to influence the exchange rate for their currency.

Fixing the Exchange Rate

When a country's exchange rate appreciates—increases in value—it has 2 distinct effects:

1. The increased value of the exchange rate makes imports less expensive for the residents of the country where the exchange rate appreciated. For example, if the U.S. dollar appreciates against the Swiss franc, Swiss watches will become less expensive for U.S. consumers. U.S. consumers would like an appreciated dollar, because it would lower their cost of living.

2. The increased value of the exchange rate makes U.S. goods more expensive on world markets. A U.S. exchange appreciation will increase imports, such as Swiss watches, but decrease exports, such as California wine.

Since exports decrease and imports increase, net exports (exports minus imports) will decrease.

When a country's exchange rate depreciates, there are 2 distinct effects:

- For example, if the U.S. dollar depreciated against the Japanese yen, Japanese imports would become more expensive in the United States, thereby raising the U.S. cost of living.

- At the same time, U.S. goods would become cheaper on world markets. With exports increasing and imports decreasing, net exports would increase.

Sometimes countries do not want their exchange rate to change. They may want to avoid sharp increases in their cost of living from an exchange rate depreciation, or they may want to avoid a reduction in net exports through an exchange rate appreciation. To prevent the value of the currency from changing, governments can enter the foreign exchange market to try to influence the price of foreign exchange. Economists call these efforts to influence the value of foreign exchange **foreign exchange market intervention**.

Foreign exchange market intervention: The purchase or sale of currencies by governments to influence the market exchange rate.

In the United States, the Treasury Department has the official responsibility for foreign exchange intervention, though in conjunction with the Federal Reserve. In other countries, governments also intervene in the foreign exchange market.

To influence the price at which one currency trades for another, governments have to affect the demand or supply for that currency. For example, to increase the value of its currency, a government must increase the demand for its currency; to decrease the value of its currency, a government must increase the supply of its currency.

In Figure 18.5, we show how governments can fix, or peg, the price of a currency. Suppose the U.S. and Swiss governments want the exchange rate to be 2 francs/dollar. The price at which demand and supply are equal, however, is currently 1.5 francs/dollar. To raise the price of dollars, the governments need to increase the demand for dollars. To do this, either government—the United States or Switzerland—or both can go into the

Figure 18.5

Intervention to Raise the Price of Dollars

To increase the price of dollars, the U.S. government sells francs in exchange for dollars. This shifts the demand curve for dollars to the right.

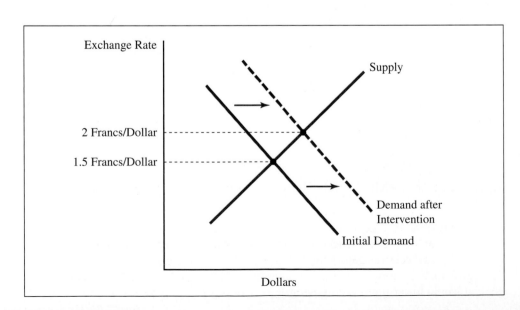

market for foreign exchange and sell francs in exchange for dollars. This will shift the demand curve for dollars to the right until the price of dollars rises to 2 francs/dollar.

In the other direction, if the free market price exceeded 2 francs/dollar, the governments would have to buy francs in exchange for dollars. By selling dollars in exchange for francs, they would increase the supply of dollars and the exchange rate would fall.

Note that to lower the price of dollars, which raises the value of the franc, the U.S. government has to buy francs in exchange for dollars. The U.S. government therefore acquires and accumulates francs anytime it tries to raise the price of francs. On the other hand, the U.S. government must sell some of the francs it has accumulated, to raise the price of dollars, which lowers the value of the franc. What would happen if the United States had no francs to sell? The United States could borrow francs from the Swiss government or persuade Switzerland to sell francs for dollars.

Fixed Versus Flexible Exchange Rates

Next, we discuss two different types of exchange rate systems. Then we take a brief look at the U.S. history on exchange rate policy and developments in exchange rates in the world today.

Fixed Exchange Rates

Whether you are in California, New York, or Indiana, all prices are quoted in dollars. No one asks whether your dollar came from San Francisco or Miami. Within the United States, a dollar is a dollar. Suppose, though, that every state in the United States had its own currency. There might be a California dollar (with a picture of the Golden Gate Bridge), an Oregon dollar (showing pictures of tall trees), and a Florida dollar (showing Disney World, of course). In principle, these dollars might trade at different rates, depending on the supply and demand of one state's dollar relative to the supply and demand for another state's dollar. For example, in one year, the Texas dollar might be worth more than the Michigan dollar, trading for 1.2 Michigan dollars.

Think how much more complicated it would be to do business if each state had different currencies. To buy goods from a mail-order company in Maine, you would have to find out the exchange rate between your state's dollar and the Maine dollar. Any large business operating in all 50 states would be overwhelmed by trying to keep track of all exchange rate movements across the states. The economy would become less efficient as individuals and businesses focused all their attention on exchange rates.

These same ideas apply across nations. Wouldn't it be nice if all countries either used the same currency or fixed their exchange rates against one another so that no one would have to worry about exchange rate movements? Currency systems in which governments try to keep constant the values of their currencies against one another are called **fixed exchange rate** systems.

In a typical fixed exchange rate system, one country stands at the center, and other countries fix, or peg, their exchange rates to the currency of this center country. Each other country must intervene in the foreign exchange market, if necessary, to keep its exchange rate constant. A government will have to intervene if, at the fixed exchange rate, the private demand and supply for its currency are not equal.

Suppose the supply of a country's currency exceeds the demand at the fixed exchange rate. An excess supply of a country's currency at the fixed exchange rate is known as a **balance of payments deficit**. A balance of payments deficit will occur whenever there is a deficit on the current account that is not matched by net sales of assets to foreigners by the private sector. (For example, a current account deficit of $100 billion with

Fixed exchange rates: A system in which governments peg exchange rates between currencies.

Balance of payments deficit: Under a fixed exchange rate system, a situation in which the supply of a country's currency exceeds the demand for the currency at the current exchange rate.

net sales of assets to foreigners of only $80 billion would mean that there is an excess supply of $20 billion.) With an excess supply of a country's currency in the currency market, that currency would fall in value without any intervention. To prevent the currency from depreciating in value and to maintain the fixed exchange rate, the government must sell foreign exchange—that means sell foreign currency—and buy its own currency. As you saw in our discussion of foreign exchange intervention, if a country sells foreign exchange, its holdings of foreign exchange will fall. So you can see that when a country runs a balance of payments deficit, it will decrease its holdings of foreign exchange.

It's also very possible that the demand for a country's currency exceeds the supply of its currency at the fixed exchange rate. An excess demand for a country's currency at the fixed exchange rate is known as a **balance of payments surplus**. A balance of payments surplus arises when there is a current account surplus that is not matched by net purchases of foreign assets by the private sector. With an excess demand for a country's currency, it would rise in value without any intervention. To prevent the currency from appreciating in value and to maintain the fixed exchange rate, the government must buy foreign exchange—buy foreign currency—and sell its own currency. Because it is buying foreign exchange, its holdings of foreign exchange will increase. From this discussion, you should be able to see that when a country runs a balance of payments surplus, it will increase its holding of foreign exchange.

Under a fixed exchange rate system, countries that run persistent balance of payments deficits or balance of payments surpluses must take corrective actions. If domestic policy actions—such as changing taxes, changing spending, or changing the supply of money—do not cure the problem, it will eventually become necessary to change the level at which the exchange rate is fixed. A country that faces a balance of payments deficit can lower the value at which the currency is pegged to increase its net exports; this is called a **devaluation**. Conversely, a country that faces a balance of payments surplus can increase the value at which its currency is pegged and reduce its net exports; this is called a **revaluation**.

The U.S. Experience with Fixed and Flexible Exchange Rates

After World War II, the countries of the world operated under a fixed exchange system known as Bretton Woods, after the town in New Hampshire where the representatives of each nation met and agreed to adopt this system. The United States operated at the center of this system: All countries fixed or pegged their currencies against the U.S. dollar.

The Bretton Woods system lasted until the early 1970s when the world abandoned it and went to the current system—a **flexible exchange rate system**—in which free markets primarily determine exchange rates. What that means is that the exchange rate of a currency is determined by the supply and demand for it.

If a fixed exchange rate system makes it easier to trade, why did it break down in the early 1970s? Fixed exchange rate systems provide benefits, but they require countries to maintain similar economic policies—especially to maintain similar inflation rates and interest rates.

To understand this, suppose the exchange rate between the United States and Germany were fixed, but the United States had an annual inflation rate of 6% compared to 0% inflation in Germany. Because prices in the United States would be rising by 6% per year, the U.S. real exchange rate against Germany would also be increasing at 6% per year. This difference in their real exchange rates over time would cause a trade deficit to emerge in the United States as U.S. goods became more expensive on world markets. As

Balance of payments surplus: Under a fixed exchange rate system, a situation in which the demand for a country's currency exceeds the supply of its currency at the current exchange rate.

Devaluation: A decrease in the exchange rate in a fixed exchange rate system.

Revaluation: An increase in the exchange rate in a fixed exchange rate system.

Flexible exchange rates: A currency system in which exchange rates are determined by free markets.

long as the differences in inflation continued and the exchange rate remained fixed, the U.S. real exchange rate would continue to appreciate, and the U.S. trade deficit would grow even worse. Clearly, this course of events could not continue.

In the late 1960s, inflation in the United States began to exceed inflation in other countries, and a U.S. balance of payments deficit emerged. In 1971, President Nixon surprised the world and devalued the U.S. dollar against the currencies of all the other countries. This was a sharp departure from the rules underlying Bretton Woods, in which the United States was at the center of the system and other countries were supposed to make adjustments, if necessary, against the dollar. Nixon hoped that a one-time devaluation of the dollar would alleviate the U.S. balance of payments deficit and maintain the underlying system of fixed exchange rates.

However, the U.S. devaluation did not stop the U.S. balance of payments deficit. Germany tried to maintain the mark's fixed exchange rate with the U.S. dollar by purchasing U.S. dollars in the foreign exchange market. What Germany was doing was importing inflation from the United States. With the U.S. balance of payments deficit continuing, Germany was required to buy U.S. dollars to keep the mark from appreciating. Germany bought U.S. dollars with German marks. Those German marks were then put into circulation. The German supply of marks in Germany increased. The increase in marks raised the inflation rate in Germany.

Private-sector investors, moreover, knew that Germany did not wish to run persistent trade surpluses and import U.S. inflation. They bet that Germany would revalue the mark against the dollar—that is, raise the value of the mark against the dollar. These speculators bought massive amounts of German assets, trading dollars for marks to purchase them. Their actions forced the German government to buy even more dollars. The flow of financial capital into Germany was so massive that the German government eventually gave up all attempts to keep its exchange rate fixed to the dollar, letting its exchange rate be determined in the free market. This was the end of the Bretton Woods system.

Exchange Rate Systems Today

The flexible exchange rate system has worked well enough since the breakdown of Bretton Woods. World trade has grown at a rapid rate. Moreover, the flexible exchange rate system has managed to handle many diverse situations, including two major oil shocks, large U.S. budget deficits in the 1980s, and large current account surpluses by the Japanese.

During the Bretton Woods period, many countries placed restrictions on flows of financial capital, for example, by not allowing their residents to purchase foreign assets or by limiting foreigners' purchases of domestic assets. By the 1970s, these restrictions began to be eliminated, and private-sector transactions in assets grew rapidly. With massive amounts of funds being traded in financial markets, it becomes very difficult to fix, or peg, an exchange rate.

Nonetheless, countries whose economies are closely tied together might want the advantages of fixed exchange rates. One way to avoid some of the difficulties of fixing exchange rates between countries is to abolish individual currencies and establish a single currency. This is precisely what a group of European countries decided to do. They adopted a single currency throughout Europe and a single central bank to control the supply of the currency. The common currency has been named the **euro**. "A Closer Look: The Euro" provides more details on this system. With a single currency, European countries hope to capture the benefits of a large market, such as the market within the United States.

Euro: The common currency in Europe.

The United Kingdom initially decided to remain outside this European single-currency system. Its currency, like the U.S. dollar and the Japanese yen, will float against each of those currencies and the euro. Many other countries have tied their exchange rate to either the dollar or the yen. Some economists believe that the world will eventually settle into three large currency blocs: the euro, the dollar, and the yen.

Managing Financial Crises

Hardly a year goes by without some international financial crisis. In 1994, Mexico experienced a severe financial crisis. In 1997, the Asian economic crisis began. How do these crises originate? What policies can be taken to prevent or alleviate them?

Let's first consider the Mexican case. During the late 1980s and early 1990s, Mexico decided to fix, or peg, its exchange to the U.S. dollar. Mexico's goal was to signal to investors throughout the world that it was serious about controlling inflation and would take the necessary steps to keep its inflation rates in line with the United States. Mexico also opened up its markets to let in foreign investors. Mexico seemed to be on a solid path to development.

However, in some sense, the policies proved to be too successful in encouraging foreign investment. As funds poured into the country, the demand for goods increased, and

A CLOSER LOOK   THE EURO

January 1, 1999, was the day that the euro, the new common European currency, made its debut. On that day, Austria, Belgium, Finland, France, Germany, Ireland, Italy, Luxembourg, Netherlands, Portugal, and Spain irrevocably fixed their exchange rates to the euro. In 2002, euro notes and coins were introduced. Beginning July 1, 2002, national currencies disappeared. French francs, German marks, Italian lire, and other currencies have ceased to exist.

A European central bank manages the monetary affairs for the single currency. It plays a role similar to the role the Federal Reserve Bank plays in the United States. The countries in the European Union no longer conduct their own independent monetary policy. With monetary policy gone, fiscal policy is their only remaining tool for macroeconomic stabilization policy.

Not all the European countries joined this system. Fearing a possible loss of independence, the United Kingdom, Denmark, and Sweden decided not to join this system initially. Greece would have liked to join, but it did not meet some of the EU's fiscal criteria necessary to join. Economists will carefully watch this experiment unfold in the twenty-first century.

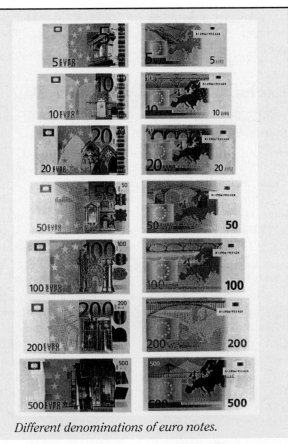

Different denominations of euro notes.

prices started to rise. This rise in prices caused an increase in Mexico's real exchange rate, and the rise in the real exchange rate caused a large trade deficit to emerge. From January 1988 to February 1994, the real exchange rate for Mexico with the United States (the price of Mexican goods relative to U.S. goods) increased by 67%.

Initially, the trade deficit did not cause any difficulties for the Mexican government. Because foreign investors were willingly trading foreign currencies for Mexican pesos to buy Mexican securities, the government in Mexico did not have any problem maintaining its pegged exchange rate with the United States. Although the Mexicans were importing more than they were exporting, they could obtain the necessary dollars to finance this trade imbalance from foreign investors who were purchasing Mexican securities. The government did not have to intervene in the foreign exchange market to keep the price of the peso constant against the dollar. In other words, Mexico did not have a balance of payments deficit.

But then, internal political difficulties arose in Mexico. Following an assassination of a political candidate and a rural uprising, foreign investors started to pull their funds out of Mexico. At this point, the Mexican government made a crucial mistake. Instead of trying to reduce its trade deficit by taking steps to reduce prices, it allowed the trade deficit to continue. Moreover, both the government and the private sector began to find that they had to borrow in dollars because foreign investors thought Mexico might be forced to devalue the peso. If a devaluation did occur, any lender in pesos would suffer a loss because the debt would be repaid at a lower exchange rate. Consequently, Mexican borrowers were forced to borrow in loans denominated in dollars.

Eventually, more political turmoil caused investors to pull out their funds, selling pesos for dollars. The Mexican central bank spent nearly $50 billion buying these pesos in an effort to keep the exchange rate constant. The $50 billion was not enough. Mexico ran out of dollars. Because it could no longer buy pesos to maintain the exchange rate, Mexico had to devalue, putting the peso more in line with its market value.

The devaluation created even more turmoil because the government and the private sector had borrowed billions in dollars. When the peso was devalued against the dollar, the burden of these debts measured in pesos increased sharply, so more pesos were needed to pay the dollar-denominated debts. Mexico faced the prospect of massive bankruptcies and the potential collapse of its economy.

To prevent a financial collapse that could easily have spread to many other developing countries, the U.S. government (along with other international financial institutions) arranged for Mexico to borrow dollars with an extended period for repayment. This allowed Mexican banks and corporations to avoid bankruptcies and prevented a major disaster. In 1996, the Mexican government was able to pay off nearly three-fourths of the loan from the United States.

The Asian crisis had a similar flavor. Economic growth had been remarkable in Asia for over 20 years, improving to a great extent the standard of living of millions of people. In the early 1990s, several Asian countries began to open up their capital markets to foreign investors and began to borrow extensively from abroad. Billions of dollars poured into Asia. In many cases, there was little financial supervision, and many of the investments proved to be unwise. Companies in both Thailand and South Korea began to lose money. Domestic investors and world investors suddenly became pessimistic and began pulling their funds out of South Korea and Thailand, among other Asian countries. The withdrawal of funds forced devaluations of currencies throughout Asia. Because many businesses had borrowed in dollars, the devaluations raised the burden of the debt and further deepened the crisis, taking its toll on other countries, including Indonesia, Malaysia, and Hong Kong. The International Monetary Fund attempted to help restore the health of these economies' financial systems, but in many cases, their policies were ineffective. The countries that undertook fiscal reforms were the quickest to recover. As

Some economists believe that the Asian crisis could have been avoided if major countries and international agencies had taken stronger action, such as large loans. Although some problems were emerging in Asia, these economists believed that the economies in Asia were fundamentally sound. However, they had borrowed extensively, and their short-term debts exceeded the foreign exchange reserves they had on hand. That made the countries *illiquid* (not having enough currency on hand) but not *insolvent* (bankrupt). In some ways, their situation was analogous to banks that never keep enough currency on hand to meet the immediate demands of their depositors.

Pursuing the banking analogy, these economists argue that the world needs a lender of last resort to prevent these crises from emerging. Such a lender (backed by the world's financial powers) could prevent unnecessary crises. However, other economists and world leaders are skeptical that such a lender would routinely be able to outguess the private markets in assessing the underlying health of the world economies. Moreover, the sums involved are so large in today's market that they could produce unacceptable risks for major financial powers.

"A Closer Look: Unnecessary Crisis?" indicates, some economists believe that the entire Asian crisis was an example of market overreaction and could have been avoided by bolder action.

These examples highlight many of the ingredients of a financial crisis. With our vast global capital markets, funds can move quickly from country to country, and economic policies sometimes do not keep pace with changing political and economic developments. It can be extremely difficult to maintain a fixed exchange rate in this environment. The flow of funds, moreover, is often so large that financial failures could cause major global disruptions in trade and commerce. The major countries of the world are searching for a reliable set of rules and institutional mechanisms to assist in financial crises. Historically, the International Monetary Fund has played a key role in assisting countries that run into financial difficulties. However, in Mexico, the sums were so large that the United States was forced to take the lead in resolving its situation. In Asia, the International Monetary Fund did not have this backing from the United States, and it was less successful. As world capital markets continue to grow, governments throughout the world will almost surely be tested through new and often unpredictable financial crises. They will need to anticipate and react to rapid changes in the economic and political environment to maintain a stable financial environment for trade.

Using the **TOOLS**

In this chapter, we developed several tools, including the demand and supply for foreign exchange, and the real exchange rate. Take this opportunity to do your own economic analysis.

1. ECONOMIC EXPERIMENT: Determining Exchange Rates

In this experiment, you will see how exchange rates are determined. The class is divided into two groups. One group will be buying a fixed number of Swiss francs. The other group will be selling a fixed number of Swiss francs. Each buyer will have a maximum price that he or she is willing to pay. Each seller will have a minimum price that he or she is willing to accept. Trade will take place in several rounds. In each round, buyers and sellers will meet individually and either negotiate a trade or not. If a trade results, the results will be reported to the instructor and then announced to the class. After each round, the instructor announces the prices at which Swiss francs were traded. After several rounds, what happens to the prices?

APPLICATIONS
2. The Real Exchange Rate Between Germany and the United States
Consider the following data for the United States and Germany:

Year	Germany GDP Deflator	U.S. GDP Deflator	Market Exchange Rate
1980	85.7	76.0	2.49 marks/dollar
1990	113.4	119.6	2.12 marks/dollar

a. By what percent did the dollar depreciate against the mark over this period?

b. Using the formula for the real exchange rate,

real exchange rate = (exchange rate × U.S. price index)/foreign price index

compute the real exchange rate for 1980 and for 1990.

c. By how much did the real exchange rate change over this period? Compare your answer to part (a).

3. Exchange Rate Depreciation and the Returns from Investing
A newspaper headline said, "Foreign Investors Fear Dollar Depreciation: U.S. Interest Rates Rise."

a. Suppose you were a Swiss citizen and had invested in a 1-year U.S. bond that yielded 6% per year. The bond cost $1,000 and paid $1,060 at the end of the year. At the time you bought the bond, the exchange rate was 2 francs/dollar. How many francs did the bond cost? If the exchange rate remained at 2 francs/dollar when you received your payment, how many francs would you have? What would be your percentage return in francs for the year?

b. Suppose the dollar fell against the franc during the year from 2 francs to 1.5 francs/dollar. At the end of the year how many francs would you have? What would be your percentage return in francs for the year?

c. Using your answers to parts (a) and (b), explain the newspaper headline.

4. Pressures on the Bank of England
During the late 1980s, the United Kingdom had fixed exchange rates with other countries in Europe, including Germany. To fight inflationary pressures after East Germany and West Germany were reunited, the Germany central bank raised interest rates sharply.

a. Let's figure out why the United Kingdom had to raise interest rates along with Germany. First, if the United Kingdom did not raise interest rates, what would investors do with their funds? Second, what effect would this movement of funds have had on the British pound? To prevent these changes in the British pound, what would the British central bank have had to do?

b. In fact, speculators in foreign exchange believed that the Bank of England would not raise interest rates. Why did speculators sell British pounds in massive amounts? Why did this force the British government to abandon its fixed exchange rate with Germany?

Summary

In this chapter, we examined the world of international finance. You saw how exchange rates are determined in markets and how governments can influence these markets. You also learned how the real exchange rate affects the trade deficit. Behind the complex world of international financial transactions are these few simple ideas:

1. Exchange rates are currently determined in foreign exchange markets by supply and demand.

2. The real exchange rate—the market exchange rate adjusted for prices—is the relative price of a country's goods and services on world markets.

3. The current account and the capital account are related as follows:
   - The current account is equal to net exports plus net income from existing investments abroad and net transfers from abroad.

- The capital account is the value of a country's sales less purchases of assets.
- The sum of the current account plus the capital account is zero.

4. Governments can attempt to change the value of currencies by buying or selling currencies in the foreign exchange market. Purchasing a currency will raise its value; selling a currency will decrease its value.

5. A system of fixed exchange rates can provide a better environment for business but requires that countries keep their inflation rates and interest rates within narrow limits.

Key Terms

appreciation, 370
balance of payments deficit, 381
balance of payments surplus, 382
capital account, 377
current account, 377
depreciation, 370
devaluation, 382

euro, 383
exchange rate, 370
fixed exchange rates, 381
flexible exchange rates, 382
foreign exchange market Intervention, 380
law of one price, 375

multilateral real exchange rate, 375
net international investment position, 379
purchasing power parity, 376
real exchange rate, 375
revaluation, 382

Problems and Discussion Questions

1. Using demand and supply analysis to assist you, what are the effects on the exchange rate between the British pound and the Japanese yen from:
   a. an increase in Japanese interest rates
   b. an increase in the price of British goods
   c. an increase in British interest rates

2. Let's estimate the exchange rate between the United States and the imaginary country of Oz. Your only information is that a Big Mac costs $2.50 in the United States and 30 ozzies in Oz. What is your estimate of the exchange rate between the dollar and the ozzie?

3. Suppose that a South American country saw its exchange rate depreciate 10% against the dollar and that prices in that country rose 12% while

prices in the United States did not change. What happened to the real exchange rate between the South American country and the United States?

4. A country had exports of $20 billion, imports of $25 billion, net transfers from abroad of –$15 billion, and –$12 billion of net income from foreign investments. What is the country's balance on the current account?

5. A country ran a current account deficit last year (measured in dollars) of $25 billion. What was its balance on the capital account?

6. Suppose the United States reported that the U.S. Treasury had increased its holdings of foreign currencies from last year. What does this tell you about the foreign exchange policies in which the United States had engaged during the last year?

7. There are rumors that there is about to be a military coup in an Eastern European country. Explain what you think will happen to the country's exchange rate.

8. What would be required before all the countries of the world could enter into a fixed exchange rate system? Do you think it is feasible?

9. Why did inflation in Mexico lead to a rise in the real exchange rate between Mexico and the United States?

10. Explain why apartments rent for different prices around the world while gold bars sell for the same price (measured in a common currency).

11. When a country depreciates its currency, initially its competitiveness in world markets increases. Then why are countries often reluctant to depreciate their currencies?

12. Until the early 1980s, Japan had required its large insurance companies to invest all their vast holdings in Japanese securities. At the prompting of the United States, Japan relaxed the restrictions and allowed the companies to invest anywhere in the world. What effect do you think this had on the yen/dollar exchange rate and the trade balance between the two countries?

13. **Web Exercise.** What are the key policy issues facing the European Central Bank? Go to the Web site of the European Central Bank [*http://www.ecb.int*]. Outline the three most important issues that are currently being debated.

14. **Web Exercise.** Use the Web to find data for a U.S. price index, a Japanese price index, and the yen/dollar exchange rate. You might start with the Web site for the Federal Reserve Bank of St. Louis [*http://www.stls.frb.org/fred*] for U.S. prices and the yen/dollar exchange rate and the Web site for the Japan Statistical Yearbook [*http://www.stat.go.jp/english/1431.htm*] for data on Japan. What has happened to the real exchange rate between the United States and Japan over the last 10 years?

Take It to the Net

We invite you to visit the O'Sullivan/Sheffrin page on the Prentice Hall Web site at: **http://www.prenhall.com/osullivan/** for additional World Wide Web exercises for this chapter.

Model Answers for This Chapter

Chapter-Opening Questions

1. An increase in U.S. interest rates will raise the value of the dollar against the Swiss franc. This increase in value of the dollar against the franc will decrease the cost for U.S. residents of a summer trip to Europe.

2. If the dollar increases in value against the Japanese yen, it will make our exports more expensive and Japanese imports less expensive. This dollar increase against the yen will reduce our trade balance with Japan.

3. Governments intervene in the market for foreign exchange because they prefer to have a different exchange rate than the one that would come from pure market transactions.

4. Many European countries have adopted a single currency because they believe that a single large market with no worries of exchange rate changes will reduce the costs of trade.

5. Financial crises emerge when private investors suddenly wish to withdraw funds from a country and, as a result, disrupt current financial arrangements.

Test Your Understanding

1. The dollar will appreciate.

2. The dollar will depreciate.

3. The dollar will depreciate.

4. The dollar will depreciate.

5. The nominal exchange rate is the market exchange rate; the real exchange rate adjusts for changes in the prices. The trade balance is related to the real exchange rate, not the market exchange rate.

6. Gold bars are easily transported and, unlike Big Macs, are not largely made and sold with nontraded goods.

Using the Tools

2. The Real Exchange Rate Between Germany and the United States

   a. The dollar fell by 14.8% [(2.12 − 2.49)/2.49 = 0.148].

   b. The real exchange rate increased from 2.208 to 2.236.

   c. Using the formula for the real exchange, we find that the real exchange rate was 2.208 in 1980 and 2.236 in 1990. That is an increase of 1.3% from 1980 to 1990. Although the dollar depreciated, prices rose more in the United States than in Germany, so the real exchange rate actually increased.

3. Exchange Rate Depreciation and the Returns from Investing

   a. At 2 francs/dollar, the bond costs 2,000 marks and pays 2,120 francs, for a 6% return.

   b. If the dollar fell to 1.5 francs/dollar, at the end of the year you would only have (1,060)(1.5) = 1,590 francs, and your return on your 2,000-franc investment would be −20.5%.

   c. If the dollar falls, returns measured in francs will decrease and foreign investors will find dollar investments less attractive. To keep investors from withdrawing funds from the United States, interest rates would have to increase.

4. Pressures on the Bank of England

   a. If the British did not raise interest rates, investors would have sold British securities to buy German securities. This would have depreciated the pound. The British government would have been forced to sell marks for pounds, decreasing the money supply and raising British interest rates.

   b. If speculators believed that Britain would not raise interest rates, the British pound would fall against the mark. To profit from the fall in the pound, speculators would sell pounds and buy German marks. The massive selling of pounds would require either massive purchases of pounds or higher interest rates. The British were not willing to do this, so they let the pound's value be determined in the market.

Glossary

Absolute advantage: The ability of one person or nation to produce a particular good at a lower absolute cost than that of another person or nation.

Accelerator theory: The theory of investment that says current investment spending depends positively on the expected future growth of real GDP.

Acid rain: Precipitation with an acidic combination of sulfur dioxides and nitrogen oxides.

Adverse-selection problem: The uninformed side of the market must choose from an undesirable or adverse selection of goods.

Aggregate demand: The relationship between the level of prices and the quantity of real GDP demanded.

Aggregate production function: Shows how much output is produced from capital and labor.

Aggregate supply: The relationship between the level of prices and the quantity of output supplied.

Anticipated inflation: Inflation that is expected.

Appreciation: An increase in the value of a currency.

Asian Pacific Economic Cooperation (APEC) organization: An organization of 18 Asian nations that attempts to reduce trade barriers between their nations.

Assets: The uses of the funds of a bank, including loans and reserves.

Asymmetric information: One side of the market—either buyers or sellers—has better information about the good than the other.

Autarky: A situation in which each country is self-sufficient, so there is no trade.

Automatic stabilizers: Taxes and transfer payments that stabilize GDP without requiring policymakers to take explicit action.

Autonomous consumption: The part of consumption that does not depend on income.

Average-cost pricing policy: A regulatory policy under which the government picks the point on the demand curve at which price equals average cost.

Average fixed cost (AFC): Fixed cost divided by the quantity produced.

Balanced budget: The situation in which total expenditures equals total revenues.

Balance of payments deficit: Under a fixed exchange rate system, a situation in which the supply of a country's currency exceeds the demand for the currency at the current exchange rate.

Balance of payments surplus: Under a fixed exchange rate system, a situation in which the demand for a country's currency exceeds the supply of the currency at the current exchange rate.

Balance sheet: An account for a bank that shows the sources of its funds (liabilities) as well as the uses for the funds (assets).

Barter: Trading goods directly for other goods.

Benefit-tax approach: The idea that a person's tax liability should depend on his or her benefits from government programs.

Board of Governors of the Federal Reserve: The seven-person governing body of the Federal Reserve system in Washington, DC.

Bond: A promise or IOU to pay money in the future in exchange for money now.

Budget deficit: The difference between a government's spending and its revenues from taxation.

Budget line: The line connecting all the combinations of two goods that exhaust a consumer's budget.

Budget set: A set of points that includes all the combinations of two goods that a consumer can afford, given the consumer's income and the prices of the two goods.

Business cycles: Another name for economic fluctuations.

Capital: See *physical capital*; see *human capital*.

Capital account: The value of a country's sales less purchases of assets. A sale of a domestic asset is a surplus item on the capital account, while a purchase of a foreign asset is a deficit item on the capital account.

Capital deepening: Increases in the stock of capital per worker.

Carbon tax: A tax based on a fuel's carbon content.

Cartel: A group of firms that coordinate their pricing decisions, often by charging the same price.

Central bank: A banker's bank; an official bank that controls the supply of money in a country.

Centrally planned economy: An economy in which a government bureaucracy decides how much of each good to produce, how to produce the goods, and how to allocate the products among consumers.

Ceteris paribus: Latin meaning "other things being equal."

Chain index: A method for calculating changes in prices that uses data from neighboring years.

Change in demand: A change in the amount of a good demanded resulting from a change in something other than the price of the good; represented graphically by a shift of a demand curve.

Change in quantity demanded: A change in the amount of a good demanded resulting from a change in the price of the good; represented graphically by a movement along a demand curve.

Change in quantity supplied: A change in the amount of a good supplied resulting from a change in the price of the good; represented graphically by a movement along a supply curve.

Change in supply: A change in the amount of a good supplied resulting from a change in something other than the price of the good; represented graphically by a shift of the supply curve.

Classical aggregate supply curve: A vertical aggregate supply curve. It reflects the idea that in the long run, output is determined solely by the factors of production.

Classical economics: A school of thought that provides insights into the economy when it operates at or near full employment.

Closed economy: An economy without international trade.

Command-and-control policy: A pollution-control policy under which the government commands each firm to produce no more than a certain volume of pollution and controls the firm's production process by forcing the firm to use a particular pollution-control technology.

Community rating: In a given community or metropolitan area, every firm pays the same price for medical insurance.

Comparative advantage: The ability of one person or nation to produce a good at an opportunity cost that is lower than the opportunity cost of another person or nation.

Complements: Two goods for which an increase in the price of one good decreases the demand for the other good.

Concentration ratio: A measure of the degree of concentration in a market; the four-firm concentration ratio is the percentage of output produced by the four largest firms.

Constant-cost industry: An industry in which the average cost of production is constant, so the long-run supply curve is horizontal.

Consumer Price Index (CPI): A price index that measures the cost of a fixed basket of goods chosen to represent the consumption pattern of individuals.

Consumer surplus: The difference between the maximum amount a consumer is willing to pay for a product and the price the consumer pays for the product.

Consumption expenditures: Purchases of newly produced goods and services by households.

Consumption function: The relationship between the level of income and consumption spending.

Consumption possibilities curve: A curve showing the combinations of two goods that can be consumed when a nation specializes in a particular good and trades with another nation.

Consumption taxation: A system of taxation which is based on the consuption, not the income, of individuals.

Contestable market: A market in which the costs of entering and leaving are very low, so the firms in the market are constantly threatened by the entry of new firms.

Contractionary policies: Government policy actions that lead to decreases in output.

Convergence: The process by which poorer countries "catch up" with richer countries in terms of real GDP per capita.

Cost-of-living adjustments: Automatic increases in wages or other payments that are tied to a price index.

Countercyclical: Moving in the opposite direction of real GDP.

Craft union: A labor organization that includes workers from a particular occupation, for example, plumbers, bakers, or electricians.

Creative destruction: The process by which competition for monopoly profits leads to technological progress.

Cross elasticity of demand: A measure of the responsiveness of the quantity demanded to changes in the price of a related good; computed by dividing the percentage change in the quantity demanded of one good (X) by the percentage change in the price of another good (Y).

Crowding in: The increase of investment (or other component of GDP) in the long run caused by a decrease in government spending.

Crowding out: The reduction in investment (or other component of GDP) in the long run caused by an increase in government spending.

Current account: The sum of net exports (exports minus imports) plus income received from investments abroad plus net transfers from abroad.

Cyclical unemployment: The component of unemployment that accompanies fluctuations in real GDP.

Deadweight loss from monopoly: A measure of the inefficiency from monopoly; equal to the difference between the consumer surplus loss from monopoly pricing and the monopoly profit.

Deadweight loss from taxation: The difference between the total burden of a tax and the amount of revenue collected by the government; also known as excess burden.

Deficit: The excess of total expenditures over total revenues.

Demand curve: See *individual demand curve*; see *market demand curve*.

Demand schedule: A table of numbers that shows the relationship between price and quantity demanded by a consumer, ceteris paribus (other things being equal).

Dependency ratio: The ratio of the population over 65 years of age to the population between 20 and 65.

Depreciation: The wear and tear of capital as it is used in production.

Depression: The common name for a severe recession.

Devaluation: A decrease in the exchange rate to which a currency is pegged in a fixed rate system.

Diminishing returns: As one input increases while the other inputs are held fixed, output increases but at a decreasing rate.

Discount rate: The interest rate at which banks can borrow from the Fed.

Discouraged workers: Workers who left the labor force because they could not find jobs.

Diseconomies of scale: A situation in which an increase in the quantity produced increases the long-run average cost of production.

Disposable personal income: The income that flows back to households, taking into account transfers and taxes.

Dominant strategy: An action that is the best choice under all circumstances.

Double coincidence of wants: The problem in a system of barter that one person may not have what the other desires.

Dumping: A situation in which the price a firm charges in a foreign market is lower than either the price it charges in its home market or the production cost.

Duopolists' dilemma: A situation in which both firms would be better off if they both chose a high price but each chooses a low price.

Durable goods: Goods that last for a long period of time, such as household appliances.

Econometric models: Mathematical computer-based models that economists build to capture the actual dynamics of the economy.

Economic cost: Explicit costs plus implicit costs.

Economic fluctuations: Movements of GDP above or below normal trends.

Economic growth: Sustained increases in the real production of an economy over a period of time.

Economic profit: Total revenue minus the total economic cost.

Economics: The study of the choices made by people who are faced with scarcity.

Economies of scale: A situation in which an increase in the quantity produced decreases the long-run average cost of production.

Elastic demand: The price elasticity is greater than one.

Employed: People who have jobs.

Entrepreneur: A person who has an idea for a business and coordinates the production and sale of goods and services, taking risks in the process.

Entrepreneurship: Effort used to coordinate the production and sale of goods and services.

Equilibrium output: The level of GDP at which the demand for output equals the amount that is produced.

Euro: The common currency in Europe.

European Union (EU): An organization of European nations that has reduced trade barriers within Europe.

Excess burden of a tax: Another name for deadweight loss from taxation.

Excess reserves: Any additional reserves that a bank holds above required reserves.

Exchange rate: The rate at which currencies trade for one another in the market.

Expansionary policies: Government policy actions that lead to increases in output.

Expectations of inflation: The beliefs held by the public about the likely path of inflation for the future.

Expectations Phillips curve: The relationship that describes the links between inflation and unemployment, taking into account expectations of inflation.

Expected real interest rate: The nominal interest rate minus the expected inflation rate.

Experience rating: Each firm pays a different price for medical insurance, depending on the past medical bills of the firm's employees.

Explicit costs: The firm's actual cash payments for its inputs.

Export: A good produced in the home country (for example, the United States) and sold in another country.

External benefit: Another term for spillover benefit.

External cost: Another term for spillover cost.

Factors of production: Labor and capital used to produce goods and services.

Federal funds market: The market in which banks borrow and lend reserves to and from one another.

Federal Open Market Committee (FOMC): The group that decides on monetary policy; it consists of the 7 members of the Board of Governors plus 5 of 12 regional bank presidents on a rotating basis.

Federal Reserve Banks: One of 12 regional banks that are an official part of the Federal Reserve System.

Financial intermediaries: Organizations that receive funds from savers and channel them to investors.

Financial liberalization: The opening of financial markets to participants from foreign countries.

Fiscal year: The calendar on which the federal government conducts its business, which runs from October 1 to September 30.

Fixed costs: Costs that do not change as the level of activity changes.

Fixed exchange rates: A system in which governments peg exchange rates.

Flexible exchange rates: A currency system in which exchange rates are determined by free markets.

Foreign exchange market: A market in which people exchange one currency for another.

Foreign exchange market intervention: The purchase or sale of currencies by governments to influence the market exchange rate.

Franchise or licensing scheme: A policy under which the government picks a single firm to sell a particular good.

Free-rider problem: Each person will try to get the benefit of a public good without paying for it, trying to get a free ride at the expense of others who do pay.

Frictional unemployment: The part of unemployment associated with the normal workings of the economy, such as searching for jobs.

Full employment: The level of employment that occurs when the unemployment rate is at the natural rate.

Full-employment or potential output: The level of output that results when the labor market is in equilibrium.

Game tree: A graphical representation of the consequences of different strategies.

General Agreement on Tariffs and Trade (GATT): An international agreement that has lowered trade barriers between the United States and other nations.

Generational accounting: Methods that assign the tax burden of debt and other programs to different generations.

Government debt: The total of all past deficits.

Government expenditure: Spending on goods and services plus transfer payments.

Government purchases: Purchases of newly produced goods and services by all levels of government.

Grim trigger: A strategy under which a firm responds to underpricing by choosing a price so low that each firm makes zero economic profit.

Gross domestic product (GDP): The total market value of all the final goods and services produced within an economy in a given year.

GDP deflator: An index that measures how the price of goods included in GDP changes over time.

Gross investment: Actual investment purchases.

Gross national product (GNP): GDP plus net income earned abroad.

Growth accounting: A method to determine the contribution to economic growth from increased capital, labor, and technological progress.

Growth rate: The percentage rate of change of a variable.

Growth version of the quantity equation: An equation that links the growth rates of money, velocity, prices, and real output.

Guaranteed price matching: A scheme under which a firm guarantees that it will match a lower price by a competitor; also known as a meet-the-competition policy.

Horizontal Equity: The idea that people in similar economic circumstances should pay similar amounts in taxes.

Household: A group of related family members and unrelated individuals who live in the same housing unit.

Human capital: The knowledge and skills acquired by a worker through education and experience and used to produce goods and services.

Hyperinflation: An inflation rate exceeding 50% per month.

Implicit costs: The opportunity cost of nonpurchased inputs.

Imports: A good produced in a foreign country and purchased by residents of the home country (for example, the United States).

Import quota: A limit on the amount of a good that can be imported.

Income effect for price change: The change in consumption resulting from an increase in the consumer's real income.

Income effect for wage change: An increase in the wage rate raises a worker's real income, increasing the demand for leisure.

Income elasticity of demand: A measure of the responsiveness of the quantity demanded to changes in consumer income; computed by dividing the percentage change in the quantity demanded by the percentage change in income.

Increasing-cost industry: An industry in which the average cost of production increases as the industry grows, so the long-run supply curve is positively sloped.

Indifference curve: A curve showing the set of combinations of goods that generate the same level of utility or satisfaction.

Indirect taxes: Sales and excise taxes.

Individual demand curve: A curve that shows the relationship between price and quantity demanded by an individual consumer, ceteris paribus (everything else held fixed).

Individual supply curve: A curve that shows the relationship between price and quantity supplied by an individual firm, ceteris paribus (everything else held fixed).

Indivisible input: An input that cannot be scaled down to produce a small quantity of output.

Industrial union: A labor organization that includes all types of workers from a single industry, for example, steelworkers or autoworkers.

Inelastic demand: The price elasticity is less than one.

Infant industry: A new industry that is protected from foreign competitors.

Inferior good: A good for which an increase in income decreases demand.

Inflation rate: The percentage rate of change of the price level in the economy.

Input-substitution effect: The change in the quantity of labor demanded resulting from a change in the relative cost of labor.

Insecure monopoly: A monopoly faced with the possibility that a second firm will enter the market.

Inside lags: Lags in implementing policy.

Intermediate good: Goods used in the production process that are not final goods or services.

International monetary fund: An organization that works closely with national governments to promote financial policies that facilitate world trade.

Invisible hand: The term that economists use to describe how the price system can efficiently coordinate economic activity without central government intervention.

Keynesian aggregate supply curve: A relatively flat horizontal supply curve. It reflects the idea that prices do not change very much in the short run and that firms adjust production to meet demand.

Keynesian economics: A school of economic thought that provides insights into the economy when it operates away from full employment.

Keynesian fiscal policy: The use of taxes and government spending to affect the level of GDP in the short run.

Kinked demand model: A model under which firms in an oligopoly match price reductions by other firms but do not match price increases.

Kyoto Agreement: An agreement among industrial nations to reduce carbon dioxide emissions.

Labor: Human effort, including both physical and mental effort, used to produce goods and services.

Labor force: The employed plus the unemployed.

Labor-force participation rate: The fraction of the population over 16 years of age that is in the labor force.

Labor productivity: Output produced per hour of work.

Labor union: An organized group of workers; the objectives of the organization are to increase job security, improve working conditions, and increase wages and benefits.

Laffer curve: A relationship between tax rates and tax revenues that illustrates that high tax rates may not always lead to high tax revenues if high tax rates discourage economic activity.

Law of demand: The lower the price, the larger the quantity demanded, ceteris paribus (other things being equal).

Law of diminishing marginal utility: As the consumption of a particular good increases, marginal utility decreases.

Law of one price: The theory that goods easily tradeable across countries, should sell at the same price, expressed in a common currency.

Law of supply: The higher the price, the larger the quantity supplied, ceteris paribus (other things being equal).

Learning by doing: Knowledge gained during production that increases productivity.

Learning effect: The increase in a person's wage resulting from the learning of skills required for certain occupations.

Lender of last resort: A central bank is the lender of last resort, the last place, all others having failed, from which banks in emergency situations can obtain loans.

Liabilities: The sources of funds for a bank, including deposits of a financial intermediary.

Limit pricing: A scheme under which a monopolist accepts a price below the normal monopoly price to deter other firms from entering the market.

Liquid: Easily convertible to money on short notice.

Liquidity demand for money: The demand for money that represents the needs and desires individuals or firms can fill on short notice without incurring excessive costs.

Liquidity trap: A situation in which interest rates are so low, they can no longer fall.

Long run: A period of time long enough that a firm can change all the factors of production, meaning that a firm can modify its existing production facility or build a new one.

Long-run average cost (LAC): Long-run total cost divided by the quantity of output produced.

Long-run demand curve for labor: A curve showing the relationship between the wage and the quantity of labor demanded over the long run, when the number of firms in the market can change and firms already in the market can modify their production facilities.

Long-run neutrality of money: An increase in the supply of money has no effect on real interest rates, investment, or output in the long run.

Long-run market supply: A curve showing the relationship between the market price and quantity supplied by all firms in the long run.

Long-run total cost: The total cost of production in the long run when a firm is perfectly flexible in its choice of all inputs and can choose a production facility of any size.

M1: The sum of currency in the hands of the public plus demand deposits plus other checkable deposits.

M2: M1 plus other assets, including deposits in savings and loans and money market mutual funds.

Macroeconomics: The branch of economics that looks at a nation's economy as a whole.

Managed competition: A health system in which organizations such as HMOs compete for patients.

Marginal benefit: The extra benefit resulting from a small increase in some activity.

Marginal cost: The additional cost resulting from a small increase in some activity.

Marginal labor cost (marginal factor cost): The increase in total labor cost resulting from hiring one more worker.

Marginal product of labor: The change in output from one additional worker.

Marginal propensity to consume (MPC): The fraction of additional income that is spent.

Marginal propensity to import: The fraction of additional income that is spent on imports.

Marginal propensity to save (MPS): The fraction of additional income that is saved.

Marginal rate of substitution (MRS): The rate at which a consumer is willing to substitute one good for another.

Marginal revenue product of labor (MRP): The extra revenue generated from one more unit of labor; equal to price of output times the marginal product of labor.

Marginal utility: The change in utility from one additional unit of the good.

Market: An arrangement that allows buyers and sellers to exchange things. A buyer exchanges money for a product, while a seller exchanges a product for money.

Market demand curve: A curve showing the relationship between price and quantity demanded by all consumers together, ceteris paribus (other things being equal).

Market equilibrium: A situation in which the quantity of a product demanded equals the quantity supplied, so there is no pressure to change the price.

Market supply curve: A curve showing the relationship between price and quantity supplied by all producers together, ceteris paribus (other things being equal).

Market supply curve for labor: A curve showing the relationship between the wage and the quantity of labor supplied.

Marketable pollution permits: A system under which the government picks a target pollution level for a particular area, issues just enough pollution permits to meet the pollution target, and allows firms to buy and sell the permits.

Median-voter rule: A rule suggesting that the choices made by government will reflect the preferences of the median voter.

Medicare: A government program that provides health benefits to those over 65 years of age.

Medium of exchange: The property of money that exchanges are made through the use of money.

Menu costs: Costs of inflation that arise from actually changing prices.

Merger: A process in which two or more firms combine their operations.

Microeconomics: The study of the choices made by consumers, firms, and government, and how these decisions affect the market for a particular good or service.

Minimum efficient scale: The output at which the long-run average cost curve becomes horizontal.

Mixed economy: A market-based economic system under which government plays an important role, including the regulation of markets, where most economic decisions are made.

Monetarists: Economists who emphasize the role of money in determining nominal income and inflation.

Monetary policy: The range of actions taken by the Federal Reserve to influence the level of GDP or the rate of inflation.

Monetizing the deficit: Purchases by a central bank of newly issued government bonds.

Money: Anything that is regularly used in exchange.

Money illusion: Confusion of real and nominal magnitudes.

Money multiplier: An initial deposit leads to a multiple expansion of deposits. In the simplified case increase in deposits = (initial deposit) × (1/reserve ratio).

Monopolistic competition: A market served by dozens of firms selling slightly different products.

Monopoly: A market in which a single firm serves the entire market.

Monopsony: A market in which there is a single buyer of an input.

Moral hazard problem: Insurance encourages risky behavior.

Multilateral real exchange rate: An index of the real exchange rate with a country's trading partners.

Multinational corporation: An organization that produces and sells goods and services throughout the world.

Multiplier: The ratio of changes in output to changes in spending. It measures the degree to which changes in spending are "multiplied" into changes in output.

Multiplier-accelerator model: A model in which a downturn in real GDP leads to a sharp fall in investment, which triggers further reductions in GDP through the multiplier.

National income: Net national product less indirect taxes.

Natural monopoly: A market in which the entry of a second firm would make price less than average cost, so a single firm serves the entire market.

Natural rate of unemployment: The level of unemployment at which there is no cyclical unemployment.

Natural resources: Things created by acts of nature and used to produce goods and services.

Negative relationship: A relationship in which an increase in the value of one variable decreases the value of the other variable.

Neoclassical theory of investment: A theory of investment that says both real interest rates and taxes are important determinants of investment.

Net exports: Exports minus imports.

Net international investment position: Domestic holdings of foreign assets minus foreign holdings of domestic assets.

Net investment: Gross investment minus depreciation.

Net national product (NNP): GNP less depreciation.

Net worth: The difference between assets and liabilities.

New growth theory: Modern theories of growth that try to explain the origins of technological progress.

Nominal GDP: The value of GDP in current dollars.

Nominal interest rates: Interest rates quoted in the market.

Nominal value: The face value of a sum of money.

Nondurable goods: Goods that last for short periods of time, such as food.

Normal good: A good for which an increase in income increases demand.

Normative economics: Analysis that answers the question, What ought to be?

North American Free Trade Agreement (NAFTA): An international agreement that lowers barriers to trade between the United States, Mexico, and Canada (signed in 1994).

Okun's law: A relationship between changes in real GDP and the unemployment rate.

Oligopoly: A market served by a few firms.

Open economy: An economy with international trade.

Open market purchases: The Fed's purchase of government bonds, which increases the money supply.

Open market sales: The Fed's sales of government bonds to the public, which decreases the money supply.

Opportunity cost: What you sacrifice to get something.

Output effect: The change in the quantity of labor demanded resulting from a change in the quantity of output.

Outside lags: The time it takes for policies to work.

Patent: The exclusive right to sell a particular good for some period of time.

Pay-as-you-go: A system that uses revenue collected this year to pay for benefits to recipients this year.

Paying efficiency wages: The firm's practice of paying wages to increase the average productivity of its workers.

Peak: The time at which a recession begins.

Perfectly competitive market: A market with a very large number of firms, each of which produces the same standardized product and takes the market price as given.

Perfectly elastic demand: The price elasticity of demand is infinite.

Perfectly elastic supply: The price elasticity of supply is infinite.

Perfectly inelastic demand: The price elasticity of demand is zero.

Perfectly inelastic supply: The price elasticity of supply is zero.

Permanent income: An estimate of a household's long-run average level of income.

Personal disposable income: Personal income after taxes.

Personal income: Income (including transfer payments) received by households.

Physical capital: Objects made by human beings and used to produce goods and services.

Political business cycle: The effects on the economy of using monetary or fiscal policy to stimulate the economy before an election to improve reelection prospects.

Pollution tax: A tax or charge equal to the spillover cost per unit of waste.

Positive economics: Analysis that answers the question, What is or what will be?

Positive relationship: A relationship in which an increase in the value of one variable increases the value of the other variable.

Poverty budget: The minimum amount the government estimates that a family needs to avoid being in poverty; equal to three times the minimum food budget.

Predatory pricing: A pricing scheme under which a firm decreases its price to drive a rival out of business, and increases the price when the other firm disappears.

Price ceiling: A maximum price; transactions above the maximum price are outlawed.

Price change formula: A formula that shows the percentage change in equilibrium price resulting from a change in demand or supply, given the values for the price elasticity of demand and the price elasticity of supply.

Price discrimination: The process under which a firm divides consumers into two or more groups and picks a different price for each group.

Price elasticity of demand: A measure of the responsiveness of the quantity demanded to changes in price; computed by dividing the percentage change in quantity demanded by the percentage change in price.

Price elasticity of supply: A measure of the responsiveness of the quantity supplied to changes in price; computed by dividing the percentage change in quantity supplied by the percentage change in price.

Price fixing: An arrangement in which two firms coordinate their pricing decisions.

Price floor: A minimum price; transactions below the minimum price are outlawed.

Price leadership: An implicit agreement under which firms in a market choose a price leader, observe that firm's price, and match it.

Price level: An average of all the prices in the economy as measured by a price index.

Price-support program: A policy under which the government specifies a minimum price above the equilibrium price.

Principle: A simple truth that most people understand and accept.

Private good: A good that is consumed by a single person or household.

Private investment expenditures: Purchases of newly produced goods and services by firms.

Privatizing: The process of selling state firms to individuals.

Procyclical: Moving in same direction as real GDP.

Producer surplus: The difference between the market price of a product and the minimum amount a producer is willing to accept for that product; alternatively, the difference between the market price and the marginal cost of production.

Product differentiation: A strategy of distinguishing one product from other similar products.

Production possibilities curve: A curve showing the combinations of two goods that can be produced by an economy, assuming that all resources are fully employed.

Protectionist policies: Rules that restrict the free flow of goods between nations, including tariffs (taxes on imports), quotas (limits on total imports), voluntary export restraints (agreements between governments to limit exports), and nontariff trade barriers (subtle practices that hinder trade).

Public choice economics: A field of economics that explores how governments actually operate.

Public good: A good that is available for everyone to consume, regardless of who pays and who doesn't.

Purchasing Power Parity: A theory of exchange rates, stating that the exchange rate between two currencies is determined by the price levels in the two countries.

Q-theory of investment: The theory of investment that links investment spending to stock prices.

Quantity demanded: The amount of a good a consumer is willing to buy.

Quantity equation: The equation that links money, velocity, prices and real output. In symbols, we have $M \times V = P \times y$.

Quantity supplied: The amount of a good a firm is willing to sell.

Rational expectations: The economic theory that analyzes how people form expectations in such a manner that, on average, they forecast the future correctly.

Real business cycle theory: The economic theory that emphasizes how shocks to technology can cause fluctuations in economic activity.

Real exchange rate: The market exchange rate adjusted for prices.

Real GDP: A measure of GDP that controls for changes in prices.

Real GDP per capita: Gross domestic product per person adjusted for changes in prices. It is the usual measure of living standards across time and between countries.

Real interest rate: The nominal interest rate minus the inflation rate.

Real value: The value of a sum of money in terms of the quantity of goods the money can buy.

Real wage: The wage paid to workers adjusted for changes in prices.

Real wages: Nominal or dollar wages adjusted for changes in purchasing power.

Recession: Six consecutive months of negative economic growth.

Rent control: A policy under which the government specifies a maximum rent that is below the equilibrium rent.

Rent seeking: The process under which a firm spends money to persuade the government to erect barriers to entry and pick the firm as the monopolist.

Required reserves: The fraction of banks' deposits that banks are legally required to hold in their vaults or as deposits at the Fed.

Reserve ratio: The ratio of reserves to deposits.

Reserves: The fraction of banks' deposits set aside in either vault cash or as deposits at the Federal Reserve.

Revaluation: An increase in the exchange rate in a fixed exchange system.

Ricardian equivalence: The proposition that it does not matter whether government expenditure is financed by taxes or by debt.

Saving: Total income minus consumption.

Savings Function: The relationship between the level of income and the level of savings.

Scarcity: A situation in which resources are limited and can be used in different ways, so we must sacrifice one thing for another.

Services: Reflect work done in which people play a prominent role in delivery, ranging from haircutting to health care.

Shoe-leather costs: Costs of inflation that arise from trying to reduce holdings of cash.

Short run: A period of time over which one or more factors of production is fixed; in most cases, a period of time over which a firm cannot modify an existing facility or build a new one.

Short-run average total cost (SATC): Short-run total cost divided by the quantity of output, equal to AFC plus AVC.

Short-run average variable cost (SAVC): Variable cost divided by the quantity produced.

Short-run demand curve for labor: A curve showing the relationship between the wage and the quantity of labor demanded in the short run, the period when the firm cannot change its production facility.

Short run in macroeconomics: The period of time that prices do not change very much.

Short-run marginal cost (SMC): The change in total cost resulting from producing one more unit of the good in the short run.

Short-run market supply curve: A curve showing the relationship between price and the quantity of output supplied by all firms in the short run.

Short-run production function: Shows how much output is produced from varying amounts of labor, holding the capital stock constant.

Short-run supply curve for a firm: A curve showing the relationship between the price of a product and the quantity of output supplied by a firm in the short run.

Shut-down price: The price at which the firm is indifferent between operating and shutting down.

Signaling effect: The increase in a person's wage resulting from the signal of productivity provided by completing college.

Slope: The change in the variable on the vertical axis resulting from a one-unit increase in the variable on the horizontal axis.

Social insurance: A system that compensates individuals for bad luck, low skills, or misfortunes.

Social Security: A government program that provides retirement, survivor, and disability benefits.

Speculative demand for money: The demand for money that reflects holding money over short periods is less risky than holding stocks or bonds.

Spillover: A cost or benefit experienced by people who are external to the decision about how much of a good to produce or consume.

Stabilization policy: Policy actions taken to bring the economy closer to full employment or potential output.

Stock of capital: The total of all the machines, equipment, and buildings in the entire economy.

Store of value: The property of money that it preserves value until it is used in an exchange.

Structural unemployment: The part of unemployment that results from the mismatch of skills and jobs.

Substitutes: Two goods related in such a way that an increase in the price of one good increases the demand for the other good.

Substitution effect for price changes: The change in consumption resulting from a change in the price of one good relative to the price of other goods.

Substitution effect for wage changes: An increase in the wage rate increases the opportunity cost of leisure and leads workers to demand less leisure and supply more labor.

Sunk cost: The cost a firm has already paid—or has agreed to pay some time in the future.

Supply curve: See *individual supply curve*; see *market supply curve*.

Supply schedule: A table of numbers that shows the relationship between price and quantity supplied, ceteris paribus (other things being equal).

Supply shocks: External events that shift the aggregate supply curve.

Supply-siders: Economists who emphasize the role of taxation for influencing economic activity.

Surplus: The excess of total revenues over total expenditures.

Tariff: A tax on an imported good.

Taxi medallion: A license to operate a taxi.

Technological progress: An increase in output without increasing inputs.

Terms of trade: The rate at which two goods will be exchanged.

Thin market: A market in which some high-quality goods are sold, but fewer than would be sold in a market with perfect information.

Tit-for-tat: A strategy under which the one firm in a duopoly starts out with the cartel price and then chooses whatever price the other firm chose in the preceding period.

Total burden of a tax: The loss in consumer surplus resulting from a tax (assuming a constant-cost industry).

Total product curve: A curve showing the relationship between the number of workers and the quantity of output produced.

Total revenue: The money the firm gets by selling its product; equal to the price times the quantity sold.

Total surplus of a market: The sum of the net benefits experienced by consumers and producers; equal to the sum of consumer surplus and producer surplus.

Total utility: The utility (measured in utils) from whatever quantity of the product the consumer gets.

Total variable cost (TVC): Cost that varies as the firm changes the quantity produced.

Trade deficit: The excess of imports over exports.

Trade surplus: The excess of exports over imports.

Transactions demand for money: The demand for money based on the desire to facilitate transactions.

Transfer payments: Payments to individuals from governments that do not correspond to the production of goods and services.

Transition: The process of shifting from a centrally planned economy toward a mixed economic system, with markets playing a greater role in the economy.

Trough: The time at which output stops falling in a recession.

Trust: An arrangement under which the owners of several companies transfer their decision-making powers to a small group of trustees, who then make decisions for all the firms in the trust.

Tying: A business practice under which a consumer of one product is required to purchase another product.

Unanticipated inflation: Inflation that is not expected.

Underemployed: Workers who hold a part-time job but prefer to work full time or hold jobs that are far below their capabilities.

Unemployed: People who are looking for work but do not have jobs.

Unemployment insurance: Payments received from the government upon becoming unemployed.

Unemployment rate: The fraction of the labor force that is unemployed.

Unitary elasticity: The price elasticity is equal to one.

Unit of account: The property of money that prices are quoted in terms of money.

Usury laws: Laws that do not allow interest rates to exceed specified ceilings.

Util: One unit of utility.

Utility: The satisfaction or pleasure the consumer experiences when he or she consumes a good, measured as the number of utils.

Utility-maximizing rule: Pick the affordable combination of consumer goods that makes the marginal utility per dollar spent on one good equal to that of a second good.

Value added: The sum of all the income (wages, interest, profits, rent) generated by an organization.

Variable: A measure of something that can take on different values.

Variable costs: Costs that vary as the quantity produced changes.

Velocity of money: Nominal GDP divided by the money supply. It is also the rate at which money turns over during the year.

Vertical equity: The idea that people with more income or wealth should pay higher taxes.

Voluntary export restraint (VER): A scheme under which an exporting country voluntarily decreases its exports.

Wage-price spiral: Changes in wages and prices causing more changes in wages and prices.

Wealth effect: The increase in spending that occurs because the real value of money increases when the price level falls.

World Trade Organization (WTO): An organization that oversees GATT and other international trade agreements.

Worldwide sourcing: The practice of buying components for a product from nations throughout the world.

Answers to Odd-Numbered Problems and Discussion Questions

Chapter 1

1. Buying a used car: It is difficult to determine the quality of the car.
   Providing health insurance: It is difficult to determine whether the customer will have large or small medical expenses.
3. The number of lectures attended, the hours of sleep the night before the exam.
5. Move along, shift.

Appendix to Chapter 1

1. a. See Figure S.1.
   b. The slope is $5.
   c. The monthly bill will increase by $15.
3. 10%, –2%, 6%.
5. The number of burglaries will decrease by 4.

Chapter 2

1. The statement ignores the opportunity cost of the time spent in college.
3. The marginal cost is the cost of equipping and paying one more officer. The officer would presumably decrease crime, and the marginal benefit is determined by the reduction in crime resulting from the additional officer. If you can measure the marginal cost and the marginal ben-efit, you should continue to hire officers until the marginal benefit equals the marginal cost.
5. In the long run, the firm can modify its production facility or build a new one.
7. Eventually, we expect output to increase at a decreasing rate because more and more workers share the espresso machine.
9. Salaries increased faster than the price of consumer goods.

Chapter 3

1. Brenda could specialize in bread. Instead of producing one shirt for herself, Brenda could use the time it would take to produce one shirt to produce two loaves of bread. If she then trades one loaf of bread for one shirt, she will have one loaf of bread left over. She gets the same number of shirts and one extra loaf of bread. Sam could specialize in shirts. Instead of producing one loaf of bread for himself, Sam could use the time it would take to produce a loaf of bread to produce two shirts. If he trades one shirt for one loaf of bread, he will have the same amount of bread but one extra shirt.
3. Professor A has a comparative advantage in the graduate course: He is twice as productive as Professor B in that course (90/45), but only 1.5 times as productive in the undergraduate course (90/60). Looking at this another way, the total performance (score in the undergraduate course plus the score in the graduate course) is 150 when Professor A teaches the graduate course and Professor B teaches the undergraduate course (90 in G plus 60 in U), compared to only 135 when Professor A teaches the undergraduate course and Professor B teaches the graduate course.
5. Mexican goods are now less costly and therefore more attractive. An American who wants to buy a good that costs 5 pesos must spend $0.25 to get the pesos to pay for the good (5 pesos times the price of $0.05 per peso), compared to $0.50 before (5 pesos times the price of $0.10 per peso). From the perspective of a Mexican consumer, American goods are now more costly and therefore less attractive. A Mexican who wants to buy a good that costs $1 must spend 20 pesos to get the dollar to pay for the good ($1 divided by the price of $0.05 per peso), compared to only 10 pesos before ($1 divided by the price of $0.10 per peso).

Chapter 4

1. a. w, $150,200 per day.
   b. demand, increase.
   c. supply, decrease.

Figure S.1 Relationship Between Hours of Tennis and the Monthly Tennis Club Bill

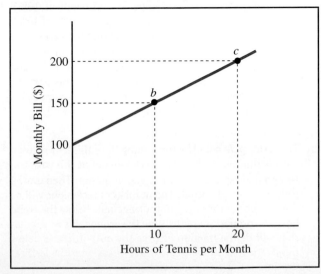

3. a. The cost of producing computers will decrease, so the production of computers will be more profitable, so firms will supply more of them. The supply curve will shift to the right, decreasing the equilibrium price.

   b. The tax increases the production cost, shifting the supply curve to the left and increasing the equilibrium price.

5. Education at private and public schools are substitutes, so the tuition hike will shift the demand for private education to the right, increasing the equilibrium price and quantity.

7. If price and quantity both increase, we know from Table 4.1 that demand has increased. We shift the demand curve to the right, increasing the price and quantity.

9. How many people switch to automobile travel as a result of the higher cost of air travel? How does the shift to automobile travel affect the number of injuries and deaths on the highways? Does the airport security system reduce the number of injuries and deaths related to air travel? If so, how many lives are saved and how many injuries are avoided?

11. The supply curve for shirts shifts to the left, increasing the equilibrium price and decreasing the equilibrium quantity.

Chapter 5

1. If we are interested in the increase in the production of goods and services, we should be interested in the growth of real GDP. If we also care about the increase in prices, we should be interested in the growth of nominal GDP.

3. We calculate the value of the goods produced in 2004 using the prices in 2004 and 2005. For 2004, the value of production is $24,000. For 2005, the value of production is $26,200. The value of production (attributable all to price changes) rose by 9.2%. If the price index for 2004 was 100, the price index for 2005 would be 1.092.

5. No, because you need to compare the price index in one year to a value in another year.

7. Refrigerators are an example of a good that depreciates. If a refrigerator costs $2,000, lasts for 10 years, and depreciates evenly over 10 years, the yearly depreciation would be $200.

9. Deterioration in air quality should be subtracted from NNP to arrive at national income. Improvements to air quality should be added.

11. If the Department of Commerce used a base year in which computer prices were high, it would overstate the growth of real GDP and understate the growth of overall prices.

Chapter 6

1. The labor force is 6 million (employed plus unemployed); the labor force participation rate is 60% (labor force divided by population 16 years and older); the unemployment rate is 8.3% (unemployed divided by labor force).

3. This belief is based on the idea that with high unemployment rates, there are likely to be discouraged workers.

5. There will always be frictional and structural unemployment.

7. The inflation rate is 11% [(60 − 55)/55].

9. The conventional unemployment rate is 7.4% (8 million/108 million). An alternative measure would add the discouraged workers to total unemployment. This would also increase the labor force by the same amount. The alternative unemployment measure would be 10.7% (12 million/112 million).

Chapter 7

1. The economists believe that high payroll taxes are the cause of high unemployment and slow employment growth.

3. With a reduction of the supply in young workers, overall wages would rise for union members.

5. Towns near the border with Mexico have more migration and hence a larger supply of labor. The result is lower wages.

7. The graph would show the demand curve for labor shifting to the right as technology improves in the economy. According to this theory, real wages therefore rise during booms and fall during recessions.

9. Today, many more women work full time and provide support for their families. The labor supply for these women is not likely to be very sensitive to changes in wages and thus is more likely to look like that of men.

11. With limited opportunities for domestic investment, savings will flow abroad. This is accomplished through a trade surplus.

Chapter 8

1. It will double in 23.3 years (70/3) and increase by a factor of 4 in 46.6 years.

3. We collect price data on many commodities in the United Kingdom and the United States in their own currencies. We then use the "exchange rate" for each commodity to calculate expenditures in dollars.

5. We measure it through growth accounting. We ask how much growth can be explained by increases in labor and capital. The remainder is attributed to technological progress.

7. Public investment increases by 5% (one-half of 10%). Private savings and investment falls by 2% (20% of 10%). Thus, total investment (public and private) increases.

9. Although income may have been increasing during this period, the fall in height suggests that basic nutrition and overall welfare may have been decreasing. This perhaps could be accounted for by rapid increases in the population of cities and the stresses of urban life in this period.

Chapter 9

1. The term *cycle* could be misleading if we think of regular, reoccurring cycles. Business cycles do not fit this pattern.

3. Draw a line representing the trend in output. Then draw a pattern of actual output. The number of recessions will be the number of times the output line falls below the trend line. The proportion of the time the economy is in a recession will be the fraction of time the output line is below trend. The magnitude of the worst recession is the farthest the output line falls below trend.

5. Rents on apartments are sticky with month-long or year-long leases. They are sticky because it is costly to move and change apartments.
7. As the classical aggregate supply curve moved to the right, prices would fall.
9. When aggregate demand fails, the aggregate demand curve shifts to the left, and prices and output fall. In the long run, the Keynesian aggregate supply curve falls to restore the economy to full employment.

Chapter 10
1. a. 800
   b. 2
   c. $S = 0.5y - 200$
   d. 200
3. The multiplier is 2.04. Therefore, investment spending needs to rise by 73.5.
5. No. Raising tax rates will also lower GDP.
7. a. GDP will rise.
   b. No. Inventories could rise because demand falls short of the expectations of producers.
9. GDP will fall because of the balanced budget multiplier.
11. More generous unemployment insurance programs put more funds into the economy in bad times and less in good times. This stabilizes consumption spending and output.

Chapter 11
1. Plant and equipment spending are governed in part by expectations of changes in GDP, which can be volatile. Housing will depend on interest rates. Inventories will be volatile because they depend on changes in demand over very short periods of time.
3. The statement is true because, with a zero rate of interest and thus no opportunity cost for invested funds, the savings in gas would ultimately pay for the costs of leveling the mountain.
5. Yes. The real cost of funds is –1%.
7. The nominal rate is 10%; the real rate is 2%.
9. This is an example of diversification, which reduces risk.

Chapter 12
1. They are accepted in exchange.
3. The opportunity cost of excess reserves is the income that could be earned by lending the reserves.
5. $13.3 million (the multiplier is 1/0.15 = 6.6).
7. An increase in the discount rate will lead banks to reduce their borrowed reserves from the Fed, and the supply of money will fall.
9. It would increase the supply of money. Any purchases by the Fed will increase reserves in banks and lead to an expansion of the supply of money.
11. They were not fully equivalent to money because they were accepted in exchange only by large banks and credit unions and not, for example, by stores or by individuals.

Chapter 13
1. You may have an opportunity to buy a rare CD at a music store and need cash on hand. You could not buy the CD with a bond.
3. You would want to sell bonds because bond prices would fall as interest rates rose.
5. It would weaken monetary policy because changes in interest rates would have less of an impact on investment.
7. Trade is more important for the economy of the Netherlands than for that of the United States. Therefore, monetary policy would have more of an effect through exchange rates in the Netherlands.
9. This would shorten the inside lag for fiscal policy. But it would give the President more political power at the expense of Congress. This could be used wisely or abused.

Chapter 14
1. They worried that unemployment had fallen below the natural rate.
3. Interest rates rise because of an increase in money demand during an economic expansion. Investment first rises because of the accelerator effect at the beginning of an expansion and falls, for the same reason, as the GDP slows down at the end of the expansion.
5. Money is neutral in the long run.
7. Tax cuts will lead to higher consumer spending. This crowds out investment in the long run through higher interest rates.
9. It is costly to guard and store large sums of money. However, interest rates are unlikely to fall too far below 0%, only perhaps a few tenths of 1%.

Chapter 15
1. High interest rates in the long run result from high inflation rates. High inflation rates occur only when there is rapid growth in the money supply.
3. Typically, firms have better access to information than workers.
5. If the government increases the money supply at a faster rate, inflation will rise. The rise in inflation will raise interest rates and the cost of holding money. Therefore, people will hold money for shorter periods of time.
7. With increased foreign aid, the government has less need to print money to finance a deficit.
9. It is true that businesses are debtors and would benefit initially from inflation that was not anticipated. However, the costs of inflation do affect businesses as well as individuals.

Chapter 16
1. The interest on the debt is $1 billion. The budget deficit (spending + interest – taxes) is $1 billion. Therefore, the debt at the end of the year is $11 billion.
3. They are more likely to need to print money, which causes rapid inflation.

5. It could induce a government to take contractionary actions during economic downturns. This could be serious if there are not sufficient escape mechanisms.

7. With a stable 2% inflation rate and full institutional adjustment, there are both menu costs and shoe-leather costs. It may be more difficult to maintain a commitment to a 2% inflation rate than to zero inflation or price stability.

9. It depends on whether individuals really increase their savings (by cutting consumption) or just shift existing funds into the tax free accounts.

Chapter 17

1. a. In Country B, the opportunity cost of 1 computer is 2 TVs, and the opportunity cost of 1 TV is 1/2 of a computer. In Country C, the opportunity cost of 1 computer is 4 TVs, and the opportunity cost of 1 TV is 1/4 of a computer. Country B has the comparative advantage of producing computers, and Country C the comparative advantage of producing TVs.

   b. The production possibility curves are straight lines for both countries, the slope being the opportunity costs and the intercepts being the maximum level of production of each good.

3. Chipland produces 120 chips and exchanges them for 70 shirts, ending up with 85 chips and 70 shirts. Shirtland produces 108 shirts and exchanges 70 of them for 35 chips, ending up with 35 chips and 35 shirts.

5. If the VERs were replaced with a tariff, the government would collect revenue. Under VERs, the importers earn large profits.

7. Consumers will benefit because prices will decrease. As each nation shifts its production to the goods for which it has a comparative advantage, workers in expanding industries will benefit, while workers in other industries will lose. The challenge for policymakers is to facilitate this transition.

9. Taxpayers will favor the shift because they will earn revenue. The firms importing goods will lobby against this because they will lose the profits they earn from the quotas. Firms may be more effective in lobbying than taxpayers because the losses are concentrated among a few firms, but the benefits are spread widely across taxpayers.

Chapter 18

1. a. The yen will appreciate.
   b. The pound will depreciate.
   c. The pound will appreciate.

3. The real exchange rate for the South American country would rise against the dollar because the percentage increase in the prices of its goods was less than the percent depreciation of its exchange rate.

5. –$25 billion.

7. This will lead to investors wishing to sell the currency and a depreciation of the exchange rate.

9. With a fixed exchange rate, the increase in Mexican prices (at a faster rate than U.S. prices increased) led to a rise in the cost of Mexican goods relative to U.S. goods or an appreciation in Mexico's real exchange rate.

11. Countries are often reluctant to depreciate their currencies because it will lead to a rise in price of imported goods and also hurt its ability to borrow money over the long run.

Index

Interest rates
    bond prices and, 275–276
    determination of, 273–275
    expected real, 236
    investment and, 276–281
    investment spending and,
        237–240
    money growth, inflation and,
        308–313
    nominal, 232, 235–237, 298
    output and, 276–281
    real, 232, 235–237
Intermediate good, 98–99
International Monetary Fund (IMF),
    52
International trade. *See* Trade
Investments, 232–235
    defined, 232
    financial intermediation in
        facilitation of, 241–245
    neoclassical theory of, 240
    Q-theory of, 240
    risks and, 242–243
Investment spending, interest rates
    and, 237–240
Invisible hand, 6
Italy, economic growth in, 156

J
Japan
    deflation in, 126
    economy in, 156, 199, 296
Job protection, costs of, 358
Johnson, Lyndon, economic policy
        under, 214
Jorgenson, Dale, 165, 240

K
Kennedy, John F., economic policy
        under, 214
Keynes, John Maynard
    on economic way of thinking, 6
    as father of Keynesian economics,
        11, 127, 180, 184, 200, 289
    on investments, 233
Keynesian aggregate supply, shifts
        in, 293
Keynesian aggregate supply curve,
        190–191, 292
Keynesian cross, 200–203
Keynesian economics, 11, 127, 180,
        186, 335

debate between classical
        economics and, 141
Keynesian fiscal policy, 209–213
    in United States history,
        213–216
Kotlikoff, Laurence, 334
Krueger, Alan, 284

L
Labor, 3, 5, 133–134
    demand and supply for,
        135–138
    marginal product of, 33
Labor force
    defined, 116
    participation rate, 116–117
Labor market, households in, 45
Labor market equilibrium, full
        employment and, 138–139
Labor productivity, 164–165
    recessions and, 165–166
Labor Statistics, Bureau of, 118,
        119
Labor supply, 135–138
    variations in, 140
Laffer, Arthur, 143
Laffer curve, capital gains and, 143
Lags, 281–282
    inside, 282–283
    outside, 282, 283–284
Laissez-faire, 56
Law of demand, 65
Law of one price, 375
Law of supply, 69
Learning by doing, 358
Lebergott, Stanley, 142, 153
Lender of last resort, 260
Liabilities, 255
Liquid, 241
Liquidity demand for money, 273
Liquidity trap, 296
Local government. *See also*
        Government
    revenue sources of, 55
Long run
    crowding out in, 300–302
    defined, 290
    diminishing returns in, 33
    output and prices in, 193–194
Long-run neutrality of money,
        298–300
Lucas, Robert E., Jr., 168–169, 316

M
M1, 252–253, 254
M2, 253–254, 273
Macroeconomics, 11–12, 126
    aggregate production function
        in, 133–134
    circular flow and, 97–98
    defined, 11, 96
    economic fluctuations and, 116
    focuses of, 96
    short run in, 186
Marginal benefit, 28
Marginal change, 9
Marginal cost, 28
Marginal principle, 27–30
    demand for labor and, 135
    output decision and, 67–68
Marginal product of labor, 33
Marginal propensity to consume,
        203
    change in, 205
Marginal propensity to import, 219
Marginal propensity to save, 203
Market(s), 5–6
    defined, 42
    government regulation of, 55–57
    international trade and, 46–47
    operation of, 44–48
    product, 45
    reasons for existence of, 42–44
Market-based economy, circular
        flow diagram in, 45
Market demand curve, 66–67
Market economy, government in,
        53–58
Market effects
    of changes in supply, 76–81
    of decrease in demand, 75–76
    of decrease in supply, 79
    of increase in demand, 74
    of increase in supply, 78
    of simultaneous changes in
        demand and supply, 80–81
Market equilibrium, 70–72
Market supply curve, 70
Martin, William McChesney, Jr., 300
McConnel, Margaret M., 183
Medical care. *See* Health care
Medium of exchange, money as, 251
Menu costs, 322
Mexico, economic growth in, 156,
        157

Photo Credits